HYDROLOGIC MODELING

OF SMALL WATERSHEDS

Edited by
C. T. Haan

Professor and Head, Agricultural Engineering Department,
Oklahoma State University, Stillwater, OK 74074

H. P. Johnson

Professor, Agricultural Engineering Department,
Iowa State University, Ames, IA 50010

D. L. Brakensiek

Research Leader, Northwest Watershed Research Center,
USDA, ARS, Boise, ID 83705

An ASAE Monograph
Number 5 in a series published by

American Society of Agricultural Engineers
2950 Niles Road, P.O. Box 410
St. Joseph, Michigan 49085
(phone 616-429-0300)

ASAE Technical Editor: James A. Basselman
1982

INTRODUCTION

In 1974 Howard P. Johnson suggested that it would be desirable to have a textbook devoted to hydrologic modeling suitable for use in graduate level courses. In discussions that followed the idea of a monograph on this topic was developed. ASAE Hydrology Group Committee SW-217, Watershed Hydraulics and Transport Processes, served as the focal point for the development of the Monograph proposal originally put forth in 1975 under the leadership of Howard P. Johnson.

The Monograph proposal was approved by ASAE and the process of developing the final outline, selecting chapter contributors and settling on the format was undertaken. Besides myself, the editors of the monograph are Howard P. Johnson and Don Brakensiek.

Selecting chapter contributors and getting a time commitment from them proved to be an easier task than anticipated. It was desired to get leading authorities to be contributors to the monograph. At the same time, it was understood that these would likely be among the busiest people. We were extremely fortunate in that our line-up of contributors reads like a who's who is small watershed modeling. Each chapter of the monograph is authored by leading hydrologists who have devoted many years of study to the topics on which they write.

The purpose of this monograph is to collect in one volume some of the latest thinking on modeling various aspects of the hydrologic cycle on small watersheds. A small watershed is taken as one in which the land phase of the hydrologic cycle predominates over the channel phase. Thus modeling the hydrology of agricultural and wild land watersheds is emphasized. Previously this material has been available only in scattered books, reports and journals. It was desired to present several levels of modeling complexity for each component of the hydrologic cycle. A rather thorough theoretical treatment is presented along with various levels of simplification.

The monograph can serve as a text for graduate students or as a reference for researchers desiring more knowledge about hydrologic modeling. It should also be a valuable reference and source book for consultants and others attempting to use hydrologic models to solve water resources problems.

ORGANIZATION OF MONOGRAPH

The monograph has 13 chapters. The monograph starts with an introductory chapter dealing with the philosophy of modeling and system synthesis. This is followed by a chapter devoted to stochastic modeling in hydrology.

Seven chapters are devoted to modeling components of the hydrologic cycle on small watersheds. These are precipitation; infiltration and percolation; surface runoff, storage and routing; evapotranspiration; subsurface flow and groundwater systems; erosion; and chemical transport processes.

These seven chapters treat the basic physical relationships governing flow and storage processes and then discuss different methods of modeling these processes. These methods range from very complete, theoretical models to simpler empirical approximations. The advantages and disadvantages, data requirements and approximations involved in each of the modeling methods are discussed.

One chapter describes how several different types of watershed models are structured by combining elements from various component models. Typical models representative of a large number of similar models are described in detail. Several levels of modeling are represented.

Two chapters are devoted to selecting, calibrating and using watershed models. Different approaches to selecting and calibrating hydrologic models are discussed. The recommended approach depends on the use to be made of the model and the degree of accuracy required.

The last chapter is a catalog of currently available models. The chapter contains a listing of the available models, their capabilities, their data requirements, and sources of information concerning them.

Originally it was planned to use a uniform notation throughout the monograph. On attempting to compile such a list of notation, it was quickly found that more confusion than clarity would result. The uniform notation idea was abandoned in favor of using notation that is more or less standard with respect to the topic being discussed. SI units have been employed.

ACKNOWLEDGMENTS

An undertaking such as this requires the cooperative efforts of many people. Howard P. Johnson deserves the credit for initiating the monograph, getting ASAE approval and support for it and serving as an editor. Don Brakensiek also has devoted a great deal of time to reviewing chapters in his role as an editor and in co-authoring the first chapter.

Charles Onstad and ASAE Committee SW-217 served as the early rallying point for the monograph. Several sessions of this committee have been devoted to providing guidance and stimulation. Hydrology Group Committees SW-212 and SW-215 have also been active supporters of the monograph. The support of the ASAE monograph committee and of James Basselman has also been appreciated.

Many members and non-members of ASAE have served as reviewers of the various chapters. Their comments have greatly improved the monograph and have helped to eliminate many potential areas of misunderstanding. The comments and suggestions of these "behind the scenes" reviewers are gratefully acknowledged.

Of course, the bulk of the work and of the credit for the monograph goes to the 13 chapter coordinators and the 15 co-authors who have devoted many days of effort to producing a quality monograph. I cannot adequately express my appreciation for the work they are doing. These people have received no monetary compensation for the work they have done. Their rewards lie in the fact that they have made a significant and lasting contribution to hydrologic modeling.

C. T. Haan

CONTRIBUTORS

C. R. Amerman	Research Hydraulic Engineer, USDA-ARS, P.O. Box 478, State Rte 621, Coshocton, OH 43812
D. L. Brakensiek	Research Hydraulic Engineer, USDA-ARS, 1175 S. Orchard Ave., Suite 116, Northwest Watershed Research, Boise, ID 83705
K. N. Brooks	Assistant Professor, Department of Forestry, University of Minnesota, St. Paul, MN 55108
S. J. Burges	Associate Professor, Department of Civil Engineering, University of Washington, Seattle, WA 98195
J. R. Burney	Head, Department of Agricultural Engineering, Technical University of Nova Scotia, Halifax, NS 00025
D. G. DeCoursey	Research Leader, P.O. Box E, USDA-ARS, Fort Collins, CO 80522
M. M. Fogel	Hydrologist and Professor, School of Renewable Natural Resources, University of Arizona, Tucson, AZ 85721
G. R. Foster	Hydraulic Engineer, USDA-ARS, and Associate Professor, Department of Agricultural Engineering, Purdue University, West Lafayette, IN 47907
M. H. Frere	Soil Scientist, USDA-ARS, Chickasha, OK 73018
L. F. Huggins	Head, Department of Agricultural Engineering, Purdue University, West Lafayette, IN 47907
T. J. Jackson	Hydrologist, USDA-ARS, Hydrology Laboratory, Beltsville, MD 20705
L. D. James	Director, Utah Water Research Laboratory, Utah State University, Logan, UT 84322
R. Khaleel	Assistant Professor, Department of Hydrology, New Mexico Institute of Mining and Technology, Socorro, NM 87801
L. J. Lane	USDA-ARS-SWC, Southwest Watershed Research Center, Tucson, AZ 85721
C. L. Larson	Professor, Department of Agricultural Engineering, University of Minnesota, St. Paul, MN 55108
R. A. Leonard	Soil Scientist, USDA-ARS, Watkinsville, GA 30677
J. L. McGuinness	Statistician (retired), USDA-ARS, North Appalachian Experimental Watershed Research, Columbus, OH 43812
M. P. Molnau	Professor, Department of Agricultural Engineering, University of Idaho, Moscow, ID 83843
J. W. Naney	Geologist, USDA-ARS, Chickasha, OK 73018
C. A. Onstad	Agricultural Engineer, USDA-ARS, NC Soil Conservation Research Center, Morris, MN 56267
H. B. Osborn	Research Hydraulic Engineer, USDA-ARS-SWC, 442 E. 7th St., Tucson, AZ 85705
W. J. Rawls	Hydrologist, USDA-ARS, BARC-W, Bldg. 007, Rm 139, Beltsville, MD 20705
K. G. Renard	Director, USDA-ARS, Southwest Watershed Research Center, 442 East 7th St., Tucson, AZ 85705
C. W. Richardson	Agricultural Engineer, USDA-ARS, Box 748, Blackland Research Center, Temple, TX 76501
H. H. Richardson	Hydraulic Engineer, 5119 Thunder Hill Road, USDA-SCS, Columbia, MD 21045
K. E. Saxton	Hydrologist, USDA-ARS, 219 Smith, Department of Agricultural Engineering, Washington State University, Pullman, WA 99164
E. H. Seely	Hydraulic Engineer, USDA-ARS, P.O. Box 2257, Sedimentation Laboratory, Oxford, MS 38655
J. C. Shaake, Jr.	Chief, Hydrological Services Division, National Weather Service, Silver Spring, MD 20910
R. W. Skaggs	Professor, Department of Biological and Agricultural Engineering, P.O. Box 5906, North Carolina State University, Raleigh, NC 27650
D. A. Woolhiser	Research Hydraulic Engineer, USDA-ARS, 442 E 7th Street, Tucson, AZ 85705

CONTENTS

CHAPTER 1— **HYDROLOGIC MODELING OF SMALL WATERSHEDS**
D. A. Woolhiser and D. L. Brakensiek

CHAPTER 2— **STOCHASTIC MODELS IN HYDROLOGY**
D. G. DeCoursey, J. C. Shaake, Jr. and E. H. Seely

CHAPTER 3— **PRECIPITATION**
H. B. Osborn, L. J. Lane, C. W. Richardson and M. P. Molnau

CHAPTER 9— MODELING THE QUALITY OF WATER FROM AGRICULTURAL LAND
M. H. Frere, E. H. Seely and R. A. Leonard

CHAPTER 10— SOME PARTICULAR WATERSHED MODELS
C. L. Larson, C. A. Onstad, H. H. Richardson and K. N. Brooks

CHAPTER 11— SELECTION, CALIBRATION, AND TESTING OF HYDROLOGIC MODELS
L. Douglas James and Stephen J. Burges

CHAPTER 12— APPLICATION AND SELECTION OF HYDROLOGIC MODELS
Thomas J. Jackson

CHAPTER 13— CURRENTLY AVAILABLE MODELS
K. G. Renard, W. J. Rawls and M. M. Fogel

chapter 1

HYDROLOGIC MODELING OF SMALL WATERSHEDS

1

HYDROLOGIC SYSTEM SYNTHESIS

by   D. A. Woolhiser, Research Hydraulic Engineer,
      USDA, ARS, Fort Collins, CO and D. L. Braken-
      siek, Research Leader, Northwest Watershed
      Research Center, USDA, ARS, Boise, ID

INTRODUCTION

Hydrologic system synthesis, prediction, and optimization are among the essential activities in the design of water resource systems. Hydrologic system synthesis involves selecting an appropriate hydrologic model and testing the operation of the model by analysis (Dooge, 1973). When the appropriate hydrologic model has been selected, it can be used to predict possible hydrologic inputs to structural components of a water-resource system. The design variables of the components or the number, location, and type of components can then be changed and the system performance evaluated so that the optimum solution can be found.

Hydrologic system synthesis is also required to answer questions such as, "What effects do agricultural land management practices have on runoff quantity and quality?" because it is infeasible to obtain experimental data for all combinations of practices, crops, and hydrologic regimes.

Hydrologic modeling inevitably requires simplification or abstraction. Indeed, man has found through experience that understanding and predicting the behavior of any significant part of his environment requires abstraction. "Abstraction consists in replacing the part of the universe under consideration by a model of simpler structure. Models, formal or intellectual on the one hand or material on the other, are thus a central necessity of scientific procedure" (Rosenbleuth and Wiener, 1945).

In designing water-resource systems and in evaluating the effects of land management techniques we require models derived from the social sciences as well as models of hydrologic systems. In this monograph, however, we are concerned with hydrologic models, more specifically hydrologic models of small agricultural watersheds. For our purposes, a small watershed is one in which agricultural or silvicultural land management practices can significantly affect the hydrologic regime. Although urban watersheds are excluded, the basic principles and many of the models described are quite applicable to urban watersheds as well.

The purpose of this chapter is to discuss the role of models in small watershed hydrology. The types of models that can be used are described and important terms are defined. Finally, hydrologic models are considered as components of water resource system models.

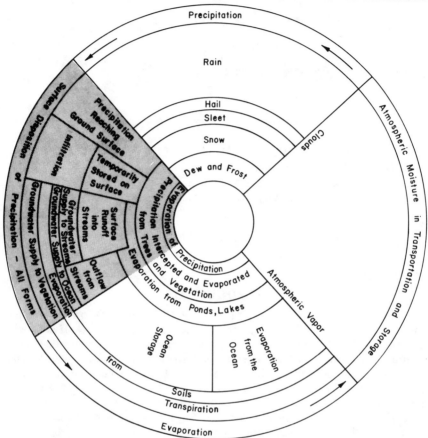

FIG. 1.1 The hydrologic cycle—a qualitative representation (shaded area pertains to the small watershed hydrology) [from Horton, 1931].

THE HYDROLOGIC CYCLE AND ITS COMPONENTS

Watershed hydrologic models obviously represent the hydrologic cycle in various and appropriate ways. The laws of conservation of mass, energy, and momentum are included in the set of theoretical principles used to explain the hydrologic cycle. One or more of these principles, along with several empirical relationships, form the basis for most models of small watersheds.

The principle of conservation of mass is frequently illustrated by the water budget for an arbitrary volume of soil. The qualitative representation of the hydrologic cycle in Fig. 1.1 introduces hydrologic terms and expresses the concept that the mass of water on earth is presumably constant. In small watershed hydrology we are concerned with the shaded part of the circle.

If we consider the sector labelled "surface disposition of precipitation - all forms" in Fig. 1.1, applied to an arbitrary volume of soil with surface area, A, and depth, d, as shown in Fig. 1.2, we can write an equation expressing the integral of the conservation of mass equation for some arbitrary time interval, Δt, as water input = water output ± change of water storage; or

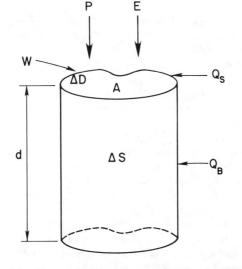

FIG. 1.2 Control volume for water balance. P = precipitation received on area A; W = water imported or exported by man; Q_s = net surface runoff; Q_B = net subsurface outflow as unsaturated or saturated porous media flow; ΔD = change in surface storage; ΔS = change in soil water storage; d = depth; and E = evaporation per unit area.

$$P + W = Q_s + Q_B + \Delta D + \Delta S + EA \quad \dots\dots\dots\dots\dots\dots\dots\dots\dots\dots\dots [1.1]$$

where

P = precipitation received on area A
W = water imported (or exported) by man
Q_S = net surface runoff
Q_B = net subsurface outflow as unsaturated or saturated porous media flow
ΔD = change in surface storage (depression and detention storage)
ΔS = change in soil water storage
E = evaporation per unit area (including evaporation from plants).

Although all dimensions should be expressed in units of mass, they are conventionally given in units of volume or volume per unit surface area. Over a long time, the differential storage terms may become relatively small, and water runoff (yield) from this control volume or from a small watershed is the difference between the total input of precipitation and the imported water and the evaporation.

The amount of evaporation is controlled by the amount of energy available at the layer of soil and air in which plants grow. A conservation of energy equation may be written at the watershed surface as net rate of incoming energy per unit area = net rate of outgoing energy per unit area, or

$$R_S(1-\rho) = R_L + G + H + LE \quad \dots\dots\dots\dots\dots\dots\dots\dots\dots\dots\dots\dots [1.2]$$

where

R_S = flux density of total shortwave radiation at the ground surface

ρ = albedo of the surface (fraction of incoming shortwave radiation that is reflected)

R_L = net flux density of longwave radiation

G = heat flux density into the ground

H = sensible heat transfer into the atmosphere

L = latent heat of vaporization of water

E = evaporation rate.

The units for all terms are heat energy per unit area per unit time. Changes in heat storage in vegetation and the heat used in photosynthesis are ignored in equation [1.2] because they are about 1 percent of R_s. Equations [1.1] and [1.2] are linked by the evaporation term E. The magnitude of E in equation [1.1] is effectively limited by the amount of heat energy delivered to the suface. A, although it also may be resitricted by stomatal resistance of vegetation or by the transport of soil water to plant roots.

Over short periods of time, the conservation of mass equation, although necessary, is not sufficient to accurately describe dynamic hydrologic phenomena such as surface runoff. In overland flow, for example, the raindrops falling on the surface are accelerated by the flowing water, and gravitational and resistance forces accelerate the flow. A second equation based on the principle of conservation of energy or momentum is required. The two equations, along with initial and boundary conditions, then describe the flow dynamics. Subsequent chapters will treat modeling the hydrologic components in more detail and will also consider the aggregation of component models into watershed models.

A CLASSIFICATION OF MODELS

By using models we can better understand or explain natural phenomena and under some conditions we can make predictions in a deterministic or probabilistic sense. What do we mean when we say we understand an event or some aspect of our environment? Hempel (1963) suggests that we understand an event or a regularity if we can give a scientific explanation of it. The essence of Hempel's definition of a scientific explanation follows: suppose that we have a statement E, which describes some phenomenon to be explained. Then, if E can be inferred from a set $L_1, L_2 \ldots L_n$ of general laws or theoretical principles and a set $C_1, C_2 \ldots C_n$ of statements of empirical circumstances, we can say that the phenomenon has been explained. From this definition it follows that formal models are required for scientific explanation.

Several different criteria have been used to develop a classification system for models. In many cases these criteria reflect the special interests or needs of a particular discipline. However, models used in any discipline can be categorized as either **formal** or **material**.

A **formal**, or intellecutal, model is a symbolic, usually mathematical representation of an idealized situation that has the important structural properties of the real system. A **material** model is a physical representation of a complex system that is assumed to be simpler than the prototype system and is also assumed to have properties similar to those of the prototype system.

Fig. 1.3 is a schematic classification of models. Material models include **iconic** or "look alike" models and analog models. An iconic model is a simplified version of the real-world system. It requires the same materials

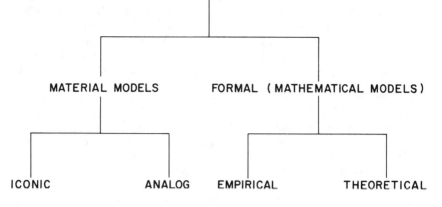

FIG. 1.3 Model Classification.

as the real system (i.e., the model of a fluid is also a fluid). Lysimeters, rainfall simulators, hydraulic flumes, and watershed experimental systems are all examples of **iconic** models. By measuring the volume of water draining from a lysimeter and weighing it periodically, we gain some insight into the relative rates of deep percolations and evapotranspiration from nearby, undisturbed areas with similar vegetation and soils. We are not interested in the model measurements in themselves, but we are interested in the insight they give us into processes occurring in the more complicated natural system. Rainfall simulators, hydraulic flumes, and watershed experimental systems may help to determine the most significant factors that should be included in mathematical models of overland flow and erosion processes. To be useful, iconic models **must** be easier to work with than the real system and must provide some information that is not a direct consequence of known and accepted mathematical models. Changes of length or time scale (or both) are frequently required to make the model useful. Because of these scale changes and other necessary simplifications, iconic models often involve distortions, and the magnitude of these distortions must be carefully considered and included in prediction equations.

In an analog model the quantities measured in the model are different physical substances than in the real (prototype) system. For example, the flow of electrical current may represent the flow of water, or the deflection of a thin membrane might represent the drawdown of a water table. The validity of an analog model depends on the existence of identical mathematical relationships describing both the real system and its analog, and so depends on the other class of models, the formal model. In watershed hydrology all formal models are mathematical; hence, we will use the term "mathematical model" or simply "model" hereafter. In this monograph we will concentrate our attention on mathematical models.

Mathematical models can be further subdivided into theoretical models and empirical models. A theoretical model includes both a set of general laws or theoretical principles **and** a set of statements of empirical circumstances. An empirical model omits the general laws and is in reality a representation of data. This distinction breaks down when we consider a model that includes some but not all of the necessary general laws. All theoretical models simplify the physical system and are, therefore, more or less incorrect. In addition, the so-called theoretical models often include obviously empirical components. All empirical relationships have some chance of being fortuitious; that is, by chance two variables may appear to be correlated when in fact they are not. In principle such relationships should not be applied outside the range of the data from which they were obtained. In modeling of small watersheds, examples of the simplification of theoretical models abound. The surface flow of water in a small watershed is generally described by the equation of conservation of mass and that of conservation of momentum, which contain an empirical hydraulic resistance term. Under certain conditions the momentum equation is greatly simplified to the so-called kinematic equation. Subsurface flow problems utilize the Darcy equation, an empirical equation. Modern infiltration modeling is based on the Green and Ampt equation, a gross simplification of the flow system. Theory and empiricism are generally so intermeshed that in actuality most or all watershed hydrology models are hybrids that include both theoretical and empirical components.

Mathematical hydrologic models as we know them today can be classified according to the following six criteria: (Ozga-Zielinska, 1976) (a) model structure and modeling subject, (b) role of the time factor, (c) cognitive value of a model, (d) character of results obtained, (e) applied approach and methods of solution, and (f) properties of operator functions.

Model Structure and Modeling Subject

Model structure and modeling subject, the first criterion, relates to what part or parts of the hydrologic cycle are included in the model and their level of abstraction in the model. The following four levels can be identified: (a) individual processes, (b) component models, (c) integrated watershed models, and (d) global watershed models. These four levels are described schematically in Fig. 1.4. An individual process model is a mathematical description of one of the physical processes involved in the hydrologic cycle. For example, models of evaporation from a free water surface, flow in unsaturated porous media, and unsteady free surface flow would be classified as individual process models. As shown in Fig. 1.4 (a) they are of the form

$$Y(t) = Q[X(t)] \quad \dots\dots\dots\dots\dots\dots\dots\dots\dots\dots\dots\dots\dots\dots \quad [1.3]$$

where

$Y(t)$ = output
$X(t)$ = input, and
Q = operator of the process.

In an evaporation model the output, $Y(t)$, would be the mass rate of transport of water vapor from the water surface and the input variables, $X(t)$, would include net radiation, wind velocity, vapor pressure deficit, and possibly other terms.

Models of components, as illustrated in Fig. 1.4(b), include linked models of individual processes with a component operator that apportions the flow of water to the individual processes in the proper order. They describe processes occurring in a particular subspace of the watershed system. Examples of component models include evapotranspiration, direct surface runoff, erosion, and subsurface flow. An evapotranspiration model, for example, would include individual process models describing interception, evaporation from the soil and from plant leaves, soil water movement, and the plant response to stress.

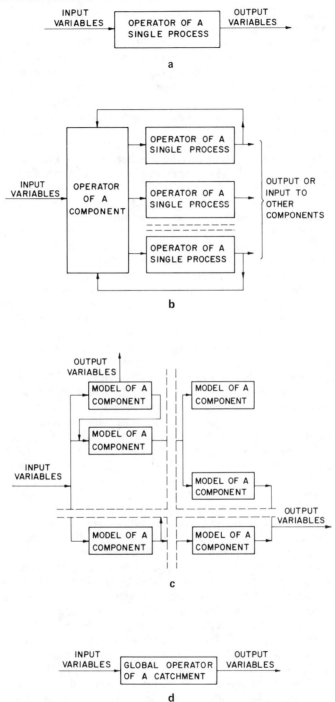

An integrated model is an example of a comprehensive watershed model. As illustrated in Fig. 1.4(c), an integrated model consists of a set of linked component models along with an operator that apportions the flow of water to the individual components in the proper order. Often integrated models include components with varying degrees of abstraction or simplification. Integrated models are developed by a process of synthesis of components and have a well-defined structure that is usually determined by the model builders' concepts of the physical nature of the watershed.

Global models are an alternative to integrated models. Their structure is much simpler—they assume that there is a functional relationship between a set of input and output variables rather than a linkage of individual components (Fig. 1.4(d)]. The nature of the system is specified in only a very simple form, such as "the system is linear, time invariant" and the operator is identified by analyzing a series of observations of input and output. This monograph emphasizes component and integrated models.

According to the second classification criterion, the **role of the time factor**, models can be classified as **static** or **dynamic**. Static models include various empirical equations and regression models in which time is not an independent variable. A regression model relating the mean annual discharge of a stream to climatic and physiographic factors is a static model. Mathematical models in which time is not a factor, i.e., steady state conditions, are also static models. Dynamic models require differential equations with time as an independent variable and thus can show the time variability of output. This monograph emphasizes dynamic models.

Three categories result when we consider the third classification criterion, the **cognitive value of a model**: (a) physically-based models, (b) conceptual models, or (c) trend models. Physically-based models are those in which the governing physical laws and the model structure are well-known and can be described by the equations of mathematical physics. Conceptual models may be utilized when the model structure and physical laws are unknown or the physically-based model is so complicated that it is more appropriate to greatly simplify the model behavior. Linear or nonlinear storage models could be classified as conceptual models.

The **character of results obtained** or output of a model can be classified as stochastic or deterministic. If any of the variables in a mathematical model are regarded as random variables having distributions in probability, then the model is **stochastic**. If all of the variables are considered to be free from random variation, then the model is **deterministic** (Clarke, 1973).

The fifth classification criterion "**applied approach and methods of solution**" overlaps somewhat with the criterion "cognitive value of the model", but introduces a different terminology. Systems can be referred to either as "black box" systems or "white box" systems, depending on whether the horizontal relationship or vertical relationship in Fig. 1.5 is followed. The horizontal relationship or "black box approach" treats the system as a system operator which transforms input into output. The "white box approach" as indicated by the vertical relationship implies that the physical laws and nature of the system are well understood and can be synthesized into a "system operation" without recourse to observations of input and output.

The last classification criterion related to mathematical **properties of the operator function**. Models may be classified as linear or nonlinear, lumped or distributed and stationary or nonstationary. According to Clark (1973), usage of the term linear has two meanings. A model is linear in the

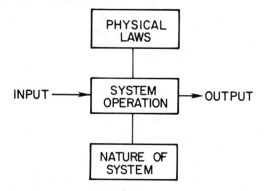

FIG. 1.5 The concept of systems operation (from Dooge, 1973).

systems theory sense if the principle of superposition is valid. The principle of superposition states that, if $y_1(t)$ and $y_2(t)$ are the system outputs corresponding to system inputs $x_1(t)$ and $x_2(t)$ respectively, then the response to $x_1(t) + x_2(t)$ is $y_1(t) + y_2(t)$. This is the most common usage in hydrology (Dooge, 1973).

An alternative meaning of linearity is linearity in the statistical sense. In this usage a model must be linear in the parameters to be estimated. For example, if an output, y, was related to an input, x, by the equation $y + a + bx$, the model is linear in the statistical sense but the principle of superposition does not hold; i.e., $y_1 + y_2 \neq a + b(x_1 + x_2)$. This particular nonlinearity is due to a threshold that is a common feature of hydrologic processes and precludes "systems" linearity in hydrologic models.

Lumped models do not explicitly take into account spatial variability of inputs, outputs or parameters and usually are represented by an ordinary differential equation or a set of linked ordinary differential equations. Distributed models include spatial variations in inputs, outputs, and parameters and often consist of a set of linked partial differential equations.

A deterministic operator is stationary if its form and parameters are invariant in time; otherwise it is nonstationary. A stochastic model is stationary if its properties do not change with absolute time. In hydrologic models, nonstationarity may be caused by periodic seasonal variations or by changes in land use that may cause transient effects in hydrologic processes and/or components.

STOCHASTIC NATURE OF HYDROLOGIC PROCESSES

A set of daily precipitation amounts arranged chronologically is an example of a time series. Other examples include daily runoff from a watershed, daily amounts of evapotranspiration, or any of the terms in equations [1.1] or [1.2] for an arbitrary time interval. An important characteristic of these series is that they are unpredictable in a deterministic sense. That is, we cannot predict with certainty how much rain will fall tomorrow or how much runoff will occur. We can only hope to describe the probability structure of such as process. These series are examples of stochastic processes, or processes developing in time in a manner controlled by probabilistic laws.

The stochastic nature of hydrologic phenomena plays a significant role in applied hydrology. For example, in flood studies one must estimate the distribution function of peak discharges before and after proposed control structures and/or land management practices are installed. Such a distribution function is an example of a functional of the stochastic run-off process. These functionals can be obtained in two ways: (a) analytical stochastic models, or (b) Monte Carlo simulation. In analytical stochastic models, the process is approximated by a mathematical model that is completely specified except for parameter values that can be estimated on the basis of an observed sample. When the parameter values are obtained, one can obtain certain probability expressions that may be valuable in decision making by analytical techniques. The analytical methods often are very elegant, but usually a price must be paid—assumptions and simplifications that must be made to obtain a mathematically tractable form.

If the stochastic process of interest is a complicated function of the input process, then either historical simulation using records of the input processes or Monte Carlo simulation must be used. Historical simulation is more straightforward, but it has the disadvantage that only one record is considered, which will certainly not be repeated in the future. In Monte Carlo simulation, sequences of inputs are simulated by random sampling from the input processes. The output series are then calculated according to the appropriate deterministic laws, and the statistical properties of the outputs can be tabulated as desired.

Three types of uncertainty exist in the distribution functions or decision variables obtained by simulation techniques: (a) model uncertainty, (b) sampling uncertainty in estimating parameters, and (c) simulation sampling uncertainty. To demonstrate these types of uncertainty, consider a stochastic model of the form:

$$\underline{Y}_t = Q(\underline{X}_t; \underline{\theta}): t \in T, T = (0,1,2...) \quad \dots\dots\dots\dots\dots\dots\dots\dots\dots\dots\dots \quad [1.4]$$

where $\underline{Y}_t = (y_1, y_2 ... y_n)$ is the output, $\underline{X}_t = (x_1, x_2 ... x_n)$ is the input, Q denotes a mathematical transformation, and $\underline{\theta} = (\theta_1, \theta_2 ...)$ are the model parameters.

Model uncertainty refers to the fact that all models are simplifications of reality and, thus, introduce distortion. Therefore, we can say that we are always working with a model $Q(\cdot)$, which is an approximation of the correct relationship $Q(\cdot)$. The parameters in the model must be estimated from data and have sampling variation. If they were calculated using different periods of record, different estimates would result. Therefore, simulations are carried out using estimated parameters $\hat{\theta}_1, \hat{\theta}_2 ....$ This parameter variation would occur even if we knew the "true" model. Finally, distribution functions obtained by Monte Carlo simulation are obtained from a finite sample and, therefore, have sampling errors. For example, let

$$F(z) = P(Y_t < z) \quad \dots\dots\dots\dots\dots\dots\dots\dots\dots\dots\dots\dots\dots\dots\dots \quad [1.5]$$

In Monte Carlo simulation n values of Y_t would be generated and $\hat{F}(z)$ would be estimated by n_z/n where n_z is the number of times that $Y_t < z$. $\hat{F}(z)$ has a sampling variance dependent on n even if Q and $\underline{\theta}$ are known with certainty.

Stochastic models in hydrology will be discussed in detail in Chapter 2.

HYDROLOGIC MODELS AS COMPONENTS OF
WATER RESOURCE SYSTEM MODELS

Although it is true that models are necessary for understanding hydrologic phenomena, in engineering we are interested in models as tools to be utilized in the optimum operation of a system, say onfarm water management or design and operation of specific watershed projects, or in guiding public policy decisions. In this context, hydrologic models of small watersheds are only components in integrated models of water resource systems. The concept of a water resource system is very general. It can include everything from an individual field up to a major river basin with many dams, water treatment plants, and other structures. A water resource system is defined as any system involving transport, storage, and change in properties (temperature or dissolved and suspended constituents) of water. Inputs to the system include controlled inputs, such as labor and materials, and uncontrolled inputs, such as precipitation and solar radiation. Outputs include water at places or times or water of a quality that is more highly valued by society than in the natural state.

Because in general there is an infinite number of combinations of input variables and output variables, some criterion is needed to choose the best set. The most generally accepted criterion states that the inputs will be chosen to maximize the welfare of those affected by the system—the so-called social welfare criterion. Therefore, models of water resource systems require not only models of hydrologic, biological, and physical systems, but also models describing the aggregate behavior and preferences of man. The social science of economics is concerned with the latter component and is obviously outside the scope of this monograph. The reader can refer to works such as Maas et al. (1962) for discussions that are relevant to the subject of watershed modeling but cannot be considered here.

Although the social welfare criterion seems very abstract, it is general enough to apply to decisions made by an individual. Suppose, for example, that a surface water reservoir is to be built for an individual farm. If the farmer is to pay the entire cost and no other people are adversely affected, the social welfare criterion simply states that the system should be designed so as to maximize the net benefits to the farmer (assuming the free market sets prices for the inputs and the crops). If both costs and benefits can be stated in monetary terms, this criterion reduces to the familiar profit maximization criterion.

Most water resource systems have external effects; i.e., situations where actions by one decision-maker adversely or beneficially affect others. Under these circumstances, decision-making is much more difficult and usually must involve the political process. Models of watershed systems may then be useful to those who establish governmental policy. The design of control measures for nonpoint agricultural pollution is an important example where modeling can be used to evaluate or compare best management practices.

Both design of individual water projects and the establishment of governmental policy dealing with water can effectively utilize the systems approach.

SYSTEMS APPROACH

The term "systems approach" has been a part of the hydrological and water resource literature for well over ten years, and its implications are generally well understood. The systems approach to a problem involves three steps:

1   describe the system,
2   describe the objective function, and
3   optimize the system.

The first step, which has already been discussed is, of course, crucially important. It involves modeling the watershed system. If the mathematical models describing the system are incomplete or badly distorted, the decisions made are likely to be incorrect.

The second step, choice of an objective function, is also extremely important. A poor choice can result in nonsensical decisions even if the system description and the optimization techniques are of the highest caliber. In water resource systems the objective function is normally stated in economic terms, e.g., "minimize the sum of damages due to flooding and costs of flood control" rather than in physical terms, "minimize flooding." A careful examination of objectives stated in physical terms usually reveals that they are not a precise statement of society's preferences and are usually ridiculous if taken to extremes.

The final step, optimization, is required if, in fact, a system is to be "best" in some sense. While the knowledge of the model builder may be useful in optimization, it is essentially a purely mathematical process and does not contribute to hydrologic theory directly.

The first step, description of the system, will be covered thoroughly in this monograph. The second two steps will be considered in less detail.

DESIGN

Those who design water resource systems are major users of watershed models. Design problems may be classified into three groups:
1   Long-run design problems,
2   intermediate-run problems, and
3   short-run problem or operating procedure.

Design of a multiple purpose reservoir is an example of a long-run design problem. A substantial capital investment must be made early in the life of the project, and benefits will be realized over a long time — perhaps 50 yr or more. An example of an intermediate-run problem is: given the quantity of water in storage in a reservoir system, what combination of irrigated crops and dry land crops should be planted next year? An example of a short-run problem is: how much water should be released from a flood control reservoir tomorrow?

Each of these problems requires hydrologic modeling. The long-run study requires information on reservoir inflows and demands for water. If records are available, stochastic models might be used to generate several sets of sequences of inputs to develop estimates of the reliability of reservoir yield for alternative reservoir capacities. Long records are usually not available for small watersheds, however, so integrated watershed models might be used in conjunction with precipitation records to estimate inflows.

The intermediate-run problem could involve the use of a static regression model, a conceptual or physically-based integrated watershed model, or possibly a global model. The short-run problem can be solved by using an integrated watershed model or a stochastic global model. Models required for design of on-farm water management systems will be much simpler than those used for larger scale design, and they may be presented in hand-book form.

Public policy decisions often require estimates of the magnitude of changes that will occur if land management practices are changed. Physically-based models are most suitable for this application.

CHOICE OF MODELS

In the following chapters models of hydrologic components as well as integrated models of watersheds will be discussed in considerable detail. Models of processes that change the properties of flowing or stored water, i.e., erosion, sediment transport, and chemical transport, will also be discussed.

A model of a system as complex as a small watershed will describe individual components with varying detail. Some components may have a strong theoretical basis, whereas others are rather crude approximations. This is a natural part of model development. As we gain more knowledge about a particular component, we tend to replace the empirical, lumped models with physically-based distributed elements. There is a limit to this process, however, because theoretical, distributed formulations require more input data and more computer time for simulation.

In most situations there will be several alternative models that could be used. The choice of the best model depends to a large extent on the problem. Obviously the best model changes as the problem changes. Objective methods of choosing the best model have not yet been developed, so this choice remains a part of the art of hydrologic modeling. Dawdy and Lichty (1968) suggest four criteria that can be used to choose between alternative models:

1 **accuracy** of prediction
2 **simplicity** of the model
3 **consistency** of parameter estimates
4 **sensitivity** of results to changes in parameter values.

Accuracy of prediction of system outputs is obviously very important. It is desirable that models developed by research be tested in such a manner that error statistics are known. All other factors being equal, the model with minimum bias and error variance would be superior. Simplicity refers to the number of parameters that must be estimated and the ease with which the model can be explained to clients or public bodies. Again, all other factors being equal, one should choose the simplest model. Consistency of parameter estimates is an important consideration in developing conceptual models using parameters estimated by optimization techniques. If the optimum values of the parameters are very sensitive to the particular period of record used, or if they vary widely between similar watersheds, the model will probably be unreliable. Finally, models should not be extremely sensitive to input variables that are difficult to measure.

Even though the above criteria are related, and obtaining an unambiguous ranking is impossible, they should be considered when a model is being chosen. In most situations there will be several alternative models that might be used. The final choice of the "best" model will depend on the problem, the resources available to the analyst, the time frame available, the input resources available, and on a number of other implicit criteria like experience and maybe even "horse sense."

In the following chapters, many of the concepts only mentioned in this chapter will be presented in detail. The reader should then be well equipped to select, evaluate, or even develop hydrologic models of small agricultural watersheds.

References

1 Clarke, R. T. 1973. Mathematical models in hydrology. Irrigation and Drainage Paper 19, Food and Agriculture Organization of the United Nations, Rome, Italy. 282 pages.

2 Dawdy, D. R., and R. W. Lichty. 1968. Methodology of hydrologic model building. *In* The use of analog and digital computers in hydrology. Int. Assoc. Sci. Hydrol. Symp. Proc., Tucson, AZ, 2(81):347-355.

3 Dooge, J. C. I. 1973. Linear theory of hydrologic systems. Technical Bull. No. 1468, USDA, ARS, Washington, DC, 327 pages.

4 Hempel, C. G. 1963. Explanation and prediction by covering laws. *In* B. Baumrin (ed.), Philosophy of science: The Delaware seminar, Interscience. John Wiley and Sons, NY and London, pp. 107-133.

5 Horton, R. E. 1931. The field, scope and status of the science of hydrology. Trans. Am. Geophys. Union 12:189-202.

6 Maas, A., M. M. Hufschmidt, R. Dorfman, T. A. Thomas, Jr., S. A. Marglin, and G. M. Fair. 1962. Design of water-resource systems. Harvard University Press, Cambridge, MA, 620 pages.

7 Ozga-Zielinska, Maria. 1976. Structure and operator functions of mathematical models of hydrologic systems. J. Hydrol. Sci. (Poland), 3(1,2):1-20.

8 Rosenblueth, A. and N. Wiener. 1945. Role of models in science. Phil. Sci. 7(4):316-321.

chapter 2 ▬▬▬▬▬▬▬▬▬▬▬

STOCHASTIC MODELS IN HYDROLOGY

2

STOCHASTIC MODELS IN HYDROLOGY

by   D. G. DeCoursey, Research Leader, Agricultural
      Research Service, USDA, Fort Collins, CO 80522;
      J. C. Shaake, Jr., Chief, Hydrological Services
      Division, National Weather Service, Silver Springs,
      MD 20910; E. H. Seely, Hydraulic Engineer,
      USDA Sedimentation Laboratory, Oxford, MS
      38655

Stochastic—from the Greek word Stochastikos meaning skillful in aiming. If an individual were shooting at a target, it is likely that the density of hits near the center would be greatest and least near the edge. The location of the hits would be random with respect to the center. Thus, the word stochastic has come to refer to the random nature of a variable. In watershed models, it refers to the spatial and temporal randomness of hydrologic processes, such as streamflow and precipitation.

INTRODUCTION

The remaining chapters of this Monograph deal with problems and approaches used in modeling hydrologic systems and components. In general, they describe the physical processes involved in the movement of water and pollutants onto, over, and through the soil surface. Quite often the hydrologic problems we face do not require a detailed discussion of the physical process, but only a time series representation of these processes. Stochastic models may be used to represent, in simplified form, these hydrologic time series. Precipitation, streamflow, temperature, and other series may be viewed as examples of stochastic processes.

Stochastic modeling places emphasis on the statistical characteristics of hydrologic processes. Some background in probability and statistics is necessary to fully understand this chapter. However, references and examples throughout the chapter should give readers with a more limited background an appreciation of the role of stochastic models in hydrology. Three very useful texts, Haan (1977) and Yevjevich (1972a and b) describe the use of stochastic processes in hydrologic modeling. Box and Jenkins (1976) and Ciriani, Maione, and Wallis (1977) and good references from which much of the material in this chapter is drawn. Lawrence and Kottegada (1977) cover the same material, as applied to streamflow, but give a more complete analytical treatment. Matalas (1975) describes the state of the art in the field of stochastic hydrology. Applications of stochastic processes in all fields of water resources are presented in an extensive compilation of articles by Shen (1976). Since this chapter concentrates on the basic concepts of stochastic processes and not on models of specific processes, details of such models are not described. Many such models are described in the Proceedings of a USDA-Agricultural Research Service sponsored Symposium on Statistical Hydrology (1974).

The material presented in this chapter can be divided into three major parts. The first part is a discussion of the statistical properties of hydrologic time series. In this part we cover such items as event time and discrete time, first and second order distribution properties, joint distribution properties, long term properties such as the Hurst effect and variance function, and different forms of asymmetry. The next part of the chapter is a discussion of the many different kinds of stochastic models that are available. The models discussed include short memory processes such as the moving average, autoregressive, mixed autoregressive moving average, and autoregressive integrated moving average. Long memory models such as fast fractional Gaussian noise, filtered fractional noise, broken-line, and some forms of the autoregressive moving average processes are described. Following a comparison of some of the short and long memory models, the generation of daily data by models such as the shot noise process is described. Finally the disaggregation process and space-time rainfall models are presented. The last part of the chapter is concerned with the subject of model selection and parameter estimation. Topics covered include incomplete data sets; properties of parameter estimates such as bias, minimum variance, and consistency; discussion of random number generators and several different methods of parameter estimation. The estimation methods described include the method of moments, method of least squares, method of maximum likelihood, and the methods of Bayesian statistics.

ROLE OF STOCHASTIC MODELS IN WATERSHED MODELING

The term "watershed modeling" has a very broad connotation. It is used here to refer to analytical simulation of the processes that take place in natural watersheds. The models are developed for many different reasons and therefore have many different forms. However, they are in general designed to meet one of two primary objectives. The role of stochastic processes is different in each.

One objective of watershed modeling is to gain a better understanding of the hydrologic phenomena operating in a watershed and of how changes in the watershed may affect these phenomena. Models created for this purpose are generally physically based, deterministic models. The hydrologic phenomena they simulate are generally defined by the laws of continuity, energy, and momentum. Such models are used primarily in the analysis of individual events, although continuous simulation models have been developed. As such these models are seldom used to generate synthetic data. Stochastic processes may be used to add the dimension of spatial and temporal variability to the various subprocesses such as infiltration, rainfall, temperature, evapotranspiration, and solar radiation. Other than some work in rainfall and infiltration, this application of stochastic processes is in its infancy and is not discussed in this chapter.

Another objective of watershed modeling is the generation of synthetic sequences of hydrologic data for facility design or for use in forecasting. Models created for these purposes vary from very deterministic forms, using much information about the physical processes involved, to "black box" forms, where the physical processes are not involved. Most of these models are of a parametric type in which some elements of the hydrologic system are combined and less detail about the internal structure of the model is presented. Stochastic inputs to such models depend upon the structure of the model.

Models that are relatively simple, for example those that calculate annual runoff from annual rainfall, have simple stochastic input requirements. In that example, a scheme for generating sequences of annual rainfall would provide the input. As models become more complex, input stochastic data also become more complex. For example, assume that a watershed model

has been designed to generate as output the entire hydrograph of flow for a period of many years. A model such as this might use hourly rainfall, windspeed, relative humidity, variable flow resistance coefficients, few of which could be considered independent. The stochastic generator for this model would very likely need to be a complex multivariate model.

Some watershed models, designed to provide synthetic sequences of hydrologic data, may be entirely stochastic. In such models little is assumed as to the internal structure of the model. They are based entirely on the statistical parameters of the historic data to which they are fitted. For example, monthly runoff at a streamflow station, synthesized by a pure stochastic process, would likely be based on the mean, standard deviation, and serial correlation of the data from the station.

STATISTICAL PROPERTIES OF HYDROLOGIC TIME SERIES

The purpose of a stochastic model is to represent important statistical properties of one or more time series. Indeed, different types of stochastic models are often studied in terms of the statistical properties of time series they generate. Examples of these properties include: trend, seasonality, mean, variance, skewness, serial correlation, covariance, cross-correlation, and long term properties such as the rescaled range and the variance function. Since the various statistical models are described in terms of these properties, the appropriate stochastic model and numerical values of the model parameters may be inferred from statistics of the observed time series. Because the above mentioned properties are well described in the references cited above, they will not be discussed here. However, before reviewing the different types of models used in hydrology, some distribution properties of stochastic processes will be discussed. These are presented because of their importance in structuring the data sets prior to model selection or fitting.

Event and Discrete Time Series

Two types of time series, event and discrete, occur most often in hydrology. Event series occur when the possible states of a system are finite. This commonly occurs in precipitation modeling, when each day is considered either wet or dry. The series of wet/dry events constitutes an event series. Discrete series occur when the random variate in the time series is continuous, but for computation and analysis purposes time is considered discrete. Streamflow, for example, is continuous but since the data are presented in hourly, daily, or monthly series, they form a discrete series.

First-order Distribution Properties

When studying hydrologic events, only one of many possible realizations of a phenomenon can ever be observed; e.g., the observed record at a streamflow measuring station. Nevertheless, to understand the theory of stochastic processes, it is necessary to assume that other realizations could have occurred but did not. The observed record plus these other, hypothetical realizations form an ensemble of records or sample functions that define the stochastic process. One way to visualize more than one sample function, from an ensemble, would be to take a very long record of streamflow data and break it up into a number of 10-year long pieces. Fig. 2-1 illustrates a few realizations (or sample functions) of such a stochastic process for annual streamflow.

If we wished to know the distribution of events that could occur at a

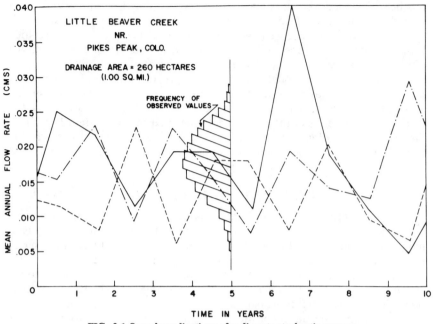

FIG. 2-1 Sample realizations of a discrete stochastic process.

given time in these sequences of events, it could be obtained by plotting a histogram of the observations at that time in the sequence (see Fig. 2-1). By letting the flow interval used to characterize the histogram be Δq, then in a limit as the number of sequences becomes very large and as the histogram interval, Δq, becomes very small, this histogram of random variables approaches a continuous function known as a first-order probability density function (pdf). Formally this can be expressed as

$$f_1(q,t) = \lim_{\substack{m \to \infty \\ q \to 0}} \frac{r}{\Delta q} \quad \dots\dots\dots\dots\dots\dots\dots\dots\dots\dots\dots\dots\dots \quad [2.1]$$

where r is the fraction of m values having, at time t, an amplitude lying between q and q + Δq (Freeman, 1963). This first order density function has the property that

$$\int_{-\infty}^{\infty} f_1(q,t) \, dq = 1 \quad \dots\dots\dots\dots\dots\dots\dots\dots\dots\dots\dots\dots \quad [2.2]$$

Although the specific properties of $f_1(q, t)$ depend on the data and application, most hydrologic data have common properties. Among these are moments of $f_1(q, t)$ which may or may not vary with time, t. Hydrologic data often have seasonal and/or other trends that cause the mean and variance to change with time.

If the mean (first moment) of the series $f_1(q, t)$ does not vary with time, the process is said to be stationary in the mean or first order stationary. If the covariance of the process is independent of time in the sequence where it is calculated, but depends only on the lag, then the series is said to be stationary in the variance and covariance. If the series is stationary in both the mean and covariance, it is said to be second order or weakly stationary. If the series is stationary on higher order moments, and also in the mean and covariance, the series is higher-order stationary; sometimes called strong stationarity or stationary in the stricter sense.

If the mean varies with time, i.e., shows a trend, the process can be expressed as the sum of two components

$$q_t = \mu_t + x_t \quad \dots\dots\dots\dots\dots\dots\dots\dots\dots\dots\dots\dots\dots \quad [2.3]$$

where μ_t is the mean, which changes with time, and x_t is a random stochastic component with zero mean. The mean, μ_t, of this process is often referred to as a deterministic component. Such deterministic components can be treated in several ways. One way is as a polynomial

$$\mu_t = \mu_0 + \sum_{i=1}^{n} \alpha_i t^i \quad \dots\dots\dots\dots\dots\dots\dots\dots\dots\dots \quad [2.4]$$

where μ_0 is a constant (the long term mean value) and α_i are coefficients; t is time. Seasonal fluctuation in the mean, variance, and higher moments may be treated in a similar fashion. If the data are in the form of monthly records, then the trend or deterministic component may very likely have an annual cyclic pattern caused by seasonal changes. Most hydrologic records, such as stream flow and temperature, show these trends. Polynomials, Fourier transformations, or other periodic functions can be used to describe these patterns and subtract them from the record, such that the remaining component is stationary in the mean.

Another way to remove seasonal effects is to standardize the original series, q_t, by forming a new series, x_t. For example, in the case of monthly data

$$x_t = \frac{q_t - \mu_i}{\sigma_i} \quad i = 1,\dots 12 \quad \dots\dots\dots\dots\dots\dots\dots\dots\dots \quad [2.5]$$

where μ_i and α_i are the monthly means and standard deviations of q_t and i is a monthly index. A major disadvantage of this approach, when compared to use of a polynomial or Fourier series, is that many more parameters are required, for example, j parameters for each month where j is the number of moments of interest.

Second-order Distribution Properties

Natural hydrologic processes are usually serially correlated. A particularly good example is stream flow during low flow periods when groundwater drainage into the channel is dominant. Serial correlation is the relation of a value at one time t_1, to values at another time, t_2. This relationship is expressed, formally, in a second-order probability density function (pdf)

$$f_2(q_1, t_1; q_2, t_2) = \lim_{\substack{m \to \infty \\ q_1 \to 0 \\ q_2 \to 0}} \frac{r}{\Delta q_1 \Delta q_2} \quad \dots\dots\dots\dots\dots\dots\dots\dots \quad [2.6]$$

where r is the proportion of m sequences having values between levels of q ranging from q_1 to $q_1 + \Delta q_1$ at time t_1, and ranging between q_2 and $q_2 + \Delta q_2$ at time t_2 (Freeman, 1965). (Note that q_1 and q_2 refer to values of q at different times not to different sample functions). Integration of the second order density function with respect to either of the two time periods leads to the first order density function at the other time

$$\int_{-\infty}^{\infty} f_2(q_1,t_1;q_2,t_2) \, dq_2 = f_1(q_1,t_1) \quad \cdots\cdots\cdots\cdots\cdots\cdots \quad [2.7]$$

The serial dependence between two values of the same processes, q_t, at times t_1 and t_2 is usually measured either in terms of the autocovariance

$$\gamma(t_1, t_2) = E \left\{ (q_{t_1} - \mu_{t_1})(q_{t_2} - \mu_{t_2}) \right\}$$

$$= \int_{-\infty}^{\infty} \int_{-\infty}^{\infty} q_{t_1} - \mu_{t_1})(q_{t_2} - \mu_{t_2})f_2(q_1,t_1;q_2,t_2)dq_1 \, dq_2 \quad \cdots\cdots \quad [2.8]$$

where E { } denotes expected value; or the autocorrelation coefficient

$$\rho(t_1, t_2) = \frac{\gamma(t_1, t_2)}{\sigma_{t_1} \cdot \sigma_{t_2}} \quad \cdots\cdots\cdots\cdots\cdots\cdots\cdots\cdots\cdots\cdots\cdots \quad [2.9]$$

Other properties of the second order pdf, $f_2(q_1, t_1; q_2, t_2)$, have not been developed to the point of practical value in hydrology; only the autocovariance and the autocorrelation are used.

As mentioned previously, if the serial dependence between values at two times, t_1 and t_2, does not depend on the time reference t_1 or t_2 but only on the differences, $t_1 - t_2$, i.e., the lag, k, the process is said to be stationary in the covariance. Stationarity in both the mean and covariance is referred to as weak or second order stationarity. Practically all useful theory of stochastic processes assumes second order stationarity.

Joint Distribution Properties

The joint probability density function described in this section concerns the probability relationship between two or more independent stochastic processes. It should not be confused with a joint pdf of stochastic processes that are not independent, such as streamflow at nearby locations. The first-order joint density function for two such processes q_t and p_t is defined by

$$f_{11}(q,t_1;p,t_2) = \lim \frac{r}{\Delta q \, \Delta p} \quad \cdots\cdots\cdots\cdots\cdots\cdots\cdots\cdots\cdots \quad [2.10]$$

$$m \to \infty$$
$$q \to o$$
$$p \to o$$

where r is the proportion of m pairs of sequences having values between q and $q + \Delta q$ at time t_1 and between p and $p + \Delta p$ at time t_2. Note that t_1 and t_2 can be the same but this is not necessary.

The serial dependence between values of the two processes at times t_1 and t_2 is usually measured in terms of the cross-covariance, $\gamma(q, t_1; p, t_2)$, or the cross-correlation, $\rho(q, t_1; p, t_2)$. If the serial dependence between p and q depends only on the difference $t_1 - t_2$, and not on a reference time t_1 or t_2, the process is stationary in the cross-variance.

If the stochastic processes are not independent, then in general, the cross-correlation between the two processes must be defined in terms of the direction of the lag, i.e., $t_1 - t_2$ or $t_2 - t_1$

$$\rho(q,t_1;p,t_2) \neq \rho(q,t_2;p,t_1). \quad \dotfill \quad [2.11]$$

In other words, the cross-correlation between, say, rainfall on day t_1 and runoff on day t_2 (say 1 day later) is not the same as the cross-correlation between rainfall on day t_2 and runoff on day t_1 (1 day earlier). This is the case even if the process is stationary.

Long-term Properties

Interest in sustaining water needs through reservoir storage, where demand approaches mean annual streamflow, and interest in extended periods of low flow both require that we investigate the long term statistical properties of hydrologic series.

The Range of Cumulative Deviations from the Mean (the Hurst Effect): The reservoir storage capacity required to supply water at the mean inflow rate during a period is related to the cumulative deviations of the flow from its long term mean. If a series of stream flow data are expressed as their deviations from the mean and these values are cumulated and plotted, the series will show maximum and minimum cumulative departures. The range of these cumulative departures, R, depends upon the length, n, of the period and is defined as

$$R = \Delta Q \max - \Delta Q \min \quad \dotfill \quad [2.12]$$

where

$$\Delta Q \max = \text{Max} \left(\sum_{t=0}^{n} (q_t - \bar{q}) \right) \quad \dotfill \quad [2.13]$$

$$\Delta Q \min = \text{Min} \left(\sum_{t=0}^{n} (q_t - \bar{q}) \right) \quad \dotfill \quad [2.14]$$

If the process is Guassian and serially uncorrelated, the expected value of the rescaled range, R/σ, divided by the standard deviation of the series is

$$E \left\{ R/\sigma \right\} = \sqrt{\frac{\pi}{2} n} = 1.25 \sqrt{n} \quad \dotfill \quad [2.15]$$

for large values of n, Siddiqui (1976). Also see the comment following equation [2-18].

Experience with sample values of this statistic from long records of streamflow data, tree ring patterns, and the thickness of annual mud layers (mud varves) in ancient lake beds show that $R/\sigma \sim n^H$ where $0.5 \leqslant H \leqslant 1.0$.

H, known as the Hurst coefficient, is named after the man who did most to establish its existence, Hurst (1950). In his analysis and that of many others, a value of H = 0.7 has been found, Lloyd (1967). The deviation of H from 0.5, which would be its value for a purely Gaussian process, has led to an extensive dialogue among hydrologists regarding long term properties of alternative stochastic models.

The relation between the range and period of record with H = 0.7 cannot be attributed to any specific physical process. It can be caused by (a) a particular type of infinite memory, not likely in most hydrologic systems; (b) nonstationarity of the mean, a very likely possibility; (c) results from various combinations of specific storage systems, a likely possibility in hydrologic systems; or (d) other processes such as a non-Gaussian distribution or temporal dependence. No matter what the cause or the argument, various mathematical schemes have been proposed to generate data that have these characteristics. Fractional Brownian noise, FB_n, discussed by Mandelbrot and Wallis (1968) is described in this chapter along with several approximations that are efficient computer algorithms. FB_n assumes a form of infinite memory. Klemes (1974) and Potter (1976) describe how nonstationarity of the mean provides a possible explanation of the Hurst phenomenon and how it can be introduced into the generating scheme. Boes and Salas (1978) proposed a mixture model for shifting levels in which Klemes' and Potter's approaches are special cases. Siddiqui (1976) argues that other statistics, in addition to H, should be considered before rejecting Gaussian models and accepting schemes designed to reproduce the Hurst phenomena.

The true cause of the Hurst Phenomenon will probably never be uncovered; however it exists, and in many cases should be considered in the generation of synthetic traces. Several of the procedures discussed in this chapter or in the literature are available to generate such traces.

The Variance Function: Of interest in watershed studies is the variance of the sum of a sequence of observations, e.g., 30 day flow accumulations. Adjusted for the mean, this statistic is known as the variance function. The variance function, $\Gamma(N)$, is the variance of the sum of N consecutive observations of a stationary, zero mean, stochastic process.

$$\Gamma(N) = \text{Var} \sum_{i=t+1}^{t+N} x_i \quad\dots\dots\dots\dots\dots\dots\dots\dots\dots\dots\dots \quad [2.16]$$

If the sequence of observations is Gaussian and serially uncorrelated, the variance function is

$$\Gamma(N) = N\sigma^2 \quad\dots\dots\dots\dots\dots\dots\dots\dots\dots\dots\dots\dots \quad [2.17]$$

where σ^2 is the variance of the N observations. Expressing equation [2-17] differently,

$$\frac{\sqrt{\Gamma(N)}}{\sigma} = \sqrt{N} \quad . \quad\dots\dots\dots\dots\dots\dots\dots\dots\dots\dots\dots \quad [2.18]$$

By comparing equations [2-15] and [2-18], we can see for the Gaussian, serially uncorrelated process that the square root of the variance function divided by the standard deviation is proportional to $E\{R/\sigma\}$, the rescaled range divided by the standard deviation.

Asymmetry

Each of the models discussed in the following sections applies to zero mean processes, equivalently, to deviations of a process about appropriate mean values. More especially, they apply only to Gaussian processes, where all random variables are normally distributed. Third and higher order moments are not accounted for. Since most hydrologic data are not Gaussian but skewed, problems of asymmetry must be addressed.

Skewed hydrologic data can come from two sources. One source is a distribution of events that has an extremely large number of either high or low events in proportion to other events in the population. The distribution of daily rainfall amounts, for example, is positively skewed—it has a long tail to the right—in the direction of large rainfall values. Another source of skewness is the occurrence of an extremely large number of events of the same magnitude—zero values of daily flow or rainfall. In some cases, a large number of events of the same magnitude may indicate the sample contains two populations that should be treated separately.

Asymmetrical Distribution of Events: There appear to be two fundamental approaches to solution of the skewness problem. One is to transform the data to produce normal variates and then model the transformed data. The other is to model the data without transformation, accounting for skewness by using skewed random deviates. Intuitively, the second approach seems more logical, but the first is more practical.

A data transformation is performed to create a new process

$$y = g(x) \dots\dots\dots\dots\dots\dots\dots\dots\dots\dots\dots\dots [2.19]$$

such that y is normally distributed. Widely used transformation in hydrology include the logarithmic transformation

$$y = \ln(x + a) \dots\dots\dots\dots\dots\dots\dots\dots\dots\dots [2.20]$$

and the Box-Cox transformation (Box and Cox, 1964)

$$y = (x + a)^b \dots\dots\dots\dots\dots\dots\dots\dots\dots\dots [2.21]$$

The coefficients a and b are selected to produce a normally distributed data set. An appropriate stochastic model is selected to represent y. Parameters of the stochastic model are estimated from the transformed historic data. Synthetic traces of x are formed from generated values of y by applying the inverse transformation.

The main argument against transforming the data before estimating model parameters is that a difference is observed between generated and historical moments, and this difference occurs in the untransformed domain. In other words the final generated values do not have the same population moments as the historical data. This occurs because analytical relationships between population moments across a variable transformation do not apply to sample moments, i.e., the moments obtained from observed records. Hence, appropriate moments to use in the transformed domain, in order to preserve exactly the original sample moments, can only be derived with the aid of these analytical relationships and the original sample moments, not from the sample moments of transformed data. This is demonstrated for the mean and standard deviation in the case of the logarithmic transformation by Matalas (1967) and Fiering (1967).

Balancing this argument are several important counter arguments. First, it is well known that moments are very inefficient statistics for parameter estimation with skewed data. In particular, the skewness coefficient for small samples is both biased and extremely unstable. Recent literature suggests the skewness coefficient to be so unreliable as to be meaningless. Therefore, whereas preserving skewness is important, preserving the exact value of the historical coefficient is not. Accordingly, to avoid making the parameters of the transformation too sensitive to the historical skewness coefficient graphical procedures can be used to normalize the data, i.e., selection of a and b in the Box-Cox transformation. Second, in the special case of streamflow generation, low flows tend to be more correlated than high flows during the same time of year. Nonlinear transformations tend to preserve this phenomenon, whereas it cannot be preserved without varying the correlation coefficient if the data are not transformed. Third, in multivariate problems there are many third moment relationships involving more than one variable. These cannot be preserved without transformation. Fourth, extremely highly skewed random deviates are sometimes needed to generate skewed data, i.e., skewness coefficients greater than 20. Last, generation of skewed random deviates is computationally inefficient.

Large Numbers of Zero Values: Quite frequently hydrologic data such as daily rainfall (amounts and intensity), evaporation, runoff from intermittent streams, and sediment loads have extensive periods of zero values. Unless the number of values is small, an attempt should be made to handle them. Analyses of daily rainfall, for example, is one case where it must be considered. The most commonly used approach in this case is to use Markov chains. Gabriel and Neuman (1962) suggested the use of a two state Markov chain of transition probabilities from a wet to dry or dry to wet conditions;

$$\begin{array}{cccc} & \text{future state} & & \\ & 0 & 1 & \\ \text{Present} & 0 \quad 1-\alpha & \alpha & \dots\dots\dots\dots\dots\dots\dots\dots\dots\dots\dots\dots\dots\dots [2.22] \\ \text{State} & 1 \quad \beta & 1-\beta & \end{array}$$

in which 1 is a wet state, 0 is a dry state, α is the probability of a wet day following a dry day, and β is the probability of a dry day following a wet day. This form of model has been used successfully by several investigators; DeCoursey and Seely (1969), Caskey (1963), Weiss (1964), Todorovic and Woolhiser (1974) and Nicks (1974). Others such as Cooke (1953) and Jorgensen (1949) were not entirely satisfied with it. Haan et al. (1976) used a 7×7 transition matrix to represent the probability of rainfall on day $j+1$ given that rainfall on day j was in any one of 7 different size classes; 0, 0-0.02, 0.03-0.06, 0.07-0.14, 0.15-0.30, 0.31-0.62, and ≥ 0.63. The method of maximum likelihood was used to find the transition probabilities. Separate matrices were defined for each month and for seven different precipitation stations. Therefore, 84 different 7×7 transition matrices were needed. Results were satisfactory with a slight overprediction of about 2.5 percent on an annual basis.

The use of transition matrices to handle dry periods of rainfall appears to be generally satisfactory for single station evaluation but extension to a multi-station situation would lead to an extremely large number of transition probabilities. For example, only a two state model would require

$$P = 2^{2n} \quad \dotfill \quad [2.23]$$

transition probabilities where n is the number of stations. Another problem with this approach is that these transition probabilities are seasonal and should be evaluated monthly, thus requiring some type of smoothing to handle inconsistencies between months.

Wiser (1974) used a negative binomial distribution to estimate aerial amounts of precipitation. Parameters of the distribution are obtained by two transformations of a "storminess" parameter. The numbers of zero-value events are a function of the transformation parameters.

In Arizona, the probability of occurrence of a significant rainfall event is extremely seasonal with almost all events falling in the period from June through October. Osborn et al. (1974) used a continuously varying probability of occurrence of an event for this period of time. The occurrence or lack of occurrence of an event on any given day is obtained by generating random numbers in the interval between 0 and 1. If the value of the generated number is less than or equal to the probability of occurrence on the given date, an event is generated.

Todorovic and Woolhiser (1974) developed a general form for the distribution of total precipitation during a given n-day period. The mean value and variance of the distribution were also determined. The expressions were applied to three different sequences of events: (a) the sequence of events is bionomial i.e., the events are identically distributed random variables, (b) the sequences of events are independent random variables, and (c) the sequence of events is the 2 state Markov chain of Gabriel and Newman (1962). In each of the three cases an analytical expression for the mean and variance of the number of events in the given n-day period is determined.

Richardson (1977) and Kelman (1977) proposed an alternative approach to modeling intermittent series, which may be applicable to a wide range of hydrologic processes. In their approach, an intermittent process of short intervals of zero values, or nonzero values as the case may be, is the truncated part of a nonintermittent, discrete time series. For example, in the case of rainfall values, the probability distribution of nonzero values is considered as the tail or a part of a truncated distribution [See Fig. 2-2, which was taken from Richardson (1977)]. Both papers describe how to estimate parameter values for multistation, time-dependent conditions, which preserve the lag and cross-correlation characteristics of the original data set. Richardson uses the multivariate procedure described by Matalas (1967) (See the section in this chapter on autoregressive models) to generate the synthetic traces that preserve both the run characteristics of zero-value days and the rainfall amounts and distribution. It is possible that this same approach can be applied to runoff processes in ephemeral channels that have zero values, especially if the runoff values are normally distributed or a transformation can be found that will fit a truncated normal distribution (See Fig. 2-3).

STOCHASTIC MODELS

Discrete stochastic models may be classified in many ways. In this chapter we subjectively decided to classify them as short memory or long

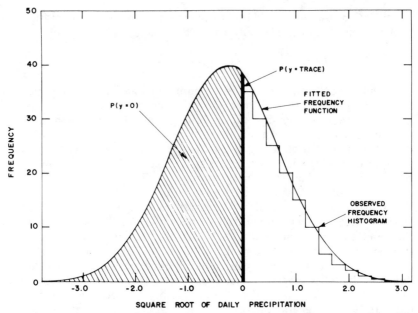

FIG. 2-2 A truncated normal distribution of daily precipitation. A square root transformation was used to normalize the precipitation (From Richardson, 1977, Fig. 2-3).

memory models. Attempts to reproduce long term characteristics such as the Hurst phenomena, previously described, distinguish the long memory from short memory models. Since these long memory models encompass an important group of processes, this classification has been used. Stochastic models may apply only to one variable or site (univariate) or simultaneously

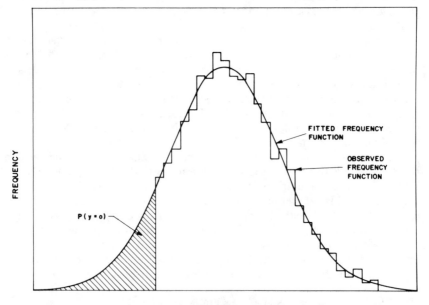

FIG. 2-3 A truncated normal distribution of monthly flow volumes. Values of monthly flow are normalized by a transformation.

to many variables or sites (multivariate); and they may or may not be sequential. Short memory models of hydrologic phenomena include the moving average processes, autoregressive processes, and mixed autoregressive-moving average (ARMA) processes. Each of these models is sequential and may be univariate or multivariate. Long memory models include fractional Gaussian-noise models; broken line processes; and, depending on parameter values, certain autoregressive integrated moving average (ARIMA) models. They may be univariate or multivariate and are sequential. A nonsequential model that may have either long or short memory and be univariate or multivariate is the disaggregation model. Finally, a different class of models dealing with space time rainfall is presented. All of these models are reviewed briefly in the following sections.

SHORT MEMORY MODELS

Moving Average Processes

The moving average has frequently been used to smooth various types of hydrologic time series such as daily or weekly air temperature, evaporation rates, wind speed, etc. The weighting factor for such smoothing was either 1 or $1/n$ where n is the number of events in the moving average. The moving average process used in the stochastic generation hydrologic data is somewhat different. In this use, the moving average process describes the deviations of a sequence of events from their mean value. The weighting factors for the sequence are not necessarily equal, nor do they need to add up to one, nor for that matter, need they be positive.

The moving average model is the simplest short memory model and expresses a sequence of events (i.e. annual flows) in terms of deviations at time t, $\tilde{z}_t$, from the mean, μ, of the process or sequence of events, z_t;

$$\tilde{z}_t = z_t - \mu \quad\dotfill\quad [2.24]$$

The deviation from the mean of the process is expressed as a finite weighted sum of elements plus a random element, a_t.

$$\tilde{z}_t = a_t - \theta_1 a_{t-1} - \theta_2 a_{t-2} - \cdots - \theta_q a_{t-q} \quad\dotfill\quad [2.25]$$

in which the θ_i are the weighted parameters and the a_{t-i} are random elements (white noise). Equation [2-25] represents a moving average process of order q. It embodies $q + 2$ parameters, μ, θ_1, ..., θ_q, and the variance of a_i, σ_a^2, that must be estimated from data sets, before it can be used in practice. In this model, the mean of $\tilde{z}_t$ is zero; μ is the mean about which the process, z_t, varies.

The lag-k auto-covariance of the process is

$$\gamma_k = E\left\{\tilde{z}_t \tilde{z}_{t-k}\right\}$$

or

$$\gamma_k = E\left\{(a_t - \theta_1 a_{t-1} - \cdots - \theta_q a_{t-q})(a_{t-k} - \theta_1 a_{t-k-1} - \cdots - \theta_q a_{t-k-q})\right\}$$

$$\dotfill\quad [2.26]$$

$$= (-\theta_k + \sum_{j=1}^{q-k} \theta_j \theta_{j+k}) \sigma_a^2 \quad 1 \leqslant k \leqslant q \quad \dots \dots \dots \dots [2.27]$$

$$= 0 \qquad\qquad\qquad k > q.$$

Since $\gamma_o = \sigma_z^2$, the variance of z_t is found by letting $k = 0$ in equation [2.26]. Because the a_i are independent random normal deviates, the E $\{a_i^2\} = \sigma_a^2$ and E $\{a_i a_j\} = 0$ for $i \neq j$. Thus the variance of $\tilde{z}_t$ is

$$\sigma_z^2 = \gamma_0 = (1 + \theta_1^2 + \theta_2^2 + \dots + \theta_q^2) \sigma_a^2 \quad \dots \dots \dots \dots \dots [2.28]$$

From this equation the variance of the deviates is found to be

$$\sigma_a^2 = \frac{\gamma_0}{(1 + \theta_1^2 + \theta_2^2 + \dots + \theta_q^2)} \quad \dots \dots \dots \dots \dots [2.29]$$

The auto-correlation function is defined as

$$\rho_k = \frac{\gamma_k}{\gamma_0} \dots \dots \dots \dots \dots \dots \dots \dots \dots \dots \dots \dots \dots [2.30]$$

which, upon substitution of equation [2-27], shows the auto-correlation function to be zero beyond lag q.

As an example, let $q = 2$, $\theta_1 = \theta_2 = 0.5$, and $\sigma_a^2 = 1$; then the variance γ_o of the process would be:

$$\gamma_0 = 1.5,$$

the lagged auto-covariances would be

$$\gamma_1 = -0.25$$

$$\gamma_2 = -0.50$$

$$\gamma_k = 0, k > 2,$$

and the auto-correlations would be

$$\rho_0 = \frac{1.5}{1.5} = 1$$

$$\rho_1 = \frac{-0.25}{1.5} = -\frac{1}{6}$$

$$\rho_2 = \frac{-0.50}{1.5} = -\frac{1}{3}$$

$$\rho_k = 0 \qquad k > 2.$$

In order to use the moving average process to generate a synthetic series, estimates, $\hat{\theta}_i$, of θ_i must be estimated. If only one or two terms are needed, graphical procedures may be used to obtain the minimum sum-of-squares estimates. See section 7.1.6 of Box and Jenkins (1976). If more than two terms are needed and a rigorous solution for the θ_i values is desirable, Box and Jenkins should be consulted. See in particular pp. 187-189, 202, 231-233, 245, 255-256, 269-273 for methods used to identify the order of the process and estimation of the model parameters.

Autoregressive Processes

Another model that has been used rather extensively in hydrologic analyses is the autoregressive model. Even though some of the models to be discussed later in this chapter offer improvements over the autoregressive model, it is still a very useful tool in the simulation of hydrologic and climatological data. As with the moving average process, this model works with deviation, $\tilde{z}_t$, from the mean, μ, of the process or sequence of events, z_t. However, the autoregressive process expresses the deviation from the mean of the process, as a finite weighted sum of previous deviation plus a random variate, a_t. Thus

$$\tilde{z}_t = \phi_1 \tilde{z}_{t-1} + \phi_2 \tilde{z}_{t-2} + \ldots + \phi_p \tilde{z}_{t-p} + a_t \quad \ldots\ldots\ldots\ldots \quad [2.31]$$

is an autoregressive process of order p. It contains $p + 2$ parameters, μ, ϕ_1, ϕ_2, ..., ϕ_p, and σ_a^2 that must be estimated from a given data set. The mean of the sequence of events is μ, the weight factors are ϕ_i, and the variance of the random variate a_i is σ_a^2.

The lag k auto-covariance, γ_k, of $\tilde{z}_t$, i.e., $\gamma_k = E\{\tilde{z}_t \tilde{z}_{t-k}\}$ can be obtained by multiplying both sides of equation [2-31] by $\tilde{z}_{t-k}$ and taking expected values

$$E\{\tilde{z}_t\tilde{z}_{t-k}\} = E\{\phi_1 \tilde{z}_{t-1}\tilde{z}_{t-k} + \phi_2\tilde{z}_{t-2}\tilde{z}_{t-k} + \ldots + \phi_p \tilde{z}_{t-p}\tilde{z}_{t-k}$$

$$+ a_t z_{t-k}\} \cdot \quad \ldots\ldots\ldots\ldots\ldots\ldots\ldots\ldots\ldots\ldots\ldots\ldots \quad [2.32]$$

This results in the lag-k auto-covariance difference equation

$$\gamma_k = \phi_1 \gamma_{k-1} + \phi_2 \gamma_{k-2} + \ldots + \phi_p \gamma_{k-p} \quad k > 0 \quad \ldots\ldots\ldots\ldots \quad [2.33]$$

The lag k autocorrelation function, p_k, is obtained by dividing equation [2-33] by γ_o, i.e., $p_k = \gamma_k/\gamma_o$

$$\rho_k = \phi_1\rho_{k-1} + \phi_2\rho_{k-2} + \ldots + \phi_p\rho_{k-p} \quad k > 0 \quad \ldots\ldots\ldots\ldots \quad [2.34]$$

The variance of $\tilde{z}_t$, σ_z^2, is obtained from equation [2-32] by setting $k = 0$

$$\sigma_z^2 = \gamma_0 = \phi_1 \gamma_{-1} + \phi_2\gamma_{-2} + \ldots \phi_p\gamma_{-p} + \sigma_a^2 \quad \ldots\ldots\ldots\ldots \quad [2.35]$$

Equation [2-35] can be used to get the variance of the deviates, σ_a^2

$$\sigma_a^2 = \sigma_z^2 - (\phi_1\gamma_{-1} + \phi_2 \gamma_{-2} + \ldots + \phi_p \gamma_{-p}) \quad \ldots\ldots\ldots\ldots \quad [2.36]$$

Alternatively, the variance of $\tilde{z}_t$, in terms of the auto-correlation coefficient, may be obtained by dividing equation [2-35] throughout by $\gamma_o = \sigma_z^2$, substituting $\gamma_k = \gamma_{-k}$, and rearranging the terms

$$\sigma_z{}^2 = \frac{\sigma_a{}^2}{1 - \rho_1\,\phi_1 - \rho_2\phi_2 - \cdots - \rho_p\phi_p} \qquad [2.37]$$

Equations [2-31], through [2-37] can be used to generate synthetic sequences, for example, annual streamflow; and to calculate statistics of the series, i.e., the variance and the lag k auto-correlation and covariance of the sequences. However, one must have estimates of the mean, the parameters ϕ_i, i = 1, 2...p, and the variance of the deviates. The mean, μ, the variance, σ_z^2, and covariance, γ_k, are estimated from historic data. Equation [2-36] is used to calculate the variance of the deviates. Values of the parameters, ϕ_i, may be calculated as described below using the Yule-Walker Equations.

Equation [2-34] is usually more efficient in solving the Yule-Walker Equations for the ϕ_i. Letting k in equation [2-34] assume values of 1, 2...p, one obtains the following set of equations

$$\rho_1 = \phi_1\,\rho_0 + \phi_2\,\rho_{-1} + \ldots + \phi_p\,\rho_{1-p}$$

$$\rho_2 = \phi_1\,\rho_1 + \phi_2\,\rho_0 + \ldots + \phi_p\,\rho_{2-p} \qquad [2.38]$$

$$\vdots$$

$$\rho_p = \phi_1\,\rho_{p-1}, \phi_2\,\rho_{p-2} + \ldots + \phi_p\,\rho_0$$

Since $\rho_o = 1.0$ and $\rho_{-1} = \rho_1$, the equation becomes

$$\rho_1 = \phi_1 + \phi_2\rho_1 + \ldots + \phi_p\rho_{p-1}$$

$$\rho_2 = \phi_1\,\rho_1 + \phi_2 + \ldots + \phi_p\rho_{p-2} \qquad [2.39]$$

$$\vdots$$

$$\rho_p = \phi_1\,\rho_{p-1} + \phi_2\,\rho_{p-2} + \ldots \phi_p$$

In matrix notation these equations are

$$[P]\,[\phi] = [\rho]$$

in which $[\mathbf{P}]$ is the p $\times$ p autocorrelation matrix, $[\phi]$ is the p $\times$ 1 vector of unknown parameters, and $[\rho]$ is the p $\times$ 1 vector of autocorrelation coefficients. By pre-multiplying both sides of equation [2-39] by $[\mathbf{P}]^{-1}$, one obtains

$$[P]^{-1}\,[P]\,[\phi] = [P]^{-1}\,[\rho] \qquad [2.40]$$

or

$$[I]\,[\phi] = [P]^{-1}\,[\rho] \qquad [2.41]$$

and

$$[\phi] = [\mathbf{P}]^{-1} [\rho]$$ .... [2.42]

where $[\mathbf{P}]^{-1}$ is the inverse of the lag-k autocorrelation matrix and $[\mathbf{I}]$ is the identity matrix.

Thus the vector of unknown coefficients $\phi_1, \phi_2, ..., \phi_p$ is obtained by pre-multiplying the vector of auto-correlation coefficients by the inverse of the auto-correlation matrix.

Box and Jenkins (1976), p. 189, 243-245, 253-254, 274-283, describe more rigorous methods of identifying the order of the process and methods of estimating the parameters, ϕ_i. Both maximum likelihood and Bayesian processes are considered.

Of particular importance in hydrologic studies are first and second order processes; very seldom are higher orders needed. Thus the following equations may be used to calculate parameters for simple first or second order autoregressive data generation schemes.

Using the previous equations, a first-order autoregressive process, $\tilde{z}_t = \phi_1 \tilde{z}_{t-1} + a_t$, has the properties

$$\sigma_z^2 = \frac{\sigma_a^2}{1 - \sigma_1^2},$$ .... [2.43]

$$\phi_1 = \rho_1 ,$$

and the lag k autocorrelation function $\rho_k = \phi^k$.

Second-order autoregressive processes, $\tilde{z}_t = \phi_1 \tilde{z}_{t-1} + \phi_2 \tilde{z}_{t-2} + a_t$, have the properties

$$\phi_z^2 = \frac{\sigma_a^2}{1-\rho_1\phi_1-\rho_2\phi_2},$$

$$\phi_1 = \frac{\rho_1 (1 - \rho_2)}{1 - \rho_1^2},$$

$$\phi_2 = \frac{\rho_2 - \rho_1^2}{1 - \rho_1^2},$$ .... [2.44]

or

$$\rho_1 = \frac{\phi_1}{1 - \phi_2},$$

$$\rho_2 = \phi_2 + \frac{\phi_1^2}{1 - \phi_2},$$

and

$$\rho_k = \phi_1 \rho_{k-1} + \phi_2 \rho_{k-2}$$

Matalas (1977) discusses the autoregressive model and some of its weaknesses as well as corrections that should be applied to the coefficients to correct for bias in estimates of the moments.

Frequently it is useful to be able to generate synthetic traces at several streamflow stations or raingage sites or the generate synthetic traces of several different meteorological parameters. Matalas (1967, 1977) discusses extension of the lag-1 autocorrelation model to the multi-(n)-site situation. The general model is

$$X(t) = AXt-1) + B\epsilon(t) \quad \dots\dots\dots\dots\dots\dots\dots\dots\dots\dots\dots\dots \quad [2.45]$$

Where $X(t)$ and $X(t-1)$ are vectors of stream flow deviates (or any other variable) from their mean at the n sites at time t and t-1 respectively, A and B are $n \times n$ matrices of coefficients, and $\epsilon(t)$ is an $n \times 1$ vector of random normal variates (one for each station). The coefficient matrices are calculated by the method of moments as follows

$$A = M(1) \ M(0)^{-1} \quad \dots\dots\dots\dots\dots\dots\dots\dots\dots\dots\dots\dots\dots \quad [2.46]$$

and

$$BB^T = M(0) - M(1) \ M(0)^{-1} \ M(1)^T = C \quad \dots\dots\dots\dots\dots\dots \quad [2.47]$$

where $M(0)$ is the (lag-zero) variance-covariance matrix of streamflow deviates (or any other variable) at the n sites, and $M(1)$ is the lag 1 cross-covariance between sites. The C matrix equal to BB^T is obtained by evaluating the right hand side of the equation. The diagonal elements of the matrix are the lag 1 autocovariance at each of the sites. Note that the lag 1 cross-covariance $\gamma(i, j)$ is not equal to $\gamma(j, i)$; that is, $M(1)$ is not symmetric. The exponents -1 and T denote the inverse and transpose of a matric, respectively. Values of the B matrix may be obtained from $BB^T = C$ by principal component analysis (Matalas, 1967).

Synthetic flows generated using equation [2-45] will resemble the corresponding historical flow sequences in terms of the means, variances and lag 1 cross-covariance. If the variance of the flow at time t, with the flow at the same station at time t-1 (the lag 1 autocovariance) and not the variance of the flow at time t with the flow at the other stations at time t-1 (the lag 1 cross-covariance) is of interest, equation [2-44] may be written as

$$X(t) = \tilde{A}X(t-1) + \tilde{B}\epsilon(t) \quad \dots\dots\dots\dots\dots\dots\dots\dots\dots\dots \quad [2.48]$$

where $\tilde{A}$ is the diagonal matrix of first order auto-correlation coefficients at the n sites and $\tilde{B}$ is defined by the solution of

$$\tilde{B}\tilde{B}^T = M(0) - \tilde{A} \ M(0) \ \tilde{A}^T \quad \dots\dots\dots\dots\dots\dots\dots\dots\dots \quad [2.49]$$

Matalas (1977).

If proper transformations are used, as described previously in the chapter, the skewness coefficients of the historic records will also be retained in the synthetic traces. See Matalas (1967, 1977) for additional discussion of these multi-site autoregressive models.

Ciriani et al. (1977) and papers by Finzi et al. (1977a, b, c) describe two computer programs (MALSAK and SPUMA) that can be used to evaluate the parameters of the autoregressive models previously described. Finzi et al. (1975) also discuss the use of SPUMA and some of the limitations of autoregressive processes. The correlation structure, means, standard deviations, extreme values, and internal consistency are all examined and examples are shown of the type of discrepancies that were observed in using a first order autoregressive model on the Arno and Tiber River Basins. These discrepancies should be noted because the SPUMA model should develop sequences that retain these characteristics.

Mejia et al. (1974b) extends the concepts used in multisite data generation to a similar concept in the multivariate generation of mixtures of normal and log-normal variables preserving the characteristics discussed by Matalas (1977).

In the previous discussion of autoregressive processes, no comment was made relative to the seasonal variations in the structure of the mean, variance, skewness and the auto and cross-correlation of variables. These variations do exist and values of model parameters can be estimated on a monthly basis. For further discussion see DeCoursey (1971), Matalas (1967, 1977), Fiering (1964, 1967), Thomas and Fiering (1962) and Yevjevich (1964). It is also possible to use Fourier Series to fit the seasonal variation in parameter values, thus reducing the total number of parameters needed to describe a hydrologic system (Richardson, 1977).

Mixed Autoregressive Moving Average (ARMA) Processes

Previous discussions of the moving average and autoregressive-type models describe methods that can be used to fit these models to a given data set. The number of elements included in both the moving average and autoregressive processes, q and p respectively, are not limited by either method. Thus, unless one knows, a priori, what model a data set conforms to, experimental error could lead to selection of a model with several parameters, whereas a much simpler model with fewer parameters would have been adequate. Use of a model containing unnecessary parameters can lead to poor estimation. Thus, in the development of a stochastic model, one should attempt to obtain an adequate but parsimonious model.

Box and Jenkins (1976) show that it is possible to express a moving average process as an autoregressive process and vice versa. For example, a single term moving average process, MA(1), can be expressed as an infinite autoregressive process. In this case, the autoregressive model would not be parsimonious. Similarly, it is not possible to represent a single term autoregressive process, AR(1), parsimoniously by a moving-average process. Thus, in the practical solution to many hydrologic problems, it may be necessary to include both autoregressive and moving average terms to obtain a parsimonious model.

Box and Jenkins (1976) describe such a composite model by expressing the deviation of a variate from its mean, $\tilde{z}_t$, as a finite weighted sum of previous deviations plus a finite weighted sum of random variates plus a random element a_t. Thus

$$\tilde{z}_t - \phi_1 \tilde{z}_{t-1} - \cdots - \phi_p \tilde{z}_{t-p} = a_t - \theta_1 a_{t-1} - \cdots - \theta_q a_{t-q} \quad \cdots \cdots \cdots [2.50]$$

is an autoregressive moving average [ARMA (p, q)] model of autoregressive order p and moving average order q.

The autocorrelation function for the ARMA process is presented in Box and Jenkins (1976, pp. 74, 75). The first q autocorrelations depend on the choice of the q-moving average parameters as well as on the p-autoregressive parameters. Beyond lag-q, the autocorrelations obey a p-th order difference equation analogous to a p-th order autoregressive process.

Of particular interest in the generation of hydrologic data is the ARMA (1, 1) process. Equation [2-50] becomes

$$\widetilde{z}_t - \phi_1 \widetilde{z}_{t-1} = a_t - \theta_1 a_{t-1} \quad \dots\dots\dots\dots\dots\dots\dots\dots\dots \quad [2.51]$$

Use of the equation requires estimates of μ, ϕ_1, θ_1, and σ_a^2. Initial estimates of these may be obtained from the fact that an ARMA (1, 1) process has the properties

$$\sigma_z^2 = \gamma_0 = \frac{1 + \theta_1^2 - 2\phi_1\theta_1}{1 - \phi_1^2} \sigma_a^2, \quad \dots\dots\dots\dots\dots\dots\dots \quad [2.52]$$

$$\rho_1 = \frac{(1 - \phi_1\theta_1)(\phi_1 - \theta_1)}{1 + \theta_1^2 - 2\phi_1\theta_1}, \quad \dots\dots\dots\dots\dots\dots\dots \quad [2.53]$$

and

$$\rho_k = \phi_1 \rho_{k-1} \quad k \geqslant 2. \quad \dots\dots\dots\dots\dots\dots\dots \quad [2.54]$$

The parameter values are bounded by $[\phi_1] < 1$ for the process to be stationary and $[\theta_1] < 1$ for the moving average operator to be invertible [Box and Jenkins (1976) p. 51 and 76]. It follows then that ρ_1 and ρ_2 must lie in the region

$$|\rho_2| < |\rho_1| \quad \dots\dots\dots\dots\dots\dots\dots\dots\dots\dots\dots \quad [2.55]$$

$$\rho_2 > \rho_1 (2\rho_1 + 1) \quad \rho_1 < 0 \quad \dots\dots\dots\dots\dots\dots\dots \quad [2.56]$$

$$\rho_2 > \rho_1 (2\rho_1 - 1) \quad \rho_1 > 0 \quad \dots\dots\dots\dots\dots\dots\dots \quad [2.57]$$

Identification of the form of a general ARMA (p, q) process is more difficult as described in Box and Jenkins (1976). In addition to a complete discussion of the identification of the general model, computer programs for parameter estimation are also described. (pages 190-192, 245, 257, 495-516) Initial estimates of parameters of simple models such as the AR(2), MA(2) or ARMA (1, 1) processes can be obtained from charts and tables (pages 201, 518-520). Matalas (1977), Finzi et al. (1977a) and O'Connell (1977b) describe the ARMA (1, 1) process, and its application in hydrology. In the following section, autoregressive integrated moving average models (ARIMA) are described. Since the ARMA model is a special case of the ARIMA model, no further discussion is presented in this section. The latter part of the next section discusses more thoroughly the estimation of parameters and applications of the ARMA as well as the ARIMA models.

Autoregressive Integrated Moving Average (ARIMA) Processes

Hydrologic data such as flow records, temperature, rainfall etc. exhibit seasonal and other cyclic patterns. These patterns can be eliminated from the data by seasonal transformation to zero mean and unit variance

$$z_t = \frac{q_t - \bar{q}_j}{\sigma_j} \qquad \dots \dots \dots \dots \dots \dots \dots \dots \dots \dots \dots \dots \dots \dots \dots \dots \quad [2.58]$$

where j denotes the jth period in the cycle. Such transformations require many parameters especially if monthly patterns are present (See previous discussion).

Many parts of the country have exhibited trends or changes in land use. Frequently this change was necessary to effectively utilize a deteriorated land resource. It can come as a gradual trend or be quite rapid. For example, many parts of the country are now in grass and timber production, that 30 to 50 years ago were in agricultural crops such as cotton, corn or small grains. The result of this change was a decrease in the volume of both water and sediment production. In the last few years the price of soybeans led to reversal of this trend, and a move from grass production to soybean production is again leading to increased runoff and sediment from the agricultural land.

Both the effects of a trend that is not seasonal and cyclic seasonal patterns in the mean can be removed by a proper differencing of the data set, i.e., the subtraction of a value from its previous value or its value j units apart. If this has been properly done, (See Box and Jenkins, 1976, or McKerchar and Delleur, 1974) then the data set will be a stationary series, and the moving average, autoregressive, or the mixed autoregressive moving average models can be used to describe the process. In this case, the mixed model is known as an autoregressive moving-average (ARIMA) model.

Box and Jenkins (1976) discuss the ARIMA (p, d, q) model expressing the d-th order differences of a series z_t as an ARMA (p, q) model. In general this type of model is of much more value in forecasting than in simulation. Therefore the bulk of the discussion concerns ARIMA (1, 0, 1) or equivalently the ARMA (1, 1) processes.

O'Connell (1977b) discusses application of ARIMA type models in synthetic hydrology. He states that in general most hydrologic phenomena, particularly runoff, can be expressed as an ARIMA (1, 0, 1) process. This process should resemble the historic sequence in terms of the mean, variance, lag-one autocorrelation and the Hurst phenomena (one significant reason for considering this model). However, in a discussion of annual flows based on short historic sequences, he shows that, even though the estimate of the mean will be unbiased, the variance, lag-one autocorrelation, and Hurst coefficient will be biased. Therefore, by using Monte Carlo methods, he developed a set of tables that can be used to select ϕ and θ such that short-run resemblance between historic and synthetic flows is maintained. See following sections of this chapter for further discussion of bias.

O'Connell (1977b) discusses the use of the ARIMA (1, 0, 1) model in generating monthly flow records that retain seasonality in the monthly means and standard deviations. The monthly data were first transformed to remove the skewness, then the transformed values were standardized using means and standard deviations of the transformed monthly data. The ARIMA (1, 0, 1) model was then applied to the standardized values. Problems often encountered in applying the Box-Jenkins moment estimation procedure for ϕ

and θ are circumvented by a simple procedure first described by Finzi et al. (1977b) and included in the MALSAK program previously mentioned.

O'Connell (1977b) also extends the ARIMA (1, 0, 1) model to multisite data generation. Solution of the matrices involved are discussed in his Ph.D. dissertation (O'Connell, 1974).

Since use of O'Connell's model is only slightly more complicated than the lag-one Markov process and includes many desirable features, it should have application in water resource planning. However, the U. S. Geological Survey, in recent experience with the multi-site model, found extending it beyond 3 sites impossible (personal communication).

Previous discussions have been directed toward use of ARIMA models in data synthesis. Some researchers have also looked at use of ARIMA models in forecasting. McKerchar and Delleur (1974) compares a second-order autoregressive model with 27 parameters, operating on standardized monthly flow data to an ARIMA model that required only 4 parameters. Forecasting with both models tended toward the monthly means as the lead time increased. The autoregressive model forecasts also tended toward the monthly standard deviations. However, because the ARIMA model did not account for seasonal variability in monthly standard deviations, the forecasting errors could not be associated with physical reality. The ARIMA model used by McKerchar and Delleur is more complex than those previously described, but is presented in their paper and in Box and Jenkins (1976).

Mejia et al. (1975) demonstrated the use of ARIMA type models in simulating or predicting fluctuations in water quality parameters of the Passaic River. Different forms of th ARIMA model were best suited to different parameters. Daily flow residuals were represented by an ARIMA (2, 1, 0) model, daily water temperature by an ARIMA (1, 0, 1) model, and daily Biochemical Oxygen Demand and oxygen deficit by ARIMA (1, 0, 0) models.

Hipel et al. (1977a) and McLeod et al. (1977) in a series of 2 papers discuss fairly completely the most recent developments in Box-Jenkins, modeling including the problems of model identification, parameter estimation, and diagnostic checking. They demonstrate these stages of model development in analyzing flow of the St. Lawrence River, annual sun-spot numbers and one of Box and Jenkins original examples, that of airline passenger data. Other applications in the field of hydrology include Carlson et al. (1970), Hipel et al. (1977b), McMichael and Hunter (1972), and Tao and Delleur (1976a). Boes and Salas (1978) propose a mixture model for shifting levels and show that the Hurst phenomena, as explained by either non-stationarity of the mean or a moving average process, is a special case of their model.

LONG MEMORY MODELS

Long memory models are specifically designed to reproduce the Hurst phenomena (Mandelbrot and Wallis, 1968). This is accomplished by several means even though the concepts or causes of the phenomena are not known. The Markov models, previously described for short memory processes, have been used successfully for the last 15 to 20 years to simulate various types of hydrologic data for one or more sites. This experience has shown that they can faithfully produce the high-frequency components of the data sets but they fail to produce the extremely low-frequency components typified by the

Hurst phenomenon. Multilag models have attempted to account for the low frequency components, but they are generally not satisfactory for the very low frequency response to which this section of the chapter is devoted.

Discrete fractional Gaussian noise (dfGn) is one of the approaches considered. It is Gaussian random processes with a kth order autocorrelation coefficient (Mandelbrot, 1971, p. 543) given by

$$\rho(k) = \frac{|k + 1|^{2H} - 2|k|^{2H} + |k - 1|^{2H}}{2} . \qquad \dots \dots \dots \dots \dots \dots \qquad [2.59]$$

It has a single parameter, H, the Hurst coefficient, which in most hydrologic applications has a value in the interval $0.5 \leqslant H \leqslant 1.0$. The process (equation [2-59]) was invented by Mandelbrot to model the variance of phenomena characterized by long run effects in which the cumulative influence of very small serial correlations between remote values is non negligible.

Construction of a sample function of dfGn involves the summation of an infinite number of components: therefore, approximations of dfGn are used to limit the number of components. However, the number of operations must be high enough to preserve the desired value of H if long term properties of a series are of interest. The order required tends to increase in proportion to the total length of period, T, to be simulated (Mandelbrot, 1971, p. 546; Fiering, 1967, p. 85, Fig. 3.8).

Mandelbrot and Wallis (1969) proposed approximations to dfGn which were referred to as Type-1 and Type-2. Type-1 has never been used because it proved to be computationally expensive. The Type-2 process, which reproduces the Hurst coefficient if the generated length of the sequences is to be considerably less than the memory of the process, did not prove to be applicable in hydrology because a large number of terms are necessary to maintain the lag 1 autocorrelation coefficients of most historical sequences. Matalas and Wallis (1971) applied a filtering procedure to minimize these deficiencies and adapted it to multisite generation of synthetic flows. The generated sequences resemble the corresponding flows in terms of station estimates of the mean, variance, skew, lag 1 autocorrelation, the Hurst coefficient and the lag-zero covariance between stations. See the discussion of filtered fractional noise (ffn) models below.

Fast fractional Gaussian noise (ffGn) processes (Mandelbrot, 1971) had also been used to approximate dfGn. Two other alternative processes for approximating dfGn processes have been proposed. One is known as the broken line process (blp). It was introduced by Mejia et al. (1972). The other is the ARIMA process previously described.

The ffGn, ffn, and blp processes are similar in that they rely on multiple, independent input series of white noise (as compared to the single input series used by the MA, AR, ARMA and ARIMA models). Each white noise series in input to a separate "subsystem" and the outputs of these subsystems are superimposed to form approximations to dfGn. The ffGn, ffn and blp differ only in detail of these subsystems; however, the blp produces a continuous approximation having some interesting crossing properties, whereas the ffn and ffGn models produced a discrete series.

In addition to the above approximations of fractional Gaussian noises, the autoregressive moving average model (ARMA) and the autoregressive integrated moving average model (ARIMA) have also been found to exhibit the

Hurst phenomenon (O'Connell, 1974, 1977b). Even though the variance, σ^2, lag 1 autocorrelation coefficient, $p(1)$, and the Hurst coefficient, H, are biased for the conventional ARIMA (1, 0, 1) process, O'Connell (1974, 1977b) describes how the parameters θ and ϕ may be selected such that resemblance of all quantities μ, σ^2, $p(1)$, and H will be retained in the synthetic flows. Tables for this purpose were generated by O'Connell using Monte Carlo methods (O'Connell, 1974). Since the ARMA and ARIMA models were discussed previously, they will not be discussed further in this section. However, a brief discussion of the ffGn, ffn, and blp models follows.

Fast Fractional Gaussian Noise Processes

Fast fractional Gaussian noise (ffGn) models are discrete approximations to theoretical fractional Gaussian noise. They are made up of three components: (a) An independent autoregressive process, $\rho_h X_h(t-1)$, used to obtain the high frequency effects, not present in the low frequency term, but necessary for discrete time fractional Brownian motion; (b) A low frequency or long-run-effects term, to reproduce the low frequency properties of the covariance function, formed by superimposing weighted outputs from a parallel set of first order autoregressive processes, $\Sigma W_j [\rho_j X_j(t-1) + \varepsilon_j(t)]$ (see Fig. 2-4); (c) A random element $\varepsilon_h(t)$. The model is defined as

$$X(H,t) = \rho_h X_h (t-1) + \sum_{j=1}^{N} W_j[\rho_j X_j(t-1) + \epsilon_j(t)] + \epsilon_h(t) \dots \dots \quad [2.60]$$

where $X(H, t)$ has mean 0 and variance 1; ε_h and ε_j are independent Gaussian processes of mean 0 and variance 1; ρ_h is a function of the Hurst coefficient, H, the number of terms used in the approximation, N, and a "base" value, B; ρ_j is a function of B only; and W_j is the weighting factor for the jth autoregressive process. Each of the autoregressive processes in the long run effects term have successively longer memories (Fig. 2-4).

The number of AR(1) processes required for the long run effects term is expressed as

$$N = \log (QT)/\log (B) \quad \dots \dots \dots \dots \dots \dots \dots \dots \dots \dots \dots \dots \quad [2.61]$$

where T is the maximum duration of the period of interest, B is the "base" value ($B > 1$) controlling the separation of individual AR(1) "decay" parameters, and Q is a "quality" parameter controlling the number of AR(1) processes needed for a given B value (see Mandelbrot (1971) for more explanation). As B approaches 1, Q increases and the approximation becomes more accurate because more AR(1) processes are included. Sufficient accuracy for most practical applications should be achieved if $Q = 6$ and $B = 3$. If these values are used, then

$$N \simeq 2 \log (6T) \quad \dots \dots \dots \dots \dots \dots \dots \dots \dots \dots \dots \dots \dots \dots \quad [2.62]$$

To place this in perspective, note that: if $T = 1000$, $N < 8$; if $T = 100$, $N < 6$; and if $T = 10$, $N < 4$.

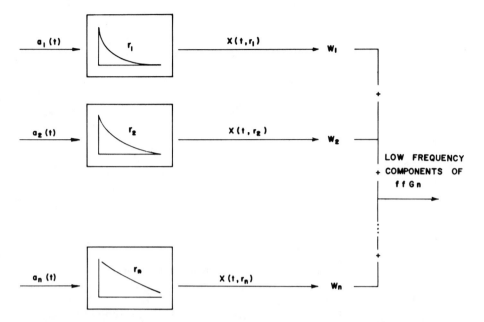

FIG. 2.4 Representation of the low frequency component of fast fractional Gaussian noise as a weighted superposition of independent lag-one autoregressive processes.

The weights applied to each autoregressive subsystem output are obtained from

$$W_n{}^2 = \frac{H(2H-1)\,(B^{1-H} - B^{H-1})}{\Gamma(3-2H)}\; B^{2(H-1)n}, \; 1 \leqslant n \leqslant N \quad \dots \dots \dots \quad [2.63]$$

where Γ denotes the Gamma function.
The autoregressive correlation parameter is

$$\rho_n = \exp(-B^{-n}) \quad \dots \dots \dots \dots \dots \dots \dots \dots \dots \dots \dots \dots \dots \quad [2.64]$$

See Mandelbrot (1971) and Lawrence and Kottegoda (1977) for additional information on B and calculation of ρ_n. Chi et al. (1973) demonstrate how to use the model in simulation and describe all of the steps necessary. Using these steps, the ffGn is probably the best of the discrete fractional Gaussian noise models.

Skewed sequences of ffGn can be generated, if desired, by the methods discussed in the section on asymmetry, that is, using log normal transformation of a normally distributed ffGn sequence (Lettenmaier and Burges, 1977b). The usual problems of maintaining the autocorrelation function through a nonlinear transformation are to be expected (Mejia and Rodriguez-Iturbe, 1974a). The transformation also causes somewhat similar problems in values of the Hurst coefficient. Burges and Lettenmaier (1975) present tables that can be used to select values of the Hurst coefficient of the normal ffGn data, H_y such that the Hurst coefficient of the transformed ffGn data, H_x, will be the desired value.

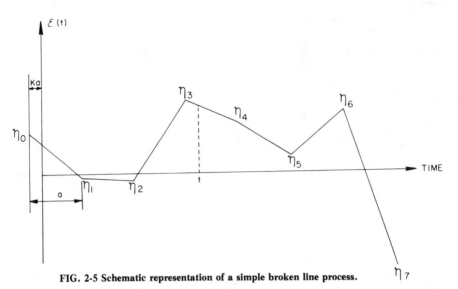

FIG. 2-5 Schematic representation of a simple broken line process.

Filtered Fractional Noise Processes

The sequence of values, X_1, X_2 ..., of a filtered fractional noise process, a modification of the Type 2 process discussed previously, are generated by applying a set of weights, W_i, successively to a sequence of independent random variables, $\varepsilon(i)$. The generating equation for the value of X at time t is

$$X_t = (H-0.5) \sum_{i=pt-M}^{pt-1} W_i \varepsilon(i) \qquad 0.5 < h < 1.0 \quad \ldots\ldots\ldots\ldots\ldots \quad [2.65]$$

where

$$W_i = (pt-i)^{H-1.5} \quad \ldots\ldots\ldots\ldots\ldots\ldots\ldots\ldots\ldots\ldots\ldots\ldots\ldots\ldots \quad [2.66]$$

where M, the memory of the system, (usually much longer than the period to be generated, that is several thousand) is a function of the Hurst coefficient, H, and the lag-k autocorrelation coefficient; p is an integer greater than one. The weights, $(pt-i)^{H-1.5}$, vary in value from nearly zero to one. Matalas and Wallis (1971) derived values of the mean, variance, skewness, and lag-one autocorrelation coefficient for this model and expressed equation [2-65] in terms of these parameters. Estimated values of the parameters plus the value of H may then be used to generate synthetic sequences. However, if short sequences are generated, values of the variance, skew, lag-one autocorrelation and Hurst coefficients must be adjusted for bias as described by Matalas (1977). A major disadvantage of using this model is that it is computationally expensive because of the large number of terms added to produce the synthetic sequence; M may take on values from 1000 to as high as 50,000.

Broken-line Processes

A broken-line process consists of the summation of a finite number of simple broken-line processes (Mejia et al., 1972). The simple broken-line process (Fig. 2-5) is a sequence of intersecting line segments in which the time projections between intersections are of the same length, a. The values of the process $\varepsilon(t)$ at the intersections are independent and are identically distributed random variables, π, with zero mean and unit variance; that is the line segments join values of the random variables spaced at equal time intervals of length a. The starting point of the process is offset from time zero by a random value less than a, ka where k is a random variable uniformly distributed over the range 0-1. Offset of the starting point is necessary to make the process stationary. The value of the process at any time t (see Fig. 2-5) is obtained by linear interpolation along the line between values preceding and following it. The equation for the simple broken line process is given by

$$\xi(t-ka) = \sum_{n=o}^{\infty} \left\{ \eta_n + (\eta_{n+1} - \eta_n)(\frac{t-na}{a}) \right\} \cdot I_{[na,(n+1)a]}(t) \quad \cdots \quad [2.67]$$

Where the parameters are as described above. The indicator function, $I_{[na,(n+1)a]}^{[t]}$, is a term to ensure that the interpolation will take place between the proper random variable; $I_{[na,(n+1)a]}^{[t]} = 1$ when $na \leqslant t \leqslant (n+1)a$ and is zero otherwise. Using this expression, the value of the process at a given time t is equal to the value of the random variable just preceding time t: η_n plus the interpolated difference, (η_{n+1}) (t-na/a), between that point and the next.

The broken line process used for simulation consists of a summation of N simple independent processes

$$\beta(t) = \mu_\beta + \sigma_\beta \left(\frac{3}{2}\right)^{1/2} \sum_{i=1}^{N} W_i(a_i) \, \xi_{a_i}(t) \dots\dots\dots\dots\dots\dots\dots [2.68]$$

where μ_β is the mean of the process to be simulated; σ_β is the standard deviation of the process to be simulated; and $W_i(a_i)$ is the weight factor for the ith simple broken line process, $\varepsilon_{a_i}(t)$. The weight factors are normalized such that

$$\sum_{i=1}^{N} [W_i(a_i)]^2 = 1.$$

The time interval between projections, a_i, indicates that the values of both $W_i(a_i)$ and $\varepsilon_{a_i}(t)$ are functions of the value of "a" selected for the process. The factor

$$\left(\frac{3}{2}\right)^{1/2}$$

comes from the fact that the variance of a simple broken line process composed of independent and identically distributed random variables with zero mean and unit variance is

$$\frac{3}{2}$$

Thus, the multiplicative factor

$$\left(\frac{3}{2}\right)^{1/2}$$

adjusts the variance of the broken line processes to a value of 1 before being scaled by the weight factors and standard deviation of the process, σ_β.

The long memory characteristics of this process come from either the time interval between random values of each simple process a_i, the weighting factor $W_i(a_i)$, or both, being allowed to change progressively with i. This is discussed by Mejia et al. (1974a) and Lawrence and Kottegada (1977) in showing how the a_i, $W_i(a_i)$, and N are calculated to maintain the lag-one autocorrelation coefficient and the Hurst coefficient. Mejia et al. (1974a) also discuss (a) generation of the random components such that the skewness coefficient of the historic record is maintained and (b) extension of the process to multisite conditions that will retain the lag-zero cross-correlation coefficients between stations.

The greatest problem associated with use of the broken line process to generate synthetic data appears to be estimation of the parameters; it is not as straight forward as the other methods discussed. Otherwise the method appears to have some advantages, especially if continuous rather than discrete simulation is of interest.

COMPARISONS OF SHORT AND LONG MEMORY MODELS

Many papers describe the models previously discussed and their application, as the numerous references showed; however, few papers compare the various models. Two such papers are Delleur et al. (1976) and Lettenmaier and Burges (1977a). Delleur et al. studied the complexity of stochastic models used for generating or forecasting hydrologic events. They compared properties of autoregressive (AR), moving average (MA), and mixed (ARMA and ARIMA) models of increasing complexity for annual, monthly, weekly, and daily series. They compared several methods of removing seasonal nonhomogeneity of monthly series and investigated seasonality of the coefficients. They also analyzed the issue of long range and short range dependence and compared several time series models. Each of the different models was found to be superior in specific cases, depending upon the use; whether for generating or for forecasting; for short or long time intervals—annual, monthly, or daily series; or for short-range or long-range dependence.

Lettenmaier and Burges (1977a) compared reservoir storage requirements as reflected by the Hurst phenomenon, using the fractional Gaussian noise (fGn) and mixed autoregressive-moving average (ARMA (1, 1)) models. The comparison was made for effective reservoir operation lives of 40 and 100 years. They used the fast fractional Gaussian noise (ffGn) generator to represent the fGn model. At an operating life of 40 years, a value of 0.7 for the Hurst coefficient, and using skewed (three-parameter log normal) models, both models gave nearly identical storage probability distributions. At the 100 year operating life, the ARMA model results differed significantly from the fGn model. However, by combining the low frequency ARMA (1, 1) process with a high-frequency lag-1 Markov process, an ARMA-Markov process, they obtained nearly identical results. Since the mixed ARMA-Markov process is much easier to develop and uses much less computer time to run, we feel it provides an attractive alternative to the fGn model.

DAILY DATA GENERATION PROCESSES

The synthetic generation of series of daily events is an extremely complicated problem for certain types of data. Data which can be considered nearly independent from one day to the next are not particularly difficult and can be handled by any of the previously described processes. However, daily processes such as temperature, solar energy, and stream flow have characteristics that are much more difficult to model. Streamflow, for example, is extremely difficult.

The high degree of persistence, due to the drainage of flood water from the channel system within which it has been stored, makes stream flow difficult to model on a daily basis. Drainage from the channel system is generally several orders of magnitude slower than filling of the system. In some cases the rising side of the hydrograph may last an hour or so on a small watershed, whereas the recession could last as long as 2 or 3 days. During the recession, correlation between the flow for one period and that either preceding or following is very high. The magnitude of the autocorrelation (slope of the recession) is a function of many things such as the irregularity (roughness) of the channel, slope of the channel, size of the channel, temperature of the water, sediment content, and the amount and condition of vegetation on the channel banks. Changes in these factors can cause the autocorrelation coefficients to vary from event to event and seasonally over the annual cycle. Since vegetative conditions, as well as the previous history of flood events, vary from year to year, the autocorrelation coefficients may also not be the same from year to year, or even in the same season.

Streamflow is made up to two components of entirely different character. One component is surface runoff, which is precipitation that, for one reason or another, was not retained on the surface of vegetation or in depressions or did not infiltrate the soil surface. The other component is flow from below the soil surface, which is flow that follows shortly after a rainfall event or flow that may have been retained for a long period of time in deep aquifers. Surface runoff is a nonlinear response due to the high degree of control that solar energy, vegetative growth, evapotranspiration and soil moisture exercise on flow characteristics. Ground water on the other hand is much more linear in response because it acts primarily like drainage from one or more reservoirs. Streamflow can be considered as surface runoff superimposed on subsurface flow confounded by flow into and out of aquifers and channel banks caused by the rising and falling water levels in the channel. The magnitude of the different components varies considerably from one site to another. It can be entirely surface runoff, for example, where streams have small headwater catchments and are in soils of very low permeability, to entirely subsurface runoff such as is experienced in the sandhills of Nebraska or some coastal plains soils of the Southeast.

These characteristics of streamflow make the synthetic generation of daily data extremely difficult. In many respects, the best model of daily data may be obtained from watershed models that attempt to simulate, to some degree, the entire hydrologic process as discussed in other chapters of this book. Depending upon the degree of complexity of the model, stochastic inputs would be climatological features such as precipitation, solar energy, wind, etc. See DeCoursey and Seely (1969) for an example of such a system.

Shot Noise Processes

Examination of a continuous streamflow record shows series of spikes of various heights, followed by exponential decays. Weiss (1973a) used this observation in proposing the use of shot-noise model to represent daily flow records as a stochastic process.

The shot noise model is a continuous time model that assumes the temporal distribution between events and the magnitude of the jump in flow

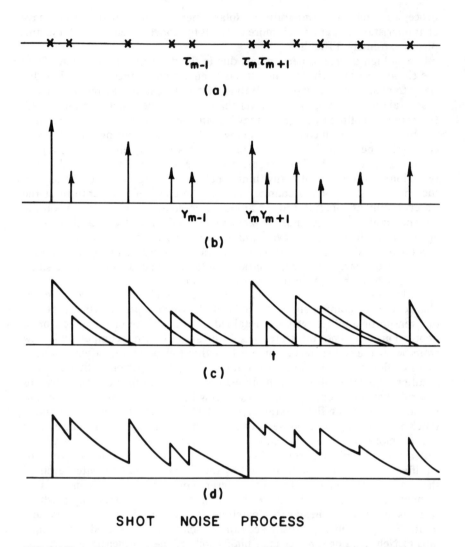

SHOT   NOISE   PROCESS

FIG. 2-6 Shot noise process (a) Events..., τ_m, ... from a Poisson process with rate ν. (b) Jumps..., y_m, ... from an exponential distribution with mean θ. (c) Pulses with values ..., $y_m e^{-b(t-\tau_m)}$..., at time t. (d) Schematic plot of continuous single shot noise process (From O'Connell, 1977, Fig. 2).

values associated with each event, the peak or spike, are exponentially distributed (See Fig. 2-6 taken from O'Connell, 1977a). The absolute value of the flow on any given date is assumed to be a fraction of all previous events (the flow rate on the previous day multiplied by a decay parameter) plus any increase from an event that may have occurred since the previous day. Since the process is continuous in time, more than one event may be generated in the time interval of one day. The generating equations accumulate these, and then discrete values, which are assumed to be based on a daily average, are calculated.

To use the model in generating synthetic data, two highly interrelated processes must be modeled. One is the incremental increase in flow rate

denoted by, x_{t+1}, and the other is the discretized value of the continuous process denoted by, $x(t+1)$, for example, the daily flow values. The following
equations taken from Weiss (1977) describe the two processes. The incremental increase in flow rate is given by

$$x_{t+1} = \frac{1}{b}(1-e^{-b}) x(t) + \sum_{m=N(t)}^{N(t+1)} \frac{1}{b} \left\{ 1-e^{[-b(t+1-\tau_m)]} \right\} y_m \cdots\cdots\cdots \quad [2.69]$$

and the discretized continuous (daily) process is given by

$$x(t+1) = e^{-b}x(t) + \sum_{m=N(t)}^{N(t+1)} e^{[-b(t+1-\tau_m)]} y_m \cdots\cdots\cdots\cdots\cdots \quad [2.70]$$

In equations [2-69] and [2-70], b is the "decay" rate; τ_m is the time of an
event, within the time interval of 1 day, and is calculated as $\tau_{m+1} = \tau_m + E$
where E is pseudorandomly generated from an exponential distribution with
mean $1/v$ (more than one event per day may occur); y_m is the magnitude of
the spike at time τ_m and is generated pseudorandomly from an exponential
distribution with mean Θ; m is a number used to keep track of the number of
events, if any, within the daily interval t to $t+1$; and $N(t)$ is a Poisson process
with rate v. The first term in both equations is the effect of previous events
and the second is the innovation term. Equations [2-69] and [2-70] describe a
continuous time process; however, daily flow values that are normally used in
hydrologic evaluation are average values over the 24 hour period of a day.
Therefore, moments of equation [2-70] that are used for fitting the model to
a data set must be modified to reflect the averaging. Modified values of the
moments are given below. Values of v, Θ and b are calculated from moments
of mean daily flow as

$$\mu_x = \frac{v\theta}{b}, \cdots\cdots\cdots\cdots\cdots\cdots\cdots\cdots\cdots\cdots\cdots\cdots\cdots\cdots\cdots\cdots\cdots \quad [2.71]$$

$$\sigma_x^2 = \frac{v\theta^2}{b} \left(\frac{2(b-(1-e^{-b}))}{b^2} \right), \cdots\cdots\cdots\cdots\cdots\cdots\cdots\cdots\cdots \quad [2.72]$$

and

$$\rho_x(1) = \frac{(1-e^{-b})^2}{2(b-(1-e^{-b}))}; \cdots\cdots\cdots\cdots\cdots\cdots\cdots\cdots\cdots \quad [2.73]$$

where μ_x, σ_x^2, and $\rho_x(1)$ are the mean, variance and lag-1 autocorrelation coefficient respectively of the mean daily flow values, (Weiss, 1973; O'Connell, 1977a). If one were working with instantaneous values from a continuous time process rather than average values, then equations [2-71], [2-72], and [2-73] should not be used. See Weiss (1977) for the correct equations.

Performance of the model as described was not entirely satisfactory because (a) seasonality or periodic structure of μ_x^2, and $\rho_x(1)$ was not adequately modeled and (b) the model did not have the long sustained recessions usually associated with drainage of subsurface aquifers. Therefore, Weiss (1973b, 1977), and O'Connell (1977a) modified the shot noise model by using a Fourier transform to describe the periodic structure of the mean and variance. The recession parameter b was not assumed to be periodic.

A sustained recession was obtained by assuming that streamflow is the sum of two shot noise processes

$$x(t) = x_1(t) + x_2(t) \quad\dots\dots\dots\dots\dots\dots\dots\dots\dots\dots\dots\dots\dots\dots\dots \quad [2.74]$$

where $x_1(t)$ is a rapid response system typical of surface runoff and $x_2(t)$ is a much slower response typical of ground water flow. Three different methods were used to describe such a process, a Second-Order Shot Noise (SOSN) Model, in which the events of the two processes are simultaneous ($\nu_1 = \nu_2$); a Double Shot Noise (DSN) Model, in which the events of the two processes are assumed to be completely independent (a fast and slow process with $\nu_1 > \nu_2$); and a Modified Second Order Shot Noise (MSOSN) Model, which was a compromise between the SOSN and DSN models, Weiss (1977). The MSOSN model was generally superior. In this model $\nu_1 > \nu_2$ and the events of the slow process occur simultaneously with some of the events of the fast process, and the jumps in flow are related by $y_1/y_2 = \Theta_1/\Theta_2$. These parameters are as defined previously.

The various Second Order or Double Shot Noise Models were combined with the seasonal structure and even extended to multi-site conditions that preserved the lag-zero cross correlation coefficients between stations (Weiss, 1973b, 1977). Fitting of such a model to daily hydrologic data is quite complex and can be a laborious task. Therefore, one should seriously consider the use of a watershed model, perhaps with stochastic input rather than a completely stochastic model of daily flow. No matter what approach is taken in the generation of daily synthetic flows, consideration must be given to the physical nature of the streamflow process.

DISAGGREGATION PROCESSES

Many of the models previously discussed cannot be used to generate monthly or shorter time interval data. For example the fGn models, which are based on assumptions of stationarity, cannot preserve seasonal variation. Some of the autoregressive processes take into account seasonal variation by standardization on a seasonal or monthly basis. The ARIMA processes can remove seasonal fluctuation by working with differenced data. But in general, the models that offer the most potential for simulating both the long term and short term properties of hydrologic processes do not preserve seasonal variation. The disaggregation model (a general autoregressive model of which all other autoregressive models are a special case) discussed below is capable of using the output of any model as input and generating a parallel series of seasonal events that aggregate to the original series. Furthermore the model may feed upon itself to further disaggregate the series to monthly, weekly, daily, and hourly events. Structure of the output series is based entirely on the statistical characteristics of the original data set; thus, the model cannot reproduce physical characteristics of a daily streamflow series. It can be used, however, for such things as the generation of hourly rainfall.

Fundamentally, the model disaggregates the annual series into seasonal values by using statistical data that show what fraction of the annual series is attributed to each season. It is made up of two components, a deterministic element that is proportional to the correlation of each season with the annual values, and a random element.

The disaggregation model takes the form (Valencia and Schaake, 1973)

$$Y(t) = AX(t) - BV(t) \quad \dots\dots\dots\dots\dots\dots\dots\dots\dots\dots\dots\dots\dots\dots \quad [2.75]$$

where $Y(t)$ is an $n \times 1$ vector of seasonal values for the tth year, n is the number of seasons in a year (for example, 12 if monthly values are to be generated), $X(t)$ is the value of the annual series for the tth year, $V(t)$ is an $n \times 1$ vector of independently distributed standard normal deviates, A is an $n \times 1$ vector of coefficients, and B is an $n \times n$ matrix of coefficients. The vector A and matrix B are obtained by analysis of N years of the historic data that relate the seasonal to annual values

$$\hat{A} = \hat{S}_{YX}\hat{S}_{XX}^{-1} \quad \dots\dots\dots\dots\dots\dots\dots\dots\dots\dots\dots\dots\dots\dots\dots \quad [2.76]$$

where $\hat{A}$ is the estimated A vector; $\hat{S}_{YX}$ is the $(n \times 1)$ cross products matrix (proportional to the covariance matrix) between the n seasonal observation, Y, and the annual values, X, summed over the N years of record used to evaluate the coefficients. $\hat{S}_{XX}^{-1}$ is the inverse of the sum of squares matrix of the N years of observed, annual values, X.

$$\hat{B}\hat{B}^T = \hat{S}_{YY} - \hat{S}_{YX}\hat{S}_{XX}^{-1}\hat{S}_{XY} \quad \dots\dots\dots\dots\dots\dots\dots\dots\dots\dots\dots \quad [2.77]$$

where $\hat{B}\hat{B}^T$ is the best estimate of the product of the B matrix and its transpose; $\hat{S}_{YY}$ is the sum of squares matrix over N years of the n seasonal values Y; $\hat{S}_{YY}$ and $\hat{S}_{XX}^{-1}$ are as described above; and $\hat{S}_{XY}$ is the cross products matrix between the annual values, X, and the n seasonal values Y summed over N years. The matrix, $\hat{B}$, can be calculated from $\hat{B}\hat{B}^T$ by the techniques of principle component analysis (Matalas, 1967).

Valencia and Schaake (1973) show that the parameter matrices A and B preserve continuity between seasonal and annual values;

$$X_i = \sum_{j=1}^{n} Y_{ij} \quad \dots\dots\dots\dots\dots\dots\dots\dots\dots\dots\dots\dots\dots\dots\dots \quad [2.78]$$

Equations [2-76] and [2-77] are used with historic data to solve the A and B matrices respectively. These matrices are used in equation [2-75] along with a random number generator and the annual series to develop seasonal values for the annual series. These values may, in turn, be further disaggregated to form sequences of any desired time interval, for example, hourly values of rainfall.

The model has been used for rainfall generation in Puerto Rico, for streamflow generation in Argentina and the United States, and for generation of hourly water demands in the Boston water distribution system.

Equation [2-75], described for a single station disaggregation model, has been extended to multisite data generation (Tao and Delleur, 1976b). In this case, the vectors X and Y become matrices of annual and seasonal values, respectively, extending across as many stations as desired. Vector A becomes a matrix of coefficients that dissaggregates each of the stations' annual series into average seasonal values. Matrix B is a coefficient matrix that preserves the covariance and cross-covariance structure of the residuals introduced in the vector, V. Tao and Delleur (1976b) show that continuity is preserved in this form of the model just as it is in the original model of Valencia and Schaake (1973). They used the model for both single and multistation disaggregation and evaluated the model performance with respect to preservation of both first and second order moments. They found these moments to be fully preserved; however, they found skewness of the generated data to be biased and proposed a possible explanation. Tao and Delleur (1976b) also showed how the model can be used to generate annual and monthly runoff volumes from annual rainfall. Mejia and Rousselle (1976) modified the disaggregation model to preserve correlations of the last season of one year with seasons of the following year.

Since the model can be used along with any annual data generation model, it has many applications in watershed modeling, especially where the long range properties of the annual series are of interest. A major disadvantage of the model is the need to calculate the large number of parameters, for the A and B matrices.

MISCELLANEOUS MODELS

The models of some hydrologic processes are such that they cannot be classified into any of the previous categories. Several rainfall models fall into this group. Since these are quite important from the standpoint of stochastic models, they are mentioned here. However, since they were developed to model a specific process and are not general models, they will not be described extensively.

Rainfall models will be divided into the following categories for presentation in this chapter: (a) point rainfall processes that generate time sequences at a single point; (b) multivariate rainfall models that consider several raingages simultaneously; and (c) areal or multidimensional models that attempt to characterize the phenomenon at any point over an area. Bras and Rodriguez-Iturbe (1976) further described each of these categories as consisting of storm exteriors and interiors. Rainfall exterior models are those that generate storm characteristics like total depth, duration of event, and time between events. Rainfall interior models generate the time distribution of the total rainfall depth within each event.

In the previous discussion of Asymmetry and Large Numbers of Zero Values, several rainfall models of point processes were described because of the approach used to generate large numbers of zero values. Todorovic and Yevjevich (1969) gave a comprehensive analysis of point rainfall processes. The time series at a given point depends upon six descriptors of the generation process: (a) the number of storms in a time interval; (b) the maximum number of storms after a reference time, with their total precipitation not ex-

below is capable of using the output of any model as input and generating a parallel series of seasonal events that aggregate to the original series. Furthermore the model may feed upon itself to further disaggregate the series to monthly, weekly, daily, and hourly events. Structure of the output series is based entirely on the statistical characteristics of the original data set; thus, the model cannot reproduce physical characteristics of a daily streamflow series. It can be used, however, for such things as the generation of hourly rainfall.

Fundamentally, the model disaggregates the annual series into seasonal values by using statistical data that show what fraction of the annual series is attributed to each season. It is made up of two components, a deterministic element that is proportional to the correlation of each season with the annual values, and a random element.

The disaggregation model takes the form (Valencia and Schaake, 1973)

$$Y(t) = AX(t) - BV(t) \quad\dotfill\quad [2.75]$$

where $\mathbf{Y}(t)$ is an $n \times 1$ vector of seasonal values for the tth year, n is the number of seasons in a year (for example, 12 if monthly values are to be generated), $\mathbf{X}(t)$ is the value of the annual series for the tth year, $\mathbf{V}(t)$ is an $n \times 1$ vector of independently distributed standard normal deviates, $\mathbf{A}$ is an $n \times 1$ vector of coefficients, and $\mathbf{B}$ is an $n \times n$ matrix of coefficients. The vector $\mathbf{A}$ and matrix $\mathbf{B}$ are obtained by analysis of N years of the historic data that relate the seasonal to annual values

$$\hat{\mathbf{A}} = \hat{\mathbf{S}}_{YX}\hat{\mathbf{S}}_{XX}^{-1} \quad\dotfill\quad [2.76]$$

where $\hat{\mathbf{A}}$ is the estimated $\mathbf{A}$ vector; $\hat{\mathbf{S}}_{YX}$ is the $(n \times 1)$ cross products matrix (proportional to the covariance matrix) between the n seasonal observation, Y, and the annual values, X, summed over the N years of record used to evaluate the coefficients. $\hat{\mathbf{S}}_{XX}^{-1}$ is the inverse of the sum of squares matrix of the N years of observed, annual values, X.

$$\hat{\mathbf{B}}\mathbf{B}^T = \hat{\mathbf{S}}_{YY} - \hat{\mathbf{S}}_{YX}\hat{\mathbf{S}}_{XX}^{-1}\hat{\mathbf{S}}_{XY} \quad\dotfill\quad [2.77]$$

where $\hat{\mathbf{B}}\mathbf{B}^T$ is the best estimate of the product of the $\mathbf{B}$ matrix and its transpose; $\hat{\mathbf{S}}_{YY}$ is the sum of squares matrix over N years of the n seasonal values Y; $\hat{\mathbf{S}}_{YY}$ and $\hat{\mathbf{S}}_{XX}^{-1}$ are as described above; and $\hat{\mathbf{S}}_{XY}$ is the cross products matrix between the annual values, X, and the n seasonal values Y summed over N years. The matrix, $\hat{\mathbf{B}}$, can be calculated from $\mathbf{B}\mathbf{B}^T$ by the techniques of principle component analysis (Matalas, 1967).

Valencia and Schaake (1973) show that the parameter matrices $\mathbf{A}$ and $\mathbf{B}$ preserve continuity between seasonal and annual values;

$$X_i = \sum_{j=1}^{n} Y_{ij} \quad\dotfill\quad [2.78]$$

Equations [2-76] and [2-77] are used with historic data to solve the $\mathbf{A}$ and $\mathbf{B}$ matrices respectively. These matrices are used in equation [2-75] along with a random number generator and the annual series to develop seasonal values for the annual series. These values may, in turn, be further disaggregated to form sequences of any desired time interval, for example, hourly values of rainfall.

The model has been used for rainfall generation in Puerto Rico, for streamflow generation in Argentina and the United States, and for generation of hourly water demands in the Boston water distribution system.

Equation [2-75], described for a single station disaggregation model, has been extended to multisite data generation (Tao and Delleur, 1976b). In this case, the vectors **X** and **Y** become matrices of annual and seasonal values, respectively, extending across as many stations as desired. Vector **A** becomes a matrix of coefficients that dissaggregates each of the stations' annual series into average seasonal values. Matrix **B** is a coefficient matrix that preserves the covariance and cross-covariance structure of the residuals introduced in the vector, **V**. Tao and Delleur (1976b) show that continuity is preserved in this form of the model just as it is in the original model of Valencia and Schaake (1973). They used the model for both single and multistation disaggregation and evaluated the model performance with respect to preservation of both first and second order moments. They found these moments to be fully preserved; however, they found skewness of the generated data to be biased and proposed a possible explanation. Tao and Delleur (1976b) also showed how the model can be used to generate annual and monthly runoff volumes from annual rainfall. Mejia and Rousselle (1976) modified the disaggregation model to preserve correlations of the last season of one year with seasons of the following year.

Since the model can be used along with any annual data generation model, it has many applications in watershed modeling, especially where the long range properties of the annual series are of interest. A major disadvantage of the model is the need to calculate the large number of parameters, for the **A** and **B** matrices.

MISCELLANEOUS MODELS

The models of some hydrologic processes are such that they cannot be classified into any of the previous categories. Several rainfall models fall into this group. Since these are quite important from the standpoint of stochastic models, they are mentioned here. However, since they were developed to model a specific process and are not general models, they will not be described extensively.

Rainfall models will be divided into the following categories for presentation in this chapter: (a) point rainfall processes that generate time sequences at a single point; (b) multivariate rainfall models that consider several raingages simultaneously; and (c) areal or multidimensional models that attempt to characterize the phenomenon at any point over an area. Bras and Rodriguez-Iturbe (1976) further described each of these categories as consisting of storm exteriors and interiors. Rainfall exterior models are those that generate storm characteristics like total depth, duration of event, and time between events. Rainfall interior models generate the time distribution of the total rainfall depth within each event.

In the previous discussion of Asymmetry and Large Numbers of Zero Values, several rainfall models of point processes were described because of the approach used to generate large numbers of zero values. Todorovic and Yevjevich (1969) gave a comprehensive analysis of point rainfall processes. The time series at a given point depends upon six descriptors of the generation process: (a) the number of storms in a time interval; (b) the maximum number of storms after a reference time, with their total precipitation not exceeding a given value; (c) the lapse time between a reference time and the end of a storm; (d) the total precipitation for a given number of storms; (e) the total precipitation for the last storm of a sequence; and (f) the total precipitation for a given interval of time. Two parameters are important in deriving probability distributions of the six descriptors. They are the average number of storms per unit time interval, and the yield characteristics of the storms. Both parameters are periodic functions of time. Several examples are used to illustrate the method. The generated sequences of one of the examples is on an hourly basis, which would be considered as an interior model according to the definition of Bras and Rodriguez-Iturbe (1976). The Disaggregation Processes, which was previously described, could be used to generate such "interiors" for other point rainfall process models.

In the discussion of autoregressive processes, techniques for extending the stochastic data generation of point processes to the situation of multi-site conditions are presented. Thus the methods used to generate point rainfall processes may be extended to multistation situations (Richardson, 1977). Mejia and Rodriguez-Iturbe (1974b) established a fundamental relationship between the spatial correlation function of rainfall and the spectrum of rainfall processes. However, it is limited to areas where the rainfall can be considered fairly uniform, although it can consider variations caused by changes in altitude. By assuming a correlation function suitable for characterizing rainfall and modifying it to reflect radial spectral density and distribution, rainfall estimates at any point can be generated.

The model of Mejia and Rodriguez-Iturbe (1974b) falls some where between the second type, multivariate rainfall models, and the third type, areal multivariate models. The third type, which attempts to characterize the rainfall at any point over an area, is perhaps the most important group of rainfall models. Lenton and Rodriguez-Iturbe (1977) extended the work of Mejia and Rodriguez-Iturbe (1974b) to generate the areal average of total rainfall depth instead of point values. The model preserves the areal covariance structure but uses point covariance of corresponding point rainfall rather than areal covariance as input. Lenton and Rodriguez-Iturbe (1977) presented an example showing a numerical application of the model. Fogel et al. (1974) assumed a geometric probability for depth of point rainfall and, by assuming that amounts measured in any two raingages are from different cloudbursts, inferred that the system has spatial independence and temporal dependence. Thus, the areal rainfall can be shown to have a negative binomial distribution. By assuming a Poisson distribution for the number of events in a season and by using the areal rainfall distribution, they generated total seasonal rainfall and simulated series of events. These values were then converted to runoff and water yield. In the paper, shortcomings of some of the assumptions were discussed.

Osborn et al. (1974) analyzed thunderstorm rainfall in the Southwest and proposed an areal and temporal distribution of rainfall amounts based on the occurrence and development of synthetic storm cells. The occurrence of a rainfall event is determined by Bernoulli sampling from a smoothed curve of significant rainfall probability. The Bernoulli variable is 0 if there is no rainfall on a day and 1 if there is rainfall. The probability of drawing a 1 or 0 on any given day is equal to the rainfall probability for that day; thus uniform random numbers are used for the sampling. The areal rainfall amount is determined by the spatially random occurrence of circular cells of constant radius R. Even though studies of individual cells in Arizona indicated the average shape is an ellipse with axes in a ratio of 1 1/2:1, a circular pattern was selected for simplicity in this modeling effort. The rainfall within the cell is determined by a functional relation with distance from the cell center and maximum amount, D_o, at the center. Both R and D_o are considered constant within each cell. A negative exponential distribution is used to generate D_o. Since the total storm pattern consists of several such cells, two other basic storm parameters are used: the average number of cells per storm, $\overline{N}$, and the preferred direction of cell placement, Θ_0. The number of cells is assumed to be Poisson distributed with a minimum of 3 cells and probability of having more than 7 very small. The directional component of subsequent cells, $\Delta\Theta_i$, is assumed to be normally distributed about the initial value Θ. With a mean of 0 deg and standard deviation of 60 deg. Both the location of the first cell and direction of movement to locate the second cell are truly random. The location of the second and subsequent cells is a function of a uniform random number. Osborn et al. (1974) illustrated their model with several examples and also discussed improvements and weaknesses of the model.

Bras and Rodriguez-Iturbe (1976) presented an analytical treatment of a modeling of the interior of a storm. The model is nonstationary, dynamic, and multidimensional. Inputs to the model include time between events, storm duration, areal average total depth, storm velocities and direction, distribution of storm types, undimensional storm pattern for each type, and form of the space and time correlation of each type. Distribution functions of the input parameters are described and steps of the generation algorithm are outlined. The generation of areal average values as well as point values at any desired location are discussed. The model of Lenton and Rodriguez-Iturbe (1977) is used to obtain aerial averages. A simple numerical example illustrated the rainfall generator.

Of all of the models of areal rainfall, the work of Gupta and Waymire (1979) is perhaps the most physically based. They viewed the synoptic area of a storm as enclosing large mesoscale areas (LMSA). The LMSA, ranging in size from 10^3 to 10^4 km^2, build and dissipate within a synoptic area in a matter of several hours. The number of LMSA in a synoptic area range from 1 to 6 and they move in relation to the moving synoptic region. Intensity within the LMSA is higher than the area surrounding it. Within the LMSA convective cells, 10-30 km^2 in extent, build and dissipate with a life span of several minutes to about half an hour. The cells generally occur in clusters and undergo motion relative to the LMSA. Intensity of rainfall is higher within the cluster than in the area surrounding it. It has been observed in some storms that cells are also found in small mesoscale precipitation areas (SMSA) ranging in size from 10^2 to 10^3 km^2. The rainfall intensity in the SMSA is higher than that in the LMSA. Gupta and Waymire (1979) developed a kinematic stochastic formulation of the mesoscale precipitation processes. This consisted of (a) a description of the different components of a LMSA that govern the structure of precipitation, (b) explicit statements on postulates of the various components in the LMSA, and (c) synthesis of the first two steps which gives a mathematical representation of the precipitation field. The postulates lead to representation of the rainfall field as a stochastic integral consisting of two embedded auxiliary stochastic fields. Each of these can be interpreted physically. In applying the results of the development, expressions for the mean, variance, and one-dimensional characteristic function of rainfall intensity are derived. The model is particularly well suited to the study of subsynoptic space-time rainfall patterns. The paper concludes with a good discussion of the need for further research in this area.

The applications of stochastic models in the previous description of rainfall models illustrates a use of stochastic processes somewhat different from that presented in previous sections of this chapter. They were presented because this use of stochastic processes is becoming more important. Other applications of stochastic models include models for bedload transport (Hung and Shen, 1974), sediment yield of ephemeral streams (Woolhiser and Todorovic, 1974), hydrologic aspects of water harvesting (Hanson et al., 1974), and water harvesting from and along highways (Evans et al., 1974).

PROBLEMS ASSOCIATED
WITH MOST STOCHASTIC HYDROLOGIC MODELS

Incomplete data sets

In the analysis of hydrologic data one seldom finds a complete data set. Thus, some approach must be selected for handling these incomplete data sets. The usual tendency is to fill in missing periods with synthesized data. If the missing data are not extensive and they are to be used for such things as flow duration curves or depth-area relations, then use of a regression equation, or some other method for estimating the missing period, is satisfactory. However, if the data are to be used in the development of a stochastic process, then this method of data synthesis will bias the record and it is not advisable.

Historic data sequences, especially those associated with multistation evaluation, are not likely to be concurrent and of equal length. With such incomplete data sets, the lag-zero variance-covariance matrix, M(0), may be inconsistent—not positive semi-definite. Since the inverse of this matrix is used in the autoregressive Markov model to calculate the A matrix, equation [2-46], it must be consistent. If it is inconsistent, then its eigenvalues will not all be positive and some of the elements in A will be complex numbers. Fiering (1968) stated that if all of the eigenvalues M(0) are positive and they sum to the order of the matrix, then the matrix is consistent. If the matrix is inconsistent, he described two methods for handling it. One method consists of manipulating the eigenvalues according to some predetermined scheme or algorithm. The second method consists of adjusting the matrix by use of random sampling technique. The first method is considered by Fiering to be the most useful; see Fiering (1968) for further discussion.

Crosby and Maddock (1970) noted that even if the M(0) and M(1) matrices are consistent, the BB^T matrix, equation [2-47], of the lag-one autoregressive model may be inconsistent. If the data sequences are monotone, or continuous from their inception to the end of the analysis period, even though each of the sequences may have originated at different points in time, the BB^T matrix may be made consistent by a technique they describe.

Statistical Similarity of Generated Sequences

In the previous material we have commented about correction for bias. In this section we will elaborate more on the subject of parameter bias and how to correct for it. Additional information on bias is presented in the section of this chapter on parameter estimation.

The parameters used to characterize hydrologic phenomena and generate synthetic sequences by the various methods are (parentheses give station indices) the mean, i.e., μ_p, the variance, σ_p^2, the skew, g_p, the lag-one autocorrelation, $\rho_p(1)$, the lag-zero cross correlation, $\rho_{p,q}(0)$, the lag-one cross correlation, $\rho_{p,q}(1)$, and the Hurst coefficient H_p. In the study of hydrologic process, true population values of these parameters are not known. Thus, we must estimate their values from historical records. Very seldom will this "relatively short" historic record yield values close to the true population values. It is very important, therefore, in recognizing that these calculated values are not necessarily true values, to calculate confidence levels on these values. Methods for this purpose are available in most statistical texts, for example, Mood et al., (1974), and Miller and Freund (1977), who discussed confidence intervals with numerous examples. Both references discussed confidence intervals of regression coefficients, which are also important in model evaluation. Haan (1977) and Yevjevich (1972a, b) discussed confidence intervals as they apply to hydrologic processes.

In addition to recognizing the possible departure of a sample statistic from its true population value, one must correct the various parameters for bias so that generated sequences will resemble historic data. Statistical resemblance is defined both in the long run (for sequences whose length approaches infinity) and in the short run (for sequences that are about as long as the historic record).

Designate ω to be a parameter characterizing a particular hydrologic phenomenon. Even though it is an unknown value, historic data may be used to estimate its value: $\hat{\omega}$. If this parameter is used in the generation of synthetic sequences, then it in effect becomes a population value. That is, given a generated sequence, of length, $\tilde{n}$, the parameter will take on a value $\tilde{\omega}$ which, as $\tilde{n} \to \infty$, will approach the historic value $\hat{\omega}$. In this case, the synthetic sequences are said to resemble the historic flows in the long run with respect to $\hat{\omega}$. If the run length, $\tilde{n}$, is finite and L sequences each of length $\tilde{n}$ are generated, then each sequence will provide an estimate of $\hat{\omega}$, denoted $\tilde{\omega}$. The mean of these values is $\tilde{\omega}^*$ as $n \to \infty$. If the expected value of $\tilde{\omega}$ which is equal to $\tilde{\omega}^*$ is equal to $\hat{\omega}$, then the synthetic sequences are said to resemble the historic flows in the short run with respect to $\hat{\omega}$. In general short run resemblance implies long run resemblance but long run resemblance does not necessarily imply short run resemblance. In fact, most parameters $\tilde{\omega}$ are biased estimates of $\hat{\omega}$ and short run resemblance does not hold. Thus, to obtain short run resemblance, parameter values must be adjusted before being used in the models (Matalas, 1977). Only the value of $\hat{\mu}$ as an estimate of the mean, μ, in the above parameters is unbiased.

The correction for bias in all other parameters depends upon the length of synthetic sequences to be generated, the mathematical structure of the synthetic data generator, and the distribution function used to generate the random input to the generator. Analytical expressions for the corrections have not been developed. However, Monte Carlo procedures have been used to estimate the bias correction. Matalas (1977) describes corrections for the standard deviation, autocorrelation coefficient, and the Hurst parameter for single site Markov (autoregressive) and filtered fractional noise (type 2) processes. Tables are presented to aid in making the corrections. In Monte Carlo development of the corrections, the distribution function of random inputs was assumed to be normal, and a synthetic flow sequence of length 100 was used. O'Connell (1977b) described parameter estimation and bias correction for the ARIMA (1, 0, 1) process using Monte Carlo procedures. Values of ϕ and θ, the autoregressive and moving average parameters respectively, are selected such that bias in the estimated value of the Hurst coefficient and lag one autocorrelation coefficients is removed. Values of sequence length, autocorrection coefficient, and ϕ are then used to correct the variance. In the development of these tables, the random input to the model was assumed to be a normal process. For more information and tables of these corrections see Matalas and Wallis (1974), Wallis et al. (1974), Box and Jenkins (1976), and O'Connell (1974). Even though methods for bias correction have not been developed for all of the models presented in this chapter, the corrections discussed above apply to the models most often used in hydrologic evaluation.

Random Number Generators

The use of stochastic models will very likely involve generation of sequences of random numbers or random vectors. This generation is not trivial because computer-generated random numbers are pseudorandom numbers which can have properties that differ from the ideal in significant ways. The trusting use of "canned" random number generators can cause unfortunate differences between expected and observed distributions.

Areas where differences may show up include: frequency, autocorrelation, and minimum and maximum values. Other important problem areas include computational speed of the generator, period of the generator, and sparseness in n-space for multidimensional random number generators.

The user of a random number generator should test it or ensure that it has been tested for significant differences from theoretical values, especially those problem areas that may be significant in the analysis. Lewis and Payne (1973) listed some tests that might be used and described a generator that has some desirable properties. The generalized feedback shift generator they described can be made computationally very fast, has an arbitrarily low period, generating an extremely large number of values before repeating itself, is independent of computer work size, gives similar sequences on different machines, and has good properties for random vectors (or at least doesn't have the bad properties of some generators). The article lists Fortran programs to utilize the generators.

MODEL SELECTION

In the previous sections of this chapter several different stochastic models of hydrologic processes have been discussed. On the basis of the examples that have been presented and comments that have been made, the user may have a good concept of the model that best fits his needs. However, this may not yet be clear; unfortunately not enough effort has been given to the process of model selection. Items that should be considered in the selection process include (a) the nature of the physical processes involved, (b) the use to be made of the model, (c) the quality of the data available and (d) the decisions that rest on the outcome of the model's use.

In examining the nature of the physical processes involved, one should ask and attempt to answer such questions as: What are the processes that interact to produce the phenomenon under investigation? Are they amenable to solution by stochastic processes? Are they independent processes? Are they independent of time? Are values of the parameters likely to change with time, i.e., are they seasonal? Is the process stationary? Must future man-induced changes be represented; if so, how?

In addition to studying the nature of the processes involved, the use to be made of the model must also be considered. How much information is needed concerning the process being modeled? Do the data need to be presented in short time intervals or is monthly or annual data sufficient? How important are such things as the Hurst phenomenon? Is it worth the extra cost to incorporate it in the model? The user of a stochastic model is most likely interested in the aggregate behavior of a process rather than a detailed description of the process. Thus, he needs to filter processes that are critical to him out of all the complex processes.

The quality of hydrologic data describing a phenomenon affects the problem of filtering useful information from complex processes that produced the phenomenon. Several models may be capable of describing the same process, and, to a great extent, selection of the one to be used depends upon a comparison of sampled data and model output. The modeler needs to analyze the nature of the differences between the two. Part of the error may be in the structure of the model. It may not agree with the structure of the real process. The addition of model components can, in some instances, improve the model. But in some cases, the addition of more components forces model parameters to assume some of the variability associated with random processes. Measurement errors, which may not be truly random but which may be biased, can also lead to an apparent error in model performance. Attempts should be made to assess the magnitude of these errors. Another source of poor model performance is error in parameter estimation. This type is caused by the necessity for basing parameter values on the historic record, and it may be unrepresentative or very short. As the sample size increases, these errors should become smaller.

Finally, in model selection, decisions that may rest upon the outcome of the model's use must be considered. To a great extent, these decisions will dictate the criteria that should be used to judge the quality of a model's performance. As an example, suppose that streamflow sequences will be used to determine the size of a dam to be used for a water supply. In this case, the model is selected and its parameters estimated in such a way as to minimize the costs of uncertainty inherent in decisions regarding the size of the dam. Alternatively, suppose aerial rainfall data were to be used to study the spatial variability of soil moisture in assessing crop conditions. In this case the model and its parameters must be selected to minimize the costs inherent in either overirrigation or losses in productivity brought on by drought induced growth stress. These are rather simplistic examples, but they serve to show the needs of the decision-maker, who may not know how to judge the quality of a model's response.

PARAMETER ESTIMATION

Parameter estimation is a problem not uniquely associated with stochastic models; it is a problem associated with most models discussed in this monograph. The only difference in fitting parameters of stochastic models, as opposed to those of the other models, lies in the fact that all of the parameters of a stochastic model are properties of a probability distribution.

In previous sections of this chapter, methods of estimating parameters are mentioned, but, it seems advisable to discuss the general topic of parameter estimation and some of the properties of these estimates.

Properties of Parameter Estimates

To appreciate the strengths and weaknesses of the various estimation techniques, the concepts of minimum variance and unbiasedness, consistency, efficiency, and sufficiency as they relate to parameter estimation will be briefly discussed. These terms will be used to describe the performance of three methods of parameter estimation; the method of moments, the method of least squares, and the method of maximum likelihood. Finally, Bayes Theorem will be investigated as a technique that can be used to improve estimates of parameter values when other data or conditions dictate its use. Much more detail concerning all of these processes is available by consulting the index of most texts on mathematical statistics and the references cited in the introduction to this chapter.

Minimum Variance and Unbiasedness: The populations of hydrologic variables that describe the many systems of interest to us are not known. Because only sample realizations from these populations are available, these variables must be considered random variables. Since we do not know the populations, we do not know the parameters, θ_i, describing the populations, i.e., the parameters needed for our models. We must estimate the values from the sample realizations available. There are several ways to estimate these parameters; thus some means or criteria is needed to judge the performance of the estimators.

Several criteria may be used to judge performance. Intuitively, the best estimate of a parameter $\hat{\nu}$ must be a function $T(x, \theta)$ of the observations (x_1, ..., x_n) such that it is closest to the true value in some sense. Since our observations are random variables, then the function $T(x, \theta)$ of these variables is also a random variable and will have a distribution function. Knowledge of this distribution is needed before the performance of the estimate can be assessed. If the expected value of our estimate $\hat{\theta}$ based on the function $T(x, \theta)$ is equal to θ, i.e., $E(\hat{\theta}) = \theta$, then the estimate of the parameter is said to be unbiased. If bias exists, then the value of the bias is $E(\hat{\theta}) - \theta$. A statement of unbiasedness means that if there were many independent sample realizations and an estimate of θ for each, then the average of these estimates will equal θ. It does not mean that the specific estimate $\hat{\theta}$ is equal to θ.

One measure of the closeness of a parameter estimate to its true value is its variance. Different functions, T, used to estimate θ will of course have different distributions. And the best distribution is the one that has a minimum variance, because, if the estimate is unbiased, values of $\hat{\theta}$ are concentrated near θ and have a better chance of being close to the value of θ than those with a larger variance. If the variance is our criteria for closeness of fit, then good estimator performance would be indicated by minimum variance and unbiasedness. It is not always possible to have both; at times a subjective decision is needed to determine which is more important.

The performance of an estimate of θ based on a function, $T(x, \hat{\theta})$, of the sample is measured by the mean square error (m.s.e.). $E(\hat{\theta} - \theta)^2$. By expanding this expression we can show that it contains both the variance of the function, $T(x, \hat{\theta})$, and bias.

$$E(\hat{\theta}-\theta)^2 = E(\hat{\theta}^2 - 2\hat{\theta}\theta+\theta^2) \quad\dots\dots\dots\dots\dots\dots\dots\dots \quad [2.79]$$

$$= E(\hat{\theta}^2) - 2\theta E(\hat{\theta}) + \theta^2$$

by both subtracting and adding $E(\hat{\theta})^2$ to the right hand side

$$E(\hat{\theta}-\theta)^2 = E(\hat{\theta}^2) - E(\hat{\theta})^2 + E(\hat{\theta})^2 - 2\theta E(\hat{\theta}) + \theta^2$$

$$= E(\hat{\theta}^2) - E(\hat{\theta})^2 + (E(\hat{\theta})-\theta)^2$$

$$= V(\hat{\theta}) + [\text{bias}(\hat{\theta})]^2 \quad\dots\dots\dots\dots\dots\dots\dots\dots \quad [2.80]$$

where $V(\hat{\theta})$ is the variance of the parameter estimate based on the function $T(x, \hat{\theta})$. Our best estimate of θ would be one where the mean square error is a minimum. This can be shown by letting any other estimate of θ. $\hat{\theta}'$, be estimated by $T'(x, \theta)$; then if $\hat{\theta}$ is unbiased,

$$E(\hat{\theta}-\theta)^2 \leqslant E(\hat{\theta}'-\theta)^2 \quad\dots\dots\dots\dots\dots\dots\dots\dots \quad [2.81]$$

for all $T'(x, \theta)$ and if the estimate of $\hat{\theta}$ is a minimum variance unbiased estimate,

$$V(\hat{\theta}) \leqslant V(\hat{\theta}'). \quad\dots\dots\dots\dots\dots\dots\dots\dots \quad [2.82]$$

As examples, consider the mean and variance, two parameters characterizing a normal distribution. Several methods can be used to estimate these parameters. Three estimates of the variance will be considered. Only one estimate of the mean (discussed below) is useful, however; others such as the average of the maximum and minimum values of a sample, the median, or the mode are of little value.

It can be shown that

$$E(\bar{x}) = \mu \quad\dots\dots\dots\dots\dots\dots\dots\dots \quad [2.83]$$

and that

$$E(s^2) = \sigma^2 \quad\dots\dots\dots\dots\dots\dots\dots\dots \quad [2.84]$$

if $\bar{x}$ and s^2 are defined as

$$\bar{x} = \frac{\sum_{i=1}^{n} x_i}{n} \quad\dots\dots\dots\dots\dots\dots\dots\dots \quad [2.85]$$

and

$$s^2 = \frac{\sum_{i=1}^{n} (x_i-\bar{x})^2}{n-1} \quad\dots\dots\dots\dots\dots\dots\dots\dots \quad [2.86]$$

Thus both $\bar{x}$ and s_2, as defined above, are unbiased estimates of μ and σ^2 respectively. As mentioned previously, a measure of the closeness of fit is the variance of the parameter estimates. It can be shown that these values are

$$V(\bar{x}) = \frac{\sigma^2}{n} \quad \dots\dots\dots\dots\dots\dots\dots\dots\dots\dots\dots\dots\dots\dots\dots\dots \quad [2.87]$$

and

$$V(s^2) = \frac{2(n-1)\sigma^4}{n^2} \quad \dots\dots\dots\dots\dots\dots\dots\dots\dots\dots\dots\dots\dots \quad [2.88]$$

Since both of these parameters are unbiased, substitution in equation [2-80] shows that the mean square errors (of the mean and variance estimates, using equations [2-85] and [2-86] as parameter definitions), are equal to the variance of the parameter estimates as given by equation [2-87] and [2-88] respectively. However, these estimates are not necessarily the minimum variance estimates. Two other estimates for the variance, σ^2, can be shown to have a lower variance than equation [2-86]. One is the variance estimated by the method of maximum likelihood (to be discussed later in this section)

$$s_1{}^2 = \frac{\sum\limits_{i=1}^{n} (x_i - \bar{x})^2}{n} \quad ; \quad \dots\dots\dots\dots\dots\dots\dots\dots\dots\dots\dots\dots \quad [2.89]$$

the other estimate of σ^2 is given by

$$s_2{}^2 = \frac{\sum\limits_{i=1}^{n} (x_i - \bar{x})^2}{n+1} \quad \dots\dots\dots\dots\dots\dots\dots\dots\dots\dots\dots\dots \quad [2.90]$$

It can be shown that equation [2-90] is the minimum variance estimate of s^2 provided $n < 4$. Both of these estimates of σ^2 are biased, but the variances of both are low enough that substituting into equation [2-80] and adding the bias leads to mean square errors less than those obtained using the unbiased estimates. See pages 255-256 of Rao (1967). Note that as $n \to \infty$ all three estimates converge, thus large samples are less subject to problems of parameter estimation than are small samples. Yevjevich (1972a), chapter 9, presented equations defining other moments for both of these parameters and also for the coefficients of variation, skewness, and kurtosis.

Exact distribution functions of the mean, standard deviation, and skewness coefficient for small samples, representative of those used in hydrology, cannot be calculated directly for most distribution functions. Therefore, Wallis et al. (1974) used Monte Carlo experiments to estimate distribution functions for three parameters for sample sizes of 10-90 for some of the most common probability distributions. Bias factors for these are presented in his paper. Graphs are available on microfiche (Wallis et al., 1974).

These comparisons of different estimators of the variance were presented to show how the mean square error of an estimate and the concepts of minimum variance and unbiasedness are related. In some cases it may be advisable to investigate these errors, however, in general, certain methods of estimation have been found to be better than others. These comparisons are discussed after each method of parameter estimation is presented.

Consistency, Efficiency, and Sufficiency: In the previous section, the terms unbiasedness and minimum error variance are used to characterize a parameter estimate. If a parameter is unbiased, then the average value of the parameter, estimated from a large number of sample realizations, would converge to the population value. Consistency is similar to unbiasedness except that given one sample realization, the parameter estimate would converge to the population value as the sample size approached infinity. Thus if a parameter estimate is consistent, then we can expect to have better estimates as the sample size increases.

Parameter efficiency relates to the variance of the estimate. If the estimate is unbiased and has the smallest possible variance, i.e., a smaller variance than any other estimate, then it is an efficient estimate. Thus a minimum-variance, unbiased estimate as previously discussed is an efficient estimate.

Sufficiency is a term applied to the amount of information contained in a sample that is used to estimate a parameter value. If all of the information contained in a sample is used, then the estimate is said to be sufficient.

General Comments on the Use of Statistics of Estimated Parameters: In the previous two sections, we have discussed terminology, with examples and a few comments, used to describe the probability distributions of parameter estimates. In this section we will elaborate on the value of these statistics and the need for their careful evaluation. Other than providing a means for evaluating various methods of parameter estimation, perhaps the most important use of the parameter statistic is in establishing confidence intervals on parameter estimates. Simply stated, confidence intervals on a parameter, θ, define the range of values that the parameter may take that we can be 100 $(1-\alpha)$ percent confident will contain the true parameter value. The intervals are defined by the variance of the parameter estimate; thus they depend upon the method of parameter estimation. The most efficient estimator will of course have the narrowest confidence intervals. Yevjevich (1972a), chapter 9, gave an excellent discussion of confidence intervals and the related subject of tolerance. Since most of the models we will be developing contain more than one parameter, the modeler needs to consider the joint confidence limits of all parameters (Yevjevich, 1972a). Both confidence limits and tolerance levels are extremely important to the model user; therefore, careful attention should be given to their development.

A subject that we will not attempt to discuss, because ample discussion is available in the literature, is the area of hypotheses testing and goodness of fit. If the reader is not familiar with this material he should review it, because it will be needed to evaluate such things as the significance of apparent trends, seasonal differences in parameter values, model comparison, goodness of fit, etc. For specific examples in the area of watershed hydrology, the reader is referred to chapters in both Yevjevich (1972a) and Haan (1977).

Frequently, the data series to be generated by a stochastic process will not consist of independent data, but serially correlated data. In this case, the sample size cannot be used directly in assessing the accuracy of prediction. If a first order autoregressive process is assumed, then the effective sample size, N_e, for estimating the distribution properties of the mean is given by Yevjevich (1972a) as:

$$N_e = N \frac{1-\rho(1)}{1+\rho(1)} \quad \dots\dots\dots\dots\dots\dots\dots\dots\dots\dots\dots\dots \quad [2.91]$$

where $\rho(1)$ is the lag 1 autocorrelation coefficient and N is the sample size. The value of N_e should replace N in estimating the distribution properties of the mean. A somewhat similar relation is needed in estimating the distribution properties of the variance

$$N_e = N \frac{1-\rho^2(1)}{1+\rho^2(1)} \quad \dots\dots\dots\dots\dots\dots\dots\dots\dots\dots\dots\dots \quad [2.92]$$

In discussion of bias and minimum error variance, information was presented that demonstrates some of the problems of parameter estimation where both unbiased and minimum variance estimates are desired. In many cases it isn't possible to have both. Since most estimates are consistent, biased estimates of parameter values can be tolerated when the sample size N is greater than 30. This isn't undesirable because, as shown in the section on estimation methods, quite frequently biased estimates are the most efficient estimates. But for sample sizes less than 30, it is recommended that unbiased estimates be used. A summary of the computational tools using both of these criteria are presented in Yevjevich (1972a) on pages 185 and 186.

Method of Moments

This section begins a discussion of (a) three methods used to obtain parameter estimates, (b) comparisons of these estimates, and (c) statements concerning the parameter distributions in the terms previously described. Computer programs are readily available in most user libraries to aid in fitting distributions by these methods.

Because the method of moments is perhaps the easiest method to use in parameter estimation, it will be discussed first. To use the method of moments, it must be assumed that the sample data has been generated by a particular type of process. For example, assume that a sequence of independently distributed random variates was generated from a distribution having a density function $f(x; \theta_1, \theta_2, ..., \theta_m)$ where x is the random variable, and $\theta_1, \theta_2, ..., \theta_m$ are parameters of the density function. The m parameter values are calculated by equating m moments of the density function with corresponding moments of the sample. Moments of the density function are

$$m_j = \int_0^\infty x^j f(x)\, dx = E(x^j) \quad \dots\dots\dots\dots\dots\dots\dots\dots\dots\dots \quad [2.93]$$

and those of the sample are

$$\hat{m}_j = \frac{1}{n} \sum_{i=1}^n x_i^j \quad \dots\dots\dots\dots\dots\dots\dots\dots\dots\dots\dots\dots \quad [2.94]$$

where the x_i are defined as deviates from their mean.

Any of the sample moments or a combination of them could be used to estimate a parameter or number of parameters. However, since higher order moments are extremely sensitive to the distribution properties of the sample, that is, to the tails of the distribution and thus extreme values in a sample, it is always advisable to use the lowest order moments.

Using the exponential distribution as an example

$$f(x,\alpha) = \alpha e^{-\alpha x} \quad \dots \dots \dots \dots \dots \dots \dots \dots \dots \dots \dots \dots \dots \quad [2.95]$$

the jth moment is given by

$$m_j = \int_0^\infty x^j \alpha e^{-\alpha x}\, dx \quad \dots \dots \dots \dots \dots \dots \dots \dots \dots \dots \quad [2.96]$$

thus $m_1 = 1/\alpha$, $m_2 = 2/\alpha^2$ etc.

If these moments are calculated from the sample, then either one of the moments could be used to estimate the coefficient α,

$$\hat{\alpha}_{(1)} = \frac{1}{\hat{m}_1} \quad \dots \dots \dots \dots \dots \dots \dots \dots \dots \dots \dots \dots \dots \quad [2.97]$$

or

$$\hat{\alpha}_{(2)} = \sqrt{2/\hat{m}_2} \quad \dots \dots \dots \dots \dots \dots \dots \dots \dots \dots \dots \quad [2.98]$$

Since these estimates will be different, it would be advisable to use the estimate based on the first moment, $\hat{\alpha}_{(1)}$, because, as previously mentioned, it is less sensitive to distribution properties of the sample.

In general the method of moments is easy to use and according to Yev-jevich (1972a), values obtained are distributed asymptotically normal, with both bias and variance proportional to $1/n$. It has also been shown, for skew-ed distributions, that the efficiency of estimation is less than one; that is, there are more efficient estimators than the method of moments. However, if the underlying distribution $f(x; \theta_1, \theta_2, \dots, \theta_n)$ is normal, the efficiency of the method is one, that is, the parameter estimates are as good as those obtained by any other method. Thus it is not advantageous to use least squares or maximum likelihood methods. However, most hydrologic data appear to come from skewed distributions. Thus, even though bias can be corrected, efficiency of parameter estimation by the method of moments is poor.

Method of Least Squares

The method of least squares is a term applied to a variety of estimation methods. In its simplest form it consists of fitting a linear theoretical func-tion or probability density function to an empirical distribution or set of sam-ple observations. If the assumed linear functions is $f(x; \theta_1, \theta_2, \dots, \theta_m)$, where x is the random variable and $\theta_1, \theta_2, \dots, \theta_m$ are parameters of the assumed function; then the method of least squares provides estimates of the parameters by minimizing the error sum of squares, S^2, between the observ-ed, y_i, and functional, y, values

$$S^2 = \sum_{i=1}^n (y_i - y)^2 \quad \dots \dots \dots \dots \dots \dots \dots \dots \dots \dots \dots \quad [2.99]$$

$$= \sum_{i=1}^n [y_i - f(x_i; \theta_1, \theta_2, \dots, \theta_m)]^2 \quad \dots \dots \dots \dots \dots \dots [2.100]$$

By taking partial derivatives of S^2 with respect to each of the parameters, m equations in m unknowns are obtained. Optimum solution is obtained when the functions are a minimum, thus

$$\frac{\partial \sum\limits_{i=1}^{n} [y_i - f(x_i; \theta_1, \theta_2, \ldots, \theta_m)]^2}{\partial \theta_j} = 0 \quad j = 1, 2, \ldots, m \quad \ldots\ldots\ldots [2.101]$$

These m equations in m unknowns are linear and can be solved simultaneously for estimates of the parameters.

In order for the method to be efficient (Yevjevich, 1972a; Overton and Meadows, 1976), (a) the input data are assumed to be error free, (b) the distribution errors must be normal, and (c) the variance of the errors must be constant and independent of position along the equal value line. If these criteria are not met, a transformation must be applied to the data to correct the deficiencies. For a normal distribution it can be shown that estimates obtained by the method of least squares are identical to those obtained by the method of maximum likelihood.

If the data to be fitted to the linear functional relation are grouped into r class intervals, then a modification of equation (2-100) can be used to estimate parameter values. Assume the observed relative frequency of occurrence within the r_i class intervals in f_i, and that the density function is $f(x; \theta_1, \theta_2, \ldots, \theta_m)$. In this case, optimum parameter estimates are obtained by minimizing the error sum of squares between the observed and assumed density function values across all class intervals

$$\chi^2 = \sum_{i=1}^{r} \frac{1}{p_i} (f_i - p_i)^2 \ldots\ldots\ldots\ldots\ldots\ldots\ldots\ldots\ldots\ldots\ldots [2.102]$$

where the p_i are the probabilities of occurrence in each of the r class intervals of the density function $f(x; \theta_1, \theta_2, \ldots, \theta_m)$. The value $1/p_i$ is a weighting function to account for irregularity of class interval size. Values of the parameters are obtained by taking partial derivatives of χ^2 with respect to each of the parameters thus obtaining m equations in m unknowns that can be solved simultaneously. This approach is sometimes referred to as the minimum χ^2 method (Yevjevich, 1972a).

Further modifications of this approach, referred to as nonlinear least squares (DeCoursey and Snyder, 1969), have been suggested for use on either linear or nonlinear functional relations, $f(x; \theta_1, \theta_2, \ldots, \theta_m)$. In this approach, all parameters are given initial estimated values $\hat{\theta}_i$. It may be shown that the error, e_i, between observations, y_i, and functional estimates, $f(x_i, \hat{\theta}_1, \hat{\theta}_2, \ldots, \hat{\theta}_m)$

$$e_i = y_i - f(x_i; \hat{\theta}_1, \hat{\theta}_2 \ldots \hat{\theta}_m) \quad \ldots\ldots\ldots\ldots\ldots\ldots\ldots\ldots [2.103]$$

may be partitioned to each of the unknown parameters by using the partial derivatives of the function with respect to each of the parameters as weighting functions. This is shown mathematically as

$$e_i = h_i \left[\frac{\partial f(x_i; \hat{\theta}_1, \hat{\theta}_2, \ldots, \hat{\theta}_m)}{\partial \hat{\theta}_1} \right] + \ldots +$$

$$h_m \left[\frac{\partial f(x_i; \hat{\theta}_1, \hat{\theta}_2, \ldots, \hat{\theta}_m)}{\partial \hat{\theta}_m} \right] \quad \ldots \ldots \ldots \ldots \ldots \ldots \quad [2.104]$$

where $h_{1,2, \ldots, m}$ are corrections to the initial estimates of the parameter values. Values of h_i can be obtained by minimizing the error sum of squares

$$\text{minimize} \left[\sum_{i=1}^{n} e_i^2 \right] \quad \ldots \ldots \ldots \ldots \ldots \ldots \ldots \ldots \quad [2.105]$$

Equation [2-104] is linear; therefore, solution to equation [2-105] may be obtained by ordinary least squares with h_i being the β coefficients, and the $\partial f / \partial \theta$ being the known x's. However, since the partial derivatives may be hard to obtain in some cases, and the parameters related, DeCoursey and Snyder (1969) replaced the partial derivatives with delta functions and used components regression rather than least squares to solve the linear equations. Equation [2-104] was obtained by dropping small terms in a Taylor series expansion. Using this method, new values of the parameters, obtained by adding the corrections, that is, $\hat{\theta}_i' = \hat{\theta}_i + h_i$, are in themselves estimates. Thus, the optimization process is repeated. If the functional relations are well formed, the solution requires only a few iterations to reach an optimum. DeCoursey (1968) illustrates use of nonlinear least squares by applying it to several hydrologic problems.

Method of Maximum Likelihood

In the last few years, the most popular method of fitting parameters has been the method of maximum likelihood. To illustrate the method, we will assume that we have a random sample of observations $x_1, x_2, \ldots, x_n$ from some unknown population. We will also assume that we know the form of the density function, $f(x; \theta)$, from which the observations come, but we do not know the value of the parameter (or vector of parameter values). Since we know the density function $f(x; \theta)$, then each observation has a certain probability of occurrence $f(x_i; \theta)$, and this probability depends upon the parameter θ in the function. The joint distribution of all sample observations, $f(\underline{x}; \theta)$ is the product of the individual probabilities over all observations n,

$$f(\underline{x}; \theta) = f(x_1, x_2, \ldots, x_n; \theta) = \prod_{i=1}^{n} f(x_i; \theta) \quad \ldots \ldots \ldots \ldots \ldots \quad [2.106]$$

$f(\underline{x}; \theta)$ is known as the likelihood function.

The method of maximum likelihood is based on the premise that the most likely value of θ is the value that leads to a maximum value of the joint probability $f(\underline{x}; \theta)$. Heuristically this may be interpreted as being that value of θ such that the individual probabilities of occurrence, $f(x; \theta)$, will be clustered together as closely as possible about the mean value. This value of θ will lead to a joint product of individual probabilities that is a maximum.

The maximum likelihood solution thus becomes the value of θ such that

$$\frac{\partial\, f(\underline{x};\theta)}{\partial\theta} = 0 \quad \dots\dots\dots\dots\dots\dots\dots\dots\dots\dots\dots\dots \quad [2.107]$$

As an example assume that we have n observations from an exponential distribution, $f(x,\, \alpha) = \alpha e^{-\alpha x}$. The joint density function of the n observations thus becomes

$$f(\underline{x};\alpha) = \prod_{i=1}^{n} \alpha e^{-\alpha x_i} = \alpha^n \exp(-\alpha \sum_{i=1}^{n} x_i) \quad \dots\dots\dots\dots\dots\dots \quad [2.108]$$

and

$$\frac{\partial f(\underline{x},\alpha)}{\partial\alpha} = (n - \sum_{i=1}^{n} x_i)\, \alpha^{n-1} \exp(-\alpha \sum_{i=1}^{n} x_i) = 0 \quad \dots\dots\dots\dots \quad [2.109]$$

from which we find that a maximum is obtained when

$$\alpha = \frac{n}{\sum\limits_{i=1}^{n} x_i} = \frac{1}{\bar{x}} \, .$$

Quite frequently, probability distributions involve an exponential function. Thus, it is much easier to work with the natural logarithm of the likelihood function $\ln[f(\underline{x};\, \theta)]$. Since the logarithmic function is monotonic, values of θ that maximize the logarithm of the likelihood function also maximize the likelihood function. This can be illustrated using the above example

$$\ln[\, f(\underline{x};\alpha)] = n\ln\alpha - \sum_{i=1}^{n} x_i \quad \dots\dots\dots\dots\dots\dots\dots\dots \quad [2.110]$$

$$\frac{\partial\, \{\ln[\, f(\underline{x};\alpha)]\}}{\partial\alpha} = \frac{n}{\alpha} - \sum_{i=1}^{n} x_i = 0 \quad \dots\dots\dots\dots\dots\dots\dots \quad [2.111]$$

$$\hat{\alpha} = \frac{n}{\sum\limits_{i=1}^{n} x_i} = \frac{1}{\bar{x}} \quad \dots\dots\dots\dots\dots\dots\dots\dots\dots\dots\dots\dots \quad [2.112]$$

which is the same as the result obtained using equation [2-109].

If the density function contains a vector of m parameters, solution for all parameters is obtained by setting the partial derivatives of the likelihood function with respect to each parameter to zero and simultaneously solving the m equations in m unknowns.

Estimates obtained by the maximum likelihood method in some cases may be biased but they are all asymptotically unbiased. If efficient estimates exist for the parameters, then maximum likelihood method will produce them. If sufficient estimates exist, solutions of the likelihood equations will be functions of these sufficient estimates. Finally, if the likelihood solution converges to the true population value, as it often does, then the estimate is consistent.

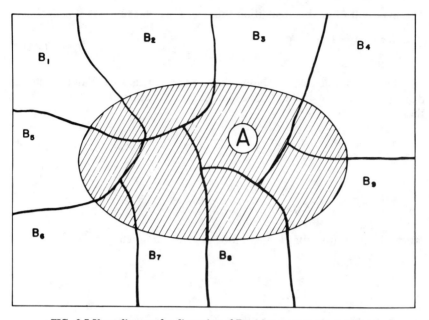

FIG. 2-7 Venn diagram for discussion of Bayesian concepts fo statistics.

For examples of the application of this method to hydrologic problems, the reader is referred to chapter 8 in Yevjevich (1972a) and chapter 3 in Haan (1977). Haan (1977) in chapter 6 also presents the maximum likelihood solutions of parameters of most of the common continuous distribution functions. These equations can be used directly to obtain the maximum likelihood solution for parameters of the functions.

The Methods of Bayesian Statistics

Quite often the hydrologist is faced with the problem of generating a synthetic trace of hydrologic data at a site or at multiple sites and he has only a very short period of record, or sample, upon which to base the values of parameters of his model. It is possible to considerably reduce error in estimates of the parameters by taking into account other information that may be available. For example, regional estimates of the parameters or data from sites close by. Techniques to use these data are based on the concepts of Bayesian statistics.

The rule of Bayes is simple and easy to comprehend if we start from basic probability concepts using a Venn diagram. Total sample space of two independent events A and B are shown in the Venn diagram of Fig. 2-7. The elements of B are mutually exclusive such that the probability of event A occurring is given by

$$P(A) = \sum_{i=1}^{n} P(A \cap B_i) \quad \dots\dots\dots\dots\dots\dots\dots\dots\dots\dots\dots\dots\dots\dots\dots \quad [2.113]$$

where $A \cap B_i$ means the intersection of A and B_i, and n is the number of elements in B. The probability of the intersection of A and B_i can be expressed in one of two different ways

$$P(A \cap B_i) = P(B_i) \cdot P(A | B_i) = P(A) \cdot P(B_i | A) \quad \dots\dots\dots\dots\dots\dots\dots \quad [2.114]$$

where $P(A|B_i)$ and $P(B_i|A)$ mean the probability of A given B_i has occurred and the probability of B_i given A has occurred respectively. Using the first expression for the probability of the intersection leads to

$$P(A) = \sum_{i=1}^{n} P(B_i) \cdot P(A|B_i) \quad \dots\dots\dots\dots\dots\dots\dots\dots\dots\dots\dots [2.115]$$

Here we have expressed the probability of an event A as the sum of several independent events. Suppose that we know event A has occurred and would like to know the probability that it came from one of the events, B_j, i.e. $P(B_j|A)$. In hydrology this would be analogous to knowing that we have a flood on a river with three major tributaries and would like to know the probability that it came from one specific tributary. Using the second expression of equation [2-114], this may be written as

$$P(B_j|A) = \frac{P(A \cap B_j)}{P(A)} \quad \dots\dots\dots\dots\dots\dots\dots\dots\dots\dots\dots [2.116]$$

Substituting the first expression of equation [2-114] for the $P(A \cap B_j)$ and equation [2-115] for the $P(A)$ in equation [2-116] leads to,

$$P(B_j|A) = \frac{P(B_j) \cdot P(A|B_j)}{\sum_{i=1}^{n} P(B_i) \cdot P(A|B_i)} \quad \dots\dots\dots\dots\dots\dots\dots\dots\dots\dots [2.117]$$

Equation [2-117] is known as Bayes rule or Bayes theorem. Another way of interpreting this equation, and one that is applicable to the estimation of parameters in a model, is that B_j is one of the parameters θ that we want to estimate and that A is the totality of our observed sample $\underline{x}$. If this is the case, then we can rewrite equation [2-117] substituting θ for $\overline{B}$, $\underline{x}$ for A, the functional f for the probability distribution P, and an integral over the parameter space for the summation. The resulting equation expresses the value of the parameters given the observed sample $f(\theta|\underline{x})$, the posterior distribution of θ, as a function of the prior estimate of the parameters and the joint density of the sample given the prior estimates

$$f(\theta|\underline{x}) = \frac{f(\theta) \, f(\underline{x}|\theta)}{\int f(\theta) \, f(\underline{x}|\theta) d\theta} \quad \dots\dots\dots\dots\dots\dots\dots\dots\dots\dots [2.118]$$

Using this interpretation, $f(\theta)$ is an estimate of parameter values prior to obtaining the data sample and $f(\underline{x}|\theta)$ is the joint density function for the sample given the prior estimates of the parameters.

A comparison of $f(\underline{x}|\theta)$ with equation [2-106] shows that the joint distribution of our sample, given prior parameter values, can be interpreted as the likelihood function. If we let

$$g(\theta) = f(\theta)f(\underline{x}|\theta) \quad \dots\dots\dots\dots\dots\dots\dots\dots\dots\dots\dots [2.119]$$

then the posterior distribution of θ is equal to the product of the likelihood function and the prior distribution of θ rescaled

$$f(\theta|\underline{x}) = \frac{g(\theta)}{\int g(\theta)d\theta} \cdot \quad \dots\dots\dots\dots\dots\dots\dots\dots\dots\dots [2.120]$$

As an example of the Bayesian approach, assume that we wish to generate a synthetic sequence of annual events at a stream flow station. We have available only $n < 25$ years of record upon which to base our parameter estimates but the data are good enough to indicate that a log-normal distribution appears to adequately represent the frequency distribution of annual values. Assume these data have a log-normal mean $\bar{x}$ and standard deviation s. However, assume that regional data are complete enough to provide estimates of the mean and variance $\bar{x}_o$ and s_s respectively. Since we have assumed that the sample is log-normally distributed, the distribution of the mean is also log-normal with parameters μ and $\sigma/\sqrt{n}$. It can be shown that the posterior distribution (the conditional distribution of the population mean, given the observed sample) of the population mean is also log-normal; its mean and standard deviation are

$$\hat{\mu}_{\bar{x}} = \frac{n\bar{x}\,s_o^2 + \bar{x}_o s^2}{ns_o^2 + s^2} \quad\cdots\cdots\cdots\cdots\cdots\cdots\cdots\cdots\cdots\cdots\cdots\cdots\cdots \quad [2.121]$$

and

$$\hat{\sigma}_{\bar{x}} = \frac{s^2\,s_o^2}{n\,s_o^2 + s^2} \quad\cdots\cdots\cdots\cdots\cdots\cdots\cdots\cdots\cdots\cdots\cdots\cdots \quad [2.122]$$

The significance of these two equations can be shown by a simple example (Table 2-1). Assume that sample record lengths of 1, 5, 10, 20, and 30 years are available and that the means and standard deviations of logarithms of the data in the samples were 3.0 and 2.0 respectively. Further assume that the prior estimate (based on the regional data) of the mean is 5.0. Two different values of the prior standard deviation, 1.0 and 4.0, were assumed, to examine the effect of size of the standard deviation of the sample on estimates of the mean as compared with the prior estimate of the mean. A value of 1 for the prior standard deviation means that our prior estimate is only 1/2 that of the sample, whereas a value of 4 means that it is twice the sample value. Since we have assumed a log-normal distribution, our

TABLE 2.1. A COMPARISON OF MAXIMUM LIKELIHOOD
AND BAYESIAN ESTIMATES OF THE MEAN AND
STANDARD DEVIATION OF THE POPULATION MEAN
FOR SAMPLE SIZE

Sample size	Maximum likelihood		Bayesian			
			$s_o = 1.0$		$s_o = 4.0$	
n	$\hat{\mu}_{\bar{x}}$	$\hat{\sigma}_{\bar{x}}$	$\hat{\mu}_{\bar{x}}$	$\hat{\sigma}_{\bar{x}}$	$\hat{\mu}_{\bar{x}}$	$\hat{\sigma}_{\bar{x}}$
1	3.0	2.0	4.6	0.89	3.4	1.79
5	3.0	0.89	3.9	0.67	3.1	0.87
10	3.0	0.63	3.6	0.53	3.1	0.62
20	3.0	0.45	3.3	0.41	3.0	0.44
30	3.0	0.37	3.2	0.34	3.0	0.36

Note:

Prior estimates $\quad \bar{x}_o = 5.0 \qquad\qquad s_o = 1.0$ and $s_o = 4.0$

Sample estimates $\quad \bar{x} = 3.0 \qquad\qquad s = 2.0$

Maximum likelihood estimates of $\hat{\mu}_{\bar{x}}$ and $\hat{\sigma}_{\bar{x}}$ based on the sample only used equations [2.123] and [2.124] respectively.

Bayesian estimates of $\hat{\mu}_{\bar{x}}$ and $\hat{\sigma}_{\bar{x}}$ based on the sample and prior estimates used equations [2.121] and [2.122] respectively.

estimates of the mean and standard deviation of the mean based only on the samples would be given by

$$\hat{\mu}_{\bar{x}} = \bar{x} \quad \dots\dots\dots\dots\dots\dots\dots\dots\dots\dots\dots\dots\dots\dots\dots\dots \quad [2.123]$$

and

$$\hat{\sigma}_{\bar{x}} = s/\sqrt{n} \quad \dots\dots\dots\dots\dots\dots\dots\dots\dots\dots\dots\dots\dots\dots \quad [2.124]$$

Table 2-1 compares values of $\hat{\mu}_{\bar{x}}$ and $\hat{\sigma}_{\bar{x}}$ based on the sample only with Bayesian estimates in which the prior estimates of the standard deviation were 1/2 and 2 times the sample values. In Table 2-1, a comparison of columns two, four, and six shows, for small samples (<10) that when the prior estimate of the variance is small compared with the sample value, the posterior estimate is significantly influenced by the prior estimate. However when the sample size gets to be 20, there is little difference between the Bayesian posterior estimates and the maximum likelihood value of 3.0 based on the sample only. A comparison between columns three, five, and seven shows a somewhat similar condition for the standard deviation of the population mean. If sample sizes are ⩾20 there is very little difference between either of the Bayesian posterior estimates and the Maximum Likelihood estimate based on the sample only. In summary, prior estimates of the standard deviation that are lower than the sample significantly influence the posterior estimate for sample sizes of less than <10, but large prior estimates have little influence on the sample estimate.

The results of this comparison cannot be generalized, but they serve to illustrate the concept of Bayesian estimation of model parameters. Information similar to that presented but for other parameters such as the mean and variance of the population standard deviation show similar results (Vicens et al., 1975a). These analyses may be summarized as follows: (a) Posterior information is a weighted combination of the prior and the sample information; (b) as the historical sample size increases, the sample information is weighted more heavily than the prior information; (c) as the total information increases, the parameter uncertainty, as measured by their posterior variance, is reduced; and, most important, (d) the posterior variances are lower than those of either the prior estimate or the sample alone. Thus, combining both information sources reduces parameter uncertainty; the Bayesian estimators are more efficient than either of the individual estimators.

Equation [2-120], which defines the posterior distribution in terms of the likelihood function and the prior distribution of θ, gives us a convenient way of expressing our uncertainty about the value of θ, but it also gives us a rational way of accounting for the information about θ that is inherent in the sample.

Risk: The value of knowing $f(\theta|\underline{x})$ is greatly increased if we wish to analyze the economic consequences of our parameter estimation techniques and our data collection policies. For example, suppose we are planning to build a water supply reservoir and have a limited set of streamflow data, $\underline{x}$. The true average streamflow rate θ is unknown, but the relative likelihood of different values of θ being the true value is given by $f(\theta|\underline{x})$. In designing the reservoir, we must estimate θ so we select $\hat{\theta}$. Since $\hat{\theta}$ is certain not equal θ exactly, the net benefits of the project are going to depend on the relationship between θ and $\hat{\theta}$. We will let $r(\theta; \hat{\theta})$ denote the "regret" (loss of possible net benefits because θ was not known exactly) when we design the system for $\hat{\theta}$ when the true state of nature turns out to be θ. If the likely range of θ is not too large, the regret is essentially a linear function of the difference between θ and $\hat{\theta}$, $(r'(\theta - \hat{\theta}))$.

$$r(\theta;\hat{\theta}) = r'(\theta-\hat{\theta}) \quad \dots\dots\dots\dots\dots\dots\dots\dots\dots\dots\dots [2.125]$$

In the reservoir example, selecting $\hat{\theta} < \theta$ would mean that the flow was underestimated and a reservoir larger than actually necessary would be provided to meet demands. Conversely, if $\hat{\theta} > \theta$, the mean flow would be overestimated and a reservoir would be provided that was too small to supply the water requirements. It is easy to see from this example that the regret function may be different for overestimation than for underestimation.

Since the marginal increase in regret increases, usually as the error in parameter estimates increase, another commonly used regret function is

$$r(\theta;\hat{\theta}) = r''((\theta-\hat{\theta})^2) \quad \dots\dots\dots\dots\dots\dots\dots\dots\dots\dots .[2.126]$$

In this formulation, the regret function is proportional to the error sum of squares between the estimated parameter value $\hat{\theta}$ and the true value θ.

The expected value of the regret, which is what we need to design a system, is called the risk, $R(\hat{\theta})$, and is computed as the product of the regret function and the likelihood of a value, $\hat{\theta}$; integrated over the range of possible values of $\hat{\theta}$

$$R(\hat{\theta}) = \int r(\theta,\hat{\theta}) \, f(\theta \mid x)d\theta \quad \dots\dots\dots\dots\dots\dots\dots\dots\dots [2.127]$$

Obviously the objective of our design is to minimize the risk $R(\hat{\theta})$. Discussion of methods used to obtain values of the parameter, $\hat{\theta}$, from equation [2-127], so as to minimize the risk, is too lengthy to include in this chapter. Neither have we attempted to discuss the relation between the distribution properties of the parameters and the coefficients of the underlying functional forms used for various regret functions. Finally, there are many similar forms of the risk function that we have not discussed. The procedures used to parameterize these functions are beyond the scope of this chapter.

Several good references are available that describe applications of the Bayesian approach to models such as those described in this chapter. For example, Lenton et al. (1974) described the application of the Bayesian approach to estimation of ρ in a first-order autoregressive model. They examined several approaches to the derivation of the posterior probability density function and discussed the risk function extensively. Wood and Rodriguez-Iturbe, in two papers (1975a, b), used Bayesian analyses to examine several flood excedence models. A composite linear model consisting of the Bayesian distributions of the individual models weighted by the posterior model was proposed. Extensive evaluation of the risk function and hydrologic uncertainty lead to procedures that can be used to make engineering decisions. Two other papers by Vicens et al. (1975a, b) discussed the applications of Bayesian analyses to hydrologic models in general. The use of regional information to define the prior distribution is described. The second paper discussed specifically a first order autoregressive process. Finally Valdes et al. (1977) extends the concepts of Bayesian estimation to the multivariate generation of synthetic streamflows.

SUMMARY

The material presented in this chapter was divided into three major areas. The first part was a discussion of the statistical properties of hydrologic time series. This included event time and discrete time, first and second order distribution properties, joint distribution properties, long term properties such as the Hurst effect and the variance function, and different forms of asymmetry. The next part of the chapter was a discussion of available stochastic models. These included short memory processes such as the moving average, autoregressive, mixed autoregressive, moving average, and autoregressive, integrated, moving average. Long memory models such as fast fractional Gaussian noise, filtered fractional noise, broken-line, and some forms of the autoregressive moving average processes were then described. Following a comparison of some of the short and long memory models, the generation of daily data by models such as the shot noise process was described. Finally the disaggregation process and space-time rainfall models were presented. The last part of the chapter was concerned with the subject of model selection and parameter estimation. Topics covered included incomplete data sets; properties of parameter estimates such as bias, minimum variance, and consistency; discussion of random number generators; and several different methods of parameter estimation. The estimation methods described included the method of moments, method of least squares, method of maximum likelihood, and the methods of Bayesian statistics.

In this chapter we have described the types of stochastic models most often used in hydrology. It should help guide a reader in model selection and model evaluation, and in making him aware of some of the concerns the model builder faces. Statistical texts referenced in the Introduction and numerous references throughout the chapter guide the reader to less frequently used models and to further study of particular issues.

References

1 Boes, C. B. and J. D. Salas. 1978. Nonstationarity of the mean and the Hurst phenomenon. Water Resources Research (14, 1):135-143.

2 Box, G. E. P. and D. R. Cox. 1964. An analysis of transformations. Jour. Royal Stat. Soc. B26, 211.

3 Box, G. E. P. and G. M. Jenkins. 1976. Time series analysis: Forecasting and control, Revised edition. Holden-Day, Inc., San Francisco, CA.

4 Bras, R. L. and I. Rodriguez-Iturbe. 1976. Rainfall generation: A nonstationary time-varying multidimensional model. Water Resources Research 12(3):450-456.

5 Burges, S. J. and D. P. Lettenmaier. 1975. Operational Comparison of stochastic streamflow generation procedures. Tech. Rep. 45, Harris Hydraul. Lab., Dept. of Civil Eng., Univ. of Washington, Seattle.

6 Carlson, R. F., A. J. A. MacCormick and D. G. Watts. 1970. Application of linear random models to four annual streamflow series. Water Research Res. 6(4).

7 Caskey, J. E., Jr. and A. Markov. 1963. Chain model for the probability of precipitation occurrence in intervals of various length. Monthly Weather Rev. 91:298-301.

8 Chi, M., E. Neal and G. K. Young. 1973. Practical application of fractional Brownian motion and noise to synthetic Hydrology. Water Resources Res. 9(6):1523-1533.

9 Ciriani, T. A., U. Maione and J. P. Wallis. 1977. Mathematical models for surface water Hydrology. John Wiley and Sons.

10 Cooke, D. S. 1953. The duration of wet and dry spells at Moncton, New Brunswick. Quart. Roy. Meteorol. Soc. 79(342):536-538.

11   Crosby, D. S. and T. Maddock, III. 1970. Estimating coefficients of a flow generator for monotone samples of data. Water Resources Research 6(4):1079-1086.

12   DeCoursey, D. G. 1968. An application of computer technology to hydrologic model building. IASH Symposium on "The Use of Analog and Digital Computers in Hydrology," Tucson, AZ, Pub. No. 80, AIRS Vol. 1, pp. 233-239.

13   DeCoursey, D. G. 1971. The stochastic approach to watershed modeling Nordic Hydrology. 1971, II pp. 186-216.

14   DeCoursey, D. G. and E. H. Seely. 1969. Indirect determination of synthetic runoff. Proc. Thirteenth Congr. Int. Assoc. Hydraulic Res. Vol. 1, 31 Aug.-5 Sept. Kyoto, Japan.

15   DeCoursey, D. G. and W. M. Snyder. 1969. Computer oriented method of optimizing hydrologic model parameters. J. Hydrology 9:34-56.

16   Delleur, J. W., P. C. Tao and L. L. Kavvas. 1976. On evaluation of the practicability and complexity of some rainfall and runoff time series models. Water Resources Res. 12(5):953-970.

17   Evans, C. E., D. A. Woolhiser and F. Rauzi. 1974. Opportunity for harvesting water from and along highways in rangeland areas of Wyoming. Proceedings of the Water Harvesting Symposium, Phoenix, AZ, USDA-ARSW-22, pp. 293-301.

18   Fiering, M. B. 1964. Multivariate technique for synthetic hydrology. J. Hydraulics Div., Amer. Soc. Civil Engrs. 90(HY5):43-60.

19   Fiering, M. B. 1967. Streamflow synthesis. Harvard University Press, Cambridge, Mass.

20   Fiering, M. B. 1968. Schemes for handling inconsistent matrices. Water Resources Res. 4(2):291-298.

21   Finzi, G., E. Todini and J. R. Wallis. 1975. Comment upon multivariate synthetic hydrology. Water Resources Res. 11(6).

22   Finzi, G., E. Todini and J. R. Wallis. 1977a. Comment upon multivariate synthetic hydrology. In: Mathematical models for surface water hydrology by Ciriani, Maione and Wallis. John Wiley and Sons. pp. 2950.

23   Finzi, G., E. Todini and J. R. Wallis. 1977b. MALSAK: Markov and least squares ARMA kernels. In: Mathematical Models for surface water hydrology by Ciriani, Maione and Wallis. John Wiley and Sons. pp. 223-248.

24   Finzi, G., E. Todini and J. R. Wallis. 1977c. SPUMA: Simulation package using matalas algorithm. In: Mathematical models for surface water hydrology by Ciriani, Maione and Wallis. John Wiley and Sons. pp. 249-276.

25   Fogel, M. M., L. Duckstein and J. L. Sanders. 1974. An event-based stochastic model of areal rainfall and runoff. Proceedings of the Symposium on Statistical Hydrology, Tucson, AZ, USDA-ARS Misc. Pub. No. 1275, pp. 247-261.

26   Freeman, H. A. 1963. Introduction to statistical inference. Addison-Wesley Pub. Co. 445 p.

27   Gabriel, K. R. and J. Newmann. 1962. A Markov chain model for daily rainfall occurrence at Tel Aviv. Quart. Jour. Roy. Met. Soc. Vol. 88, pp. 90-95.

28   Gupta, V. K. and E. C. Waymire. 1979. A stochastic kinematic study of subsynoptic space-time rainfall. Water Resources Research 15(3):637-644.

29   Haan, C. T., D. M. Allen and J. O. Street. 1976. A Markov chain model of daily rainfall. Water Resources Research 12(3):443-449.

30   Haan, C. T. 1977. Statistical methods in hydrology. Iowa University Press, Ames.

31   Hanson, C. L., E. L. Neff and D. A. Woolhiser. 1974. Hydrologic aspects of water harvesting in the Northern Great Plains. Proceedings of the Water Harvesting Symposium, Phoenix, AZ, USDA-ARSW-22, pp. 129-140.

32   Hipel, K. W., A. I. McLeod and W. C. Lennoz. 1977a. Advances in Box-Jenkins Modeling, 1. Model construction. Water Resources Res. 13(2).

33   Hipel, K. W., A. I. McLeod and E. A. MacBean. 1977b. Stochastic modeling of the effects of reservoir operation. J. Hydrology 32, pp. 97-113.

34   Hung, C. S. and H. W. Shen. 1974. Research in stochastic models for bedload transport. Proceedings of the Symposium on Statistical Hydrology, Tucson, AZ, USDA-ARS Misc. Pub. No. 1275, pp. 262-286.

35   Hurst, H. E. 1951. Long-term storage capacity of reservoirs. Trans. Amer. Soc. Civil Eng. 116, pp. 776-808.

36   Jorgensen, D. L. 1949. Persistency of rain and no-rain periods during the winter of San Francisco. Monthly Weather Rev. 77, 303-307.

37   Kelman, J. 1977. Stochastic modeling of hydrologic intermittent daily processes. Hydrology Papers No. 89, Colorado State University, Fort Collins, CO.

38   Klemes, V. 1974. The Hurst phenomenon: A puzzle? Water Resources Research 10(4):675-688.

39   Lawrence, A. J. and N. T. Kottegada. 1977. Stochastic modeling of riverflow fine series. J. R. Statist. Soc. A, 140, Part I, pp. 1, 47.

40 Lenton, R. L., I. Rodriguez-Iturbe and J. C. Schaake, Jr. 1974. The estimation of ρ in the first-order autoregressive model: A Bayesian approach. Water Resources Research 10(2):227-241.

41 Lenton, R. L. and I. Rodriguez-Iturbe. 1977. A multidimensional model for the synthesis of processes of areal rainfall averages. Water Resources Research 12(3):605-612.

42 Lettenmaier, D. P. and S. J. Burges. 1977a. Operational assessment of hydrologic models of long-term persistence. Water Resources Research 13(1):113-124.

43 Lettenmaier, D. P. and S. J. Burges. 1977b. An operational approach to preserving skew in hydrologic models of long-term persistence. Water Resources Research 13(2).

44 Lewis, T. G. and Walt Payne. 1973. Generalized feedback shift register pseudorandom number algorithm. Journal of Assoc. for Computing Machinery 20(3):456-468.

45 Lloyd, E. H. 1967. Stochastic reservoir theory. Advan. Hydroscience, 4, pp. 281-339.

46 Osborn, H. B., L. J. Lane and R. S. Kagan. 1974. Stochastic models of spatial and temporal distribution of thunderstorm rainfall. Proceedings Symposium on Statistical Hydrology, USDA Misc. Pub. No. 1275, pp. 211-231.

47 Mandelbrot, B. B. and J. R. Wallis. 1968. Noah, Joseph, and operational hydrology. Water Resources Research 4(5):909-918.

48 Mandelbrot, B. B. and J. R. Wallis. 1969. Computer experiments with fractional Gaussian noises, 1, Averages and Variances. Water Resources Res. 5(1):228-241.

49 Mandelbrot, B. B. 1971. A fast fractional Gaussian noise generator. Water Resources Research 7(3):543-553.

50 Matalas, N. C. 1967. Mathematical assessment of synthetic hydrology. Water Resources Research 3(4):937-945.

51 Matalas, N. C. 1975. Developments in stochastic hydrology. Review of Geophysics and Space Physics 13(3):67-73.

52 Matalas, N. C. 1977. Generation of multivariate synthetic flows. In: Mathematical models for surface water hydrology by Ciriani, Maione, and Wallis. John Wiley and Sons, pp. 27-38.

53 Matalas, N. C. and J. R. Wallis. 1971. Statistical properties of multivariate fractional noise processes. Water Resources Res. 7(6):1460-1468.

54 Matalas, N. C. and J. R. Wallis. 1974. Generation of synthetic flow sequences. In: Systems approach to water management (A. K. Biswas, ed.). McGraw Hill, NY.

55 Mckerchar, A. I. and J. W. Delleur. 1974. Application of seasonal parametric linear stochastic models to monthly flow data. Water Resources Res. 10(2).

56 McLeod, A. I., K. W. Hipel and W. C. Lennox. 1977. Advances in Box-Jenkins modeling, 2. Applications. Water Resources Res. 13(3).

57 McMichael, F. C. and J. S. Hunter. 1972. Stochastic modeling of temperature and flow in rivers. Water Resources Res. 8(1).

58 Mejia, J. M., I. Rodriguez-Iturbe and D. R. Dawdy. 1972. Streamflow Simulation. 2. The broken line process as a potential model for hydrologic simulation. Water Resources Res. 8(4):931-941.

59 Mejia, J. M. and I. Rodriguez-Iturbe. 1974a. Correlation links between normal and log normal processes. Water Resources Res. 10(4):689-690.

60 Mejia, J. M. and I. Rodriguez-Iturbe. 1974b. On the synthesis of random field sampling from the spectrum: An application to the generation of hydrologic spatial processes. Water Resources Research 10(4):705-712.

61 Mejia, J. M, D. R. Dawdy and C. F. Nordin. 1974a. Streamflow simulation 3. The broken line process and operational hydrology. Water Resources Res. 10:242-245.

62 Mejia, J. M., I. Rodriguez-Iturbe and J. R. Cordova. 1974b. Multivariate generation of mixtures of normal and log normal variables. Water Resources Res. 10(4).

63 Mejia, J. M., R. C. Ahlert and S. L. Yu. 1975. Stochastic variation of water quality of the Passaic River. Water Resources Res. 11(2).

64 Mejia, J. M. and J. Rousselle. 1976. Disaggregation models in hydrology revisited. Water Resources Research 12(2):185-186.

65 Miller, I. and J. E. Freund. 1977. Probability and statistics for engineers. Second Edition. Prentice-Hall, Inc. Englewood Cliffs, NJ.

66 Mood, A. M., F. A. Graybill and D. C. Boes. 1974. Introduction to the theory of statistics. Third Edition, McGraw-Hill, NY.

67 Nicks, A. D. 1974. Stochastic generation of the occurrence pattern, and location of maximum amount of daily ranfall. Proceedings Symposium on Statistical Hydrology, USDA Misc. Pub. No. 1275, pp. 154-171.

68 O'Connell, P. E. 1974. Stochastic modeling of long-term persistence in streamflow se-

quences. Ph.D. Thesis. Imperial College, University of London. 284 pp.

69   O'Connell, P. E. 1977a. Shot noise models in synthetic hydrology. In: Mathematical models for surface water hydrology by Ciriani, Maione, and Wallis. John Wiley and Sons. pp. 19-26.

70   O'Connell, P. E. 1977b. ARIMA models in synthetic hydrology. In: Mathematical models for surface water hydrology by Ciriani, Maione, and Wallis. John Wiley and Sons. pp. 51-70.

71   Overton, D. E. and M. E. Meadows. 1976. Stormwater modeling. Academc Press, NY.

72   Potter, K. W. 1976. Evidence for nonstationarity as a physical explanation of the Hurst phenomenon. Water Resources Research 12(5):1047-1052.

73   Rao, C. R. 1967. Linear statistical inference and its applications. John Wiley and Sons, NY.

74   Richardson, C. W. 1977. A model of stochastic structure of daily precipitation over an area. Hydrology Paper No. 91, Colorado State University, Fort Collins.

75   Shen, H. W. 1976. Stochastic approaches to water resources. Volumes I and II, Pub. by H. W. Shen, P.O. Box 606, Fort Collins, CO 80521, 28 chapters.

76   Siddiqui, M. M. 1976. The asymptotic distribution of the range and other functions of partial sums of stationary processes. Water Resources Research 12(6):1271-1276.

77   Tao, P. C. and J. W. Delleur. 1976a. Seasonal and nonseasonal ARMA models in hydrology. J. Hydraulics Div. Amer. Soc. Civil Engr. HY10, 1541-1559.

78   Tao, P. C. and J. W. Delleur. 1976b. Multistation, multiyear synthesis of hydrologic time series by disaggregation. Water Resources Research 12(6):1303.

79   Thomas, H. A., Jr. and M. B. Fiering. 1962. The mathematical synthesis of streamflow sequences. In: The design of water resource systems, ed. Arthur Mass. Harvard University Press, Cambridge, Mass.

80   Todorovic, P. and V. Yevjevich. 1969. Stochastic process of precipitation. Hydrology Paper No. 35, Colorado State Universtiy, Fort Collins, CO, 61 pp.

81   Todorovic, P. and D. Woolhiser. 1974. Stochastic model of daily rainfall. Proceedings Symposium on Statistical Hydrology, USDA Misc. Pub. No. 1275, pp. 232-246.

82   USDA-Agricultural Research Service. 1974. Proceedings Symposium on Statistical Hydrology, Tucson, AZ. Aug. 31-Sept. 2, 1971. USDA Misc. Pub. 1275, pp. 386.

83   Valdes, J. B., I. Rodriguez-Iturbe and G. J. Vicens. 1977. Bayesian generation of synthetic streamflows. 2. The multivariate Case. Water Resources Research 13(2):291-295.

84   Valencia, R. D. and J. C. Schaake, Jr. 1973. Disaggregation processes in stochastic hydrology. Water Resources Research 9(3):580-585.

85   Vicens, G. J., I. Rodriguez-Iturbe and J. C. Schaake, Jr. 1975a. A Bayesian framework for the use of regional information in hydrology. Water Resources Research 11(3):405-414.

86   Vicens, G. J. and I. Rodriguez-Iturbe and J. C. Schaake, Jr. 1975b. Bayesian generation of synthetic streamflows. Water Resources Research 11(6):827-838.

87   Wallis, J. R., N. C. Matalas and J. R. Slack. 1974. Just a moment! Water Resources Research 10(2):211-219.

88   Weiss, G. 1973a. Shot noise models for synthetic generation of multisite daily streamflow data. Symposium UNESCO World Meteorol. Organization, Intr. Assoc. of Hydrol. Sci., Madrid.

89   Weiss, G. 1973b. Filtered poisson processes as models for daily streamflow data. Ph.D. Thesis, Imp. College of Sci. and Technol., London.

90   Weiss, G. 1977. Shot noise models for the generation of synthetic streamflow data. Water Resources Research 13(1).

91   Weiss, L. L. 1964. Sequences of wet and dry described by a Markov chain probability model. Monthly Weather Rev. 92, 169-176.

92   Wiser, E. H. 1974. A precipitation data simulator using a second order autoregressive scheme. Proceedings Symposium on Statistical Hydrology, USDA Misc. Pub. No. 1275, pp. 120-134.

93   Wood, E. F. and I. Rodriguez-Iturbe. 1975a. Bayesian inference and decision making for extreme hydrologic events. Water Resources Research 11(4):533-542.

94   Wood, E. F. and I. Rodriguez-Iturbe. 1975b. A Bayesian approach to analyzing uncertainty among flood frequency models. Water Resources Research 11(6):839-843.

95   Woolhiser, D. A. and P. Todorovic. 1974. A stochastic model of sediment yield for ephemeral streams. Proceedings of the Symposium on Statistical Hydrology, Tucson, AZ, USDA-ARS Misc. Pub. No. 1275, pp. 295-308.

96   Yevjevich, V. M. 1964. Fluctuations of wet and dry years. Part II. Analysis by serial correlation. Colorado State University, Paper No. 4, Ft. Collins, CO.

97 Yevjevich, V. M. 1972a. Probability and statistics in hydrology. Water Resources Publication, Fort Collins, CO.

98 Yevjevich, V. M. 1972b. Stochastic processes in hydrology. Water Resources Publication, Fort Collins, CO.

LIST OF SYMBOLS

English Letters

a	Subscript, superscript, coefficient, normally distributed random variable, or interval spacing between random variables in a simple broken line process
b	coefficient or "decay" rate in shor noise models
d	order of differencing in ARIMA models
e	base of natural logarithms
e_i	error of the ith predicted value
f( )	a functional
g	sample coefficient of skewness
g( )	a functional
h	subscript to indicate high frequency terms in ffGn models, or correction to parameter estimates
f	subscript or superscript
k	a random variable used to designate the lag between elements in the correlation or covariance
l	a specific generated sequence of events
m	population size, number of parameters in a density function, or number of events per day in shot noise models
m_j	j^{th} moment of a distribution function
n	subscript, superscript, population size, period of record, number of seasons in a year, or a subset of the population
$\tilde{n}$	generated sequence of length n
p	integer, random variable, or order of an autoregressive process
q	random variable or order of a moving average process
r	relative fraction of values in one element of a histogram
r( )	regret function
s	sample standard deviation
t	time
$\underline{x}$	observed sample
x	random variable
$\bar{x}$	sample mean
y	magnitude of a spike in a shot noise model (generated from an exponential distribution or random variable usually a transformation of another random variable)
z	random variable
$\tilde{z}$	deviations of a random variable from the mean
A	element of a subset of independent events
B	a "base" parameter for separation of AR(1) processes in an FFGN process or element of a subset of independent events
D_o	maximum point amount of rainfall in a storm cell
E	random variable with an exponential distribution (shot noise models)
E( )	expect value of the element within the parentheses
H	Hurst coefficient
I[ ]	indicator function to insure proper interpolation in simple broken line process
L	number of generated sequences
M	memory of a system
N	population size, period of record, number of AR terms in an ffGn process, or number of cells in a storm cluster
N_e	effective sample size
P	number of transitional probabilities in a given model
Q	a "quality" parameter in controlling the number of AR(1) processes in an ffGn process
R	range of cumulative departures from the mean and radius of rainfall cells
R( )	risk function
S^2	error sum of squares
T	designates the transpose of a matrix, or maximum duration of period of interest in ffGn processes
T(x,)	general function expressing the distribution of random variable, x, as defined by parameter
V( )	variance of parameter in parentheses

W	weighting factor
X	random variable
$\underset{\sim}{A}$	matrix or vector of coefficients
$\tilde{A}$	matrix of coefficients
$\hat{A}$	estimate of the A matrix
B	matrix of coefficients
$\tilde{B}$	matrix of coefficients
$\hat{B}$	estimate of the B matrix
C	matrix
$[I]$	identity matrix
$M(k)$	variance covariance matrix of lag k
$[P]$	autocorrelation matrix
$\hat{S}_{YX}$	sample cross products matrix between seasonal Y and annual X values
$\hat{S}_{XX}$	sample sums of squares matrix of annual values, X
$\hat{S}_{XY}$	sample cross products matrix between annual, X, and seasonal Y value
$\hat{S}_{YY}$	sample of squares matrix of seasonal values, Y
$V(t)$	vector of independently distributed standard normal deviates
$X(t)$	vector of random deviates at time t
$Y(t)$	matrix of seasonal values in a disaggregation of annual values for year t

Greek Letters

α	coefficient or conditional probability
$\hat{\alpha}$	estimated value of coefficient
γ	covariance
η	normal distributed random variables, mean o and variance 1
θ	moving average coefficient or a population parameter
$\hat{\theta}$	estimate of moving average coefficient or estimate of population parameter
μ	population mean
$\hat{\mu}$	estimated value of the mean
ν	parameter, inversely related to the mean of the exponential distribution used to generate the time intervals between events in a shot noise model
$\xi(t)$	value of a simple broken line process at t
p	correlation coefficient
σ	population standard deviation
$\hat{\sigma}$	estimated value of the standard deviation
τ	time of an event within the interval of 1 day (shot noise models)
ϕ	autoregressive coefficient
$\hat{\phi}$	estimate of autoregressive coefficient
x^2	error sum of squares across class intervals
ω	hydrologic parameters
$\hat{\omega}$	estimate of a hydrologic parameter
$\tilde{\omega}$	hydrologic parameter based on an artificially generated sequence of events
β	conditional probability
$\beta(t)$	value of a broken line process at time t
$\Gamma( )$	variance function (variance of the number of consecutive observations in the parentheses) or the gamma function
$\varepsilon(t)$	normally distributed random variable, mean o and variance 1 at time t
Θ	mean of the exponential distribution used to generate the spike in shot noise models or parameter indicating storm cell placement
$\varepsilon[t]$	vector of random normal variates at time t
$[p]$	vector of autocorrelation coefficients
$[\phi]$	vector of autoregressive coefficients
∂	partial derivative

chapter 3 ████████████████████████

PRECIPITATION

3

3

PRECIPITATION

by   H. B. Osborn and L. J. Lane, USDA-ARS-SWC,
     Southwest Watershed Research Center, Tucson,
     AZ, C. W. Richardson, USDA-ARS, Grassland-
     Forage Research Center, Temple, TX and M.
     Molnau, Agricultural Engineering Department,
     University of Idaho, Moscow, ID.

INTRODUCTION

The input to most hydrologic models is precipitation, and rain and snow are the forms of precipitation of primary interest in the hydrologic modeling of small watersheds. Reasons for precipitation modeling include estimating annual and seasonal water yields, engineering design based on predicting flood peaks, erosion, sedimentation and chemical transport, and estimating crop yields from dry and irrigated croplands, and from range and pasture lands.

The proposed use of a hydrologic model dictates the needed detail and complexity of precipitation input. Economic considerations usually determine whether the desired sampling detail is actually achieved. For example, data from a single standard raingage may be sufficient to determine average annual or seasonal rainfall on a small watershed. A single recording raingage may provide enough information to predict average annual erosion and surface water yield. A network of recording gages is needed to describe the variation of precipitation in time and space. Data from a network of recording gages may be needed to estimate flood peaks, erosion, and sedimentation from individual events, or spatial variability of runoff production. Other hydrologic measurements, like temperature, humidity, solar radiation, evapotranspiration, and antecedent soil moisture, may be needed as well as precipitation for accurate water balance calculations or accurate crop yield estimates.

In this chapter, we will describe rainfall and snowfall models and rainfall and snowmelt as input to more complex hydrologic models. We tried to identify some hydrologic models that are widely used as well as some models or modeling efforts, that are less widely used but seem to show potential for future development. We made no effort to describe all hydrologic models or models which include precipitation.

RAINFALL

Significant Features

Rainfall is extremely variable, both in time and space. The extreme variability in mean annual precipitation and seasonal patterns of precipitation are illustrated in Fig. 3.1 by typical seasonal distribution graphs for

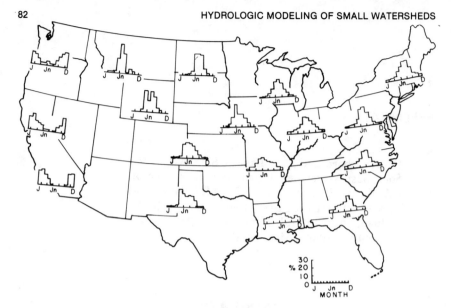

FIG. 3.1 Typical monthly distribution of precipitation in various climatic regions (after Linsley, et al., 1949).

selected stations in the United States. The spatial variability of precipitation amounts for a given event is illustrated in Fig. 3.2. Obviously, a model which describes rainfall, even for the most general low intensity rain, would be extremely complex. Therefore, the description of rainfall must be simplified to be useful in modeling. The nature of the rainfall, the required sophistication of the output, and the available resources will determine the amount of simplification.

There are three major directions in hydrologic analysis of rainfall: (a) determining the optimum sampling in time and space to answer specific questions, (b) determining the accuracy of precipitation estimates based on existing sampling systems, and (c) simulating precipitation patterns in varying degrees of complexity based on existing sampling systems for input to hydrologic models for gaged and ungaged watersheds. Input to

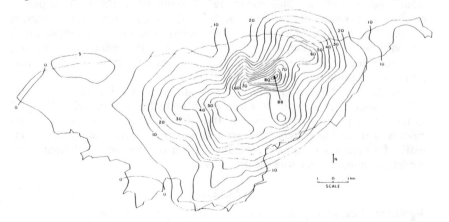

FIG. 3.2 Spatial variability of precipitation amounts for a given event (after Osborn, et al., 1974).

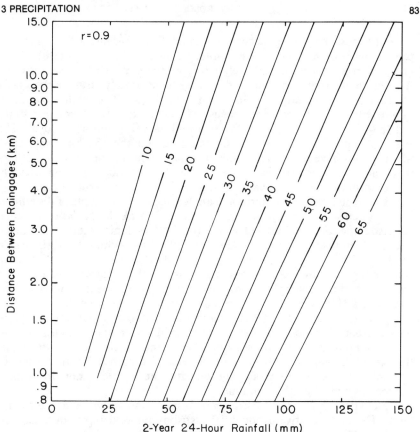

FIG. 3.3 Diagram for estimating the distance between gages as a function of the 2-yr 24-h and 2-yr 1-h rainfall (after Hershfield, 1965).

hydrologic models can be based on existing sampling systems (when available) or on simulated input. Most rainfall models are simulation models that have been developed based on data from existing sampling systems.

Optimum Sampling

In general, most analyses to determine optimum sampling systems to answer specific hydrologic questions are based on depth-area-duration relationships of rainfall. In the past, much anguish could have been avoided by thoroughly analyzing the sampling requirements for a planned hydrologic project, and by objectively choosing between available funds and sampling needs early in the project life. Many researchers have investigated network design: a sampling of these efforts follow.

Hershfield (1965) analyzed the spacing of 15 raingage networks in different climatic regions in the United States. He selected 15 major storms for each of the 15 watershed networks. Gage densities varied from 3 per 1 km² to 1 per 16 km². From these data, Hershfield developed a relationship (based on an arbitrary, but reasonable standard, r = 0.9) as a function of the 2-yr, 24-h and 2-yr, 1-h rainfall to aid in establishing gage density (Fig. 3.3). The relationship indicated that gages should be more closely spaced, as short duration rainfall intensities increase. Although the relationship was developed from a limited amount of data, it can be used as a first approximation of raingage spacing.

At times, the desired accuracy of rainfall measurement for a specified project or study may be unreasonable. For example, Osborn et al. (1972) analyzed records from a relatively dense raingage network in southeastern Arizona to determine the required spacing to accurately estimate the spatial variability of maximum 15-min storm rainfall (which is highly correlated to peak runoff from small watersheds). Using an arbitrary correlation standard (r = 0.9) between gages, the required gage spacing was 300 m. This spacing would have required 1400 raingages on the 150 km² watershed, which would have been completely unmanageable. In this case and others, there must be a compromise between desired and actual sampling. Usually, the compromise results in sparser sampling for a longer period of time.

Eagleson (1967) used harmonic analyses and the concepts of distributed linear systems to study the sensitivity of runoff peak discharge to the characteristic spatial variability of convective and cyclonic rainfall. He determined theoretical general relations for optimum rainfall network density for flood-forecasting purposes. He found that including watershed characteristics in the overall network design reduced the number of necessary gages, and that in simpler cases, for example when mean annual rainfall was required for a 3240 km² watershed, only two gages were needed.

Hendrick and Comer (1970) found statistical correlations among gages on a northern Vermont watershed based on distance and azimuth between gages, rainfall amount, and season. They found no correlation with elevation within a range of 400 m. They developed a correlation field function with which to determine raingage density and configuration for similar watersheds and climatic conditions.

Stol (1972) investigated correlations between rainfall gages in the Netherlands. He used negative exponential distributions utilizing both linear and quadratic distances between gages. Although the records from gages were often highly correlated, he found that extrapolating from one gage to another did not result in a correlation of 1.

Most efforts have been based primarily on large basins or regions, and are unnecessarily complex for small watershed design. However, observations on space and time correlation between number of gages and network watershed geometry is valid for all but the smallest watersheds in most regions, and probably valid for any but the smallest watersheds in regions where thunderstorm rainfall produces most of the runoff.

Effect of Rainfall Variability on Streamflow Simulation

Nash (1958) stated that the relationship between rainfall and runoff can be considered in three parts: (a) the relationship between volume of storm rainfall and the resulting volume of storm runoff, (b) the more complex manner in which the distribution of the rainfall in time affects the resulting runoff, and (c) the relationship between frequency of all rainfall occurrences and the occurrences of runoff-producing rainfall. The effects of spatial variability in rainfall on runoff might be considered as a fourth and most difficult relationship to define.

In discussing computer models, Linsley (1967) stated that with adequate amounts of the proper kinds of hydrologic data, streamflow hydrographs can be reproduced which are as accurate as the input supplied. For small watersheds, the input with the greatest variability is rainfall. Therefore, the accuracy of streamflow simulation depends primarily on how well this variability can be defined in a specific case.

Dawdy and Bergmann (1969) used data from a 15 km² watershed with three recording raingages to study the effects of data errors on simulations of flood hydrograhs and peaks. Their model required input of daily rainfall and evaporation (to evaluate antecedent conditions) as well as storm rainfall and a "R" factor for estimating rainfall excess. They found that the combined effects of differences in the time distribution of rainfall at different points as well as the spatial distribution over the watershed limited the accuracy of simulation.

Fogel (1969) reported on the effects of storm rainfall variability on runoff from small watersheds in the Southwest. He pointed out that runoff is a complicated process at best, and becomes much more complicated when the input is high intensity, short duration thunderstorm rainfall of limited areal extent. Again, although thunderstorm rains are more significant on small semiarid rangeland watersheds, they also produce significant runoff in more humid regions. Fogel pointed out that most current methods for estimating runoff volumes require knowledge of only total rainfall depth, which can lead to significant errors in estimating runoff.

Obsorn and Lane (1969) studied the relative sensitivity of rainfall variables and watershed characteristics on runoff from intense, short duration thunderstorm rainfall. They found that for four very small watersheds (less than 5 ha) runoff volume was most strongly correlated to total rainfall, that peak runoff rate was best correlated to maximum 15-min rainfall, that flow duration was best correlated to watershed length, and that lag time was best correlated to watershed area. Watershed characteristics did not add significantly to estimates of peaks or volume of runoff. In other words, for the data analyzed, the variability in rainfall dominated the relationships and indicated the difficulty in identifying significant variables other than rainfall in modeling runoff from small rangeland watersheds.

Wei and Larson (1971) presented a comprehensive analysis of the effects of areal and time distribution of rainfall on runoff hydrographs from small watersheds in southern Minnesota. They worked with a 2-phase model (Fig. 3.4) with precipitation as the input to the land phase portion, phase 1, of the model. Direct precipitation input to the channel, phase 2, can be considered insignificant for small watersheds, and only phase 1 is considered here. Five different triangular-shaped patterns of excess rainfall were selected to study the effects of time distribution, while three different rainfall patterns (concentrated on the upper, middle, and lower zones, respectively) were used to study the effects of areal distribution on runoff hydrographs. The results of the study were described in detail, and generally indicated significant difference in peak discharges for varying time and areal distributions of rainfall. For most small watersheds and design practices, this level of sophistication probably is not necessary, but in cases where relatively small differences in estimates of peak discharge can have economic impact, the work by Wei and Larson would be worth studying in detail.

The time and space distribution of heavy storm rainfall in Illinois were investigated by Huff (1967, 1968). His investigation was based on a network of 49 recording raingages on 1000 km² with subareas of 130, 260, and 520 km². His criteria for "heavy" storm rainfall was a mean depth of at least 12 mm, and a point value equal to or greater than that of a 2-yr frequency.

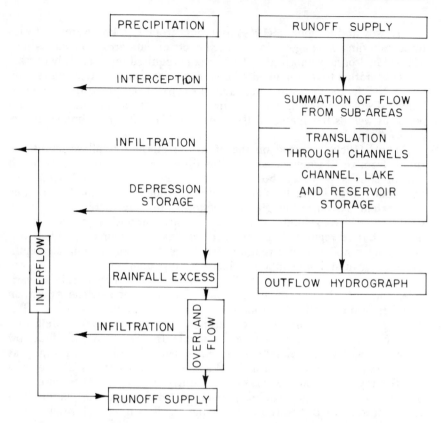

FIG. 3.4 The surface runoff process in two phases (after Wei and Larson, 1971).

For time distribution, he found that the relations could be represented by relating the percent of storm rainfall to storm duration and grouping the data according to the section in which rainfall was heaviest. These results were applicable to hydrologic modeling in the Midwest. For spatial distribution, he tested eight different statistical distributions for best fit. The most sensitive variables were: area, mean rainfall, and storm duration. The results were presented as probability distributions for different sets of conditions with respect to area, storm duration, and rainfall amount. Both investigations would be useful for hydrologic modeling for summer rainfall in Midwestern watersheds.

Effect of Elevation

Generally, elevation differences have little influence on rainfall occurrence and magnitude on small watersheds, or at least possible rainfall differences are difficult to identify on small watersheds with elevation differences of less than 500 m (Chang, 1977). For most hydrologic modeling of small watersheds, possible elevation effects on rainfall can be ignored. For mountainous terrain, both the number of events and amount of rainfall per event generally increase with elevation. Duckstein et al. (1973) used an event-based stochastic rainfall model and empirical data to investigate elevation effects on summer rainfall in the Santa Catalina Mountains in southern Arizona. Their results indicated an increase in the number of storms and the amount of rainfall per storm with deviation and apply to many Western mountain ranges where summer thunderstorm rainfall produces significant runoff. Therefore, for long, narrow mountain watersheds with elevation differences of about 500 m or more, elevation may be considered as a significant variable affecting rainfall.

Sensitivity Analysis

In developing models to solve hydrologic problems, many variables may influence the model output significantly. Generally, however, a model is far more sensitive to a few variables (or possibly just one) than to others. For example, within narrow ranges, differences in total storm rainfall may have considerably less effect on runoff estimates than differences in the maximum amount of rainfall for a shorter duration within the storm, or changes in watershed characteristics, like vegetation, may have much less influence on runoff than rainfall intensity.

Sensitivity analysis should be a part of every effort in hydrologic modeling of small watersheds. For precipitation, sensitivity analysis requires varying selected parameters individually through an expected range of values and then comparing the range of output values from each input variable. The relative sensitivity of parameters is important in all phases of modeling — formation, calibration, and verification. Several persons have addressed themselves to this problem. McCuen (1973) used a variety of simplified models to demonstrate the importance of sensitivity analysis in all phases of modeling. Osborn et al. (1972) showed the relative sensitivity of rainfall parameters in runoff prediction. These efforts were only two of the many examples illustrating the often overlooked value of sensitivity analysis as an aid in hydrologic modeling.

Frequency Analysis

The primary objectives of frequency analysis are to determine the return periods of events of known magnitude, and then to estimate the magnitude of events for design return periods beyond the recorded history (Kite, 1975). The statistical tool used to extrapolate the known record is the probability distribution. An empirical probability distribution is often used with observed precipitation data to determine precipitation amouns for design return periods. The frequency of occurrence of rainfall amounts are determined by ranking the observed data, computing a plotting position, and plotting the rainfall amount and position on probability paper. Several plotting position formulas are available. Some have been described by Chow (1964) and Yevjevich (1972). The most practical and widely used plotting position formula is

$$P(y) = \frac{m}{N+1} \quad \dots \dots \dots \dots \dots \dots \dots \dots \dots \dots \dots \quad [3.1]$$

where

y = the rainfall value
$P(y)$ = is the plotting position
m = the rank of the rainfall value, and
N = the number of observations.

The return period, or recurrence interval, is given by the inverse of $P(y)$.

When a few data series must be analyzed various frequency papers can be examined and knowledge of probability and processes used to glean maximum design information (Reich, 1976, 1978). When data from many stations are used to calculate the parameters for a preselected probability distribution, or to determine the best disribution (Alexander et al., 1969; Goodridge, 1976) for the particular data type, electronic computers are essential.

The selected distribution is then used to extrapolate to return periods greater than the record period. The predicted values are subject to considerable error, depending primarily on the length of record available (Bell, 1969).

There is no general agreement as to which distribution, or distributions, should be used for rainfall frequency analysis. The National Weather Service (NWS) used a modified version of the Gumbel extreme value distribution (W.M.O., 1974) regressed against topographic features surrounding all gages to develop a rainfall frequency atlas (NOAA Atlas 2) for the United States. It reduces some of the areal smoothing in Hershfield's (1961) TP40. The atlas is widely used to select point rainfall amounts for varying storm durations and return periods for small watershed runoff design. More recently, Frederick et al. (1977) produced maps for 5- through 60-min rains for the 37 eastern United States by mathematically fitting this distribution, which has the synonym Fisher-Tippett Type I. Examinations of single-state data include those by Goodridge (1976) and Reich et al. (1970) for California and Pennsylvania.

Bell (1969) pointed out that the design floods from small watersheds were generally the result of high intensity rains of short duration and limited areal extent. Rainfall frequencies are based on point records, and do not represent either the maximum rainfall that may occur on a watershed or the average watershed rainfall (Fogel and Duckstein, 1969). The NWS has published (also in NOAA Atlas 2) point-to-area relationships as a family of curves to be used to indicate the reduction in average areal rainfall for a given point value. These curves are generally valid for watersheds larger than 2 or 3 km², but should be used with caution on long, narrow watersheds or in regions where runoff is dominated by air-mass thunderstorms.

For regions dominated by air-mass thunderstorm rainfall (like southern Arizona), Osborn et al. (1979) published a family of curves indicating significantly larger reductions in average watershed rainfall than those published in the NOAA Atlas. Also, typical relationships between point and watershed maximum rainfall for given return periods were developed. For all but the smallest watersheds, the maximum rainfall that can occur about once in 100 years somewhere on the watershed, is significantly greater than that expected at any specific point within the watershed for the same return period.

HYDROLOGIC RAINFALL MODELS

Most rainfall models were not developed specifically for small watershed design. However, such models usually are applicable to small watersheds, and in fact, are often better suited to the smaller watersheds because of the difficulty of explaining rainfall variability in space and time on large watersheds. Most rainfall models are designed with runoff prediction in mind.

Recent modeling efforts have centered on autoregressive and Markov chain methods to describe persistence in time series of rainfall. Each model assumes one or more probability distributions to fit the stochastic distribution of observed rainfall. Both point occurrence and amount of rainfall have been simulated for varying time intervals. Early models were simple and assumed constant correlation coefficients and homogeneous rainfall populations. Current efforts are directed towards segmented multipopulation models.

To date, none of the many available models has had wide usage. Some models are scholarly efforts which may lead to practical designs in the future. Others are used by individuals or groups in one locality or region. All models have parameters whose values must be evaluated from rainfall data. A sample of the available models along with a brief history of their development follows.

Gringorten's (1966) observation, that persistence is often as important as variability in rainfall occurrence, has guided most of the efforts to model precipitation.

Rainfall for short time intervals, like a day or an hour, has been difficult to model because of the sequential persistence between rainfall amounts, and because the time series are dominated by zero values (intermittent process). The occurrence or nonoccurrence of rainfall for such short intervals have normally been described by Markov chains. With the Markov chain approach, the probabilities of transition from one state (wet or dry) to the other state are determined. A wet-dry sequence is then generated using the transition matrix. When a rainfall occurrence is determined, the precipitation amount is drawn from a probability distribution describing precipitation amounts given the occurrence of rainfall.

Gabriel and Neumann (1962) seemed to be the first to successfully describe the occurrence or nonoccurrence of daily rainfall with a Markov chain model. Additional evidence of the feasibility of using a Markov chain to describe the occurrence of sequences of wet or dry days was given by Caskey (1963), Weiss (1964), and Hopkins and Robillard (1964). Feyerman and Bark (1965) suggested that the matrix of Markov chain transition probabilities should be estimated to reflect seasonal variations.

Gringorten (1966) demonstrated that a simple Markov chain could be a useful device for making estimates of the frequencies of a large variety of weather events for durations ranging from several hours to several weeks. He used a normal or Gaussian distribution y $(N|0, 1)$ where y has a mean of zero and variance 1.0 and cumulative probability P(y) so that

$$P(y) = \frac{1}{2\pi} \int_{-\infty}^{y} \exp\left(-\frac{t^2}{2}\right) dt \dots\dots\dots\dots\dots\dots\dots [3.2]$$

He assumed that successive hourly values of y are generated by a stationary Markov process with constant correlation ρ between successive values. The i~th value of y becomes

$$y_o = N_o \qquad\qquad i = 0$$

$$y_i = \rho y_{i-1} + \sqrt{1 - \rho^2} \cdot N_i, \, i \geqslant 1 \dots\dots\dots\dots\dots\dots [3.3]$$

where N_i is the i~th normal number selected at random from the population. If $\rho = 0$, the m-hour minimum has a cumulative distribution F(y) so that

$$F(y) = 1 - [1 - P(y)]^m \dots\dots\dots\dots\dots\dots\dots\dots [3.4]$$

To solve practical problems, Gringorten found it necessary to simulate probability distributions by a Monte Carlo method. He presented eight examples which he felt illustrated the value of the method. Only one of the eight examples concerned precipitation, and that was an estimate of the frequency of heavy snowfall in January at Boston, MA. His examples do illustrate the wide variety of stochastic processes that can be modeled.

Later efforts are more or less similar to Gringorten's work. Several groups of investigators have developed models to simulate daily point rainfall occurrences, amounts, daily maximums within selected periods, and cumulative amounts of daily rainfall. Such models have wide applicability, but generally should be used only in the climatic regime in which they were developed.

Todorovic and Woolhiser (1974) described an application of stochastic processes for the description and analysis of daily precipitation. The total amount of precipitation during an n-day period was assumed as a discrete parameter stochastic process. The most general form of the distribution functions, mathematical expectation, and variance were determined. Special cases were considered for (a) the sequence of independent identically distributed random variables, (b) the sequence of independent random variables, and (c) the Markov chain. Presented were numerical examples based on rainfall records from Austin, TX, assuming daily rainfall amounts were exponentially distributed.

Todorovic and Woolhiser (1975) carried their work one step further by developing a stochastic model of n-day precipitation. General expressions were derived for the distribution functions of the total amount of precipitation, and the largest daily precipitation occurring in an n-day period. They compared two cases — one assuming persistence (Markov chain) and the other assuming no persistence (Bernoulli) — and found the persistence model gave a better fit to the data.

Hanson et al. (1974) coupled a stochastic model for daily rainfall with a threshold value for runoff production to develop a stochastic model for runoff volume. The ratio of daily runoff to daily rainfall, assuming the rainfall threshold to produce runoff is exceeded, was modeled using the beta distribution. This ratio was then multiplied by the daily rainfall to produce a sequence of synthetic runoff data. The synthetic runoff data were then used as input data in simulation studies to design stock ponds. This analysis provides an excellent example of the use of stochastic models in hydrologic design problems for agricultural structures.

Allen and Haan (1975) and Haan et al. (1976) pointed out that the design of many water resources projects requires knowledge of possible long-term rainfall patterns. To help in design of such projects, they developed a stochastic model based on a first-order Markov chain to simulate daily rainfall at a point. The model used historical data in Kentucky to estimate Markov transition probabilities. A separate matrix was estimated for each month of the year. The model is capable of simulating a daily rainfall record of any length, based on the estimated transition probabilities and frequency distributions of rainfall amounts. Although based on Kentucky rainfall records, the model probably is applicable within a larger region in the mideastern United States.

Raudkivi and Lawgrin (1972, 1974) developed a technique to simulate rainfall sequences based on 10-min time units. The serial correlation of the historical data was modeled by an autoregressive scheme, and the skewness described by the Pearson Type 3 distribution functions. The model was tested with rainfall data at Aukland, New Zealand, so the extent of applicability is uncertain. The method could be tested in other areas.

Smith and Schreiber (1974) investigated daily point rainfall records in southeastern Arizona to see how these daily records could be associated with short duration thunderstorm rainfalls. They found that a segmented Markov chain model gave a good fit to historical data from three independent point records. They also pointed out that yearly variations in the process require additional probabilistic description, indicated by annual variance in number of rain days and significant changes in autocorrelation properties, before the model could be used in simulation.

Chin (1977), in a very ambitious project, looked at daily rainfall occurrences from records of 25 yrs or longer at over 100 stations in the United States. He investigated the use of increasing orders to Markov chains to model daily rainfall occurrences. He found that the orders depended primarily on season and geographical locations, which in turn could be related to storm type. He concluded that the common practice of using the Markov chain order as the only model was unjustified without further testing. At the same time, however, he admitted that short records could mislead one into using a more complex model than justified. A specific example of a case in which a third-order Markov chain is applicable is given.

Osborn and Davis (1977) developed a three-parameter model to simulate rainfall occurrence in Arizona and New Mexico. The model was an effort, with simplifying assumptions, to follow what actually happens physically to produce rainfall in Arizona and New Mexico. The three parameters, latitude, longitude, and elevation can be determined easily for any point or small watershed. A flow diagram of the model (Fig. 3.5) follows through a logical sequence in determining if rainfall occurs. The model also allows for differences in storm types (frontal, convective, and frontal-convective) which may be important in areas where significant precipitation occurs from more than one storm type.

In Arizona and New Mexico, the principal sources of moisture for runoff-producing rainfall are from the Southeast — the Gulf of Mexico (SE), and the Southwest—the Gulf of California/Pacific Ocean (SW). Cold fronts also can trigger precipitation in the Southwest, and the combination of a cold front and warmer moist air from either the Southeast or the Southwest can result in exceptionally heavy rainfall. The model has eight outcomes based on the two sources of moisture and frontal activity. All probabilities for each of the three systems were determined independently (Fig. 3.5), and the "combination events were assumed to represent the less frequent, exceptional rainfalls." The model can be used to estimate rainfall occurrence for input to a more complex rainfall/runoff model or for a water balance model, as well as to indicate the variability in daily, seasonal, and annual water supply for agricultural users. The model is regional only; other types of models may work better in other regions.

Bras and Rodriguez-Iturbe (1976) pointed out that most rainfall models concentrate on storm exteriors or single fixed points. Very few models attempt to generate exterior and interior rainfall characteristics in space and time, and those that do have limiting assumptions of stationary behavior at all levels of storm activity. Unfortunately, simplification is essential in developing practical models of natural processes.

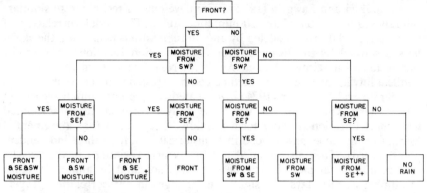

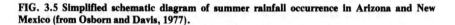

+ AREAL RAINFALL GENERATED WITH ALAMOGORDO CREEK THUNDERSTORM RAINFALL MODEL.
+ + AREAL RAINFALL GENERATED WITH WALNUT GULCH AIR-MASS THUNDERSTORM RAINFALL MODEL.

FIG. 3.5 Simplified schematic diagram of summer rainfall occurrence in Arizona and New Mexico (from Osborn and Davis, 1977).

Several investigators have developed models that include spatial distribution of rainfall. Bras and Rodriquez-Iturbe (1976) suggested a non-stationary multidimensional rainfall generator capable of simulating storm rainfall over an area, assuming the validity of Taylor's hypothesis (Taylor, 1937) of turbulence within the storm's interior. The method is fairly complex, but may be practical in the future if both watershed and storm characteristics can be better defined.

Areal representation of rainfall becomes more important in regions where convective storms of short duration and limited areal extent produce significant runoff-producing rainfall, and where it may be necessary to predict differences in runoff due to changes in watershed characteristics (like urbanization). Duckstein et al. (1972) introduced a stochastic model of runoff-producing rainfall for summer-type storms in the southwestern United states. They pointed out that modifications in runoff occur either naturally or through human influences, and that in either case, rainfall input must be properly modeled to determine actual changes in runoff with changes in watershed characteristics. They considered summer precipitation as an intermittent stochastic phenomenon, and obtained the probability distribution of areal rainfall by convoluting a Poisson distribution number of events with a geometric or negative binomial probability of rainfall amount. They then used their rainfall model in several rainfall-runoff relationships to illustrate the practical value of the method.

In the first example, they successfully used a linear rain model of their own design (Fogel and Duckstein, 1970) to illustrate the accuracy of their rainfall model. In the second, and most interesting, case they looked at the Soil Conservation Service (SCS) formula (SCS, 1964):

$$Q' = \frac{(R-A)^2}{(R-A) + S} \dots \dots \dots \dots \dots \dots \dots \dots \dots \dots \dots \dots \dots \dots \dots \dots [3.5]$$

where
$$A = \text{initial abstractions,}$$
$$S = \text{watershed factor,}$$
$$R = \text{rainfall, and}$$
$$Q' = \text{runoff volume,}$$

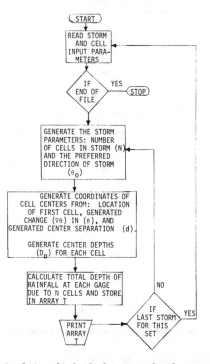

FIG. 3.6 Flow chart for simulation of individual air-mass thunderstorm rainfalls (from Osborn, Lane and Kagan, 1974).

and showed how their rainfall model could be combined successfully with the SCS model. In the final example, they used rainfall data from New Orleans to suggest that their model was more than regional.

Osborn et al. (1974) developed a simplified stochastic model (Fig. 3.6) based on airmass thunderstorm rainfall data from a dense network of recording raingages in southeastern Arizona. Probability distributions were used to model random variables — storm cell number, spatial distribution, and center depth. Storm rainfall could be simulated for any length of record. The principle purpose of this model was to predict peak discharge from rangeland watersheds. A Bernoulli random variable based on seasonal occurrences described the occurrence of the runoff-producing events. When more persistence was included in the model, the major events became too closely spaced — illustrating a modeling problem, i.e., it may be difficult to model all rainfall occurrences with equal accuracy for all uses. This model has been combined with the occurrence model (Osborn and Davis, 1977) to provide input to rainfall/runoff models to predict peak discharges from rangeland watersheds.

Smith and Schreiber (1974) proposed a probabilistic relationship among the point depth of rainfall, the local probability distribution of storm cell, maximum rainfall depth, and the dimensionless expression of storm depth-area pattern for air-mass thunderstorms in the Southwest. In a sample test, the expression was successfully used to reproduce point rainfall depth probability from storm maximum depth distribution and depth-area data from Tombstone, AZ.

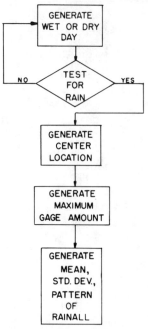

FIG. 3.7 Flow chart of the rainfall generating system (from A. D. Nicks, 1974).

Nicks (1974) used a four-stage stochastic generation technique to synthesize the daily rainfall for a 4000 km² area in central Oklahoma. Spatial
patterns of rainfall input to a hydrologic model were constructed by stochastically generating: (a) the occurrence or nonoccurrence of rainfall on
each day, (b) the location of the central or maximum rainfall amount within
the area, (c) the maximum rainfall amount, and (d) the pattern of rainfall
over the area corresponding to the central rainfall amount. Each phase in
the generating sequence is shown in Fig. 3.7. Tests were presented for the
representativeness and consistency of the generated data. The Markov chain
model used for generating rainy day sequences and the method of generating mean rainfall were both satisfactory. The author is further refining
this model.

Richardson (1977) used the multivariate normal distribution to model
daily precipitation over an area (Fig. 3.8). Square roots of daily precipitation at a point were found to approximate a sample from a univariate normal
distribution that had been truncated to zero. Zero daily precipitation amounts
were considered negative amounts of unknown quantity. The method of
moments could not be used to estimate the mean and standard deviation
of the normal distribution because the data were truncated at zero. A method
for estimating the mean and variance of truncated normal populations was
used to estimate the parameters. The model was tested on a study region
in Texas. Seasonal variation of the means and standard deviations were
described with Fourier series. Fourier coefficients were related to position
within the study region. Lag-one autocorrelation coefficients were found
to be a function of interstation distance. The model is capable of being used
to generate sequences of daily precipitation over a network of rain gages
at any location in the study region given only the latitude and longitude of
each station. The model can also be used for areas outside the study region
if the model parameters are defined using historical data. Richardson (1978)

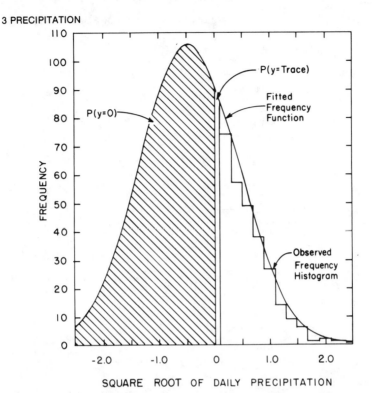

FIG. 3.8 The truncated normal distribution of daily precipitation with a square root transformation (from Richardson, 1977).

demonstrated the applicability of the model by generating precipitation sequences for an area in Texas and an area in Nebraska. The generated data contained many of the statistical characteristics observed in the historical data that are important from hydrologic design considerations.

Finally, Corotis (1976) presented a "universal" stochastic mesoscale model (STORM) based on regeneration of convective rainfall-producing cells, to be used to predict thunderstorm activity, generate rainfall for watershed models, like the Stanford watershed models (Crawford and Linsley, 1962; Ross, 1970), or contribute to a more complete theoretical understanding of the thunderstorm process. The user of the STORM program must define the basin or watershed area, and stipulate whether the storm is to be an air-mass or band-type thunderstorm. The beginning time and number of cells are simulated from a Poisson distribution. The program has been written to allow the user to specify any of several decay formulas for the depth-area relationship of the cells. The model was developed for hourly increments. A flow diagram of the STORM program is given in Figs. 3.9 and 3.10, and a complete listing of the Fortran deck, along with a description of the input, may be obtained from the writer. The user may wish to work with the author to shorten the rainfall interval to more accurately define air mass thunderstorm rainfall.

None of the proposed areal rainfall models should be considered for practical use without thorough study. The models fall roughly into two groups — those based on specific data from specific locations, and those that are primarily theoretical. Both types are relatively complex and are not easily verified. The value of the data-based models may be limited to the regions in which they were developed, and the theoretical models may be most valuable in the future as research tools.

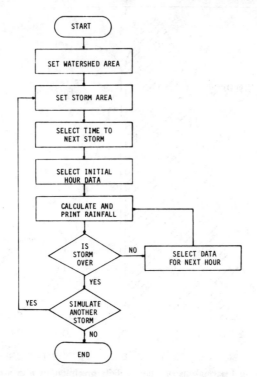

FIG. 3.9 Overall flow diagram for STORM program (from Corotis, 1976).

RAINFALL AS PART OF HYDROLOGIC MODELS

Rainfall data are required as input for most hydrologic or erosion models. The model output largely determines the form of the rainfall data input. For example, annual water or sediment yield models generally require estimates of annual or seasonal rainfall amounts. Models used to predict runoff peaks require rainfall inputs of relatively short duration (minutes or hours). Storage models require time dependent rainfall (or snowmelt) input. Models that predict erosion, sediment transport, and chemical transport on a storm basis usually require rainfall input on a storm basis.

Amounts of rainfall for given durations are usually based on point rainfall records, and some estimation procedure is used to compute average rainfall over a watershed area. On the other hand, models used to predict or estimate events of specified frequencies do not require input of actual rainfall data. In those cases, rainfall is usually based on regional estimates for the desired frequency (e.g. the 100-yr storm) and the output is that amount which will occur, on the average, once during the interval. Finally, some models may include simulation of time dependent rainfall amounts as input to deterministic models. These models predict a hydrologic series resulting from the simulated rainfall. The output of such models is stochastic.

Many hydrologic and erosion models have been developed that use rainfall data as input. Several of the most widely used models will be described to illustrate the type of rainfall data that are needed for various models.

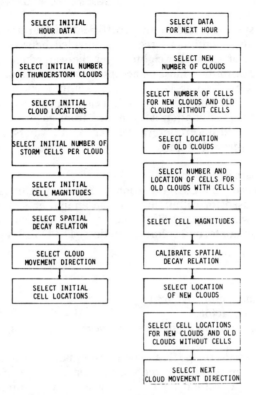

FIG. 3.10 Flow diagram for (a) Initial hour of STORM program; (b) Hourly computation of STORM program (from Corotis, 1976).

Stanford Watershed Model

The Stanford Watershed model is a digital computer program used to synthesize continuous streamflow hydrographs (Crawford and Linsley, 1962; Ross, 1970). The model has many applications and has been used to produce continuous hydrographs, evaluate runoff coefficients, evaluate the effects of urbanization on flood peaks and volumes, and estimate infrequent flood peaks on natural watersheds. The program is relatively simple to operate and can give useful practical output.

Input to the model includes hourly rainfall amounts at selected points over the watershed. Rainfall is assumed evenly distributed in space and time. Other model parameters are varied to produce a best fit to known runoff data, and then the model may be used on similar ungaged watersheds. Some parameter fitting may actually offset rainfall variability, in which case simulation for an ungaged watershed will have added uncertainty. Obviously, the greater the temporal and spatial variability of rainfall, the greater the uncertainty. Users of the model should be aware of the probable errors in simulation because of the input errors, and should allow for these in their analyses.

USDA Hydrograph Laboratory (USDAHL) Watershed Model

The mathematical model of watershed hydrology developed at the USDA Hydrograph Laboratory, Beltsville, MD, is a collection of subroutines designed to estimate runoff from precipitation data on small watersheds (Holtan et al., 1975). Variables include precipitation, land use, infiltration, evapotranspiration, and routing coefficients. Input precipitation to the model consists of a continuous record subdivided between obvious break points of rainfall or snowfall weighted over the watershed. Unknown variations in areal distribution must be accepted as error, although these errors may be reduced by dividing larger watersheds into small areas and independently applying the model to rainfall measurements on each small area. Usually, however, precipitation is estimated from gages outside the watershed, so input is still uncertain even on very small watersheds. The model can be run for any period of time.

Universal Soil Loss Equation

The Universal Soil Loss Equation (USLE) (Wischmeier and Smith, 1965) is widely used for estimating average annual erosion from field-size watersheds (Stewart et al., 1975). The equation parameters account for soil, vegetation, climate, and cultural practices. The USLE is given as

$$A = RKLSCP \dotfill [3.6]$$

where

A = estimated soil loss, and
R = rainfall factor.

The other parameters describe the soil, vegetation, topography, and cultural practices.

A good estimate of the R factor is essential. Wischmeier and Smith (1965) presented an iso-erodent map of the eastern United States. Ateshian (1974) developed a method for estimating R for the entire United States based on two distributions and 2-yr, 6-h point rainfall amounts. Average annual values of the rainfall-erosivity factor, R, for the entire United States were developed by Wischmeier in 1975 (Stewart et al., 1975). The USLE, based on R values from iso-erodent maps, is acceptably accurate in many cases for estimating average annual erosion rates for long periods of time. However, for shorter periods (like 1 or 2 yr or for individual events) in the eastern United States, and for any length of record in many areas of the western United States, estimates of erosion based on R values from regional or national maps may be very inaccurate (Wischmeier, 1976; Renard and Simanton, 1975).

The inaccuracies are due primarily to the short duration and extreme spatial and temporal variability of intense runoff-producing thunderstorm rainfall. To compensate for the time variability in rainfall intensity, Wischmeier and Smith (1958) suggested using rainfall energy (E) times rainfall intensity (I) for more accurate estimates of R in the USLE when recording raingage records were available. More recent work (Renard and Simanton, 1975) indicated that, particularly for intense widely scattered thunderstorm rainfall when recording raingage records are available, the EI index gives a much better estimate of R than available maps of average R values.

Wischmeier and Smith (1958) provided a table of kinetic energies for given rainfall intensities (Table 3.1), and explained their method in detail. Rainfall intensities (I) are determined for the shortest reasonable durations and energy values are determined from the table and accumulated for each storm. The total accumulated energy (t-m/ha/cm) is multiplied by the maximum 30-min intensity (cm/h) and the product divided by 100 to give the R factor for the storm.

TABLE 3.1 KINETIC ENERGY OF NATURAL RAINFALL (METRIC TON-METERS
PER HECTARE PER CM) (MODIFIED FROM WISCHMEIER AND SMITH, 1958)

Intensity cm/h	0.0	0.1	0.2	0.3	0.4	0.5	0.6	0.7	0.8	0.9
0	0	121	148	163	175	184	191	197	202	206
1.	210	214	217	220	223	226	228	231	233	235
2.	237	239	241	242	244	246	247	249	250	251
3.	253	254	255	256	258	259	260	261	262	263
4.	264	265	266	267	268	268	269	270	271	272
5.	273	273	274	275	275	276	277	278	278	279
6.	280	280	281	281	282	283	283	284	284	285
7.	286	286	287	287	288	288	289	289	290	290
8.	291	291	292	292	293	293	294			

Unfortunately, this method provides a good estimate of R only if a recording raingage is located on or very near the watershed. The accuracy of erosion estimates for short periods of record, based on single-gage precipitation records, decreases rapidly with distances between gages and watershed. Serious errors may occur if gages and watershed are separated by as much as 2 km. For watersheds without recording raingages, average annual R values can be used (Fig. 3.11), but erosion estimates must be for relatively long periods (Stewart et al., 1975).

Rational Method

There are many empirical rainfall-runoff models of similar form that require input of rainfall estimates for storms of given frequencies. Possibly the best known is the simple and aptly named Rational formula (Linsley et al., 1949). This model is the most widely used empirical equation for predicting peak discharge from a small watershed. The equation is:

$$q = CiA_i \dots\dots\dots\dots\dots\dots\dots\dots\dots\dots\dots\dots\dots\dots\dots [3.7]$$

Where

q = peak discharge in ft^3/s
i = rainfall intensity in in./h for the given frequency
A_i = the area in acres, and
C = a runoff coefficient.

(Because of the unique 1 to 1 relationship between i and A_i, the rational equation is not neatly converted to metric, although it can be by adding a constant.) The equation is rational and useful as long as the rainfall intensity is for a duration equal to the time of concentration and the area is small enough to ensure relatively homogeneous rainfall and watershed characteristics. Analyses suggested that, although the method can result in large errors in any given case, it may, on the average, give reasonable design results (Shaake et al., 1967).

SCS Methods

SCS has developed two methods for estimating volume and rate of runoff from agricultural watersheds in the United States. The older method (NEH-4), which is described in the National Engineering Handbook, Section 4, Hydrology, is now used generally for watersheds larger than 800 ha (SCS, 1972). The more recent method (TR-20), which is described in SCS-TP-149, is now used for establishing conservation practices for drainage on individual farms and ranches up to 800 ha (Kent, 1973). The two methods are closely allied.

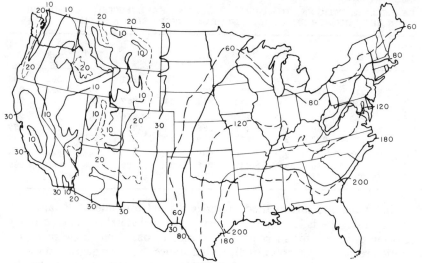

FIG. 3.11 Average annual values of the rainfall-erosivity factor, R (from Stewart et al., 1975).

The NEH-4 method is based on 24-h rainfall, since almost all rainfall data available at the time the method was developed were from standard nonrecording raingages. Both methods still use 24-h rainfall as the base for calculating watershed input. Both methods are fairly complex, involving estimates of watershed characteristics including slope, area, soil type, and cover. The NEH-4 method provides for development of a complete hydrograph, whereas TR-20 has been simplified with computer programming to develop a series of graphs which can be used directly for most small watershed designs. The methods leading to the development of the graphs are described in detail in SCS-TP-149 (1972). The graphs can be used for drainage up to 800 ha, peak discharges of 0.14 to 56 m³/s, 24-h rainfall depths from 25 to 300 mm, curve numbers (based on watershed characteristics) from 60 to 90, and three general slope classifications, flat (1 percent), moderate (4 percent), and steep (16 percent). One can interpolate between the three given slopes.

There are three detailed examples in TP-149 of a more complex method to aid in determining peak discharges in cases that do not fit into the general categories. In most cases, however, the differences one obtains in peak discharge by following through the more complex and tedious method are not large enough to warrant the extra effort. Use of this method in a few specific cases will soon give the planner confidence in using the more simplified method.

It was recognized that 24-h rainfall is not evenly distributed in time and space, and that some adjustments were necessary to simulate reasonable peaks and volumes of runoff. The "adjustments" in 24-h rainfall are of primary interest here.

The adjustments were confined to the time distribution of rainfall. It was believed that areal variability on small watersheds was small enough to be ignored. More recent research suggests that in many cases, areal variability will have a greater affect on peak discharge than the time distribution of rainfall. However, much more information is available on time distribution at a point than on the variability of rainfall, both in time and space over an area.

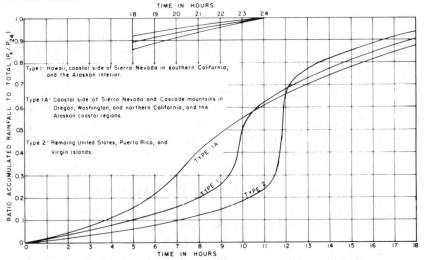

FIG. 3.12 Twenty-four-hour rainfall distributions (after SCS TP-149, 1973).

Two major climatic regions were identified in TP-149. Runoff from small watersheds in the first region was assumed most strongly influenced by maritime climate and rainfall was classed as Type I (Fig. 3.12). Runoff from small watersheds in the second region was assumed most strongly correlated to thunderstorm rainfall which was classed as Type II (Fig. 3.12). In the first case (Type I), the maximum 30-min rainfall was concentrated at about 10 h within a 24-h period of rainfall, while the second (Type II) was concentrated at about 12 h, and was more intense. The selection of the period of maximum intensity for both distributions was based on design considerations, rather than on meteorological factors (Kent, 1973).

In practice, the location of the intense rainfall within the 24-h period makes little difference, since peak discharge for most small drainages is highly correlated to the maximum 30-min rainfall. Using the Type II distribution will give somewhat larger peaks, and would represent a more conservative design. Since thunderstorms occur almost everywhere, the user must decide whether or not they occur often enough in a particular area to use the Type II distribution rather than the Type I.

The sparse runoff data available in the western United States when the original SCS method was developed limited the verification of curve numbers for conditions in arid and semiarid regions. For example, analysis of rainfall-runoff data in the Southwest indicates that the high intensity and the limited areal extent of thunderstorm rainfall, which are not included in the SCS method, are dominant factors in predicting runoff production from semiarid rangelands (Simanton et al., 1973).

Others

The synthesis of a flood hydrograph is often based on characteristics of a design storm. Time distributions of 1,623 flood producing rains of 30 min to 48 h were studied (Kerr et al., 1970) at 46 sites across Pennsylvania. After examining many combinations, the storms were classified into eight dimensionless patterns based upon storm amount, duration, and season. Geographic differences could not be verified. The resultant design procedure was incorporated into Lee's et al. (1974) double triangle unit hydrograph manual.

Analysis of 69 large flood hydrographs from 17 varied watersheds of 10 to 500 km² suggested that a 1-h single triangular hydrograph can be developed from the area and percentage of wooded area. Reich and Wolf (1973) suggested tentative design hydrographs may thus be estimated in hilly terrain, like that in the Appalachians with long summer humid continental or east coast continental climates, and mean annual precipitations between 850 through 1200 mm. Some generalization for estimating 1-h maximum rainfalls, which would be necessary input to this approximate flood-runoff model were generalized for remote parts of the world (Reich, 1963), and have been improved meanwhile through data analysis.

SNOW IN SMALL WATERSHED MODELING

Snow and snowfall play a significant part in the hydrologic regime of agricultural areas in many parts of the world.

In this section, we will discuss those aspects of snow hydrology that are important in modeling accumulation and melt on small watersheds — primarily shallow packs in non-mountainous areas, since both deep and shallow packs in mountainous areas are already well covered in the literature (Corps of Engineers, 1956; Leaf and Brink, 1973; Anderson, 1973).

Snow has received attention as a water resource, primarily in the northern parts of North America, Europe, and Asia. All of Canada receives snow in hydrologically significant amounts (Gray, 1968; McKay and Thompson, 1968), while some portions of the United States receive very little snow, particularly in the Southeast.

Potter (1965) defined snow cover as 25 mm or more of snow on the ground without regard to the water content of the snow. For hydrologic purposes, the water content is more important than depth, unless one is interested in the insulating properties of the snow as in soil freezing studies. Thus, maps, like those by Kuzmin (1963) and McKay and Thompson (1968) which show snow water equivalent and snow density, are more useful for hydrologic modeling. Frost on plants is also a significant factor in some regions where snowfall may not be present in large amounts. If enough days of frost formation occur, much of the water budget for an area may be unaccounted for unless frost formation and subsequent melt and sublimation are modeled (Makkink and van Heemst, 1975).

Snow Properties

Small watershed snow packs characteristically will be shallow (depth < 1 m), have relatively uniform density, and exhibit some degree of redistribution of snow during and after snowfall. The more important snow properties and characteristics, which are used in simulation, are snow water equivalent, density or specific gravity, depth, optical properties, and areal extent of the snow cover. The water equivalent of snowpack, W, is the depth of water contained in the ice and liquid water present in a snowpack. The density of the snowpack, P, is then defined as the mass of water per unit volume of snow (Martinec, 1976), but is conventionally expressed as a specific gravity and is measured simply by weighing a known volume of snow. In conventional snow surveys, both the depth, D, and water equivalent, W, are determined (Soil Conservation Service, 1972). Then

$$P = W/D \qquad \dots\dots\dots\dots\dots\dots\dots\dots\dots\dots\dots\dots\dots\dots\dots\dots \quad [3.8]$$

Typically, the density increases with time as the pack settles (Ffolliott and Thorud, 1969; Gray, 1968; Garstka, 1944). Density values usually range between 0.15 to 0.45 (150 to 450 mg/m³), with the lower values early in the accumulation season or immediately after snowfall, while higher values prevail after a period of partial melting or blowing snow.

The density can be simulated by estimating the density of snow at the time it falls, and then by a bookkeeping technique for accounting for the water equivalent and depth of snow on the ground. Garstka (1964) gave a range of 0.01 to 0.15 units for newly fallen snow, while the average density for the United States is 0.10 units. In eastern Colorado, a 19-yr average was 0.119 units (Greb, 1975). In its most simple form, the density of newly fallen snow can be assumed to be 0.10 units, or an equation for specific gravity, like the following may be used to calculate newly fallen snow density (Hydrocomp, 1969):

$$P = P_o + (T/100)^2 \quad\dotfill\quad [3.9]$$

P = specific gravity when $T = 0°C$
P_0 = specific gravity at $-18\ °C$
T = current air temperature $(-18\ °C)$

The remaining problem then is to determine if the precipitation is rain or snow. This can be done in several ways. The most simple is to assume that all precipitation is either rain or snow based on a temperature of 0 °C or some similar value. The SCS Model TR-20 (1965) for river basin planning uses 1.7 °C as the dividing line between rain and snow. It is reasonable to assume an air temperature greater than 0 °C at the ground level since the snow is formed at considerable heights in the atmosphere.

Another method used by Shih et al. (1972) apportions a percentage of the day's precipitation to rain, and the remainder to snow when the model time period is 1 day and the mean daily temperatures are used. Hydrocomp (1969) uses a combination of dry bulb and dew point temperatures to determine if rain or snow is falling.

Anderson (1976) used the basic equations governing mass and energy transfer to derive equations that express the increase in density of snow on the ground due to the increase in weight of the snow with new snowfall and crystal metamorphism. These equations, while more exact, require extensive calibration, and would apply to only one point. Thus, they are not really practical, but deserve further study as more sophisticated models are developed and better results needed.

It is generally accepted that the areal density of snow in shallow packs does not vary as much as the depth. Ffolliott and Thorud (1969) measured 195 points within a 170-ha watershed with an average water equivalent of 84 mm. The 5 percent confidence interval was 9 mm, whereas the density was 0.24 ± 0.01 units. The figures for the peak melt season was 0.36 ± 0.07 units. McKay and Thompson (1968) present a map of Manitoba and eastern Saskatchewan showing an average density of 0.16 to 0.22 units. McKay (1968) says that areas that have uniform topography and vegetation could be measured using a large number of snow stakes and a few density measurements. This would indicate that for much agricultural land the density could be more accurately modeled than the water equivalent. Hegedus and Szesztaz (1969) found that for Hungary, the coefficient of variation (C_V) of the density was less than 0.08 for the entire winter, while for depth, C_V was 0.8 to 0.20 units. Adams (1976) also observed that over a 206-ha area the depth was much more variable (100-200 mm) than the density (0.27 - 0.30 unit).

The areal extent of the snow cover during the melt period is needed to calculate the effective contributing area of melt. The most common methods for doing this are to assume the area not covered with snow is a function of time since the last general snowfall, or as a function of a percentage of seasonal runoff.

The fraction area not covered with snow is given by Martinec (1960) as:

$$A = 1/(1 + e^{-bt}) \quad \dots\dots\dots\dots\dots\dots\dots\dots\dots\dots\dots\dots\dots\dots\dots \quad [3.10]$$

where

A = fraction of total area snow free
t = time since arbitrary origin
b = calibration coefficient.

An estimate of the total melt time is necessary. For small watersheds, this will normally be quite short, depending on the water equivalent, area, topography, and cover of the watershed. This may be only a few days after a snowfall event (Garstka, 1944; Druffel, 1973). If the snow covered area is related to the percent of seasonal runoff, the only initial estimate to be made is the total runoff expected (Corps of Engineers, 1972; Kim et al., 1974). Since the generated runoff could also be related to the water equivalent in the basin, the area could also be related to the water equivalent remaining on the watershed (Anderson, 1973). In either case, the shape of the curves relating area to either runoff or water equivalent must be determined for each basin, but each will often have an exponential shape.

Another snowpack property of prime importance to modelers is water holding capacity. Any water above this capacity will drain from the pack. The amount of water in the snowpack is thermal quality of the pack, B, and is defined as the ratio of heat necessary to produce a given volume of water from a snowpack to that required to produce the same volume of water from ice. This ratio also is the same as the fraction of the snowpack that is ice.

$$B = 1 - f_p \quad \dots\dots\dots\dots\dots\dots\dots\dots\dots\dots\dots\dots\dots\dots\dots\dots\dots\dots \quad [3.11]$$

where

f_p = liquid water content of the snowpack as a fraction of W.
Values of B ranged from 0.78 to slightly over 1 in a 1.4 m deep pack in California (Gerdel, 1945). He also found that a 0.76 m pack probably could not hold more than 10 percent of the water equivalent as free water ($f_p = 0.10$). Anderson (1976) used values of $f_{pmin} = 0.03$ and $f_{pmax} = 0.1$, and interpolated between these values as a function of density. Kovzel (1969) found that the water holding capacity of snow was related to the snow density as $(0.11/P) - 0.11$ for a range of density of 0.13 to 0.45. Dunne et al. (1976) used a value of $f_p = 0.08$ to calculate water movement through ice and snow. Colbeck (1974) found that for a ripe pack ($P - 0.56$) f_{pmin} was not 0.07 times the pore volume. In many cases, shallow packs will not be able to hold much water, since even for a 1 m deep pack with $f_p = 0.03$ and $P = 0.50$, this would only be 15 mm of water, not a very large amount as compared with the 500 mm stored in the ice.

MODELS OF SNOWMELT

Most models of snowmelt use variations of the energy balance method pioneered by Wilson (1941) in which he outlined the sources of energy that cause snowmelt. In this section, the use of the energy balance method and its simplifications are first outlined, and secondly, the application of various techniques of snowmelt calculations as incorporated into currently used models are described.

Energy Balance Techniques

The use of the energy balance technique results in a model which may be very close to being correct, but which may be unwieldly to use, except in very specialized, highly instrumented situations (Anderson, 1976; Corps of Engineers, 1972; Gray and O'Neill, 1974; Obled and Rosse, 1977). This section begins with an overview of the energy budget, and then goes on to deal with usable simplifications and problems encountered in modeling shallow packs on small watersheds.

Energy Budget

The energy budget for a snowpack is commonly given as (Gray and O'Neill, 1974; Corps of Engineers, 1956; Anderson, 1968; Kuzmin, 1973):

$$H = H_c + H_e + H_g + H_p + H_{rl} + H_{rs} \quad \dots\dots\dots\dots\dots\dots\dots\dots\dots\dots [3.12]$$

H = net heat transfer to snowpack from its environment
H_c = convective or sensible heat transfer from the air
H_e = latent heat transfer from condensation - evaporation - sublimation
H_g = conduction of heat across the soil-snow interface
H_p = heat transfer due to heat content of rain drops
H_{rl} = net longwave radiation exchange between the snowpack and its surroundings
H_{rs} = net shortwave radiation exchange between the snowpack and its surroundings.

For shallow snowpacks, Gray and O'Neill (1974) add a term, H_{gs}, the heat transferred to the soil surface by solar radiation penetrating the snowpack. If H is the total net change in energy, the melt, M, is calculated as H/L_f where L_f is the latent heat of fusion of ice. If liquid water is present in the snowpack (B < 1), then the calculated melt must be divided by B to determine true melt.

The sensible and latent heat transfer are often treated together because they have some elements in common. One of the more common methods for calculating evaporation from a snow surface is the mass-transfer method (Corps of Engineers, 1956 and 1960).

$$L_e = f(v) \, (e_s - e_a) \quad \dots\dots\dots\dots\dots\dots\dots\dots\dots\dots\dots\dots\dots\dots\dots [3.13]$$

L_e = loss of mass from or to the snow by evaporation or condensation
v = wind speed
e_s = snow surface vapor pressure
e_a = air vapor pressure.

Other methods used for evaporation from water surfaces are also used for evaporation from snow. These can be characterized by the profile methods. An example is (Munn, 1966):

$$H_e = L_v k_e \rho_a \, \partial q / \partial z \quad \dots\dots\dots\dots\dots\dots\dots\dots\dots\dots\dots\dots\dots [3.14]$$

L_v = latent heat of vaporization
k_e = diffusivity coefficient
ρa = density of air
q = specific humidity
z = height above surface.

For a shallow pack site at Ottawa, Ontario, Gold and Williams (1961) found 25 percent of a pack, containing 134 mm of water, was lost to evaporation over a 2-wk period. Lemmela (1973) found 2.0 to 9.8 percent of total water equivalent was lost to evaporation. Norum et al. (1976), as well as other researchers, contend that sublimation is low for most snowpacks, and so can be ignored.

Since sensible heat transfer is similar to evaporation, the following equation from Anderson (1976) is:

$$H_c = -\rho_a C_p k_c \partial T_a / \partial_a \quad \dots\dots\dots\dots\dots\dots\dots\dots\dots\dots\dots\dots\dots [3.15]$$

C_p = specific heat of air at constant pressure
k_c = eddy transfer coefficient
T_a = air temperature.

Conduction of heat from the ground is many times ignored as the values are expected to be small. This may not always be the case, since Obled and Rosse (1977) reported 0.8 mm/day melt into a lysimeter from ground heat. The Corps of Engineers (1960) used 0.5 mm/day over an entire basin. Investigating a shallow prairie snow pack, Norum et al. (1973) felt that the net transfer from soil to snow may not be enough to cause appreciable melting. Most modelers assume a constant value for this heat movement both because of the difficulty of determining good values of the heat conduction coefficient of wet or frozen soil and the smallness of the heat value as compared with other heat fluxes.

The conduction of heat within a snowpack has an effect on the heat storage within a pack. During actual melt, the snowpack is isothermal, and there is no change in heat content of the snowpack due to temperature changes. However, in many cases during the accumulation season and for some packs during the melt season, there is a temperature gradient in that snowpack — particularly for shallow snowpacks and for the top 30-50 mm of deeper packs, where the liquid water will refreeze each evening (Obled and Rosse, 1977).

Allen (1976) divided the snow temperature calculations into three classes based on water equivalent. In all cases, the snow surface temperature is assumed less than or equal to the air temperature, but never greater than 0 °C. If the water equivalent is less than 50 mm, the mean snowpack temperature is equal to the mean daily air temperature, but never more than 0 °C. If $50 < W < 114$ mm, then the snowpack temperature is 1.5 times the snow surface temperature plus the previous day's ground surface temperature. For $W > 114$ mm, the diffusion equation is used, and the snowpack is not assumed to be isothermal. He found the thermal diffusivity, ∞, equal to $0.025/(2.75 - p_s)$ cm³/s/k.

The purpose of calculating snowpack temperature is to calculate the cold content of the snowpack. This is the amount of energy it would take to bring the temperature to 0 °C, and is calculated as (Eagleson, 1970):

$$H_{cc} = \int T_s \rho_s c_p \, dz \quad\dots\dots\dots\dots\dots\dots\dots\dots\dots\dots\dots\dots [3.16]$$

H_{cc} = heat deficit (cold content) of snowpack.

For a shallow pack, it should be possible to assume some average temperature. The amount of cold content is not great, since an average value for nighttime radiational cooling is about 2 mm of water (Eagleson, 1970). The depth of water corresponding to H_{cc} is:

$$H_{cc} = L_f \rho_w d_{cc} \quad\dots\dots\dots\dots\dots\dots\dots\dots\dots\dots\dots\dots\dots [3.17]$$

d_{cc} = depth equivalent of water at 0 °C
ρ_w = density of water.

For a pack with a depth of 320 mm, with conditions of a pack at an average temperature of −16.4 °C, and density of 0.173 gm/cm³, H_{cc} = −45 cal/cm² or 5.7 mm of water at 0 °C would have to be added to the pack to bring its temperature up to 0 °C (Kuzmin, 1972). This calculation is always necessary to obtain a complete heat balance of a snowpack since this energy must be supplied before melting can begin. This is particularly important with energy and advection to the snowpack by rain.

Net radiation is the sum of all the radiation fluxes, and is the most important component in the energy balance of a snowpack during accumulation and periods of continuous snowcover (Allen, 1976; Gray and O'Neill, 1974; Male and Gray, 1975). Net radiation is:

$$H_r = H_{rs} - H_{rl} \quad\dots\dots\dots\dots\dots\dots\dots\dots\dots\dots\dots\dots\dots [3.18]$$

For research watersheds with continuous snowcover and little relief, it is possible to measure H_r, since both short and longwave radiation tend to be fairly uniform over large areas. Usually, however, L_i, shortwave incoming radiation, or R_d, longwave incoming radiation, or both, are measured, so several approximations must be made — H_{rs} can be calculated as $H_{rs} = L_i(1 - a)$ where a = albedo of the snow. The albedo is usually calculated as a decay function since last snowfall. Only the surface "active layer" (about top 100 mm) has an effect on the albedo and absorption of solar radiation (Anderson, 1976; O'Neill and Gray, 1973a; Obled and Rosse, 1977). For deeper snowpacks, the Corps of Engineers (1956 and 1960) recommends that the albedo be decreased from 0.80 to 0.40 after about 20 days. Eggleston et al. (1971) developed a decay function for albedo as a function of time, whereas Anderson (1976) uses an equation based on snow surface density. Bergen (1975) also suggested that for surface grain sizes over 1.5 mm, the albedo is a function of density rather than grain size. O'Neill and Gray (1973a) found only a small variation (0.65 to 0.85) in albedo during the non-melt season, but a much sharper decrease in albedo during the melt season than that indicated by the Corps of Engineers (1956). This was perhaps due to a much shallower snowpack. O'Neill and Gray (1973b) showed little effect of snow depth on albedo for depths greater than 30 or 40 mm, which is the depth 5 percent of the incident radiation could penetrate. Gerdel (1948) found that 5 percent of the radiation penetrated to a depth of 180 mm in the Central Sierras. Usually, a is decreased to 0.4 after a rainfall.

Kuzmin (1973), Allen (1976), and Eagleson (1970), as well as many others, extensively discussed solar radiation calculation on inclined surfaces, like hills and gullies. Without measured values, these calculated values may be used, but can have large errors associated with them, especially for areas with some dust or cloud cover. Allen (1976) does not allow the shortwave radiation on any slope to decrease below 5 percent of the measured value.

Longwave radiation can be calculated from the Stephen-Boltzmann Law. Since this radiation is radiated uniformly from the sky, the effect of topography is not felt as in shortwave radiation. For clear sky conditions, the emissivity is commonly taken as a constant, whereas the moisture in the air is ignored (Bengtsson, 1976; Corps of Engineers, 1956). For areas with crop or forest cover, the computations are carried out separately for the covered and uncovered area, with the canopy temperature usually taken as equal to the air temperature.

The melt due to rain falling on a snow pack is not very large, but is very important because of its roles of increasing the snow temperature to 0 °C and filling the available water holding capacity of the snowpack. For shallow packs, this capacity can be very small. The actual heat content of rain is (Anderson, 1976):

$$H_p = \rho_w C_v (T_w - T_s)P \dots \dots \dots \dots \dots \dots \dots \dots \dots \dots \dots [3.19]$$

where
C_v = specific heat of rain water
T_w = wet bulb of air (often assumed $= T_a$)
T_s = snow temperature
ρ_w = density of rain water
P = depth of rainfall.

If the precipitation is actually snow at a temperature below 0 °C, the temperature profile of the snowpack will be rearranged, and its cold content increased.

Simplifications

Several investigators have studied the relative importance of the various energy balance components. This greatly aids in simplifying the computations when the situation justifies it or more detailed data are not available.

Zuzel and Cox (1975) measured daily values of wind, air temperature, vapor pressure, net radiation, and melt at a point. They found that for an area with continuous snow cover, vapor pressure, net radiation, and wind run explained 78 percent of the variations in melt, whereas air temperature and net radiation explained 60 percent. Temperature had a coefficient of determination of 0.51, and net radiation was 0.40.

Raffelson (1974) investigated the energy balance of isolated snowdrifts in Wyoming during melt. He found the sensible and latent heat components were about the same size, and both substantially larger than the radiation component. O'Neill (1972) and Gray and O'Neill (1974) found that net radiation was the predominant energy source for snowmelt for the Canadian Prairies when the snow cover was continuous, supplying 93 percent of the melt energy. For non-continuous cover, advection of heat from bare ground to isolated drifts caused 44 percent of the melt energy to be supplied by sensible heat transfer and 56 percent by net radiation. For an isolated drift,

Cox and Zuzel (1976) found that 69 percent of the energy available for melt and evaporation came from sensible heat input. The Corps of Engineers (1960) assigned a constant value to shortwave radiation during rain periods. King and Molnau (1976) noted that temperature index methods seem to work well for calculating snowmelt during overcast periods, indicating that radiation was relatively unimportant during those periods. Kuzmin (1973) explored five different simplifications of the basic energy budget method. He found that the use of temperature was possible for plains, but only if the mean daily temperature was greater than 2 °C.

Emphasis has been put on determining snowmelt by use of air temperature or a temperature index because of the ease of obtaining air temperatures and because temperature is the most easily extrapolated of meteorological variables. Usually, an air temperature equation has the form of

$$M = k(T_a - T_b) \dots\dots\dots\dots\dots\dots\dots\dots\dots\dots\dots\dots\dots [3.20]$$

where

k = degree day coefficient millimeter/day/°C
T_b = a base temperature, °C
M = melt, millimeter/day.

For most cases, T_b is assumed to be a constant. Granger and Male (1977) used $T_b = 0$ while observing that k increased during the melt season. They felt that this was due to the effect of radiation on air temperature during clear periods. Anderson (1973) used the degree-day method for clear weather melt periods and a simplified energy balance during rain periods when radiation factors can be more easily calculated. The melt factor is allowed to vary from a minimum on December 21 to a maximum on June 21, using a sine curve. For an Iowa watershed with no forest cover, the melt factor ranged from 7.3 to 3.6 mm/°C/day. Martinec (1960) developed a relationship between k and density for an open area in Bohemia.

McKay (1968) presents curves of degree-day factors for a shallow prairie snowpack. Gartska (1944) noted a strong correspondence between cumulative runoff and cumulative degree-hours above 0 °C. This relationship seemed consistent within a storm, but varied between storms. The SSARR model (Corps of Engineers, 1972) uses a table input of degree-day factor versus cumulative runoff. This did not work well for SSARR tests in the large Minnesota River basin (Kim et al., 1974). They used functions of the degree-day factor versus percentage of snowpack depleted as well as cumulative degree-days. Both methods seemed to work well for these large basins with shallow packs. King (1976) used the degree-day method on small watersheds in the Palouse Prairie. He used k as a function of cumulative degree-hours with good success. However, he found that different functions may be needed for basins with different aspects because of the rolling topography. Jolley (1973) also found that the summation of degree days gave good correlation to snowmelt runoff on a watershed near Ottawa, Ontario which was half grassland and half forested.

Bengtsson (1976) developed the idea of an equilibrium temperature to use in place of the base temperature. This is the temperature at which no net transfer of heat between the air and snow takes place. By equating the energy balance approach with the degree-day factor, he found that k could be determined as a function of wind speed for a forested watershed and a function of solar radiation for nonforested areas.

Following the degree-day method of simplified snowmelt calculation in popularity are the Corps of Engineer equations as outlined in their publications of 1956 and 1960. While developed using data from deep mountain snowpacks, these equations have been used in New Brunswick (Davar, 1970), Minnesota (Kim et al., 1974), as well as in areas of deeper snowpacks. Good results for these equations were reported in a comparison of several watershed models with snowmelt routines (NWS, 1972). These equations for open or partly forested areas include air temperature, a wind speed function, rainfall, and a constant radiational component for rainfall periods. For rain-free periods, forest cover, solar radiation, and computed longwave radiation are added to the equations.

Full derivation and use of the equations can be found in various publications (Corps of Engineers, 1956, 1960). It is worth noting that the most complicated equation is one in which the land is open or partly forested, as in most agricultural lands.

In some operational and many research situations, it may be possible to measure melt directly, rather than rely on equations for the snowmelt input to mathematical models of small watersheds. These have also been used successfully in testing snowmelt equations. Lysimeters measure the meltwaters directly, and are reported by Thompson et al. (1975), Davar (1970), Haupt (1969), and Corps of Engineers (1955). Others have used a lysimeter-snow pillow to obtain both the change in snow water equivalent and water from the bottom of the pack, and used these measurements for actual forecasting (Cox and Zuzel, 1973; Cox, 1971; Molnau, 1971).

Vegetative and Topographic Influences

Vegetation and topography influence the accumulation and melt of snow. Attempts to manage the snow by use of windbreaks or snow fences have given new insight into the influence of natural features on melt of snowdrifts.

Saulmon (1973) found that water loss from induced drifts in eastern Montana averaged 50 percent, but total water yield was increased an average of 112 mm. McCool (1976) used snow fences to keep drifts from forming in high erosion hazard areas. If such drifts are formed on an area to be modeled, consideration must be given to models of drifts. The different cropping patterns or growth of windbreaks will also greatly influence snow catch and drifting (Greb, 1975; Tabler, 1975a; Tabler, 1975b; Willis et al., 1969; Frank and George, 1975). Since large drifts normally form in areas of rolling topography, the differential melting due to the varying influence of solar radiation on melt must be considered (Dunne and Black, 1971; Cox and Zuzel, 1976).

SNOWMELT IN HYDROLOGIC MODELS

Many hydrologic models include routines which will compute the amount of snowmelt by any one or combination of methods mentioned in previous sections. Very few models have been designed primarily as snowmelt models; normally, the snowmelt routine is added to the precipitation section where the water input to the main part of the hydrologic model is determined. Thus, the following sections describe snowmelt routines from several different types of hydrologic models which have been used in a wide variety of situations and may be applicable to small watersheds.

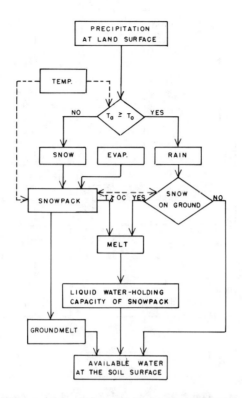

FIG. 3.13 Snow accumulation and ablation (from Riley et al., 1969).

In general, all comments in previous sections about areal variability of rainfall input to hydrologic models also apply to snowfall input. With few exceptions, some type of temperature function is used to determine the forms of precipitation. Snowfall is usually more uniform over an area than is rainfall because of the nature of the weather systems which cause snow to form. However, it is not the snowfall but the melt from the snow on the ground that is of interest. This snow may be very unevenly distributed, particularly in areas of rolling terrain or vegetation variation that can cause drifts to form. In these cases, the watershed may have to be divided up into areas corresponding to the major drift areas, rather than some other hydrologic unit.

US Department of Agriculture Hydrograph Laboratory (USDAHL)

The USDAHL model (Holtan et al., 1975) is an example of the use of a minimal amount of snow data. Precipitation input to the model must be tagged as either rain or snow, and the watershed is considered to be completely snow covered or not covered. Snow is melted by use of a single degree-day type equation. In an attempt to overcome the limitations of this equation, King and Molnau (1976) added a separate subroutine that would allow the program to use daily maximum and minimum temperature to determine if the precipitation was rain or snow, and treated each zone separately. The melt was based on a degree-day melt factor which varied with the accumulated degree days above 0 °C.

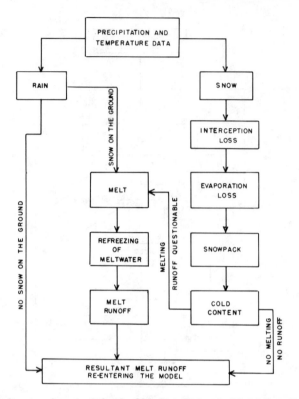

FIG. 3.14 Block diagram of snowmelt for the Ohio State University Model (from Ricca, 1972).

SSARR

The Streamflow Synthesis and Reservoir Regulation (SSARR) model, developed by the Corps of Engineers (1972) for use in forecasts in the Columbia River Basin, uses an extensive set of options for snowmelt. These include calculating melt on the entire basin, a split basin (snow on part only), or by elevation band. The methods of calculation can be by the generalized energy budget equations or by a degree-day equation. The degree-day factor may be entered in a table for variability throughout the year, or it may be a function of accumulated seasonal runoff. The snow covered area can be entered on a table of values or computed as a function of accumulated runoff. The University of Minnesota (Kim et al., 1974) modified SSARR to also include the option of varying the degree-day factor with the accumulated degree-day above the base temperature.

Utah Water Research Laboratory

The flow chart for this hybrid model (Eggleston et al., 1971; Riley et al., 1969) is shown in Fig. 3.13. This is a routine used in a hybrid computer model and illustrates some of the necessary steps in a mass budget of snow on the ground. This model has been used successfully in mountain snowpack situations, but there is nothing in its development which suggests it would not work on agricultural watersheds. It includes sections for dealing with steeply sloping areas where a radiation index is used to compute actual radiation on a slope.

National Weather Service

The National Weather Service model for forecasting streamflow has been tested on several types of watersheds, including those of primarily agricultural character (National Weather Service, 1972; Anderson, 1973; Kim et al., 1974). When the temperature is above freezing, a degree-day approach is used, but when more than 2.5 mm of rain falls in a 6-h period, an energy balance equation is used to compute melt. There is a negative melt factor included to lower the pack temperature when the air temperature is less than freezing.

Ohio State University Model

The Ohio State University Model (OSUM) (Fig. 3.14) is derived from the Kentucky Watershed Model (KWM) (Ricca, 1972; James, 1972). The OSUM includes a snowmelt routine developed specifically for agricultural watersheds and was tested on the Coshocton Watersheds. The model includes simplified versions of each of the energy balance terms and requires daily average dewpoint, wind run, solar radiation, and maximum and minimum temperature. A factor for increasing or decreasing the rate of cold content change, essentially a thermal conductivity index, is included, which is very important in shallow snowpacks.

Other Models

Based on the above models, there are other models which are used for various application. Some of these that may prove useful in small watershed studies are those of Allen (1976) and Obled and Rosse (1977). Development of a model for the prairies of Canada is underway at the University of Saskatchewan, which specifically addresses the problem of shallow snowpacks, frozen ground, and other problems associated with small agricultural watersheds (Male and Gray, 1975; Norum et al., 1976).

References

I. RAIN

1   Alexander, G. N., A. Karoly, and A.B. Susts. 1969. Equivalent distributions with application to rainfall as an upper bound to flood distributions. J. Hydrol. 9:322.

2   Allen, D. M. and C. T. Haan. 1975. Stochastic simulation of daily rainfall. Report 82, WRRI, Univ. of Kentucky.

3   Ateshian, J. K. H. 1974. Estimation of rainfall erosion index. J. Irrig. and Drain. Div., ASCE 100(IR3):293-307.

4   Bell, F. C. 1969. Generalized rainfall-duration frequency relationship. J. Hydraul. Div., ASCE 95(1):311-328.

5   Bras, R. L., and I. Rodriguez-Iturbe. 1976. Rainfall generation: A non-stationary time-varying multidimensional model. WRR 12(3):450-456.

6   Caskey, J. E. Jr. 1963. A Markov chain model for the probability of precipitation occurrence in intervals of various lengths. Monthly Weather Review 91:298-301.

7   Chang, M. 1977. An evaluation of precipitation gage density in a mountain terrain. Water Resour. Bull. 13(1):39-46.

8   Chin, E. H. 1977. Modeling daily precipitation occurrence process with Markov chain. Water Resour. Res. 13(6):949-956.

9   Chow, V. T. 1964. Handbook of Applied Hydrology. McGraw-Hill Book Co., New York. 1479 pp.

10   Corotis, R. B. 1976. Stochastic considerations in thunderstorm modeling. J. Hydraul. Div., ASCE 102(HY7):865-879.

11   Crawford, N. H., and R. K. Linsley. 1962. The synthesis of continuous streamflow hydrographs on a digital computer. Tech. Rept. 12, Stanford Univ., July.

12   Dawdy, D. R., and J. M. Bergmann. 1969. Effect of rainfall variability on stream flow simulation. WRR 5(5):958-966.

13   Duckstein, L., M. M. Fogel, and C. C. Kisiel. 1972. A stochastic model of runoff-producing rainfall for summer type storms. WRR 8(2):410-420.

14   Duckstein, L., M. M. Fogel, and J. C. Thames. 1973. Elevation effects on rainfall: A stochastic model. J. Hydrol. 18:21-35.

15   Eagleson, P. S. 1967. Optimum density of rainfall networks. WRR 3(4):1021-1034.

16   Feyerman, A. M. and L. D. Bark. 1965. Statistical methods for persistent precipitation patterns. J. Appl. Meteor. 4:320-328.

17   Fogel, M. M. 1969. Effect of storm rainfall variability on runoff from small semiarid watersheds. TRANSACTIONS of the ASAE 12(6):808-812.

18   Fogel, M. M. and L. Duckstein. 1969. Point rainfall frequencies in convective storms. WRR 5(6):1229-1237.

19   Fogel, M. M. and L. Duckstein. 1970. Prediction of convective storm runoff in semiarid regions. Int. Assoc. Sci. Hydrol. Publ. 96:465-478.

20   Frederick, R. H., V. A. Meyer, E. P. Auciello. 1977. Five- to 60-minute precipitation frequency maps for the Eastern and Central US. NOAA Tech. Memo NWF HYDRO 35.

21   Gabriel, K. R., and J. Neuman. 1962. A Markov chain model for daily rainfall occurrence at Tel Aviv, Quart. J. Royal Meteor Soc. 88:90-95.

22   Goodridge, J. D. 1976a. Rainfall Analysis for Drainage Design, Vol. I: Short Duration Precipitation Frequency. DWR Bull. No. 195, California Dept. of Water Resour., Sacramento. 671 p.

23   Goodridge, J. D. 1976b. Selection of frequency distributions. Dept. of Water Resources, California. 85 p.

24   Gringorten, I. I. 1966. A stochastic model of the frequency and duration of weather events. J. Appl. Meteor. 5(5):606-624.

25   Haan, C. T., D. M. Allen, and J. O. Street. 1976. A Markov chain model of daily rainfall. WRR 12(3):443-449.

26   Hanson, C. L., E. L. Heff, and D. A. Woolhiser. 1974. Hydrologic aspects of water harvesting in the northern Great Plains. Water Harvesting Symp. Proc. Phoenix, AZ, March 26-28, pp. 129-140.

27   Hendrick, R. L. and G. H. Comer. 1970. Space variations of precipitation and implications for raingage network design. J. Hydrol. 10:151-163.

28   Hershfield, D. M. 1961. Rainfall frequency atlas of the US for durations from 30 min to 24 h and return periods from 1 to 100 yr. Tech. Paper No. 40, USWB. 61 p.

29   Hershfield, D. M. 1965. On the spacing of raingages. IASH Publ. 67, Symp. Design of Hydrol. Networks. pp. 72-79.

30   Holtan, H. N, G. J. Stiltner, W. H. Henson, and N. C. Lopez. 1975. USDAHL-74. Revised model of watershed hydrology. Tech. Bull. 1518, USDA Agricultural Research Service, Washington, DC.

31   Hopkins, J. W. and P. Robillard. 1964. Some statistics of daily rainfall occurrence for the Canadian prairie provinces. J. Appl. Meteor. 3:600-602.

32   Huff, F. A. 1967. Time distribution of rainfall in heavy storms. WRR 3(4):1007-1020.

33   Huff, F. A. 1968. Spatial distribution of heavy storm rainfall in Illinois. WRR 4(1):47-54.

34   Kent, K. M. 1973. A method for estimating volume and rate of runoff in small watersheds, Soil Conserv. Serv. TP-149, USDA, SCS. 62 pp.

35   Kerr, R. L., D. F. McGinnis, B. M. Reich, and T. M. Rachford. 1970. Analysis of rainfall-duration-frequency for Pennsylvania. I.R.L.&W.R., Pennsylvania State University, Research Publ. 70. 152 p., Aug.

36   Kite, G. W. 1975. Confidence limits for design events. WRR 11(1):48-53.

37   Lee, B. H., B. M. Reich, T. M. Rachford, and G. Aron. 1974. Flood Hydrograph Synthesis for Rural Pennsylvania Watersheds. The Pennsylvania State University, I.R.L.&W.R., Res. Rept., 94 p. June.

38   Linsley, R. K. 1967. The relation between rainfall and runoff. J. Hydrol. 5:297-371.

39   Linsley, R. K., M. A. Kohler, and J. L. H. Paulhus. 1949. Applied Hydrology. McGraw-Hill Co., New York, 689 pp.

40   McCuen, R. H. 1973. The role of sensitivity analysis in hydrologic modeling. J. Hydrol. 18:37-53.

41   Nash, J. E. 1958. Determining runoff from rainfall. Proc. Inst. Civ. Eng. 10:163-185.

42   Nicks, A. D. 1974. Stochastic generation of the occurrence, pattern, nd location of maximum amount of daily rainfall. USDA Misc. Publ. 1275:154-171.

43   Osborn, H. B. and L. J. Lane. 1969. Precipitation-runoff relationships for very small semiarid rangeland watersheds. WRR 5(2):419-429.

44   Osborn, H. B., L. J. Lane and J. F. Hundley. 1972. Optimum gaging of thunderstorm rainfall in southeastern Arizona. Water Res. Res. AGU 8(1):259-265.

45   Osborn, H. B., L. J. Lane, and V. A. Myers. 1978. Two useful rainfall/runoff relationships for Southwestern thunderstorms. Accepted for publication, TRANSACTIONS of the ASAE.

46   Osborn, H. B., W. C. Mills and L. J. Lane. 1972. Uncertainties in estimating runoff-producing rainfall for the thunderstorm rainfall runoff models. Proc. Int. Symp. on Uncertainties in Hydrol. and Water Res. Sup. 2.6:1-13.

47   Osborn, H. B., L. J. Lane and R. S. Kagan. 1974. Stochastic models of spatial and temporal distribution of thunderstorm rainfall. USDA Misc. Publ. 1275:211-231.

48   Osborn, H. B. and D. R. Davis. 1977. Simulation of summer rainfall occurrence in Arizona and New Mexico. Proc. Joint Meet. Ariz. Sec., AWRA-Hydrol. Sec., Ariz. Acad. Sci., April. 7:153-162.

49   Raudkivi, A. J. and N. Lawgrin. 1972. Generation of serially correlated nonnormally distributed rainfall duration. WRR 8(2):398-409.

50   Raudkivi, A. J. and N. Lawgrin. 1974. Simulation of rainfall sequence. J. Hydrol. 22:271-294.

51   Reich, B. M. 1963. Short-duration rainfall intensity estimates and other design aids for regions of sparse data. J. Hydrol. 1:3-28.

52   Reich, B. M., D. M. McGinnis, and R. L. Kerr. 1970. Design procedures for rainfall-duration-frequency in Pennsylvania. Publ. No. 65, I.R.L.&W.R., The Pennsylvania State University. 60 p.

53   Reich, B. M. 1978. Rainfall intensity-duration-frequency curves developed from, not by, computer output. Transportation Res. Record, 9 p.

54   Reich, B. M. 1976. Magnitude and frequency of floods. CRC Critical Reviews in Environmental Control 6:297-348.

55   Renard, K. G. and J. R. Simanton. 1975. Thunderstorm precipitation effects on the rainfall-erosion index of the USLE. Proc. Ariz. Sec., AWRA-Hydrol. Sec., Ariz. Acad. Sci., Tempe, AZ. 5:47-56.

56   Richardson, C. W. 1977. A model of stochastic structure of daily precipitation over an area. Colorado State University Hydrology Paper No. 91, 45 pp.

57   Richardson, C. W. 1978. Generation of daily precipitation over an area. Water Resour. Bull. 14 (In press).

58   Ross, G. A. 1970. The Stanford Watershed Model: The correlation of parameter values selected by a computerized procedure with measurable physical characteristics of the watershed. Res. Rept. 35, WRRI, Univ. of Kentucky.

59   Shaake, J. C., J. C. Geyer, and J. W. Knapp. 1967. Experimental examination of the rational method. J. Hydrol. Div., ASCE 93(6):353-370.

60   Simanton, J. R., K. G. Renard, and N. C. Sutter. 1973. Procedure for identifying parameters affecting storm runoff volumes in a semiarid environment. USDA, ARS-W-1.

61   Smith, R. E., and H. A. Schreiber. 1974. Point process of seasonal thunderstorm rainfall. I. Distribution of rainfall events, WRR 9(4):871-884, 1973; II. Rainfall depth probabilities, WRR 10(3):424-426.

62   Soil Conservation Service Handbook. 1964. Revised 1972. National Engineering Handbook. Section 4, Hydrol.

63   Stol, P. T. 1972. The relative efficiency of the density of raingage networks. J. Hydrol. 15:193-208.

64   Stewart, B. A., D. A. Woolhiser, W. H. Wischmeier, J. H. Caro, and M. H. Frere. 1975. Control of water pollution from cropland. Vol. 1. A manual for guideline development. USDA, ARS, US. Environmental Protection Agency Report No. EPA-600/2-75-026a.

65   Taylor, G. I. 1937. Statistical theory of turbulence. Proc. Royal Society Series A, 151.

66   Todorovic, P., and D. A. Woolhiser. 1974. Stochastic model of daily rainfall. USDA Misc. Publ. 1275.

67   Todorovic, P., and D. A. Woolhiser. 1975. A stochastic model of n-day precipitation. J. Appl. Meteor. 14(1):17-24.

68   Wei, T. C. and C. C. Larson. 1971. Effects of areal and time distribution of rainfall on small watershed runoff hydrographs. Bull. 30, Water Res. Ctr., Univ. of Minn., March.

69   Weiss, L. L. 1964. Sequences of wet and dry days described by a Markov chain probability model. Monthly Weather Rev. 92:169-176.

70   Wischmeier, W. H. 1976. Use and misuse of the USLE. J. Soil and Water Conserv. 31(1):5-9.

71   Wischmeier, W. H., and D. D. Smith. 1958. Rainfall energy and its relationship to soil loss. Trans. AGU, 39(2):285-291.

77   Wischmeier, W. H., and D. D. Smith. 1965. Predicting rainfall-erosion losses from cropland east of the Rocky Mountains. Agr. Handb. 282, USDA, ARS, Wash., DC.

73   World Meteorological Organization. 1974. Guide to hydrologic practices. 3rd ed. WMO No. 168:5.18-5.30.

74   Yevjevich, V. 1972. Probability and Statistics in Hydrology. Water Resour. Publ., Ft. Collins, CO.

II. SNOW

75 Adams, W. P. 1976. Areal differentiation of snow cover in east-central Ontario. Water Resour. Res 12(6):1226-1234.

76 Allen, Louis E. 1976. A subalpine snowmelt runoff model. University of Wyoming, Wyoming Water Resources Research Center, Water Resour. Ser. No. 65.

77 Anderson, E. A. 1968. Development and testing of snow pack energy balance equation. Water Resour. Res. 4(1):19-37.

78 Anderson, E. A. 1973. National Weather Service river forecast system-snow accumulation and ablation model. US Department of Commerce, National Oceanic and Atmospheric Administration, National Weather Service, NOAA Technical Memorandum NWS HYDRO-17.

79 Anderson, E. A. 1976. A point energy and mass balance model of snow cover. US Department of Commerce, National Oceanic and Atmospheric Administration, National Weather Service, NOAA Tech. Rept. NWS 19.

80 Bengtsson, L. 1976. Snowmelt estimated from energy budget studies. Nordic Hydrol. 7:3-18.

81 Colbeck, S. C. 1971. One-dimensional water flow through snow. US Army Corps of Engineers, Cold Region Research and Engineering Laboratory, Res. Rept. 296.

82 Colbeck, S. C. 1974. Capillary effects on water percolation in homogenous snow. Glaciology 13:85-97.

83 Corps of Engineers. 1955. Lysimeter studies of snowmelt. US Army Corps of Engineers, North Pacific Division, Snow Investigations Res. Note No. 25.

84 Corps of Engineers. 1956. Snow hydrology, summary report of the snow investigation. U.S. Army Corps of Engineers, North Pacific Division, Portland.

85 Corps of Engineers. 1960. Runoff from snowmelt. US Army Corps of Engineers, Engineering and Design Manual EM 1110-2-1406.

86 Corps of Engineers. 1972. Program description and users manual for SSARR. Program 724-K5-60010, US Army Engineer Division, North Pacific Division.

87 Cox, L. M. 1971. Field performance of the universal surface precipitation gage. Western Snow Conf. Proc. 39:84-88.

88 Cox, L. M. and J. F. Zuzel. 1973. Forecasting runoff universal surface gage snowmelt measurements. Soil and Water Conser. 28(3):131-134.

89 Cox, L. M., and J. F. Zuzel. 1976. A method for determining sensible heat transfer to late-lying snowdrifts. Western Snow Conf. Proc. 44:23-28.

90 Davar, K. S. 1970. Snowmelt measurements and their use in synthesizing snowmelt hydrographs. Eastern Snow Conf. Proc. 15:87-97.

91 Druffel, L. 1973. Characteristics and prediction of soil erosion on a watershed in the Palouse. Master of Science Thesis, University of Idaho.

92 Dunne, T. and R. D. Black. 1971. Runoff processes during snowmelt. Water Resour. Res. 7(5):1160-1172.

93 Dunne, T., A. G. Price and S. C. Colbeck. 1976. The generation of runoff from subarctic snowpacks. Water Resour. Res. 12(4):677-685.

94 Eagleson, P. S. 1970. Dynamic Hydrology. McGraw-Hill. 462 pp.

95 Eggleston, K. O., E. K. Israelson, and J. P. Riley. 1971. Hybrid computer simulation of the accumulation and melt process in a snowpack. Utah State University, Water Research Laboratory, PRWG65-1.

96 Ffolliott, P. F., and D. B. Thorud. 1969. Snowpack density, water content and runoff on a small Arizona watershed. Western Snow Conf. Proc. 37:12-18.

97 Frank, A. B., and E. J. George. 1975. Windbreaks for snow management in North Dakota. In: Snow Management on the Great Plains, Great Plains Agricultural Council, Publ. No. 73.

98 Garstka, W. U. 1944. Hydrology of small watersheds under winter conditions of snow cover and frozen soil. Geophys. Union Trans., Part 6:838-871.

99 Garstka, W. U. 1964. Section 10. Snow and snow survey. In: Ven Te Chow (ed.) Handb. of Applied Hydrol., McGraw-Hill.

100 Gerdel, R. W. 1945. Dynamics of liquid water in deep snowpacks. American Geophys. Union Trans. 26:83-90.

101 Gerdel, R. W. 1948. Penetration of radiation into the snowpack. American Geophys. Union Trans. 29(3):366-374.

102 Gold, L. W., and G. P. Williams. 1961. Energy balance during the snowmelt period at an Ottawa site. Int. Assoc. of Hydrol. Sci. Publ. 54:233-294.

103 Granger, R. J., and D. H. Male. 1977. Melting of a prairie snowpack. American Meteorological Society, Proc. 2nd Conf. on Hydrometeorol. pp. 261-268.

104 Gray, D. M. 1968. Snow hydrology of a prairie environment. In: Snow Hydrology, Proc. Workshop Seminar, Canadian Nat. Comm. for the Int. Hydrol. Decade, pp. 21-32.

105   Gray, D. M. and A. D. J. O'Neill. 1974. Application of the energy budget for predicting snowmelt runoff. In: Henry S. Santeford and James L. Smith (ed.), Advanced Concepts and Techniques in the Study of Snow and Ice Resources, National Academy of Sciences.

106   Greb, B. W. 1975. Snowfall characteristics and snowmelt storage at Akron, CO. In: Snow Management on the Great Plains, Great Plains Agricultural Council Publication No. 73.

107   Haupt, H. F. 1969. A 2-yr evaluation of the snowmelt lysimeter. Western Snow Conf. Proc. 37:97-101.

108   Hegedus, M. and K. Szesztaz. 1969. Some problems of determining the water equivalent of snow cover. In: Floods and Their Computation. Proc. the Leningrad Symp., 1967. UNESCO Studies and Reports in Hydrol. 2(3):616-628.

109   Holtan, H. N., G. J. Stiltner, W. H. Hensen, and N. C. Lopez. 1975. USDAHL-74 revised model of watershed hydrology. US Department of Agriculture, Tech. Bull. 1518.

110   Hydrocomp, Inc. 1969. Hydrocomp simulation programming operation manual (2nd ed). Hydrocomp, Inc., Palo Alto, CA.

111   James, L. D. 1972. Hydrologic modeling, parameter estimation and watershed characteristics. J. Hydrol. 17:283-307.

112   Jolley, J. P. 1973. Influence of air temperature and solar radiation on snowmelt ripening and runoff. Eastern Snow Conf. Proc. 18:114-119.

113   Kim, Kwonshik, Chung-Sang Chu, C. E. Bowers, and D. G. Baker. 1974. Forecasting rainfall and snowmelt floods on upper midwest watersheds. University of Minnesota, St. Anthony Falls Hydraul. Lab. Project Rept. No. 151.

114   King, D. L. 1976. Simulation of the snow hydrology of the Palouse prairie. University of Idaho, Master of Science Thesis.

115   King, D. L., and M. Molnau. 1976. Snowmelt simulation in the Palouse prairie. Paper presented at the 49th Meet. Northwest Sci. Assoc., Cheney, WA.

116   Kovzel, A. G. 1969. A method for the computation of water yield from snow during snowmelt period. In: Floods and Their Computation, Proc. Leningrad Symp., 1967. UNESCO Studies and Reports in Hydrol. 2(3):598-607.

117   Kraus, H. 1975. An energy balance model for ablation in mountainous areas. In: Proceedings of the Moscow Symposium, Snow and Ice. Int. Assoc. of Hydrol. Sci. Publ. No. 104.

118   Kuzmin, P. P. 1973. Melting of the snow cover. Israel Program for Scientific Translation, published for National Science Foundation, Translation TT 71-50095.

119   Leaf, C. F., and G. F. Brink. 1973. Computer simulation of snowmelt within a Colorado subalpine watershed. US Department of Agriculture, Forest Service, Research Paper RM-99.

120   Laugham, E. J. 1974. The occurrence and movement of liquid water in the snowpack. In: Henry S. Santeford and James L. Smith (ed), Advanced Concepts and Techniques in the Study of Snow and Ice Resources, National Academy of Science.

121   Lemmela, R. 1973. Measurement of evaporation-condensation and melting from a snow cover. Proceedings of the Banff Symposium, 1972, Int. Assoc. of HYDROLOGIC Sci. Publ. 107, 2:670-679.

127   Makkink, G. F. and H. D. J. Van Heemst. 1975. Simulation of the water balance of arable land and pastures. Centre for Agricultural Publishing and Documentation, Wageningen, 79 p.

123   Male, D. H., and D. M. Gray. 1975. Problems in developing a physically based snowmelt model. Canadian J. Civ. Eng. 2(4):474-488.

124   Martinec, J. 1960. The degree-day factor for snowmelt-runoff forecasting. Int. Assoc. of Sci. Hydrol. Pub. 51, pp. 468-477.

125   McCool, D. K. 1976. Effect of windbreak density and placement on snow deposition on the Palouse hills. Paper presented at the 21st Annual Meeting, Pacific Northwest Region, ASAE, Penticton, BC.

126   McKay, G. A., and H. A. Thompson. 1968. Snowcover in the prairie provinces of Canada. TRANSACTIONS of the ASAE 11(6):812-815.

127   McKay, G. A. 1968. Problems of measuring and evaluating snow-cover. In: Snow Hydrology, Proc. of Workshop Seminar, Canadian Nat. Comm. for the Int. Hydrol. Decade, pp. 49-65.

128   McKay, G. A. 1976. Hydrological mapping. In: John C. Rodda (ed), Facets of Hydrology, John Wiley and Sons, 368 p.

129   Molnau, M. 1971. Comparison of runoff from a catchment snow pillow and a small forested watershed. Western Snow Conf. Proc. 39:39-43.

130   Munn, R. E. 1966. Descriptive Micrometeorology. Advances in Geophysics, Supplement 1, Academic Press, 245 p.

131   National Weather Service. 1972. National Weather Service river forecast procedures. US Department of Commerce, National Oceanic and Atmospheric Administration, National Weather Service, NOAA Technical Memorandum NWS HYDRO-14.

132   National Weather Service. 1973. NOAA Atlas 2. Precipitation frequency atlas of the western United States. US Dept. of Commerce, NOAA, Silver Spring, MD. 43 pp.

133   Norum, D. J., D. M. Gray, and D. H. Male. 1976. Melt of shallow prairie snowpacks: basis for a physical model. Canadian Agri. Eng. 18(1):2-6.

134   Obled, C., and B. Rosse. 1977. Mathematical models of a melting snowpack at an index plot. J. Hydrol. 32:139-163.

135   O'Neill, A. D. J. 1972. The energetics of shallow prairie snowpacks. University of Saskatchewan, PhD. Dissertation.

136   O'Neill, A. D. J., and D. M. Gray. 1973a. Solar radiation penetration through snow. Int. Assoc. of Hydrol. Sci. Publ. 107, 1:227-241.

137   O'Neill, A. D. J., and D. M. Gray. 1973b. Spatial and temporal variation in the albedo of a snowpack. Int. Assoc. of Hydrol. Sci. Publ. 107, 1:176-186.

138   Potter, J. G. 1965. Snow cover. Canadian Department of Transport, Meteorological Branch, Climatic Studies No. 3.

139   Raffelson, C. N. 1974. Evaporation from snowdrifts under oasis conditions. University of Wyoming, Master of Science Thesis.

140   Ricca, V. T. 1972. The Ohio State University version of the Stanford streamflow simulation model: Part 1 — Technical aspects. Ohio State University, Water Resources Center.

141   Riley, J. P., D. G. Chadwick, and K. O. Eggleston. 1969. Snowmelt simulation. Western Snow Conf. Proc. 37:49-56.

142   Ross, G. A. 1970. The Stanford watershed model: the correlation of parameter values selected by a computerized procedure with measurable physical characteristics of the watershed. Res. Rept. No. 35, Water Resour. Institute, University of Kentucky.

143   Saulmon, R. W. 1973. Snowdrift management can increase water harvesting yield. J. Soil and Water Conserv. 28(3):118-121.

144   Scott, R. F. 1964. Heat exchange at the ground surface. US Army Material Command, Cold Region Research and Engineering Laboratory, Cold Region Science and Engineering II-A1.

145   Shih, G. B., R. H. Hawkins, and M. D. Chambers. 1972. Computer modeling of a coniferous forest watershed. In: Age of Changing Priorities for Land and Water, ASCE.

146   Soil Conservation Service. 1965. TR-20 project formulation hydrology. USDA, SCS Central Technical Center, Portland, OR.

147   Soil Conservation Service. 1972. Snow survey and water supply forecasting. Soil Conservation Service. Nat. Eng. Hardb. Section 22, USDA, SCS.

148   Tabler, R. D. 1975a. Estimating the transport and evaporation of blowing snow. In: Snow Management on the Great Plains, Great Plains Agricultural Council, Publ. No. 73.

149   Tabler, R. D. 1975b. Predicting profiles of snowdrifts in topographic catchments. Western Snow Conf. Proc. 43:87-97.

150   Thompson, K., J. DeVries, and J. Amorocho. 1975. Snowmelt lysimeter. Western Snow Conf. Proc. 43:35-40.

151   Willis, W. O., H. J. Hass, and C. W. Carlson. 1969. Snowpack runoff as affected by stubble height. Soil Sci. 107:256-259.

152   Wilson, Walter T. 1941. An outline of the thermodynamics of snowmelt. Am. Geophys. Union Trans., Part 1:182-195.

153   Yen, Yin-Chao. 1969. Recent studies on snow properties. Adv. Hydrosci. 5:173-214.

154   Zuzel, J. F., and L. M. Cox. 1975. Relative importance of meteorological variables in snowmelt. Water Resour. Res. 11(1):174-176.

chapter 4 ▐█████████████████

INFILTRATION

4

INFILTRATION

by R. W. Skaggs, Professor of Biological and Agricultural Engineering, North Carolina State University, Raleigh, North Carolina 27650 and R. Khaleel, Assistant Professor Hydrology, New Mexico Institute of Mining and Technology, Socorro, New Mexico 87801.

INTRODUCTION

Infiltration is defined as the entry of water from the surface into the soil profile. It is an important hydrologic process which must be carefully considered in models or procedures for describing the hydrology of a watershed. For example, it is the infiltration capacity of the soil that determines for a given storm, the amount and time distribution of rainfall excess that is available for runoff and surface storage. The same soil related factors that control infiltration also govern soil water movement and distribution during and after the infiltration process. Hence an understanding of infiltration and the factors affecting it is important to the determination of surface runoff as well as the subsurface movement and storage of water within the watershed. Philip (1969), Hillel (1971), and Morel-Seytoux (1973) have presented excellent reviews of the infiltration processes. Many aspects of infiltration and percolation are also treated in detail in a compilation by Hadas et al. (1973).

Although infiltration may involve soil water movement in two or three dimensions, such as rainfall on a hillside, it is often treated as one-dimensional vertical flow and it is this process that will be emphasized here. The discussion will begin with a general description of the infiltration process. This will be followed by a review of theoretical methods that have been proposed for characterizing infiltration and subsequant soil water movement under various initial and boundary conditions. Solutions to the governing equations are used to demonstrate the effects of factors such as initial soil water content and application rates on infiltration. The influence of other factors such as surface sealing and resistance to air movement are also considered. Approximate methods for predicting infiltration using simplified algebraic equations are presented and discussed.

GENERAL DESCRIPTION

Consider infiltration into a deep, homogeneous soil column with a uniform initial water content. At time t = 0, water is ponded at a shallow depth on the soil surface and is continually added at a rate to keep the ponded depth constant. The flux or the rate water enters the soil surface is called the infiltration rate, f. Infiltration rates, for cases where air flow effects are negligible, decrease with time as shown schematically in Fig. 4.1. The decrease is primarily due to reduction in the hydraulic gradients at the surface but may also be affected by other factors such as surface sealing and

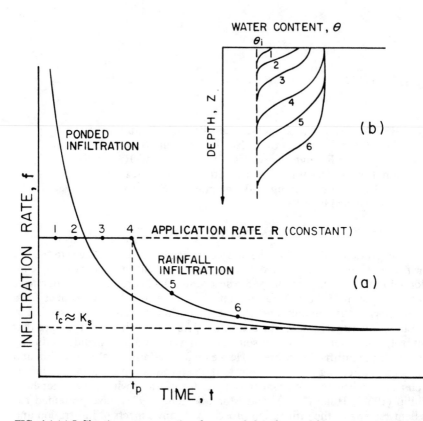

FIG. 4.1 (a) Infiltration rate versus time for a ponded surface and for a constant application rate, R (effects of air flow are neglected). (b) Water content versus depths at times denoted by 1, 2, 3, ...6 in Fig. 4.1a for the constant application rate. NOTE: At times 1, 2 and 3, infiltration capacity > R so infiltration rate limited by rainfall rate; at time 4 infiltration capacity = R; and at times 5 and 6 the infiltration capacity < R, the wetted depth increases in thickness and water is available for runoff and/or surface storage.

crusting. If the measurements are continued for a sufficiently long time, the infiltration rate will approach a constant rate, f_c. The constant f_c is generally assumed to be equal to the saturated hydraulic conductivity, K_o, but will actually be somewhat less than K_o due to entrapped air. In most cases f_c is more accurately approximated by K_s, the hydraulic conductivity at residual air saturation.

Since water is always ponded on the surface in our hypothetical experiment, the infiltration rate is limited only by soil-related factors. The rate that water will infiltrate as limited by soil factors is often called the infiltration capacity (f_p) of the soil. Hillel (1971) noted that the term, capacity, is generally used to denote an amount or volume and can be misleading when applied to a time-rate process. He proposed the term soil infiltrability rather than infiltration capacity.

Now consider the same soil column as described above with water applied at a constant rate, R, to the surface. For this case the infiltration rate during the early stages of the event (points 1, 2 and 3 in Fig. 4.1a and curves 1, 2 and 3 in Fig. 4.1b) will be equal to R and is limited by the application rate rather than soil conditions and properties. As long as the application rate is less than the infiltration capacity, water will infiltrate as fast as it is supplied and the infiltration rate will be controlled by the application rate ($f = R$). As infiltration continues, f_p decreases until it is just equal to the application rate (point 4 in Fig. 4.1a and curve 4 in Fig. 4.1b). For later times the infiltration capacity will be less than R (points 5 and 6 in Fig. 4.1a and curves 5 and 6 in Fig. 4.1b). The surface will become ponded and the infiltration rate will be controlled by the soil profile ($f = f_p$). Water supplied in excess of the infiltration capacity will become available for surface storage and/or runoff.

Infiltration rate is normally expressed in units of length per unit time (or volume per unit area per unit time, $L^3L^{-2}T^{-1}$), e.g., cm/h, mm/h. Total infiltration volume or cumulative infiltration, $F = F(t)$, is the total amount of water infiltrated (L) at any time t and may be expressed as,

$$F(t) = \int_0^t f(t)\, dt \quad \dots\dots\dots\dots\dots\dots\dots\dots\dots\dots\dots\dots\dots \quad [4.1]$$

where f is the infiltration rate which may or may not be equal to infiltration capacity as discussed above.

The soil water distribution during infiltration from a ponded surface into a uniform, relatively dry soil was first presented by Bodman and Coleman (1943). They showed that the profile could be divided into the four zones shown schematically in Fig. 4.2. The saturated zone extended from the surface to a maximum depth of approximately 1.5 cm. The transition zone, a region of rapid decrease of soil water content, extended from the zone of saturation to the transmission zone, a zone of nearly constant water content which lengthens as infiltration proceeds. The wetting zone maintains a nearly constant shape during infiltration and culminates in the wetting front which is the visible limit of water penetration into the soil. Except for the saturation and transition zones, the results of Bodman and Coleman have been generally confirmed by other investigators. While there has been considerable disagreement in the literature, it is generally agreed that, in most cases, the

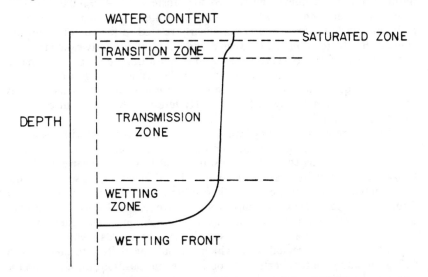

FIG. 4.2 The infiltration zones of Bodman and Coleman (1943).

soil will not be completely saturated at the surface due to air entrappment and possible counterflow of the air phase. Most theories of soil water movement do not predict the transition zone. However, McWhorter (1976) showed that an abrupt steepening of the profile near the surface would be predicted for rainfall infiltration if the resistance to air movement is considered.

GOVERNING EQUATIONS

Infiltration is primarily controlled by the factors governing water movement in soil. In this section we will examine the basic laws governing soil water movement and the use of these laws to characterize infiltration in terms of soil properties and boundary conditions. The basic relationship for describing soil water movement was derived from experiments by Darcy in 1856 who found that the flow rate in porous materials is directly proportional to the hydraulic gradient. Darcy's law may be written as

$$q_s = -K \, \partial H/\partial s \qquad \qquad [4.2]$$

where q_s is the flux, or volume of water moving through the soil in the s-direction per unit area per unit time ($L^3 L^{-2} T^{-1}$); and $\partial H/\partial s$ is the hydraulic gradient in the s-direction. The proportionality factor, K, is the hydraulic conductivity (L/T), which depends on both properties of the fluid and the porous medium. H is the total potential head (L) which is the sum of several component potentials discussed in detail by Day et al. (1967). For our purposes, H may be considered equal to the hydraulic head which is the sum of the pressure head, h, and the distance above the datum plane or the elevation-head, z. Taking the datum plane at the soil surface,

$$H = h - z \qquad \qquad [4.3]$$

where z is the distance measured positively downward from the surface.

For positive pressure heads, water content, θ, is usually constant and the soil is assumed saturated. However, saturation is rarely complete under natural conditions due to entrapped air. Instead, $\theta = \theta_s$, the apparent saturated water content, for $h > 0$. For unsaturated soils, the pressure head, h, is inherently negative and is nonlinearly related to the volumetric water content, θ. The relationship between h and θ is a soil property called the soil-water characteristic. However, $h = h(\theta)$ is not a unique function in that h depends not only on θ, but also on whether the soil is wetting or draining at the point in question. That is, the soil water characteristic exhibits hysteresis as is shown schematically in Fig. 4.3. Hysteresis is discussed in detail by Childs (1969) and by Nielsen, et al. (1972).

For saturated soils, the hydraulic conductivity is constant with respect to h. Whenever the hydraulic conductivity at a given water content varies from point to point in the soil mass, the soil is said to be heterogeneous. If the hydraulic conductivity does not depend on location within the soil mass, the soil is homogeneous. If the hydraulic conductivity is dependent on the flow direction, the soil is said to be anisotropic. Isotropic soils have hydraulic conductivity functions which are independent of direction. An excellent discussion of Darcy's law for anisotropic soils is given by Childs (1969).

For regions of the soil mass which are only partially saturated and in which the water content varies with both time and position, the equation for flux may be written as,

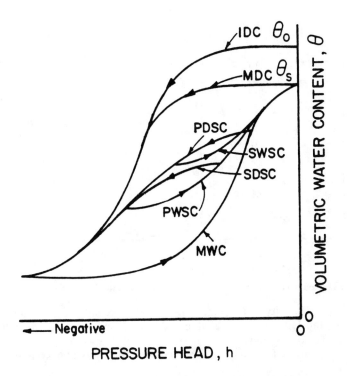

FIG. 4.3 Diagram of typical hysteresis curves, where IDC is the initial drainage curve, MWC and MDC are main wetting and drainage curves respectively, PWSC and PDSC are primary wetting and drainage scanning curves, and SWSC and SCSC are secondary wetting and drainage scanning curves. From Gillham, 1972, cited by Rawlins, 1976.

$$q_s = - K(\theta) \frac{\partial H}{\partial s} \quad \dotfill \quad [4.4]$$

where the hydraulic conductivity, K, is a function of water content, θ. Since the relationship $\theta = \theta(h)$ is a property of the soil (albeit also dependent on the wetting and drying history due to hysteresis), we may write $K = K(h)$, and

$$q_s = -K(h) \frac{\partial H}{\partial s} . \quad \dotfill \quad [4.5]$$

For unsaturated soils the water moves primarily in small pores and through films located around and between solid particles. As the water content decreases, the cross-sectional area of the films also decreases and the flow paths become more limited. The result is a hydraulic conductivity function that decreases rapidly with water content as shown schematically in Fig. 4.4. In most cases hysteresis in the $K(\theta)$ relationship is small. However, when $K = K(h)$ is used as in equation [4.5], hysteresis may be quite pronounced due to hysteresis in the $h(\theta)$ relationship (Fig. 4.3). As noted earlier, natural soils are usually not completely saturated because of air entrappment during the wetting process. Thus, even for apparently saturated regions below the water table, the volumetric water content may equal θ_r, the water content at residual air saturation rather than the total porosity. The corresponding

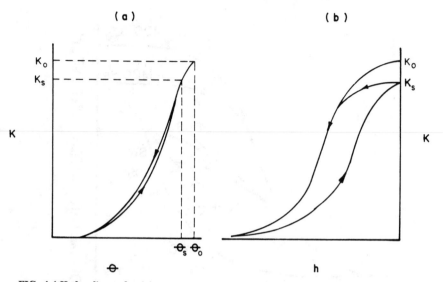

FIG. 4.4 Hydraulic conductivity versus water content (a) and soil water pressure head (b).

hydraulic conductivity is K_s (Fig. 4.4a) which may still be considered constant in regions below the water table and is sometimes referred to as the apparent saturated conductivity.

The principle of conservation of mass for the soil water system may be written as

$$\partial\theta/\partial t = - \nabla \cdot \overline{q} \dotfill [4.6]$$

where $\overline{q}$ is the flux vector, t is time (T) and θ is the volumetric soil water content (L^3/L^3). For flow in the vertical z direction only, equation [4.6] may be written as

$$\partial\theta/\partial t = - \partial q_z/\partial z \dotfill [4.7]$$

Combining equations [4.7] and [4.5] and taking the datum at the surface so that $H = h - z$ yields the Richards equation for the vertical direction:

$$C(h)\partial h/\partial t = \frac{\partial}{\partial z} [K(h)\partial h/\partial z] - \partial K/\partial z \dotfill [4.8]$$

where the soil water capacity, $C(h)$, may be obtained from the soil water characteristic as

$$C(h) = d\theta/dh \dotfill [4.9]$$

Note that the use of equation [4.8] assumes that there is no resistance to soil air movement and the air pressure remains constant throughout the profile. This is often not the case and will be discussed in a subsequent section.

Equation [4.8] can be expanded to include two-dimensional flow by adding the term $\partial/\partial x (K(h) \partial h/\partial x)$ to the right side of the equation. It can also be written with the water content, θ, as the dependent variable by defining soil water diffusivity as $D(\theta) = K(h) dh/d\theta$ so that

$$\frac{\partial\theta}{\partial t} = \frac{\partial}{\partial z} [D(\theta) \frac{\partial\theta}{\partial z}] - \frac{\partial K}{\partial z} \dotfill [4.10]$$

Equations [4.8] and [4.10] were first derived by Richards (1931) and are referred to as forms of the Richards equation (Swartzendruber, 1969).

Both forms of the Richards equation for flow in the vertical direction contain two soil parameters; the θ-based equation contains $D(\theta)$ and $K(\theta)$, and the h-based equation contains $C(h)$ and $K(h)$. These parameters are related for unsaturated soil by $D = K/C$. For most soils, all three parameters vary markedly with water content or pressure head. The pronounced nonlinearity of these parameters is the prime source of difficulty in solving the Richards equation subject to boundary conditions pertinent to infiltration.

Advantages can be stated for both the h-based and θ-based equations in describing the movement of water in unsaturated soil. When saturated conditions are reached, the h-based equation is reduced to the familiar Laplace equation describing saturated flow. For saturated flow, $K(h)$ reaches a constant value, $C(h) = 0$, and the pressure head, h, changes from a negative to a positive quantity. For cases where both saturated and unsaturated flow conditions exist, the solution to the h-based equation will be valid; however, the θ-based equation does not hold for saturated conditions as $D(\theta)$ tends to infinity. On the other hand, there are advantages to the θ-based equation for describing completely unsaturated flow as the changes in both θ and D are typically an order of magnitude less than corresponding changes in h and C. In general, round off errors in numerical solutions to the θ-based equation are of lesser consequence than for the h-based equation.

SOLUTIONS TO THE RICHARDS EQUATION

In order to characterize the infiltration process using the Richards equation, it is first necessary to solve the equation for existing boundary conditions. As an example, the boundary and initial conditions for ponded infiltration may be written as

$$h = \delta, \quad z = 0, \quad t > 0$$
$$h = h_i, \quad z \to \infty, \quad t \geq 0$$
$$h = h_i, \quad z \geq 0, \quad t = 0$$

where δ is the ponded water depth and h_i is the soil water pressure head corresponding to the initial water content. The solution obtained will yield $h = h(z,t)$ either in functional form, if obtained analytically, or in tabular form if obtained numerically. The infiltration rate can then be determined at any time by simply applying Darcy's law at the surface. Thus, both the pressure head distribution at any time during the process and the infiltration rate may be determined by solving the Richards equation.

The nonlinearity of the soil properties K, D and C has prevented exact analytical solutions of equations [4.8] and [4.10] except for a few limited cases. However, many numerical techniques have been developed for solution of the equations subject to various boundary conditions of interest.

Numerical methods as well as approximate techniques for solving the governing equations will be discussed in some detail in later sections of this chapter. In the following section, numerical solutions to the Richards equation are used to examine effects of various factors, such as soil properties and boundary conditions, on the infiltration process.

FACTORS AFFECTING INFILTRATION

Soil Properties

It may be concluded from the previous discussion (equations [4.8] and [4.10]) that infiltration is dependent on the soil properties $K(h)$, $C(h)$ and $D(\theta)$. Knowledge of these relationships (either $K(h)$ and $C(h)$ or $K(\theta)$ and $D(\theta)$) is necessary to solve the Richards equation for a given set of initial and boundary conditions. For layered soils, these properties must be known for each layer and, for multi-dimensional flow in anisotropic soils, the properties must be known as a function of flow direction.

Infiltration rate-time relationships as predicted from numerical solutions of equation [4.8] for vertical infiltration from a ponded surface into deep homogeneous soil profiles are plotted in Fig. 4.5 for six example soils. Corresponding plots for cumulative infiltration are given in Fig. 4.6. Inasmuch as the infiltration rate asymptotically approaches K_s, one of the most important variables controlling infiltration is the hydraulic conductivity. However, during early stages of infiltration, the soil structure or the pore size distribution has a significant effect. As the soil behind the wetting front approaches saturation, the hydraulic gradient approaches unity and the hydraulic conductivity begins to control the flow rate. Generally speaking, the wider the range of pore sizes the more gradual the change in the infiltration rate.

The influence of the shapes of the soil water characteristic and the hydraulic conductivity-water content relationships on infiltration was studied by Hanks and Bowers (1963). They showed that variations in the soil-water diffusivity at low water contents had negligible effect on infiltration from a

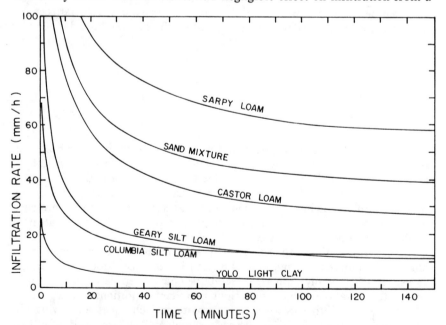

FIG. 4.5 Predicted infiltration rates from numerical solutions to the Richards equation for deep soils with a shallow ponded surface. Soil properties were obtained from the literature as follows: Sarpy 1. and Geary s.l. - Hanks and Bowers (1962); Castor 1. - Staple and Gupta (1966); Yolo l.c. - Philip (1957a); Sand m. - Skaggs, et al. (1969); Columbia s.l. - Kirkham and Powers (1972).

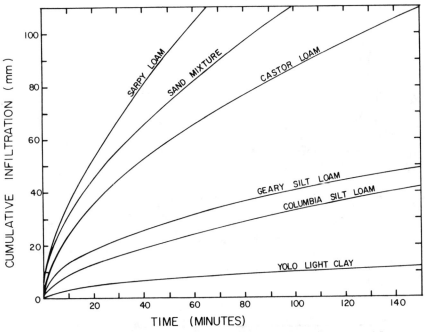

FIG. 4.6 Predicted cumulative infiltration relationships for the soils in Fig. 4.5.

ponded water surface. However, variations in either the diffusivity or soil-water characteristic at water contents near saturation have a very strong influence on predicted infiltration. Therefore, errors in measuring the hydraulic soil properties are of far greater consequence for water contents near saturation than for drier conditions so far as infiltration is concerned.

Initial Water Content (θ_i)

One of the important factors influencing infiltration of water into the soil profile is the initial water content. Fig. 4.7 shows predicted influx curves for infiltration from a shallow ponded surface into a deep Columbia silt loam. The four solutions were obtained by numerically solving Richards equation for the uniform initial water contents given. Soil properties used were those reported by Kirkham and Powers (1972). Note that infiltration rates are high for drier initial conditions but that the dependence on initial water content decreases with time. If infiltration is allowed to continue indefinitely, the infiltration rate will eventually approach K_s regardless of the initial water content. Infiltration rates are higher at low initial water contents because of higher hydraulic gradients and more available storage volume.

Changes in the initial water content have much the same effect on the infiltration rate as do changes in the pore size distribution or the soil structure. The higher the initial water content, the lower the initial infiltration rate and the more quickly the rate approaches the asymptote, K_s. In other words, high initial water contents reduce the effective porosity and the range of pore sizes available for infiltrating water. Philip (1957c) showed that for all times during infiltration, the wetting front advances more rapidly for higher initial water contents. Again this is the same effect that reduction in the total porosity would have on the wetting front advance, providing the hydraulic conductivity remains unchanged.

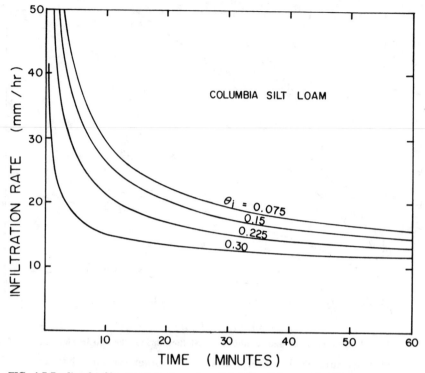

FIG. 4.7 Predicted infiltration rates for a deep Columbia silt loam with different initial water contents. Saturated volumetric water content for this soil is $\theta_s = 0.34$.

Rainfall Rates

As noted earlier, infiltration depends on the rate of water application as well as soil conditions. For example, if the rainfall rate, R, is less than K_s for a deep homogeneous soil, infiltration may continue indefinitely at a rate equal to the rainfall rate without ponding at the surface (curve for R = 3 mm/h in Fig. 4.8). The water content of the soil in this case does not reach saturation at any point but approaches a limiting value which depends on rainfall intensity. Specifically, for a given rainfall intensity, R, the soil profile approaches a uniform water content, θ_L; where θ_L is the water content for which the hydraulic conductivity is equal to R, i.e. $K(\theta_L) = R$. Because the unsaturated hydraulic conductivity decreases with decreasing θ, the lower the rain intensity, the lower the value of θ_L. Detailed investigations of rainfall infiltration have been conducted by Rubin and his co-workers (Rubin and Steinhardt, 1963, 1964; Rubin et al., 1964; and Rubin, 1966). Note that the above discussion for $R<K_s$ is valid only for deep homogeneous soils. For soils with restricting layers, infiltration at $R<K_s$ will not always continue indefinitely without surface ponding. When the wetting front reaches the restricting layer, water contents above the layer will increase and surface ponding *may* result even though the rainfall rate is less than K_s of the surface layer. Whether or not surface ponding and runoff occurs under such conditions depends on the soil properties of the restricting layer, its initial water content and lower boundary condition as well as the rate of drainage in the lateral direction.

The effect of rainfall rates greater than the saturated conductivity

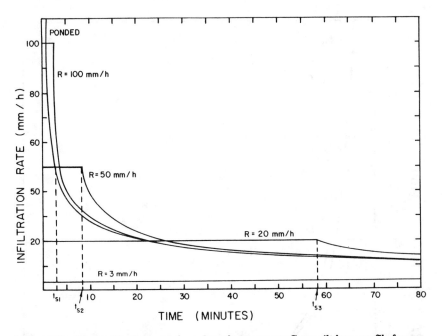

FIG. 4.8 Predicted infiltration rates for a deep, homogeneous Geary silt loam profile for constant surface application rates and for a shallow ponded surface. The initial water content was uniform at $\theta_i = 0.26$ which corresponds to $h_i = -750$ cm of water.

(R>K$_s$) on infiltration rate is shown in Fig. 4.8 for Geary silt loam. Initially, water infiltrates at the application rate. After some time, t_s, the infiltration capacity falls below R, surface ponding begins and water becomes available for runoff. The time of surface ponding decreases with increasing R and the infiltration rate-time relationships are clearly dependent on the rainfall intensity (Fig. 4.8).

If the infiltration rate is plotted versus cumulative infiltration, F, (Fig. 4.9) rather than time, the resulting relationships are much less dependent on R. In fact, for approximate purposes, the relationships may be assumed to be independent of R and a single curve used for all application rates greater than K$_s$. This assumption is inherent in the Green-Ampt methods used to predict time of ponding by Mein and Larson (1973) and in the parametric model presented by R. Smith (1972). Smith (1972) proposed that this assumption could be extended to the case of erratic rainfall where the unsteady rainfall or application rate dropped below the infiltration capacity for period of time followed by a high intensity application. Reeves and Miller (1975) made the same hypothesis. They obtained numerical solutions to the Richards equation which considered hysteresis and surface crusting. Their investigations showed that the infiltration capacity could be approximated as a simple function of cumulative infiltration, regardless of the rainfall rate-time history. Such findings are important in application in that parameters for approximate methods such as the Green-Ampt equations are not dependent on the rainfall rate and hence only have to be defined for different initial conditions. This considerably reduces input requirements and makes such methods easier to use.

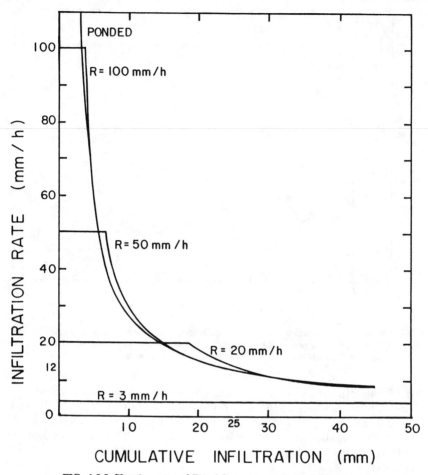

FIG. 4.9 Infiltration rates of Fig. 4.8 versus cumulative infiltration.

Surface Sealing and Crusting

In the preceding discussions we have assumed that the soil matrix or skeleton is rigid and does not change with time. Actually the hydraulic properties at the soil surface may change dramatically during the application of water. Such changes, which depend on the surface cover, have a stronger influence on the rate of infiltration than some of the other factors discussed. Indeed in some of the early studies of infiltration, the exponential decay of infiltration rate with time was assumed to be due to slaking of aggregates and swelling of colloids which progressively sealed the soil (Horton, 1939).

Edwards and Larson (1969) used the theory of soil-water movement to investigate the influence of surface seal development on infiltration of water into a tilled soil. They determined the saturated hydraulic conductivity of a surface layer 0.5 cm thick as a function of time of exposure to simulated rainfall. In one example, the saturated hydraulic conductivity of the surface layer decreased from 1.9 cm/h to 0.2 cm/h after 2 h of simulated rainfall applied at a rate of 7 cm/h. The predicted cumulative infiltration for the 2-h period was reduced by about 50 percent and the infiltration rate from 25 to 10 mm/h because of surface sealing. Greater reduction in infiltration rate did not occur because of an increase of the suction gradient at the surface as the seal was formed. Hillel and Gardner (1969, 1970) used approximate analytical methods to evaluate the effect of surface sealing on steady state and transient infiltration processes. They showed that infiltration into a crusted profile may be approximated by assuming that water enters the soil layer below the crust at a nearly constant suction, the magnitude of which depends on the conductivity and thickness of the crust and the hydraulic properties of the underlying soil.

Morin and Benyamini (1977) concluded that the crust formed by raindrop impact is the dominant factor influencing the infiltration capacity of a bare Hamra soil. In order to characterize the infiltration process they considered three different initial soil conditions, uncrusted dry soil, crusted wet soil and crusted dry soil. For each different initial condition the infiltration capacity could be described in terms of the cumulative rainfall striking the surface rather than cumulative infiltration as in Fig. 4.9. When treated in this way, infiltration capacity was found to be independent of the rainfall intensity for field tests on each of the three initial conditions. When simulated rainfall was applied at a rate of 130 mm/h, the infiltration capacity of a bare Hamra soil decreased to 8 mm/h after 60 min as opposed to a continuous rate of 130 mm/h when the surface was protected by a straw mulch.

Because of the complex nature of the sealing process and the difficulty of describing the manner in which hydraulic properties of the surface layer change with time, there have been few attempts to use the theory of soil-water movement to analyze the phenomena. However, the results of numerous experimental investigations indicating the importance of surface sealing have been reported. An example of the effect that surface conditions have on the infiltration rate-time relationship is shown in Fig. 4.10 for a Zanesville silt loam. These measurements were obtained from rainulator plot data as

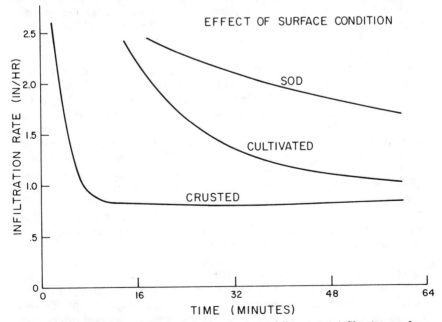

FIG. 4.10 Effect of surface sealing and crusting due to rainfall impact on infiltration rate for a Zanesville silt loam soil.

described by Skaggs et al. (1969). The data for crusted soil were obtained from cultivated plots which had been subjected to simulated rainfall for two hours, and then tested in a dry condition at a later date. Identical treatment of a sod plot had no effect on the infiltration relationship.

Mannering and Meyer (1963) showed that straw mulch applied at densities of greater than one ton per acre prevented surface sealing due to rainfall impact. For mulch densities of 1/2 ton or less per acre, surface sealing occurred and cumulative infiltration was reduced from approximately 32 mm to 12 mm for a 30-min test on Wea silt loam. Corresponding final infiltration rates were reduced from about 6 to 2 mm/h. Other studies of the influence of rainfall energy and various soil factors on surface sealing and infiltration have been reported by Moldenhauer and Long (1964), Burwell and Larson (1969), Koon et al. (1970), Horton (1940), and Duley (1939). Clearly, surface sealing and crusting has a significant, perhaps dominant effect on infiltration in bare or unprotected soils. It is therefore necessary to consider this factor when predicting infiltration under rainfall conditions. This is particularly important for soils with only partial surface cover such as row crop lands during seedbed preparation and the early part of the growing season.

Layered Soils

The Richards equation was solved by Hanks and Bowers (1962) for infiltration from a ponded surface into a two-layered soil. A continuous pressure head distribution was predicted at the layer boundaries, but the predicted water content distributions were discontinuous because of the difference in the soil-water characteristics of the two soils. For a coarse over a fine soil, infiltration proceeded exactly as for a coarse soil alone until the wetting front arrived at the boundary between the two layers. Then the progress of the wetting front was slowed, a positive pressure head developed in the top layer and the infiltration rate approached that predicted for the fine soil alone. The infiltration rate-time relationship predicted for fine over coarse soils was nearly the same as that predicted for a uniform fine-textured soil except for a decrease in the infiltration rate when the wetting front reached the coarse layer. Whisler and Klute (1966) obtained similar solutions for coarse textured soils over fine soils, fine textured lenses in coarse soils and coarse textured lenses in fine soils. Their solutions for a coarse textured lens in fine soil predicted that the wetting front would be held up for a period before entering the coarse layer. The pressure head at the wetting front is nearly always negative. Therefore, the larger pores in a coarse textured layer do not fill with water, resulting in only partial saturation and low hydraulic conductivity in the layer. The result is a sharp decrease in the infiltration rate followed by a partial recovery when the wetting front moves into the coarse layer. This effect was observed by Miller and Gardner (1962) for infiltration into air dry stratified soils. Thus, a thin layer of soil of either coarser or finer texture than the otherwise uniform profile serves to cause a decrease in infiltration rate when the wetting front reaches that layer.

Movement and Entrapment of Soil Air

It was stated in an earlier section that the derivation of the Richards equation assumes that displaced soil air moves through the profile with negligible resistance and that the air pressure remains constant throughout. The Richards equation will be written for nonconstant air pressure later in this section. However as long as it is written in terms of h, constant air pressure must be assumed. This assumption is usually justified by the small viscosity of air relative to that of water and by assuming that air can escape through large pores that remain partially open during infiltration. While these assumptions may hold in some instances, there are numerous cases where air is trapped by infiltrating water causing an air pressure buildup in advance of the wetting front and a reduction of the infiltration rate. Even for deep profiles, air pressure buildup causes infiltration rates to be less than would occur if resistance to air movement was truly negligible.

Entrapment of a certain amount of air within individual soil pores usually occurs during infiltration whether or not there is an air pressure buildup in advance of the wetting front. Pores containing entrapped air are unavailable for the transport of water and result in a hydraulic conductivity of K_s rather than K_o as discussed previously. The difference in K_s and K_o depends on the number and size of pores blocked by entrapped air. Wilson and Luthin (1963) suggested that entrapment occurs primarily in the larger pores. Slack (1978) presented a method for evaluating K_s for different amounts of air trapped in large pores. Using his methods for a total air entrapment of 10 percent ($\theta_s = 0.9\ \theta_o$) would predict an 80 to 90 percent reduction in hydraulic conductivity. Thus air entrapment in individual pores may have a significant effect on K_s and on the infiltration process.

The fact that air movement may significantly affect infiltration has been recognized for many years (e.g., Free and Palmer, 1940). Studies showing the effects of air pressure buildup and the flow of air on the infiltration process have been conducted by Wilson and Luthin (1963), Peck (1965) and Adrian and Franzini (1966). A particularly detailed study of this phenomena with oil as the infiltrating liquid was reported by McWhorter (1971). He conducted infiltration experiments for conditions representing both semi-infinite and finite profile depths as well as presented analytical methods for predicting the effects of two-phase flow.

Most of the literature concerning multiphase immiscible flow equations is found in petroleum engineering journals. Breitenbach et al. (1968a, b) developed multiphase flow equations for oil, water and gas phases, and described numerical techniques for solving those equations in petroleum reservoirs. The petroleum engineering approach of multiphase fluid flow modeling was applied in describing two-phase (air-water) movement in unsaturated porous medium (Green et al., 1970; Phuc and Morel-Seytoux, 1972). Analytical procedures were also developed for handling the two-phase equations (McWhorter, 1971, 1976; Brustkern and Morel-Seytoux, 1970, 1975; Noblanc and Morel-Seytoux, 1972; Sonu and Morel-Seytoux, 1976).

The nonlinear partial differential equations for transient, two-phase flow through unsaturated porous medium are obtained by combining: (a) the continuity equation for each fluid phase, (b) Darcy's law for each phase, (c) a fluid conservation equation, (d) an equation defining the capillary pressure, and (e) an equation of state for the air phase. The following assumptions are made: (a) Darcy's law is valid for both wetting (water) and nonwetting (air) phases, (b) the two fluids, air and water, are homogeneous and immiscible, (c) the water as a wetting phase is incompressible and the air as a nonwetting phase is compressible and (d) the flow is isothermal. The continuity equations for the two phases are water phase,

$$\frac{\partial q}{\partial z} = -\phi \frac{\partial S_w}{\partial t}$$ .... [4.11a]

and air phase,

$$\frac{\partial}{\partial z}(\rho_a q_a) = -\phi \frac{\partial}{\partial t}(\rho_a S_a)$$ .... [4.11b]

where the subscript a refers to the air phase, S = fluid saturation = θ/ϕ, ϕ = porosity, and ρ = fluid density.

Darcy's law for the two phases may be expressed as:
water phase,

$$q = -\frac{kk_r}{\mu}(\frac{\partial P}{\partial z} - \rho g)$$ .... [4.12a]

and air phase,

$$q_a = -\frac{kk_{ra}}{\mu_a}(\frac{\partial P_a}{\partial z} - \rho_a g)$$ .... [4.12b]

where k = absolute or saturated permeability (L^2) in the z-direction (the hydraulic conductivity can be defined as K = $k\rho g/\mu$); k_r, k_{ra} = relative permeabilities for water and air, respectively; μ, μ_a = viscosities for water and air, respectively ($ML^{-1}T^{-1}$); g = acceleration of gravity (LT^{-2}); and P = fluid pressure ($ML^{-1}T^{-2}$). The fluid conservation equation states

$$S_w + S_a = 1$$ .... [4.13]

Using the definition of capillary pressure, P_c, in a partially saturated medium

$$P_c = P_a - P$$ .... [4.14]

Air is assumed to behave as a perfect gas, and the gas law yields density of air as a function of air pressure

$$\rho_a = P_a/(R_o T)$$ .... [4.15]

where R_o = universal gas constant, and T = temperature.

The relative permeability of each fluid phase is assumed to be a known function of saturation of the liquid phase:

$$k_r = k_r(S_w)$$ .... [4.16a]

and

$$k_{ra} = k_{ra}(S_a) = k_{ra}(1-S_w)$$ .... [4.16b]

Combining equations [4.11] through [4.15] yields the air pressure equation [4.17a], water saturation equation [4.17b], and the air saturation equation [4.17c].

The air pressure equation is

$$\frac{\partial}{\partial z}\left[\frac{kk_r}{\mu}\left(\frac{\partial P_a}{\partial z} - \frac{\partial P_c}{\partial z} - \rho\,g\right)\right] + \frac{1}{P_a}\frac{\partial}{\partial z}\left[\frac{kk_{ra}\rho_a}{\mu_a}\left(\frac{\partial P_a}{\partial z} - \rho_a g\right)\right]$$

$$= \frac{\phi S_a}{P_a}\frac{\partial P_a}{\partial t} \quad\dotfill\quad [4.17a]$$

The water saturation equation is

$$\frac{\partial S_w}{\partial t} = \frac{1}{(\phi)}\frac{\partial}{\partial z}\left[\frac{kk_r}{\mu}\left(\frac{\partial P}{\partial z} - \rho g\right)\right] \quad\dotfill\quad [4.17b]$$

The air saturation equation is

$$\frac{\partial S_a}{\partial_t} = \frac{1}{(\phi\rho_a)}\frac{\partial}{\partial z}\left[\frac{kk_{ra}\rho_a}{\mu_a}\left(\frac{\partial P_a}{\partial z} - \rho_a g\right)\right] - \frac{S_a}{P_a}\frac{\partial P_a}{\partial t} \quad\dotfill\quad [4.17c]$$

Equation [4.17a] is solved implicitly for air pressures at time $t+1$. Equations [4.17b] and [4.17c] are solved explicitly for water and air saturations, respectively (Khaleel and Reddell, 1976).

Brustkern and Morel-Seytoux (1970) developed an analytical approach to the solution of the two-phase flow equations. Their procedure reduces the system of two complex partial differential equations to (a) a water saturation equation, i.e., equation [4.18] and (b) an integral equation, i.e., equation [4.19]:

$$\phi\frac{\partial S_w}{\partial t} + \overline{V}\frac{\partial I}{\partial z} = 0 \quad\dotfill\quad [4.18]$$

and

$$\overline{V} = \left[(P_{a1} - P_{a2}) + g\rho\int_1^2 i_w dz + \int_1^2 i_w dP_c\right]\Big/\left[\int_1^2 \frac{dz}{k\left(\frac{k_{ra}}{\mu_a} + \frac{k_r}{\mu}\right)}\right] \quad\dotfill\quad [4.19]$$

where

$\overline{V}$ = average total velocity and is the algebraic sum of water and air fluxes; i.e., $\overrightarrow{V} = q + q_a$;

I = fractional flow function and is the ratio of water flow to total flow, i.e., $I = q/\overline{V}$;

P_{a1}, P_{a2} = air pressures at location 1 (ground surface) and at location 2 (ahead of wetting front); and

i_w = $\dfrac{1}{\left[1 + \dfrac{k_{ra}}{\mu_a}\dfrac{\mu}{k_r}\right]}$.

Equations [4.18] and [4.19] are solved for the unknowns $S_w(z,t)$ and $\overline{V}$. Equation [4.19] involves integration of known functions of saturation and coordinates. The value of $\overline{V}$ as calculated from equation [4.19] applies strictly only at time t. Thus the size of the time step, Δt, must be small enough so that the value of $\overline{V}$ changes only slightly during the time interval (Brustkern

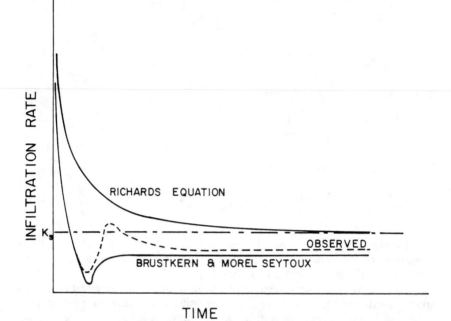

FIG. 4.11. Schematic of the effect of the air phase on infiltration as predicted by solution of the Richards equation by the methods of Brustkern and Morel-Seytoux (1970) and as observed by McWhorter (1971).

and Morel-Seytoux, 1970). Once $\overline{V}$ is calculated from equation [4.19], equation [4.18] can be integrated explicitly to give a new saturation profile at time $t + \Delta t$. The procedure is repeated as long as desired. The effect of air movement on infiltration as predicted by methods presented by Brustkern and Morel-Seytoux (1970) is shown schematically in Fig. 4.11 for a soil with a water table or restrictive layer at a relatively shallow depth. When the air phase is neglected, the infiltration rate predicted by solution of the Richards equation asymptotically approaches K_s, the hydraulic conductivity at residual saturation. However, when air is entrapped between the wetting front and the water table or a restrictive layer, air pressure increases causing a rapid reduction in infiltration rate. As air pressure increases, upward flow of the air phase begins followed by escape of air from the surface and an increase in the infiltration rate. This predicted infiltration rate also asymptotically approaches a constant value but this value is significantly less than K_s. The predicted 'dips' in the infiltration rate curve occur sooner and are more pronounced for smaller depths to the water table or restricting layers, which is consistant with the observations of McWhorter (1971). However, McWhorter observed that when air began to escape from the surface, the infiltration rate increased to values higher than the final rate (shown schematically by the broken curve in Fig. 4.11), then decreased. A disturbance of the surface zone was observed at the time air began to escape and the increase was attributed to deformation of the soil matrix resulting in higher hydraulic conductivity of the surface layers. As an example of the effect of the air phase, McWhorter's data for a 1.85-m long, closed column of

Poudre sand shows that the long-term infiltration rate asympotically approaches a value that is approximately 60 percent of K_s.

McWhorter (1976) presented approximate methods for characterizing two-phase flow during steady infiltration as occurs during rainfall or sprinkler irrigation. His analysis, which assumed that air is incompressible and thus tended to predict the maximum effect of the air phase on infiltration, showed that the time required for surface ponding may be much smaller than that predicted from a single phase flow analysis. Furthermore, resistance to air flow will cause ponding to occur at infiltration rates that would persist indefinitely if resistance to air movement could truly be neglected. In one example the maximum sustainable infiltration rate (i.e. without surface ponding) was only 32 percent of that predicted from single phase flow theory.

In the above discussion we have considered movement of water and air in a homogeneous soil or in layers of homogeneous materials. However natural soils are seldom homogeneous and often are permeated, especially in the surface layers, by relatively large channels formed by roots, cracking due to shrinkage, and worm holes. Obviously such channels would have a great effect on infiltration as they would provide both pathways for rapid inflow of ponded water and an escape route for air as the wetting front advances. The effect of macropores on infiltration has been studied by Dixon and Peterson (1971) and by Dixon and Linden (1972). They found that large pores, open to the soil surface, can contribute greatly to infiltration, in some cases raising total infiltration by a factor of 10 or more. However, small soil air pressures can block this contribution so large pores close to the surface, but not open, have a much smaller effect on infiltration. Thus infiltration can be increased by using cultural practices designed to prevent the sealing of large pores near the surface.

APPROXIMATE INFILTRATION MODELS

Infiltration can be characterized for most initial and boundary conditions of interest by solving the governing differential equations using numerical methods. These solutions, which will be discussed in detail in a subsequent section, provide a physically consistent means of quantifying infiltration in terms of the soil properties governing movement of water and air. However such elaborate procedures are rarely used in practice. One reason is that numerical solutions are usually expensive due to computational requirements. A more severe limitation is the difficulty of obtaining necessary soil property data. Variation of the soil properties, both with depth and from point to point in the field, causes numerous measurements to be required to adequately describe field conditions. Present methods of determining the properties are difficult and such data are only available for a limited number of soils. Thus, while the numerical prediction methods are extremely valuable in analyzing the effects of various factors on the infiltration process, they have so far been of limited value for production scale applications in modeling watershed hydrology.

Attempts to characterize infiltration for field applications have usually involved simplified concepts which permit the infiltration rate or cumulative infiltration volume to be expressed algebraically in terms of time and certain soil parameters. Some of the approximate models have been developed by applying the principles governing soil water movement for simplified boundary and initial conditions. The parameters in such models can be determined from soil water properties, when they are available. Other models are strictly empirical and the parameters must be obtained from measured infiltration data or estimated using more approximate procedures. The most obvious characteristic of the infiltration process is that for ponded surfaces the rate decreases rapidly with time during the early part of an infiltration event. Although attributed to different physical phenomena, this characteristic is reflected by all of the approximate infiltration equations.

Kostiakov Equation

One of the simplest infiltration equations was proposed by Kostiakov (1932),

$$f_p = K_k \, \bar{t}^\alpha \dotfill [4.20]$$

where f_p is the infiltration capacity, t is time after infiltration starts, and K_k and α are constants which depend on the soil and initial conditions. The parameters in this equation have no physical interpretation and must be evaluated from experimental data.

Horton Equation

Horton (1939, 1940) presented a three parameter infiltration equation which may be written as,

$$f_p = f_c + (f_o - f_c) \, e^{-\beta t} \dotfill [4.21]$$

where f_c is the final constant infiltration rate, f_o is the infiltration capacity at t = 0, and β is a soil parameter which controls the rate of decrease of infiltration rate. The parameters f_o and β must depend on the initial water content as well as the application rate, and for homogeneous profiles, f_c will be somewhat smaller than the saturated hydraulic conductivity. Again the equation parameters must usually be evaluated from experimental infiltration data.

Philip Equation

Philip (1957b) proposed that the first two terms of his series solution for infiltration from a ponded surface into a deep homogeneous soil be used as a concise infiltration equation. The equation may be written for infiltration rate as,

$$f_p = \frac{S}{2} \, t^{-1/2} + C_a \dotfill [4.22]$$

where S is a parameter called sorptivity which, along with C_a can be evaluated numerically using procedures given by Philip if the soil properties $D(\theta)$ and $h(\theta)$ are known. The resulting value for C_a will be approximately $K_s/3$ (Youngs, 1968) so the equation will not be physically consistent for large times if Philip's methods are used to define C_a. A regression fit to experimental data will tend to give $C_a = f_c$, however. Youngs (1968) showed that C_a could be approximated as $C_a = 2K_s/3$ and $S = (2M \, K_s S_f)^{1/2}$ where M is the fillable porosity, $M = \theta_s - \theta_i$, and S_f is the effective suction at the wetting front.

Holtan Equation

An empirical equation based on a storage concept was described by Holtan (1961). After several modifications of the original form, the equation for infiltration capacity in inches/h may be written as (Holtan and Lopez, 1971),

$$f_p = GI \cdot a \cdot SA^{1.4} + f_c \quad\quad\quad\quad\quad\quad [4.23]$$

where SA is the available storage in the surface layer (inches), GI is the growth index of crop in percent of maturity, a is an index (in./h per (in.)$^{1.4}$ of storage) of surface connected porosity which is a function of surface conditions and the density of plant roots, and f_c is the constant or steady state infiltration rate, which is estimated from the hydrologic soil group.

The procedure in applying the Holtan equation is to measure or predict the initial soil water content θ_i, and compute the initial available storage SA $= (\theta_s - \theta_i)d$ where d is the surface layer depth. The infiltration capacity may then be predicted from equation [4.23]. The infiltrated water will reduce the value of SA, but this value will recover in part during the same time, due to drainage from the surface layer at a rate of f_c up to the limit of SA$_o$ and by evapotranspiration (ET) through plants. That is, after a period of time Δt, SA $=$ SA$_o$ - F + $f_c \Delta t$ + ET Δt, where F is the amount of infiltration during Δt.

The values adopted for f_c are based on a range of values for each of the hydrology groups (Table 4.1). The hydrologic soil group for a given soil type can be obtained from the SCS National Engineering Handbook (1965). Estimates for the parameter, a, in terms of crop or surface cover conditions are given in Table 4.2 (after Frere et al., 1975).

Advantages of the Holtan equation are that it is relatively easy to use for rainfall infiltration and the input parameters can be obtained from a rather general description of the soil type and crop conditions. A major difficulty with the Holtan equation is the determination of the control depth on which to base SA. Holtan and Creitz (1967) suggested using the depth of the plow layer or the depth to the first impeding layer; however, Huggins and Monke (1966) found that the effective control depth was highly dependent on both the surface condition and cultural practices used in preparing the seed bed. Smith (1976) argued that the infiltration curves are physically related to gradients and hydraulic conductivity far more than to soil porosity and that we should not expect the Holtan equation to adequately describe the process. Experience with the Holtan equation indicates that, because of the generality of the inputs, its accuracy is questionable on a local or point by point basis in the watershed.

TABLE 4.1. ESTIMATES BY
HYDROLOGY GROUP FOR THE
FINAL INFILTRATION RATE, f_c IN
THE HOLTAN EQUATION (AFTER
MUSGRAVE, 1955)

Hydrologic soil group	f_c (in./h)
A	0.45-0.30
B	0.30-0.15
C	0.15-0.05
D	0.05-0

TABLE 4.2. ESTIMATES OF VEGETATIVE
PARAMETER "a" IN THE HOLTAN
INFILTRATION EQUATION (AFTER
FRERE, ET AL., 1975)

| Land use or cover | Basal area rating* | |
	Poor condition	Good condition
Fallow†	0.10	0.30
Row crops	0.10	0.20
Small grains	0.20	0.30
Hay (legumes)	0.20	0.40
Hay (sod)	0.40	0.60
Pasture (Bunch grass)	0.20	0.40
Temporary pasture (sod)	0.20	0.60
Permanent pasture (sod)	0.80	1.00
Woods and forests	0.80	1.00

*Adjustments needed for "weeds" and "grazing."
†For fallow land only, poor condition means
"After row crop," and good condition means
"After sod."

Green-Ampt Model

An approximate model utilizing Darcy's law was proposed by Green and Ampt (1911). The original equation was derived for infiltration from a ponded surface into a deep homogeneous soil with a uniform initial water content. Water is assumed to enter the soil as slug flow resulting in a sharply defined wetting front which separates a zone that has been wetted from a totally unwetted zone (Fig. 4.12). Direct application of Darcy's law yields the following form of the Green-Ampt equation.

$$f_p = K_s(H_o + S_f + L_F)/L_F \qquad [4.24]$$

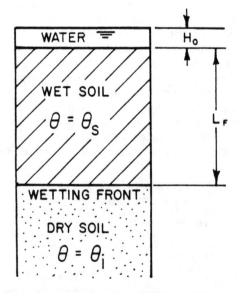

FIG. 4.12 The Green-Ampt model assumes slug flow with a sharp wetting front between the infiltrated zone and soil at the initial water content. The wet zone increases in length as infiltration progresses.

where K_s is the hydraulic conductivity of the transmission zone, H_o is the depth of water ponded on the surface, S_f is the effective suction at the wetting front, and L_F is the distance from the surface to the wetting front. Expressing the cumulative infiltration as $F = (\theta_s - \theta_i)L_F = M \, L_F$ and assuming the depth of ponding at the surface is shallow so that $H_o \approx 0$ equation [4.24] may be written as,

$$f_p = K_s + K_sM \, S_f/F \dotfill [4.25]$$

where the initial soil water deficit (or fillable porosity) M, is the difference between initial and final volumetric water contents, $M = \theta_s - \theta_i$. Although the original derivation by Green and Ampt assumed total saturation behind the wetting front, this requirement was in effect relaxed by Philip (1954). He assumed the water content θ_s, was constant but not necessarily equal to the total porosity. Likewise, K_s is expected to be less than the saturated hydraulic conductivity.

Substituting $f_p = dF/dt$ in equation [4.25] and integrating, with the condition $F = 0$ at $t = 0$, yields

$$K_st = F - S_fM \ln (1 + F/MS_f) \dotfill [4.26]$$

This form of the Green-Ampt equation relates infiltration volume to time from the start of infiltration and is more convenient than equation [4.25] for some applications. Note that the derivation of equation [4.26] assumes a ponded surface so that infiltration rate is equal to infiltration capacity at all times. This is not the case for rainfall infiltration and equation [4.26] will require modification as will be discussed below.

In addition to uniform profiles for which it was originally derived, the Green-Ampt equation has been used with good results for profiles that become denser with depth (Childs and Bybordi, 1969), for profiles where hydraulic conductivity increases with depth (Bouwer, 1976), and for soils with partially sealed surfaces (Hillel and Gardner, 1970). Bouwer (1969) showed that it may also be used for nonuniform initial water contents. Morel-Seytoux and Khanji (1974) found that the form of equation [4.25] remained the same when simultaneous movement of both water and air is considered. They substituted H_c, the effective matric drive, for S_f and accounted for the resistance to air movement by the introduction of a viscous resistance correction factor, β, which was defined as a function of the soil and fluid properties. The Green-Ampt equation as modified by Morel-Seytoux and Khanji (1974) may be written as,

$$f_p = K_s/\beta + K_sM \, H_c/\beta F \dotfill [4.27]$$

Calculated values of β for five soils showed a range from 1.1 to 1.7 as opposed to an assumed value of $\beta = 1$ when the air phase is neglected. Neglecting the air phase for the five soils considered would have resulted in overpredicting the infiltration rates by 10 to 40 percent. However this only holds if the equation parameters are defined from basic soil properties rather than from infiltration measurements. If K_s is determined from field infiltration data the effect of air resistance will be reflected in the K_s value obtained and equations [4.25] and [4.26] will give reliable predictions for large times.

Determination of parameters in the Green-Ampt model: Bouwer (1966, 1969) showed that the hydraulic conductivity parameter in the Green-Ampt equation should be less than the saturated value, K_o, because of entrapped air. He described air-entry permeameter which can be used in the field for measuring K_s, the conductivity at residual air saturation, and the air entry suction. When measured values are not available, Bouwer (1966) suggested that K_s may be approximated as $K_s = 0.5\ K_o$. The effective suction at the wetting front, S_f, is somewhat more difficult to determine. Bouwer (1969) used the water entry suction, h_{ce}, for S_f in equation [4.25] and suggested that it can be approximated as one-half of the air entry value. Mein and Larson (1973) used the unsaturated hydraulic conductivity as a weighting factor and defined the average suction at the wetting front as:

$$S_{av} = \int_0^1 \psi\ dK_r \quad\dotfill\quad [4.28a]$$

where ψ is the soil water suction, $(\psi = -h)$, ψ_i is the suction at the initial water content, θ_i, and K_r is the relative hydraulic conductivity, $K_r = K(\psi)/K_s$. Neuman (1976) obtained the following theoretical expression for S_{av} by relating it to the physical characteristics of the soil:

$$S_{av} = \int_0^{\psi_i} K_r\ d\psi \quad\dotfill\quad [4.28b]$$

An expression, identical to equation [4.28b], was proposed by Bouwer (1964) for 'critical pressure head' in cases of horizontal flow systems above the water table. Morel-Seytoux and Khanji (1974) introduced the concept of effective matric drive, H_c, which is dependent on the relative conductivities of both air and water. However, for most cases the value of S_{av} given by equation [4.28a] or [4.28b] is a reasonable approximation of H_c (Morel-Seytoux and Khanji, 1974).

One of the problems of using equations [4.28] to obtain S_{av} is the requirement of the unsaturated hydraulic conductivity function $K(\psi)$. Some investigators have used prediction methods to estimate $K(\psi)$ and then determine S_{av} from equations [4.28]. Brakensiek (1977) used prediction methods by Brooks and Corey (1964) and Jackson (1972) to determine S_{av} for the five soils originally investigated by Mein and Larson (1973). He showed that, for the Brooks and Corey (1964) model, equation [4.28] may be integrated to give,

$$S_{av} = h_{ce}\ \eta/(\eta-1) \quad\dotfill\quad [4.29]$$

where h_{ce} is water entry (or air exit) suction approximately equal to one-half of the air entry value (bubbling pressure). The bubbling pressure and the parameter η may be obtained with the graphical procedures outlined by Brooks and Corey (1964). Brakensiek (1977) found that S_{av} values computed from the two prediction methods were in good agreement with the original values obtained by Mein and Larson using actual K_r data and with H_c values computed by Morel-Seytoux and Khanji (1974) for the same five soils. Idike et al. (1977) obtained similar results by using the hydraulic conductivity prediction method of Campbell (1974) and equation [4.28] to calculate S_{av} for these soils. Brakensiek (1977) also found that the simple equation $S_{av} = 0.76\ P_b$, where P_b is the desorption bubbling pressure, is an acceptable approximation for the soils investigated.

The flexibility of the Green-Ampt equations for describing infiltration under varied initial, boundary and soil profile conditions makes it an attractive method for field applications. The fact that the equation parameters have physical significance and can be computed from soil properties is an added advantage. However it will usually prove advantageous to determine the equation parameters from field measurements by fitting measured infiltration data. Such measurements tend to lump the effects of heterogeneities, worm holes, crusting, etc. in the equation parameters. This will usually result in more reliable infiltration predictions than if the parameters are determined from basic soil property measurements. Methods for determining Green-Ampt equation parameters by fitting infiltrometer data were presented by Brakensiek and Onstad (1977). They considered spatial variation of the estimated parameters and presented methods for averaging the values to give lumped parameter values for watershed modeling. A sensitivity analysis for the equation parameters showed that predicted infiltration and runoff amounts and rates were most sensitive to the errors in fillable porosity, M, and K_s and less sensitive to errors in S_{av}.

Application of the Green-Ampt model to rainfall infiltration—The Mein and Larson equation: We noted previously that, although the infiltration capacity-time relationship is dependent on the application rate (Fig. 4.8), the relationship between infiltration capacity and cumulative infiltration is approximately independent of rainfall intensity (Fig. 4.9). Therefore it seems logical that the Green-Ampt equation [4.25] could be applied directly for rainfall conditions. On the other hand, the time based equations (e.g., Kostiakov, Horton and Philip) would be more difficult to apply because of the dependence of the equation parameters on rainfall intensity. Mein and Larson (1973) applied the Green-Ampt model for rainfall conditions by determining cumulative infiltration ($F = F_p$) at the time of surface ponding ($t = t_p$) from equation [4.25].

$$f = f_p = R = K_s + K_s M \, S_{av}/F_p$$

Then substituting S_{av} for S_f and solving for F_p, the Mein and Larson equation may be written as,

$$F_p = \frac{S_{av} M}{R/K_s - 1} \quad \dots\dots\dots\dots\dots\dots\dots\dots\dots\dots\dots\dots\dots\dots \text{[4.30]}$$

where S_{av} is the average suction at the wetting front as discussed above. Since $f = R$ prior to surface ponding, $F_p = R \, t_p$, where t_p is the time of surface ponding. Then for steady rainfall the infiltration rate may be expressed as,

$$f = R \qquad \text{for } t < t_p \quad \dots\dots\dots\dots\dots\dots\dots\dots\dots\dots\dots \text{[4.31a]}$$

$$f = f_p = K_s + K_s S_{av} M/F_p \qquad \text{for } t > t_p \dots\dots\dots\dots\dots\dots \text{[4.31b]}$$

where $t_p = F_p/R$ and F_p is defined by equation [4.30]. If $R < K_s$, surface ponding will not occur (providing the profile is deep and homogeneous as was assumed in the derivation of the equations) and $f = R$.

An equation for rainfall infiltration analogous to equation [4.26] was obtained by Mein and Larson (1971):

$$K_s(t - t_p + t_p') = F - M\, S_{av} \ln (1 + F/M\, S_{av}) \dots\dots\dots\dots\dots\dots [4.32]$$

where t_p' is the equivalent time to infiltrate volume F_p under initially ponded surface conditions and may be calculated directly from equations [4.26]. Application of the Green-Ampt model can be made by using either equations [4.31] or [4.32]. Since equation [4.32] is implicit in F, it may be desirable to increment F and solve directly for time, t, and then for f from equation [4.31].

Example for steady rain: Rainfall at a constant intensity of 0.5 cm/h occurs on a deep Yolo light clay which has an initial uniform water content of θ_i = 0.25. There is no surface depressional storage so runoff begins when ponding is initiated. The following soil property data were given by Mein and Larson (1971) for Yolo light clay: $\theta_s = 0.499$, $K_s = 0.044$ cm/h, and $S_{av} = 22.4$ cm. S_{av} was estimated from equation [4.28] using the imbibition hydraulic conductivity data given by Moore (1939).

Prediction of Time of Surface Ponding, t_p: The soil water deficit $M = \theta_s - \theta_i = 0.499 - 0.25 = 0.249$. Infiltration volume at the time of surface ponding, F_p, is obtained from equation [4.30] as,

$$F_p = \frac{S_{av}\, M}{R/K_s - 1} = \frac{22.4 \times 0.249}{\dfrac{0.5}{0.044} - 1} = 0.54 \text{ cm}$$

At $t = t_p$, $f = R$ and $F = Rt_p$ so

$$t_p = F_p/R = 0.54/0.5 = 1.07 \text{ h}$$

Prediction of Infiltration After Surface Ponding: Equation [4.32] can be used to determine the F(t) relationship after surface ponding. If the surface had been ponded at $t = 0$, the time, t_p', required to infiltrate $F_p = 0.54$ cm is (from equation [4.26]),

$$t_p' = \frac{0.54}{0.044} - \frac{22.4\,(0.249)}{0.044} \ln (1 + \frac{0.54}{0.249 \times 22.4})$$

$$t_p' = 0.56 \text{ h}$$

Then from equation [4.32],

$$t = t_p - t_p' + F/K_s - \frac{M\, S_{av}}{K_s} \ln (1 + F/M\, S_{av})$$

or

$$t = 0.51 + F/0.044 - \frac{0.249 \times 22.4}{0.044} \ln (1 + \frac{F}{0.249 \times 22.4})$$

Then for $F = 0.75$ cm

$$t = 0.51 + 0.75/0.044 - 127 \ln (1 + \frac{0.75}{5.58})$$

$$t = 1.53 \text{ h}$$

The infiltration rate at this time can be calculated from equation [4.31b] as,

$f = 0.044 + 0.044 \times 22.4 \times 0.249/0.75 = 0.37$ cm/h.

By repeating the above procedure for successive values of F the infiltration volume and rate as a function of time can be easily obtained (Table 4.3). The infiltration - time relationship can be obtained directly from equation [4.32] by simply incrementing F as in Table 4.3 and noting that $\Delta F = \bar{f} \Delta t$ where $\bar{f}$ is the average infiltration rate and Δt is the time required to infiltrate ΔF. For example, consider the increment from $F = 0.54$ where $f = 0.5$ cm/h to $F = 0.75$ where $f = 0.37$ cm/h (Table 4.3). Here $\Delta F = 0.21$ cm and $\bar{f} = (0.5 + 0.37)/2 = 0.43$, so $\Delta t = 0.21/0.43 = 0.48$ h. Then the time for $F = 0.75$ cm would be $1.07 + 0.48 = 1.55$ h as opposed to 1.53 h calculated from equation [4.32]. While there may be advantages to using the incremental procedure for some applications, ΔF must be kept small to permit an accurate estimate of $\bar{f}$.

Use of the Green-Ampt model for unsteady rain: The validity of the Green-Ampt model for unsteady rainfall appears to be dependent on the degree of unsteadiness. Results of Reeves' and Miller's (1975) study support the use of the Green-Ampt equation for unsteady rainfall, although they did not specifically consider the equation in any form. They found that the infiltration capacity (f_p) for unsteady rainfall could be approximated as a function of cumulative infiltration (F) regardless of the application rate versus time history. Since the Green-Ampt equation expresses f_p as a function of F for steady rainfall, which is a special case of unsteady rainfall, it follows that the equation should hold for the unsteady case. Chu (1978) used the Green-Ampt equation for unsteady rainfall and obtained good agreement between predicted rainfall excess and measured runoff from a 113-acre watershed. On the other hand, James and Larson (1976) found that a model consisting of the Green-Ampt equations, in combination with components for describing soil water redistribution, consistently over-predicted infiltration capacities for intermittent rainfall. The soil water was redistributed during relatively long periods of zero application and a new soil water distribution was considered when rainfall restarted.

Based on the results of studies reported in the literature, it appears that the Green-Ampt equation will give a good approximation of infiltration for unsteady rainfall that results in an extension of the wetted profile. However, if the rainfall distribution includes relatively long periods of low intensity or zero rainfall, the wetted profile will redistribute and the Green-Ampt equa-

TABLE 4.3. INFILTRATION INTO A YOLO
LIGHT CLAY AS A FUNCTION OF TIME
FOR A STEADY RAINFALL RATE OF
0.5 cm/h

t (hours)	F (cm)	f (cm/h)
0	0	0.5
1.07	0.54	0.5
1.53	0.75	0.37
2.30	1.0	0.29
3.04	1.2	0.25
3.89	1.4	0.22
4.85	1.6	0.20
7.06	2.0	0.17

tions will not be reliable for later times.

Example for unsteady rainfall: Rainfall occurs at the following intensities on the Yolo soil of the previous example:

$$R = 1.5 \, \text{cm/h}, \quad 0 \leqslant t \leqslant 1 \, \text{h}$$
$$R = 0.10 \, \text{cm/h}, \quad 1 < t \leqslant 4 \, \text{h}$$
$$R = 0.50 \, \text{cm/h}, \quad 4 < t \leqslant 6 \, \text{h}$$
$$R = 0.0 \, \text{for} \quad t > 6 \, \text{h}.$$

Again $K_s = 0.044$ cm/h, $S_{av} = 22.4$ cm and $M = \theta_s - \theta_i = 0.249$. However in this case a surface retention storage of 0.50 cm must be filled before runoff can begin. That is, when infiltration capacity falls below rainfall intensity, water will be ponded on the surface until the ponded depth reaches a maximum of $s = s_m = 0.5$ cm. After this time rainfall in excess of infiltration will be available for runoff. When rainfall ceases, water ponded on the surface will continue to infiltrate until the stored water is removed from the surface. This problem can be solved by applying equations [4.30] through [4.32] in combination with a water balance at the surface. Neglecting evaporation, the water balance at the surface may be expressed as

$$\Delta P = \Delta F + \Delta s + RO \quad \dots \dots \dots \dots \dots \dots \dots \dots \dots \dots \dots \dots \dots \dots \dots \dots \quad [4.33]$$

where $\Delta P = R\Delta t$, the rainfall during Δt; ΔF is cumulative infiltration; Δs is the change in surface storage; and RO is surface runoff during time, Δt.

Chu (1978) presented a systematic approach for using the Green-Ampt equations together with a water balance at the surface to predict infiltration for unsteady rainfall. A simplified approach will be used in this example. The reader is referred to Chu's (1978) paper for a more detailed treatment of infiltration for unsteady rainfall.

Time of surface ponding: Cumulative infiltration at the initiation of surface ponding is (equation [4.30]).

$$F_p = \frac{22.4 \times 0.249}{\dfrac{1.5}{0.044} - 1} = 0.17 \, \text{cm}.$$

Then $t_p = F_p/R = 0.17$ cm/1.5 cm/h $= 0.11$ h. Note that if the rainfall rate had been low so that surface ponding did not occur, t_p would have been greater than the duration of the first rainfall period, i.e., $t_p > 1$h.

Infiltration after surface ponding: The equivalent time, t_p', required to infiltrate 0.17 cm under initially ponded conditions is (from equation [4.26]) $t_p' = 0.0025$ h. Then infiltration for the remainder of the first rainfall period may be expressed implicitly as (equation [4.32]).

$$F - 5.58 \ln (1 + F/5.58) = 0.044 \, (t - 0.11 + 0.0025)$$

The value of F at the end of the first rainfall period, or at any other time during that period, can be easily determined from the graphical solution of equation [4.32] given in Fig. 4.13. When the equations are programmed for computer solution, t is determined directly for small increments of F or iteration is used to obtain F for a specified t. Using Fig. 4.13 for t = 1 h, F =

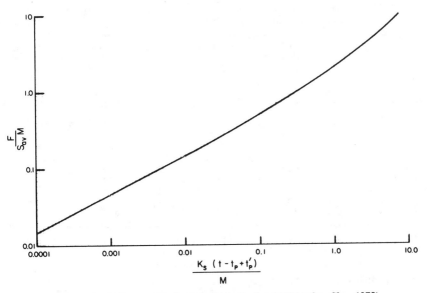

FIG. 4.13 Plot for graphical solution of equation [4.32] (after Chu, 1978).

0.67 cm. Then a water balance between $t = t_p = 0.11$ h and $t = 1$ h is (equation [4.33]),

$$1.5 (1 - 0.11) = (0.67 - 0.17) + \Delta s + RO$$
$$\Delta s + RO = 0.83 \text{ cm}.$$

Since the maximum surface storage is $s_m = 0.5$ cm and $s = 0$ at $t = 0.11$ h, $\Delta s = 0.5$ cm and $RO = 0.83 - 0.5 = 0.33$ cm. The infiltration rate at $t = 1$ h as obtained from equation [4.31b] is $f = 0.41$ cm/h.

Infiltration during the second rainfall period: The surface is ponded at the beginning of the second period so $f = f_p$ and equation [4.32] holds until the 0.5 cm of water stored on the surface is infiltrated. Let t_1 be the time that infiltration of the ponded water is completed. Then for the period $\Delta t = t_1 - 1$, $\Delta s = -0.5$ and $\Delta P = 0.1\Delta t = 0.1(t_1 - 1)$. Since $RO = 0$ during this period, equation [4.33] can be solved for ΔF as, $\Delta F = 0.1 (t_1 - 1.0) + 0.5$. That is $\Delta F =$ rainfall during Δt plus the 0.5 cm of water stored on the surface at $t = 1$ h. Infiltration volume at $t = t_1$ is, $F = 0.67 + \Delta F = 1.17 + 0.1 (t_1 - 1.0)$. Substituting this value for F along with $t = t_1$ in equation [4.32] and solving by iteration gives $t_1 = 3.7$ h, at which time $F = 1.42$ cm and $f = 0.21$ cm/h. After t_1 the infiltration rate is $f = R = 0.1$ cm/h (equation [4.31a]) until $t = 4$ h when the rainfall rate increases to 0.5 cm/h. At $t = 4$ h, $F = 1.42 + 0.1 (4-3.5) = 1.47$ cm and the infiltration capacity is $f_p = 0.21$ cm/h.

Infiltration during the third rainfall period: At $t = 4$ h the rainfall rate increases to 0.5 cm/h; but $f_p = 0.21$ cm/h so surface ponding begins immediately. A new t_p' is calculated and substituted into equation [4.32] and infiltration is predicted in the same manner as in the first period. A summary of the calculations for the total infiltration event is given in Table 4.4. At the cessation of rainfall, $t = 6$ h, 0.5 cm of water remains ponded on the surface and infiltration continues for an additional 2.81 h while the surface water infiltrates. Rainfall and infiltration rates are plotted in Fig. 4.14. Corresponding plots for cumulative volumes are given in Fig. 4.15.

TABLE 4.4. SUMMARY OF INFILTRATION CALCULATIONS WITH
THE GREEN-AMPT EQUATIONS FOR UNSTEADY RAINFALL

t(h)*	$t_p(h)$	$t'_p(h)$	R(cm/h)	P(cm)	F(cm)	f_p(cm/h)	f(cm/h)	s(cm)	RO(cm)
0.0	—	—	1.50	0.0	0.0	0.0	1.5	0.0	0.0
0.11	0.11	0.002	1.50	0.17	0.17	1.5	1.5	0.0	0.0
0.71	0.11	0.002	1.50	1.06	0.56	0.48	0.48	0.50	0.0
1.0	0.11	0.002	1.50	1.5	0.67	0.41	0.41	0.50	0.33
1.00^+	0.11	0.002	0.10	1.5	0.67	0.41	0.41	0.50	0.33
2.00	0.11	0.002	0.10	1.6	0.98	0.29	0.29	0.29	0.33
3.70	0.11	0.002	0.10	1.77	1.44	0.21	0.21	0.0	0.33
3.70^+	—	—	0.10	1.77	1.44	0.21	0.10	0.0	0.33
4.00	—	—	0.10	1.80	1.47	0.21	0.10	0.0	0.33
4.00^+	4.00	3.75	0.50	1.80	1.47	0.21	0.21	0.0	0.33
5.00	4.00	3.75	0.50	2.30	1.67	0.19	0.19	0.30	0.33
6.00	4.00	3.75	0.50	2.80	1.81	0.18	0.18	0.50	0.49
6.00^+	4.00	3.75	0.00	2.80	1.81	0.18	0.18	0.50	0.49
8.81	4.00	3.75	0.00	2.80	2.31	0.15	0.15	0.0	0.49

*A (+) superscript means just to the positive side of the time, while a (-) superscript means
just less, or to the negative side, of the time.

Smith's Infiltration Envelope

Smith (1972) reported on extensive numerical experiments based on
Richards equation for a range of soils from fine clay with swelling properties
to a moderately uniform sand. The infiltration model as shown in Fig. 4.16
resulted from analysis of simulation using a constant rainfall rate for six
soils. Initially, the infiltration rate is limited by the rainfall rate, R. Then, the
soil water pressure head at the surface goes to zero and surface storage or
runoff begins at the time denoted t_p in Fig. 4.16. This time marks the beginning of the infiltration decay-type function that has the form:

$$f_p = f_\infty + A(t - t_o)^{-\alpha} \quad \dots\dots\dots\dots\dots\dots\dots\dots\dots\dots\dots\dots \quad [4.34]$$

where $f_\infty = K_s$ by theory; and A, t_o and α are parameters unique to a soil, initial moisture and rainfall rate. For infiltration from an instantaneously
ponded surface, $t_o = 0$ and equation [4.34] is very similar to the Kostiakov

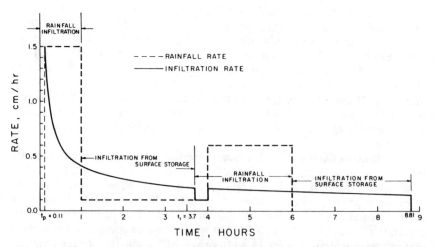

FIG. 4.14 Infiltration rate as a function of time for an unsteady rainfall event. Note that surface
retention storage causes infiltration to continue after the cessation of rainfall at t = 6 h.

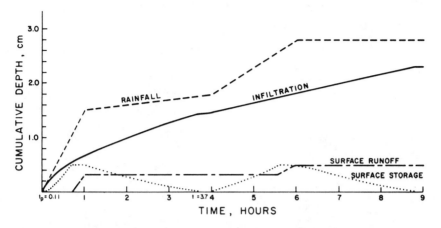

FIG. 4.15 Relationships between cumulative rainfall, infiltration, surface runoff and surface storage for the unsteady rainfall event of Fig. 4.14.

infiltration equation (equation [4.20]). Smith found that use of dimensionless variables would result in a normalized equation,

$$f_* = 1 + (1 - \alpha)(t_* - t_{o*})^{-\alpha} \quad \dots\dots\dots\dots\dots\dots\dots\dots\dots [4.35]$$

where $f_* = f_p/f_\infty$, $t_* = t/T_o$; T_o = normalizing time given by Smith (1972) as,

$$T_O = \left[\frac{A}{(1-\alpha)f_\infty}\right]^{1/\alpha} \quad \dots\dots\dots\dots\dots\dots\dots\dots\dots\dots [4.36a]$$

and

$$t_o* = t_p* = \left[\frac{1-\alpha}{R_*-1}\right]^{1/2} \quad \dots\dots\dots\dots\dots\dots\dots\dots\dots\dots [4.36b]$$

where $t_{p*} = t_p/T_o$ and $R_* = R/f_\infty$.

Use of equation [4.35] to describe rainfall infiltration requires determination of four parameters; f_∞, α, T_o, and t_{o*}. Alternately, equation [4.34] requires values for f_∞, A, α, and t_o. A numerical example illustrates the estimation of the four dimensioned parameters from infiltrometer data.

Example (after Rovey et al., 1977): Consider that an infiltrometer experiment has been performed on a given soil, and the data shown in Table 4.5 have been obtained (Rovey et al., 1977). The parameters are obtained from this infiltrometer data in the following manner.

First, an initial estimate of f_∞ is the apparent long-time asymptote in an arithmetic plot of f versus t. Apparently, f_∞ is less than 0.028 cm/min (Table 4.5). Second, t_o is selected as that value for which (f = f_∞) versus (t-t_o) is most closely a straight line on a log-log plot. Finally, t_o and f_∞ are varied to obtain a reasonably straight line. The process is aided by noting that estimates of f_∞ that are too large or too small affect the curve at the lower end (t large) of the data, and conversely, the curve is sensitive to estimates of t_o at the opposite (t small) end. The user is cautioned that large infiltrometer

TABLE 4.5. EXAMPLE INFILTROMETER
DATA
R = 0.1596 cm per min (after Rovey et al.,
1977)

Time, minutes	Infiltration rate, cm/min
0	0.1596
1	0.1596
2	0.1596
3	0.150
4	0.106
5	0.099
7	0.076
9	0.073
12	0.068
15	0.062
20	0.053
30	0.047
50	0.034
100	0.028

plots incorporate considerable storage delay into measurements of the plot outflow, which will bias the infiltration parameters if not corrected. This as well as natural soil variability cause response curves typically *not* to exhibit the sharp break at $t = t_p$ shown in Fig. 4.16.

As shown in Fig. 4.17, a line has been fitted to the data of Table 4.5 using $t_o = 1.3$ min and $f_\infty = 0.01$ cm/min. The intersection of this line with the horizontal line representing $R = 0.1596$ cm/min is at $t - t_o \cong 1.45$, or $t_p = 2.75$ min. The slope of the line is $\alpha = -0.51$ and A is the value of $f - f_\infty$ when $t - t_o = 1.0$, here found to be 0.185 cm/min. Using the derived parameters, equation [4.34] is then,

$$f = f_p = 0.01 + 0.185 \ (t - 1.3)^{0.51} \ ; \text{for } t > 2.75 \text{ min} \quad \cdots\cdots\cdots\cdots \quad [4.37]$$

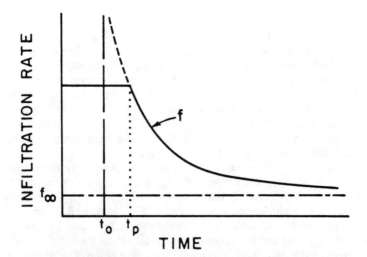

FIG. 4.16 Schematic for Smith's (1972) infiltration envelope model.

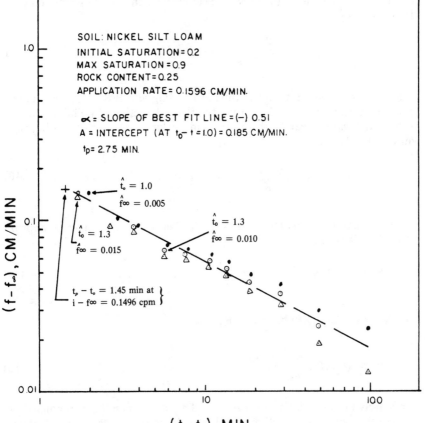

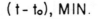

FIG. 4.17 Graphical fitting of infiltrometer data to determine infiltration parameters α, A, T_o, and f_∞ (after Rovey et al., 1977).

where f is in cm/min and t in minutes. From equations [4.36] and following, values for T_o and the nondimensional parameters may be calculated:

$$T_0 = 1240 \text{ min.}$$
$$t_p* = 0.002$$
$$t_o* = 0.001$$
$$R_* = 16.0$$

Then the infiltration rate equation [4.35] may be written as,

$$f_* = 1 + (0.49)(t_* - 0.001)^{-0.51} ; t_* > 0.002 \quad \dots \dots \dots \dots \dots \quad [4.38]$$

Smith and Parlange Model

Smith and Parlange (1978) started with the Richards equation and derived an infiltration model for arbitrary rainfall rates. Their model can be used to predict both ponding time and infiltration capacity after ponding in terms of only two parameters. Both parameters may be calculated from measurable soil properties or determined from infiltrometer experiments.

For soils in which $K(\theta)$ varies slowly near θ_s, the ponding time may be determined by

$$\int_0^{t_p} R dt = \frac{B(\theta_i)}{R_p - K_s} \approx \frac{S^2/2}{R_p - K_s} \quad \dots\dots\dots\dots\dots\dots\dots\dots\dots \quad [4.39]$$

where R_p = rainfall rate at the time of ponding and $B(\theta_i)$ is approximately equal to $S^2/2$ where S is the sorptivity originally defined by Philip (1957b). When $K(\theta)$ varies near K_s the Smith and Parlange model for ponding time may be written as,

$$\int_0^{t_p} R dt = \frac{A}{K_s} \ln \frac{R_p}{R_p - K_s} \quad \dots\dots\dots\dots\dots\dots\dots\dots\dots \quad [4.40]$$

Again A may be estimated as $A = S^2/2$. The value of S^2 may be approximated as (Parlange, 1975),

$$S^2 \approx 2 \int_{\theta_i}^{\theta_s} (\theta - \theta_i) D(\theta) \, d\theta \quad \dots\dots\dots\dots\dots\dots\dots\dots \quad [4.41a]$$

for slowly varying $D(\theta)$ near $\theta = \theta_s$, and

$$S^2 = 2(\theta_s - \theta_i) \int_{\theta_i}^{\theta_s} D(\theta) \, d\theta \quad \dots\dots\dots\dots\dots\dots\dots\dots \quad [4.41b]$$

for rapidly varying $D(\theta)$ near saturation. The time of ponding is predicted for either case (equations [4.39] or [4.40]) by calculating the value of $\int_0^{t_p} R dt$ and comparing it to the value of the right side as rainfall progresses. Ponding is predicted at the time when the two sides are equal.

For $t > t_p$, Smith and Parlange obtained an equation for the case of slowly varying $K(\theta)$ which was directly analogous to the Green-Ampt equation

$$f_p = K_s \left(\frac{C_o}{K_s F} + 1 \right) \quad \dots\dots\dots\dots\dots\dots\dots\dots\dots \quad [4.42]$$

where

$$C_o \approx (R_p - K_s) \int_0^{t_p} R \, dt \approx S^2/2. \quad \dots\dots\dots\dots\dots\dots\dots \quad [4.43]$$

By substituting

$$\int_0^{t_p} R \, dt = F_p = \frac{S_{av} M K_s}{R_p - K_s}$$

from equation [4.30] into equation [4.43] we get $C_o = S_{av} M K_s$ which is the definition of C_o in the Green-Ampt equation.

For rapidly varying $K(\theta)$ near saturation, Smith and Parlange presented the following equation

$$\frac{C_O}{K_s} \ln \frac{f_p}{f_p - K_s} = F \quad \dots\dots\dots\dots\dots\dots\dots\dots\dots\dots\dots \quad [4.44]$$

which is the same as derived earlier by Parlange (1975).

In both cases (equations [4.42] and [4.43]) the equations hold for rainfall and for an initially ponded surface. The equation forms are simple and involve only two parameters which can be obtained from infiltration data although nonlinear regression methods may be required.

NUMERICAL METHODS

The approximate and analytical equations described in the previous sections can be used to characterize the infiltration process with rather simple, straight-forward methods. However, in most cases these equations were developed for idealized situations with specific boundary and initial conditions. In the general case infiltration problems may involve nonuniform initial water contents, time dependent boundary conditions, hysteresis and heterogeneous and anisotropic porous media. These factors can be considered by using numerical methods to solve the governing equations subject to appropriate initial and boundary conditions. Philip (1957a) presented a rapidly converging numerical procedure for ponded infiltration into a deep homogeneous soil with uniform initial water content. Other numerical procedures which were more general in application but which required the use of the digital computer followed. Whisler and Klute (1965) used an iterative procedure to solve equation [4.8] subject to a nonuniform initial water content. Their technique took into account hysteresis, a factor that was also included in the numerical technique of Staple (1966). Whisler and Klute (1966) presented a method to solve equation [4.8] for infiltration into a layered soil of arbitrary depth and initial head distribution. The method is also valid for rainfall surface conditions. Techniques for solving equations [4.8] and [4.10] subject to rainfall boundary conditions were presented by Rubin (1966) and Rubin and Steinhardt (1963). The technique given by Rubin (1966) can also be used to account for the effects of non-zero air entry suction. Smith and Woolhiser (1971a) solved the Richards equation for rainfall-ponding surface conditions. The solutions were used in combination with solutions for unsteady overland flow to predict infiltration and runoff from sloping soils. Theoretical predictions were in good agreement with the results of both laboratory anf field experiments.

Numerical (finite difference) procedures for solving the Richards equation for two and three dimensional flow have been developed by Rubin (1968), Amerman (1969) and Freeze (1971). The application of the finite element technique to infiltration problems, especially for complex flow domains, is rather recent but is gaining recognition. However, for simple flow geometries, finite difference techniques are most commonly used. Discussion in this section will deal with the application of finite difference methods to solve the Richards equation for infiltration and redistribution of soil water.

Discretization

Discretization schemes frequently used to obtain finite difference ap-

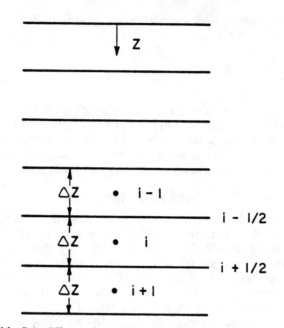

FIG. 4.18 Grid for finite difference formulation of the Richards equation for flow in the vertical direction.

proximations to the Richards equation are: (a) Explicit scheme; (b) Implicit scheme; and (c) Crank-Nicolson (C-N) approximation.

   Explicit scheme: Using the grid system as shown in Fig. 4.18, an explicit formulation of equation [4.8] yields,

$$h_i^{j+1} = h_i^j + \frac{\Delta t}{C_i^j \Delta z} \left[K_{i+1/2}^j \left(\frac{h_{i+1}^j - h_i^j}{\Delta_z} - 1 \right) - K_{i-1/2}^j \left(\frac{h_i^j - h_{i-1}^j}{\Delta_z} - 1 \right) \right]$$

$$\dotfill [4.45]$$

where the subscript i refers to the spatial increment and the superscript j refers to time increment. Procedures for obtaining estimates for $K_{i\pm1/2}$ are discussed later.

   Equation [4.45] can now be solved explicitly for the unknown h_o^{j+1} at the $j+1$ time level. The explicit scheme has been used by Ibrahim (1967) for a ponded boundary condition problem and by Staple (1966) in solving infiltration and redistribution problems. Although the explicit scheme is as simple computationally as one could desire, the method is stable and convergent only if (Richtmeyer, 1957)

$$\Delta t \leqslant 0.25 \, \Delta z^2 \, C/K \dotfill [4.46]$$

   Implicit scheme: An implicit formulation of equation [4.8] is obtained by replacing the space derivatives with their finite difference analogs at the $j+1$ time level. The approximation at each node involves three unknown values at the $j+1$ time level and one known value at the j-th time level. When applied to all nodes, the result is a system of simultaneous linear algebraic equations with unknowns at the $j+1$ time level. The system of equations form a tridiagonal matrix and solutions are obtained by Gaussian elimination (an algorithm is available in Remson et al., 1971, pp. 166-171). For an interior node (non-boundary grid), the implicit scheme yields

$$a_i h_{i+1}^{j+1} + b_i h_i^{j+1} + c_i h_{i-1}^{j+1} = RHS_i \dots\dots\dots\dots\dots\dots\dots\dots\dots\dots \quad [4.47]$$

where

$$a_i = K_{i+1/2}^j / \Delta z^2 \quad \dots\dots\dots\dots\dots\dots\dots\dots\dots\dots\dots\dots\dots\dots\dots \quad [4.48a]$$

$$b_i = -[(K_{i+1/2}^j + K_{i-1/2}^j)/\Delta z^2 + C_i^j/\Delta t] \quad \dots\dots\dots\dots\dots\dots\dots\dots \quad [4.48b]$$

$$c_i = K_{i-1/2}^j / \Delta z^2 \quad \dots\dots\dots\dots\dots\dots\dots\dots\dots\dots\dots\dots\dots\dots\dots \quad [4.48c]$$

$$RHS_i = (K_{i+1/2}^j - K_{i-1/2}^j)/\Delta z - C_i^j h_i^j/\Delta t \quad \dots\dots\dots\dots\dots\dots \quad [4.48d]$$

Equation [4.47] is not "fully implicit" since the variables C_i^j and $K_{i\pm1/2}^j$ are still represented at the j-th time level. In a fully implicit scheme, C_i^j and $K_{i\pm1/2}^j$ would be replaced by their estimates at the $j+1$ time level, i.e., by C_i^{j+1} and $K_{i\pm1/2}^{j+1}$. Such schemes are described later.

Crank-Nicolson (C-N) approximation: The C-N approximation averages the space derivatives at the $j+1$ and j-th time levels to obtain an approximation at the $j+1/2$ level. A C-N formulation of equation [4.8] yields,

$$C_i^{j+1/2} \frac{(h_i^{j+1} - h_i^j)}{\Delta t} = \frac{K_{i+1/2}^{j+1/2}}{2(\Delta z)^2} (h_{i+1}^{j+1} + h_{i+1}^j - h_i^{j+1} - h_i^j - 2\Delta z) -$$

$$\frac{K_{i-1/2}^{j+1/2}}{2(\Delta z)^2} (h_i^{j+1} + h_i^j - h_{i-1}^{j+1} - h_{i-1}^j - 2\Delta z) \quad \dots\dots\dots\dots\dots\dots \quad [4.49]$$

The system of equations generated by equation [4.49] are tridiagonal. Equation [4.49] was used by Hanks and Bowers (1962) for studying infiltration into layered soils and by Smith and Woolhiser (1971b) for infiltration from a ponded or rainfall upper boundary. Estimates of $K_{i\pm1/2}^{j+1/2}$ and $C_i^{j+1/2}$ are obtained by linearization techniques as discussed in the following section.

Implicit methods generally use much larger time steps than the explicit methods, but their stability conditions have to be determined by trial and error, as they depend upon the nonlinearity of the equations (Haverkamp et al., 1977). Also the programming is more involved than for the explicit method.

Linearization Techniques

In equations [4.47] and [4.48], the values of $C(h)$ and $K(h)$ can be obtained explicitly from the $h(\theta)$ and $K(\theta)$ relationships since these values are referred to the preceding time level, j. Such a method is known as implicit scheme with explicit linearization. In a fully implicit scheme, the values for C(h) and K(h) are either referred at the time level $j+1/2$, or at $j+1$ time level. The predictor-corrector technique is used for implicit evaluation of the coefficients at the $j+1/2$ time level while an iterative procedure is used for evaluation at the $j+1$ time level.

Predictor-corrector method: The Douglas-Jones (1963) predictor-corrector method involves the use of a predictor to compute values for K and C at the $j+1/2$ time level. Then a corrector is used to compute the pressure distribution at the $j+1$ time level. Implicit evaluation of the coefficients at the $j+1/2$ level requires that the tridiagonal system of equations be solved twice for each time step: first at time level $j+1/2$ (i.e., $t + 1/2\Delta t$) to obtain values for K and C, then at time level $j+1$ (i.e., $t + \Delta t$) to evaluate the pressure distribution. Implicit finite difference formulations and solutions of equation [4.8] using the predictor-corrector method are given by Remson et al. (1971), Molz and Remson (1970) and Havercamp et al. (1977).

Iteration: The following procedure was suggested by Smith and Woolhiser (1971b) for iteration within a time step: (a) an initial estimate of h_i^{j+1} (i = 1 ..n, where n is the number of grids) is made and "estimates" of K_i^{j+1} and C_i^{j+1} are obtained using $h(\theta)$ and $K(\theta)$ relationships; (b) the coefficients a, b and c are computed (equations [4.48]) and the resulting linear equations are solved for "estimates" of h_i^{j+1} using the tridiagonal algorithm; (c) the most recent "estimates" of h_i^{j+1} are compared with the estimates used in step (a) for h_i^{j+1} for i = 1, ...n, and if each agrees within a given error criterion, the tridiagonal system of equations is considered solved for the time step; (d) if the estimated h_i^{j+1} are significantly different from step (b), the new values of h_i^{j+1} are used to calculate new a_i, b_i and c_i and step (b) is repeated.

The iterative procedure has been used, among others, by Whisler and Klute (1965) and Smith and Woolhiser (1971b). The method is time consuming and the nature of convergence or divergence of such a scheme appears to be dependent on the type of the difference equation used, the finite grid dimensions and the local shape of the θ-h-K relationships (Smith and Woolhiser, 1971b).

Other linearization techniques used in infiltration problems are: (a) extrapolation, and (b) Kirchhoff transformation. Rubin and Steinhardt (1963) and Rubin (1967) used linear extrapolation from time levels to estimate K_i^{j+1} and C_i^{j+1}. In order to overcome stability problems due to the presence of very high pressure head gradients near the wetting front during infiltration into a dry material, the Kirchhoff integral transformation has been used (Rubin, 1966, Havercamp et al., 1977).

Gauss-Seidel (G-S) and Successive Over Relaxation (S.O.R.) Techniques

The Gauss-Seidel and Successive Over Relaxation iterative techniques are ideal for the solution of sparse matrices (when the matrix of coefficients consists mainly of zeros) generated by the finite difference forms of equation [4.8].

G-S method: The G-S form of equation [4.8] for an interior grid (Fig. 4.17) is:

$$h_i^{m+1} = [K_{i+1/2}^m(h_{i+1}^m - \Delta z) + K_{i-1/2}^m (h_{i-1}^{m+1} + \Delta z) + \underset{r}{C_i^m h_i^j}]/(K_{i+1/2}^m$$

$$+ \underset{r}{K_{i-1/2}^m + C_i^m}) \dots\dots\dots\dots\dots\dots\dots\dots\dots\dots\dots\dots\dots [4.50]$$

where m = values obtained during the preceding iteration within a time step; m+1 = values obtained during the current iteration; and r = $\Delta t/\Delta z^2$. In equation [4.50], the most recent iterates are used, as soon as they become available, by replacing h_i^m by h_i^{m+1} immediately after they are computed. As can be seen, equation [4.50] is easier to program on a digital computer compared to the Gaussian elimination techniques discussed earlier. Several investigators have used the G-S method in studying infiltration and redistribution problems (Remson et al., 1965; Remson et al., 1967; Rubin, 1967).

S.O.R. method: By adding and subtracting h_i^m to the right hand side of equation [4.50] rearranging, and defining a parameter ω called the relaxation factor to accelerate convergence, the S.O.R. form of equation [4.50] may be expressed as,

$$h_i^{m+1} = h_i^m + \omega [\{ K_{i+1/2}^m(h_{i+1}^m - \Delta z) + K_{i-1/2}^m(h_{i-1}^{m+1} + \Delta z)$$

$$+ \underset{r}{C_i^m h_i^j} \} /(K_{i+1/2}^m + K_{i-1/2}^m + \underset{r}{C_i^m}) - h_i^m] \dots\dots\dots\dots [4.51]$$

The expression in the { } is the increase given to h_i^m by one G-S iteration. The parameter ω lies between 1 and 2 and the S.O.R. method converges almost twice as fast as the G-S method (G. Smith, 1965). Amerman (1976) applied the S.O.R. method in studying a two-dimensional, steady flow problem.

Boundary Conditions

The upper boundary conditions in one-dimensional infiltration problems usually take the form of (a) a constant flux at the surface, i.e., q (0, t) = constant; (b) a ponded surface, i.e., h(0,t) = constant; or (c) a constant water content at the surface, i.e., θ(0,t) = constant. An example illustrating the incorporation of a flux boundary condition in the numerical procedure is given below. For infiltration of rainfall at rate, R, (before ponding), the upper B.C. is

$$q = R = - K (\frac{\partial h}{\partial z} - 1) \qquad \text{at } z = 0, 0 \leqslant t \leqslant t_p \dots\dots\dots\dots [4.52]$$

Defining the grid system as shown in Fig. 4.18 and using the flux B.C. given by equation [4.52], the implicit finite-difference form of equation [4.8] for grid number 1 is

$$\frac{C_i^j(h_1^{j+1} - h_1^j)}{\Delta t} = \frac{K_{1+1/2}^j}{\Delta z} (\frac{\partial h}{\partial z} - 1)_{1+1/2} + \frac{R}{\Delta z} \dots\dots\dots\dots [4.53]$$

Equation [4.47] for grid number 1 then becomes

$$a_1 h_2 + b_1 h_1 = RHS_1 \quad \dots\dots\dots\dots\dots\dots\dots\dots\dots\dots\dots \quad [4.54]$$

where

$$a_1 = K_{1+1/2}/\Delta z^2 \quad \dots\dots\dots\dots\dots\dots\dots\dots\dots\dots\dots \quad [4.55a]$$

$$b_1 = -\left(\frac{K_{1+1/2}}{\Delta z^2} + \frac{C_1}{\Delta t}\right) \quad \dots\dots\dots\dots\dots\dots\dots\dots\dots \quad [4.55b]$$

and

$$RHS_1 = -\frac{C_1 h_1^j}{\Delta t} + (K_{1+1/2} - R)/\Delta z \dots\dots\dots\dots\dots\dots \quad [4.55c]$$

Equation [4.47] may be written for each interior node, i = 2, 3, 4, ... n-1 giving n-2 equations with n unknowns. With equation [4.54] and a similar equation for the bottom boundary condition we have n equations in n unknowns. This system of equations may then solve for h_i at every node point by Gaussian elimination or other procedures discussed above.

Selection of Interblock Hydraulic Conductivity

The interblock hydraulic conductivity between two adjacent grids (Fig. 4.18) may be computed in several ways. Haverkamp and Vauclin (1979) used nine different methods of weighting interblock hydraulic conductivity values in studying two test problems using different types of soil and boundary conditions. Some of their weighting schemes were:

1   **Arithmetic mean** taken over adjacent grid point conductivity values, i.e.

$$K_{i\pm1/2} = 0.5 (K_i + K_{i\pm1}) \quad \dots\dots\dots\dots\dots\dots\dots\dots\dots \quad [4.56]$$

This scheme is most frequently used in classical finite-difference methods (Whisler and Klute, 1965; Rubin, 1968; Amerman, 1976).

2   **Harmonic mean** i.e.

$$K_{i\pm1/2} = \frac{2K_i K_{i\pm1}}{K_i + K_{i\pm1}} \quad \dots\dots\dots\dots\dots\dots\dots\dots\dots \quad [4.57]$$

The harmonic mean has been used by Smith and Woolhiser (197ab) and Reddell and Sunada (1970).

3   **Geometric mean** i.e.

$$K_{i\pm1/2} = (K_i \cdot K_{i\pm1})^{1/2} \quad \dots\dots\dots\dots\dots\dots\dots\dots\dots \quad [4.58]$$

4   **"Upstream mobility"** concept where the conductivity of the grid from which the fluid originates is used (Phuc, 1969; Brutsaert et al., 1971; Khaleel and Reddell, 1976). In cases where the flow is originating from upstream grids

$$K_{i+1/2} = K_i \text{ and } K_{i-1/2} = K_{i-1}. \quad \dots\dots\dots\dots\dots\dots\dots\dots \quad [4.59]$$

Other weighting schemes include taking arithmetic mean, harmonic mean or geometric mean of adjacent grid point pressure head values, and then using the K(h) relationship to determine the effective K value (Haverkamp and Vauclin, 1979). For example, for the arithmetic mean using adjacent grid point pressure head values

$$K_{i\pm1/2} = K(0.5 (h_i + h_{i\pm1})) \qquad\qquad\qquad\qquad [4.60]$$

Haverkamp and Vauclin also give two other schemes based on finite-difference linear interpolation and linear extrapolation to upstream conductivity values. They found that the use of different weighting approximations in finite difference methods introduces weighting errors of critical influence on the accuracy of the solution. For the test problem studied, the geometric mean method generated the least weighting error.

Comparison of Different Numerical Methods

Haverkamp et al. (1977) compared six different numerical schemes in terms of execution times and mass balance errors for constant flux infiltration into a uniform soil column. Table 4.6 presents data on execution time and the mass balance at t = 0.80 h, after 10.95 cm of water had infiltrated into the soil. The execution time was defined as the total time required for execution of the program, including compilation. The mass balance deviation is defined as the percentage difference between the water infiltrated and the water in the column at the end of infiltration, minus the water initially present, and corrected for drainage out of the profile. Model 1 uses a continuous simulation language, CSMP employed by Bhuiyan et al. (1971), de Wit and van Keulen (1972) and others for infiltration problems. Model 1 in effect is a θ explicit formulation of the θ-based equation [4.10]. The two explicit models, model 1 and model 2, used between 5 and 10 times more time than the implicit models. Except for model 5, all the methods had an excellent mass balance (from 0.2 to 0.4 percent deviation). Haverkamp et al. (1977) reasoned that for the type of soil used the Kirchhoff transformation integral changed too drastically with time during infiltration resulting in a poor mass balance for model 5. For this particular problem, Kirchhoff's integral transformation models (Models 5 and 6) were no better than those obtained

TABLE 4.6. COMPARISON BETWEEN EXECUTION TIMES AND MASS BALANCE
FOR THE VARIOUS MODELS (AFTER HAVERCAMP ET AL., 1977)

Reference	Type of discretization	Linearization	Time and depth intervals	Execution time, s,	Mass balance deviation, %
Model 1	C.S.M.P.	Explicit	$\Delta t = 0.4$ s	209	0.21
Model 2	Explicit (eq. [4.45])	Explicit	$\Delta z = 1$ cm	223	0.23
Model 3	Implicit (eq. [4.47])	Explicit		23	0.41
Model 4	Implicit	Implicit with Predictor-corrector	$\Delta t = 5$ s	43	0.28
Model 5	Implicit with Kirchhoff transformation	Explicit		29	1.80
Model 6	Implicit with Kirchhoff transformation	Implicit with Predictor-corrector	$\Delta z = 1$ cm	58	0.33

with the implicit model (Model 4) with implicit linearization of the hydraulic conductivity and water capacity functions. All models yielded excellent agreement with water content profiles measured at various times in a sand column.

SUMMARY

This chapter presents a discussion of the infiltration of water into the soil profile and of methods, both approximate and exact, for modeling the process. The exact methods involve application of laws governing the movement of water and air in porous media. These basic relationships are presented and methods for solving the governing equations are discussed. Solutions to the governing equations are used to examine the effects of factors such as soil properties, initial water content and rainfall rate on infiltration.

While the exact approach may be used to characterize infiltration for most initial and boundary conditions, its application is difficult because of computational and input data requirements. Numerous approximate methods have been developed over the years in an attempt to apply rather simple, easy-to-use models to describe the infiltration process. Several approximate methods are discussed in this chapter. They include empirical models such as those proposed by Kostiakov (1932), Horton (1939) and Holtan (1961) and models derived by application of the theory of soil water movement with certain simplifications or assumptions. Examples in the latter category are the models of Green and Ampt (1911), Philip (1957), Smith (1972) and Smith and Parlange (1978). The Green-Ampt model has been modified and applied to many different conditions during recent years and it is discussed in detail herein. Methods for determining the Green-Ampt equation parameters are examined and examples of its application are presented. The chapter concludes with a discussion of several numerical methods that have been used to solve the governing infiltration equations.

References

1 Adrian, D. D. and J. B. Franzini. 1966. Impedance to infiltration by pressure build-up ahead of the wetting front. J. Geophysical Research 71(24):5857-5863.

2 Amerman, C. R. 1969. Finite difference solutions of unsteady, two-dimensional, partially saturated porous media flow. Ph.D. Thesis, Purdue University, Lafayette, IN.

3 Amerman, C. R. 1976. Soil water modeling I: A generalized simulator of steady, two-dimensional flow. TRANSACTIONS of the ASAE 19(3):466-470.

4 Bhuiyan, S. I., E. A. Hiler, C. H. M. van Bavel, and A. R. Aston. 1971. Dynamic simulation of vertical infiltration into unsaturated soils. Water Resour. Res. 7(6):1597-1606.

5 Bodman, G. B. and E. A. Coleman. 1943. Moisture and energy conditions during downward entry of water into soils. Soil Sci. Soc. Am. Proc. 7:116-122.

6 Bouwer, H. 1964. Unsaturated flow in groundwater hydraulics. J. Hydraulics Div. ASCE 90(HY5):121-144.

7 Bouwer, H. 1966. Rapid field measurement of air-entry value and hydraulic conductivity of soil as significant parameters in flow system analysis. Water Resour. Res. 2:729-738.

8 Bouwer, H. 1969. Infiltration of water into nonuniform soil. J. Irrigation and Drainage Division, ASCE 95(IR4):451-462.

9 Bouwer, H. 1976. Infiltration into increasingly permeable soils. J. Irrigation and Drainage Div. ASCE 102(IR1):127-136.

10 Bouwer, H. and R. D. Jackson. 1974. Determining soil properties, p. 611-672. In van Schilfgaarde, J. (ed), Drainage for Agriculture, American Society of Agronomy, Madison, WI.

11 Brakensiek, D. L. 1977. Estimating the effective capillary pressure in the Green and Ampt infiltration equation. Water Resour. Res. 13(3):680-682.

12 Brakensiek, D. L. and C. Onstad. 1977. Parameter estimation of the Green and

Ampt infiltration equation. Water Resour. Res. 13(6):1009-1012.

13   Breitenbach, E. A., D. H. Thurnau, and H. K. van Poollen. 1968a. The fluid flow simulation equations. Preprint SPE 2020. Society of Petroleum Engrs. of AIME, Dallas Meeting, April 22-23. 11 p.

14   Breitenbach, E. A., D. H. Thurnau, and H. K. van Poollen. 1968b. Solution of the immiscible fluid flow simulation equations. Preprint SPE 2021. Society of Petroleum Engrs. of AIME, Dallas Meeting. April 22-23. 13 pp.

15   Brooks, R. H. and A. T. Corey. 1964. Hydraulic properties of porous media. Hydrology Paper No. 3. Colorado State Univ., Fort Collins.

16   Brustkern, R. L. and H. J. Morel-Seytoux. 1970. Analytical treatment of two-phase infiltration. J. Hydraulics Div. ASCE 96(HY12):2535-2548.

17   Brustkern, R. L. and H. J. Morel-Seytoux. 1975. Description of water and air movements of soils. J. Hydrol. 24:21-35.

18   Brutsaert, W. F., E. A. Breitenbach, and D. K. Sunada. 1971. Computer analysis of free surface well flow. J. Irrigation and Drainage Div. ASCE 97(IR3):405-420.

19   Burwell, R. E. and W. E. Larson. 1969. Infiltration as influenced by tillage-induced random roughness and pore space. Soil Sci. Soc. Am. Proc. 33:449-452.

20   Campbell, G. S. 1974. A simple method for determining unsaturated conductivity from moisture retention data. Soil Sci. 117(6):311-314.

21   Childs, E. C. 1969. An introduction to the physical basis of soil water phenomena. John Wiley & Sons, New York. 493 pp.

22   Childs, E. C. and M. Bybordi. 1969. The vertical movement of water in stratified porous material—1. Infiltration. Water Resour. Res. 5(2):446-459.

23   Chu, S. T. 1978. Infiltration during unsteady rain. Water Resour. Res. 14(3):461-466.

24   Day, P. R., G. H. Bolt and D. M. Anderson. 1967. Nature of soil water, Ch. 12. In "Irrigation of Agricultural Land" (R. M. Hagan, ed.) Am. Soc. Agron., Madison, WI, pp. 193-208.

25   DeWit, C. T. and H. van Keulen. 1972. Simulation of transport processes in soils. Cent. Agric. Publ. Doc. Pudoc. Wageningen, Netherlands.

26   Dixon, R. M. and D. R. Linden. 1972. Soil-air pressure and water infiltration under border irrigation. Soil Sci. Soc. Am. Proc. 36(5):948-953.

27   Dixon, R. M. and A. E. Peterson. 1971. Water infiltration control: a channel system concept. Soil Sci. Soc. Am. Proc. 35(6):968-973.

28   Douglas, J., Jr. and B. F. Jones. 1963. On predictor-corrector method for nonlinear parabolic differential equations. J. SIAM 11:195-204.

29   Duley, F. L. 1939. Surface factors affecting the rate of intake of water by soils. Soil Sci. Soc. Am. Proc. 4:60-64.

30   Edwards, W. M. and W. D. Larson. 1969. Infiltration of water into soils as influenced by surface seal development. TRANSACTIONS of the ASAE 12:463-465, 470.

31   Free, G. R. and V. J. Palmer. 1940. Interrelationship of infiltration, air movement, and pore size in graded silica sand. Soil Sci. Soc. Am. Proc. 5:390-398.

32   Freeze, R. A. 1971. Three-dimensional, transient, saturated-unsaturated flow in a groundwater basin. Water Resour. Res. 7:347-366.

33   Frere, M. H., C. A. Onstad, and H. N. Holtan. 1975. ACTMO, an agricultural chemical transport model. ARS-H-3, USDA-ARS. 54 pp.

34   Green, D. W., H. Dabiri, and C. F. Weinaug. 1970. Numerical modeling of unsaturated groundwater flow and comparison of the model to a field experiment. Water Resour. Res. 6(3):362-374.

35   Green, R. E. and J. C. Corey. 1971. Calculation of hydraulic conductivity: a further evaluation of some predictive methods. Soil Sci. Soc. Am. Proc. 35:3-8

36   Green, W. H. and G. Ampt. 1911. Studies of soil physics, part I. - the flow of air and water through soils. J. Agricultural Science 4:1-24.

37   Hadas, A. D. Swartzendruber, P. E. Rijtema, M. Fuchs and B. Yaron. Physical aspects of soil water and salts in ecosystems. Springer-Verlag, New York, Chs. A1, A3, A5, A9, A10.

38   Hanks, R. J. and S. A. Bowers. 1963. Influence in variations in the diffusivity-water content relation on infiltration. Soil Sci. Soc. Am. Proc. 27:263-265.

39   Hanks, R. J. and S. A. Bowers. 1962. A numerical solution of the moisture flow equation for infiltration into layered soils. Soil Sci. Soc. Am. Proc. 26:530-534.

40   Haverkamp, R. and M. Vauclin. 1979. A note on estimating finite difference interblock hydraulic conductivity values for transient unsaturated flow problems. Water Resour. Res. 15(1):181-188.

41   Haverkamp, R., M. Vauclin, J. Touma, P. J. Wierenga and G. Vachaud. 1977. A comparison of numerical simulation models for one-dimensional infiltration. Soil. Sci. Soc. Am. Proc. 41:285-294.

42   Hillel, D. 1971. Soil and water—physical principles and processes. Academic Press, New York.

43   Hillel, D. and W. R. Gardner. 1969. Steady infiltration into crust topped profiles. Soil Science 108:137-142.

44   Hillel, D. and W. R. Gardner. 1970. Transient infiltration into crust topped profiles. Soil Science 109:69-76.

45   Holtan, H. N. 1961. A concept for infiltration estimates in watershed engineering. USDA ARS Bull. 41-51, 25 pp.

46   Holtan, H. N. and N. R. Creitz. 1967. Influence of soils, vegetation and geomorphology on elements of the flood hydrograph. Proc. Symposium on floods and their computation, Leningrad, Russia.

47   Holtan, H. N., C. B. England and V. O. Shanholtz. 1967. Concepts in hydrologic soil grouping. TRANSACTIONS of the ASAE 10(3):407-410.

48   Holtan, H. N. and N. C. Lopez. 1971. USDAHL-70 Model of watershed hydrology. Tech. Bull. No. 1435. USDA-ARS.

49   Horton, R. E. 1939. Analysis of runoff plot experiments with varying infiltration capacity. Trans. Am. Geophys. Union, Part IV:693-694.

50   Horton, R. E. 1940. An approach toward a physical interpretation of infiltration-capacity. Soil Sci. Soc. Am. Proc. 5:399-417.

51   Huggins, L. F. and E. J. Monke. 1966. The mathematical simulation of the hydrology of small watersheds. TR1, Purdue Water Resources Research Center, Lafayette, IN. 129 pp.

52   Ibrahim, H. A. 1967. Hysteresis and intermittent vertical infiltration in unsaturated porous media. Unpublished Ph.D. thesis, Cornell Univ., Ithaca, NY.

53   Idike, L., C. L. Larson, D. C. Slack and R. A. Young. 1977. Experimental evaluation of two infiltration equations. ASAE Paper 77-2558. ASAE, St. Joseph, MI 49085. 21 pp.

54   Jackson, Ray D. 1972. On the calculation of hydraulic conductivity. Soil Sci. Soc. Am. Proc. 36:380-382.

55   James, L. G. and C. L. Larson. 1976. Modeling infiltration and redistribution of soil water during intermittent application. TRANSACTIONS of the ASAE 19(3):482-488.

56   Khaleel, R. and D. L. Reddell. 1976. Simulation of pollutant movement in groundwater aquifers. Texas Water Resour. Institute Tech. Rept. TR-81. Texas A&M Univ., College Sta., TX. 248 pp.

57   Kirkham, Don and W. L. Powers. 1972. Advanced soil physics. Wiley-Interscience, New York.

58   Koon, J. L., J. G. Hendrick and R. E. Hermanson. 1970. Some effects of surface cover geometry on infiltration rate. Water Resour. Res. 6:246-253.

59   Kostiakov, A. N. 1932. On the dynamics of the coefficient of water-percolation in soils and on the necessity for studying it from a dynamic point of view for purposes of amelioration. Trans. 6th Comm. Intern. Soil Sci. Soc., Russian Part A:17-21.

60   Mannering, J. V. and L. D. Meyer. 1963. The effects of various rates of surface mulch on infiltration and erosion. Soil Sci. Soc. Am. Proc. 27:84-86.

61   McWhorter, D. B. 1976. Vertical flow of air and water with a flux boundary condition. TRANSACTIONS of the ASAE 19(2):259-261, 265.

62   McWhorter, D. B. 1971. Infiltration affected by flow of air. Hydrology Paper No. 49. Colorado State Univ., Fort Collins.

63   Mein, R. G. and C. L. Larson. 1973. Modeling infiltration during a steady rain. Water Resour. Res. 9(2):384-394.

64   Mein, R. G. and C. L. Larson. 1971. Modeling infiltration component of the rainfall-runoff process. Bulletin 43, Water Resour. Research Center, University of Minnesota, Minneapolis, MN. 72 pp.

65   Miller, D. E. and W. H. Gardner. 1962. Water infiltration into stratified soil. Soil Sci. Soc. Am. Proc. 26:115-118.

66   Moldenhauer, W. C. and D. C. Long. 1964. Influence of rainfall energy on soil loss and infiltration rates: I. Effect over range of texture. Soil Sci. Soc. Am. Proc. 28:813-817.

67   Molz, F. J. and I. Remson. 1970. Extraction term models of soil moisture use by transpiring plants. Water Resour. Res. 6(5):1346-1356.

68   Moore, R. E. 1939. Water conduction from shallow water tables. Hilgardia 6:383-426.

69   Morel-Seytoux, H. J. 1973. Two phase flows in porous media. Advances in Hydroscience 9:119-202.

70 Morel-Seytoux, H. J. and J. Khanji. 1974. Derivation of an equation of infiltration. Water Resour. Res. 10(4):795-800.

71 Morin, J. and Y. Benyamini. 1977. Rainfall infiltration into bare soils. Water Resour. Res. 13(5):813-817.

72 Musgrave, G. W. 1955. How much of the rain enters the soil? In: USDA Yearbook of Agriculture, Water, 1955:151-159.

73 Neuman, S. P. 1976. Wetting front pressure head in the infiltration model of Green and Ampt. Water Resources Research 12(3):564-566.

74 Nielsen, D. R., R. D. Jackson, J. W. Cary and D. D. Evans. (Eds.) 1972. Soil water. Am. Soc. Agron., Madison, WI. 175 pp.

75 Nielsen, D. R., J. W. Biggar, and K. T. Erh. 1973. Spatial variability of field-measured soil-water properties. Hilgardia 42(7):215-260.

76 Noblanc, A. and H. J. Morel-Seytoux. 1972. A perturbation analysis of two-phase infiltration. J. Hydraulics Div. ASCE 98(HY9):1527-1541.

77 Parlange, J.-Y. 1975. A note on the Green-Ampt equation. Soil Sci. 119(6):460-467.

78 Parlange, J.-Y. 1971. Theory of water movement in soils: 2, one-dimensional infiltration. Soil Sci. 111(3):170-174.

79 Peck, A. J. 1965. Moisture profile development and air compression during water uptake by bounded porous bodies. 3: vertical columns. Soil Sci. 100(1):44-51.

80 Philip, J. R. 1954. An infiltration equation with physical significance. Soil Sci. 77:153-157.

81 Philip, J. R. 1957a. The theory of infiltration: 1. The infiltration equation and its solution. Soil Sci. 83:435-448.

82 Philip, J. R. 1957b. The theory of infiltration: 4. Sorptivity and algebraic infiltration equations. Soil Sci. 84:257-264.

83 Philip, J. R. 1957c. The theory of infiltration: 5. The influence of initial water content. Soil Sci. 84:329-339.

84 Philip, J. R. 1969. Theory of infiltration. Advances in hydroscience 5:215-296.

85 Phuc, Le van. 1969. General one-dimensional model for infiltration. Unpublished M.S. thesis. Colorado State Univ., Fort Collins, CO.

86 Phuc, Le van and H. J. Morel-Seytoux. 1972. Effect of soil air movement and compressibility on infiltration rates. Soil Sci. Soc. Am. Proc. 36(2):237-241.

87 Rawlins, S. L. 1976. Measurement of water content and the state of water in soils. In: Water deficits and plant growth IV. Academic Press, N.Y. pp. 1-55.

88 Reddell, D. L. and D. K. Sunada. 1970. Numerical simulation of dispersion in groundwater aquifers. Hydrology Paper No. 41. Colorado State Univ., Fort Collins, CO. 79 p.

89 Reeves, M. and E. E. Miller. 1975. Estimating infiltration for erratic rainfall. Water Resour. Res. 11(1):102-110.

90 Remson, I., R. L. Drake, S. S. McNeary, and E. M. Wallo. 1965. Vertical drainage of an unsaturated soil. J. Hydraulic Div. ASCE 91(HY1):55-74.

91 Remson, I., A. A. Fungaroli, and G. M. Hornberger. 1967. Numerical analysis of soil-moisture systems. J. Irrigation and Drainage Div. ASCE 93(IR3):153-166.

92 Remson, I., G. M. Hornberger, and F. J. Molz. 1971. Numerical methods in subsurface hydrology. Wiley-Interscience, Inc., N.Y. 389 p.

93 Richards, L. A. 1931. Capillary conductiion through porous mediums. Physics 1:313-318.

94 Richtmeyer, R. D. 1957. Difference methods for initial value problems. Interscience Publ., New York.

95 Rovey, E. W., D. A. Woolhiser, and R. E. Smith. 1977. A distributed kinematic model of upland watersheds. Hydrology Paper No. 93. Colorado State Univ., Fort Collins, CO. 52 p.

96 Rubin, J. 1968. Theoretical analysis of two-dimensional, transient flow of water in unsaturated and partly unsaturated soils. Soil Sci. Soc. Am. Proc. 32:607-615.

97 Rubin, J. 1966. Theory of rainfall uptake by soils initially drier than their field capacity and its applications. Water Resour. Res. 2(4):739-749.

98 Rubin, J. 1967. Numerical methods for analyzing hysteresis affected post infiltration redistribution of soil moisture. Soil Sci. Soc. Am. Proc. 31:13-20.

99 Rubin, J. and R. Steinhardt. 1963. Soil water relations during rain infiltration: I. Theory. Soil Sci. Soc. Am. Proc. 27:246-251.

100 Rubin, J. and R. Steinhardt. 1964. Soil water relations during rain infiltration: III. Water uptake at incipient ponding. Soil Sci. Soc. Am. Proc. 28:614-619.

101 Rubin, J., R. Steinhardt and P. Reiniger. 1964. Soil water relations during rain in-

filtration: II. Moisture content profiles during rains of low intensities. Soil Sci. Soc. Am. Proc. 28:1-5.

102   Skaggs, R. W., L. F. Huggins, E. J. Monke, and G. R. Foster. 1969. Experimental evaluation of infiltration equations. TRANSACTIONS of the ASAE 12(6):822-828.

103   Slack, D. C. 1978. Predicting ponding under moving irrigation systems. ASCE Journal of the Irrigation and Drainage Division 104(IR4)/446-451.

104   Smith, G. D. 1965. Numerical solution of partial differential equations. Oxford Univ. Press., N.Y. 179 pp.

105   Smith, R. E. 1976. Approximations for vertical infiltration rate patterns. TRANSACTIONS of the ASAE 19(3):505-509.

106   Smith, R. E. 1972. The infiltration envelope: Results from a theoretical infiltrometer. Journal of Hydrology 17:1-21.

107   Smith, R. E. and J.-Y. Parlange. 1978. A parameter-efficient hydrologic infiltration model. Water Resour. Res. 14(3):533-538.

108   Smith, R. E. and D. A. Woolhiser. 1971a. Overland flow on an infiltrating surface. Water Resour. Res. 7(4):899-913.

109   Smith, R. E. and D. A. Woolhiser. 1971b. Mathematical simulation of infiltrating watersheds. Hydrol. Paper 47, Colorado State Univ., Fort Collins.

110   Sonu, J. and H. J. Morel-Seytoux. 1976. Water and air movement in a bounded deep homogeneous soil. J. Hydrol. 29:23-42.

111   Staple, W. J. 1966. Infiltration and redistribution of water in vertical columns of loam soil. Soil Sci. Soc. Am. Proc. 30:533-558.

112   Staple, W. J. and R. P. Gupta. 1966. Infiltration into homogeneous and layered columns of aggregated loam, silt loam, and clay soil. Can. J. Soil Sci. 46:293-305.

113   Swartzendruber, D. 1969. The flow of water in unsaturated soils. p. 215-292. In: R. M. DeWiest (ed.) Flow through porous media. Academic Press, New York.

114   Swartzendruber, D. and E. G. Youngs. 1974. A comparison of physically based infiltration equations. Soil Science 117(3):165-167.

115   U.S. Dept. Agr., Soil Conservation Serv. 1965. Hydrology, Part IV, SCS National Engrg. Handbook. USDA.

116   Whisler, F. D. and H. Bouwer. 1970. Comparison of methods for calculating vertical drainage and infiltration for soils. Journal of Hydrology 10:1-19.

117   Whisler, F. D. and A. Klute. 1965. The numerical analysis of infiltration, considering hysteresis, into a vertical soil column at equilibrium under gravity. Soil Sci. Soc. Am. Proc. 29:489-494.

118   Whisler, F. D. and A. Klute. 1966. Analysis of infiltration into stratified soil columns. Symposium on water in the unsaturated zone, Wageningen, The Netherlands.

119   Wilson, L. G. and J. N. Luthin. 1963. Effect of air flow ahead of the wetting front on infiltration. Soil Sci. 92(2):136-143.

120   Youngs, E. G. 1968. An estimation of sorptivity for infiltration studies from moisture movement considerations. Soil Sci. 106:157-163.

chapter 5 ▮▮▮▮▮▮▮▮▮

SURFACE RUNOFF, STORAGE AND ROUTING

5

5

SURFACE RUNOFF, STORAGE
AND ROUTING

by   L. F. Huggins, Head, Department of Agricultural
Engineering, Purdue University, West Lafayette,
IN and J. R. Burney, Head, Department of
Agricultural Engineering, Technical University of
Nova Scotia, Halifax, N.S.

Surface runoff is that portion of precipitation which, during and immediately following a storm event, ultimately appears as flowing water in the drainage network of a watershed. Such flow may result from direct movement of water over the ground surface, precipitation in excess of abstraction demands, or it may result from emergence of soil water into drainageways. Methods of quantifying these physical processes are outlined in this chapter.

In order to select a method of modeling any of the several hydrologic components of which a watershed model is composed, it is essential to recognize the impossibility of basing a selection only on considerations concerning the physics of a particular component. The point was made in earlier chapters that all modeling procedures, especially those concerned with something as complex as the hydrology of watersheds, involve varying degrees of approximation to the real situation. When deciding which approximations are the most appropriate, i.e. the most accurate for a feasible computational effort, it is necessary to first chose an overall framework for the complete watershed model. It is only from the viewpoint of the overall model structure and the manner in which interactions between components are accounted for that rational judgments can be made about modeling the surface runoff component.

WATERSHED MODELING APPROACHES

A comprehensive classification of watershed models was presented in Chapter 1. For the purposes of this chapter, only a subset of these various forms is considered.

The first, and most essential, classification involves whether the model will employ a phenomenologic or transfer function, i.e., "black box", approach. The former attempts to quantify individual component physical processes which are known to occur. The latter attempts to avoid the difficulties of describing several complex, interacting processes by treating the catchment as a single entity which transforms input (precipitation) into output (runoff) according to an overall mathematical function which does not directly recognize component physical processes (Amorocho and Orlob, 1961). It relies on the availability of a period of gaged precipitation-runoff records to identify a system transfer function and to optimize coefficient values. While this approach offers several advantages, especially for large catchments, it will not receive more attention because it does not require surface storage or runoff relationships and because it has several significant disadvantages including: necessity of a historical rainfall-runoff record, dependence on similarity of past and future hydrologic conditions in the catchment of interest and, therefore, an inability to assess impacts of major land use changes.

Unfortunately, eliminating transfer function models from further consideration still leaves a wide spectrum of modeling approaches that must be considered before appropriate component relationships can be selected. The remaining spectrum is bounded at one end by lumped modeling approaches and at the other extreme by distributed models.

A lumped parameter model is one which attempts to evaluate impacts of spatial variability of governing parameters by using a procedure to calculate "effective values" for the entire area. The most commonly employed procedure is an area-weighted average. With this approach, the model builder attempts to condense, i.e., to lump, all influences of spatial non-uniformities into mathematically equivalent point coefficient values. This approach is founded on the law of the mean in differential calculus. That theorem essentially says that, for any continuous functional relationship which is differentiable over any specified range, an equivalent or mean value exists which can be substituted in place of the functional relationship itself. Thus, the primary advantage of a lumped model over a distributed one is computational efficiency.

A distributed parameter modeling approach is one which attempts to incorporate, to the degree practical, data concerning the areal distribution of parameter variations together with computational algorithms to evaluate the influence of this distribution on simulated behavior. A pure distributed approach would require development of rigorous partial differential equations for every hydrologic component and specification of an infinite number of boundary conditions applicable to each equation. Thus, all practical distributed modeling approaches utilize approximations to spatial variability which can legitimately be called lumping approximations. While it is therefore possible to view this classification scheme as simply a matter of degree, such a view does not adequately differentiate the fundamental differences between these two philosophies. A continuum of models does exist which represents all levels of combining these two approaches. Nevertheless, a sufficient degree of distributive analysis is practical to require substantially different component relations. Subsequent material in this chapter is developed using lumped versus distributed modeling requirements as fundamentally different methodologies.

The primary emphasis of this chapter concerns quantifying runoff that occurs from a specific hydrologic event rather than "continuous flow" modeling which is generally preferred by those primarily interested in estimating water yields instead of storm runoff hydrographs. This emphasis has been chosen because event-oriented models provide a direct means of continuous simulation. Continuous simulations can be obtained by specifying a continuous precipitation input; albeit, normally at the expense of computational efficiency.

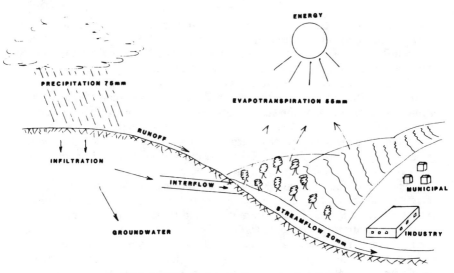

FIG. 5.1 Hydrologic cycle for a natural watershed.

COMPONENT CONCEPTUALIZATION

Since it is necessary to maintain a system viewpoint when choosing model components, it is desirable to begin the discussion of runoff modeling by conceptually describing all component processes which subsequently must be modeled with mathematical relations. While there is duplication of material presented in other chapters, this discussion is intended to point out the high degree of interaction between component processes and to demonstrate why it is essential to chose an overall model framework before selecting methods to quantify its internal parts. Furthermore, this discussion serves to establish a frame of reference from which the adequacy of proposed modeling methodologies can be measured; just how well do specific relations account for mechanisms intuitively known to have a role in surface runoff.

Fig. 5.1 depicts the hydrologic cycle for a natural catchment. It represents the system's overview that must be kept in mind when a model is being developed. Those hydrologic components of particular interest include: interception, surface retention, infiltration, surface detention and surface runoff. The precipitation component is assumed as a specified input, while erosion processes and chemical transport are outside the scope of this chapter. Evapotranspiration is assumed to influence only antecedent moisture conditions at the beginning of a storm event. For situations where a resulting event-oriented model is to be used to simulate continuous streamflow, relationships must be added to continuously simulate evapotranspiration.

It should be clear from Fig. 5.1 that each component is dependent on others which control its inputs. This interdependence should be even clearer upon examination of those parameters which can be hypothesized to control each component process.

Interception

Interception is precipitation which collects on the plant canopy. It ultimately evaporates back into the atmosphere and is generally lost as far as surface runoff is concerned. However, it represents an abstraction from precipitation and must ultimately be quantified. The four primary factors which influence the amount of interception are: species of vegetation, growth stage of vegetation, season of year and wind velocity.

Certainly the type of vegetation growing on an area will have a marked influence on the amount of water it can intercept. The second factor which influences interception is the stage of growth of vegetation at the time of concern. Small, immature crops will have practically no interception while at a later stage of growth, a very significant amount of precipitation may be intercepted by that crop. Season of the year has a considerable impact on the leaf canopy which is present on a given vegetal species.

The fourth factor, wind velocity, is important for two reasons. First, it affects the amount of evaporation that occurs from leaf surfaces. One might expect that, because of high humidity conditions during a precipitation event, evaporation might be negligible. Experiments have indicated such is not the case. There is such a vast surface area involved in some of the denser vegetative canopies, e.g. forest covers, that a significant amount of water is evaporated from these surfaces during a precipitation event. As the velocity of wind increases the amount of evaporation occurring from these surfaces increases. Wind velocity has another effect on vegetation: mechanical movement of that vegetation. As wind velocity increases, turbulence in the air and movement of air through the canopy cause agitation of leaves which shakes off some water. Thus, the canopy is capable of holding a smaller interception volume as wind velocity increases.

Surface Retention

This is water retained on the ground surface in micro-depressions. At the end of the storm, this water will either evaporate or infiltrate into the soil profile. There is a small probability that some surface retention will become surface runoff if, in the process of infiltration, it becomes interflow water as it moves through the soil profile. Factors which control the amount of surface retention are micro-topography and surface macro-slope.

The primary physical factor influencing the magnitude of surface retention is the surface micro-relief of the area and any factors which have a bearing on that micro-relief. The three most important ones which could be considered as a subcategory are: cultural practices, season of the year and erosion patterns. Cultural practices include both tillage techniques and how these are influenced by the vegetation grown. These cultural practices are seasonal in nature; consequently, season of the year influences retention. Another important influence is the erosion pattern that occurs due to previous storms and whether or not this pattern has been changed or obliterated by a tillage operation.

The second broad factor listed is surface macro-slope. As the average slope of a surface increases for a given roughness, the volume of surface retention will usually decrease. Generally, macro-slope is of secondary importance to micro-relief characteristics.

Surface Detention

This is water temporarily detained on the surface that is a necessary requirement for surface runoff to occur. Therefore, it could logically be considered as an integral part of the surface runoff component rather than a separate process. For purposes of clarity it is discussed separately. The most significant factors controlling surface detention include: surface micro-relief, vegetation, surface macro-slope, rainfall excess distribution and the general topography of a catchment.

Surface micro-relief controls cross-sectional shapes of overland flow "channels" that transmit surface water to smaller tributaries and ultimately down to the main channel. Thus, any items listed as a subcategory of micro-relief influences on surface retention must also be included as a subcategory for detention factors. Vegetation must be included because it also determines cultural practices employed and because plant stems can influence the hydraulic roughness of a surface. Surface macro-slope also has a strong bearing on the amount of surface detention volume that will occur. The steeper the average slope, the higher the flow velocity and the lower the detention volume required to sustain a given flow rate.

The general topography of the watershed is the last item. It affects the amount of water coming onto an elemental area from adjacent areas. Since water for surface runoff is supplied from both rainfall and runoff from adjacent areas, detention volume is strongly influenced by general topographic features of the catchment.

The influence of general watershed topography on runoff relationships can serve to illustrate the point made earlier concerning the necessity of developing a watershed model from a system's perspective. A depth-runoff rate relationship can be developed which considers only localized, i.e. "point", parameters, e.g. Manning's equation. However, consider the situation near the upper elevations of a large depression in a catchment. At the beginning of a storm, before any surface water has accumulated in the depressions, the point depth-runoff relationship can accurately simulate surface runoff at locations throughout the depressional area. If the storm has sufficient intensity and duration to cause the entire depression to become flooded, the surface runoff rate at any point within the depression is no longer controlled by its local characteristics; rather the outlet condition for the entire depression becomes the flow control point. Thus localized characteristics often cannot be considered without taking global properties into account.

Infiltration

For many watersheds, infiltration is the most important hydrologic component determining the shape of the runoff hydrograph from the area. The major controlling factors are: soil type, surface crusting, season of the year, antecedent moisture conditions, rainfall hyetograph and subsurface moisture conditions.

Soil type is the prime factor to consider when modeling moisture infiltration. Soil typing is simply a classification scheme used to characterize certain physical properties of a particular soil. If the classification is accurately done, soils with similar physical characteristics will be identified by the same type "name" regardless of geographic location. Thus, soils of the same type name should have similar infiltration characteristics.

The second item affecting infiltration is surface crusting. Experiments have indicated the first few millimeters of the soil profile have a profound influence upon the rate at which water can infiltrate. Any factor which affects the surface crust will have an influence upon infiltration. Three important subcategory factors are: cultural practices, the type of vegetation (because it protects the soil surface from raindrop impact) and rainfall intensity itself (because this has a strong bearing upon the size of raindrops that occur). The average size of raindrops generally tends to increase with increasing rainfall intensity. Larger drops have a higher energy and tend to do more damage to the surface structure, thereby affecting the surface crust.

Season of the year has particularly marked effects on infiltration, not only because it affects vegetation, but because the presence or absence of frozen ground is critical. It is possible for frozen ground to have a non-zero infiltration rate. This rate depends on the nature of freezing, moisture content of the soil at the time it was frozen, soil type and other factors. Certainly freezing will normally drastically decrease the rate of infiltration, but some water will usually infiltrate.

The rate at which water infiltrates into the soil profile is highly dependent upon the moisture content present in that soil. Consequenly, antecedent moisture conditions, i.e. the amount of moisture present at the beginning of a storm event, will greatly influence infiltration rates during that storm.

The rainfall hyetograph itself also influences infiltration properties. Soil at a particular moisture content has the capacity to infiltrate water at a certain rate. This is referred to as its infiltration capacity. However, it may well be that the rate of rainfall at that time is less than the infiltration capacity of the soil. Obviously, water cannot infiltrate into soil faster than the rate at which it is being supplied. So even though a soil has a high infiltration capacity, the actual rate of infiltration may be limited by the rate at which water from rainfall and surface runoff from adjacent areas is coming onto the area. Therefore, unsteady rainfall rates during which the supply fluctuates below and above the infiltration capacity greatly complicate predictions of instantaneous infiltration rates.

The last factor affecting infiltration is subsurface moisture content. In reality, this refers to the hydrologic component of interflow rather than infiltration, per se. Interflow is the re-emergence of subsurface moisture onto the surface, usually at an elevation lower than that at which it entered the soil profile. However, it is possible to incorporate the subject of interflow into the overall characterization of the rate of infiltration by defining interflow as negative infiltration. If one adopts that concept (this is generally done for computational convenience in actual models), the subsurface moisture distribution is quite important in predicting the rate and amount of water that will re-emerge onto the soil surface. The geology of subsurface strata is an important factor controlling interflow.

Surface Runoff

In order to obtain a prediction of surface runoff it is necessary to quantitatively characterize all other components discussed. Often these other components are viewed simply as abstractions from the precipitation input.

Factors that specifically influence the rate at which water runs off an elemental area are: the hydraulic roughness of the surface as influenced by micro-relief, the surface macro-slope (in general, the steeper the surface the more quickly water runs off), and finally, the depth of flow in that elemental area. Generally, if only localized or "point" properties are considered, as the depth of flow increases, so does the rate at which water runs off.

CONCEPTUAL HYDROGRAPH DEVELOPMENT

All hydrologic components—physical processes—occurring within a watershed during a storm event, together with their major controlling parameters, have been identified. Before attempting to develop quantifying relationships it is necessary to have a clear concept of how these processes occur and interact as a function of time from the beginning of a precipitation event. Conceptual models simply define in qualitative terms the manner of occurrence of those physical processes intuitively known to exist. Admittedly, it's a big step to go from a conceptual model which includes all factors known to influence hydrologic behavior to the implementation stage requiring quantifying relationships and predictive coefficients. However, a firm conceptual ideal of what the model must simulate is essential in order to provide a frame of reference against which to judge the adequacy of particular models. This section attempts to describe the temporal sequence of processes that occur in an elemental area (a few square meters) within a hypothetical catchment.

As indicated earlier, none of the hydrologic models currently being used or proposed are rigorous; they all represent gross approximations to the many complex physical processes involved. Because they are approximations, the user must decide how satisfactorily a given model simulates what actually occurs. With a thorough understanding and a standard of comparison, a rational choice can be made concerning which analysis is the most satisfactory for a given application.

Idealized Surfaces

What happens when precipitation falls on a very small, flat surface that is completely impervious? Fig. 5.2 depicts those physical processes which occur and the expected response of a "slab" of uniform hydraulic roughness with surface area, A.

The situation shown in Fig. 5.2 can be rigorously analyzed. The primary governing equation for analyzing this problem is the equation of continuity. In order to solve that differential equation some additional information is needed. Basically, a functional relationship is required which characterizes the rate of runoff at any given point. That rate will depend upon the depth of flow at a point, x, the slope of the flow surface, the hydraulic roughness

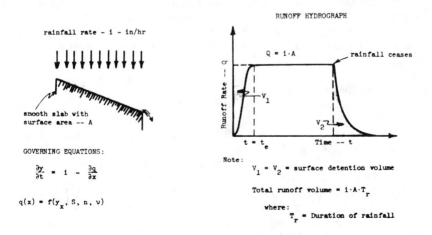

FIG. 5.2 Runoff from an impervious surface.

characteristic of the surface and a characteristic which describes the viscosity of the fluid. In addition to such a functional relationship, often referred to as a discharge function, initial and boundary conditions must be specified.

When the above approach is applied to the differential continuity equation the expected solution, as shown on the right hand portion of Fig. 5.2, is obtained. The left-hand portion of this hydrograph shows flow begins at time $= 0$ and gradually increases until it reaches an almost linear rate of increase. Ultimately, the runoff rate asymptotically approaches an equilibrium rate of runoff, Q, which equals the product of i, the rainfall intensity, times the area over which rainfall is being applied. That rate of runoff continues indefinitely until such time as the rate of rainfall changes. If rainfall abruptly ceases, water stored on the surface eventually runs off and the rate of outflow from the element asymptotically decreases to zero.

A couple of additional characteristics of the runoff hydrograph are worth noting. First of all, the regions labeled V_1 and V_2 are of equal area. Continuity of mass requires all rainfall coming onto the surface must eventually flow off, assuming no evaporation. Thus, during the initial unsteady state portion of the hydrograph when the rate of runoff is increasing, water falling onto the surface that has not yet reached the outlet is stored as an accumulating film of water. This is the surface detention volume. Once rainfall ceases, that stored volume of water ultimately runs off. The volume of runoff that occurs from the time at which rainfall ceases until the surface becomes completely dry, again assuming no surface tension effects or evaporation, exactly equals the surface detention volume built up during the initial unsteady portion of the hydrograph. Due to the comparatively smooth surface texture, surface retention is negligible.

A second hydrograph property worth noting concerns the total runoff volume. It corresponds to the area under the runoff hydrograph. It is equal to i x A (which is the rate of runoff, Q) x the total time, T_r, during which rainfall persists. This again is a direct consequence of the continuity of mass condition which says the total volume of runoff must eventually equal the total volume of water that falls on the surface.

The flat impervious surface considered represents a situation much simpler than occurs on natural watersheds. Only a few applications, a parking lot for example, are concerned with predicting the runoff volume or hydrograph that might be reasonably analogous to the situation just depicted. It's necessary to complicate the situation somewhat to understand processes that occur in an agricultural watershed and to obtain a more realistic conceptual model.

Agricultural Elemental Areas

Fig. 5.3 shows a schematic diagram of a physical situation which is more typical of natural watersheds. The conceptual model developed below attempts to describe those physical processes likely to occur when such an area is subjected to a precipitation event.

It is still necessary to put some stringent restrictions on the conceptual model to be developed. The areal size is assumed to be very small, at most a few square meters in size; specifically, one that is sufficiently small that it is realistic to assume a uniform type of soil. Furthermore, it is assumed that vegetal cover is constant and that the element has a constant or overall surface slope. This restriction doesn't mean actual point slopes must be con-

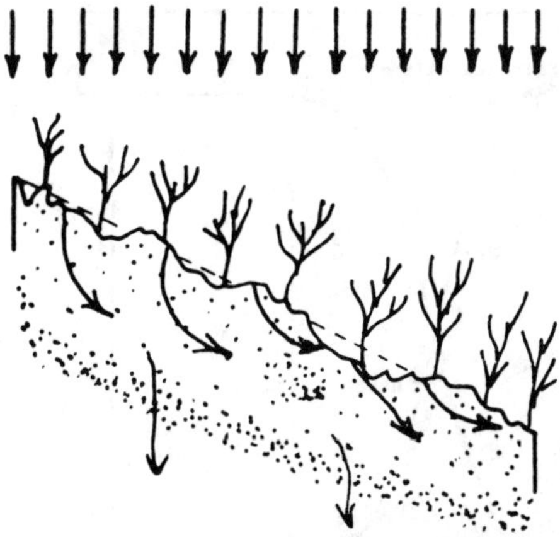

FIG. 5.3 Profile of a natural elemental area.

stant, but that a plane surface must exist which would approximate the macro-slope of the elemental area. Because of the small size of the element it is realistic to assume a uniform areal distribution of precipitation during a natural storm event.

Consider a situation similar to the previous one where at time = 0 rainfall is applied to the elemental area. As soon as rain begins to fall, vegetation growing on the area is going to prevent some of it from striking the ground surface. This physical process is referred to as interception. Part of the rain, if there isn't complete canopy covering the area, will immediately begin reaching the surface. Once rain reaches the soil surface, a portion begins to infiltrate into the profile while the remainder begins to fill up small depressions or micro-relief areas on the rough surface. Once the combined demands for filling depressional storage, satisfying interception, and the continuing demand for infiltration are exceeded water begins to accumulate in a surface detention condition and runoff begins.

The black dots in Fig. 5.3 are intended to depict soil density conditions. Very close spacing of the black dots represent a more dense or tighter soil in terms of its infiltration characteristics. Fig. 5.3 corresponds to a situation in which a layer has developed somewhat under the surface of the soil. This layer is more dense and more restrictive to infiltration and movement of subsurface water through the soil than the upper layer. One of the things likely to occur in such situations, which are common in agricultural fields subjected to annual plowing and cultivation, is a significant reduction in steady-state infiltration. In addition, a portion of the water that moves into the soil profile is likely to move horizontally as well as vertically downward and may, at some lower elevation in the watershed, re-emerge as interflow onto the surface of the ground to again become overland flow.

A composite hydrograph of all these hydrologic components as a function of time is shown in Fig. 5.4. This fairly complex graph attempts to portray the interacting components as they vary with time from the beginning of precipitation. The ordinate of the graph is labeled rate per unit area. This could be rate of rainfall, rate of runoff, rate of infiltration, or whatever, since it is used as the rate scale for all physical processes. This graph attempts to portray the rate of a particular hydrologic component at a given instant as

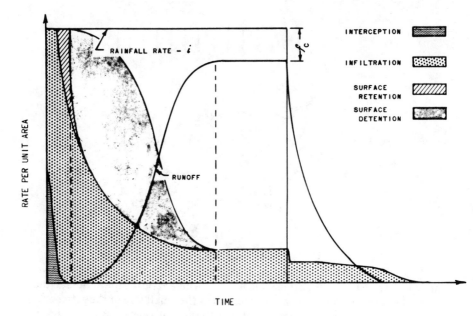

FIG. 5.4 Hydrologic response of a natural elemental area.

the height of the area designated by a particular shading. In other words, each component, except rainfall and runoff rate which both are referenced to the X-axis, utilizes a variable base line for its ordinate.

Consider interception first. The X-axis is its base line and the rate at which water is intercepted at any time is depicted simply as the orginate of the correspondingly shaded area. At time $= 0$ a certain percentage of the rate at which rainfall is being applied is abstracted as interception. In general, the initial rate could be estimated by multiplying the rainfall rate by the percent of the surface area covered by plant canopy, i.e. the projected area of the canopy. That means, if 50 percent of the area is covered by the canopy's vertical projection, approximately one-half of the rainfall would initially be used in satisfying interception storage. Usually, this rate of abstraction would decrease quickly because the total interception demand of the plant surfaces is generally small; something on the order of 0.25 mm to possibly as high as 1.5 mm of precipitation might be expected as the total interception capacity for an agricultural crop canopy.

Rainfall not being used to satisfy interception at time $= 0$ is next utilized to satisfy infiltration capacity demands. Fig. 5.4 was drawn with the assumption that the initial infiltration capacity of the soil was greater than the rate at which water was being supplied to the area minus the rate at which it was being intercepted. This is indicated by noting that the correspondingly shaded area reaches the rate of application of rainfall. This means that at time $= 0$ the rainfall supply was being entirely utilized satisfying two demands: interception and a portion of the infiltration capacity demand. The actual height of the uniquely shaded area on the graph (rather than the height between the top of shading and the X-axis) represents the infiltration rate into the soil.

As time increases a condition is reached at which the combined demands for interception and infiltration capacity are less than the rate at which rainfall is being supplied to the area. At that time, a start can be made toward satisfying surface retention storage needs. Water not required for infiltration and interception demands will begin filling up micro-relief depressions.

Moving further along the time axis, a dotted vertical line may be noted. By this time interception demands have decreasing essentially to zero. Although a very low rate of abstraction for interception due to evaporation could have been shown, it was assumed negligible in comparison to the rates of rainfall, infiltration, etc. At the time corresponding to the first vertical dotted line on the graph, the combined demands for infiltration capacity and surface retention storage are decreasing and become equal to the rate of application of rainfall. This is the first time water is available for surface detention storage and the first surface runoff occurs from the area.

Proceeding still further along the time axis, infiltration capacity continues to decrease with time. This is consistent with infiltration experiments on most soils. The infiltration capacity of dry soil is quite high. As rainfall is applied and moisture moves into the subsurface profile, infiltration capacity tends to decrease with time until ultimately, if rainfall continues at a rate in excess of the infiltration capacity, the rate of infiltration into the soil profile eventually becomes relatively constant and remains so for an indefinite period of time. That is the situation sketched on Fig. 5.4. The infiltration rate into the soil profile is shown decreasing continuously until the second dotted line is reached. At that time the infiltration capacity reaches a constant value. While the infiltration capacity is decreasing, increasing amounts of rainfall become available to satisfy surface detention needs and the rate of runoff continues to increase.

As surface detention demands are continually being satisfied and as the infiltration capacity decreases to a constant rate, the runoff rate gradually increases until, at a time corresponding to the second vertical dotted line shown in Fig. 5.4, the infiltration capacity demand and runoff rate become constant. This also corresponds to the time at which surface detention demands decrease to zero. If rain continues beyond this point at a constant rate as shown in Fig. 5.4, runoff will continue at a constant rate equal to the rate of rainfall, I, minus the rate at which water is continuing to infiltrate into the soil profile. This rate is labeled f_c; therefore, the difference in the rate of application of rainfall and the steady state rate of runoff also equals f_c. The rate of rainfall minus the rate of all the permanent abstractions is given a specific name in hydrologic analyses, it's referred to as the rainfall excess rate. Similarly, the total volume of runoff from a storm is often referred to simply as the rainfall excess.

Sustained equilibrium conditions are relatively simple and of little interest at this time, but the recession portion of the hydrograph is interesting. Once rainfall ceases the runoff rate begins to decrease rapidly as shown in Fig. 5.4. Only surface retention and detention storage are available to sustain infiltration and runoff. The infiltration rate is shown undergoing a very rapid decrease because this process is primarily one of vertical water movement. When rainfall is no longer supplying the entire surface area it is common for only 10 to 15 percent of the surface to be inundated. Because infiltration continues at full capacity on only this small percentage of the total area, the overall rate at which water infiltrates over the entire element drops very quickly to a fraction of its rate during rainfall. Surface runoff continues until the detention storage volume is exhausted. Infiltration will continue beyond this point until the surface retention water has all infiltrated or evaporated.

Scaling Considerations

The concepts outlined above have been predicated on the assumption that the area under consideration is very small, an elemental area. What additional factors need to be accounted for if a watershed sized area is to be modeled? First, it should be pointed out that, in theory, there is really no difference in the processes which occur on an elemental scale as opposed to a watershed scale. In other words, the conceptual model developed above applies just as accurately to large waterhsheds as it does to small ones. Differences between techniques applied to large and small catchments arise when approximate quantitative relationships are delineated to characterize those complex physical processes that were conceptualized.

In the process of developing approximate techniques for modeling hydrologic processes some factors dominant for small watersheds may become relatively unimportant as the watershed size increases. Conversely, some factors dominant in controlling predictions for large watersheds may be relatively minor for predictions on smaller areas. Since modeling techniques are usually rather crude approximations, the accuracy with which any given model can simulate a hydrologic event depends on the size of the watershed to which it is applied. Factors for which the relative significance is especially likely to change with watershed size include: areal precipitation distribution, interflow, and overland versus channel flow considerations.

Certainly the impact or importance of the areal distribution of precipitation will tend to increase as the size of the watershed increases. As catchment size becomes smaller it's more feasible to assume the rate of application of rainfall is uniform at a particular instant in time over the entire area. Conversely, as watershed size increases it may be important to worry about the path that a particular storm follows.

The relative importance of interflow changes quite drastically as the size of the watershed increases. For many small watersheds, particularly agricultural areas located in upland regions of a large watershed, interflow is often negligible. For large waterhsheds the interflow factor may be the major contributing factor, especially if one is concerned about total volumes of runoff rather than a storm hydrograph. The relative importance of interflow also tends to be much greater on forested watersheds than developed land. This is generally thought to result from the enhanced surface infiltration associated with forest litter which often allows all rainfall to infiltrate (Hewlett and Troendle, 1975).

Channel flow conditions tend to dominate overland flow considerations for large watersheds. As the size of a watershed increases it's necessary to employ rigorous flood routing procedures to determine the path and rate of movement of flows from various subwatersheds.

Conversely, some factors that are of greater importance for small watersheds than larger watersheds include: vegetal cover, surface microtopography and soil type distribution. For example, vegetal cover variations tend to be averaged out and often are negligible as the watershed area becomes quite large. Factors such as soil type and micro-relief, because they vary so widely, can be lumped without major accuracy loss as catchment area becomes larger. In contrast, because these factors have such a dominant localized effect they can frequently not be neglected for smaller watersheds. Overland flow relationships can be crucial to the accuracy of models used for small, agricultural catchments.

Conclusions

The general concepts presented in this section need to be kept in mind when evaluating specific analytical techniques that will simulate the hydrologic behavior of a watershed for a given storm event. The suitability of various quantitative techniques employed needs to be judged against conceptual models developed. These concepts are intended to describe all physical processes that occur in a watershed. If a numerical or analytical technique for predicting watershed response is to be accurate it must take into account these conceptual factors. The more accurately these factors are accounted for, the more accurate the resulting predictions.

Finally, the justification for the admonition concerning use of a system's perspective when developing or selecting watershed models should now be more clear. The degree of interaction between hydrologic components as well as the discussion concerning scaling considerations illustrate the futility of trying to establish quantifying relationships for each hydrologic component independently of others. The necessary compromises between accuracy and computational feasibility that must always be made when constructing a model make anything but the system's viewpoint irrational.

OVERLAND FLOW THEORY

The theoretical basis for developing equations describing overland flow have all evolved from the field of hydromechanics. The purpose of this section is to outline those developments in order that they may be utilized where appropriate to develop quantifying runoff relationships.

Surface water flow in its natural unregulated state is hydraulically classified as unsteady, nonuniform flow, i.e. the velocity and flow depth vary in both time and space. Furthermore, the type of flow ranges over a continuum from the shallow sheet flow of excess rain on a parking lot, through the divided flow over an agricultural land to rill flow with concentration in small channels which join and eventually form channel flow in streams and rivers.

The theoretical hydrodynamic equations governing this flow are generally attributed to Barre de St. Venant and were formulated in the latter part of the 19th century. However, because of their nature no closed form solution is possible. Prior to the advent of high-speed computers and numerical analysis techniques, varying simplified forms were used to solve specific problems.

Hydrodynamic Equations

The St. Venant equations are based on the fundamental laws governing conservation of mass (continuity) and conservation of linear momentum applied to a control volume or fixed section of channel.

Basic Continuity Equation. The basic equation of mass conservation or continuity is:

$$\iint \rho \bar{v} \, d\bar{A} = \frac{\partial}{\partial t} \iiint \rho \, dV \dots \dots \dots \dots \dots \dots [5.1]$$

in which

ρ = fluid density
$\bar{v}$ = velocity vector
$\bar{A}$ = area vector, positive outward
t = time
V = volume.

    The term on the left represents the net rate of efflux through the surface of the control volume and the equation states that by the law of conservation of mass this rate of loss is equal to the rate of change of mass within the control volume. The area vector $\bar{A}$ is oriented in an outward direction normal to the control surface and the scaler dot product $\bar{v} \, d\bar{A}$ is positive if the vectors $\bar{v}$ and $d\bar{A}$ are in the same direction. The left hand term then represents the difference between the mass outflow from the control volume and the mass inflow, by integration over the whole surface. The term $\rho \, dV$ on the right represents an elementary mass which is integrated throughout the control volume and differentiated with respect to time, i.e. the time rate of change of mass within the control volume.

    Basic Momentum Equation. The law of conservation of linear momentum may be expressed as:

$$\bar{F} + \iiint \bar{B}\rho \, dV = \iint \bar{v}(\rho \bar{v} \, d\bar{A}) + \frac{\partial}{\partial t} \iiint \bar{v}\rho \, dV \dots \dots \dots \dots \dots [5.2]$$

in which the additional symbols are:

$\bar{F}$ = sum of all surface force on the control volume
$\bar{B}$ = sum of all internal forces per unit mass.

The terms on the left of the equation represent forces affecting the control volume and, by the law of conservation of momentum, this is equal to the time rate of change by momentum.

    The first term on the left, $\bar{F}$, represents the hydrostatic and shear forces on the surface of the control volume. The second term represents gravitational and centrifugal forces on each elemental volume summed over the control volume. On the right of the equation, the first term is the net rate of efflux of momentum across the control surface, while the second term represents the time rate of change of momentum within the control volume.

    St. Venant Equations. In applying the above two equations to a section of open channel, it is generally assumed that the flow is one-dimensional, the channel is straight and the slope is gradual. These simplifying assumptions enable a uniform velocity distribution (Coriolis coefficient = 1) and a hydrostatic pressure distribution to be assumed.

    The derivation of the continuity and momentum equations as they apply to problems of unsteady nonuniform flow will not be repeated here. Strelkoff (1969) presents a rigorous derivation including a consideration of the implications of assumptions inherent in the formulation. After substitution of the appropriate terms in the basic equations given above for a unit width of channel, the continuity equation reduces to:

$$\frac{\partial y}{\partial t} + \frac{\partial Q}{\partial x} = q - f \dots \dots \dots \dots \dots \dots \dots \dots \dots \dots \dots \dots \dots \dots [5.3]$$

and the momentum equation becomes:

$$\frac{\partial v}{\partial t} + v\frac{\partial v}{\partial x} + g\frac{\partial y}{\partial x} = g(S_O - S_f) - qv/y \dots \dots \dots \dots \dots \dots \dots \dots [5.4]$$

in which:
- y = local depth of flow
- Q = discharge per unit width
- q = lateral inflow per unit length and width of channel
- f = lateral outflow per unit length and width of channel
- v = velocity
- g = gravitational constant
- S_o = bed slope
- S_f = friction slope
- x = flow direction axis.

In applying these quasi-linear partial differential equations to the solution of flood wave problems, the initial flow profile condition is assumed known as are the boundary conditions of the upstream inflow hydrograph and the downstream rating curve for the reach in question. This type of problem, known as a Cauchy problem, has an open solution domain on the x, t-plane over which are sought the y and v surfaces.

The solution is obtained by the method of characteristics (outlined for the simpler kinematic wave equations in the following section) in which the characteristic curves in the x, t-plane represent the loci of discontinuities in the derivatives of v and y with respect to x and t. These characteristic curves physically represent lines along which disturbances of the water surface profile are propagated. As the propagation velocity is equal to the celerity plus or minus the velocity, both characteristic curves will be oriented in a downstream direction for supercritical flow. For subcritical flow, both an upstream and a downstream characteristic curve will exist at any point in the x, t-plane. The backward characteristic curves are necessary to the solution for conditions in which backwater effects occur into tributaries and for reflected waves from the faces of downstream reservoirs.

A graphical solution to the St. Venant equations is presented by Chow (1959). However, this type of solution has been superceded by numerical techniques based on the use of digital computers. A review of finite differencing schemes used in the solution of the St. Venant equations is presented by Strelkoff (1970).

Kinematic Equation

Lighthill and Whitham (1955) proposed that the dynamic terms in the momentum equation had negligible influence for cases in which backwater effects were absent. This quasi-steady approach, known as the kinematic wave approximation, results in the replacement of the St. Venant equations by the much simpler kinematic equations, viz. the continuity equation (equation [5.3]), and a depth-discharge equation of the generalized form:

$$Q = \alpha y^m \dotfill [5.5]$$

in which α and m are parameters.

From studies of the influence exerted on the rising limb of an overland flow hydrograph by parameters in a dimensionless form of the St. Venant equations, Woolhiser and Liggett (1967) showed that the effect of neglecting dynamic terms in the momentum equation could be assessed by the value of a single dimensionless parameter k, defined as,

$$k = \frac{S_0 L}{HF^2} \dotfill [5.6]$$

in which:

  L = length of bed slope
  H = equilibrium flow depth at outlet
  F = equilibrium Froude number for flow at outlet.

For values of k greater than 10, very little advantage in accuracy is gained by using the momentum equation in place of a depth-discharge relationship. Since k is usually much greater than 10 in virtually all overland flow conditions, the kinematic wave equations generally provide an adequate representation of the overland flow hydrograph. Kinematic equations do not include the effect of the Froude number and also neglect any surface profile changes due to dynamic effects. Boundary and initial conditions apply only to the solution of the continuity equation, and changes in the surface water profile can only be caused by changes in the supply rate. Effects of these changes are propagated only in a downstream direction, i.e. the equations do not allow for upstream wave effects.

As shown by Eagleson (1970), application of the method of characteristics to the kinematic equations leads to ordinary differential equations which may be easily integrated along the single forward characteristic curve or path of wave propagation. By definition, a characteristic curve is the locus of discontinuity in partial derivatives with respect to space and time.

Letting $q_e = q - f$, the rainfall excess in the continuity equation (equation [5.3]), and taking the time derivative of the depth-discharge equation, the kinematic equations may be re-written as:

$$\frac{\partial y}{\partial t} + \frac{\partial Q}{\partial x} = q_e \dotfill [5.7]$$

and,

$$\alpha m y^{m-1} \frac{\partial y}{\partial t} - \frac{\partial Q}{\partial t} = 0 \dotfill [5.8]$$

In addition, total derivatives of the depth and flow rate are given by:

$$\frac{\partial y}{\partial x}dx + \frac{\partial y}{\partial t}dt = dy \dotfill [5.9]$$

and,

$$\frac{\partial Q}{\partial x}dx + \frac{\partial Q}{\partial t}dt = dQ. \dotfill [5.10]$$

In matrix form, equations [5.7] through [5.10] may be written as:

$$\begin{vmatrix} 1 & 0 & 0 & 1 \\ \alpha m y^{m-1} & 0 & -1 & 0 \\ dt & dx & 0 & 0 \\ 0 & 0 & dt & dx \end{vmatrix} \begin{vmatrix} \partial y/\partial t \\ \partial y/\partial x \\ \partial Q/\partial t \\ \partial Q/\partial x \end{vmatrix} = \begin{vmatrix} q_e \\ 0 \\ dy \\ dQ \end{vmatrix} \dotfill [5.11]$$

Application of the method of characteristics means that a discontinuity is sought in the solution of the four partial derivatives. From Cramer's rule, such a discontinuity, or indeterminacy, is the result of a zero numerator and denominator determinant in the solution of equation [5.11].

Setting the determinant (denominator) equal to zero yields:

$$\left|\frac{dx}{dt}\right|^2 - \alpha m y^{m-1}\frac{dx}{dt} = 0. \dotfill [5.12]$$

which has two solutions for the wave speed c:

$$\frac{dx}{dt} = c = \alpha m y^{m-1} = mv \dotfill [5.13]$$

and the trivial solution,

$$\frac{dx}{dt} = c = 0 \dotfill [5.14]$$

There is therefore only one characteristic direction given by equation [5.13], of which equation [5.14] is a zero depth special case. The positive sign indicates that the wave propagation is only in a downstream direction and it may be noted that the propagation velocity, c, exceeds the stream velocity, v.

If now, each column in the determinant is replaced in turn by the column vector on the right of equation [5.11], each of these numerator determinants is set equal to zero, and using equation [5.13], the resulting equations are:

$$\frac{dQ}{dt} = cq_e \dotfill [5.15]$$

$$\frac{dQ}{dx} = v = q_e \quad \dotfill \quad [5.16]$$

$$\frac{dy}{dt} = q_e \quad \dotfill \quad [5.17]$$

and,

$$\frac{dy}{dx} = \frac{q_e}{c} \quad \dotfill \quad [5.18]$$

Equations [5.15] through [5.18] apply only along the characteristic curves defined by equation [5.13]. Assuming a constant rainfall excess on a plane of length L, equation [5.17] yields,

$$y = q_e t \quad \dotfill \quad [5.19]$$

and substitution in equation [5.13], followed by integration, results in the equation of the characteristic curves:

$$x - x_0 = \alpha q_e^{m-1} (t - t_0)^m \quad \dotfill \quad [5.20]$$

for an initially dry surface in which x_0 and t_0 are space and time values on their respective axes. The characteristic curves given by equation [5.20] are illustrated in Fig. 5.5 and trace the space-time path of flow disturbances.

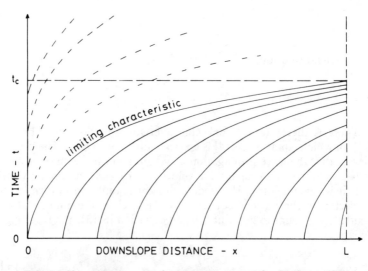

FIG. 5.5 Characteristic curves for kinematic waves (after Eagleson, 1970).

As shown in Fig. 5.5, the limiting characteristic originates at the space-time origin and substituting $x_o = 0$ and $t_o = 0$ in equation [5.20], with $x = L$, the time for a flow distrubance to travel the length of the plane, or the time of concentration for an excess rainfall duration of at least equal magnitude is:

$$t_c = \left| \frac{Lq_e^{1-m}}{\alpha} \right|^{1/m} \quad \dots\dots\dots\dots\dots\dots\dots\dots\dots\dots\dots\dots\dots [5.21]$$

The kinematic equations therefore exhibit a nonlinear behavior, since the time of concentration is a function of rainfall excess.

A detailed application of the kinematic equations to conditions of varying rainfall durations, infiltration and interflow on a plane, and to idealized catchment models is lucidly presented by Eagleson (1970). Two particular results relevant to hydrograph generation are especially illustrative and are briefly discussed below:

(a) **Plane outflow hydrographs.** Assuming the depth of rainfall excess, D, to be constant, i.e.,

$$D = q_e t_r \dots\dots\dots\dots\dots\dots\dots\dots\dots\dots\dots\dots\dots\dots\dots\dots [5.22]$$

the hydrographs illustrated in Fig. 5.6 may be generated by allowing the rainfall duration, t_r, to vary in applications of the kinematic equations.

For $t_r = 0$, an infinite pulse of excess rainfall is dumped uniformly on the catchment. The resulting hydrograph (OABC in Fig. 5.6) is the impulse transfer function of instantaneous hydrograph. If D is 1 unit in depth, the hydrograph is known as the instantaneous unit hydrograph. The outflow is seen to remain constant during the time, AB, in which a disturbance travels

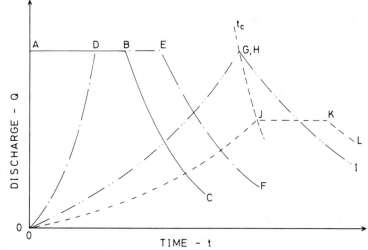

FIG. 5.6 Outflow hydrographs for a plane.

the length of the plane at the constant depth D. As may be noted from Fig. 5.6, this time will be shorter than the time of concentration due to the initial non-zero flow depth.

As the excess rainfall duration increases, but remains less than the time of concentration, t_c, the peak flow occurs at a time equal to the rainfall duration, retains the same magnitude, but is of increasingly shorter duration (as shown by curve ODEF). In the limit, for $t_r = t_c$, (curve OGHI), the hydrograph peak only instantaneously reaches the discharge magnitude. For excess rainfall durations greater than the time of concentration, the value of t_c will increase according to equation [5.21], since the intensity of the excess rainfall decreases for the assumed constant depth. As shown by curve OJKL, the peak discharge is reached at the time of concentration and remains constant until rainfall cessation.

A comparison may be made with the Rational Formula method for calculating flood peaks, in which the peak discharge is assumed to occur at a rainfall duration equal to the time of concentration. Natural rainfall intensity-duration curves, furthermore, indicate an increase in intensity and a decrease in amount with decreasing duration. The above analysis, using the kinematic equations, substantiates the logical reasoning of the Rational Formula in that, even for a fixed amount of rainfall, durations shorter than the time of concentration do not result in a higher peak discharge. Rainfall durations longer than the time of concentration result in a decreased peak discharge. However, since depth increases with duration in natural rainfall events, the peak discharge may be expected to decrease more slowly than the idealized fixed amount condition described for these kinematic equations.

(b) **Simple catchment model.** An idealized catchment model may be conceived as consisting of a plane whose outflow enters a transversely flowing stream channel, as shown in Fig. 5.7. Defining $\lambda = t_s/t_c$, i.e. the ratio of the time of concentration in the stream to that on the plane, and assuming a constant rainfall excess depth, D, the effect of a varying rainfall duration predicted by applying the kinematic wave equation to the catchment is illustrated in Fig. 5.8.

For small values of λ the stream response is relatively rapid and, as illustrated in Fig. 5.7, the isochrones (lines of equal travel time to the stream outlet) tend to run parallel to the stream and exhibit characteristics of the

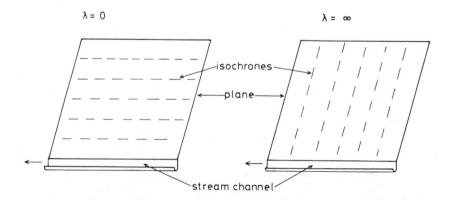

FIG. 5.7 Conceptual catchments.

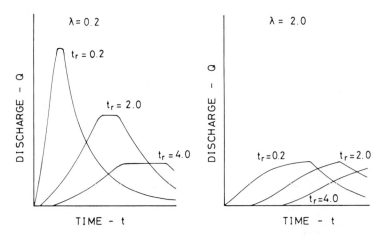

FIG. 5.8 Outflow hydrographs for simple catchment model.

plane alone. This latter feature is illustrated by a comparison of the graph on the left in Fig. 5.8 and the curves in Fig. 5.6. As λ increases the isochrones move toward a direction perpendicular to the stream. In addition, as shown on the right in Fig. 5.8, the flood peaks caused by short duration rainfall events decrease appreciably as cessation of rainfall occurs before the full catchment contributes to outflow. For longer duration storms the duration of the flood peak decreases as the peak is only reached at a later time. In fact, peak discharge tends to become independent of storm duration as λ increases.

Numerical Solution. The finite difference approximations to the partial derivatives in the continuity equation (equation [5.7]), based on the space-time grid shown in Fig. 5.9, may be written as:

$$\frac{\partial Q}{\partial x} = \frac{(Q_4 - Q_2)}{\Delta x} \quad \dots \dots \dots \dots \dots \dots \dots \dots \dots \dots \dots \dots \dots \dots \dots [5.23]$$

$$\frac{\partial y}{\partial t} = \frac{y_4 + y_2 - y_3 - y_1}{2\Delta t} \quad \dots \dots \dots \dots \dots \dots \dots \dots \dots \dots \dots \dots [5.24]$$

and the average lateral inflow:

$$q_e = (q_4 + q_2)/2 \dots \dots \dots \dots \dots \dots \dots \dots \dots \dots \dots \dots \dots [5.25]$$

Substituting equations [5.23] and [5.24] in equation [5.7] and re-arranging:

$$Q_4 - Q_2 + (y_4 + y_2 - y_3 - y_1)\Delta x / (2\Delta t) = q_e \dots \dots \dots \dots \dots \dots [5.26]$$

Equations [5.5], [5.25] and [5.26] may be successively used to develop a solution in the x, t-plane (Brakensiek, 1967).

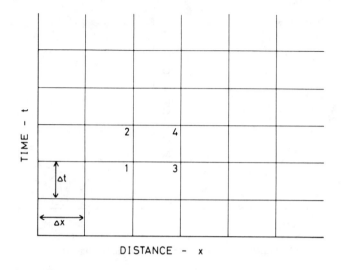

FIG. 5.9 Space-time grid for finite difference form of continuity equation.

Since Q_4 = outflow (O), $Q_2 + q_e$ = net inflow (I), $(y_4 + y_2)\Delta x/2$ = storage (S_2) and $(y_3 + y_1)\Delta x/2$ = storage (S_1), equation [5.26] may be re-written as:

$$I - O = (S_2 - S_1)/\Delta t = \Delta S/\Delta t \dots\dots\dots\dots\dots\dots\dots [5.27]$$

Equation [5.27] is the form of the hydrologic continuity equation commonly used in reservoir and channel routing calculations.

In advancing the solution parallel to the time axis, i.e. to generate the outflow hydrograph for the reservoir or reach in question, the depth-discharge equation (equation [5.5]) may be considered to have the forms:

$$S_2 = f(O_2) \dots\dots\dots\dots\dots\dots\dots\dots\dots\dots\dots\dots\dots\dots\dots [5.28]$$

or,

$$S_2 = g(O_2, I_2) \dots\dots\dots\dots\dots\dots\dots\dots\dots\dots\dots\dots\dots\dots [5.29]$$

Use of equation [5.28] together with equation [5.27] is known as level pool flood routing and assumes instantaneous dispersion of inflow wave effects into storage. Equation [5.29] assumes a wedge storage effect as, for example, in the Muskingham routing procedure.

Huggins and Monke (1966) applied equations [5.27] and [5.28] to the modeling of outflow hydrographs from small agricultural catchments. They idealized a catchment as a matrix of square planar surfaces with outflow and inflow between adjacent surfaces. By applying these equations to all elements at successive time intervals this distributed parameter model produces a spatially integrated hydrograph.

STEADY-STATE OVERLAND FLOW

Overland flow occurs as a result of rainfall in excess of the soil infiltration capacity and the storage capacity of depressions. On natural land surfaces flow follows a myriad of interlinking and constantly changing flow paths as soil and dead vegetation are entrained and deposited. The complexity over even a small sample area, at any point in time, is such that a direct mathematical or deterministic approach to defining the transit storage (detention)—discharge relationship is not feasible. Consequently, a holistic approach is generally adopted and overland flow is envisaged as a shallow sheet of average depth. This approach allows the interpretation of overland flow as that of wide channel flow having an "effective" wetted perimeter. Average depth is often defined as the volume per unit area for surface water in excess of retention (depression) storage.

The assumption of wide channel flow as an approximation enables the characterization of the depth—discharge relationship to be defined in terms of theoretical laminar flow equation or the well-established empirical channel flow equations of Chezy or Manning. However, in spite of these simplifying assumptions, a decision remains in selecting the applicable equation, and for the most commonly assumed case of turbulent flow, a roughness coefficient.

These problems are often of academic interest in large watersheds with well-defined drainage channels, because of the modulating effect of channel storage on the resulting catchment discharge. However, channel storage is generally absent, or of minor influence, in small agricultural catchments. Most mathematical models of the hydrology of such catchments have exhibited, as may be expected, a high degree of sensitivity to the overland flow depth—discharge relationship selected. As illustrated by Huggins and Monke (1966), an overestimate of discharge for a given average depth results in an unrealistically sharp and early predicted hydrograph peak.

The recent use of a "piggy-back" approach to non-point source pollution modeling, by associating pollutant detachment and transport with overland flow in existing established hydrological models, has increased the necessity for an accurate predictive method for the overland flow detention—discharge relationship. This relationship determines flow velocity, and as detachment and transport of soil particles and other pollutant material has generally been found to be proportional to a power of flow velocity greater than unity, resultant pollutant concentration—time curves exhibit extreme sensitivity to predicted flow.

In general, a period of calibration consisting of at least one full year of gaged record must be used to establish values of non-measurable parameters in a hydrologic model for a given catchment. These parameters may be determined by trial-and-error or by an optimizing technique such as that used by James (1970) for a version of the Stanford Watershed Model. The remaining period of gaged record, used for model verification illustrates, or by some statistical measure quantifies, the model's applicability to the selected catchment.

The true test of any hydrologic model, however, is the confidence with which it may be applied to an ungaged catchment. In this sense, parameters have to be estimated and parameters in the overland flow equation selected are among the most sensitive. Rainfall simulator tests on small field plots and hydrological models have, moreover, indicated that a wide variation in hydraulic roughness occurs on natural land surfaces. To enable models to be used confidently for predictive purposes on ungaged catchments, it is essential that a physical measure of the micro-topography be related to the hydraulic roughness.

Theory

The most common depth-discharge relationships used in hydrologic models are the classical equations of laminar and turbulent hydraulics applied to wide, open channels.

Laminar Flow. The laminar flow equation, for conditions under which viscosity is dominant, may be derived by considering a depth of flow, y_x, as shown in Fig. 5.10, in which water molecules are assumed to flow parallel to the bed surface. At a distance, y_x, from the bed surface the relationship between the dynamic viscosity, μ, and the shear stress, τ, is given by Newton's law of viscosity, viz.,

$$\tau = \mu \frac{dv_x}{dy_x}. \dots\dots\dots\dots\dots\dots\dots\dots\dots\dots\dots [5.30]$$

in which v_x is the velocity at depth y_x.

Along the XX' plane the shear stress is equal to the gravitational force of the overlying water and, defining the unit force of water as w, and the bed slope as 1 in S_o,

$$\mu \frac{dv_x}{dy_x} = \tau = w(y - y_x)S_o \dots\dots\dots\dots\dots\dots\dots\dots\dots\dots [5.31]$$

If w is replaced by the product of the density of water, p, and the gravitational constant, g, and introducing the kinematic viscosity, $v = \mu/p$, equation [5.31] may be rewritten as

$$dv_x = \left| \frac{gS_o}{v} \right| (y - y_x)\, dy_x \dots\dots\dots\dots\dots\dots\dots\dots\dots [5.32]$$

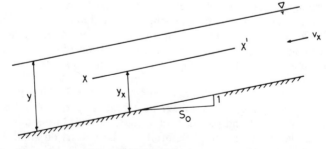

FIG. 5.10 Laminar flow.

Integrating the velocity, v_x, on the **XX'** plane a distance y_x above the surface gives

$$v_x = \left| \frac{gS_oy}{\nu} \right| \left| y - \frac{y_x}{2} \right| \dots \dots \dots \dots \dots \dots \dots \dots \dots \dots \dots \dots \dots [5.33]$$

The average flow velocity is evaluated by summing the velocity on each plane over the depth of flow and dividing by the total flow depth, i.e.,

$$v = \frac{1}{y} \int_0^y \left| gS_o \frac{y_x}{\nu} \right| \left| y \frac{y_x}{2} \right| dy_x = \frac{gS_oy^2}{3\nu} \dots \dots \dots \dots \dots \dots \dots [5.34]$$

The discharge per unit width, Q, then is the product of the average velocity and depth of flow, or

$$Q = \left| \frac{gS_o}{3\nu} \right| y^3 \dots \dots \dots \dots \dots \dots \dots \dots \dots \dots \dots \dots \dots \dots [5.35]$$

For uniform flow as described above, the water surface is parallel to the bed slope and the friction slope is therefore equal to the bed slope, i.e. $S_f = S_o$. When used under nonuniform flow conditions, this is not true and the slope term in the above equations is the friction slope, S_f.

Turbulent Flow. An increase in surface roughness and depth of flow tend to produce eddying and the flow then changes from planar to turbulent. Surface roughness tends to increase in dominance as the flow regime passes through the transitional region of Reynold's number. The depth-discharge relationship in the turbulent flow regime is commonly defined by the Chezy, Darcy-Wiesbach or Manning equations. For a unit flow width in a wide, open channel having a hydraulic radius equal to the flow depth, these are respectively:

$$Q = C \sqrt{S_f} \, y^{3/2} \dots \dots \dots \dots \dots \dots \dots \dots \dots \dots \dots \dots \dots \dots [5.36]$$

$$Q = \sqrt{\frac{2gS_f}{f}} \, y^{3/2} \dots \dots \dots \dots \dots \dots \dots \dots \dots \dots \dots \dots [5.37]$$

and,

$$Q = \left| \frac{\sqrt{S_f}}{n} \right| y^{5/3} \dots \dots \dots \dots \dots \dots \dots \dots \dots \dots \dots \dots \dots [5.38]$$

The corresponding hydraulic roughness coefficients are C, f and n.

Discussion. In generalized form, the laminar and turbulent flow equations, equations [5.35] through [5.38], may be written as,

$$Q = X_1 S_f^{Y_1} y^m \dots\dots\dots\dots\dots\dots\dots\dots\dots\dots\dots\dots\dots\dots\dots [5.39]$$

in which X_1, Y_1 and m are parameters. A simpler form often used in the development of the kinematic flow theory combines $X_1 S_f$ into a single parameter, α, as given by equation [5.5].

Equation [5.39] is not amenable to direct evaluation under natural surface conditions since the friction slope is implicitly defined by the equation and the local depth, y, varies with bed surface irregularities. The approach normally adopted is to replace the local depth, y, with a measurable average depth, d (water volume per unit area), and the friction slope, S_f, with the known surface slope, S_o. Changing those variables and combining the terms $X_1 S_o^{Y_1} = K$ yields:

$$Q = K d^m \dots\dots\dots\dots\dots\dots\dots\dots\dots\dots\dots\dots\dots\dots\dots\dots\dots\dots [5.40]$$

Horton (1938) suggested the use of equation [5.40] in analyzing results of field plot experiments for both natural and simulated rainfall-runoff. The values of K and "m" were obtained from a log-log plot of Q against d. Horton found the value of m to generally be about 2; a condition representing a mixture of laminar and turbulent flow. This graphical technique was used extensively for both field plots (Izzard, 1942 and Hicks, 1944) and small agricultural and urban catchments (Sharp and Holtan, 1942 and Horner and Jens, 1943). An average value of 2 for the parameter m was generally substantiated for a wide range of surfaces from asphalt to short grass.

A value of 2 for m has great appeal because of its simplicity in utilizing the general equation (equation [5.40]) in theoretical analyses and in repeated computations in digital computer models. However, the value of K has been found to have a wide variation. This parameter incorporates effects of surface slope, surface form and grain roughness as well as many other undefined factors of influence.

Laboratory Studies

As natural land surfaces exhibit a continually changing surface form due to erosion and deposition, and are subject to only indirectly estimable infiltration losses, laboratory studies have been conducted on "fixed" impervious surfaces to attempt to relate physical form with shallow flow hydraulic roughness under controlled and accurately measurable conditions.

Tests conducted on the rough side of a hardboard surface have indicated that Manning's "n" tended to increase with a decrease in depth (Woo, 1956 and Harbaugh and Chow, 1967). Chow (1959) also noted that measurements in river channels indicated the same trend.

In an attempt to relate hydraulic roughness to a measureable topographic parameter, a series of artificially created, but full-size prototype "natural" surfaces were tested on a 4.2 m square bed laboratory rainfall simulator (Das, 1970; Kundu, 1971; Burney and Huggins, 1973 and Pod-

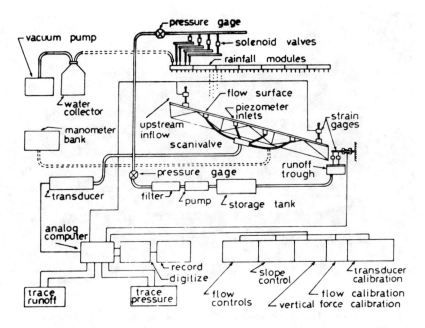

FIG. 5.11 Purdue laboratory rainfall simulator—overland flow table (Kundu, 1971).

more, 1975). As shown in Fig. 5.11, the equipment consisted primarily of an instantaneous on-off rainfall generator, an upslope surface flow generator and instrumentation to control the operation and record the flow-surface mass (dead load plus retention and detention) and the runoff rate. The flow surface could be inclined on any slope between 0 and 5 percent. Rainfall rates could be varied in 13 mm/h increments between 0 and 190 mm/h, and the upslope flow rate could be varied from 0 to 460 mm/h. Greater detail on the design and operation is given by Das (1970) and Kundu (1971).

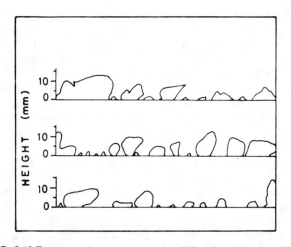

FIG. 5.12 Representative cross-sections on K3 surface (Kundu, 1971).

FIG. 5.13 Naturally eroded surface B3 (Burney and Huggins, 1973).

Surfaces Tested. A variety of artificially created surface roughness conditions were generated to simulate roughness of the order of those that occur under natural field conditions. These included three combinations of stone sizes glued to a flat bed surface to produce uniform-type roughnesses (surfaces K1 — K3; Das, 1970 and Kundu, 1971) and three erosion patterns of varying grain roughness and rill development formed in an initially leveled sand bed (surfaces B3, B4 and T1; Burney and Huggins, 1973 and Podmore, 1975). Examples of the types of roughness represented by these two categories are shown in Figs. 5.12 and 5.13. Foster (1975), using similar laboratory facilities, studied a surface, F1, having a single dominant rill.

Physical Surface Measurements. Measurements of the microtopography of field surfaces have been recorded to obtain quantitative physical data relating to tillage effectiveness (Kuipers, 1957, Burwell et al, 1963 and Currence and Lovely, 1970), vibration in off-road vehicles, depression storage (Huggins and Monke, 1966 and Mitchell, 1970) and overland flow roughness (Heermann et al, 1969 and Merva et al, 1970). The spacing of elevation readings has in turn reflected the intended use. However, much of the instrumentation and methods of analysis developed for other purposes may be selectively applied to quantifying surface roughness for hydraulic applications.

A board with sliding probe needles mounted at evenly spaced intervals has proved to be a single and effective instrument. Huggins and Monke (1966) inserted a sheet of thin metal into plowed land and sprayed paint on the exposed section to obtain an indirectly measurable cross-section of the surface microtopography. Indirect measurements of a flume bed (Squarer, 1968) and a river bed (Annambhotla, 1969) have been obtaned at spacings down to 6 mm by using Sonar. Laboratory micro-relief meters having an

FIG. 5.14 Micro-relief meter (Burney and Huggins, 1973).

automated moving probe have been constructed by Burney and Huggins (1973), Fig. 5.14, to record elevation readings at 2.5 mm intervals over 0.6 m square sample areas, and by Podmore (1975) to record at spacings as small as 0.25 mm intervals on a 1.8 m line.

Analysis of Physical Surface Measurements. A commonly used measure quantifying the degree of roughness of a natural surface is the variance, or standard error, of elevation readings. However, as stated by Merva et al (1970), such a parameter does not account for the configuration of the surface, i.e. whether the surface is smooth with wide, shallow rills or rough with closely spaced gravel particles. Discrete readings on two such differing surfaces may conceivably result in the same variance but those surfaces may also be expected to result in differing hydraulic responses.

Spectral analysis of elevations facilitates a breakdown of the variance into components contributed by specific frequencies over the surface area. The resultant plot of spectral power against frequency, as illustrated in Fig. 5.15, indicates the nature of the surface configuration. A corrugated surface, for example, would have a single spike at the frequency of the corrugations indicating that the variance is accounted for by a single sine wave of this frequency. The variance is twice the area under the positive frequency section of the spectral curve (the mathematical analysis also produces a mirror image, negative frequency curve). Consequently, an advocated parameter for characterizing the surface has been average wavelength.

Burney and Huggins (1973) recorded two-dimensional elevation readings at six sample positions on surface B3 and at three positions on surface B4. The elevation readings from each of these sample areas were subjected to two-dimensional spectral analyses in which the variance was distributed over multi-directional frequencies. The resultant elliptical contour plots, an example of which is shown in Fig. 5.15, provided considerable

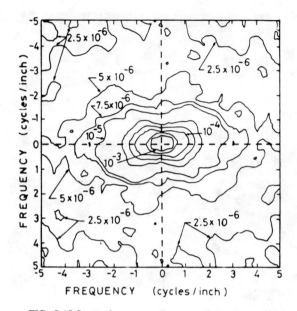

FIG. 5.15 Spectral contours (Burney and Huggins, 1973).

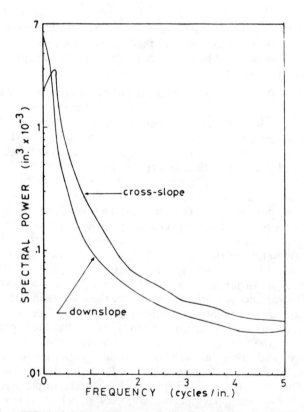

FIG. 5.16 Collapsed line spectra (Burney and Huggins, 1973).

detail about the nature of the sample areas but could not readily be condensed to provide a single defining parameter which could be related to hydraulic roughness. Averaged line spectra, as shown in Fig. 5.16 were obtained by summing on the up-slope and cross-slope axes.

Podmore (1975) obtained line spectra for elevation readings taken across the full width of the B4 and T1 surfaces. Six cross-slope and three downslope sets of readings were made on each surface. He fitted the equation:

$$S_p = \gamma f_s^{\eta} \qquad\qquad\qquad\qquad\qquad\qquad\qquad\qquad\qquad [5.41]$$

to each of the resultant spectra. In equation [5.41], S_p is the spectral power, f_s the frequency and γ and η surface characterizing parameters. Correlation coefficients in excess of 0.9 were obtained. However, the value of η obtained was approximately -2, indicating a strong randomness for all profiles. Surface T1 and the cross-slope spectra for both surfaces B4 and T1 exhibited higher η-values indicating a steeper spectrum, or larger average wavelength. However, considerable variation existed between sample areas.

Podmore also analyzed his surface elevation data by an amplitude—frequency distribution concept developed by Brickman et al. (1971) to analyze road profile data in relation to riding comfort. While spectral analysis indicates only average roughness at a particular frequency, amplitide—frequency analysis produces a joint probability table of "events" occurring in finite intervals of amplitude and frequency. An "event" is defined as the occurrence of two points of equal elevation, the amplitude then being the elevation deviation from the mean and the frequency being the inverse of twice the separation distance. A typical tabulation is presented in Fig. 5.17. Amplitude plots were made by summing across the frequencies and indicated clearly the presence of localized rilling.

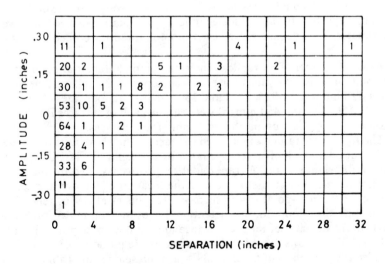

FIG. 5.17 Amplitude-separation distribution for surface T1 (Huggins et al., 1976).

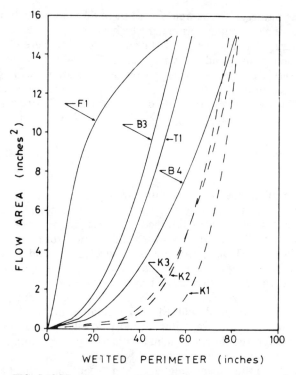

FIG. 5.18 Mean area to wetted perimeter on cross-sections of surfaces (Huggins et al., 1976).

The validity of the assumption of overland flow being equivalent to flow in a wide, open channel with a hydraulic radius equal to the depth was also investigated by Podmore. The resulting plot is shown in Fig. 5.18. Surfaces K1, K2 and K3, having increasing sand and gravel roughness, exhibited an increasing departure from the wide channel approximation of a constant wetted perimeter. This departure was even more marked for eroded surfaces.

Hydraulic Tests. Two replications of a complete factorial set of treatment combinations consisting of five surface slopes (1, 2, 3, 4 and 5 percent), four rainfall intensities (0, 50, 100 and 150 mm/h) and four rates of up-slope inflow (0, 150, 300 and 450 mm/h) were run on each of surfaces B3, B4 and T1. Similar tests were run on the remaining four surfaces.

The full hydrograph was recorded for each of the above tests and steady state detention and runoff rates evaluated by averaging the last 20 readings of this equilibrium section. A trapezoidal shape was assumed for the steady state flow profile, i.e. an assumption of the location of the average surface detention at the mid-point of the surface. Huggins et al (1976) related the discharge at this point to the detention by using non-linear regression analysis to fit the data set for each surface to a number of depth—discharge equations. The results for Manning's equation (equation [5.38]) and the generalized equation (equation [5.39]) are presented in Table 5.1 for discharge, Q, in units of cumecs/m width, detention, d, in units of cu.m/sq.m surface area and bed slope, S_o, in units of m/m.

TABLE 5.1. OPTIMIZED PARAMETERS IN THE MANNING
AND GENERALIZED EQUATIONS (HUGGINS ET AL, 1976)

Surface	Manning's equation		General regression equation			
	n	Correlation coefficient (r^2)	X_1	Y_1	m	Correlation coefficient (r^2)
K1	0.036	0.990	107.	1.95	0.465	0.998
K2	0.054	0.994	16.	1.68	0.465	0.998
K3	0.064	0.979	104.	2.09	0.478	0.996
B3	0.024	0.956	525.	1.81	0.939	0.996
B4	0.030	0.986	68.	1.77	0.520	0.993
T1	0.027	0.989	31.	1.57	0.537	0.992
F1	0.024	0.989	47.	1.38	0.715	0.996

Conclusions

The shallow flow experiments discussed above were carried out over a range of surfaces from rough stones to a large rill. Analyses of the hydraulic data resulted in a wide variation in parameters required to regress a generalized stage-discharge equation (equation [5.40]). Moreover, regression analyses of subsets for each surface, including those with no rainfall, gave little deviation from parameter values presented in Table 1, indicating a remarkable consistency for each surface as evidenced by high correlation coefficients (greater than 0.99). However, no consistency emerged between hydraulic parameter values and physical form coefficients for the surfaces tested. Discharge tended to be proportional to depth to a power varying around the Manning equation value of 1.67.

A multi-parameter equation such as equation [5.40] is necessary as an experimental tool to attempt to quantify physical surface effects. However, it would appear that parameters are not independent and, in addition, tend to vary widely from surface to surface. When Manning's equation was fitted to the same data, correlation coefficients dropped but, as shown in Table 5.1, were still very high. While a multi-parameter equation will provide a better fit for experimentally measured data, the problem in practical application is one of parameter estimation. Manning's equation, having only one parameter to estimate, viz. the hydraulic roughness "n", is currently as suitable as any other means for characterizing the depth-discharge relationship in shallow overland flow although it should be recognized that the relationship is no more than an approximation.

Field values of Manning's "n" have varied widely. No direct measurement of flow depth is feasible and inaccuracies in analysis of rainfall simulator experiments could account for a large portion of variations reported. Relatively smooth fallow surfaces have generally been reported as having "n" values between 0.030 and 0.100, row crops between 0.07 and 0.400 and broadcast crops between 0.040 and 0.900.

SIMULATING SURFACE RUNOFF WITH LUMPED MODELS

A lumped approach to the modeling of surface runoff considers the catchment as a spatially singular entity which transforms rainfall excess into an outflow hydrograph. This approach ranges from the use of a mathematical transfer function, or "black-box" approach, to a modeling of the detailed interrelationship of processes using area-weighted average values for hydrologically significant phenomena.

The regularly shaped hydrographs of large catchments are often amendable to the fitting of mathematical functions, i.e. identification of the system's transfer function. However, the modulating influence (reservoir effect) of channel storage diminishes rapidly with a decrease in catchment size and overland flow assumes an ever increasing influence on the form of the outflow hydrograph. Typical agricultural catchments of concern are under 10 km² in area and respond rapidly to overland flow variations. Hydrographs tend to be "noisy", i.e. reflecting multiple peaks of the rainfall hyetograph in their outputs. Thus, these smaller watersheds are much less amenable to transfer function analysis.

The several different types of lumped mathematical models all share one significant strength, computational efficiency. Thus despite difficulties in applying certain of the methodologies to small catchments and even though they often yield less comprehensive information concerning watershed behavior, they represent one of the most important classes of models. Furthermore, the vast majority of field tested models come under this category.

Unit Hydrograph Theory

The selection, analysis and use of recorded hydrographs for direct simulation purposes are reflected in variations of the unit hydrograph technique. This technique, which assumes a linearity of the transfer function, is computationally attractive and often sufficiently accurate. Unit hydrograph techniques may be applied to synthesize hydrographs either from recorded rainfall events or from specific return period storms extracted from intensity-duration-return period curves and hypothetical time distribution patterns.

Catchments having appreciable channel storge effects, or subjected to short duration, high intensity rainfall, give rise to well-formed skewed bell-shaped flood hydrographs. For a given catchment the duration of the hydrograph tends to be relatively constant and independent of the storm duration. Peak flows tend to be proportional to the flow volume in excess of the base flow.

Recognizing the above characteristics of flood hydrographs, Sherman (1932) proposed the basis for the unit hydrograph theory. The unit hydrograph is defined as the hydrograph of direct runoff (runoff less baseflow) resulting from 1 unit of rainfall excess falling uniformly over the basin at a constant rate during a specified period of time.

Application of this technique presupposes five assumptions, viz.:

1   Rainfall is spatially uniform over the drainage basin during the specified time period.

2   The rainfall rate is constant.

3   The time base of the hydrograph of direct runoff is constant.

4   Discharge at any given time, for the same time base, is directly proportional to the total amount of direct runoff.

5   The hydrograph reflects all combined physical characteristics of the given drainage basin.

In applying the technique, events selected for generation of the characteristic unit hydrograph should be single peak hydrographs resulting from widespread, high intensity storms of short duration. This is particularly necessary for smaller catchments whose hydrographs tend to replicate variations in rainfall intensity. In addition, the rainfall duration must not exceed the time of concentraion of the catchment. With regard to assumptions inplicit in the theory, as set out above, the following general comments are germane to each condition in the order given:

1   In order to ensure reasonably uniform spatial distribution of rainfall, the catchment should not be too large. If the area exceeds approximately 5,000 km², it should be sub-divided into sub-basins with channel routing.

2   In order to satisfy the requirement of constant rainfall intensity, the rainfall duration should be short. As will be illustrated later, this assumption is not necessary for the instantaneous unit hydrograph.

3   The base time of the direct runoff hydrograph is usually unknown and depends on the method of base flow separation used.

4   The proportionality of ordinates of the direct runoff hydrograph assumes the principle of linearity or superposition, i.e. that excess rainfall effects are additive.

5   The assumption that the hydrograph reflects the influence of catchment characteristics assumes a time invariance of the catchment. This means that the catchment is always assumed to behave in the same manner to a given rainfall event, independent of season, prior rainfall or, in the longer term, any hydrologically significant physical modifications. This assumption is particularly restrictive in small agricultural catchments.

Basic Unit Hydrograph. Having selected a recorded discharge hydrograph and the concomitant rainfall hyetograph for analysis, it is necessary to separate out the rainfall excess hyetograph and the direct runoff hydrograph prior to establishing the unit hydrograph. No exact method for accomplishing either of these functions exists since the separate components are unknown. However, a multiplicity of approximation methods have been proposed, based to varying degrees on known physical relationships. Rainfall excess represents the fraction of rainfall which gives rise to the direct runoff hydrograph by either overland flow or interflow. In general, assuming the catchment in question is neither impervious nor saturated, this fraction will increase during the storm as the infiltration capacity of the soil decreases, as shown in Fig. 5.19.

Methods used to determine the rainfall loss curve include the threshold concept, infiltration curves and functional relationships between accumulated rainfall and runoff:

1   The threshold concept envisages the catchment surface as a storage reservoir having a maximum soil moisture storage, S. As evapotranspiration depletes its reservoir, a deficit, d, having a maximum value of S develops. This deficit is decreased by infiltration from rainfall. Evapotranspiration is assumed to occur at a rate less than the potential rate and a typical assumption is,

$$E_a = \left| \frac{S - d}{S} \right| E_p \dots \dots \dots [5.42]$$

in which, E_a is actual evapotranspiration, E_p is potential evapotranspiration and (S - d) represents the available moisture, An assumption is required to define the manner in which the soil moisture is replenished. The common assumption that excess rainfall does not start until the deficit, d, is satisfied

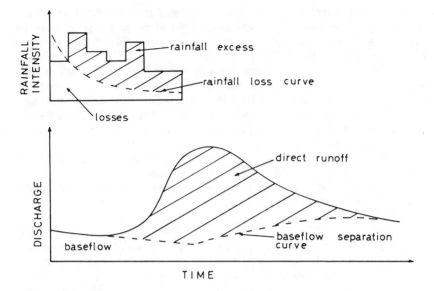

FIG. 5.19 Excess rainfall and direct runoff separation.

and that all following rainfall is excess rainfall, creates an unrealistic vertical sub-division of the hyetograph.

In order to more closely reproduce the decay loss curve, the conceptualized soil storage model may be considered to be subdivided both vertically and by soil series. Each soil type then has several levels of storage with each level representing a soil horizon. Assumptions usually made are that each reservoir is depleted according to equation [5.42] with succeedingly lower level reservoirs maintaining full storage until the soil horizon immediately above is fully depleted. During replenishment by rainfall each soil type is satisfied at a different time, resulting in a step function rainfall loss curve.

2   The infiltration approach to positioning the rainfall loss curve assumes the curve to be that of an average basin infiltration capacity curve. While this approach produces the desired shape, and is the most theoretically sound, the problem in application is the estimation of relevant parameters in the infiltration equation adopted and the position of the curve following periods during which rainfall intensity is less than infiltration capacity.

3   Among the many functional relationships proposed to predict rainfall excess, the most commonly used is that of the U.S. Soil Conservation Service. This method is described in greater detail below in the section on the SCS triangular hydrograph procedure.

While the latter method provides the most definitive means for separating out excess rainfall, it may be noted that, in common with many other suggested methods (the infiltration curve approach is an exception), the time distribution of the rainfall is not considered. Both a high and a low intensity rainfall of the same depth is predicted to produce the same volume of excess rainfall, contrary to the known time dependence of rainfall losses.

A recorded hydrograph results from combined effects of surface runoff, interflow and groundwater flow. Since groundwater, or baseflow, substantially lags surface flow, produces a non-resultant additive effect and causes a long exponential tail on the recession curve beyond the time period of interest, it must necessarily be separated out. The remaining hydrograph is the direct runoff hydrograph and reflects effects of overland flow and quick-return interflow.

A baseflow separation line is drawn on the hydrograph from the point of upturn on the rising limb to a point on the recession curve. In general, the initial point is easily identified. However, both the shape of the separation curve and the ending point on the hydrograph recession limb are speculative. Commonly used shapes are a slightly rising straight line or a continuation of the initial baseflow line to a point below the hydrograph peak, followed by an S curve to join the recession curve asymptotically. A technique in which a master curve of baseflow recession is used to position the end point of the separation line is described in detail by Wilson (1974). Since the volume of excess rainfall is, by definition, equal to the volume of direct runoff, some adjustments will be required in the locations of the rainfall and hydrograph separation curves derived by the estimation techniques used.

Finally, a basic unit hydrograph may be simply produced by dividing ordinates of the direct runoff hydrograph by the runoff depth (area under the direct runoff hydrograph expressed as an equivalent catchment depth).

It is desirable that more than one unit hydrograph be derived for a catchment in order that a more typical average unit hydrograph may be developed for application. Methods used to average unit hydrographs of the

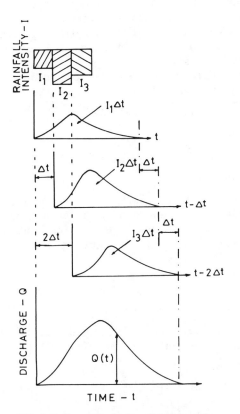

FIG. 5.20 Composite basic unit hydrograph.

same time base and to produce unit hydrographs of different time bases for differing rainfall durations are described by Chow (1964) and Wilson (1974) in addition to many other texts and are not reproduced here.

In applying the basic unit hydrograph technique to produce composite direct runoff hydrographs from excess rainfall hyetographs the linearity principle is utilized. As shown in Fig. 5.20, each block of excess rainfall is assumed to produce its own direct runoff hydrograph; summation of ordinates of separate hydrographs produces a composite hydrograph.

If $u(\Delta t, t)$ represents the ordinate of the unit hydrograph for a rainfall duration of Δt at any time, t, then by superposition the ordinate for a block of rainfall of intensity I for a time t is $u(\Delta t, t)$ I Δt. Treating each block of rainfall in Fig. 5.20 as a separate event, i.e. displacing the direct runoff hydrographs, the ordinates of the composite direct runoff hydrograph are,

$$Q(t) = \sum_{i=1}^{n} u \left| \Delta t, t - (i-1)\Delta t \right| I_i \Delta t \dots \dots \dots \dots \dots \dots \dots [5.43]$$

Instantaneous Unit Hydrograph (IUH). If the rainfall blocks in the composite hydrograph shown in the previous section are imagined to be continually subdivided, the duration of each sub-block will approach zero. Each block may then be conceived as an instantaneous application of excess rainfall to the catchment. The resulting hydrograph produced by each rainfall pulse is known as the instantaneous hydrograph, or more commonly for a unit depth of excess rainfall, the IUH. The IUH approach eliminates the dependence of the unit hydrograph on the rainfall duration and is better suited to theoretical analyses.

Utilizing the IUH technique, the composite discretely-derived hydrograph shown in Fig. 5.20 is replaced by the functionally-derived hydrograph in Fig. 5.21. In the limit equation [5.43] becomes,

$$Q(t) = \int_{0}^{t' \leqslant t_0} u(t - \tau) \, I(\tau) \, d\tau \dots \dots \dots \dots \dots \dots \dots \dots \dots [5.44]$$

The integral in equation [5.44] is known as the convolution, or Duhamel, integral and is common to all linear systems. The expression $u(t - \tau)$ is the kernel function and $I(\tau)$ is the input function. By definition, the integral under the curve is equal to unity, i.e.

$$\int_{0}^{\infty} u(t) \, dt = 1 \dots \dots \dots \dots \dots \dots \dots \dots \dots \text{ from equation } [5.44]$$

In addition, the first moment of the IUH is equal to the time lag, t_L (time between the centroids of the rainfall and runoff curves), i.e.,

$$\int_{0}^{\infty} u(t) \, t \, dt = t_L \dots \dots \dots \dots \dots \dots \dots \dots \dots \dots \dots [5.45]$$

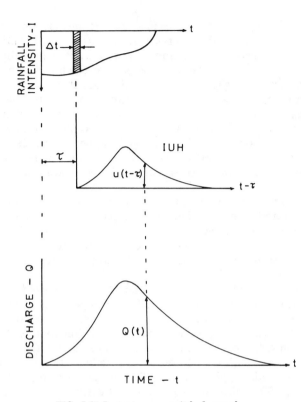

FIG. 5.21 Instantaneous unit hydrograph.

In applying the IUH technique it is necessary to first derive the IUH from a given input and associated output (system identification), after which the IUH may be used to predict output for given excess rainfall input functions (system prediction). Methods used include application of orthogonal functions (Fourier series and Lagurre functions), Laplace transforms, autocorrelation techniques and direct discrete numerical convolution (Delleur, 1971). Some of these techniques are described by Chow (1964) and by Delleur and Rao (1971).

Because of the difficulty of applying any of the above techniques prior to the development and current wide-spread application of relevant digital computer programs, conceptual models were developed for generating catchment IUHs. Although these models are no longer necessary in this context, they lead naturally to a consideration of spatial as well as temporal influences on the direct runoff hydrograph and are presented later.

SCS (Triangular) Synthetic Hydrograph

For many catchments, rainfall and concomitant runoff recordings do not exist, or the small size of the catchment makes difficult the application of unit hydrograph techniques described above. Chow (1964) and Wilson (1974) provide detailed descriptions for deriving synthetic unit hydrographs from catchment physiographic characteristics for use in such cases. In addition, Schwab, et al (1981) illustrate a "typical" dimensionless unit hydrograph derived from unit hydrographs of a large variety of catchments.

A more commonly used practice in small catchments is one developed by the U.S. Soil Conservation Service which uses a triangular shaped hydrograph to approximate the unit hydrograph. It is probably the most widely used of currently available methods for predicting a complete runoff hydrograph from ungaged agricultural watersheds. The triangular hydrograph procedure per se, which constitutes the flow routing portion of the analysis, is based upon the assumption that a time distribution of the manner in which storm rainfall is translated into rainfall excess, i.e. surface runoff volume, is available. Thus, normal application procedures involve first applying a Direct Runoff analysis, also developed by the Soil Conservation Service, to obtain this necessary direct runoff distribution.

Direct Runoff Analaysis. This model starts with total precipitation from a storm event and translates that rainfall, according to empirical relationships obtained from multiple correlation analyses, into a runoff volume. The method attempts to account for effects of: (a) total precipitation, (b) an initial rainfall abstraction, (c) a time-variable infiltration rate, and (d) antecedent soil moisture.

In terms of those hydrologic components defined above for the conceptual hydrologic model, the Direct Runoff analysis attempts to account for an initial rainfall abstration which is a combination of interception storage, infiltration before runoff begins, and surface retention volume. In addition, the infiltration rate during a storm event has been accounted for by using a function, never explicitly defined, which is variable with respect to time and becomes asymptotic to zero as rainfall continues for an indefinitely long period of time. The third, and heretofore not defined, concept employed is called the maximum potential difference between runoff and precipitation. This is an attempt to quantify the influence of antecedent moisture on the predicted runoff volume from a particular storm event. This factor is also a function of the average type of soil present throughout a watershed as well as vegetal cover and cultural practices present in that catchment.

The actual manner in which these various factors have been quantified is essentially empirical, as are all multiple correlation techniques. Data from all over the United States was assembled from a variety of gaged watersheds and were correlated with various physical factors of those watersheds that relate to the runoff volume that occurred during gaged events. This unpublished data came primarily from watersheds which might be classified as medium to large catchments (from several square kilometers up to several scores of square kilometers). Furthermore, storms included were generally of fairly long duration. This means substantial errors might be expected in predictions of runoff volume from brief thundershower type events on small areas.

Based on trends observed in the collected data, the basic relationship developed to translate precipatation into rainfall excess (direct runoff volume) is:

$$\frac{P - I_a - Q}{S} = \frac{Q}{P - I_a} \dotfill [5.46]$$

where:

P = is the precipitation from the storm being analyzed,

I_a = is the abstraction corresponding to losses from a combination of early infiltration, interception and surface retention volume,

Q = is the total volume of runoff, the rainfall excess, from the event, and

S = is the maximum potential difference between P and Q.

A close examination of the left-hand-side of the equation [5.46] indicates that, conceptually, it is a ratio between actual and potential difference between precipitation and runoff. P minus I_a minus Q is the actual difference in potential runoff at a given instant and S is the maximum potential difference that will occur by the end of the storm. This ratio is equated to the right-hand-side which is the ratio between the actual amount of runoff, Q, that has occurred at any given time and the maximum potential amount of runoff that can occur. The particular hypothesis of an equality between these two rations can be justified only on an empirical basis.

Accepting the previous ratio relationship on the basis of empirical trends, an equation can be obtained which translates precipitation directly into runoff volume, Q. When $P < I_a$, Q = 0; otherwise, it is given by:

$$Q = \frac{(P - I_a)^2}{P - I_a + S} \dots\dots\dots\dots\dots\dots\dots\dots\dots\dots\dots\dots\dots\dots\dots\dots [5.47]$$

A further empirical evaluation was made on the basis of trends in the data base. The initial abstraction value, I_a, was found to correlate with S. The resulting coefficient value recommended is $I_a = 0.2S$.

Application of the Direct Runoff analysis to a particular catchment involves the use of several tables which relate physical watershed characteristics such as soil type, vegetation and antecedent moisture conditions to the parameter S (normally this is done through an indirect parameter called the curve number). Comprehensive tables suitable for design analysis may be found in several references, Design of Small Dams (1972) and Schwab, et al (1981). The influence of spatial variability in watershed characteristics is normally accounted for by an area-weighted average of curve number values applicable to uniform sub-regions of the entire catchment.

In order to obtain a simulated runoff hydrograph it is necessary to somehow include the element of time, both from the standpoint of precipitation input and hydraulic transport, into the runoff analysis. The correlation approach which produced equation [5.46] was based on relating total precipitation from a given storm to the total resulting runoff. Nevertheless, a plausible extension of that relationship was made by assuming it could also be used to predict the time distribution of runoff by applying it on a continuous basis to the rainfall hyetograph, i.e. inferring that the amount of runoff resulting from precipitation occurring prior to any given point in time was obtainable by substituting P as a function of time into equation [5.47].

Time of Concentration. With a model now defined to characterize translation of precipitation as a function of time into rainfall excess, the only remaining process requiring characterization in order to simulate a runoff hydrograph concerns time lags associated with water flowing to the outlet. While this could theoretically be done by using rigorous hydrodynamic equations, the application of these boundary-value dependent equations to a natural watershed with its infinite flow patterns is clearly impractical. Instead, a single, conceptually simple parameter was introduced for the purpose of integrating all flow induced time delays. That parameter was the time of concentration, the time for runoff from the hydrologically most remote point in the watershed to flow to the outlet.

While a time of concentration parameter is conceptually straightforward, the assignment of a numeric value to a term which encompasses so many complex physical conditions of a watershed is subject to substantial inaccuracies. One of the first, and still most widely used, relationships proposed for use with ungaged watersheds was developed primarily for flow in well defined channels by C. E. Ramser (1927).

$$T_C = 0.02 L_C^{0.77} S_C^{-0.385} \quad \dotfill \quad [5.48]$$

where:
T_c = time of concentration, min
L_c = length of channel reach, m
S_c = average slope of channel reach, m/m.
This relationship tends to correlate poorly with gaged runoff measurements of the time of concentration for very small (less than 5 sq. km.) catchments. This result should be expected since small catchments are dominated by overland (shallow) flow conditions rather than having a well defined network of channels.

Kerby (1959) developed a flow travel time based upon an overland flow equation:

$$T_C = \left| \frac{2.2 n L_O}{\sqrt{S_O}} \right|^{0.467} \quad \dotfill \quad [5.49]$$

where:
L_o = length of overland flow, m
S_o = slope along that path, m/m
n = Manning-type roughness coefficient
When applied on a watershed scale, this overland flow phase effectively has a maximum travel time because erosion experiments and other field and laboratory investigations have consistently shown that oveland flow conditions can seldom be maintained for a distance longer than 100-150 meters.

Almost all surface runoff starts out not as channel flow, but as shallow flow over a surface. Thus, the equation recommended to compute a time of concentration is the sum of equations [5.48] and [5.49], namely:

$$T_C = 0.02 L_C^{0.77} S_C^{-0.385} + \left| \frac{2 n L_O}{\sqrt{S_O}} \right|^{0.467} \quad \dotfill \quad [5.50]$$

The second half of equation [5.50] has a maximum value regardless of watershed size because of the upper limits specified for L_o. On the other hand, as the size of a watershed increases the maximum length of channel flow, L_c,

TABLE 5.2. OVERLAND FLOW
ROUGHNESS COEFFICIENTS
(FROM W. S. KERBY)

Surface	n
Smooth, impervious surface	0.02
Smooth, bare packed soil	0.10
Poor grass, cultivated row crops of moderately rough bare soil	0.20
Pasture or average grass	0.40
Deciduous timberland	0.60
Timberland with deep forest litter or dense grass	0.80

tends to continually increase. This implies that, as watershed size becomes large, the channel flow portion of the time of concentration equation will dominate the overall value. Thus, the above equation is recommended for **all** watersheds since it is more appropriate for small areas and is also entirely valid for large areas.

A couple of additional precautions relative to computing T_c values for actual watersheds should be mentioned. First, it is necessary to determine the maximum travel time for water to move along any flow path to the outlet, not just the time of travel along the physically longest path. While these are often one and the same, for watersheds with more than one major tributary it may be necessary to calculate a travel time for more than one flow path in order to determine which has the longest travel time (because of different slopes and roughness values along each path). Secondly, it is not a correct procedure to break the channel flow reach into smaller segments and then sum the resulting travel times that could be computed by applying the channel flow part of the time of concentration equation to each channel segment. Instead, sum the total length along the channel and use the fall along the total channel length to compute the channel slope, S_c. This segmenting of a channel reach into small pieces and then adding travel times is not correct because of non-linearities in the T_c equation.

Hydrograph Development. Fig. 5-22 serves as a conceptual model of how an increment of rainfall excess is translated by a watershed's hydraulic

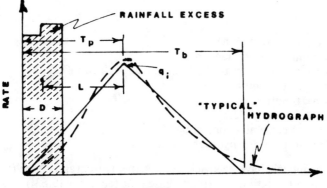

FIG. 5.22 Triangular shape approximation.

processes into an incremental runoff hydrograph. It is the basis for the SCS Triangular Hydrograph analysis procedure. This model is based upon empirical observation of how natural watersheds "typically" respond to rainfall in excess of the rate at which it can infiltrate.

Certain quantities can by defined from the triangular hydrograph based on the fact that rainfall excess must, be definition, equal runoff volume. The lag, L, is defined as the time between the centroid of the rainfall excess and the peak of the triangular unit graph of runoff. The base of this unit graph is called T_b. The runoff rate, q_i, is the peak instantaneous rate resulting from the application of rainfall excess.

Strictly on the basis of empirical relationships established from examining unpublished data from a large variety of watersheds and storms, certain correlations have been established between watershed characteristics and these three parameters. L and T_b were correlated to the time of concentration of a watershed. That data indicated the lag time, L, was approximately 0.6 of the time of concentration for many watersheds. T_b has been found experimentally to be approximately 2.67 times the time to peak, which is actually $D/2 + L$. Where gaged runoff records are available, these coefficients may be determined specifically for the watershed of interest; otherwise, the above values are recommended for ungaged catchments.

Interrelationships required to transform an incremental volume of runoff into an incremental runoff hydrograph may be summarized as:

$$L = 0.6T_c \dots \dots \dots \dots \dots \dots \dots \dots \dots \dots \dots \dots \dots \dots [5.51]$$

$$T_p = D/2 + L \dots \dots \dots \dots \dots \dots \dots \dots \dots \dots \dots \dots \dots [5.52]$$

$$T_b = 2.67T_p \dots \dots \dots \dots \dots \dots \dots \dots \dots \dots \dots \dots \dots \dots [5.53]$$

$$q_i = 16.7A \, Q/T_p \dots \dots \dots \dots \dots \dots \dots \dots \dots \dots \dots \dots \dots [5.54]$$

where:
A = watershed area, km²
D = rainfall excess period, min
L = lag time from centroid of rainfall to peak runoff, min
Q = total runoff, mm
q_i = peak runoff rate, m³/s
T_b = base time of hydrograph, min
T_c = time of concentration, min
T_p = time to peak for hydrograph, min

Once models have been selected for the hydrograph shape (triangular), time-to-peak (equation [5.52]) and base time (equation [5.53]), the peak rate of runoff may be computed. The area under the hydrograph is the volume of runoff and it must be equal to the rainfall excess. Equating these two quan-

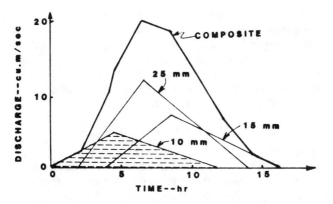

FIG. 5.23 Synthetic hydrograph development.

tities yields a relationship for the peak rate of runoff, equation [5.54]. The constant 16.7 is dependent only upon the system of units being used.

Because the time of concentration is influenced by numerous physical characteristics of a catchment, it represents, in some crude sense, an overall indication of all hydraulic transfer properties of the catchment. At least, as should be apparent from the last set of equations, that is the manner in which it is used by the Triangular Hydrograph analysis; as the single integrator and parameter which defines the manner in which direct runoff, i.e. rainfall excess, is translated into a hydrograph.

Fig. 5.23 depicts how these basic relationships are applied to yield a synthetic hydrograph predicted for any real or hypothetical storm event. The procedure begins with a distribution of rainfall excess as predicted by a Direct Runoff analysis for a known or assumed rainfall distribution. The time increment to use for representing a storm will vary with catchment size and storm duration. For the example shown in Fig. 5.23, that rainfall excess distribution is given in the upper left corner.

The rainfall excess distribution for a storm is computed according to the total accumulated precipitation distribution. From this time distribution of total runoff, incremental runoff volumes as shown for a two-hour time interval in Fig. 5.23 can be computed.

The example shown in Fig. 5.23 has 10 mm of runoff occurring from the first two hours of the precipitation event, 25 mm from precipitation occurring between hours 2-4 and 15 mm from the last two hours of the storm. The hypothetical watershed for this example is assumed to have an area of 8 sq. km. and a time of concentration of 350 min.

The triangular hydrograph shape and the previously developed relationships, equations [5.51] through [5.54], are used to approximate the manner in which an incremental volume of rainfall excess is translated into a time distribution of runoff at the watershed's outlet. This translation is shown in Fig. 5.23 for the first 10 mm of runoff as a shaded triangle. This infers that the first 10 mm of rainfall excess, if it were totally isolated, would produce the corresponding triangular runoff hydrograph at the watershed's outlet.

Runoff hydrographs that could be expected from each of the three increments of rainfall excess are shown in a correspondingly labeled manner in Fig. 5.23. The hydrograph from the second rainfall excess increment starts at time = 2 h while that for the third increment begins at time = 4 h. The total runoff hydrograph predicted to occur from the storm is then obtained by the principle of superposition, i.e. in reality an assumption that the watershed behaves as a linear system. Thus, to compute the actual predicted runoff rate at any time, at time = 5 h for example, the ordinates of the three elemental triangular hydrograph must be summed to yield a value of $1.7 + 4.7 + 8.1 = 14.5$ m³/s as the predicted runoff rate for the composite hydrograph.

COMBINATION MODELS

Lumped models which include spatial effects do so only indirectly by use of average or "effective" parameters intended to account for spatial variability of actual physical variables. Conversely, distributed models are spatially multiparametered and integrate the spatially varied runoff within a time increment. Although no clean-cut boundaries may be assigned, a class of models which include limited spatial influences, albeit generally conceptual rather than physical, exists between these two extremes. These models may be classified as combination models.

This class of combination models arose not throught the development of spatial incorporation into modeling, but rather as a consequence of the difficulty of directly deriving instantaneous unit hydrographs (IUHs). The influence of a catchment in transferring rainfall excess into direct runoff was viewed conceptually as equivalent to transferal through a series of reservoirs linked by channels. In particular, the conceptual elements of the linear reservoir and the linear channel proved to be valuable building blocks in combination model development.

Prior to a consideration of specific models and their application, it is necessary to define and elaborate on the linear reservoir and the linear channel:

1   A linear reservoir is a conceptual reservoir in which the storage, S, is directly proportional to the outflow, Q, or

$$S = KQ \dots\dots\dots\dots\dots [5.55]$$

The proportionality constant, K, is known as the storage coefficient. The difference between inflow, I, and outflow is the time rate of change in storage, i.e. by continuity,

$$I - Q = dS/dt \dots\dots\dots\dots\dots [5.56]$$

Substituting equation [5.55] in equation [5.56],

$$I - Q = K \, dQ/dt. \dots\dots\dots\dots\dots [5.57]$$

or,

$$dQ/dt + Q/K = I/K. \dots\dots\dots\dots\dots [5.58]$$

the solution for which is:

$$Q = I\left(1 - e^{-t/K}\right) \quad \dots \dots \dots \dots \dots \dots \dots \dots \dots \dots \dots [5.59]$$

It may be noted that when t approaches infinity the outflow tends to the inflow, i.e. an equilibrium condition. If the inflow stops at time $t = t_o$ at which time the outflow $Q = Q_o$, then from equation [5.57] with $I = 0$ and $\tau = t\text{-}t_o$,

$$dQ/d\tau + Q/K = 0 \quad \dots \dots \dots \dots \dots \dots \dots \dots \dots \dots \dots \dots \dots [5.60]$$

for which the solution is:

$$Q = Q_o e^{-\tau/K} \quad \dots \dots \dots \dots \dots \dots \dots \dots \dots \dots \dots \dots \dots \dots [5.61]$$

For an instantaneous inflow which fills a reservoir of storage S_o in time $t_o = 0$,

$$Q_o = S_o/K \quad \dots \dots \dots \dots \dots \dots \dots \dots \dots \dots \dots \dots \dots \dots \dots [5.62]$$

Combining equations [5.61] and [5.62], and since $\tau = t$,

$$Q = (S_o/K)e^{-t/K} \quad \dots \dots \dots \dots \dots \dots \dots \dots \dots \dots \dots \dots \dots [5.63]$$

The IUH for a linear reservoir, in which $S_o = 1$ and inflow is instantaneous, is

$$u(t) = (1/K)e^{-t/K} \quad \dots \dots \dots \dots \dots \dots \dots \dots \dots \dots \dots \dots \dots [5.64]$$

as shown in Fig. 5.24.

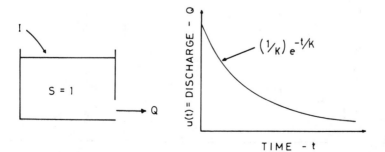

FIG. 5.24 IUH for a linear reservoir.

2 A linear channel is a fictitious channel in which the cross-sectional flow area at a section is proportional to the discharge, or

$$A = CQ \dots \dots \dots \dots \dots \dots \dots \dots \dots \dots \dots \dots \dots \dots \dots [5.65]$$

The proportionality constant, C, is known as the translation coefficient. The velocity at a section of the channel therefore remains constant, but may vary from section to section. An inflow hydrograph or excess rainfall hyetograph routed through a linear channel remains unchanged in shape and is merely translated in time, as shown in Fig. 5.25. The IUH is a Dirac-delta function (a spike of infinitesimally small time and unit area) at a time equal to the channel travel time, T, and is generally written as $\delta(t)$.

Cascaded Reservoirs

A conceptual model of a catchment having the same hydrologic response as a series of n linear reservoirs, each having the same storage coefficeint, K, was formulated by Nash (1957). This model has proved to be a simple but effective method for deriving catchment IUHs.

As shown diagrammatically in Fig. 5.26, a hydrograph-shaped outflow curve is developed and modified by successively routing the outflow from one reservoir as inflow to the next lower reservoir. Catchments having considerable impervious area, such as small urban catchments, commonly exhibit IUHs of the one or two reservoir shape due to the rapid response. Conversely, large flat agricultural catchments having little channel formation exhibit the considerable lag of a large number of reservoir routings.

Assuming instantaneous unit input into the initial reservoir, the outflow from this reservoir (previously developed as equation [5.64]) may in turn be considered as input to the second reservoir. Using τ as the variable in the convolution integral, the outflow from the second reservoir may be obtained as

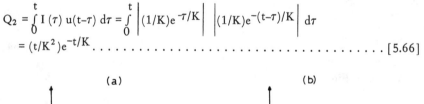

$$= (t/K^2)e^{-t/K} \dots \dots \dots \dots \dots \dots \dots \dots \dots \dots \dots \dots \dots \dots [5.66]$$

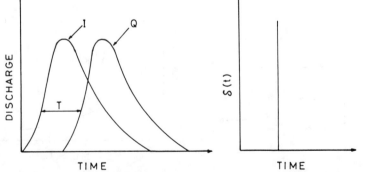

FIG. 5.25 Linear channel (a) inflow and outflow translation (b) IUH.

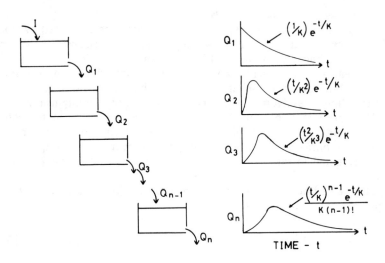

FIG. 5.26 Cascaded reservoirs of the Nash model.

For n repetitions of the above convolution, the generalized formula for the IUH of the conceptualized drainage basin may be derived as

$$Q_n = u(t) = \frac{1}{K(n-1)!}(t/K)^{n-1}e^{-t/K} \dots \dots \dots \dots [5.67]$$

in which the value n is not necessarily an integer.

The two parameters, K, the storage constant for each of the reservoirs and n, the number of reservoirs, may be simply evaluated by taking incremental moments of the excess rainfall hyetograph (ERH) and the direct runoff hydrograph (DRH), and substituting in the formulas

$$M_{D1} - M_{E1} = nK \dots \dots \dots \dots \dots \dots \dots [5.68]$$

and,

$$M_{D2} - M_{E2} = n(n+1)K^2 + 2nKM_{E1} \dots \dots \dots \dots [5.69]$$

in which:
M_{D1} = first moment of the unit area DRH
M_{D2} = second moment of the unit area DRH
M_{E1} = first moment of the unit area ERH
M_{E2} = second moment of the unit area ERH.

The value nk, as indicated by equation [5.68], represents the time lag between centroids of the rainfall and runoff curves and is also equal to the first moment of the IUH (equation [5.45]).

Cascaded Reservoirs and Channels

The general theory of these conceptual models was developed by Dooge (1964). He envisaged a catchment as being conceptually equivalent to a series of alternating linear reservoirs and linear channels. While this formulation enabled realistic catchment shape effects to be introduced, by dividing a catchment into sub-areas each having a linear channel with rainfall excess input and a linear reservoir, the general equation is not readily usable.

The approach is presented briefly below because of the many models, developed both before and following Dooge's presentation, which may be viewed as simplified modifications of his general theory. For example, Nash's model presented in the previous section is a special case of the generalized model.

The single linear reservoir equation (equation [5.58]) may be re-written in operator notation as

$$(1 + KD)Q(t) = I(t) \quad\dots\dots\dots\dots\dots\dots\dots\dots\dots\dots\dots\dots\dots [5.70]$$

in which D is the time derivative, d/dt.

For a series of n reservoirs, having storage coefficients $K, K_2, \dots, K_n$ in an upstream direction, the final outflow equation in operator form may be derived as:

$$Q_n(t) = \frac{I(t)}{\displaystyle\prod_{k=1}^{n} (1 + K_k D)} \quad\dots\dots\dots\dots\dots\dots\dots\dots\dots\dots\dots\dots\dots [5.71]$$

If now a catchment is sub-divided by isochrones (lines of equal travel time to the outlet) into a number of elemental areas, and if τ_j is the translation time between the j-th upstream elemental area and the catchment outlet, then the outflow contributed by this elementary catchment is given by:

$$Q_j(t) = \frac{\delta(t-\tau_j) I_j \, \Delta A}{\displaystyle\prod_{k=1}^{j} (1 + K_k D)} \quad\dots\dots\dots\dots\dots\dots\dots\dots\dots\dots\dots [5.72]$$

The quantity I_j represents the ratio of the rainfall intensity falling on the j-th upstream area element to the catchment average intensity, and $\delta(t-\tau_j)$ is the linear channel translation effect.

Summing over the whole catchment, the IUH is given by the equation:

$$u(t) = \frac{1}{A} \int_{0}^{A(t)} \frac{\delta\left| t - \tau(A) \right| I(A) \, dA}{\displaystyle\prod_{k=1}^{k(A)} (1 + K_k D)} \quad\dots\dots\dots\dots\dots\dots\dots\dots\dots\dots [5.73]$$

The above equation is mathematically complicated because of the integration over an area. Assuming a constant rainfall distribution, and multiplying top and bottom by $T_c d\tau$ in which T_c is the catchment time of concentration yields,

$$u(t) = \frac{1}{AT_c} \int_0^{t \leqslant T_c} \frac{\delta(t-\tau)}{k(\tau) \prod_{k=1}^{\infty} (1 + K_k D)} \frac{T_c}{d\tau} \frac{dA}{d\tau} d\tau \dots \dots \dots \dots [5.74]$$

The quantity $dA/d\tau$ represents the length of an isochrone and may be obtained from a time-area diagram, i.e. a plot of area against travel time to the outlet. The quantity $(T_c dA)/(A \, d\tau)$ is the dimensionless form of the ordinate of a time-area diagram and is commonly written as $w(\tau/T_c)$ in equation [5.74] as given by Chow (1964).

The general equation (equation [5.74]) is not directly usable. However, as previously mentioned, a number of simplified models may be related to it. Chow (1964) describes briefly some conceptual models, both linear and nonlinear, which have evolved as variations of Dooge's general model.

One particular variation of Dooge's model is the so-called improved rational method. This method utilizes Dooge's model under the assumption of no reservoir storage. Equation [5.74] then reduces to a linear channel effect for which

$$u(t) = w(\tau/T_c)/T_c \dots \dots \dots \dots \dots \dots \dots \dots \dots [5.75]$$

In the original form of the rational formula the storm is selected to have a duration equal to the catchment time of concentration. In the improved rational method the critical storm is one which maximizes the peak of the convolution of the rainfall excess and the time-area diagrams.

DISTRIBUTED WATERSHED MODELING OF SURFACE RUNOFF

Detailed system models of catchment behavior represent the opposite end of the modeling spectrum to transfer function models. Such models only became feasible with the availability of modern digital computers. Computational labor no longer precluded the adoption of algorithms requiring detailed and lengthy calculations.

A truly distributed hydrologic model would require the development and solution of a comprehensive set of partial differential hydrodynamic and porous media flow equations. The solution of such equations is highly boundary value dependent. A detailed description of the infinite variety of boundary conditions present in a natural watershed is not currently feasible. Therefore, those models that are currently classified as distributed parameter models only approximate this approach. Thus, while it is possible to view this category as simply a reduced degree of lumping, such a perspective does not adequately differentiate the fundamental differences between these two modeling philosophies.

Models can be classified as distributed when they utilize data concerning the spatial distribution of controlling parameter variations in conjunction with computational algorithms to evaluate the influence of this distribution on simulated behavior. Such models attempt to increase the accuracy of the simulation by preserving and utilizing information concerning the areal distribution of all spatially non-uniform processes characterized by the model.

This increased accuracy, if it is indeed attained, usually comes at the expense of increased computational and data preparation effort. A watershed model typical of the distributed parameter philosophy was originally outlined by Huggins and Monke (1966) and then expanded to incorporate non-point pollution processes as described in Lake and Morrison (1977). That deterministic model, identified by the acronym ANSWERS, is based upon the hypothesis that:

At every point within a watershed a fundamental relationship exists between the rate of surface runoff and those hydrologic parameters which influence runoff, e.g., rainfall intensity, infiltration, typography, soil type, etc.

An important concept of the above hypothesis is its applicability on a "point" basis. In order to make this hypothesis useable on a watershed scale, the point concept must be relaxed to refer instead to an "elemental area". A watershed element is defined as a square contiguous region within which all hydrologically significant parameters are uniform.

A watershed to be modeled is conceptualized as being made up of a collection of square elements. While parameter values must be assumed uniform within each element, they are allowed to vary in an unrestricted manner between elements. Thus, any degree of spatial variability within a watershed is easily represented.

The distributed concept of the ANSWERS model comes about by defining mathematical relationships for all simulated processes as they apply to an element in the watershed. These relationships are based upon the conceptual model outlined near the beginning of this chapter. Coefficients (parameters) for these relationships must then be specified for each element. The variation of coefficient values between elements defines the spatial characteristics unique to a given catchment. The collective behavior of individual elements is simulated by integration of the continuity equation which treats outflow from

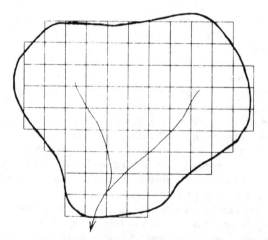

FIG. 5.27 Hypothetical watershed subdivided into elements.

an individual element as inflow into its adjacent elements. Flow is assumed to be governed by kinematic equations and Manning's equation is used as the stage-discharge relationship.

A major advantage of a distributed model approach is the ability to incorporate component relationships developed from small "plot-sized" studies to yield predictions on a watershed scale. It is generally much easier to formulate individual process modeling relations as independent equations applicable on a "point" basis and then depend upon integration algorithms to simulate effects of spatial and temporal variations than it is to develop complex weighting functions for lumped models. Thus, distributed models are much less dependent upon calibration data to "adapt" the model to widely differing geographic regions than are lumped models.

Distributed models can easily be expanded to incorporate numerous component processes and their interactions without changing the fundamental model structure, Overton (1976). Likewise, stochastic effects, Haan (1977), can readily be incorporated into individual component relationships on a case-by-case basis.

A distributed analysis is very flexible and can accommodate a wide range of superficially similar, but totally different models. The concept of a grid pattern to accommodate spatial effects was proposed long before the availability of computers made the approach practical, Bernard (1936). Solomon and Gupta (1977) have used the same basic catchment grid concept as the ANSWERS model on a river basin scale. Naturally, the principle of small, uniform elements is no longer applicable; consequently, the component relationships incorporated into their model are totally different from those developed for smaller areas.

Models developed by Kuh, Reddell and Hiler (1976) and by Kling and Olson (1974), while designed as distributed models for use on small catchments, are also superficially similar in approach but each entirely different in terms of their component relationships and flow routing procedures.

Recently the mathematical technique known as finite element analysis has been applied to distributed watershed modeling. The works of Ross, et al (1978) and of Kuh, et al (1978) are representative of such efforts. Finite element analysis can readily accommodate irregular shaped areas; therefore, these models subdivide a watershed into a collection of irregular but hydrologically similar areas known as "hydrologic response units" prior to simulation computations. One of the primary advantages of finite element algorithms over the spatial-time integration of square elements is improved computational efficiency. Beasley, et al (1980) contrast results available from a finite element model and the more conventional approach to a distributed parameter model.

SELECTING COMPONENT RELATIONSHIPS AND MODELS

The chapter introduction indicated it was not possible to choose among alternative component relationships for modeling overland flow or any of the other hydrologic components without first selecting an overall model structure. A vast number of models and component relationships have and are being developed. Why should such a multitude of models exist and how can a rational selection be made between them?

First, the large number of component relationships and watershed models exist because of the great complexity of processes being simulated and the resulting gross approximations that are necessary to obtain practical models. Each model builder uses a somewhat different set of objectives to establish the relative importance of various components. This results from the fact that most models are developed to address a certain class of problems. While most model builders have special biases for any model they helped develop, most would concede there is no single "best" model. Specific models are better than others for certain purposes, but no single model currently comes close to quantifying all processes encompassed under the subject of watershed simulation. Furthermore, no single model is likely to be forthcoming in the near future.

Despite the wide range of models available, it is possible to develop some general considerations which should assist in the task of selecting from among them. However, all considerations to be developed must be viewed in terms of the intended use of the model. It is currently advisable that one choose from among a group of models that has been specifically designed for the subclass of problems of primary concern, e.g., certain models minimize inaccuracy in predicting annual flow volume while others concentrate on storm runoff rates.

At least four general criteria can be identified for model evaluation and selection: (a) the accuracy, detail and type of information required of the model output, (b) the cost of operating the model, (c) the amount and type of data required by the model, and (d) especially for applications involving simulating non-point source pollution impacts, the accuracy with which influences of the spatial distribution of parameters can be evaluated on a storm by storm (event) basis. Each of these four criteria merit further elaboration.

The first criteria, required accuracy/detail, is, to a considerable degree, a restatement of the overriding consideration of intended use of the model. However, it is essential to remember that any model is only an approximation of reality. Each model is strongly influenced by the preconceived notions of its designer concerning the relative importance of processes it purports to characterize. Therefore, a model will often quantify some processes very well while simultaneously simulating others poorly. Likewise, the detail of output information varies widely, but is often constrained by the fundamental nature of the model's structure.

A second factor to be considered in choosing a model, and one which requires little additional elaboration, is operational costs. Operational costs can be expected to increase somewhat as the detail of the output provided by a model increases. It is the user's responsibility to decide if the additional information justifies its cost.

Data requirements of any model being considered are an important and frequently an inadequately appreciated factor. Everyone should certainly be aware that valid information must be supplied to any model if meaningful results are to be expected. However, while the statement "garbage in—garbage out" is a modeling axiom, it must be pointed out that its converse, good data in—good results out, is not necessarily true. The following statement is a more complete description of the attitude that should prevail when selecting a model:

> The accuracy of any model's prediction is limited by both the validity of its input data and the adequacy of the relationships (mathematical) of which it is composed.

In short: the best of input data cannot compensate for an inadequately structured or incomplete model. The governing processes and the relationships incorporated into a model to simulate those processes have a profound influence upon the ultimate accuracy with which it can characterize the system of interest.

One additional point needs to be made concerning the assessment of data requirements of a model. It is easy to develop a false sense of complacency about a model which requires little parametric data. Just because a specific model does not require input data about a variety of catchment characteristics does not automatically make those characteristics unimportant to the real system nor does it relieve the model user of responsibility for those characteristics. Precluding the use of a model which requires some parameter values which are not readily available can be very unwise. It is valid and generally preferable to assume values for missing data needed by a detailed model than to select a model which does not "require" such data. Models which do not require data concerning parameters which influence simulated processes impose acceptance of the model builder's *a priori* assumption that either (a) those parameters are negligible or (b) they can be accounted for in some simple manner using internal fixed constants to characterize those processes. In contrast, when hard data for a detailed model are not available, it is a simple task to utilize the model itself to evaluate the sensitivity of the output to a feasible range of values for missing data.

Based on the above statements, it is recommended a model be chosen on the basis of its inherent relevance to specific needs of the given application. Next, put as much effort into assembling a data base as the application warrants. Assume a range of reasonable values for any remaining parameters and test how critical those values are for predicted results. If the output doesn't change significantly, any reasonable values are satisfactory. If the results are very sensitive to those values, some additional effort may be warranted to obtain a firmer basis for assigning numerical values. Furthermore, if the latter situation occurs something is inferred about alternative models. Either the detailed model is very inaccurate about the manner in which it simulates the influence of this parameter or the simpler model which doesn't require that data is grossly in error by neglecting to require it (or both).

Finally, one of the fundamental choices that must be made concerns selecting a lumped or distributed parameter model. Generally, the primary advantage of a lumped model is computational efficiency. The relative significance of this factor tends to increase for larger catchments. For large basin studies the only viable alternative are often a choice between a lumped model or statistical extrapolations of distributed parameter simulations for smaller representative subwatersheds.

For the increasing number of applications dealing with problems of pollution which originate from diffuse sources, it is essential that the model(s) selected be able to assess the influence of the areal distribution of controlling parameters and of proposed remedial measures. Very few physiochemical processes important to non-point pollution behave as linear systems. Therefore, the use of arithmetic averages to represent an "effective" value for non-uniform conditions is often only a crude approximation of the influence of the spatial distribution of interacting factors such as soil type, topography, and land use, Overcash and Davidson (1980).

The majority of non-point pollution problems, both from agricultural as well as urban areas, are storm induced. Thus, studies designed to evaluate the severity of such problems or the effectiveness of methods for curing them should be capable of simulating a watershed's response to individual real or hypothetical storms (technically referred to as event-oriented models). This does not infer that continuous simulations and long-term averages are not germane. Instead, it is a recognition that a comparatively large percentage of the pollution, especially that associated with soil erosion from agricultural areas, results from a small percentage of the annual precipitation associated with infrequent, but intense storms. An accurate assessment of the impact of proposed treatment practices on these storms is essential for determining long-term benefits.

References

Amorocho, J. and G.T. Orlob. 1961. Nonlinear analysis of nonlinear systems. Univ. of Calif., Water Res. Ctr. Contribution No. 40.

Annambhotla, V.S.S., 1969. Statistical properties of bed forms in alluvial channels in relation to flow resistance. Ph.D. Dissertation, Univ. of Iowa, Iowa City, Iowa.

Beasley, D.B., B.B. Ross, V.O. Shanholtz and L.F. Huggins. 1980. Comparison of Two Distributed Parameter Watershed Models. Proc. Hydrologic Modeling Symposium. ASAE Pub. No. 4-80. pp 196-205.

Bernard, M. 1936. Giving Areal Significance to Hydrologic Research on Small Areas. **Headwaters Control and Use.** Upstream Engr. Conf. U.S. Gov. Printing Office. pp. 5075.

Brakensiek, D.L., 1967. Kinematic flood routing. Trans. Am. Soc. Agr. Eng. 10(3): 340-343.

Brakensiek, D.L. and C.A. Onstad. 1968. The synthesis of distributed inputs for hydrograph predictions. Water Resources Res. 4(1): 79-85.

Brickman, A.D., J.C. Wambold and J.R. Zimmerman. 1971. An amplitude - frequency description of road roughness. Highway Research Board Special Report 116: 53-67.

Burney, J.R. and L.F. Huggins. 1973. Hydraulics of shallow flows over stable eroded sand surfaces defined by area spectra. Water Resources Res. Center Tech. Rept. No. 36, Purdue Univ., West Lafayette, IN.

Burwell, R.E., R.R. Allmaras and M. Amemiya. 1963. A field measurement of total porosity and surface microrelief of soils. Proc. Soil Sci. Soc. Amer. 27: 697-700.

Chow, V.T., 1959. Open channel hydraulics. McGraw-Hill, New York.

Chow, V.T., 1964. Runoff. In Chow, V.T. (ed), Handbook of applied hydrology, McGraw-Hill, New York.

Crawford, N.H and R.K. Linsley. 1966. Digital simulation in hydrology: Stanford watershed model IV. Dept. Civil Eng. Tech. Rept. 39, Stanford Univ., Palo Alto, CA.

Currence, H.D. and W.G. Lovely. 1970. The analysis of soil surface roughness. Trans. ASAE 13(6): 710-714.

Das, K.C., 1970. Laboratory modelling and overland flow analysis. Ph.D. Dissertation, Purdue Univ., West Lafayette, IN.

Delleur, J.W., 1971. Personal communication.

Delleur, J.W. and R.A. Rao, 1971. Linear systems analysis in hydrology - the transform approach, the kernel oscillations and the effect of noise. U.S.-Japan Bi-Lateral Sem. in Hydrol., Honolulu, Hawaii.

Dooge, J.C.I., 1959. A general theory of the unit hydrograph. J. Geophys. Res. 64(1): 241-256.

Eagleson, P.S., 1970. Dynamic hydrology. McGraw-Hill, New York.

Foster, G.R., 1975. Hydraulics of flow in a rill. PhD. Dissertation, Purdue Univ., West Lafayette, IN.

Haan, C.T. 1977. **Statistical Methods in Hydrology.** Iowa State Univ. Press

Harbaugh, T.E. and V.T. Chow. 1967. A study of the roughness of conceptual river systems of watersheds. Proc. 12th Cong. I.A.H.R.: 9-17.

Heermann, D.F., R.J. Wenstrom and N.A. Evans. 1969. Prediction of flow resistance in furrows from soil roughness. Trans. ASAE 12 (4): 482-485, 489.

Hewlett, J.D. and C.A. Troendle, 1975. Non-point and diffused water sources: a variable source area problem. Watershed Management. ASCE Proceedings, Aug. 11-13. pp. 21-45.

Hicks, W.I., 1944. A method of computing urban runoff. Trans. ASCE 1217-1268.

Horner, W.W. and S.W. Jens. 1943. Surface runoff determination from rainfall without using coefficients. Trans. ASCE 107: 1039-1117.

Horton, R.E., 1938. The interpretation and application of runoff plat experiments with reference to soil erosion problems. Soil Sci. Soc. Amer. Proc. 3: 340-349.

Huggins, L.F. and E.J. Monke. 1966. The mathematical simulation of the hydrology of small watersheds. Water Resources Res. Center Tech. Rept. No. 1, Purdue Univ., West Lafayette, IN.

Huggins, L.F., J.R. Burney, P.S. Kundu and E.J. Monke. 1973. Simulation of the hydrology of ungaged watersheds. Water Resources Res. Center Tech. Rept. No. 38, Purdue Univ., West Lafayette, IN.

Huggins, L.F., T.H. Podmore and C.F. Hood. 1976. Hydrologic simulation using distributed parameters. Water Resources Res. Center. Tech. Rept. No. 82, Purdue Univ., West Lafayette, IN.

Izzard, C.F., 1942. Runoff from flight strips. Proc. Highway Res. Board 22: 94-99.

James, D.L., 1970. An evaluation of relationships between streamflow patterns and watershed characteristics through the use of OPSET a self calibrating version of the Stanford Watershed Model. Research Rept. No. 36, Water Resources Institute, Univ. of KY., Lexington, KY.

Kling, G.F. and G.W. Olson. 1974. The sediment transport computer model. Cornell Agronomy Mimeo 74011, Dept. Agron., Cornell Univ., Ithaca, NY.

Kuh, H., D.L. Reddell and E.A. Hiler. 1976. Two-dimensional model of erosion from a watershed. ASAE Paper 76-2539. Am. Soc. of Agr. Engrs., St. Joseph, MI.

Kuipers, H., 1957. A relief meter for soil cultivation studies. Netherlands Jour. of Agr. Sci. 50: 255-262.

Kundu, P.S., 1971. Mechanics of flow over very rough surfaces. Ph.D. Dissertation, Purdue Univ., West Lafayette, IN.

Lake, J. and J. Morrison, ed. 1977. Environmental impact of land use on water quality: Final report on the Black Creek project—tech. rept. EPA-905/9-77-007-B. pp. 177-203.

Lighthill, M.J. and G.B. Whitham, 1955. On kinematic waves 1. Proc. Royal Soc., London, Ser. A, Vol 229: 281-316.

Linsley, R.K. Kohler and Paulus, 1969. Applied hydrology.

Merva, G.E., R.D. Brazee, G.O. Schwab and R.B. Curry. 1970. Theoretical considerations of watershed surface description. Trans. ASAE 13(4): 462-465.

Mitchell, J.K., 1970. Micro-relief surface depression storage. Ph.D. Dissertation Univ. of IL, Urbana, IL.

Nash, J.E., 1957. The form of the instantaneous unit hydrograph. Int'l. Assoc. Sci. Hydrol. Pub. 45, Vol. 3: 114-121.

Overcash, M.R. and J.M. Davidson. 1980. **Environmental Impact of Nonpoint Source Pollution.** Ann Arbor Science Publishers, Inc.

Overton, D.E. 1976. **Stormwater Modeling.** Academic Press, Inc.

Podmore, T.H., 1975. Surface roughness effects on overland flow. Ph.D. Dissertation, Purdue Univ., West Lafayette, IN.

Ross, B.B., V.O. Shanholtz, D.N. Contractor and J.C. Carr. 1978. A model for evaluating the effect of land uses on flood flows. Bull. 85, Virginia Water Resources Res. Ctr., Blacksburg.

Schwab, G.O., R.K. Frevert, T.W. Edminster and K.K. Barnes. 1981. **Soil and water conservation engineering.** 3rd Ed. J. Wiley & Sons.

Sharp, A.L. and H.N. Holtan. 1942. Extension of graphic analysis of sprinkled-plot and small homogeneous watersheds. Trans. Amer. Geophys. Un. 23: 578-593.

Sherman, L.K., 1932. Stream flow from rainfall by the unit-graph method. Eng. News-Rec. 108: 501-505.

Solomon, S.I. and S.K. Gupta. 1977. Distributed numerical model for estimating runoff and sediment discharge of ungaged rivers. II. Model development. Water Resources Res. v13, n3, pp. 619-629.

Squarer, D., 1968. An analysis of relationships between flow conditions and statistical measures of bed configurations in straight and curved alluvial channels. Ph.D. Dissertation, Univ. of Iowa, Iowa City, IA.

Strelkoff, T., 1969. One-dimensional equations of open channel flow. Trans. Hyd. Div. ASCE 95 (HY3): 861-876.

Strelkoff, T., 1970. Numerical solution of St. Venant equations. Jour. Hyd. Div. ASCE 96 (HY1): 223-252.

U.S. Bureau of Reclamation, 1972. Design of small dams. 2nd Ed. U.S. Gov. Printing Office.

Wilson, E.M., 1974. Engineering hydrology. 2nd Ed. Macmillan, London.

Woo, D., 1956. Study of overland flow. Ph.D. Dissertation, Univ. of MI, Ann Arbor, MI.

Woolhiser, D.A. and J.A. Liggett, 1967. Unsteady one-dimensional flow over a plane-the rising hydrograph. Water Resources Res. 3(3): 753-771.

chapter 6 ▰

EVAPOTRANSPIRATION

6

6

EVAPOTRANSPIRATION

by K. E. Saxton, Hydrologist, Agricultural Research
    Service, USDA, Department of Agricultural
    Engineering, Wash. State Univ., Pullman, WA
    99164; J. L. McGuinness, Statistician (retired),
    Agricultural Research Service, USDA, North Ap-
    palachian Experimental Watershed Research, Col-
    umbus, OH 43812

INTRODUCTION

Evapotranspiration (ET) is the conversion of water to vapor and the transport of that vapor away from the watershed surface into the atmosphere.
The amount of liquid water and the energy to vaporize it will vary both in
space and time over the watershed surface. Water is available at plant surfaces, soil surfaces, streams and ponds, or snowpacks. Solar radiation is
the main energy source.

Evapotranspiration flux moves large quantities of water from the soil
back to the atmosphere. In humid zones, about 750 to 900 mm/yr (30 to
35 in./yr) of water may be vaporized. In subhumid areas, receiving only
natural precipitation and experiencing dry surfaces more frequently, 550
to 700 mm/yr (22 to 28 in./yr) commonly evaporate from vegetated surfaces.
In drier regions, where evaporative demands are even higher, most if not all
of the precipitation is returned to the atmosphere through this process.
Leupold and Langbein (1960) estimated that 70 percent of the precipitation
falling on the United States is returned to the atmosphere through ET.

Accurate spatial and temporal predictions of ET are required for hydrologic models of small watersheds. Soil moisture reserves are largely determined by the difference between infiltration and ET; but, in turn, infiltration, percolation, evapotranspiration, and other hydrologic variables
are highly dependent on the soil moisture quantities and distributions. The
important influence of ET in hydrology has been shown and discussed by
Woolhiser (1971, 1973), McGuinness and Harrold (1962), Knisel et al.
(1969), and Parmele (1972). However, Betson (1973) noted that the inability
to accurately estimate ET does not negate many practical results of hydrologic modeling.

Although ET varies at each watershed point and continuously throughout the day, a spatially averaged daily ET quantity is often adequate for
many small area applications. Climatic variables usually do not vary significantly over small areas and only major changes in crops or soils are often
important. In the discussion that follows, we maintain this view of time
and space requirements which results in many important details being simplified, averaged, or omitted in the interest of application for hydrologic
predictions.

Predicting ET from agricultural watersheds requires considering many atmospheric variables, plant characteristics, and soil parameters. Some useful estimation methods avoid direct consideration of some or most of these factors, usually at the expense of detail, accuracy, and understanding. When a modeler chooses from the several available methods, he must carefully consider his purpose. A highly detailed and comprehensive ET prediction method is not usually needed in a model to predict peak flow rates from small watersheds. This chapter is intended to help the modeler understand the ET mechanism and intelligently choose from the variety of prediction methods available.

PERSPECTIVE

The transfer of water back to the atmosphere has intrigued and fascinated scientists since early recorded history (Biswas, 1970). By 346 BC, when Aristotle wrote the first treatise on meteorology, evaporation was already generally associated with the sun's heat (Biswas, 1970, p. 65). Leonardo da Vinci, in the late 1400's wrote: "where there is life there is heat, and where vital heat is, there is movement of vapor (Biswas, 1970, p. 141)". By the late 1700's, pan evaporation was measured much as it is now; and in 1795, Dalton constructed a lysimeter complete with runoff and drainage measurement (Biswas, 1970, p. 275).

The Nineteenth Century was a period of scientific observations like those of Fitzgerald (1886) who identified many of the important quantities and variables related to pan and lake evaporation. Rohwer (1931) reported very similar studies. Hydrologic techniques before the mid-Twentieth Century can be characterized by the statement of Thornthwaite and Holzman (1942, p. 63): "But the measurement of evaporation has continued to be impossible, despite the fact that it has become increasingly necessary as measurements of rainfall, runoff, and infiltration have improved." A bibliography on evaporation and evapotranspiration, emphasizing papers from the United States since the early 1800's, was published by Robinson and Johnson (1961).

Development during the past three decades have been significant. This era was initiated by theoretical work, like that of Penman (1948) in which he combined the vertical energy budget with horizontal wind effects; and lysimeter studies, like as those of Harrold and Dreibelbis (1958, 1967), which identified the plant characteristic effects. Penman model improvements and adaptations were made by Tanner and Fuchs (1968), van Bavel (1966), Monteith (1965), Rijtema (1965) and others by including direct net radiation estimates and improved wind profile theory. The effects of plants on ET have been vigorously investigated and reported by Gates and Hanks (1967), Kozlowski (1968), Monteith (1976), and many others. Plant roots and soil moisture have received considerable attention in recent years (Hillel and Talpaz, 1976; Feddes et al., 1976b).

Wartena (1974) provided a useful summary of the past century of research on ET. He concluded that, although results have been impressive, several basic problems are yet to be solved, like the effect of turbulent air and the influence of soil water content and root development. Despite these and other limitations, we can make many useful predictions for hydrology and irrigation.

We have come to an understanding that ET from vegetated surfaces is the result of several processes like radiation exchanges, vapor transport, and biological growth, operating within a system involving the atmosphere, plants, and soil. Thus, much of the contemporary research and development of prediction methods involves or recognizes the variables within such a system. Models reported by Saxton et al. (1974a,b), Ritchie (1972), van Keulen (1975), Hanks et al. (1969), Baier (1967), Lemon et al. (1973), and van Bavel and Ahmed (1976) are typical examples of this integrated systems approach.

PRINCIPLES OF ET

Evapotranspiration from vegetated surfaces requires energy inputs, water availability, and a transport process from the surface into the atmosphere. The flux of water vapor is largely limited by one or more of these requirements (Weigand and Taylor, 1961). Several researchers have provided good descriptions of these primary variables which determine ET rates (Tanner, 1957; Goodell, 1966; Penman et al., 1967; Gray, 1970; Campbell, 1977). Because ET is a phase change of water, large energy inputs are required. At a nominal value of 580 cal g^{-1}, a daily ET of 5 mm (0.2 in.) will require 47.3 million Btu, or the equivalent of 4480 kg/ha (2 t/a) coal. Solar radiation usually supplies 80 to 100 percent of this energy, and is often the factor limiting ET.

For non-irrigated agriculture, water availability to the evaporating plant and soil surfaces also often limits ET. Thus, the rate of ET is limited to the diffusion rate of soil water to the soil surface and to the plant roots and through the plant system. In these circumstances, adsorbed radiant energy (incoming minus reflected) in excess of that required to transform the available water is dissipated primarily by an increase of sensible heat in the air and soil.

The aerodynamic transport process of water vapor upward from the evaporating surface for most vegetated situations does not often significantly limit the ET process. Although molecular diffusion is involved at the soil and plant surfaces, turbulent diffusion predominates and is caused mostly by wind shear but also by thermal convection under calmer conditions. The diffusion of water vapor from the soil and plant surfaces and within their structures is highly complex when examined in detail, but essential to the ET mechanism.

The horizontal advection of sensible heat from areas of excess energy to areas of limited energy is another important energy source for ET. This is often called the "clothes line" or "oasis" effect and is best exemplified by a wet vegetated field downwind of a dry desert area, like that reported by Davenport and Hudson (1967). Significant advection effects are often encountered in much less obvious circumstances and over large areas (Rosenberg, 1969a).

Evapotranspiration varies spatially as a result of variations in climate, crops, or soils. Climatic variables related to ET tend to be conservative and often do not change rapidly or significantly over considerable distance. However, we cannot make generalizations because local elevations, aspects, orographic effects, and cropping patterns can cause large ET changes. The variation of crops and soils over a region in question will need to be treated either by separate considerations of major combinations or broad scale averages. Some spatial averaging is implicit in every ET estimate and the user must acknowledge and quantify the effects with respect to the application.

The daily ET data presented in Fig. 6.1 are indicative of the annual distribution and daily variation of ET values. A summary of similar data

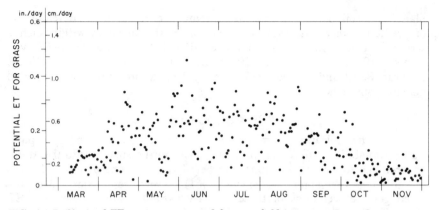

FIG. 6.1 Daily actual ET amounts computed for corn field in western Iowa (Saxton et al., 1974b).

is shown in Fig. 6.2 for a 10-yr period of daily values obtained for frequently irrigated, frequently mowed (8 to 10 cm) grass cover grown at Davis, CA. The considerable daily variation within each month demonstrates the dynamic behavior of ET values. If crop cover and soil moisture characteristics also vary widely during the measurements, the ET values will vary more, as demonstrated by Tanner (1967, p. 557) using data from Coshocton, OH. These and many other data demonstrate the variability and complexity of the ET process.

The soil-plant-atmosphere system may be represented schematically as shown in Fig. 6.3. Of the water-flow paths illustrated, ET is the next major component of the water budget after precipitation. The interaction of ET with the other components, like rooting and soil moisture profiles,

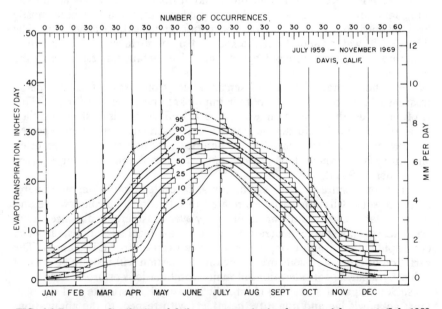

FIG. 6.2 Frequency distribution of daily evapotranspiration for perennial ryegrass (July 1959-Sept. 1963) and Alta Fescue grass (June 1964-Nov. 1969) (Pruitt, et al., 1972b).

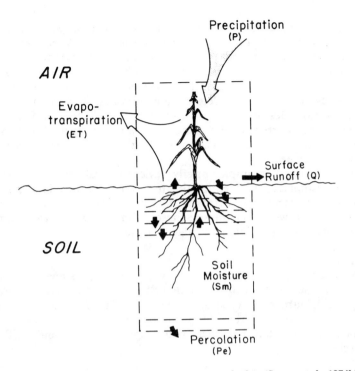

FIG. 6.3 Schematic of the soil-plant-air system water budget (Saxton et al., 1974b).

and the dynamic nature of these many components with time becomes readily apparent as the water budget of this system is computed.

Many methods of estimating ET, whether for hydrologic models or irrigation scheduling, follow a concept of a vertical water budget within a system like that in Fig. 6.3. In general, the procedure is to first estimate or measure a potential for ET based on meteorological factors, then compute the amount of that potential that is utilized by the actual ET processes, given the current status of the plant- and soil-water-related characteristics. To apply such a procedure requires three sets of variables to be considered: (a) those for the potential ET determinations; (b) plant-water-related characteristics; and (c) soil-water-related characteristics. Each of these is the subject of the next three sections, followed by a fourth section where the concepts are combined to predict actual ET.

POTENTIAL ET METHODS

The potential for ET, PET, is usually defined as an atmospheric determined quantity, which assumes that the ET flux will not exceed the available energy from both radiant and convection sources. This definition of PET works well for most modeling concepts because it allows consideration of the atmospheric variable somewhat separate from the plant and soil effects, even though interactions and feedback from these to the atmosphere do not allow complete isolation.

Techniques for estimating PET are based on one or more atmospheric variables, like solar or net radiation and air temperature and humidity, or some measurement related to these variables, like pan evaporation. Direct measurement or prediction of some variables such as vapor or heat flux is difficult and not yet practical for most applications. Variables like net radiation have only been routinely measureable for a relatively few years and are not yet normally available. As a result, most procedures for estimating PET make empirical use of atmospheric related measurements or methods to estimate those non-determinant variables. Because the causative atmospheric variables are relatively conservative in space, PET estimates can often be transferred some distance with minimal error. For most hydrologic applications, this is necessary because data are rarely available on the area where needed.

The following paragraphs briefly review several frequently applied methods for estimating PET. Estimating techniques for periods shorter than 1 day usually demand more extensive data or considerable diurnal adjustment. As a result, we will emphasize those techniques which use commonly available data inputs for periods of 1 day or longer.

Pan Evaporation

Measured evaporation from a shallow pan of water is one of the oldest and most common methods of estimating PET. It is an indirect integration of the principal atmospheric variables related to ET. Given some standardization of pan shape, environmental setting, and operation, good correlations have been developed between pan evaporation, E_p, and PET by a simple relation

$$PET = C_{ET} \cdot E_p \quad \dots \dots \dots \dots \dots \dots \dots \dots \dots \dots \dots \dots \dots \dots \quad [6.1]$$

where C_{ET} is a coefficient.

Pan-to-PET coefficients (C_{ET}) are necessary because evaporation for a pan is generally more than that from a well-wetted vegetated surface, or even a pond, due to the pan's excessive exposure and lower reflectance of solar radiation. The US Weather Bureau Class A pan is a metal pan 122 cm in diameter, 25 cm high and mounted with its bottom about 10 cm above the surrounding soil. Thus, it is capable of receiving and utilizing more atmospheric energy than larger, less exposed surfaces and the pan water often becomes quite warm. These coefficients are influenced by the pan surroundings, fetch, relative humidity, and wind speed (Jensen, 1973, p. 74; Hanson and Rauzi, 1977). As these variables change, values of C_{ET} can range from 0.5 to 0.8. However, over several days and for other than extreme or unusual conditions, a much more stable value will prevail. Many examples of pan-to-PET coefficients can be found in texts and publications (Hargreaves, 1966; Richardson and Ritchie, 1973; Saxton et al. 1974a).

Although specific coefficient values for application to any given situation or pan may have to be found by calibration, representative values from other studies will provide good guidance. Mean monthly values are graphically shown by Jensen (1973, p. 79) for 10 widely separate locations over the world. For the eight locations with a uniform grass cover, the mean annual coefficients varied from 0.72 to 0.83 and averaged 0.77.

Several researchers have obtained best results by applying seasonally varied coefficients, like those shown in Table 6.1. This seasonal variation reflects only the difference in climatic response between the evaporating

TABLE 6.1. EXAMPLE RATIO VALUES
OF PET/PAN EVAPORATION

Month		PET/PAN	
January	0.55*	0.59†	0.62‡
February	0.70	0.69	0.60
March	0.78	0.75	0.60
April	0.84	0.76	0.65
May	0.88	0.78	0.71
June	0.88	0.78	0.72
July	0.88	0.77	0.71
August	0.86	0.75	0.71
September	0.80	0.72	0.69
October	0.70	0.67	0.69
November	0.58	0.60	0.67
December	0.53	0.56	0.62
Mean	0.75	0.70	0.67

*Saxton et al. (1974a).
†Mustonen and McGuinness (1968) p. 77.
‡Fleming (1975) p. 62.

pan and vegetated surface and not other effects like crop maturation, or moisture stress. For many hydrologic applications, we can use a mean annual value of 0.70 to 0.80 with an annual distribution similar to those of Table 6.1, to obtain good results.

When selecting or developing pan coefficients, we must identify what effects are included in the coefficients. Many coefficients relate pan evaporation to actual ET from cropped surfaces, thus the effects of plant growth characteristics and average water availability are also included. This is particularly true for irrigation design and consumptive-use estimates (Blaney and Criddle, 1966; Hargreaves, 1966).

Measurements or estimates of pan evaporation are available from many US Weather Bureau reporting stations, research stations, and meteorologic offices of other agencies. Most measurements are from the standardized US Weather Bureau Class A pan, although many other pan types, like sunken, screened, floating, and insulated pans, have been used. Data from each of these pans is unique and will relate to PET by a different set of coefficients.

Generalized maps of Class A pan and pond evaporation are available to estimate average conditions. Kohler et al. (1959) and Nordenson (1962) provided maps and seasonal distributions. These were also presented by Veihmeyer (1964).

Methods to calculate pan evaporation from meteorologic data are given by Penman (1948), Kohler et al. (1955), Christiansen (1966, 1968) and Kohler and Parmele (1967). The method of Christiansen (1968) relates pan evaporation, E_p, to extraterrestrial solar radiation, R_t, (in equivalent depth of evaporation) by the relation

$$E_p = 0.324 \, R_t \, C_T \, C_W \, C_H \, C_S \, C_E \qquad \qquad \text{[6.2]}$$

or to incoming solar radiation, R_S (in equivalent depth of evaporation) by

$$E_p = 0.482 \, R_S \, C_T \, C_W \, C_H \qquad \qquad \text{[6.3]}$$

TABLE 6.2. MEAN MONTHLY SOLAR RADIATION AT THE TOP OF THE ATMOSPHERE, R_t, IN UNITS OF EQUIVALENT DEPTH OF EVAPORATION (cm) AT 20°C*

Latitude	Jan	Feb	Mar	Apr	May	June	July	Aug	Sept	Oct	Nov	Dec
North												
50	11.7	16.7	28.6	38.4	48.3	50.3	50.1	43.0	31.7	22.1	13.1	9.7
40	19.1	23.4	34.8	42.1	49.7	50.5	50.8	45.8	36.7	29.1	20.4	16.9
30	26.7	29.5	39.8	44.6	50.0	49.8	50.5	47.4	40.7	35.0	27.4	24.5
20	33.9	34.8	43.7	46.0	49.1	47.9	49.1	47.8	43.5	40.0	33.9	32.0
10	40.2	39.1	46.2	45.9	46.9	44.8	46.4	46.8	44.8	44.1	39.5	39.0
Equator	45.3	42.2	47.3	44.5	43.5	40.6	42.4	44.5	44.9	46.8	44.1	45.0
South												
10	49.3	44.2	46.9	41.7	38.9	35.4	37.4	40.9	43.6	47.8	47.5	49.6
20	52.1	44.9	45.2	37.8	33.3	29.4	31.5	36.1	40.9	47.5	49.7	52.7
30	53.7	44.6	42.2	32.7	26.9	22.7	24.8	30.5	37.1	46.2	50.4	54.8
40	53.9	42.8	37.9	26.6	19.8	15.7	17.7	24.1	32.2	43.5	49.9	55.5
50	53.0	39.7	32.2	20.3	12.9	9.1	10.6	16.0	26.2	39.2	48.4	55.0

*Adapted from Christiansen (1966, p. 216). Multiply by 584.9 cal/cm^3 to obtain Langleys (cal/cm^2).

Monthly values of solar radiation at the top of the earth's atmosphere, R_t, have been calculated for various latitudes; Table 6.2 is an abbreviated example. Incoming solar radiation, R_S, is measured at many first order weather stations and usually reported in cal/cm^2/day which must be divided by the latent heat of vaporization (584.9 cal/g at 20 °C) to obtain equivalent cm depths. The coefficients for equations [6.2] and [6.3] are obtained by the relationships:

$$C_T = 0.463 + 0.425 \, (T/T_o) + 0.112(T/T_o)^2 \quad \dots\dots\dots\dots\dots\dots [6.4]$$

$$C_W = 0.672 + 0.406(W/W_o) - 0.078(W/W_o)^2 \dots\dots\dots\dots\dots\dots [6.5]$$

$$C_H = 1.035 + 0.240(H/H_o)^2 - 0.275(H/H_o)^3 \dots\dots\dots\dots\dots\dots [6.6]$$

$$C_S = 0.340 + 0.856(S/S_o) - 0.196(S/S_o)^2 \quad \dots\dots\dots\dots\dots\dots [6.7]$$

$$C_E = 0.970 + 0.030(E/E_o) \quad \dots\dots\dots\dots\dots\dots\dots\dots\dots\dots\dots [6.8]$$

where
T = mean air temperature
T_o = 20 °C
W = mean wind velocity 2 m above ground
W_o = 6.7 km/hr
H = mean relative humidity expressed decimally
H_o = 0.60
S = mean sunshine percentage expressed decimally
S_o = 0.80

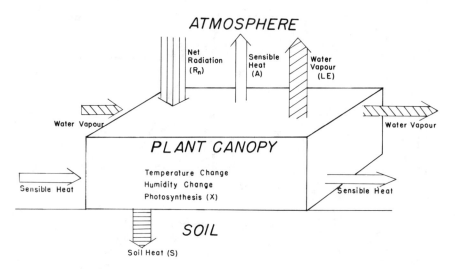

FIG. 6.4 Energy balance over a vegetated surface (Gray, 1970).

E = elevation, and
E_0 = 305 m.
The coefficient equations are presented as a ratio of a selected standard value so that if data are not available, the coefficient reverts to a value of 1.0 when the standard is assumed and pan evaporation can be estimated using what data are available.

Energy Budget
Methods of estimating PET based on the vertical energy budget of a vegetated surface have a physical basis because energy limits evaporation where moisture is readily available and the necessary vapor transport occurs. Fig. 6.4 shows the major components of the energy budget which form the basis for the several methods that use this approach. Except for cases of significant advection, like field edges and oasis effects, the horizontal components are usually negligible. The budget (in cal/cm²/min), except as noted, of the major vertical components may be expressed as

$$R_n = A + LE + S + X \quad \dots\dots\dots\dots\dots\dots\dots\dots\dots\dots\dots [6.9a]$$

and

$$R_n = R_s - aR_s + R_l - R_{lr} \quad \dots\dots\dots\dots\dots\dots\dots\dots\dots\dots [6.9b]$$

where
R_s = incoming solar radiation (short wave)
aR_s = solar radiation reflected
R_l = incoming radiation (long wave)
R_{lr} = emitted long wave radiation
R_n = net radiation
A   = sensible heat of air

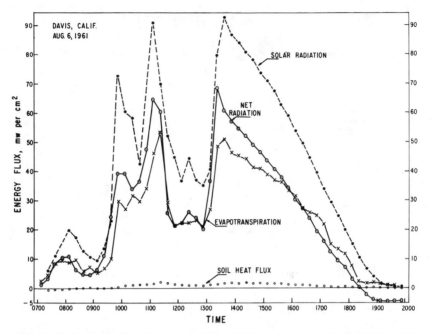

FIG. 6.5 Daily distribution of net and solar radiation, evapotranspiration, and soil flux for a well-irrigated grass turf 10-15 cm tall (Pruitt, 1964).

LE = latent heat of water vapor
   L = latent heat of vaporization cal/cm³ or cal/g¹, and
   E = depth of evaporative water, cm³/cm²/min
S = soil heat
X = miscellaneous heat sinks, like plant and air heat storage, and photosynthesis.

Tanner (1957) summarized the heat budget for agricultural surfaces, and Brown and Covey (1966) demonstrated the use of this approach for a cornfield.

Fig. 6.5 shows a typical diurnal distribution and relative magnitude of some of the terms in equation [6.9]. A portion of the incoming radiation $(R_s + R_l)$ is emitted or reflected $(aR_s + R_{lr})$, providing a net radiation balance (R_n). Soil heat flux utilizes a very small quantity of available energy during daytime, and this is almost balanced with nighttime radiation loss. The miscellaneous terms account for an even smaller quantity. The result is that net radiation is primarily used in ET or sensible heat where water is readily available at the surface, like the situation demonstrated in Fig. 6.5, where about 80 percent of R_n is used by ET. If water had not been readily available, ET would have been reduced and the sensible heat component increased. For cases of advected energy, ET may exceed R_n because in this case R_n is not the only significant energy source.

Recognizing that A and LE terms are of much greater magnitude than S and X, Bowen (1926) proposed using the ratio of sensible to latent heat

$$\beta = \frac{A}{LE}$$ .... [6.10]

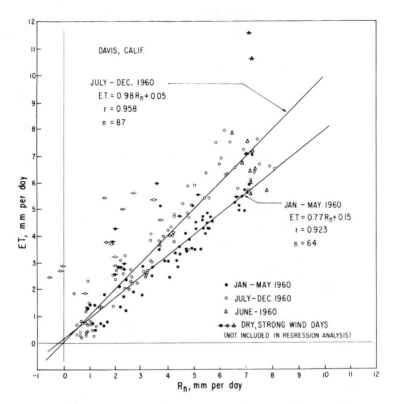

FIG. 6.6 Daily ET for irrigated ryegrass versus net radiation (Pruitt, 1964).

where β is commonly referred to as the Bowen ratio. Equation [6.9] with S and X neglected and equation [6.10] substituted becomes

$$LE = \frac{R_n}{1 + \beta} \quad \dots \dots \dots \dots \dots \dots \dots \dots \dots \dots \dots \dots \dots \dots [6.11]$$

The value of β can be calculated from gradients of air temperature and vapor pressure above the evaporating surface, which is a relatively difficult measurement usually made only at research installations (Fritschen, 1966; Parmele and Jacoby, 1975). Typical β values range from 0.1 to 0.3 for moist conditions.

The correlation of R_n with PET is the basis for several estimating techniques. A typical correlation, shown in Fig. 6.6 for daily values from a well-watered grass cover (Pruitt, 1964), shows ET is near or slightly less than R_n, which would be as expected if the vertical energy balance held. Days with apparent advection deviate considerably from the regression line. Saxton et al. (1974a,b) showed a similar relation for net radiation and PET computed by the combination method, and Rosenberg (1972) showed LE/R_n ratio values. In all cases, scatter due to other affecting variables is considerable. Graham and King (1961) reported very similar results with corn near Guelph, Ontario. Data by Rosenberg (1972) taken in Nebraska showed

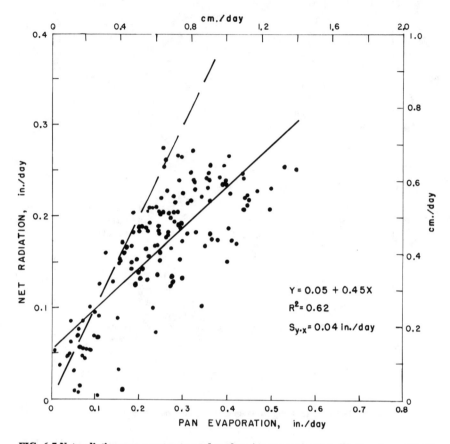

FIG. 6.7 Net radiation over grass compared to class A pan evaporation, Western Iowa, March 15 to October 30, 1970 (Saxton, 1972).

PET averaged more than R_n indicating horizontal advection often experienced in that region (Rosenberg, 1969a). van Bavel (1967) in the desert climate of Phoenix, AR found LE for tall alfalfa exceeded R_n almost every day. Ritchie (1971) showed LE/R_n ratios near to 1.0 for crops in Texas after nearly full canopy had developed.

The relationship of R_n to pan evaporation in Fig. 6.7 indicated that both of these variables have a basis for estimating PET. However, the slope of the regression is not unity, thus different coefficients are required to relate R_n and pan evaporation to PET.

For estimates of 5 days or longer, Jensen and Haise (1963) developed the following prediction equation:

$$PET = (0.025\,T + 0.078)R_s \qquad\qquad\qquad [6.12]$$

where:

    PET = potential ET (30-50 cm alfalfa) (cm/day)
    T   = mean air temperature (°C), and
    R_s = solar radiation (cm/day).

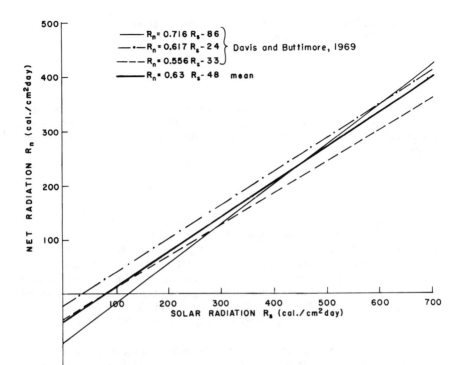

FIG. 6.8 Relationships between net and solar radiation pooled for various crops and locations.

The Jensen-Haise method was related to PET for a full cover crop, like alfalfa, and other crop coefficients developed for use by the US Bureau of Reclamation for irrigation designs (Robb, 1966). Other applications have been made for irrigation scheduling (Jensen, 1973).

Turc (1961) proposed a similar empirical equation for PET based on radiation and temperature of:

$$PET = 0.40\ T\ (R_s + 50)/(T + 15) \quad \dots\dots\dots\dots\dots\dots\dots\dots\dots [6.13]$$

where T is °C, R_S is in ly, and PET is in mm/month. Aslung (1974), using data from near Copenhagen, showed strong linear relationships between both ET and plant production with global radiation.

Obtaining reliable radiation values by either measurement or estimation often becomes the key to successful applications of energy budget methods. Direct radiation measurements are usually one of two types: (a) total incoming solar, R_S, (e.g., by Epply pyrohelieometer) or (b) all wave net radiation, R_n, (e.g., by Fritchen type net radiometer). Net radiation can be used directly to predict PET. Solar radiation, which is the most common measurement at meteorologic stations, can be used to estimate R_n taking into account the albedo and heating coefficients of the plant and soil surfaces. Albedo and emittance vary with stage of plant growth, soil color, degree of wetness, crop and soil temperature, sun angle, and other factors. Davies and Buttimor (1969) presented the relationships shown in Fig. 6.8 which are pooled for many crops and world locations and concluded that many surfaces are similar enough that mean values can be quite useful. The mean of their relationships is

$$R_n = 0.63 R_s - 48 \quad \dots\dots\dots\dots\dots\dots\dots\dots\dots\dots\dots \quad [6.14]$$

Jensen (1973) in his Table B1 also summarizes radiation measurements from 28 diverse locations and sites. Almost all results had a correlation coefficient greater than 0.90, many above 0.95. The means for these data provide the relationship

$$R_n = 0.65 R_s - 45 \quad \dots\dots\dots\dots\dots\dots\dots\dots\dots\dots\dots \quad [6.15]$$

which is almost identical with equation [6.14]. Saxton (1972) reported a relationship very similar to those of equations [6.14] and [6.15], however, he further showed a seasonal trend in the R_n/R_s ratio, which ranged from about 0.40 at mid-March and November to about 0.55 in mid-July. Other data and summaries relating net and solar radiation have been reported by Reifsnyder and Lull (1965), Stanhill et al. (1966), Fritschen (1967), Linacre (1968), Idso (1971), Fitzpatrick and Stern (1973), and Coulson (1975).

The rate of incoming solar radiation reaching an inclined plane on the Earth's surface, depends upon complex celestial and terrestial geometry and interactions as the radiation traverses through about 150 km of the Earth's atmosphere. The sun supplies an average radiation of 1.94 ly/min to the outer edge of the atmosphere (solar constant) with variations from 2.01 ly/min on Dec. 21 to 1.88 ly/min on June 21 due to change in the Earth-to-Sun distance. Much of this radiation is adsorbed and scattered as it passes through the atmosphere by the ozone, water vapor, carbon dioxide, dust and gas molecules. If R_s is not measured within a reasonable distance from the area in question, methods to estimate values based on the solar constant, solar geometry, and atmospheric variables are described by Frank and Lee (1966), Kreith (1973), ASHRAE (1974), Coulson (1975), Hanson (1976), Thompson (1976), and Reufeim (1976).

The Christiansen (1968) method (equation [6.2]) expresses the radiation balance empirically by solving the geometric relationships for the site's location with data as in Table 6.2, then correcting for atmospheric conditions. For mean conditions when each coefficient of equation [6.2] equals one, 32 percent of the potential solar radiation would reach the Earth's surface during the month on a horizontal surface.

The slope and aspect of a plane at the Earth's surface may introduce considerable variation to the incident radiation as compared with a horizontal plane. A watershed is composed of a multitude of individual facets, but the average slope-aspect effect can be determined from the view that all incoming radiation must pass through a plane defined by points on the watershed boundary, thus this single plane can be used for some objectives. The slope and orientation will be particularly important for relatively small, steep watersheds. Frank and Lee (1966) provided many calculations of slope-aspect effects on solar radiation. Tables 6.3 and 6.4 briefly summarizes the interactions among slope, aspect, date of year, and latitude. Mathematical

TABLE 6.3. ASPECT AND SCOPE EFFECTS ON TOTAL ANNUAL
POTENTIAL SOLAR RADIATION, R_{sp}, RECEIVED BY A
SURFACE, THOUSANDS OF LANGLEYS*

Latitude	slope, percent	Aspect		
		N	E-W	S
30 deg N	0	282	282	282
	10	266	282	295
	20	248	280	305
	30	230	278	312
	40	210	275	316
	50	192	271	318
40 deg N	0	254	254	254
	10	234	253	271
	20	214	253	285
	30	193	251	296
	40	172	250	305
	50	153	248	310
50 deg N	0	220	220	220
	10	198	220	239
	20	176	220	257
	30	156	220	272
	40	138	220	284
	50	123	220	293

*Compiled from Frank and Lee (1966). Potential radiation is
defined as incoming direct-beam radiation with no atmospheric
attenuation.

and graphical methods have been presented by Gloyne (1965), Jackson
(1967), and Romanova (1974).

Temperature Based Methods

There is some correlation between the climatic variables causing PET
and air temperature. And air temperature is one of the most readily available climatic variables. Several methods have been developed for predicting
PET based on average air temperatures or accumulated degree-days (Veihmeyer,
1964, Table 11-2).

The Blaney-Criddle (1966) method has been widely applied for irrigation designs in the western US. The basic equation is

$$u = k\,p\,\frac{45.7\,t + 813}{100} \quad\dots\dots\dots\dots\dots\dots\dots\dots\dots\dots\dots\dots\dots [6.16]$$

where

u = estimated monthly evapotranspiration in mm
k = an empirical consumptive-use coefficient
p = mean monthly percentage of annual daytime hours of the year, and
t = mean monthly air temperature, °C.

Values of k and p are shown in Tables 6.5 and 6.6. For hydrologic
predictions, the k values must be carefully assessed for the meteorologic and
crop effects they represent (Jensen, 1973, p. 84). This method was developed
for irrigated conditions where soil moisture is not limiting.

Pelton et al. (1960) provided an evaluation of temperature-based methods. Experience has shown the results of energy budgets are usually more

TABLE 6.4. ASPECT AND TIME EFFECT ON TOTAL DAILY POTENTIAL SOLAR RADIATION, R_{sp}, RECEIVED BY A SURFACE, LANGLEYS*

Latitude	Date		10 percent slope Aspect			Horizontal surface
			N	E-w	S	
30 deg N	Jun 22		1017	1002	985	1005
	Jun 1 and	Jul 12	1002	992	979	995
	May 18	Jul 27	976	973	968	976
	May 3	Aug. 10	936	945	950	947
	Apr 19	Aug 25	883	905	922	907
	Apr 4	Sep 9	819	845	884	856
	Mar 21	Sep 23	745	793	836	794
	Mar 7	Oct 8	666	726	781	727
	Feb 20	Oct 22	588	658	723	658
	Feb 7	Nov 7	517	594	666	594
	Jan 23	Nov 19	459	541	618	541
	Jan 10	Dec 3	418	502	583	502
	Dec 22					
40 deg N	Jan 22		1022	1020	1015	1023
	Jan 1 and	Jul 13	998	1002	1001	1004
	May 18	Jul 27	957	969	977	972
	May 3	Aug 10	898	922	940	924
	Apr 19	Aug 25	823	859	890	861
	Apr 4	Sep 9	736	785	829	786
	Mar 21	Sep 23	640	702	758	702
	Mar 7	Oct 8	544	616	682	616
	Feb 20	Oct 22	453	532	606	532
	Feb 7	Nov 7	373	457	536	456
	Jan 23	Nov 19	311	397	479	396
	Jan 10	Dec 3	268	354	438	354
	Dec 22		243	330	414	329
50 deg N	Jun 22		1011	1019	1024	1021
	Jun 1 and	Jul 12	977	991	1002	993
	May 18	Jul 27	920	943	962	945
	May 3	Aug 10	839	875	906	876
	Apr 19	Aug 25	741	790	834	791
	Apr 4	Sep 9	631	694	749	694
	Mar 21	Sep 23	517	590	656	590
	Mar 7	Oct 8	406	487	562	486
	Feb 20	Oct 22	307	393	472	391
	Feb 7	Nov 7	225	311	393	310
	Jan 23	Nov 19	164	249	330	247
	Jan 10	Dec 3	124	206	286	205
	Dec 22		102	182	261	181

*Compiled from Frank and Lee (1966). Potential radiation is defined as incoming direct beam with no atmospheric attenuation.

reliable than temperature-based methods, and the latter should be used only in cases of quite limited data. Temperature methods may be useful for broadscale planning but not for daily models which represent hydrologic processes.

Aerodynamic Profile Methods

The measurement of water vapor, as it is transported away from an evaporating surface, offers the potential of the most direct measurement of ET. The approach usually involves measuring temperature and vapor pressure of the air at two or more heights above the evaporating crop and a profile of wind velocities to define moisture and temperature gradients and wind transport, or fluctuations of vertical velocity and humidity at a single height. The measurements are all quite sensitive and the amount

TABLE 6.5. SEASONAL CONSUMPTIVE-USE COEFFICIENTS k
IN BLANEY-CRIDDLE EQUATION FOR IRRIGATION CROPS
IN WESTERN UNITED STATES
(BLANEY AND CRIDDLE, 1966)

Crop	Length of growing season or period	k
Alfalfa	Between frosts	0.80 - 0.90
Beans	3 months	0.60 - 0.70
Corn	4 months	0.75 - 0.85
Cotton	7 months	0.60 - 0.70
Grains, small	3 months	0.75 - 0.85
Sorghums	4-5 months	0.70 - 0.80
Pasture, grass	Between frosts	0.75 - 0.85

of required data is voluminous.

Considerable research has been conducted with sophisticated instrumentation, like that described by Dyer (1961) for the mass transfer-eddy flux method or that of Parmele and Jacoby (1975) for the Bowen ratio measurements. Good results have been obtained as compared with lysimeters, but instrumentation and techniques for hydrologic measurements or predictions are not yet developed to the point that these methods can be applied for other than research purposes.

Combination Method

Neither the vertical energy budget nor the aerodynamic methods are capable of predicting PET without assumptions and limitations. Penman (1948, 1956) developed a method to combine these two theories which removed some of these limitations and his equation is widely used. With diffinement and testing (Businger, 1956; Tanner and Pelton, 1960; van Bavel, 1966), it now represents one of the more reliable techniques for predicting PET from climatic data.

The complete derivation of the combination equation is quite lengthy and involves many micrometeorologic concepts. The derivation can be divided into the following steps: (a) define the vertical energy budget of the soil or plant surface, (b) apply the Dalton-type transport function to obtain Bowen's ratio, (c) apply Penman's psychrometric simplification to eliminate the need for surface temperature, and (d) apply the vertical transport equation obtained from turbulent transport theory. A complete development for each of these steps is given by Saxton (1972, Appendix A) and abbreviated derivations are found in many sources (e.g., Jensen, 1973, p. 70).

TABLE 6.6. DAYTIME-HOURS, PERCENTAGE (OR 100p) IN BLANEY-CRIDDLE
EQUATION (ANNUAL VALUE OF p = 1.00)
(VEIHMEYER, 1964; BLANEY AND CRIDDLE, 1966)

Latitude deg, N	Jan	Feb	Mar	Apr	May	June	July	Aug	Sept	Oct	Nov	Dec
20	7.74	7.25	8.41	8.52	9.15	9.00	9.25	8.96	8.30	8.18	7.58	7.66
30	7.30	7.03	8.38	8.72	9.53	9.49	9.67	9.22	8.33	7.99	7.19	7.15
40	6.76	6.72	8.33	8.95	10.02	10.08	10.22	9.54	8.39	7.75	6.72	6.52
50	5.98	6.30	8.24	9.24	10.68	10.91	10.99	10.00	8.46	7.45	6.10	5.65

Several assumptions are made in the course of the derivation, like air thermal stability and equal transport coefficients of momentum and vapor, but these seem to have neglegible effects for most applications.

The combination equation may be written:

$$LE = \frac{(\Delta/\Upsilon)\, R_n + \dfrac{(K\, L\, d_a\, u_a)}{[\ln(\frac{z_a - d}{z_o})]^2}}{1 + (\Delta/\Upsilon)} \quad\dots\dots\dots\dots\dots\dots\dots\dots\dots \text{[6.17]}$$

$$K = \frac{\rho\, k^2 \epsilon}{p} \quad\dots\dots\dots\dots\dots\dots\dots\dots\dots\dots\dots\dots\dots\dots \text{[6.18]}$$

where

E = potential evapotranspiration rate (cm/day)
Δ = slope of psychrometric saturation line (mbars/°C)
γ = psychrometric constant (mbars/°C)
R_n = net radiation flux (cal/cm²/day)
L = latent heat of vaporization (cal/g)
d_a = saturation vapor pressure deficit of air (e_0 - e_1 (mbars)
u_a = windspeed at elevation z_a (m/day)
z_a = anemometer height above soil (cm)
d = wind profile displacement height (cm)
z_o = wind profile roughness height (cm)
ρ = air density (g/cm³)
k = von Karman coefficient (0.41)
ϵ = water/air molecular ratio (0.622), and
p = ambient air pressure (mbars).

All terms of K and the value of L are treated as constants in most applications. Care must be exercised to maintain consistent units throughout.

Application of the combination equation [6.17] requires measurements or estimates of four variables—net radiation, air temperature, air humidity, and horizontal wind movement—plus appropriate values for the other parameters which can usually be treated as constants for a given site. Net radiation can be assessed the same as for the energy budget approach. The (Δ/γ) term is a function of air temperature and tabled values are available (van Bavel, 1966). A polynominal equation will represent these values as

$$(\Delta/\Upsilon) = 0.672 + 4.28 \times 10^{-2}\, T + 1.13 \times 10^{-3}\, T^2$$

$$+ 1.66 \times 10^{-5} T^3 + 1.70 \times 10^{-7}\, T^4 \quad\dots\dots\dots\dots\dots\dots \text{[6.19]}$$

where T is air temperature (°C), (Saxton, 1972). Atmospheric pressure will cause about a 5 percent change from sea level to 1500-m (4921 ft) elevation (Jensen, 1973, p. 69). Vapor pressure deficit can be calculated using ambient air temperature and either relative humidity or dew point temperature with appropriate psychrometric calculations. Horizontal wind travel must be from a height in the wind profile appropriately represented by the logarithmic wind profile terms.

The logarithmic wind profile values are difficult to define, particularly z_0, for surfaces other than open water or flat close-cut vegetation (Szeicz et al., 1969). A sensitivity analyses (Saxton, 1975) showed LE is not highly sensitive to these terms, but large errors in z_0 and d are possible, which then result in significant LE errors. When used as a calibrating parameter, z_0 normally should not be larger than 1 cm for daily estimates, and would be from 0.25 to 0.5 cm when using mean monthly meterologic data (Jensen, 1973, p. 70). For daily estimates, Saxton (1972, 1974a) showed z_0 values of about 0.5 cm for pasture and about 2.0 cm for mature corn after finding that the total wind term of $[\ln (z_a - d)/z_0]^2$ had a value of about 25 to 30 for both crops with some seasonal variation within this range. Parmele and Jacoby (1975) showed z_0 values of 0.5 to 2.0 cm for corn. The wind profile displacement height, d, is about equivalent to crop height.

There is a requirement that the variables Δ/γ, R_n, d_a and u_a correctly represent the time increment being computed so that the LE value for the total increment is a close integration of shorter time increments if they had been calculated. For example, a daily average d_a from max-min values multiplied times the daily wind run will not provide the same value as the average of hourly d_a values times hourly wind run. Data availability rarely allows computations for short time periods, but the consequences must be recognized and the data averaged accordingly (Tanner and Pelton, 1960; van Bavel, 1966; Pruitt and Doorenbos, 1977).

Several other modifications and simplifications have been made to the combination method since its introduction by Penman (1948). Monteith (1965) added a term to account for vapor movement resistance from the evaporating surface and similarly Tanner and Fuchs (1968) incorporated a surface temperature value. Improved calculation methods have been developed (Messem, 1975; Lowe, 1977) and Thom and Oliver (1977) suggested a different ventilation term. Doorenbos and Pruitt (1975) provided empirical adjustments for predicting ET based on a study by an FAO consultation group using data from 10 sites with widely different climates.

Applications of the combination equation have generally been successful when tested with measured data inputs over monitored evaporating surfaces (e.g., van Bavel, 1966). Comparison of predicted PET using the combination model versus measured Class A pan evaporation is shown in Fig. 6.9 (Saxton, 1974). These same evaporation data were compared with R_n in Fig. 6.7. The improved correlation of PET over R_n can largely be related to the added consideration of the aerodynamic terms in the combination equation.

Sensitivity Analysis

It is necessary to evaluate the relative effect of the several variables that cause PET to assess the accuracy of PET predictions. Sensitivity analyses help to determine the required accuracy of instrumentation for measurements and calculations needed for estimating PET. No single answer is possible because evaporation for each period is the result of a unique set of variable effects, but average guidelines have been developed (McCuen, 1974; Saxton, 1975; Coleman and DeCoursey, 1976). In general, vertical

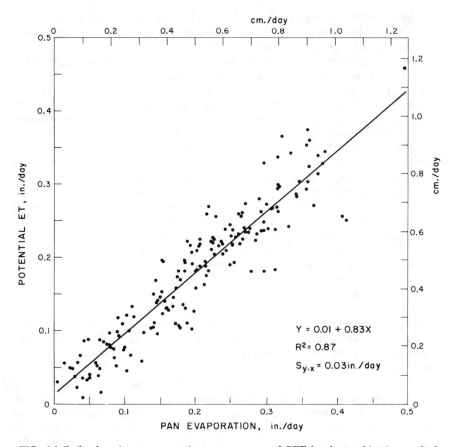

FIG. 6.9 Daily class A pan evaporation versus computed PET by the combination method near Treynor, Iowa (Saxton et al., 1974a).

energy related variables, particularly R_n, are most important. Aerodynamic variables are usually less important, except when there are very dry winds.

Advection

The horizontal transport of energy and humidity can be quite significant under some circumstances and is difficult to measure or estimate without an extensive instrumentation network. Energy is advected by sensible heat moving downwind from areas where energy is greater than that which the plant can utilize, which usually means air movement from dry areas to areas with more moisture available for evaporation. High vapor deficits also increase the evaporative ability of this foreign air. Large humid areas experience little advection effect. The effect in semihumid and semiarid regions is quite variable but occasionally significant, either because of local advection or regional air mass transport. Rosenberg (1969a) and Hanks et al. (1971) discussed advection and Blad and Rosenberg (1974) showed that advected energy supplied about 20 percent of the total energy during 4 wks midsummer in eastern Nebraska. The aerodynamic portion of the combination equation, which contains wind travel and vapor deficit, will account for advection effects if the terms are correctly represented (van Bavel, 1966).

Millar (1964), Davenport and Hudson (1967) and Rider et al. (1963) discussed the basis of advection.

Spatial Variation

Climatologic variables which determine PET tend to vary slowly with distance given that major land form features are reasonably similar. For some applications, when data are transferred from off-site, the effects of aspect and slope may be important. The methods for predicting radiation on differing slopes and aspects, which was presented previously, will provide relative values. Foyster (1973) described a grid technique to determine regional PET, and the method of computing actual ET in the Stanford hydrology model (Crawford and Linsley, 1966) contains an empirical adjustment for spatial variation over larger watersheds.

Comparison of Methods

The selection of a method for PET estimates depends on several criteria. Data availability often dominates. Accuracy required and time available to develop accurate estimates from available data sources are important. Whether the estimates are in retrospect, current time, or projections will often dictate time and data availability.

Studies comparing the results of several methods were reported by McGuinness and Bordne (1972), Bordne and McGuinness (1973), and Parmele and McGuinness (1974). Doorenbos and Pruitt (1975) and Burman (1976) showed similar comparisons for a variety of stations.

The comparison values in Table 6.7 (Parmele and McGuinnes, 1974) showed that data inputs and location of equation development account for much of the differences. Blaney-Criddle used only mean daily air temperature; Jensen-Haise used solar radiation and air temperature, and Christensen used all available data. The Penman, van Bavel, and Weather Bureau methods are all related developments and require air temperature, air humidity, wind and radiation. The Mustonen-McGuinness method adds soil moisture data to the Weather Bureau method. The first three methods were developed for irrigated areas of western US. The more simple and direct methods which use only net radiation and pan evaporation provide almost equally accurate estimates as those requiring more data, although they are more empirical and thus subject to increased variations, particularly in the drier climates. Pruitt and Doorenbos (1977) made comparisons over a wide range of climates and concluded that there is a very strong need for local calibration of all equations.

In a review of 15 methods for estimating PET, including those just discussed, Jensen (1973, Table 7.3) showed that only the combination equations of Penman or its modifications by van Bavel and others and the R_n based method of Jensen-Haise would be recommended for periods of 5 days or less. He noted that the availability of meteorological data alone should not be the sole criterion in selecting a method, since some of the needed data can be estimated with sufficient accuracy to permit using one of the better methods. He concluded that in general, energy balance or energy balance-aerodynamic equations will provide the most accurate results of the various meteorological methods because they are based on physical laws and rational relationships.

TABLE 6.7. CORRELATION AND REGRESSION STATISTICS FOR MEASURED
VERSUS COMPUTED DAILY EVAPOTRANSPIRATION (ET) FOR MIXED MEADOW
GRASS AT COSHOCTON, OHIO USING 1968 ON-SITE METEOROLOGICAL DATA
(6/23-9/14/68) (PARMELE AND McGUINNESS, 1974)

Calculation method	Avg. calc. daily ET, mm/day*	Diff. from lysimeter, percent	Intercept a, mm/day	Slope b, mm/day	Standard error, mm/day	Correlation coefficient, r
Blaney-Criddle	5.36	+25.6	1.83	11.5	1.55	0.31
Jensen-Haise	4.50	+ 5.4	0.76	19.8	0.86	0.85
Christiansen	5.74	+34.5	0.41	20.7	1.09	0.74
Penman	3.78	-11.3	0.64	24.3	0.91	0.82
van Bavel	4.14	- 3.0	0.86	20.8	0.99	0.81
W.B. Class A Pan	4.34	+ 1.8	1.02	19.1	0.84	0.86
W.B. lake	3.23	-24.4	1.12	24.8	0.81	0.87
Net radiation	4.04	- 5.4	0.81	21.3	0.97	0.80
Mustonen-McGuinness	3.84	-10.1	1.08	21.2	0.79	0.88

*Average ET by lysimeter = 4.27 mm/day for n = 70.

Data Sources

Data for PET calculations are often scattered and difficult to assemble into continuous reliable sets for consistent calculations. Published reviews of data sources are provided by the US Weather Bureau (now a part of National Oceanic and Atmospheric Administration, NOAA) (US Dept. of Commerce, 1964; 1968). Broader scale summaries and climatic atlases are also available (Thorthwaite Assoc., 1964; Caprio, 1974; Bryson and Hare, 1974). Generalized maps of evaporation, like those by Kohler et al. (1959) and Nordenson (1962), are often useful although any measured data from within a reasonable distance would provide better average and time-distributed inputs to hydrologic models.

PLANT TRANSPIRATION

Plants control a large number of the processes that determine ET rates, either by their use of radiant energy, stomatal control of leaf transpiration, or root interaction with available soil water. Plant effects have received more emphasis in recent years. Federer (1975) noted the change of recent research from ET as a physically controlled process to ET as a physiologically controlled process. This is a particularly important development for hydrologic predictions because watershed vegetation in many climates seldom transpires at a potential rate. This emphasis has been carried over to application through system models of ET from crops with incomplete canopies where transpiration and soil evaporation are calculated separately (Ritchie, 1972; Saxton, et al., 1974a; Tanner and Jury, 1976).

The effects of plants on ET can be divided into the main categories of: (a) canopy, (b) phenology, (c) root distribution, and (d) water stress. Obviously there are many interactions among these categories, but they represent major considerations for computational purposes and provide a convenient framework for discussion. Often, several of these effects have been combined into crop coefficient curves.

Many of the basic interactions of crops with the atmosphere and soil are provided by Monteith (1976), Kramer (1969) and Slatyer (1967). Details on modeling basic plant processes are given by Thornley (1976). New developments in modeling plant growth may eventually provide significant inputs related to plant functions and ET.

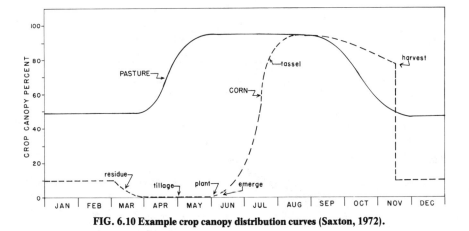

FIG. 6.10 Example crop canopy distribution curves (Saxton, 1972).

Canopy

The dynamic development, maturation, and decay of crop canopies significantly influence plant transpiration effects. For annual crops, like corn or cotton, the canopy very rapidly develops from nothing to nearly full soil cover and then matures and is harvested. The canopy of any particular day largely determines the amount of intercepted solar radiation or adsorbed advection, thus hydrology models must provide a representation of this dynamic plant behavior.

A direct approach is to graph the canopy growth curve versus time to represent the percent of ground shading throughout the year. Example curves based on visual observations are shown in Fig. 6.10. To define crop canopy curves requires knowledge or observations about normal planting dates, emergence times, rate of development, tasselling or blooming dates, harvest dates, and residue conditions. Representing canopy as average daily soil shading primarily is a partitioning of the radiant energy between plant and soil, thus modifications need to be considered if advection is expected to play a significant role. Although not highly accurate, an empirical canopy curve based on local knowledge of crop growth will often adequately represent crop canopy effects.

Recent research on crop effects has used the ratio of leaf area divided by soil surface area as a leaf area index (LAI) to relate measured ET to effective canopy. This measure compares canopy effects of different crops, although it has not been entirely satisfactory among crops of widely differing canopy structures. Ritchie and Burnett (1971) and Kristensen (1974) showed very similar curves for barley, sugarbeets, long and short grass, corn, and sorghum, as shown in Fig. 6.11. For almost all cases, the actual-to-potential ET (AET/PET) ratio approached 1.0 as the LAI approached 3.0. Although LAI values relate closely to the AET/PET ratio and provide a direct measure of crop canopy, they are difficult to predict, and estimates of canopy cover as a percent of the soil shading may yet be the most practical (Adams et al., 1976).

Phenology

The phenological development of plants often modifies a plant's ability to transpire. As a crop matures, its need for water and ability to transpire are diminished. Because phenological changes may occur independent of

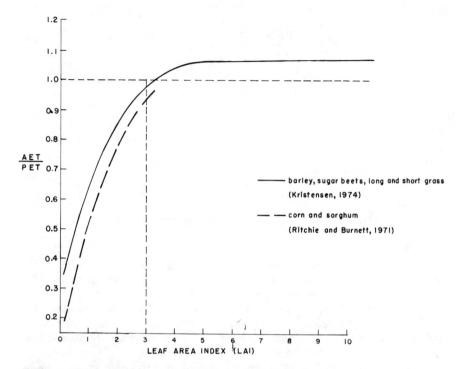

FIG. 6.11 Relationship between leaf area index (LAI) and actual over potential evapotranspiration to define the influence of crop canopy.

the crop canopy present, this effect must be an added consideration.

As with canopy, a time distribution graph of the relative ability of a plant canopy to transpire will often be adequate for hydrologic models. The effect being represented is the expected transpiration ability of the canopy existing at any time as compared with that of a fully transpiring, equal canopy. Example curves are shown in Fig. 6.12. Crop maturation is the principal cause for loss of ability, but drying of leaves from stress of heat, moisture, or insects may also cause modifications. For example, cool season grasses may mature and become somewhat dormant during midseason, as shown in Fig. 6.12, then recover as fall cooling begins.

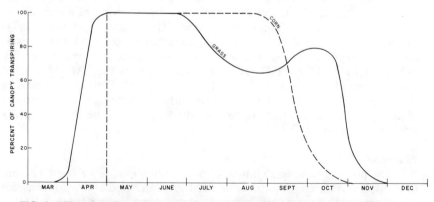

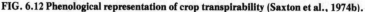

FIG. 6.12 Phenological representation of crop transpirability (Saxton et al., 1974b).

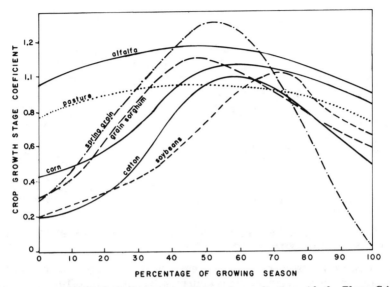

FIG. 6.13 Seasonal distribution of crop coefficients for application with the Blaney-Criddle Equation (USDA, Soil Conservation Service, 1967).

Crop residues pose a special canopy situation since they intercept radiation but have no ability to utilize that energy for evaporation unless intercepted precipitation is present. This can be considered a special case of crop phenology where the crop has lost all ability to transpire, or the residues may be considered as part of the soil evaporation process. Nevertheless the residues change characteristics over time through decay and destruction by tillage and must be dynamically represented.

Crop Coefficients

The crop effects on ET have often been represented by crop coefficients, either as average seasonal values or as seasonal distributions. Most often the coefficients account for the combined effects of crop canopy, phenological development, and soil evaporation. This general approach has largely been used for irrigation ET predictions where there is less need for separation of the ET processes. In the same sense, these empirical relationships can be quite useful for simplified hydrologic models and general guidance to crop performance because they often represent tested experience.

The representation and application of crop coefficients varies considerably, thus each data set must be examined to ensure all assumptions are met. The representative curves in Fig. 6.13 were developed to be used only with the Blaney-Criddle equation (equation [6.16]), and essentially all crop and soil effects are included. The growing season is approximately defined as planting to harvesting.

Another set of coefficients presented in Fig. 6.14 also relate the AET/PET ratio to crop development, but in this case PET is defined as that from a well-watered grass surface (which will relate closely to an atmospheric determined PET). The approximate number of days to effective cover (approximately full soil shading) is 85 days for corn, 35 days for beans, and at heading for small grain. Alfalfa reaches effective cover at first harvest, where the coefficient decreases to 0.5, then recovers to a value of 1.0 in 20

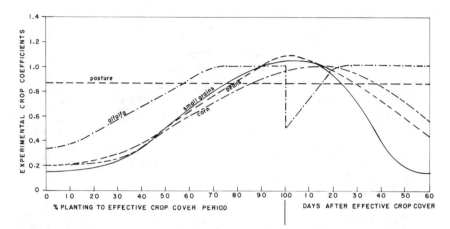

FIG. 6.14 Crop coefficients relating AET/PET ratio to crop stage where PET is defined as that from well-watered grass surface (Jensen, 1973).

days. Pasture is assumed a constant coefficient, although this may not be accurate for full year computations as demonstrated in Fig. 6.10.

The example relationships of Figs. 6.13 and 6.14 show the variability among crops in their development and ET demand. Such relationships have been developed from research data and experience, thus the accuracy and variation year-to-year may be considerable. Relationships for other crops and locations may be found in Denmead and Shaw (1959), USDA Soil Conservation Service (1967), Pruitt et al. (1972a), Shaw (1963), Mustonen and McGuinness (1967), Hanks et al. (1968), and Luebs et al. (1975). Doorenbos and Pruitt (1975) provided a method to develop crop-coefficient curves for many crops under a wide range of growing season lengths and climates.

When translating crop coefficients to hydrologic model applications, care must be exercised to define any expected differences between irrigated or non-irrigated situations; seasonal dates; management practices like planting, cutting and harvesting; and other crop characteristics. Particular care to maintain separation of hydrologic processes must be taken in models where canopy, phenology, soil evaporation, roots and moisture stress are considered.

Roots

Crop roots are as important as canopy in the process of connecting soil water with atmospheric energy and the resulting transpiration. However, root distribution and their effectiveness are more difficult to study and quantify. Much work has been done to quantify the root development of major crops. Corn roots were studied by Linscott et al. (1962), Taylor and Klepper (1973), and Mengel and Barker (1974). Soybean data were reported by Allmaras et al. (1975a, 1975b) and Stone et al. (1976). Cotton roots were considered by Taylor and Klepper (1974). Some information is available on most crops and basic relationships are presented in texts like those of Whittington (1968) and de Roo (1968).

Many hydrologic models have simply considered depth of maximum rooting as a predetermined parameter or fitted coefficient. For more physically related modeling, the time and depth of rooting density is required,

TABLE 6.8. DISTRIBUTIONS OF WATER EXTRACTION FROM SOIL LAYERS BY TRANSPIRATION, PERCENTAGE OF TOTAL (SAXTON ET AL., 1974b)

Depth of soil layer, cm	Beginning date of each distribution*									Grass, all season
	5/10	6/7	6/14	6/27	7/4	7/11	7/18	7/25	8/1	
0.0 - 15.2	100	50	40	35	35	35	35	35	30	35
15.2 - 30.5		50	27	25	25	25	25	25	25	30
30.5 - 45.7			20	20	18	15	10	8	8	20
45.7 - 61.0			13	10	10	8	8	7	7	10
61.0 - 76.2				10	7	7	7	5	5	3
76.2 - 91.4					5	5	5	5	5	2
91.4 - 106.7						5	5	5	5	
106.7 - 121.9							5	5	5	
121.9 - 137.2								5	5	
137.2 - 152.4									5	

*Planting date about May 1-15.

especially for annual crops which establish a complete new root system each year. Only in this way can soil moisture profiles and their interaction with the root profiles be modeled. This becomes very important when large differences in moisture contents exist with soil depth. Crop transpiration may be severely limited if the rooting patterns do not coincide with available moisture in the soil profile.

The water uptake by plants and the mathematical representation of this phenomena have received considerable attention in recent years (Klute and Peters, 1969; Feddes et al., 1976a, 1976b; Hillel and Talpaz, 1976; Slack et al., 1977). In addition to representing time and depth of rooting densities, several approaches of calculating the resistance of water to the root, then through the root, stems, and leaves have been proposed (Goldstein and Mankin, 1972). Root age and location seem to be quite important. Taylor and Klepper (1973) speculated that the deeper, less dense roots may be more effective for water uptake because they are younger and usually in wetter soil. Studies in this level of detail have not yet provided additional hydrologic prediction capability; thus, including basic root-density dynamics for interaction with available soil water may be the most sophistication now warranted.

Saxton et al. (1974b) obtained satisfactory results using nine depth-percentage distributions to represent soil water extraction by corn throughout the growing season, and a single distribution for an established pasture. These distributions, shown in Table 6.8, represent the expected water extraction given adequate water throughout the profile and may only approximately reflect actual root densities.

Most crops have a genetic rooting characteristic that will provide estimates of root density distributions with depth and time; and, in turn, estimates of water extraction. Older roots are less efficient in water extraction, thus root quantity distributions must be modified. Characteristic rooting patterns can be significantly modified by the soil root environment like dense layers, poor aeration, very dry or wet, and chemicals. Some deep-rooted plants, like alfalfa or trees, may extract water from deep wet layers or shallow groundwater and pose special modeling problems.

Water Stress

It has long been recognized that transpiration is reduced at some level of deficiency of soil water and will eventually cease if water is severely limited.

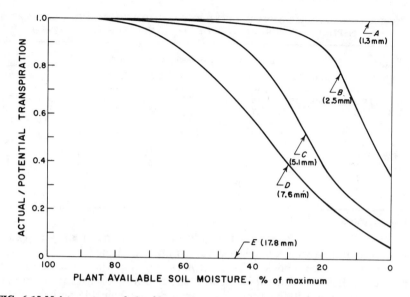

FIG. 6.15 Moisture stress relationships used to compute actual transpiration. Curves A to E represent potential ET demand rates (mm/day) with values in parentheses suggested for corn in western Iowa (Saxton et al., 1974b).

This process has not been quantified with any significant degree of confidence. Many studies have been conducted, but their results are often contradictory, or at least not comparable due to crop, soil, or technique differences.

Mustonen and McGuinness (1968) and Baier (1969) summarized several relationships between plant-available soil water and actual/potential transpiration ratio. There were wide differences of opinion. Some of these relationships are derived for unusual conditions, like deep-rooted crops in sandy soil. Other relationships are simple mathematical expressions for expediency. The variation of soil depth used to define the quantity of available water also caused some differences.

Denmead and Shaw (1962) developed basic plant-stress data using a large-container study. They later used these results for predicting transpiration from corn (Shaw, 1963) and meadow (Shaw, 1964). Holmes and Robertson (1963) showed similar relationships. Ritchie (1973) did not obtain similar results, but he defined available water using the entire soil profile — not that related only to current plant roots — which thus precluded a direct comparison.

It is generally agreed that both plant-available soil moisture and the atmospheric demand determine what proportion of potential transpiration a plant will achieve, i.e., the actual/potential ratio. Given a moderate available soil water status, a plant under low atmospheric demand may achieve nearly all of that demand, but the same moisture level and a high atmospheric demand may result in moisture stress and a significant reduction of transpiration from the potential.

A relationship of this process is given in Fig. 6.15 where each curve represents an AET/PET versus plant-available soil moisture relationship for a specific atmospheric potential. This approach, designed after that of Shaw (1964), was applied by Saxton et al. (1974b) to individual 15-cm soil layers.

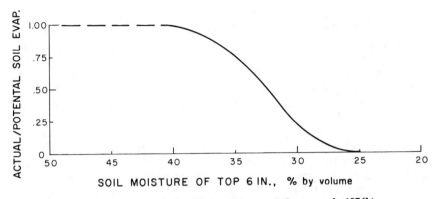

FIG. 6.16 Soil evaporation relationship for silt loam soil (Saxton et al., 1974b).

Potential daily demand values associated with curves A through E (low to high PET) were determined for corn and grass crops by calibration. Those for corn are shown in parentheses on the curves. Interpolations were made between the curves as defined by daily PET.

The application of relationships like those in Fig. 6.15 will require calibration for each soil depth used to define the available soil moisture, each crop, and perhaps for each soil. Soil water pressures (capillary suction) may be a better measure than plant available water. Additional effects which have been investigated, like soil conductivity near the roots and plant water pressure, may eventually reduce the need for calibration (Ritchie et al., 1972; Ritchie and Jordan, 1972; Yang and de Jung, 1972; Sheperd, 1975). Some recent simulations have attempted to treat the movement of water through the soil to the roots and through the roots and canopy as a series of conduits with internal and boundary resistances, but this approach will require further development and testing before it can be readily applied (Szeicz and Long, 1969; Denmead and Millar, 1976; Campbell, 1977; Slack et al., 1977).

SOIL WATER EVAPORATION

The evaporation of water from a soil surface is very similar to transpiration from a plant. Weigand and Taylor (1961) in their review of evaporation from porous media noted that for an analysis to describe evaporation accurately, it must deal with the rate limiting process like energy, heat transfer, unsaturated flow, or molecular diffusion of vapor. The principles again are the availability of energy and water at the soil surface and the transport of water vapor into the atmosphere.

Soil evaporation is often described as occurring at three separate stages beginning with wet soil (Gardner and Hillel, 1962; Idso et al., 1974). In the first stage, the drying rate is limited by and equals the evaporative demand (available energy). During the second stage, water availability progressively becomes more limiting. The third stage is described as an extension of the second stage but is limited to a more constant rate. Studies utilizing the concept of concurrent flow of heat and water by van Bavel and Hillel (1976) clearly demonstrated the first two stages but did not support the notion of a third stage.

A relationship incorporating the first two stages for reducing potential soil-water evaporation to actual is shown in Fig. 6.16. This curve was developed by Saxton et al. (1974b) from those suggested in the literature (Holmes and Robertson, 1963) and field calibration in a silt loam soil. This relationship resembles the C and D curves used to represent crop water stress in Fig. 6.15. However, unlike plants, soil lacks the ability to compensate for stress and thus a more straight-forward approach to a description of soil evaporation is possible. The approach by Hillel (1975, 1977) and van Bavel and Hillel (1976) of simultaneous heat and water flux at the soil surface and within the soil profile provides a more detailed and accurate prediction of soil evaporation but requires significantly more data input and computational time. An intermediate, and perhaps more feasible approach, is to consider intercepted and ponded water at or near the soil surface for stage one drying and upward unsaturated flow for stage two.

Considerable effort has been made to explain many influences on soil evaporation, like mulches, residues, wetting methods, crust formation, and tillage (Unger and Parker, 1976; Adams et al., 1976; Bond and Willis, 1970, 1971; Bresler and Kemper, 1970). Each of these effects can be significant, but the cause can usually be attributed to one of the physical limitations. Soil cracking and dew formation potentially influence evaporation, although neither seems to be of significant magnitude (Ritchie and Adams, 1974; Rosenberg, 1969b). Average dew during 11 days at midsummer in eastern Nebraska was only 0.14 mm/day (0.005 in./day). Thus, for hydrologic predictions, separating the atmospheric potential reaching the soil surface from that going to the vegetation and accounting for the moisture availability limitations will provide first estimates of soil evaporation with some calibration yet necessary.

ACTUAL ET METHODS

Modeling the actual ET component of the hydrologic cycle of small watersheds may be approached in many ways depending upon the data available, the degree of detail desired in the representation, major crops to be considered, and relative emphasis among the several processes that determine ET. A large number of systems have been developed in recent years for actual ET predictions—each has its own requirements and emphases. For application to small watershed hydrology, a method should account for climatic, crop, and soil variables in some reasonable fashion under a range of moisture regimes. The methods discussed in the following paragraphs range from quite simple to very complex, and their success in accurate representations is somewhat proportional to complexity; thus each hydrologist will need to select a method based upon objectives.

A simple daily water budget based on an equation of the type

$$ARI_i = (ARI_{i-1} + R_{i-1})\,K \quad\dots\dots\dots\dots\dots\dots\dots\dots\dots\dots\dots\dots \quad [6.20]$$

where
    ARI = antecedent retention index for day i
    R = daily retention (infiltration), and
    K = a seasonally varied coefficient less than 1.0,
was adopted from an exponential antecedent precipitation index (Saxton and Lenz, 1967). Daily estimates of actual ET provided reasonable estimates of antecedent soil moisture as compared with observed soil moisture data. Guidelines for estimating K coefficients were provided.

Haan (1972) simulated daily ET in a model written to estimate monthly streamflow from daily precipitation by the relationship

$$E = E_p(M/C) \quad \dotsfill \quad [6.21]$$

where
- E = actual ET (mm/day)
- E_p = potential ET by the Thornthwaite method (mm/day)
- M = available soil moisture (mm), and
- C = maximum available soil moisture (mm).

Twentyfive mm (1 in.) of soil moisture was made readily available and the ratio M/C was set to 1.0 until that was depleted. On days with rainfall, E_p was divided by 2 to account for cloudy conditions. Such a simplified scheme will only work well where monthly or seasonal results are being analyzed and only then with calibration for crop and soil conditions.

A somewhat more complex soil moisture budgeting equation was reported by Bair and Robertson (1966) as

$$AE_i = \sum_{j=1}^{n} k_j \, \frac{S_i}{S_j} \, Z_j \, PE_i \, e^{-w(PE_i - \overline{PE})} \quad \dotsfill \quad [6.22]$$

where
- AE = actual ET (mm/day)
- k = coefficient for soil and plant characteristics
- S_i = available soil moisture (mm)
- S_j = capacity for available water (mm)
- Z_j = factor for different types of soil dryness curves
- w = factor for effects of varying PE rates on AE/PE ratio
- PE_i = potential ET (mm/day), and
- $\overline{PE}$ = average for month or season (mm/day).

The equation is summed for soil layers j for each day i. The coefficient k_j largely depends on plant roots in each layer, Z_j adjusts for nonlinearity in the relation of AE/PE versus soil moisture (like those in Fig. 6.14), and w makes a similar adjustment and can be estimated by $w = 7.91 - 0.011$ (S_i/S_j). Using coefficient values obtained by calibration and experience, an equation of this type will provide reasonably good daily actual ET estimates because most major effects are considered. The need for calibration causes difficulty in general application, particularly by those who do not have much experience with the equation.

A similar single equation approach was applied by Holtan et al. (1975) and England (1975). Their equation is

$$ET = (GI) \, k \, E_p \, [S-SA)/S]^x \quad \dotsfill \quad [6.23]$$

where

- ET = actual ET (mm/day)
- GI = growth index of crop (percent)

k = ratio of ET to pan evaporation for full canopy
E_p = pan evaporation (mm/day)
S = total soil porosity (percent)
SA = available soil porosity (percent), and
x = exponent estimated to be 0.10.

The GI values reflect crop growth and harvest and are time dependent. The soil storage values S and SA for the root zone approximate water stress although a more precise representation which includes root development and crop stress would significantly improve this aspect. Betson (1976) used a modification of this approach for monthly ET estimates.

Soil moisture depletions (actual ET) for irrigation scheduling have been estimated by Jensen et al., (1971) by the relationship

$$E_t = K_c\,E_{tp} \qquad \dotfill \qquad [6.24]$$

where

E_t = actual ET (mm/day)
E_{tp} = potential ET (mm/day), and
K_c = a coefficient representing the combined effects of the resistance of water movement from the soil to the various evaporating surfaces, the resistance to the diffusion of water vapor from the surfaces to the atmosphere, and the relative amount of radiant energy available as compared with the reference crop. This inclusive coefficient was estimated as

$$K_c = K_{co}\,K_a + K_s \qquad \dotfill \qquad [6.25]$$

where

K_{co} = mean crop coefficient based on experimental data (soil moisture not limiting)
K_a = ln (AW + 1)/ln 101
AW = remaining available soil moisture (in.), and
K_s = the increase when the soil surface is wetted and equals $(0.9 - K_c)$ times 0.8, 0.5, and 0.3 for day 1, 2 and 3 after wetting. This method has worked successfully for irrigated conditions where soil water seldom limits transpiration and considerable calibration of the several coefficients has been conducted.

Ritchie (1972) composed a series of equations to represent actual ET beginning with the Penman equation to define potential ET, then separately calculated soil and plant evaporation. The potential soil evaporation (first-stage drying) was determined by the relationship

$$E = [\Delta/\Delta + \Upsilon]\,R_n \exp (- 0.398\ LAI) \qquad \dotfill \qquad [6.26]$$

where

E = potential soil evaporation (mm/day)
Δ = slope of the saturation vapor pressure curve at mean air temperature
γ = psychrometric constant (mbars/°C)
R_n = net radiation (cal/cm²/day), and
LAI = leaf area index.

The soil evaporation proceeds at potential rate until soil water transport restricts the water quantity. The amount of drying before this occurs was determined for each soil. A second stage soil evaporation was computed by the relation

$$E = \alpha\, t^{1/2} \quad \dots\dots\dots\dots\dots\dots\dots\dots\dots\dots\dots\dots\dots\dots\dots \quad [6.27]$$

where
  E = soil evaporation (mm/day)
  t = time (days), and
  α = a coefficient to be determined experimentally.
  Plant transpiration in the Ritchie model was represented by the empirical relation

$$E_p = E_o(-0.21 + 0.70\, \text{LAI}^{1/2}) \quad \dots\dots\dots\dots\dots\dots\dots\dots\dots\dots \quad [6.28]$$

where
  E_p = transpiration (mm/day)
  E_o = potential ET (mm/day), and
  LAI = leaf area index.
This equation is valid only for conditions where water is not limiting and LAI varies from 0.1 to 2.7. For LAI > 2.7, $E_p = E_o$. The equation has been tested on cotton and grain sorghum.

This model was later adapted to field conditions where soil water was limiting. In one case, a relationship of the type

$$E_p = \overline{E}_o[1-(t/t_1)^{1/2}] \quad \dots\dots\dots\dots\dots\dots\dots\dots\dots\dots\dots\dots\dots \quad [6.29]$$

was attempted where

  E_p = transpiration (mm/day)
  $\overline{E}_o$ = monthly average potential ET (mm/day)

  t = time after lower limit of soil water content for potential ET (days), and
  t_1 = time to deplete remaining available water after t begins (days).
Computed values were divided by 3 where LAI < 3 to provide improved results. A second attempt reported by Ritchie et al. (1976) used equation [6.29] multiplied by the ratio of current extractable soil water divided by potential extractable soil water within the soil profile.

A comprehensive model to compute daily actual ET from small watersheds was developed and reported by Saxton et al. (1974b). This model, shown schematically in Fig. 6.17, separates the major climatic, crop, and soil effects into a calculation procedure with emphasis on graphical representation of principle relationships. Calculated amounts of interception evaporation, soil evaporation, and plant transpiration are combined to provide daily actual ET estimates.

Beginning at the top of Fig. 6.17, intercepted water at the plant and soil surfaces is considered to have first use of the potential ET energy, and no limits are imposed. Remaining potential ET is divided between soil water evaporation or plant transpiration according to plant canopy present. Actual soil evaporation is the potential limited by soil water content at the surface,

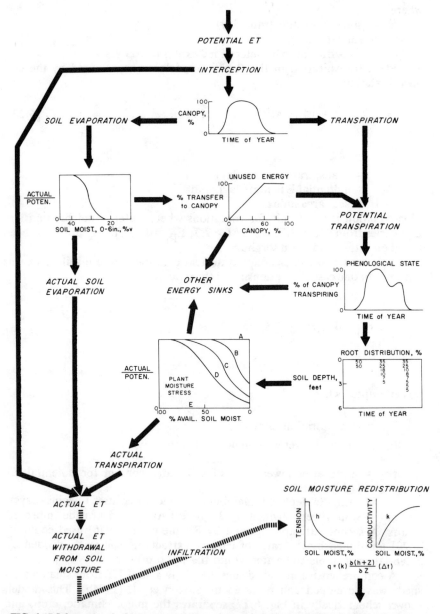

FIG. 6.17 Schematic calculation sequence for computing daily actual ET and soil water changes (Saxton et al., 1974b).

except in the very wet range, thus representing the traditional two-stage drying sequence by the relationship of Fig. 6.16. For dry soil with a plant canopy, a percent of the unused soil evaporation potential is returned to the plant transpiration potential to account for re-radiated energy from the heated soil and air. Actual transpiration is computed through sequential consideration of plant phenology to describe the transpirability of the existing canopy (Fig. 6.12), a root distribution to reflect where in the soil profile the plant is attempting to obtain water (Table 6.8), and a water stress relationship which is applied to each soil layer and is a function of the plant available water of that soil layer and the atmospheric demand on the plant (Fig. 6.15). The soil water is adjusted by abstracting the daily actual ET from each rooting layer, adding daily infiltration computed from daily precipitation minus measured or estimated runoff, and estimating soil water redistribution and percolation by a Darcy-type unsaturated flow computation.

This model has been successfully calibrated and applied to corn and grass on loessial soils, and has the flexibility to be adapted to many types of crops and soils. Fig. 6.18 shows an example of results with this method for selected soil layers of a 1.8-m (6-ft) soil profile throughout the growing season after calibration for the corn crop and silt loam soil. The predicted values were set equal to observed only at the first observation date. Campbell and Johnson (1975), Anderson (1975) and Koelliker et al. (1976) have successfully applied modified versions of this method of wet lands of Iowa, drylands of Iowa, and the semiarid region of western Kansas, respectively. Like most ET methods, this method represents a single crop and soil combination for the computed vertical water balance, thus watersheds with several crops and/or soils would require multiple applications per daily calculation or average crop and soil representations.

Several methods have been reported which apply best to basin hydrology or specific land uses. The ET method applied by Crawford and Linsley (1966) in their Stanford Watershed Model IV considers the effect of areal variation through a coefficient which estimates percent of area which attains varying percentages of an evaporative opportunity, which is in turn a function of a time-dependent coefficient to represent crop growth. Using pan evaporation as a potential ET, this model combines estimated actual ET from interception, two soil zones, and groundwater to estimate a total daily actual ET. No attempt is made to separate soil evaporation from transpiration, and calibration parameters are obtained by fitting to observed watershed data. Fleming (1975, p. 137) provided further details and explanation.

Morton (1975, 1976) presented a method based on regional climatic data and showed its application to many large basins in the United States and Canada. Hanson (1976) and Aase et al. (1973) have developed ET prediction equations for native rangeland of the western US. Grigel and Hubbard (1971) describe an empirical ET model, SOGGY.

Other methods have restricted their data inputs to readily available climatologic data which often makes them more practical than more sophisticated methods. Eagleman (1967) described a method based on air temperature and humidity. Brun et al. (1972), Kanemasu et al. (1976), and Rosenthal et al. (1977), described methods using air temperature, R_n, and LAI. Jensen et al. (1971) discussed a similar practical approach for irrigation scheduling, but the technique can be modified and applied to hydrologic needs.

Several methods have been developed which describe the ET processes within the soil-plant-atmosphere system. The soil-plant-atmosphere model (SPAM) described by Lemon et al. (1973) and Shawcroft et al. (1974) treats the ET and plant growth characteristics in detail. A similar model reported by Hanks et al. (1969) and Nimah and Hanks (1973a, 1973b) concentrates more on the soil moisture and its plant interaction. A model by Goldstein and Mankin (1972), PROSPER, represents this same system with emphasis on forested watersheds.

Even more sophisticated models are being developed as new capability

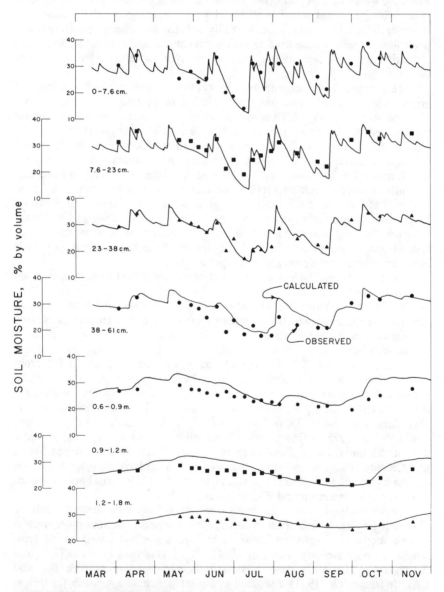

FIG. 6.18 Soil moisture distributions observed and calculated using the method of Saxton et al. (1974b), for corn on silt loam soil during 1970.

in computing capacity and ease of programming is available. Kristensen and Jensen (1975) applied a detailed ET model to the crops of barley, sugarbeets, and grass over a 4-yr period with reported accuracy of 10 percent. van Bavel and Ahmed (1976) described a model of the soil moisture flow and root uptake programmed in CSMP. Hansen (1975) reported a more general model of the soil-plant-atmosphere system programmed in DYNAMO II. Lambert et al. (1973) presented a model of the ET system called TROIKA. H. van Keulen (1975) presented a model programmed in CSMP with all details well described, and Makkink and van Heemst (1974) showed the application results of a similar model.

Not all recent methods of modeling ET have been cited. Those that are presented vary widely in their objectives, the amount of detail required, computation time, and availability of data. Comparison of the several methods shows that the best results are obtained when the soil-plant-atmosphere system is represented by dynamic simulations of the major processes determining ET. Performance of a water yield model will be quite sensitive to the ET method used, whereas a flood peak model may be indifferent to the ET method used. Each ET application must match the prediction method to the objectives.

References

1 Aase, J. K., J. R. Wight and F. H. Siddoway. 1973. Estimating soil water content on native rangeland. Agr. Meteorol. 12(2):185-191.

2 Adams, J. E., G. F. Arkin and J. T. Ritchie. 1976. Influence of row spacing and straw mulch on first stage drying. Soil Sci. Soc. Am. J. 40(3):436-442.

3 Allmaras, R. R., W. W. Nelson and W. B. Vorhees. 1975a. Soybean and corn rooting in southwestern Minnesota, USA, Part 1: Water uptake sink. Soil. Sci. Soc. Am. Proc. 39(4):764-771.

4 Allmaras, R. R., W. W. Nelson and W. B. Vorhees. 1975b. Soybean and corn rooting in southwestern Minnesota, USA, Part 2: Root distributions and related water inflow. Soil Sci. Soc. Am. Proc. 39(4):771-777.

5 ASAE. 1966. Evapotranspiration and its role in water resources management. Conf. Proc., Chicago, IL. ASAE, St. Joseph, MI 49085.

6 Am. Soc. Civil Engr. 1966. Methods for estimating evapotranspiration. Proc. Irrig. & Drain., Specialty Conf., Las Vegas, NV, Nov. 2-4, ASCE, NY.

7 Am. Soc. of Heating, Refrigeration, and Air-Conditioning Engineers (ASRAE). 1974. Applications handbook. George Banta Co., Menasha, WI.

8 Anderson, C. E. 1975. A water balance model of agricultural watersheds on deep loess soils. Ph.D. Dissertation, Dept. of Agronomy, Kansas State University, Manhattan.

9 Aslyng, H. C. 1974. Evapotranspiration and plant production directly related to global radiation. Nordic Hydro. 5:247-256.

10 Baier, W. and G. W. Robertson. 1966. A new versatile soil moisture budget. Can. J. Plant Sci. 46:299-315.

11 Baier, W. 1967. Relationships between soil moisture, actual and potential evapotranspiration. Nat. Res. Coun. of Canada Hydro. Symp. Proc. No. 6, Nov. pp. 155-204.

12 Baier, W. 1969. Concepts of soil moisture availability and their effect on soil moisture estimates from a meteorological budget. Agr. Meteorol. 6:165-178.

13 Betson, R. P. 1973. Evapotranspiration information needs from the viewpoint of hydrologic modeling. Presentation at the San Francisco Fall meeting, Am. Geophysical Union.

14 Betson, R. 1976. Urban hydrology—a systems study in Knoxville, TN. Tennessee Valley Authority, Div. Water Manage., 138 pp., June.

15 Biswas, A. K. 1970. History of hydrology. North-Holland Pub. Co., New York, NY.

16 Blad, B. L. and N. J. Rosenberg. 1974. Evapotranspiration by subirrigated alfalfa and pasture in the east central great plains. Agron. J. 66(2):248-252.

17 Blaney, H. F. and W. D. Criddle. 1966. Determining consumptive use for water developments. ASCE Irrig. and Drain. Spec. Conf., Proc. Nov. 2-4. pp. 1-34.

18 Bloemen, G. W. 1974. On the evolution of parameter values in water balance models. Tech. Bull. 92, Inst. for Land and Water Manage. Res., Wageningen, The Netherlands, 100 pp.

19 Bond, J. J. and W. O. Willis. 1970. Soil water evaporation: first stage drying as influenced by surface residue and evaporation potential. Soil Sci. of Am. Proc. 34(5): 924-928.

20 Bond, J. J. and W. O. Willis. 1971. Soil water evaporation: Long-term drying as influenced by surface residue and evaporation potential. Soil Sci. Soc. of Am. Proc. 35(6): 984-987.

21 Bordne, E. F. and J. L. McGuinness. 1973. Some procedures for calculating potential evapotranspiration. Prof. Geographer 25(1):22-28.

22 Bowen, I. S. 1926. The ratio of heat losses by conduction and by evaporation from any water surface. Phys. Rev. 27:779-787.

23 Bresler, E. and W. D. Kemper. 1970. Soil water evaporation as affected by wetting methods and crust formation. Soil Sci. Soc. Am. Proc. 34(2):3-8.

24 Brown, K. W. and W. Covey. 1966. The energy-budget evaluation of the micrometeorological transfer process within a cornfield. Agr. Meteorol. 3:73-96.

25 Brun, L. J., E. T. Kanemasu, and W. L. Powers. 1972. Evapotranspiration from soybean and sorghum fields. Agron. J. 64(2):145-148.

26 Bryson, R. A. and F. K. Hare (ed.). 1974. Climates of North America. World survey of climatology, Vol. II. Elsevier, NY.

27 Businger, J. A. 1956. Some remarks on Penman's equation for the evapotranspiration. Neth. J. Agr. Sci. 4:77-80.

28 Burman, R. D. 1976. Intercontinental comparison of evaporation estimates. Am. Soc. Civ. Engr. Proc. 102(IR1):109-118.

29 Campbell, G. S. 1977. An introduction to environmental biophysics. Springer-Verlag. New York, NY.

30 Campbell, K. and H. P. Johnson. 1975. Hydrologic simulation of watersheds with artificial drainage. Water Resour. Res. 11(1):120-126.

31 Caprio, M. 1974. World maps of potential evapotranspiration, plant development and spring greening and autumn browning of vegetation, based on the solar thermal unit model. Montana Agr. Exp. Sta. Res. Rep. 60.

32 Christiansen, J. E. 1966. Estimating pan evaporation and evapotranspiration from climatic data. ASCE Irig. and Drain. Spec. Conf. Proc., Nov. 24, pp. 193-231.

33 Christiansen, J. E. 1968. Pan evaporation and evapotranspiration from climatic data. ASCE, J. Irrig. and Drain. Div. 94:243-265.

34 Coleman, G. and D. C. DeCoursey. 1976. Sensitivity and model variance analysis applied to some evaporation and evapotranspiration models. Water Resour. Res. 12(5):873-879.

35 Coulson, K. L. 1975. Solar and terrestrial radiation. Academic Press, New York, NY.

36 Crawford, N. H. and R. K. Linsley. 1966. Digital simulation in hydrology: Stanford watershed model IV. Tech. Rept. No. 39, Dept. Civ. Engr. Stanford Univ., Palo Alto, CA.

37 Davenport, D. C. and J. P. Hudson. 1967. Changes in evaporation rates along a 17-km transect in the Sudan Gezira. Agr. Meteor. 4:339-352.

38 Davies, J. A. and P. H. Buttimor. 1969. Reflection coefficients, heating coefficients, and net radiation at Simcoe, southern Ontario. Agr. Meteorol. 6:373-386.

39 Denmead, O. T. and R. H. Shaw. 1959. Evapotranspiration in relation to the development of the corn crop. Agron. J. 51:725-726.

40 Denmead, O. T. and R. H. Shaw. 1962. Availability of soil water to plants as affected by soil moisture content and meteorological conditions. Agron. J. 45:385-390.

41 Denmead, O. T. and B. D. Millar. 1976. Field studies of the conductance of wheat leaves and transpiration. Agron. J. 68(2):307-311.

42 deRoo, H. C. 1968. Tillage and root depth. Root growth. W. J. Whittington, ed. London, England. pp. 339-358.

43 Doorenbos, J. and W. D. Pruitt. 1975. Crop water requirements. Irrig. and Drain. Paper No. 24, FAO, Rome, 179 pp. (Revised 1977, 144 pp.)

44 Dyer, A. J. 1961. Measurements of evaporation and heat transfer in the lower atmosphere by an automatic eddy-convection technique. Q. J. Royal Meteor. Soc. 87:401-412.

45 Eagleman, J. R. 1967. Pan evaporation, potential and actual evapotranspiration. J. Applied Meteor. 6:482-488.

46 England, C. B. 1975. Soil moisture accounting component of the USDAHL-74 model of watershed hydrology. Water Resour. Bul. 11(3):559-567.

47 Feddes, R. A., P. Kowalik, K. Kolinska-Malinka and H. Zaradny. 1976a. Simulation of field water uptake by plants using a soil water dependent root extraction function. J. Hydrol. (Amst.) 31(1-2):13-26.

48 Feddes, R. A., P. Kowalik, S. P. Neuman and E. Bresler. 1976b. Finite difference and finite element simulation of field water uptake by plants. Hydrol. Sci. Bul. 21(1):81-98.

49 Federer, C. A. 1975. Evapotranspiration (Lit. Review 1971-1974). Reviews of Geo-
-physics and Space Physics 13(3):442-445.
50 Fitzgerald, D. 1886. Evaporation. Trans. ASCE. 15:581-646.
51 Fitzpatrick, E.A., and W. R. Stern. 1973. Net radiation estimated from global
solar radiation. Plant response to climatic factors. Proc. of the Uppsala Sym. (UNESCO,
Paris). pp. 403-410.
52 Fleming, G. 1975. Computer simulation techniques in hydrology. Elsevier Pub.
Co., New York, NY. 333 pp.
53 Foyster, A. M. 1973. Application of the grid square technique to mapping of evapotranspiration. J. Hydrology 19(3):205-226.
54 Frank, E. C., and R. Lee. 1966. Potential solar beam irradiation on slopes: tables
for 30 ° to 50 ° latitude. US Forest Service Res. Paper RM-18, Rocky Mtn. Forest and Range
Expt. Sta., Fort Collins, CO.
55 Fritschen, L. J. 1966. Evapotranspiration rates of field crops determined by the
Bowen ratio method. Agron. J. 58:339-342.
56 Fritschen, L. J. 1967. Net and solar radiation relations over irrigated field crops.
Agr. Meteorol. 4(1):55-62.
57 Gardner, W. R. and D. I. Hillel. 1962. The relation of external evaporative conditions to the drying of soils. J. Geophys. Res. 67(11):4319-4325.
58 Gates, D. M. and R. J. Hanks. 1967. Plant factors affecting evapotranspiration.
Chapt. 27, Am. Soc. Agron. No. 11.
59 Gloyne, R. W. 1965. A method for calculating the angle of indicence of the direct
beam of the sun on a plane surface of any slope and aspect. Agr. Meteorology 2:401-410.
60 Goldstein, R. A. and J. B. Mankin. 1972. PROSPER: a model of atmosphere-soil-
plant water flow. Summer Computer Simulation Conf. Proc., San Diego, CA, pp. 176-181.
61 Goodell, B. C. 1966. Watershed treatment effects on evapotranspiration. Int. Symp.
on Forest Hydrology, Penn. State Univ. Aug. 29-Sept. 10, 1965. Pergaman Press, New York, NY.
62 Graham, W. G. and K. M. King. 1961. Fraction of net radiation utilized in evapotranspiration from a corn crop. Soil Sci. Soc. Am. Proc. 25:158-160.
63 Gray, D. M. (Ed.). 1970. Handbook on the principles of hydrology. Nat. Res.
Coun. of Canada. Water Information Center, Port Washington, NY.
64 Grigel, D. F. and J. E. Hubbard. 1971. SOGGY: An empirical evapotranspiration
model for soils. 1971 Summer Simulation Conf. Proc., July 19-21, 1971, Boston, MA. pp.
795-800.
65 Haan, C. T. 1972. A water yield model for small watersheds. Water Resour. Res.
8(1):58-69.
66 Hanks, R. J., H. R. Gardner and R. L. Florian. 1968. Evapotranspiration-climatic
relations for several crops in the central great plains. Agron. J. 60(5):538-542.
67 Hanks, R. J., A. Klute and E. Bresler. 1969. A numeric method for estimating
infiltration, redistribution, drainage, and evaporation of water from soil. Water Resour. Res.
5(5):1064-1069.
68 Hanks, R. J., L. H. Allen and H. R. Gardner. 1971. Advection and evapotranspiration of wide-row sorghum in the central great plains. Agron. J. 62:520-527.
67 Hansen, G. K. 1975. A dynamic continuous simulation model of water state and
transportation in the soil-plant-atmosphere system. Acta Agricultura Scandinavica 25:129-149.
70 Hanson, C. L. 1976. Model for predicting evapotranspiration from native rangelands in the northern great plains. TRANSACTIONS of the ASAE 19(3):471-477.
71 Hanson, C. L. and F. Rauzi. 1977. Class A pan evaporation as affected by shelter,
and a daily prediction equation. Agr. Meteorol. 18:27-35.
72 Hanson, K. J. 1976. New estimate of solar irradiance at the earth's surface on
zonal and global scales. J. Geophys. Res. 81(24):4435-4443.
73 Hargreaves, G. H. 1966. Consumptive use computations from evaporation pan
data. Am. Soc. Civ. Engr. Irrig. & Drain. Spec. Conf. Proc., Nov. 2-4, pp. 35-62.
74 Harrold, L. L. and F. R. Dreibelbis. 1958. Evaluation of agricultural hydrology
by monolith lysimeters, 1944-55. USDA Tech. Bul. No. 1179, 166 pp.
75 Harrold, L. L. and F. R. Dreibelbis. 1967. Evaluation of agricultural hydrology
by monolith lysimeters, 1956-62. USDA Tech. Bul. No. 1367, 123 pp.
76 Hillel, D. 1975. Simulation of evaporation from bare soil under steady and di-
urnally fluctuating evaporativity. Soil Sci. 120(3):230-237.
77 Hillel, D. 1977. Computer simulation of soil-water dynamics. Int. Develop. Res.
Centre, Box 8500, Ottawa, Canada.
78 Hillel, D. and H. Talpaz. 1976. Simulation of root growth and its effect on the
pattern of soil water uptake by a nonuniform root system. Soil Sci. 121(5):307-312.

79   Holmes, R. M. and G. W. Robertson. 1963. Application of the relationship between actual and potential evapotranspiration in dry land agriculture. TRANSACTIONS of the ASAE 6(1):65-67.

80   Holtan, H. N., G. J. Stiltner, W. H. Hensen, and N. C. Lopez. 1975. USDAHL-74 revised model of watershed hydrology. USDA Tech. Bul. 1518, 99 pp.

81   Idso, S. B. 1971. Relations between net and solar radiation. J. Meteor. Soc. Japan 49(1):1-12.

82   Idso, S. B.; R. J. Reginato and R. D. Jackson. 1974. The three stages of drying of a field soil. Soil Sci. Soc. Am. Proc. 38(5):831-837.

83   Jackson, R. J. 1967. The effect of slope, aspect, and albedo on potential evapotranspiration from hillslopes and catchments. J. Hydrol. (New Zealand) 6(2):60-69.

84   Jensen, M. E. (Ed.). 1973. Consumptive Use of Water and Irrigation Water Requirements. ASCE, New York, NY. 215 pp.

85   Jensen, M. E. and R. H. Haise. 1963. Estimating evapotranspiration from solar radiation. ASCE Proc. 89(IR4): 15-41.

86   Jensen, M. E., J. L. Wright and B. J. Pratt. 1971. Estimating soil moisture depletion from climate, crop, and soil data. TRANSACTIONS of the ASAE 14(5):954-959.

87   Kanemasu, E. T., L. R. Stone and W. L. Powers. 1976. Evapotranspiration model tested for soybean and sorghum. Agron. J. 68(4):569-572.

88   Klute, A. and D. B. Peters. 1969. Water uptake and root growth. In: Root growth, W. J. Whittington (ed.). Plenum Press, NY.

89   Knisel, W. G., R. W. Baird and M. A. Hartman. 1969. Runoff volume prediction from daily climatic data. Water Resour. Res. 5(1):84-94.

90   Koelliker, J. K., W. H. Neibling and F. E. Ohmes. 1976. Land forming systems to improve water use efficiency. Principal investigators report to Kansas Water Resources Research Institute, Manhattan, KS, 70 pp.

91   Kohler, M. A., T. J. Nordenson and W. E. Fox. 1955. Evaporation from pans and lakes. US Weather Bureau Res. paper 38, 21 pp.

92   Kohler, M. A., T. J. Nordenson and D. R. Baker. 1959. Evaporation maps for the United States. Tech. paper No. 37, US Weather Bureau, Washington, DC.

93   Kohler, M. A. and L. H. Parmele. 1967. Generalized estimates of free-water evaporation. Water Resour. 3(4):997-1005.

94   Kozlowski, T. T. (ed.) 1968. Water deficits and plant growth. Academic Press, New York, NY, Vol. 1, 390 pp.; Vol. 2, 333 pp.

95   Kramer, P. J. 1969. Plant and soil water relationships. McGraw-Hill Book Co., New York, NY.

96   Kreith, F. 1973. Principles of heat transfer. Intext Press, New York, NY.

97   Kristensen, K. J. 1974. Actual evapotranspiration in relation to leaf area. Nordic Hydrol. 5:173-182.

98   Kristensen, K. J. and S. E. Jensen. 1975. A model for estimating actual evapotranspiration from potential evapotranspiration. Nordic Hydrol. 6:170-188.

99   Lambert, J. R. and F. W. T. Penning deVries. 1973. Dynamics of water in the soil-plant-atmosphere system: a model named TROIKA. In: J. Jacobs, O. L. Lange, J. S. Olson, and W. Wieser (Ed.). Ecological Studies. Analysis and Synthesis. Springer-Verlag. New York, NY. 4:257-273.

100   Lemon, E. R., D. W. Stewart, R. W. Shawcroft and S. E. Jensen. 1973. Experiments in predicting evapotranspiration by simulation with a soil-plant-atmosphere model (SPAM). In: R. R. Bruce, K. W. Flach, and H. M. Taylor (Ed.). Field Soil Water Regine, Soil Sci. Soc. Am., Madison, WI. pp. 57-74.

101   Leupold, L. B. and W. B. Langbein. 1960. A primer on water. US Geol. Survey. 50 pp.

102   Linacre, E. T. 1968. Estimating the net-radiation flux. Agr. Meteorol. 5:49-63.

103   Linscott, D. L., R. L. Fox and R. C. Lipps. 1962. Corn root distribution and moisture extraction in relation to nitrogen fertilization and soil properties. Agron. J. 54(3):185-189.

104   Lowe, P. R. 1977. An approximating polynomial for the computation of saturation vapor pressure. J. App. Meteorol. 16(1):100-103.

105   Luebs, R. E., A. E. Laag and P. A. Nash. 1975. Evapotranspiration of dryland barley with different plant spacing patterns. Agron. J. 67(3):339-342.

106   Makkink, G. F. and H. D. J. van Heemst. 1974. Simulation of the water balance of arable land and pastures. Centre for Agr. Publishing and Documentation. Wageningen, The Netherlands.

107   McCuen, R. H. 1974. Sensitivity and error analysis of procedures used for estimating evaporation. Water Resour. Bul. 10(3):486-497.

108   McGuinness, J. L. and E. F. Bordne. 1972. A comparison of lysimeter-derived potential evapotranspiration with computed values. USDA Tech Bul. No. 1452.

109   McGuinness, J. L. and L. L. Harrold. 1962. Seasonal and areal effects on small-watershed streamflow. J. Geophys. Res. 67(11):4327-4334.

110   Mengel, D. B. and S. A. Barker. 1974. Development and distribution of the corn root system under field conditions. Agron. J. 66(3):341-344.

111   Messem, A. B. 1975. A rapid method for the determination of potential transpiration derived from the Penman combination model. Agr. Meteorol. 14(3):369-384.

112   Millar, B. D. 1964. Effects of local advection on evapotranspiration rate and plant water status. Aust. J. Agr. Res. 15:85-90.

113   Monteith, J. L. 1965. Evaporation and environment. In: Fogg, G. E. (Ed.). The state and movement of water in living organism. Academic Press, New York, NY, pp. 205-234.

114   Monteith, J. L. (Ed.). 1976. Vegetation and the atmosphere. Academic Press. New York, NY.

115   Morton, F. I. 1975. Estimating evaporation and transpiration from climatological observations. J. App. Meteor. 14:488-497.

116   Morton, F. I. 1976. Climatological estimates of evapotranspiration. Am. Soc. Civ. Engr. Proc. 102(HY3):275-291.

117   Mustonen, S. E. and J. L. McGuinness. 1967. Lysimeter and watershed evapotranspiration. Water Resour. Res. 3(4):989-996.

118   Mustonen, S. E. and J. L. McGuinness. 1968. Estimating evapotranspiration in a humid region. USDA Tech. Bul. No. 1389, 123 pp.

119   Nimah, M. N. and R. J. Hanks. 1973a. Model for estimating soil water, plant, and atmospheric interrelations—1. Description and sensitivity. Soil Sci. Soc. Am. Proc. 37(4): 522-527.

120   Nimah, M. N. and R. J. Hanks. 1973b. Model for estimating soil water, plant, and atmospheric interrelations—2. Field test of model. Soil Sci. Soc. Am. Proc. 37(4):528-532.

121   Nordenson, T. J. 1962. Evaporation from the 17 western states. Geological Survey Professional paper 272-D. US Govt. Printing Office, Washington, DC.

122   Parmele, L. H. 1972. Errors in output of hydrologic models due to errors in input potential evapotranspiration. Water Resour. Res. 8(2):348-359.

123   Parmele, L. H. and J. L. McGuinness. 1974. Comparisons of measured and estimated daily potential evapotranspiration in a humid region. J. Hydrol. 22(3-4):239-251.

124   Parmele, L. H. and E. L. Jacoby. 1975. Estimating evapotranspiration under non-homogeneous field conditions. USDA Agr. Res. Serv. Rep. No. ARS-NE-51.

125   Pelton, W. L., K. M. King and C. B. Tanner. 1960. An evaluation of the Thornthwaite and mean temperature method for determining potential ET. Agron. J. 52:387-395.

126   Penman, H. L. 1948. Natural evaporation from open water, bare soil, and grass. Proc. Royal Soc. Ser. A, No. 1032, 193:120-145.

127   Penman, H. L. 1956. Estimating Evaporation. Am. Geophys. Union 4(1):9-29.

128   Penman, H. L., D. E. Angus and C. H. M. van Bavel. 1967. Microclimatic factors affecting evaporation and transpiration. Chapt. 26, In: R. M. Hagan, H. R. Haise and T. W. Edminister, (Ed.). Am. Soc. Agron. No. 11. Irrigation of Agricultural Lands.

129   Pruitt, W. O. 1964. Cyclic relations between evapotranspiration and radiation. TRANSACTIONS of the ASAE 7(3):271-275.

130   Pruitt, W. O., F. J. Lourence and S. von Oettingen. 1972a. Water use by crops as affected by climate and plant factors. CA Agr.

131   Pruitt, W. O., S. von Oettingen and D. L. Morgan. 1972b. Central California evapotranspiration frequencies. ASCE Proc. 98(IR2):177-184.

132   Pruitt, W. O. and J. Doorenbos. 1977. Empirical calibration, a requisite for evapotranspiration formulae based on daily or longer mean climatic data. Proc. of the International Round Table Conference on "Evapotranspiration" Budapest, Hungary. May 26-28.

133   Reifsnyder, W. E. and H. W. Lull. 1965. Radiant energy in relation to forests. USDA Tech. Bul. No. 1344. 111 pp.

134   Reufeim, K. J. A. 1976. Solar radiation at a site of known orientation on the earth's surface. J. Appl. Meteor. 15:651-656.

135   Richardson, C. W. and J. T. Ritchie. 1973. Soil water balance for small watersheds. TRANSACTIONS of the ASAE 16(1):72-77.

136   Rider, N. E., J. R. Philip, and E. F. Bradley. 1963. The horizontal transport of heat and moisture—a micrometeorological study. Q. J. Roy. Meteor. Soc. 89:507-531.

137   Rijtema, P. E. 1965. An analysis of actual evapotranspiration. Agr. Res. Rep. 689, Pudoc, Wageningen, The Netherlands. 107 pp.

138 Ritchie, J. T. 1971. Dryland evaporative flux in a subhumid climate: I. Micrometeorological influences. Agron. J. 63(1):51-55.

139 Ritchie, J. T. 1972. Model for predicting evaporation from a row crop with incomplete cover. Water Resour. Res. 8(5):1204-1213.

140 Ritchie, J. T. 1973. Influence of soil water status and meteorological conditions on evaporation from a corn canopy. Agron. J. 65(6):893-897.

141 Ritchie, J. T. and E. Burnett. 1971. Dryland evaporative flux in a subhumid climate: II. Plant influences. Agron. J. 63:56-62.

142 Ritchie, J. T., E. Burnett and R. C. Henderson. 1972. Dryland evaporative flux in a subhumid climate: III. Soil water influence. Agron. J. 64(2):168-173.

143 Ritchie, J. T. and J. E. Adams. 1974. Field measurement of exaporation from soil shrinkage cracks. Soil Sci. Soc. Am. Proc. 38(1):131-134.

144 Ritchie, J. T. and W. R. Jordan. 1972. Dryland evaporative flux in a subhumid climate: IV. Relation to plant water status. Agron. J. 64(2):173-176.

145 Ritchie, J. T., E. D. Rhoades, and C. W. Richardson. 1976. Calculating evaporation from native grassland watersheds. TRANSACTIONS of the ASAE 19(6):1098-1103.

146 Robb, D. C. N. 1966. Consumptive use estimates from solar radiation and temperature. In: Irrig. and Drainage Speciality Conf., Las Vegas, NV, Nov. 2-4. Methods for estimating evaporation. ASCE. pp. 169-191.

147 Robinson, T. W. and A. I. Johnson. 1961. Selected bibliography on evaporation and evapotranspiration. US. Geol. Survey Water-Supply Paper 1539-R, 25 pp.

148 Rohwer, C. 1931. Evaporation from free water surfaces. USDA Tech. Bul. No. 271.

149 Romanova, Y. N. 1974. Variation in evaporative power on slopes of different exposure and steepness in the USSR. Sov. Hydrol. 5:334-343.

150 Rosenberg, N. J. 1969a. Advective contribution of energy utilized in evapotranspiration by alfalfa in the east central great plains. Agr. Meteor. 6(3):179-184.

151 Rosenberg, N. J. 1969b. Evaporation and condensation on bare soil under irrigation in the east central great plains. Agron. J. 61:557-561.

152 Rosenberg, N. J. 1972. Frequency of potential evapotranspiration rates in central great plains. ASCE Proc. 98(IR2):203-206.

153 Rosenthal, W. D., E. T. Kanemasu, R. J. Raney and L. R. Stone. 1977. Evaluation of an evapotranspiration model for corn. Agron. J. 69:461-464.

154 Saxton, K. E. 1972. Watershed evapotranspiration by the combination method. Unpublished Ph.D. Thesis, Iowa State Univ. Lib., Ames, IA (Dissertation Abst. Int. 33(4): 1514b-1515b. 1972).

155 Saxton, K. E. 1975. Sensitivity analyses of the combination evapotranspiration equation. Agr. Meteorol. 15:343-353.

156 Saxton, K. E. and A. T. Lenz. 1967. Antecedent retention indexes predict soil moisture. ASCE Proc. 93(HY4):223-241.

157 Saxton, K. E., H. P. Johnson and R. H. Shaw. 1974a. Watershed evapotranspiration estimated by the combination method. TRANSACTIONS of the ASAE 17(4):668-672.

158 Saxton, K. E., H. P. Johnson and R. H. Shaw. 1974b. Modeling evapotranspiration and soil moisture. TRANSACTIONS of the ASAE 17(4):673-677.

159 Shaw, R. H. 1963. Estimation of soil moisture under corn. Agric. and Home Econ. Expt. Sta., Iowa State Univ., Ames, IA. Bul. 520. pp. 968-980.

160 Shaw, R. H. 1964. Prediction of soil moisture under meadow. Agron. J. 56(3): 320-324.

161 Shawcroft, R. W., E. R. Lemon, L. H. Allen, D. W. Stewart and S. E. Jensen. 1974. The soil-plant-atmosphere model and some of its predictions. Agr. Meteorol. 14(1/2): 287-307.

162 Shephard, W. 1975. Inclusion of plant moisture status in combination method estimates of pasture evaporation. J. Hydrol. 26(3/4):199-208.

163 Slack, D. C., C. T. Haan and L. G. Wells. 1977. Modeling soil water movement into plant roots. TRANSACTIONS of the ASAE 20(5):919-927.

164 Slatyer, R. O. 1967. Plant-water relationships. Academic Press, New York, NY.

165 Stanhill, G., G. J. Hofstede and J. D. Kalma. 1966. Radiation balance of natural and agricultural vegetation. Q.J. Roy. Met. Soc. 92:128-140.

166 Stone, L. R., I. D. Teare, C. D. Nickell and W. C. Mayaki. 1976. Soybean root development and soil water depletion. Agron. J. 68(4):677-680.

167 Szeicz, G., S. Tajchman and G. Endrodi. 1969. Aerodynamic and surface factors in evaporation. Water Resour. Res. 5(2):380-393.

168 Szeicz, G. and I. F. Long. 1969. Surface resistance of crop canopies. Water Resources Res. 5(3):622-633.

169 Tanner, C. B. 1957. Factors affecting evaporation from plants and soils. J. Soil and Water Conserv. 12(5):221-227.

170 Tanner, C. B. 1967. Measurement of evapotranspiration. Chapter 29 in: R. M. Hagan, H. R. Haise and T. W. Edminster (eds). Am. Soc. Agron. No. 11.

171 Tanner, C. B. and M. Fuchs. 1968. Evaporation from unsaturated surfaces: a generalized combination method. J. Geophys. Res. 73(4):1299-1304.

172 Tanner, C. B. and W. A. Jury. 1976. Estimating evaporation and transpiration from a row crop during incomplete cover. Agron. J. 68(2):239-243.

173 Tanner, C. B. and W. L. Pelton. 1960. Potential evapotranspiration estimates by the approximate energy balance method of Penman. J. Geophys. Res. 63(10):3391-3413.

174 Taylor, H. M. and B. Klepper. 1973. Rooting density and water extraction patterns for corn (Zea maysL). Agron. J. 65:965-968.

175 Taylor, H. M. and B. Klepper. 1974. Water relations of cotton. I. Root growth and water use as related to top growth and soil water content. Agron. J. 66(4):584-588.

176 Thom, A. S. and H. R. Oliver. 1977. On Penman's equation for estimating regional evaporation. Q. J. Roy. Met. Soc. 103:345-357.

177 Thompson, E. S. 1976. Computation of solar radiation from sky cover. Water Resour. Res. 12(5):859-865.

178 Thornley, J. H. M. 1976. Mathematical models in plant physiology. Academic Press, New York, NY.

179 Thornthwaite, C. W. and B. Holzman. 1942. Measurement of evaporation from land and water sources. USDA Tech. Bul. No. 817, 143 pp.

180 Thornthwaite Assoc. 1964. Average climatic water balance data of the continents. Part VII. United States. Publications in Climatology 17(3).

181 Turc, L. 1961. Evaluation Des Besoins en Eau d'irrigation, evapotranspiration potentielle. Ann. Agron. 12(1):13-49.

182 Unger, P. W. and J. J. Parker. 1976. Evaporation reduction from soil with wheat, sorghum, and cotton residues. Soil Sci. Soc. Am. J. 40(6):938-942.

183 US Dept. of Commerce. 1964. Selective guide to published climatic data sources prepared by US Weather Bureau. US Govt. Printing Office. Washington, DC.

184 US Dept. of Commerce. 1968. Climatic atlas of the United States. US Govt. Printing Office, Washington, DC. (National Climatic Center, Asheville, NC), 80 pp.

185 USDA, Soil Conservation Service. 1967. Irrigation water requirements. Tech. Release No. 21, 88 pp.

186 van Bavel, C. H. M. 1966. Potential evaporation; the combination concept and its experimental verification. Water Resour. Res. 12(3):455-467.

187 van Bavel, C. H. M. 1967. Changes in canopy resistance to water loss from alfalfa induced by soil water depletion. Agr. Meteor. 4:165-176.

188 van Bavel, C. H. M. and J. Ahmed. 1976. Dynamic simulation of water depletion in the root zone. Ecol. Modelling 2:189-212.

189 van Bavel, C. H. M. and D. I. Hillel. 1976. Calculating potential and actual evapotranspiration from a bare soil surface by simulation of concurrent flow of water and heat. Agr. Meteor. 17:453-476.

190 van Keulen, H. 1975. Simulation of water use and herbage growth in arid regions. Simulation Monogr., Pudoc, Wageningen, The Netherlands.

191 Veihmeyer, F. J. 1964. Evapotranspiration. Sect. 11. In: Chow, V. T. (Ed.), Handbook of Applied Hydrology, McGraw-Hill Book Co., New York, NY.

192 Ward, R. C. 1972. Checks on the water balance of a small catchment. Nordic Hydrology 3:44-63.

193 Wartena, L. 1974. Basic difficulties in predicting evaporation. J. Hydrol. 23(1/2):159-177.

194 Weigand, C. L. and S. A. Taylor. 1961. Evaporative drying of porous media. Utah State Univ. Agr. Expt. Sta. Spec. Rep. 15, Logan, UT.

195 Whittington, W. J. 1968. Root growth. Plenum Press, New York, NY.

196 Woolhiser, D. A. 1971. Deterministic approach to watershed modeling. Nordic Hydrol. II:146-166.

197 Woolhiser, D. A. 1973. Hydrologic and watershed modeling—state of the art. TRANSACTIONS of the ASAE 553-559.

198 Yang, S. J. and E. deJung. 1972. Effect of aerial environment and soil water potential on the transpiration and energy status of water in wheat plants. Agron. J. 64(5):574-578.

SYMBOL DEFINITIONS

a	solar radiation reflectance coefficient	—
A	sensible heat flux to air	cal/cm²/day
AE	actual ET	mm/day
ARI	antecedent retention index	cm
AW	available soil water (equation [25])	in.
C	maximum available soil moisture	mm
C_E	elevation coefficient (equation [2])	—
C_{ET}	pan coefficient for reduction to PET	—
C_H	humidity coefficient (equation [2]	—
C_p	specific heat of air flux	cal/cm²/day
C_s	sunshine coefficient (equation [2]	—
C_T	temperature coefficient (equation [2])	—
C_w	wind coefficient (equation [2])	—
d	wind profile displacement height	cm
d_a	saturation vapor deficit of air	mbars
e_o	saturation vapor pressure	mbars
e_t	existing vapor pressure	mbars
E	elevation (equation [8])	m
	actual ET (equation [21])	mm/day
	potential soil evaporation (equation [26])	mm/day
E_o	potential ET (equation [28])	mm/day
E_p	potential ET by Thornthwaite (equation [21])	mm/day
	pan evaporation	mm/day
	transpiration (equation [28])	mm/day
E_t	actual ET (equation [24])	mm/day
ET	evapotranspiration	mm/day
E_{tp}	potential ET (equation [24])	mm/day
GI	growth index of crop (equation [23])	—
H	mean relative humidity	percent
k	von Karman coefficient (equation [18])	—
	Blaney-Criddle coefficient (equation [16])	—
	antecedent retention coefficient (equation [20])	—
	Bair and Robertson coefficient (equation [22])	—
	ratio of ET to pan evaporation (equation [23])	—
K_a	available water coefficient (equation [25])	—
K_c	resistance coefficient (equation [24])	—
K_{co}	mean crop coefficient (equation [25])	—
K_s	wetted soil coefficient (equation [25])	—
L	latent heat of vaporization	cal/g
LAI	leaf area index	—
LE	latent heat of vaporization	cal/day
M	available soil moisture (equation [21])	mm
p	ambient air pressure	mbars
	mean monthly percent of annual sunshine (equation [16])	percent
PE	potential ET (equation [22])	mm/day
PET	potential ET	mm/day
PE	average PE for month or season	mm/day
Q	surface runoff	mm
R	daily retention	mm
R_l	incoming long wave radiation	cal/cm²/day
R_{lr}	emitted long wave radiation	cal/cm²/day
R_n	net radiation	cal/cm²/day
R_s	solar radiation	cal/cm²/day
	incoming solar radiation (equation [3])	cm
R_t	extra terrestrial solar radiation (equation [2])	cm
S	total porosity	percent
	available soil moisture (equation [22])	mm
	soil heat flux	cal/cm²/day
	mean sunshine percentage	percent
SA	available soil porosity (equation [23])	percent
SM	soil moisture	percent

t	time	day
	mean monthly air temperature (equation [16])	°C
T	air temperature	°C
u	estimated monthly ET (equation [16])	mm
u	estimated monthly ET (equation [16])	mm
u_a	horizontal windspeed at elevation z_a	m/day
x	empirical exponent (equation [23])	—
X	miscellaneous heat sinks	cal/cm²/day
z_0	wind profile roughness height	cm
z	soil type coefficient (equation [22])	—
z_a	anemometer height above soil	cm
w	factor for PE rates (equation [22])	—
∝	empirical coefficient (equation [27])	—
β	Bowen ratio	—
δ	psychrometric constant	—
p	air density	g/cm³
Δ	slope of saturated psychrometric curve	mbars/°C
ε	water/air molecular ratio	—

chapter 7

SUBSURFACE FLOW AND GROUND WATER SYSTEMS

7

SUBSURFACE FLOW AND
GROUNDWATER SYSTEMS

7

SUBSURFACE FLOW AND GROUND WATER SYSTEMS

by   C. R. Amerman and J. W. Naney, Research Hydraulic Engineer, USDA, ARS, Coshocton, OH, and Geologist, USDA, ARS, Chickasha, OK, respectively.

INTRODUCTORY CONCEPTS

Subsurface water includes all water beneath the Earth's surface. It is recharged by infiltration either directly on the land surface or in the beds of streams, lakes, and oceans. Man occasionally enhances recharge with recharge wells and seepage beds. Subsurface water is discharged through the processes of evaporation and transpiration or from springs and seeps either on the land surface or in the beds of surface bodies of water. Man adds other discharge mechanisms, such as pumped wells and gravity drains.

The subsurface environment consists of some arrangement of porous materials. Water moves within the pores of these materials—pores which account for as much as 50 percent of the total volume in some soils. Soil flora and fauna share this pore space with water. Most terrestrial hydrologic activity takes place within the root zone. Todd (1970) reported that an average of 70 percent of precipitation in the continental United States is returned to the atmosphere via evapotranspiration (ET). A comparison of two maps of the United States—one of the distribution of potential ET (Hamon, 1961) and the other of the distribution of precipitation (Linsley et al., 1949)— showed that in the humid eastern United States, ET can account for from about 50 percent to as much as 80 percent of precipitation. Although some of this is direct evaporation from surface water, most is water that has been in the root zone.

Soil water is often conceptually subdivided into at least three parts (Buckman and Brady, 1969)—superfluous or drainable water, plant-available water, and unavailable water. The volume of water released from the soil between a soil water pressure head (h) of about −1/3 bar (called field capacity) and about −15 bars (called the wilting point) is considered plant-available water. This water is detained in storage by capillary forces. Drainable water, as the name implies, is thought of as water that readily drains from soil under the influence of gravity. It is often considered as the water occupying pores larger than capillary size. Unavailable water is mostly hygroscopic water—water held tightly in films around individual soil

Contribution of the Watershed Research Unit, U.S. Department of Agriculture, Science and Education Administration, Agricultural Research, Columbia, MO, in cooperation with the Missouri Agricultural Experiment Station, Columbia.

particles. From a practical standpoint, most drainage probably occurs when soil water pressures are higher than −1/3 bar, and most transpiration probably occurs when soil water pressures are lower, so this subdivision of soil water has some conceptual utility. There is, however, no hydraulic reason to classify soil water into different pressure zones.

Water moves in response to gradients, ΔH, in total hydraulic head, H. In soils and other porous media, the relationship between water movement and hydraulic head gradient is expressed as Darcy's law (equation [4.2]). As discussed in connection with equation [4.3], H in most media has only two effective components: h and z (z is the elevation or gravity head). Fig. 4.3 of Chapter 4 shows the relation between h and Θ (soil water content). For vertical flow, the gradient of z, dz/ds, is constant with magnitude of unity in the downward direction regardless of soil water content. On the other hand, a gradient in h occurs only if there is a gradient in Θ. Thus, in soils where water content varies smoothly and gradually, the gravity component may dominate regardless of the average water content. Hydraulic conductivity, K, as shown in Fig. 4.4 of Chapter 4, drops rapidly as Θ decreases. In that figure, the Θ-scale is arithmetic, and the K-scale is logarithmic over several orders of magnitude. The magnitude of water flux generally drops rapidly as a soil dries, regardless of net gradient changes. Thus, the apparent division between drainable and plant-available water may be more directly associated with the general level of soil water content and with hydraulic conductivity than with capillary action per se. Of course, ET can lower upper zone soil water content enough that an upward hydraulic gradient is established, thus effectively stopping drainage.

Water enters the subsurface domain primarily by infiltration, as described in Chapter 4. In arid areas and in humid areas during much of the growing season, most infiltration events only partly replenish plant-available water. Hydraulic conductivity is generally low in this range of soil water content, and only insignificant amounts of water percolate beyond the root zone unless deep cracks or other large, continuously open pores intersect the soil surface (Bouma and Dekker, 1978; Bouma et al., 1978). Under these conditions, infiltrated water returns to the atmosphere along the relatively short route of ET.

Long-term infiltration or infiltration into previously wet soil sometimes raises the soil water content to more than field capacity. Without impeding layers or such flow interceptors as tile drains, which might alter hydraulic gradients away from the vertical, drainable water percolates out of the root zone and continues on down to join a body of ground water. When soils contain impeding layers, drainage water may form ephemeral, perched zones of saturation. Drains, a sloping impeding layer, or both, cause hydraulic gradients to incline away from the vertical, and the direction of drainage water flow has a lateral component. Lateral flow over a sloping impeding layer is often thought to be the mechanism by which interflow occurs if the lateral flow returns to the land surface or to a stream without having first found its way to a primary ground water body (Kirkby, 1978).

With few exceptions (e.g. Kazmann, 1972), most authors and dictionaries define ground water as water below a water table. A water table is defined as a surface where gage pressure is at zero and is usually conceived as separating the unsaturated zone above it from the saturated zone below it. Bouwer (1978), in a particularly clear description of ground water, noted that the zone above a water table is not always unsaturated and the zone below is not always saturated. In some materials, capillary rise can effectively saturate a zone just above the water table. On the other hand, entrapped air can cause a significant departure from saturation below the water table (Fig. 4.3, Chapter 4). The key criterion is pressure. Ground water is under positive pressure and will flow into a hole or out of a stream bank or any other intersecting surface on which the pressure is atmospheric or at least lower than that in the ground water.

In watershed modeling, baseflow is usually defined as drainage from ground water bodies, whose water tables are above the levels of the streambeds. McGuinness et al. (1961) described a hydrologic system in which several thin water bodies perched on underclays contributed to the intersecting stream system. Bathala et al. (1976) discussed the relation between a reach of the Wabash River and a deep aquifer in glacial deposits. In the southwestern United States, streambeds are often highly permeable material above a water table and streamflow percolates to ground water. Hewlett (1961) suggested that baseflow in some western North Carolina mountain watersheds is supported by the drainage of largely unsaturated soils rather than by an extensive ground water body. Subsurface water can exit into a stream only if a positive pressure zone exists at the point of exit. In Hewlett's watersheds this positive pressure or saturated zone is apparently of quite limited extent.

All flow processes occur within physical settings that exhibit an almost infinite variety of combinations of soils, geologic materials, topography, and climate. Furthermore, subsurface water movement, physical properties of the media, and boundary geometries can generally be determined only by indirect, often inadequate sampling techniques based on physical tests of questionable accuracy. Approaches to subsurface flow quantification usually entail sparse observational sampling of the system and rely upon interpolation or upon mathematical simulation techniques to extrapolate these observations to a more complete quantification of the entire system.

In the context of watershed modeling, especially small watershed modeling, a question naturally arises as to how much detail about subsurface water is necessary. The answer, of course, depends on the objective of the modeling exercise and upon the physical nature of the flow system simulated. Subsurface physical influences are often subtly reflected in surface water, so evaluation of their effects requires great care. The answer is also influenced by economy. In rural areas, few hydrologic problems justify the expenditure of very large amounts of money in seeking a solution. Although there is a considerable amount of subsurface water flow theory, and some has been incorporated into a number of ground water flow models, little is currently used in watershed modeling. The cost of mathematical simulation and of obtaining needed input data is high.

However, the uses for watershed models are broadening. For example, simulation of movement through the landscape of dissolved chemical constituents has been added to the more traditional need to simulate water quantities arriving at or passing certain points of interest. As will be discussed in greater detail in the section on empirical modeling, current methods of handling subsurface water movement in watershed models generally do not consider flow paths or times in residence and are therefore inadequate where there is a need to investigate the path a dissolved pollutant might take.

Anticipating that needs and economics will change and that more detailed subsurface water movement studies will be both needed and justified, the following section reviews the highlights of subsurface water flow theory.

SUBSURFACE WATER FLOW THEORY

In the mid 19th century, Darcy provided the key to subsurface flow quantification when he discovered that velocity of water flow in sands was proportional to the negative gradient of hydraulic head (equation [4.2]).

Darcy's law was first used in connection with saturated (or at least positive pressure) flow. Hydraulic conductivity, K, was calculated by measuring q, ΔH and ΔS with linear flow permeameters (Taylor, 1948) and solving equation [4.2]. Jacob (1950) pointed out that K includes the effects of both specific weight and viscosity of water (both temperature dependent) as well as the effects of media properties. He defined K as:

$$K = k \frac{\gamma}{\mu} \quad \dots\dots\dots\dots\dots\dots\dots\dots\dots\dots\dots\dots\dots\dots\dots\dots\dots\dots\dots \quad [7.1]$$

where

k = intrinsic permeability of the media
γ = specific weight of water
μ = viscosity of water.

Ground water temperature does not vary appreciably, and K continues to be used for most computations. Equation [7.1] should be considered when using laboratory methods for measuring K that will later be used in field simulation.

In real-world situations, subsurface flow follows curving paths, converges here, and diverges there. Simple application of Darcy's law is not practical even if it were possible—and it yields no information on the distribution of head loss in the system.

Investigators (e.g. Childs, 1969) combined Darcy's law with an equation of continuity (or conservation of mass). They assumed that water is incompressible, and that the media is isotropic. A Laplace equation resulted for saturated flow:

$$\frac{\partial^2 H}{\partial x^2} + \frac{\partial^2 H}{\partial y^2} + \frac{\partial^2 H}{\partial z^2} = 0 \quad \dots\dots\dots\dots\dots\dots\dots\dots\dots\dots\dots\dots\dots\dots\dots \quad [7.2]$$

where

x,y,z = distances parallel to the major axes of the Cartesian coordinate system.

This is a linear, elliptic partial differential equation requiring specification of boundary conditions for complete description of a given problem.

There is no general solution for the Laplace equation. Childs (1969) reviewed four methods of approaching solutions of approximations: (a) conjugate equations; (b) conformal mapping; (c) electrical or other analogs; and (d) numerical iteration. The first two methods are discussed more fully by Polubarinova-Kochina (1962) and by Harr (1962). Bouwer and Little (1959), Bouwer (1962), Thiel et al. (1962), Thiel and Bornstein (1965), Jorgensen (1975), and Getzen (1977) are among those who have used analogs. Southwell (1946) described the use of numerical techniques before the advent of high speed computers. Klute et al. (1965) have used a fifth approach, that of analytical mathematics.

All but the numerical and analog methods are generally limited to two-dimensional, idealized systems of simple geometry and soils. They have been used to study such well-defined, localized flow systems as occur under gravity dams or through earth dams and in connection with tile drains, irrigation systems, and so on. Solving a problem consists in finding the appropriate mathematical expression or transformation. Usually, a relatively small amount of computation is required, and solutions can be manually obtained.

Numerical techniques and analog methods can, in principle, be applied to three-dimensional systems of complicated geometry involving heterogeneous media, but the solutions obtained are only approximations to the solution of the Laplace equation. That is, numerical techniques and electrical analogs can be used to model the Laplace equation rather than to exactly solve it. Two numerical techniques are currently in use—finite differences and finite elements. Each requires large amounts of computation. Consequently the finite difference method described by Southwell (1946) was not much used until digital computers became available. Remson et al. (1971) discussed both numerical methods as they are applied to subsurface water movement.

The Laplace equation, [7.2], assumes that neither water nor soil is compressible. These assumptions may be reasonable for unconfined ground water bodies, i.e., water bodies whose upper boundaries are water tables. For confined aquifers, those for which upper and lower boundaries are relatively impermeable, removal of water results in a reduction of pore pressure even though the aquifer may remain saturated. Under these conditions, compressibility of both water and media must be taken into account.

Jacob (1950) gave a derivation of the equation for unsteady flow in confined, isotropic media:

$$\frac{\partial^2 H}{\partial x^2} + \frac{\partial^2 H}{\partial y^2} + \frac{\partial^2 H}{\partial z^2} = \frac{\theta \gamma_0}{K} (\beta + \frac{\alpha}{\theta}) \frac{\partial H}{\partial t} \quad \dots\dots\dots\dots\dots\dots\dots \quad [7.3]$$

where

Θ = porosity
γ_0 = specific weight of water
β = compressibility of water
α = vertical compressibility of the media
t = time.

The Dupuit-Forchheimer (1863) assumption of essentially horizontal flow in which dH/dz is insignificant was adopted in order to obtain this form. For a uniformly thick bed of horizontal flow, Jacob (1950) reduced equation [7.3] to:

$$\frac{\partial^2 H}{\partial x^2} + \frac{\partial^2 H}{\partial y^2} = \frac{S}{T} \frac{\partial H}{\partial t} \quad \dots\dots\dots\dots\dots\dots\dots\dots\dots\dots\dots\dots\dots\dots\dots \quad [7.4]$$

where

S = $\Theta \gamma_0 b (\beta + \alpha/\Theta)$
T = Kb
b = thickness of the bed.

The term S is called the coefficient of storage and is the volume of water released from storage by a unit decrease in head in a vertical column of unit cross sectional area. DeWiest (1965) gave a good conceptual explanation of S. The term T is called transmissivity or transmissibility.

Prickett and Lonnquist (1971), Trescott et al. (1976), and others added a volumetric flux term to equation [7.4], removed the assumption of isotropy, and oriented the coordinate axes parallel to the principal components of the transmissivity tensor:

$$\frac{\partial}{\partial x}(T_x \frac{\partial H}{\partial x}) + \frac{\partial}{\partial y}(T_y \frac{\partial H}{\partial y}) = S\frac{\partial H}{\partial t} + W \quad\dots\dots\dots\dots\dots\dots [7.5]$$

where T_x and T_y are the x and y components of transmissivity, respectively, and W is the volumetric flux of recharge or withdrawal per unit surface area. For steady state flow, $\partial h/\partial t = 0$ and $W = 0$. Equation [7.5] would then become a Laplace equation if the coordinates were distorted to account for anisotropy (Childs, 1969), and the solution methods previously discussed can be applied.

Prickett and Lonnquist (1971) and Trescott et al. (1976) developed two-dimensional finite difference models for the time-varying equation [7.5]. Gupta et al. (1975) presented a three-dimensional, finite element model based on equation [7.3]. There are numerous other models as well. The U.S. Geological Survey is active in the development of ground water models and has recently summarized the status of several of these models, both operational and developmental (Appel and Bredehoeft, 1976).

Four types of numerical solution, each employing finite-difference techniques for solving the ground water flow equations listed above were described by Trescott et al. (1976). These are line successive over-relaxation (LSOR), line successive over-relaxation plus two-dimensional correction (LSOR + 2DC), alternating direction implicit procedure (ADI), and strongly implicit procedure (SIP). Trescott et al. (1976) also compared numerical results of the four finite difference techniques.

Another solution to the selected flow equation is found in the finite difference technique used by Nelson (1962). Nelson used both over-relaxation and under-relaxation techniques which employed the Gauss-Seidel predictor-corrector method for a node-by-node solution of the difference equation beginning with an initial head estimate. The predictor-corrector technique is detailed by Remson et al. (1971) with a comparison of exact analytical and finite difference solution of the equation for ground water flow to a tile drain assuming the diameter of the drains is negligible and that the Dupuit-Forchheimer assumptions hold for flow to drains. This procedure is also useful for the study of unconfined ground water flow between trenches (Hornberger et al., 1969) and for the study of the interaction of water between a stream and an unconfined aquifer (Hornberger et al., 1970).

While engineers and geologists were working to develop and improve techniques for solving ground water problems, soil physicists were working on problems involving soil water in the root zone. Drainage workers approached the removal of excess water on the basis of the Laplace equation using the methods described earlier. Others approached infiltration and unsaturated flow problems on the basis of the Richards' equation as described in Chapter 4. Essential to the development of this equation was the work of Buckingham (1907), who showed that soil water pressure head (he called it capillary potential) varies with soil water content and postulated that hydraulic conductivity (he called it capillary conductivity) also varied with soil water content. Others (Richards, 1931; Moore, 1939) confirmed by experiment that K is a function of h for unsaturated conditions.

Richards' equation, [4.8], in one, two, or three dimensions applies to any region of unsaturated flow and becomes the Laplace equation when saturation prevails, as stated in Chapter 4. The fact that Richards' equation is transformed to the Laplace equation at saturation should not be taken to imply mathematical continuity, however.

Consider the general case of Richards' equation applied in three dimensions:

$$C \frac{\partial h}{\partial t} = \frac{\partial}{\partial x}(K \frac{\partial h}{\partial x}) + \frac{\partial}{\partial y}(K \frac{\partial h}{\partial y}) + \frac{\partial}{\partial z}(K \frac{\partial h}{\partial z}) - \frac{\partial K}{\partial z} \quad \dots \dots \dots \quad [7.6]$$

where the symbols are as defined in Chapter 4. At saturation $C = d\Theta/dh = 0$. If the medium is uniform and isotropic, and K is equal in all directions and $\partial K/\partial z = 0$. Equation [7.6] reduces to equation [7.2] in which the dependency of h upon t has been lost, even though h may continue to change with the passage of time.

Equations [7.6] and [7.2] are two fundamentally different equations, requiring different approaches for solution. The Richards' equation is a parabolic equation and is highly nonlinear in C and K. A particular problem is specified by boundary conditions given as values of h or as values of the gradient of h and by an initial condition (initial distribution of h).

In contrast, as stated earlier, the Laplace equation is a linear, elliptic equation. A particular problem is completely specified by boundary conditions alone and is usually considered a steady state problem. The only way to simulate an unsteady condition with the Laplace equation is to cause boundary conditions to vary with time.

Rubin (1968), Hornberger et al. (1969), Taylor and Luthin (1969), Amerman (1969), and Verma and Brutsaert (1970) followed various finite difference approaches to simultaneous solution of Richards' equation in the unsaturated zone and the Laplace equation in the saturated zone. These were generally cumbersome and expensive methods and were applicable only in near-surface conditions. Cooley (1971) modified equation [7.3] to include a degree-of-saturation term in the coefficient of $\partial H/\partial t$. He solved this parabolic equation by the finite difference method in both saturated and unsaturated zones. Being based on equation [7.3], Cooley's equation accounted for fluid and media compressibility, but was subject to the Dupuit-Forchheimer assumption. Neuman (1973) applied a finite element technique to a version of equation [7.3]. Freeze (1971a) presented a more complete equation in that he retained provisions for changes in density and thus eliminated adherence to the Dupuit-Forchheimer assumption. He solved this equation using a finite difference technique.

Narasimhan and Witherspoon (1977) derived the flow equation in integral form and included a first approximation for media deformation. Narasimhan et al. (1978) presented an integrated finite difference algorithm for solution of this equation.

The foregoing has been a brief discussion of events leading to the present state of the art of subsurface water movement simulation. To summarize, we have powerful mathematical techniques with which to address almost any subsurface water movement problem by approximating solutions using modeling. The mathematical resources may, in many cases, surpass our present needs, considering how inaccurate the physical descriptions of most subsurface flow systems are.

Freeze (1975) has injected a cautionary note regarding the real-world utility of ground water models based upon such as equations [7.3], [7.5], and [7.6]. Out of practical necessity, the application of these equations almost always involves simplification of the manner in which hydraulic properties of porous media (hydraulic conductivity, compressibility, porosity) vary in space. Usually one assumes that a given medium is uniform or that at most it consists of a finite number of zones whose properties may differ from each other, but each of which is internally uniform. One then settles in some way upon a set of "average" values for the hydraulic properties so that the model will emulate the real-world prototype.

In fact, the physical properties of soils and geologic materials vary continuously in space. Law (1944) discussed this variability from a statistical standpoint and proposed that hydraulic conductivity follows a log-normal distribution. Freeze (1975) followed up on this and other work (Warren and Price, 1961; McMillan, 1966) with an analysis of the influence of standard deviations of the three properties mentioned above upon the standard deviation of predicted hydraulic heads. He concluded that the natural standard deviation in these quantities is so great that it precludes usefully accurate prediction of hydraulic head distributions in real systems. Dagan (1976) challenged, with some justification, the applicability of the media design under which Freeze (1975) conducted his statistical experiments. But the essential question of how the natural variability of media properties affects hydraulic predictions by physically-based models remains.

A model's utility depends ultimately upon whether it simulates a prototype with reasonable accuracy. While there may be shortcomings in theory (such questions as the one just mentioned concerning media variability or those regarding entrapped air or swelling media) and problems with measurement or characterization of model input properties, there have been numerous apparently successful practical applications of porous media flow theory to real-world problems (Taylor and Luthin, 1963); Freeze and Witherspoon, 1966; Cooley, 1971; Bibby and Sunada, 1971; Freeze, 1971b; Stephenson and Freeze, 1974; Weeks et al., 1974; Jorgensen, 1975; Getzen, 1977).

SUBSURFACE FLOW THEORY AND
RECENT WATERSHED MODELING ATTEMPTS

Quantitative simulation of subsurface water discharge to streamflow is much less advanced than is the simulation of either infiltration or movement of subsurface water within its own domain. Further, except for Rovey and Richardson (1975), an important exception discussed later, no one has tried to include physically-based simulation of subsurface flow in general watershed models. Most surface hydrologic models are based mainly on empirical approaches or on the representation of one process by another, such as Dawdy's and O'Donnell's (1965) use of a series of reservoirs to represent surface storage, ground water storage, and so on. An empirical model or a reservoir model cannot be easily linked with a theoretically-based porous media flow model.

Weeks et al. (1974) made a comprehensive analysis of the projected hydrologic impact of oil shale development upon the Piceance Basin in Colorado. They used the Bredehoeft and Pinder (1970) multiaquifer model. The latter is a quasi three-dimensional model in that two-dimensional (plan view) solutions of equation [7.5] are obtained simultaneously for all aquifers in the system, and the aquifers are coupled by one-dimensional leakage through the confining layers. Weeks et al. (1974) used this model to predict changes in ground water discharge in the vicinity of the proposed mine sites. They used a digital watershed model, comprised of empirical submodels, developed by Leavesley (1973) to characterize the general hydrology of the Piceance Basin and to predict the effects of precipitation changes upon it. This model considered the effects of subsurface water by relatively simple accounting procedures. Weeks et al. (1974) did not report any attempt to interface these two models or to use the output of the ground water model in the basin-wide general hydrologic model.

Several studies have linked subsurface flow with surface hydrology. Smith and Woolhiser (1971) have simultaneously modeled infiltration and overland flow under idealized conditions. Marino (1975), using a finite difference approach, applied the one-dimensional form of equation [7.5] to study the response of a shallow, horizontal aquifer to stream stage fluctuation. Freeze (1972a, 1972b, 1978) linked a finite difference approximation of the Richards' equation to a channel flow model for the purpose of studying baseflow and interflow.

Winter (1976) modeled two-dimensional porous media flow systems for which one or more lakes were included on the upper boundary. Later (Winter, 1978) he expanded the study to include three dimensions and solved a variation of the steady state form of equation [7.5] by finite differences.

Rovey and Richardson (1975) (Rovey, 1975) have formulated what is apparently the first general hydrologic model based on solving the three-dimensional Richards' equation. In their model the aquifer is represented as a three-dimensional grid in the form of a rectangular parallelipiped with a straight channel down its middle. The two ends of the modeled reach were essentially two-dimensional; the midsection three dimensional. The river penetrated the aquifer in the two-dimensional sections, but it did not fully penetrate in the three-dimensional reach. Such quantities as precipitation, evapotranspiration, and pumping were calculated and then discretized so that appropriate values could be assigned to each surface grid element. The Dupuit-Forchheimer assumption was used by Rovey (1975) to develop the two-dimensional segment of the finite difference model. This assumption introduces errors that are negligible if the water table is nearly horizontal and water table fluctuations are small compared with the saturated thickness of the aquifer.

The models developed by Trescott et al. (1976) and by Rovey (1975) were designed primarily for the solution of large (more than 26 km²) combined stream-aquifer flow systems and contained a mechanism for modeling large ET losses. Many small watershed models (less than 26 km²) do not attempt to model evapotranspiration or baseflow and treat these parameters as single value terms.

Hall*, on the other hand, investigated ground water yield from small upland watersheds using a numerical approach. He obtained a finite difference solution to equation [7.5] by using a modified iterative alternating direction implicit (ADI) method (Prickett and Lonnquist, 1971). Hall identified a number of features important to the equation and method of solution in the present form: (a) incompressibility was assumed so that specific yield could be substituted for storativity to allow for the solution of unconfined flow problems using what is basically a confined flow model; (b) the Dupuit-Forchheimer assumption and the related assumption that there is no vertical change in head; (c) a stream can be simulated in the model either as a constant head boundary or by linkage with Darcy's law through a less permeable stream bottom; (d) ET can be incorporated as a function of depth to water table below land surface; (e) recharge to the water table can be incorporated as a constant term; and (f) the model is not driven easily into steady state. The model used a slight variation of the nondimensionality devised by Leake (1977). Hall tested it on watershed areas ranging from 30 to 156 ha that had a general geology of loess over glacial till over Pennsylvanian limestone. The thickness of the loess varies from negligible at the streambeds to as much as 30 m near watershed divides. He used characteristic vertical strips of aquifer between the divide and stream for his simulation because data were insufficient to allow the simulation of an entire watershed. Hall developed a dimensionless recession curve for the time period equivalent to 360 days and for the time required to dewater the aquifer.

EMPIRICAL MODELING OF SUBSURFACE WATER

Fleming (1975) briefly discussed subsurface processes and how hydrologic models commonly handle them. The usual method is to consider subsurface water as resident in one or more storages or reservoirs. Amounts of water in storage are tracked by relatively simple water balance or accounting equations; discharges are released according to empirical relations.

The storage balance equation is usually a simple accounting of inflows and outflows:

$$\theta_t = \theta_{t-1} + I \, \Delta t - O \, \Delta t \qquad\qquad [7.7]$$

where

θ_t = total water in storage at time t

I = a summation of such inflow rates as infiltration or inflowing seepage.

O = a summation of such outflow rates as evapotranspiration, outflowing seepage (baseflow, interflow, etc.)

Subsurface outflow rates are usually expressed as functions of the amount of subsurface water remaining in storage. Crawford and Linsley (1966), for example, computed interflow discharge during a 15-min interval as:

$$q_i = (1 - [IRC]^{1/96}) \, SRGX \qquad\qquad [7.8]$$

---

*From a presentation, "Ground-Water Yield of Small Upland Watersheds," at the AGU meeting in Miami, FL, 1978.

where

    IRC   = daily recession rates of interflow

    SRGX = volume of interflow in storage.

They computed ground water discharge for each 15-min time interval as:

$$G_g = (1 - [KK24]^{1/96})(1 + KU{\cdot}S) S_{gw} \quad \dots\dots\dots\dots\dots\dots\dots \quad [7.9]$$

where

    KK24 = minimum observed daily ground water recession constant

    KU   = variable ground water recession parameter

    S   = ground water slope

    S_{gw} = ground water storage.

Recession constants (IRC, KK24, and KU) for such equations as [7.8] and [7.9] are obtained empirically by analysis of hydrographs recorded for the streams to be modeled. Analysis often consists of separating the various subsurface components (Linsley et al., 1949) and estimating the parameters of the resulting curves (Jamieson and Amerman, 1969).

Table 7.1 shows which subsurface flow components are considered in 29 hydrologic models that have appeared since 1958. Fleming (1975) analyzed the first 17 of these models. Infiltration, the input to subsurface water, is specifically considered in all but four models. The primary subsurface output, ET, is submodeled in 16 models, only a little over half the total. Baseflow, another output, is specifically considered in only 13 models, and of these, eight also account for interflow, another possible output. Soil water and ground water volumes are identifiable storages in 19 and 11 models, respectively, and percolation is simulated as either a link between them or as a loss term in 13 models. One model also links soil water and ground water through a capillary rise algorithm.

STOCHASTIC APPROACHES

Equations [7.3], [7.5], and [7.6] are physically approximate expressions of the manner in which water moves through porous materials for given boundary conditions. In natural systems, the hydrologically active boundaries are those across which recharge and discharge occur. Thus precipitation, evapotranspiration factors, and stream stages, for example, determine the boundary conditions on the subsurface flow system. The variation of these climatic factors leads to a generally time-lagged variation in such subsurface flow factors as water table position and baseflow rate.

Like climatic data, subsurface flow data form time series whose characteristics are governed at least in part by probability laws. Subsurface flow may be analyzed and modeled as a collection of stochastic processes as well as by the deterministic and parametric methods already discussed. Yevjevich (1972) discussed stochastic processes in the context of hydrology.

Kriz (1972) statistically analyzed 70 yr of weekly ground water levels in a well in Czechoslovakia and reported certain conclusions regarding average water levels, the departures from the average, and the periodicity of extreme departures. Assuming no change in the flow system and boundary conditions (climate and man's withdrawals or inputs), these analyses indicated the probable amplitudes and periodicities of future fluctuations.

TABLE 7.1. SUBSURFACE FLOW COMPONENTS CONSIDERED IN WATERSHED MODELS

Model	Reference	F	SW	ET	IF	PERC	GW	BF	Other
SSARR	Rockwood, 1968	✓	✓	✓			✓	✓	
Stanford	Crawford and Linsley, 1966	✓	✓	✓	✓	✓	✓	✓	
BRRL	Road Research Laboratory, 1963								
Dawdy-O'Donnell	Dawdy and O'Donnell, 1965	✓	✓	✓	✓	✓	✓		Capillary rise
Boughton	Boughton, 1966	✓	✓	✓	✓				
Huggins-Monke	Huggins and Monke, 1968	✓	✓						Drainage
HSP	Hydrocomp, 1969	✓	✓	✓	✓	✓	✓	✓	
Kutchment	Kutchment and Koren, 1968	✓	✓						
Hyreuin	Schultz, 1968	✓							
Lichty et al.	Lichty et al., 1968	✓	✓	✓					Drainage
Kozak	Kozak, 1968	✓							
Mero	Mero, 1969	✓	✓	✓	✓	✓	✓		
USDAHL	Holtan and Lopez, 1971	✓	✓	✓	✓	✓		✓	Drainage
IH	Nash and Sutcliffe, 1971	✓	✓	✓				✓	Subsurface runoff
WRB-Dee	Jamieson and Wilkinson, 1972	✓	✓	✓	✓	✓	✓	✓	
UBC	Quick and Pipes, 1972	✓	✓	✓	✓	✓	✓	✓	
Shih et al.	Shih et al., 1972	✓	✓	✓	✓	✓	✓	✓	
Leaf-Brink	Leaf and Brink, 1973		✓	✓					
ANSWERS	Beasley, 1977	✓							Drainage
K. State	Anderson, 1975	✓	✓	✓	✓				
VSA	Lee and Delleur, 1976	✓							
KINGEN 75	Rovey et al., 1977	✓							
Huggins et al.	Huggins et al., 1975	✓	✓			✓			
Bloemen	Bloemen, 1974				✓	✓	✓		
Monach	Porter and McMahon, 1971		✓					✓	
Hymo	Williams and Hann, 1972	✓							
USUWSM	Bowles and Riley, 1976	✓	✓	✓	✓	✓	✓	✓	
TR 20	Maclay, 1965	✓							
HEC-1	U.S. Army Corps of Engrs., 1973	✓							

*F – Infiltration; SW – Soil water; Et – Evapotranspiration; IF – Interflow; PERC – Percolation; GW – Ground water; BF – Baseflow.

Greater sophistication can be obtained by applying the methods described by Fiering and Jackson (1971) to Kriz's data. Basically, these authors constructed time series models which yielded predicted (called synthetic) time series that preserved the statistics of the real time series used to calibrate the models. Running a model many times for a given future period yields a family of possible time series, each of which preserves the statistics of the calibration period. This family can then be analyzed for such items of interest as the likelihood of encountering extremes beyond those experienced during the period of record.

Rao et al. (1975) developed both a univariate and a multivariate autoregressive model. Each expressed well water level as a function of water levels in neighboring wells, of precipitation measured at nearby sites, and of stage in a nearby river. Functions were included to represent periodicity and randomness. Using this approach, one can infer cause and effect relationships and forecast probable future patterns of water levels.

Bathala et al. (1976) evaluated a regional aquifer using a finite dif-ference solution of equation [7.4] with stochastic inputs. Precipitation and river stages, determined both directly from historical records and from a stochastic model for each quantity, were used as inputs to the model.

SUBSURFACE WATER AND SMALL WATERSHED MODELING

Preceding sections have briefly reviewed some of the more prominent subsurface water modeling approaches available today. A pertinent question is: Where do these various approaches fit into the context of small watershed modeling? The answer lies in consideration of the purpose of a particular modeling effort, in the economics of the project, and in the context of more abstract factors, such as environmental quality and physical well-being of various lifeforms, including man.

The physically-based, deterministic approach represented by the Richards', Jacob, and Laplace equations is by far the most expensive ap-proach to subsurface water modeling. It requires detailed knowledge of system geometry, distribution of hydraulic properties within the system, and hydraulic conditions imposed on the boundaries of the system. Even with all these measurements, the models usually require some calibration—for much the same reason that a simple weir must be calibrated to determine the weir coefficient. Currently, computational expense is considerable but will prob-ably decrease as both mathematical and computer technologies advance.

On the other hand, the power of the physically-based approach far ex-ceeds that of any other. Using this approach, one can approximate such quantities as water flow paths, water content, water pressure, water velocity, time of residence in various parts of the system, and so on. These quantities are useful in answering many questions about the movement of dissolved substances through the landscape and about what chemical changes might take place along the flow paths.

Physically-based models may also be used in an iterative mode with field exploration to develop a physical description of the subsurface portion of a watershed. Sparse sampling can miss localized subsurface features that can be inferred from subsequent attempts to match model output with observed data. Further sampling can then be done in the zone or zones brought to at-tention by the model.

The empirical representations for subsurface water movement as used in many watershed models are generally inexpensive components from the com-putational standpoint. Nearly all require calibration against historical records, but they require little sampling and physical measurement in the field. None yield useful information on the hydraulics of the flow system beyond that contained in the dependent variables of the empirical equations.

Stochastic models for subsurface water are also computationally inex-pensive. They require no measurement of field properties, but they depend entirely upon the existence of a historical record. Some watershed models are developed to predict the hydrologic impact of a comtemplated change in the watershed. Because stochastic methods depend upon historical records for calibration, they are of little use for such purposes.

Empirical submodels also depend upon historical records for such pur-poses as determining the parameters of a hydrograph recession or a storage-discharge curve. These parameters have some conceptual meaning, however.

There is often a basis for exercising engineering judgment in revising them to reflect an approximation of the effect of a watershed change upon them.

A physically-based model supported by reasonably accurate data on boundary geometry and media hydraulic properties will, in principle, yield the most complete and accurate prediction of proposed watershed changes that can be expressed in terms of boundary condition or media properties.

In conclusion, there are essentially three approaches to modeling sub-surface water—stochastic, empirical, and physical-mathematical. In the context of general small watershed modeling, economic considerations justify continued reliance on stochastic or empirically-based subsurface water sub-models for applications. High-risk watershed problems may justify the physical-mathematical approach, especially where ground water quality is involved. Research and development should continue with the aim of making physically-based models practical and of linking physically-based submodels with submodels based on other approaches. Smith and Woolhiser (1971), Freeze (1972a, 1972b), Weeks et al. (1974), and Rovey and Richardson (1975) have given us a start in this direction by the conjunctive use of empirically-based and physically-based models. This may be a very good way to approach small watersheds where a general hydrologic prediction is need-ed or where detailed analysis of some specific aspect of subsurface water hydrology is needed.

References

1 Amerman, C. R. 1969. Finite difference solutions of unsteady, two-dimensional, par-tially saturated porous media flow. Unpublished Ph.D. Thesis. Purdue Univ., Lafayette, IN. Diss. Abstr. Int. 30(9):4105B-4106B.

2 Anderson, C. E. 1975. A water balance model for agricultural watersheds on deep loess soils. Ph.D. Dissertation, Kansas State Univ.

3 Appel, C. A., and J. D. Bredehoeft. 1976. Status of ground-water modeling in the U.S. Geological Survey. USGS Circular 737.

4 Bathala, C. T., J. A. Spooner, and A. R. Rao. 1976. Regional aquifer evaluation studies with stochastic inputs. Purdue Univ., Water Resources Center Tech. Report 72, West Lafayette, IN.

5 Beasley, D. B. 1977. ANSWERS: A mathematical model for simulating the effects of land use and management on water quality. Ph.D. Thesis. Purdue Univ., West Lafayette, IN.

6 Bibby, R., and D. K. Sunada. 1971. Mathematical model of leaky aquifer. Proc. ASCE, J. Irrig. and Drain. Div. 97(IR3):387-395.

7 Bloemen, G. W. 1974. On the evaluation of parameter values in water balance models. Tech. Bull. 92, Inst. for Land and Water Management Research, Wageningen, The Netherlands.

8 Boughton, W. C. 1966. A mathematical model for relating runoff to rainfall with dai-ly data. Trans. Inst. Engineers (Australia) 7:83.

9 Bouma, J., and L. W. Dekker. 1978. A case study on infiltration into dry clay soil I. Morphological observations. Geoderma 20(1):27-40. .

10 Bouma, J., L. W. Dekker, and J. H. M. Wosten. 1978. A case study on infiltration in-to dry clay soil II. Physical measurements. Geoderma 20(1):41-51.

11 Bouwer, H. 1962. Analyzing ground-water mounds by resistance network. Proc. ASCE, J. Irrig. and Drain. Div. 88(IR3):15-36.

12 Bouwer, H. 1978. Groundwater hydrology. McGraw-Hill Book Co., New York.

13 Bouwer, H., and W. C. Little. 1959. A unifying numerical solution for two-dimensional steady flow problems in porous media with an electrical resistance network. Soil Sci. Soc. Amer. Proc. 23(2):91-96.

14 Bowles, D. S., and J. P. Riley. 1976. Low flow modeling in small steep watersheds. Proc. ASCE, J. Hydraul. Div. 102(HY9):1225-1239.

15 Bredehoeft, J. D., and G. F. Pinder. 1970. Digital analysis of areal flow in multi-aquifer groundwater systems: A quasi three-dimensional model. Water Resour. Res. 6(3):883-888.

16 Buckingham, E. 1907. Studies on the movement of soil moisture. USDA Bull. 38.

17 Buckman, H. O., and N. C. Brady. 1969. The nature and properties of soils. Seventh ed., MacMillan, New York.

18 Childs, E. C. 1969. An introduction to the physical basis of soil water phenomena. John Wiley and Sons Ltd., London.

19 Cooley, R. L. 1971. A finite difference method for unsteady flow in variably saturated porous media: Application to a single pumping well. Water Resour. Res. 7(6):1607-1625.

20 Crawford, N. H., and R. K. Linsley. 1966. Digital simulation in hydrology: Stanford watershed model IV. Stanford Univ. Tech. Report 39.

21 Dagan, G. 1976. Comment on a stochastic-conceptual analysis of one-dimensional groundwater flow in nonuniform homogeneous media. Water Resour. Res. 12(3):567.

22 Dawdy, D. R., and T. O'Donnell. 1965. Mathematical models of catchment behavior. Proc. ASCE, J. Hydraul. Div. 91(HY4):123-137.

23 DeWiest, R. J. M. 1965. Geohydrology. John Wiley and Sons, New York.

24 Dupuit, J. 1863. Etude theoriques et pratiques sur le mouvement des eaux. Second ed., Dunod, Paris.

25 Fiering, M. B., and B. B. Jackson. 1971. Synthetic streamflows. Water Resources Monograph 1, pp. 1-98, American Geophysical Union.

26 Fleming, G. 1975. Computer simulation techniques in hydrology. Elsevier Publishing Co., New York.

27 Freeze, R. A. 1971a. Three-dimensional, transient, saturated-unsaturated flow in a groundwater basin. Water Resour. Res. 7(2):347-366.

28 Freeze, R. A. 1971b. Influence of the unsaturated flow domain on seepage through earth dams. Water Resour. Res. 7(4):929-941.

29 Freeze, R. A. 1972a. Role of subsurface flow in generating surface runoff. 1. Base flow contributions to channel flow. Water Resour. Res. 8(3):609-623.

30 Freeze, R. A. 1972b. Role of subsurface flow in generating surface runoff. 2. Upstream source areas. Water Resour. Res. 8(5):1272-1283.

31 Freeze, R. A. 1975. A stochastic-conceptual analysis of one-dimensional groundwater flow in nonuniform homogeneous media. Water Resour. Res. 11(5):725-741.

32 Freeze, R. A. 1978. Mathematical models of hillslope hydrology, Chapt. 6 in Kirkby, M. J. (Ed.), Hillslope Hydrology. John Wiley and Sons, New York, pp. 177-225.

33 Freeze, R. A., and P. A. Witherspoon. 1966. Theoretical analysis of regional ground-water flow: 1. Analytical and numerical solutions to the mathematical model. Water Resour. Res. 2(4):641-656.

34 Getzen, R. T. 1977. Analog-model analysis of regional three-dimensional flow in the ground-water reservoir of Long Island, New York. USGS Prof. Paper 982.

35 Gupta, S. K., K. K. Tanji, and J. N. Luthin. 1975. A three-dimensional finite element ground water model. Univ. of California-Davis, California Water Resources Center Contribution 152.

36 Hamon, W. R. 1961. Estimating potential evapotranspiration. Proc. ASCE, J. Hydraul. Div. 87(HY3):107-120.

37 Harr, M. E. 1962. Ground water and seepage. McGraw-Hill Book Co., New York.

38 Hewlett, J. D. 1961. Soil moisture as a source of base flow from steep mountain watersheds. Southeastern Forest Experiment Station Paper 132.

39 Holtan, H. N., and N. C. Lopez. 1971. USDAHL-70 model of watershed hydrology. USDA Tech. Bull. 1435.

40 Hornberger, G. M., I. Remson, and A. A. Fungaroli. 1969. Numeric studies of a composite soil moisture ground-water system. Water Resour. Res. 5(4):797-802.

41 Hornberger, G. M., J. Ebert, and I. Remson. 1970. Numerical solution of the Boussinesq equation for aquifer-stream interaction. Water Resour. Res. 6(2):601-608.

42 Huggins, L. F., and E. J. Monke. 1968. A mathematical model for simulating the hydrologic response of a watershed. Water Resour. Res. 4(3):529-539.

43 Huggins, L. F., T. H. Podmore, and C. F. Hood. 1975. Hydrologic simulation using distributed parameters. Purdue Univ., Water Resources Center Tech. Report 82.

44 Hydrocomp, Inc. 1969. Operations manual. Second ed., Hydrocomp, Palo Alto, CA.

45 Jacob, C. E. 1950. Chapter V. Flow of ground water, pp. 321-386. In: Rouse, Hunter (ed.), Engineering hydraulics, John Wiley and Sons, New York.

46 Jamieson, D. G., and C. R. Amerman. 1969. Quick-return subsurface flow. J. Hydrol. 8:122-136.

47 Jamieson, D. G., and J. C. Wilkinson. 1972. River Dee research program 3. A short-term control strategy for multi-purpose reservoir systems. Water Resour. Res. 8(4):911.

48 Jorgensen, D. G. 1975. Analog-model studies of ground-water hydrology in the Houston district, Texas. Texas Water Development Board Report 190.

49   Kazmann, R. G. 1972. Modern Hydrology. Second ed., Harper and Row, New York.

50   Kirkby, M. J. (Ed.). 1978. Hillslope hydrology. John Wiley and Sons, New York.

51   Klute, A., E. J. Scott, and F. D. Whisler. 1965. Steady state water flow in a saturated inclined soil slab. Water Resour. Res. 1(2):287-294.

52   Kozak, M. 1968. Determination of the runoff hydrograph on a deterministic basis using a digital computer. Proc. Symp. on the Use of Analogue and Digital Computers in Hydrology, Tucson, IASH/UNESCO, 1:138-151.

53   Kriz, H. 1972. Statistical processing of long-term observations of groundwaters. J. Hydrol. 16(1):17-37.

54   Kutchment, L. S., and V. I. Koren. 1968. Modelling of hydrologic processes with the aid of electronic computers. Proc. Symp. on the Use of Analogue and Digital Computers in Hydrology, Tucson, IASH/UNESCO, 2:616-624.

55   Law, J. 1944. A statistical approach to the interstitial heterogeneity of sand reservoirs. Trans. AIME 155:202-222.

56   Leaf, C. F., and G. E. Brink. 1973. Hydrologic simulation model of Colorado subalpine forest. USDA Forest Service Res. Paper RM-107.

57   Leake, S. A. 1977. Simulation of flow from an aquifer to a partially penetrating trench. J. of Res., USGS 5:535-540.

58   Leavesley, G. H. 1973. A mountain watershed simulation model. Ph.D. Dissertation. Colorado State Univ., Fort Collins, CO.

59   Lee, M. T., and J. W. Delleur. 1976. A variable source area model of the rainfall-runoff process based on the watershed stream network. Water Resour. Res. 12(5):1029-1036.

60   Lichty, R. W., D. R. Dawdy, and J. M. Bergmann. 1968. Rainfall runoff model for small basin flood hydrograph simulation. Proc. Symp. on the Use of Analogue and Digital Computers in Hydrology, Tucson, IASH/UNESCO, 2:356-367.

61   Linsley, R. K., Jr., M. A. Kohler, and J. L. H. Paulhus. 1949. Applied hydrology. McGraw-Hill Book Co., New York.

62   Maclay, R. E. 1965. Project formulation—hydrology, computer program user's manual. USDA-SCS, Washington, DC.

63   Marino, M. A. 1975. Digital simulation model of aquifer response to stream stage fluctuation. J. Hydrol. 25(1/2):51-58.

64   McGuinness, J. L., L. L. Harrold, and C. R. Amerman. 1961. Hydrogeologic nature of streamflow on small watersheds. Proc. ASCE, J. Hydraul. Div. 87(HY1):1-13.

65   McMillan, W. D. 1966. Theoretical analysis of groundwater basin operations. University of California-Berkeley, Water Resources Center Contribution 114.

66   Mero, F. 1969. An approach to daily hydrometeorological water balance computations for surface and groundwater basins. Seminar on Integrated Surveys for River Basin Development, Delft.

67   Moore, R. E. 1939. Water conduction from shallow water tables. Hilgardia 12(6):383-426.

68   Narasimhan, T. N., and P. A. Witherspoon. 1977. Numerical model for saturated-unsaturated flow in deformable porous media 1. Theory. Water Resour. Res. 13(3):657-664.

69   Narasimhan, T. N., P. A. Witherspoon, and A. L. Edwards. 1978. Numerical model for saturated-unsaturated flow in deformable porous media 2. The algorithm. Water Resour. Res. 14(2):255-261.

70   Nash, J. E., and J. V. Sutcliffe. 1971. River flow forecasting through conceptual models, Part I—A discussion of principles. J. Hydrol. 10(3):282-290.

71   Nelson, R. W. 1962. Steady Darcian transport of fluids in heterogeneous partially saturated porous media, Part I, Mathematical and numerical formulation. AEC Research and Development Report HW-72335 PT 1.

72   Neuman, S. P. 1973. Saturated-unsaturated seepage by finite elements. Proc. ASCE, J. Hydraul. Div. 99(HY12):2233-2250.

73   Polubarinova-Kochina, P. Y. 1962. Theory of ground water movement. Princeton Univ. Press, Princeton, NJ (translated by J. M. R. DeWiest).

74   Porter, J. W., and T. A. McMahon. 1971. A model for the simulation of streamflow data from climatic records. J. Hydrol. 13(4):297-324.

75   Prickett, T. A., and C. G. Lonnquist. 1971. Selected digital computer techniques for groundwater resource evaluation. Illinois State Water Survey Bull. 55.

76   Quick, M. C., and A. Pipes. 1972. Daily and seasonal runoff forecasting, with a water budget model. Interntl. Symposia on the Role of Snow and Ice in Hydrology, Measurement and Forecasting, Banff, Alberta, UNESCO/WMO.

77   Rao, A. R., R. G. S. Rao, and R. L. Kashyap. 1975. Stochastic models for ground water levels. Purdue Univ., Water Resources Research Center Tech. Report 67.

78   Remson, I., G. M. Hornberger, and F. J. Molz. 1971. Numerical methods in subsurface hydrology. Wiley-Interscience, New York.

79   Richards, L. A. 1931. Capillary conduction of liquids through porous mediums. Physics 1:318-333.

80   Road Research Laboratory. 1963. A guide for engineers to the design of storm sewer systems. Road Note 35, London, Her Majesty's Stationary Office.

81   Rockwood, D. M. 1968. Application of streamflow synthesis and reservoir regulation—SSARR—Program to lower Mekong River. Publ. No. 80, FASIT Symp., Tucson, AZ.

82   Rovey, C. E. K. 1975. Numerical model of flow in a stream-aquifer system. Hydrology Paper 74, Colorado State Univ., Fort Collins.

83   Rovey, C. E. K., and E. V. Richardson. 1975. Mathematical model of flow in a stream-aquifer system. Proc. 2nd Annual Symp. on Model Technology, San Francisco, CA (published by ASCE, New York), pp. 439-457.

84   Rovey, E. W., D. A. Woolhiser, and R. E. Smith. 1977. A distributed kinematic model of upland watersheds. Hydrology Paper 93, Colorado State Univ., Fort Collins.

85   Rubin, J. 1968. Theoretical analysis of two-dimensional, transient flow of water in unsaturated and partly unsaturated soils. Soil Sci. Soc. Amer. Proc. 32:607-615.

86   Schultz, G. A. 1968. Digital computer solutions for flood hydrograph predictions from rainfall data. Proc. Symp. on the Use of Analogue and Digital Computers in Hydrology, Tucson, IASH/UNESCO, 1:125-137.

87   Shih, G. B., R. H. Hawkins, and M. D. Chambers. 1972. Computer modelling of a coniferous forest watershed. In: Age of Changing Priorities for Land Water, ASCE, New York.

88   Smith, R. E., and D. A. Woolhiser. 1971. Mathematical simulation of infiltrating watersheds. Hydrology Paper 47, Colorado State Univ., Fort Collins.

89   Southwell, R. F. 1946. Relaxation methods in theoretical physics. Oxford Univ. Press.

90   Stephenson, G. R., and R. A. Freeze. 1974. Mathematical simulation of subsurface flow contributions to snowmelt runoff, Reynolds Creek Watershed, ID. Water Resour. Res. 10(2):284-294.

91   Taylor, D. W. 1948. Fundamentals of soil mechanics. John Wiley and Sons, New York.

92   Taylor, G. S., and J. N. Luthin. 1963. The use of electronic computers to solve subsurface drainage problems. J. Agric. Res. 34(12).

93   Taylor, G. S., and J. N. Luthin. 1969. Computer methods for transient analysis of water-table aquifers. Water Resour. Res. 5(1):144-152

94   Thiel, T. J., and J. Bornstein. 1965. Tile drainage of a sloping fragipan soil. TRANSACTIONS of the ASAE 8(4):555-557.

95   Thiel, T. J., B. S. Vimoke, and G. S. Taylor. 1962. Instrumentation and fabrication of an electrical resistance network for studying moisture flow problems. J. Agric. Eng. Res. 7(4):323-327.

96   Todd, D. K. 1970. The water encyclopedia. Water Information Center, Port Washington, NY.

97   Trescott, P. C., G. F. Pinder, and S. P. Larson. 1976. Chapter C1. Finite difference model for aquifer simulation in two dimensions with results of numerical experiments, pp. 2-33. In: Techniques of Water Resources Investigations of the U.S. Geological Survey, Box 7, Automated Data Processing and Computations, USGS.

98   U.S. Army Corps of Engineers. 1973. HEC-1, flood hydrograph package, user's manual for computer program 723-X6-L2010. U.S. Army Corps of Engineers, Hydrologic Engineering Center.

99   Verma, R. D., and W. Brutsaert. 1970. Unconfined aquifer seepage by capillary flow theory. Proc. ASCE, J. Hydraul. Div. 96(HY6):1331-1344.

100   Warren, J. E., and H. S. Price. 1961. Flow in heterogeneous porous media. Soc. Petrol. Eng. J. 1:153-169.

101   Weeks, J. B., G. H. Leavesley, F. A. Welder, and G. J. Saulnier, Jr. 1974. Simulated effects of oil-shale development on the hydrology of Piceance Basin, CO. USGS Prof. Paper 908.

102   Williams, J. R., and R. W. Hann. 1972. Hymo, a problem-oriented computer language for building hydrologic models. Water Resour. Res. 8(1):79-86.

103   Winter, T. C. 1976. Numerical simulation analysis of the interaction of lakes and ground water. USGS Prof. Paper 1001.

104   Winter, T. C. 1978. Numerical simulation of steady state three-dimensional ground-water flow near lakes. Water Resour. Res. 14(2):245-254.

105   Yevjevich, V. 1972. Stochastic processes in hydrology. Water Resources Publications, Fort Collins, CO.

chapter 8 ███████████████████

MODELING THE EROSION PROCESS

8

MODELING THE EROSION PROCESS

by   G. R. Foster, Hydraulic Engineer, USDA, and
     Associate Professor, Department of Agricultural
     Engineering, Purdue University, West Lafayette,
     Indiana 47907

INTRODUCTION TO EROSION-SEDIMENTATION SYSTEMS OF SMALL WATERSHEDS

Erosion and sedimentation by water embody the processes of detachment, transportation, and deposition of soil particles (sediment) by the erosive and transport agents of raindrop impact and runoff over the soil surface (ASCE, 1975). Detachment is the dislodging of soil particles from the soil mass by the erosive agents. Transportation is the entrainment and movement of sediment from its original location. Sediment travels from upland sources through the streams and may eventually reach the ocean (Holeman, 1968). Not all sediment reaches the ocean; some of it is deposited on the toe of slopes, in reservoirs, and on flood plains along the way (ASCE, 1975). This process is sedimentation. Some sediment is deposited only temporarily. Subsequent storm events, sometimes several years later, may reentrain the sediment and move it further along the stream system (Trimble, 1975).

Erosion and sedimentation can be major problems (ASCE, 1975). Erosion reduces productivity of cropland. Sediment degrades water quality and may carry soil absorbed polluting chemicals. Deposition in irrigation canals, stream channels, reservoirs, estuaries, harbors, and other water conveyence structures reduces the capacity of these structures and requires costly removal.

Sediment Sources and Sinks

Sediment sources produce sediment; sinks trap sediment. Classification of sources and sinks is useful for identifying and evaluating the extent of erosion and sedimentation and for recommending erosion and sedimentation controls. Sources include agricultural lands; construction sites; roadway embankments, cuts, and ditches; disturbed forest lands; surface mines; and natural geologic eroding 'badlands.' Sources may also be classified according to the dominant type of erosion: sheet, rill, gully, stream channel, or landslide (Hutchinson et al., 1976). Sheet erosion is the removal of a thin, relatively uniform layer of soil particles. Rill erosion is erosion in numerous small channels that are several millimeters wide and deep. When rills cannot be obliterated by normal tillage, they are called gullies. Stream

Contribution from Agricultural Research Service, USDA, in cooperation with the Purdue Agricultural Experiment Station. Purdue Journal Paper No. 7776.

channel erosion is by streamflow, and landslide erosion is soil movement enmasse.

Typical sediment sinks include the toe of concave slopes, strips of vegetation, flood plains, and reservoirs--areas where deposition occurs because the flow's transport capacity is reduced below its sediment load. Sediment loss to sinks reduces sediment load so that less sediment leaves a watershed than is detached. The delivery ratio concept and delivery ratios less than unity reflect the influence of sediment sinks.

Downslope or downstream erosion-sedimentation processes directly interrelate with and depend on inputs from upslope and upstream areas. A decrease or increase in runoff from upland areas will correspondingly increase or decrease detachment and transport capacity in the channels. For example, stable streams may become major sediment producers where upstream urban development drastically increases runoff (Robinson, 1976).

Sediment yield directly relates to sediment production on the upland areas for a system in quasi-equilibrium. However, control of upland erosion does not always immediately reduce sediment yield. Instead, elimination of incoming upland sediment increases the erosivity of the channel flow. If sediment is available from previous deposition or from erodible channel boundaries, sediment yield may continue for several years at a high rate before the system readjusts and responds, if it ever does completely, to the control of upland erosion (Trimble, 1975).

Consequently, an accurate estimate of sediment yield must consider the entire watershed erosion-sedimentation system. Major sediment sources and sinks must be identified and the watershed's erosion-sedimentation history determined. An assumption of channel equilibrium must be examined carefully, because most channels are dynamic, sometimes with time lags of a few decades.

Hydrology

The hydrologic processes of rainfall and runoff drive erosion and sedimentation processes. Factors that affect either rainfall or runoff directly affect erosion and sedimentation. Thus, any analysis of erosion, sediment transport, or sediment yield must consider hydrology.

Hydrologically, a watershed may be conceptualized as having overland flow, channel flow, and subsurface flow components, with overland flow and channel areas being the major ones so far as erosion and sedimentation are concerned. Although overland flow is usually analyzed as a broad sheet flow, often it concentrates in many small defineable channels (Foster, 1971). Any erosion caused by flow in these small channels (rills) is rill erosion. Erosion on areas between the rills is interrill erosion (Meyer et al., 1975b). Both interrill and rill erosion are overland flow rated processes, denoted by upland erosion, a term convenient for this discussion.

Where surface flow can not hydrologically or hydraulically be treated as overland flow, it is considered channel flow. Erosion occurring in channel flow is defined and analyzed as concentrated flow, gully, or stream channel erosion.

Rills are frequently defined as small erodible channels which can be obliterated by normal tillage (Hutchinson et al., 1976). Also, depth might be used as a criteria; for example, a rill becomes a gully if its depth exceeds 300 mm. A distinction between rills and gullies based on depth works well for erosion surveys because the field surveyor is not required to use judgment to decide if a rill is a gully. For modeling purposes, flow characteristics, rather than rill depth or size, determine whether a set of channels are rills or gullies. Usually rills infer a large number of small flow concentrations uniformly distributed over an area whereas the number of gullies or channels is small.

Sometimes in farm fields, topography concentrates overland flow into major flow concentrations where serious erosion can occur if the soil is not protected. If the watershed being analyzed is on the order of the size of the field containing the flow concentration, this erosion would be analyzed as channel erosion. If the watershed being analyzed is much larger and this source of sediment is small in relation to other sources, it could very well be included with rill erosion. Such distinctions between rill and channel erosion are ones that the modeler must make depending on the situation.

Erosion-Sedimentation Characteristics of Small Watersheds

A typical small watershed and the components that a modeling analysis might involve depends on the application and range from a uniform land profile to one having complex overland flow segments, numerous channel segments, and impoundments. The importance of particular features depends on their presence or absence and the degree to which they influence erosion and sedimentation processes. Four illustrations are given below.

1. Erosion on a Simple Land Profile

A simple land profile is chosen from a field to estimate erosion for a critical area. A conservation plan for the field might be based on the erosion estimate for this profile. The analysis involves only the selected profile and overland flow erosion processes. This simple land profile might also be a roadway embankment.

2. Sediment Yield from a Typical Farm Field

An estimate of sediment yield from a farm field having no installed structural conservation practices is required when selecting a management practice to control sediment delivery from the field. Soils probably vary over the field, as do slope lengths and steepnesses. Cropping and management might also vary over the field. Upland erosion occurs over almost the entirety of the field. In addition, the topography of this field, like that of most fields, causes overland flow to collect and concentrate in flows as wide as 1 to 2 m. Unless the soil in these flow concentrations is protected, serious erosion may occur.

This field, like most fields, also has ridges and heavy vegetation around its edges which slow runoff before it leaves the field. Or, the flow might pass through a culvert under a road as it leaves the field. Any of these features can and frequently does act as a flow control which pond the flow and cause considerable deposition of sediment.

3. Sediment Yield from a Field with Structural Conservation Practices

An objective of good conservation planning is to reduce erosion and sediment yield with practices like terraces, grass waterways, and impoundments as well as good cropping practices like conservation tillage. Rill and interrill erosion occurs on this field as in the previous examples. When overland flow reaches the terrace channels, it becomes concentrated flow and may or may not deposit sediment depending on various factors such as the inflow sediment rate from upland erosion, the discharge rate, and the terrace channel slope.

Usually terraces empty into grass waterways. Depending on their slope, vegetal cover, and incoming flow and sediment load, sediment may or may not be deposited in the waterways. Finally, the flow from the grass waterways may or may not pass through a control before it leaves the field.

If the flow passes through a tile outlet like an impoundment terrace, deposition usually occurs. However, the amount of deposition depends on a number of factors, including impoundment depth, sediment size, and detention time.

4. Complex Watershed

A complex watershed has all of the features in the first three examples occurring on a large number of subareas over the watershed; in addition, it has gullies and defined stream channels. The response of the gullies and channels directly relates to the inputs from upstream and upslope areas. If the incoming sediment load is greater than the transport capacity in the channels, deposition occurs and the channels aggrade. Conversely, if the incoming sediment load is less than the transport capacity, potentially the channels can degrade.

Upland Erosion

1. Basic Concepts

Detachment, transport, and deposition are basic processes that occur on upland areas. Detachment occurs when the erosive forces of raindrop impact or flowing water exceed the soil's resistance to erosion. Transport of detached particles is by raindrop splash and flow. Deposition occurs when the sediment load of a given particle type exceeds its corresponding transport capacity. The relative importance of these fundamental processes depends on whether the processes are occurring on interrill or rill areas and on the levels of the controlling variables.

Erosion on interrill areas is essentially independent of erosion in the rills, but erosion in the rills depends greatly on sediment inputs from the interrill areas. If sediment inflow from the interrill areas exceeds the transport capacity of flow in the rills, deposition occurs. If the sediment inflow is less than the transport capacity of flow in the rills, and if the flow's erosive forces exceed the resistance of the soil in the rills to detachment by flow, rill erosion occurs.

Most downslope movement of upland sediment is by flow in the rills. Even though excess transport capacity may exist on the interrill areas, this transport capacity does not add to the transport capacity of flow in the rills. This is subtle but a key point in using data from small experimental areas (e.g., 1 m by 1 m) to estimate parameter values for erosion models. Conversely, excess transport capacity in the rills is not available to transport sediment detached by raindrop impact on interrill areas. In most instances, sheet and interrill erosion are effectively the same. Unlike gully erosion, which is the next most severe stage of erosion after rill erosion, interrill erosion and rill erosion occur in the same stage of erosion. Sheet erosion is sometimes incorrectly classified as a less severe stage than rill erosion.

2. Major Factors Affecting Upland Erosion Processes

Detachment of soil particles is basically a function of the erosive forces of raindrop impact and flowing water, the susceptability of the soil to detachment, the presence of material that reduces the magnitude of the eroding forces, and management of the soil that makes it less susceptible to erosion. Transport is basically a function of the transport forces of the transport agents, the transportability of the detached soil particles, and the presence of material that reduces the transport forces.

Either detachment or transport capacity may limit erosion and sediment load at a location on the slope, as Fig. 8.1 shows (Ellison, 1947; Meyer and

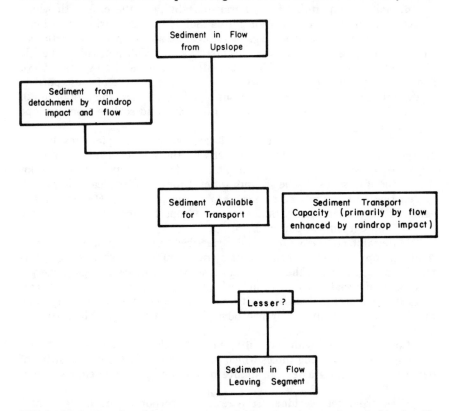

FIG. 8.1 Interaction of erosion processes at steady state on a segment of a typical land profile (Meyer and Wischmeier, 1969).

Wischmeier, 1969). At a given location on a slope, if the amount of sediment made available for transport by the detachment processes is less than transport capacity, then the sediment load moving on downslope will be the amount of detached sediment available for transport. Conversely, if the available detached sediment exceeds the transport capacity, deposition occurs and the transport capacity controls the sediment load.

a. Hydrology. Rainfall and runoff provide the basic energy input to drive the erosion process. A runoff hydrology model is assumed to be available to calculate hydrologic inputs. Later presentations will relate erosion components to rainfall and runoff characteristics.

b. Topography. Erosion is a function of a slope's length, steepness, and shape. Basically, these factors modify the energy of the hydrologic inputs.

c. Soil Erodibility. Some soils are naturally more susceptible to erosion than others (Wischmeier and Mannering, 1969). Soils also differ in their susceptibility to detachment by raindrop impact as compared with their susceptibility to detachment by flow (Meyer et al., 1975b). Freshly deposited aggregates seem to be more erodible than soil exposed to repeated wetting, drying, and compacting traffic. Erodibility can decrease over time with good management practices. Conversely, it can increase as erosion removes the surface soil and tillage brings up a more erodible subsurface soil. Continued intensive tillage breaks down soil structure and depletes organic matter, which increases erodibility.

d. Soil Transportability. Soil transportability is the ease with which detached soil particles can be transported. Soil is eroded as primary particles (sand, silt, and clay) and aggregates (conglomerates of primary particles). The size of aggregates ranges from about 2 μm to 500 μm with a specific gravity of about 1.8 (e.g., Long, 1964; Moldenhauer and Koswara, 1968). Sediment produced by upland erosion is usually a mixture of these particle types, but the proportions are functions of soil properties, the proportion of the sediment coming from interrill vs. rill areas, and sorting from upslope deposition.

e. Cover. Cover including a plant canopy, mulches, plant residue, or densely growing plants in direct contact with the soil surface has a greater impact on erosion than any other single factor. The canopy intercepts raindrops, and if it is close to the ground, water dripping off the leaves has much less energy than unhindered raindrops (Wischmeier, 1975). However, many canopies have open spaces that allow raindrops to strike the soil surface directly and detach soil particles.

Material in contact with the soil surface reduces erosion more effectively than a canopy. No detachment occurs by raindrop impact where the soil surface is covered because there is no fall distance for drops to regain energy. Also, such material slows the runoff, which increases the flow depth. This increased flow depth decreases detachment by cushioning the impact of the raindrops and reducing their hydrodynamic impact forces (Mutchler and Young, 1975).

Cover in contact with the soil surface also absorbs much of the flow's eroding and transporting forces which greatly reduces rill erosion. Strips of dense mulches and grasses can induce deposition and filter sediment from the runoff.

f. Incorporated Residue. Crop residue incorporated each year builds and maintains the soil's organic matter content thus helping to control soil loss (Wischmeier and Smith, 1978). Also, incorporation of larger pieces of mulch material like corn stalks and slash on disturbed forest lands seems to greatly reduce rill erosion. The buried pieces act like grade control structures and prevent rills from cutting very deeply especially if the pieces are close together and near the soil surface. The effect on interrill erosion is negligible, although both rill and interrill erosion decrease over time as these buried pieces are exposed. Over many years, the reduction can be substantial, like the effect of a desert pavement.

   g. Residual Land Use. Erosion at a given time depends on previous management history (Wischmeier, 1960). A field freshly plowed out of meadow is much less erodible than one continuously tilled. The fine root network and the improved soil structure from meadows are especially effective in maintaining high infiltration rates, protecting the soil against erosive forces, and decreasing the soil's susceptibility to erosion. These influences disappear in 2 to 3 yr with continued tillage (Wischmeier and Smith, 1978).

   h. Subsurface Effects. Plant roots, especially the root network of grasses and trees, hold the soil in place and increase infiltration. A well developed grass root network can reduce erosion by 75 percent (Wischmeier, 1975).

   i. Tillage. Tillage is sometimes a detachment mechanism that creates a ready supply of detached aggregates. Tillage seems to increase rill erosion much more than interrill erosion. Repeated wetting, drying, and compacting traffic causes the aggregates to form bonds, and the soil becomes less erodible. A soil that had not been tilled for 6 yr was only 40 percent as erodible as it was immediately after its last tillage (Wischmeier, 1975).

   Immediately after tillage, rill erosion may be great. As erosion progresses, the bottom of the rills may reach the bottom of the tilled layer where the soil may be relatively nonerodible. Thus erosion rate decreases with any further erosion and is a function of the extent of previous erosion.

   j. Roughness. Roughness, either in the form of pockets or obstacles that pond the flow in microponds, greatly reduces the flow's transport capacity and can cause considerable deposition. As these storage areas fill up, however, sediment delivery increases rapidly.

   k. Tillage Marks. Tillage marks straight up and down the hill generally increase rill erosion; tillage on the contour generally reduces it (Wischmeier and Smith, 1978). Flow in tillage marks on the contour has a greatly decreased effective flow gradient. A considerable amount of sediment eroded from the tillage ridges and row side slopes is often deposited in tillage channels on the contour. However, flow along the contour eventually collects in low areas. If runoff volume exceeds storage capacity behind the ridges in the low areas, the flow breaks through the ridges and causes significant rill erosion.

2. Major Factors Affecting Channel Processes

   a. Inflow from Upstream Areas. Both incoming flow and sediment affect channel bahavior. If the incoming sediment load exceeds the flow's transport capacity, depostion occurs. If incoming sediment load is less than the transport capacity, erosion can occur. In channels where deposition occurred previously during periods of excessive upland erosion, sediment yield may continue at a high rate after upland sediment is cut off because the previously deposited sediment is eroded.

   b. Soil Erodibility. Some soils are more erodible than others. Furthermore, the erodibility of deposited soil depends on the type of sediment (fine or coarse) and on wetting, drying, and compacting traffic, Also, moisture content when the soil was compacted and age since the last disturbance also influences erodibility (Grissinger, 1966).

c. Soil Transportability. Sediment in channel flow can range in size from clays to sands and from aggregates to primary particles. Some particles move as bedload and are easily deposited. Others, like the clays, move as suspended load and travel some distance before deposition. Furthermore, some aggregates may break down during transport and release primary particles.

d. Tillage. Tillage loosens the soil and seems to make it considerably more susceptible to erosion by flow.

e. Nonerodible Layer. Frequently, channels in a field will erode downward no further than the depth of tillage by an implement like a plow or disk. This greatly reduces channel erosion during subsequent storms. Similarly, nonerodible layers like rock or channel armoring developed by selective erosion decrease erosion in larger channels.

f. Cover. Vegetative cover in a channel usually greatly reduces channel erosion. Dense vegetation often induces deposition. Grass waterways are a typical example.

g. Channel Control. A channel control above the elevation of the approach channel slows the flow reducing its transport capacity. Deposition may result. A field boundary or a culvert are examples of this type of control. If the control is below the channel outlet grade, a headcut can develop and allow intense erosion as it advances upslope. Headcuts are typical of many gullies, especially those in the loess region of Southwestern Iowa (Piest et al., 1975).

h. Channel Sidewall Stability. Many channels widen by sloughing of sidewalls. The channel flow may undercut the sidewalls or moisture buildup in them may reduce their stability. Slope failure occurs and material slumps into the flow. The flow may quickly remove this sediment, or, if flow is not sufficient to erode and transport (clean out) the slumped debris, the gully becomes stable (Piest et al., 1975).

i. Channel Alignment. Intense erosion can occur on the outside of channel bends where the flow's shear stresses are high (ASCE, 1975).

MODELING UPLAND EROSION

Given an understanding of the various erosion processes, the next step is to derive and solve the mathematical expressions describing upland erosion.

Continuity

The main concept for modeling upland erosion is that sediment load is controlled by either the amount of sediment made available for transport by the detachment processes or by the transport capacity of the transport agents (Meyer and Wischmeier, 1969). Fig. 8.1 is a graphical statement of this concept and in actuality is a form of the continuity equation. The continuity equation normally used in dynamic upland erosion models is (Bennett, 1974):

$$\partial q_s / \partial x + \rho_s \, \partial(cy)/\partial t = D_r + D_1 \quad \dots \dots \dots \dots \dots \dots \dots \dots \dots \quad [8.1]$$

where q_s = sediment load (mass per unit width per unit time), x = distance along the slope, ρ_s = mass density of the sediment particles, c = concentration of the sediment in the flow (volume sediment per volume flow), y = flow depth, t = time, D_r = rill erosion rate (mass per unit area per unit time), and D_l = delivery rate of sediment from interrill areas (mass per unit area per unit time). Flow and sediment are assumed to be uniformly distributed across the slope, and therefore, variables like y are averages and q_s, D_r, and D_l are expressed on a total width or area basis although the processes can occur on a limited area. Dispersion terms have been neglected in equation [8.1]. The term $\partial q_s/\partial x$ is the buildup or loss of the sediment load with distance; $\rho_s\partial(cy)/\partial t$ is the storage rate of sediment within the flow depth; and D_r and D_l are contributions of sediment from lateral inflow.

In some cases, quasi-steady sediment movement may be assumed; this reduces the continuity equation to (Curtis, 1976; Foster and Huggins, 1977; Thomas, 1976):

$$dq_s/dx = D_r + D_1 \dots\dots\dots\dots\dots\dots\dots\dots\dots\dots\dots\dots\dots \quad [8.2]$$

which is essentially the continuity form represented by Fig. 8.1. The storage term is also dropped in bedload transport analyses (Chang and Hill, 1976).

Interrelationships between Deposition and Sediment Load

Flow depth y in equation [8.1] is assumed to be available from other hydrologic computations, but q_s, D_r and D_l are not independent variables. Rill detachment (or deposition) D_r maybe assumed to be directly proportional to the difference between the sediment transport capacity and sediment load or (Foster and Meyer, 1975; Simons et al., 1977):

$$D_r = \alpha(T_c - q_s) \dots\dots\dots\dots\dots\dots\dots\dots\dots\dots\dots\dots \quad [8.3]$$

where α = a first order reaction coefficient for deposition (length^{-1}) and T_c = flow transport capacity (mass per unit width per unit time). Foster and Meyer (1972a) rewrote the equation for erosion as:

$$(D_r/D_{rc}) + (q_s/T_c) = 1 \dots\dots\dots\dots\dots\dots\dots\dots\dots\dots \quad [8.4]$$

where D_{rc} = rill erosion detachment capacity rate (mass per unit area per unit time). Maximum rill erosion rate is assumed to occur when there is no sediment load. The coefficient α for erosion is given by D_{rc}/T_c.

Equations [8.3] and [8.4] introduce the concept that sediment load may be different from transport capacity. Deposition by flow occurs when sediment load exceeds transport capacity. Detachment by flow can occur when transport capacity exceeds sediment load. A detachment capacity can be defined based on the local conditions but the actual detachment rate depends on the degree to which the transport capacity is filled.

Equations [8.3] and [8.4] are most applicable to the deposition of suspended load. They have been reasonably well validated by Einstein (1968) for deposition of suspended silt and gravel beds in channel flow and by Foster and Huggins (1977) and Davis (1978) for deposition by overland flow. The equation is less well validated for erosion, although Apmann and Rumer

TABLE 8.1. OBSERVED VALUES FOR FIRST ORDER
REACTION COEFFICIENT FOR DEPOSITION α FOR
$D = \alpha(T_c - q_s)$. (From Foster and Huggins, 1977 and
Davis, 1978)

Particle type	Sedimentation diameter	Specific gravity	Simulated rainfall, 30 mm/h	Range for α values
	(μm)			(m^{-1})
Sand	342	2.59	No	13 to 33
Sand	342	2.59	Yes	3 to 13
Sand	150	2.59	No	13 to 33
Sand	150	2.59	Yes	3 to 13
Coal	342	1.55	No	$\cong 13$
Coal	342	1.55	Yes	$\cong 3$
Coal	156	1.65	No	$\cong 13$
Coal	156	1.56	Yes	$\cong 3$

(1970) did show a similar effect for erosion and suspension of noncohesive sediment. The equations are a simplification of the more complete continuity equation having terms for dispersion.

Based on the laboratory study by Tollner et al. (1976) of deposition in nails simulating grass, α decreases when: (1) the Reynold's number increases based on spacing of the nails (which indicates increased turbulence and decreased settling), (2) fall velocity decreases (which indicates slower settling and thus less trapping in a given distance), and (3) discharge rate increases (which indicates that a higher discharge decreases settling time).

Foster and Huggins (1977) and Davis (1978) found that α decreased when particles were more easily suspended which occurred with particles of small fall velocities and turbulence from raindrop impact. A decrease in α indicates that particles travel further before they deposit. Observed values from Foster and Huggins' and Davis' overland flow deposition experiments are given in Table 8.1.

Considering these data and Einstein's result for deposition of silt by channel flow, the following equation seems appropriate for estimating α for deposition by overland flow:

$$\alpha = 0.5V_s/q \quad \dots \dots \dots \dots \dots \dots \dots \dots \dots \dots \dots \dots \dots \dots \dots \dots \quad [8.5]$$

where V_s = fall velocity and q = discharge per unit width.

Interactions among Rill and Interrill Detachment and Sediment Load

Before the effect of sediment load on rill detachment can be described, interrill detachment and its relationship to sediment load must be considered. In areas where flow is depositing sediment over a broad area such as the toe of concave slopes, a logical assumption is that interrill detachment does not occur. However, as models are generally written, this deposition can not be distinguished from deposition that often occurs in middles between rows, especially if the rows are on a flat slope. In this chapter, interrill detachment and delivery are usually assumed to be totally unaffected by deposition by flow.

Without a mechanism to "insert" particles into the flow, most transport relationships having a critical shear stress will underestimate sediment load. Therefore, interrill delivery is assumed to occur at its capacity rate and to "insert" the interrill sediment into the flow. If the flow has no transport capacity, the interrill sediment will be deposited at a rate described by equation [8.3]. Although equation [8.3] is recommended for describing the lag effect for the deposition of fine particles, such a relationship is generally not required to describe rill detachment for cohesive soils. Since rill erosion of cohesive soils tends to be localized at headcuts and flowchutes (Meyer et al., 1975a), rill detachment is assumed to occur at capacity rate except for a few restrictions to prevent nonsensical results (Foster, 1976). If the sediment load is less than the transport capacity, rill detachment is limited by the lesser of the rate that will just fill transport capacity or rill detachment capacity. Also, detachment by flow is not allowed when deposition is occurring.

Solving the Equations

No general solution to equations [8.1] through [8.4] exists. Consequently, in the most general case, the equations are solved numerically. However, in some cases for both steady and unsteady conditions, analytical solutions are possible. Also, complex problems can sometimes be reduced to a form where analytical solutions apply. For example, a complex slope can be approximated by a series of uniform slopes where a solution is available if steady or quasi-steady conditions can be assumed. Analytical solutions can sometimes be applied piecewise for more efficient computations and for greater accuracy. Also, analytical solutions provide a check for numerical solutions.

Regardless of whether or not the problem is steady or dynamic, the independent variables for equations [8.1] through [8.4] are flow depth, y; interrill delivery rate, D_i; rill erosion detachment capacity, D_{rc}; and transport capacity, T_c. A hydrologic analysis provides flow depth. Relationships for the other variables are discussed in later sections.

1. Uniform Slope-Steady Conditions

a. Deposition with Interactions between Sediment Load and Transport Capacity. The solution to equations [8.2] and [8.3] for steady conditions, a uniform segment, and a constant α and dT_c/dx over the segment is (Foster and Meyer, 1975):

$$D_r = (dT_c/dx - D_1) + C' \cdot \exp(-\alpha x) \quad\dotsfill\quad [8.6]$$

where C' = an integration constant evaluated from:

$$C' = [D_{ru} - (dT_c/dx - D_1)] \cdot \exp(\alpha x_u) \quad\dotsfill\quad [8.7]$$

where D_{ru} = a known rate for D_r at x_u that may be estimated by:

$$D_{ru} = \alpha(T_{cu} - q_{su}) \quad\dotsfill\quad [8.8]$$

where q_{su} = the sediment load at x_u and T_{cu} = the transport capacity at x_u.

On a concave slope, rill detachment generally occurs on the upper part, deposition on the lower part. The beginning point for applying equations [8.6] through [8.8] is where $T_c = q_s$, i.e., where transport capacity equals sediment load. Deposition begins at this point, and $D_r = 0$ at this location.

Sediment load from equation [8.3] is:

$$q_s = T_c - D_r/\alpha \dots\dots\dots\dots\dots\dots\dots\dots\dots\dots \quad [8.9]$$

or combining equations:

$$q_s = T_c - \left\{ (dT_c/dx - D_1) + [D_{ru} - (dT_c/dx - D_1)] -\exp[-\alpha(x-x_u)]/\alpha \right\}$$

$$\dots\dots\dots\dots\dots\dots\dots\dots\dots\dots\dots\dots\dots \quad [8.10]$$

In the special case where $dT_c/dx = 0$ and $T_c = 0$, the solution to equations [8.2] and [8.3] is:

$$q_s = q_{su} \exp[-\alpha(x-x_u)] \dots\dots\dots\dots\dots\dots\dots \quad [8.11]$$

where q_{su} is the sediment load at x_u. Tollner et al. (1976) apparently approximated $dT_c/dx = 0$ and $T_c = 0$ experimentally because equation [8.11] closely approximates their results. Therefore, an estimate for α is:

$$\alpha = - [Ln (q_s/q_{su})]/(x-x_u)\dots\dots\dots\dots\dots\dots\dots \quad [8.12]$$

Equations [8.6] through [8.12] apply to grass as buffer strips along streams or as alternating strips in stripcropping. The grass significantly reduces transport capacity of flow at the upper edge of each strip, but upslope from the strip, transport capacity may exceed sediment load. In many cases, the reduced transport capacity at the upper edge is below the sediment load as Fig. 8.2 shows schematically. Deposition occurs in the upper part of the grass strip. If transport capacity increases within the strip, and if the strip is long enough, deposition will end and rill detachment will occur in the lower part.

The integration constant C' can be obtained from equations [8.7] and [8.8] by taking T_{cu} as the transport capacity just after its abrupt decrease. Equation [8.10] applies over the distance to where deposition ends, x_{de}, which is (Foster and Meyer, 1975):

$$x_{de} = x_u - \left\{ Ln [(D_1 - dT_c/dx)/(D_u -dT_c/dx + D_1)] \right\} /\alpha \quad \dots.. \quad [8.13]$$

b. Deposition Without Interaction between Sediment Load and Transport Capacity. In this case, equation [8.3] is not used. Where deposition occurs, sediment load is assumed to equal transport capacity. This is the condition described by Fig. 1. In this case:

$$q_s = T_c \dots\dots\dots\dots\dots\dots\dots\dots\dots\dots\dots \quad [8.14]$$

and deposition rate is the unknown given by:

$$D_r = dT_c/dx \dots\dots\dots\dots\dots\dots\dots\dots\dots\dots \quad [8.15]$$

Equation [8.15] does not apply where rill detachment occurs.

c. Rill Detachment without Interaction between Sediment Load and

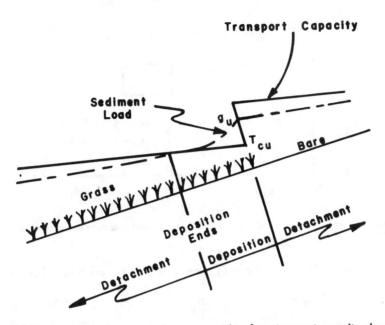

FIG. 8.2 Erosion-transport processes in a grass strip where transport capacity abruptly decreases at the upper edge.

Transport Capacity. In this case, detachment is known and sediment load is given by:

$$q_s = \int_{x1}^{x2} (D_r + D_1)dx + q_{sxl} \quad \cdots\cdots\cdots\cdots\cdots\cdots\cdots\cdots\cdots\cdots [8.16]$$

where q_{sxl} = the sediment load at $x = xl$. The average soil loss per unit area for the segment xl-$x2$ is:

$$A_{x1-x2} = [\int_{x1}^{x2} (D_r + D_1)dx]/(x_2 - x_1) \quad \cdots\cdots\cdots\cdots\cdots\cdots [8.17]$$

If functions for D_r and D_1 cannot be written and solved analytically, equations [8.16] and [8.17] are numerically integrated using the simple trapezoidal rule or other techniques.

2. Unsteady Conditions

For unsteady (dynamic) problems, the time element is added. Equations [8.1] and [8.3] have been solved analytically for uniform slopes and steady excess rainfall (Lane and Shirley, 1978). For the general case, the problem is usually solved numerically using finite difference schemes and a typical grid in time and space like the one shown in Fig. 8.3 (Li, 1977). Since, $q_s = \rho_s cq$ and $q = vy$, equation [8.1] can be rewritten as:

$$\partial q_s / \partial x + \partial(q_s/v)/\partial t = D_r + D_1 \quad \cdots\cdots\cdots\cdots\cdots\cdots\cdots\cdots [8.18]$$

where v = flow velocity. For simplification, replace q_s with g, D_r with R, and D_1 with I.

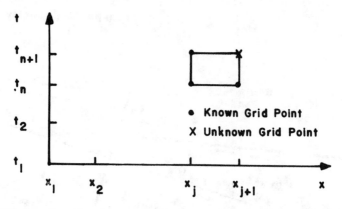

FIG. 8.3 Rectangular grid used to numerically solve erosion equations in a dynamic model (Li, 1977).

Equation [8.19] is a finite difference form of equation [8.18] (Li, 1977):

$$\left[\frac{g_{j+1}^{n+1} - g_j^{n+1}}{\Delta x}(1\text{-}a) + \frac{g_{j+1}^n - g_j^n}{\Delta x}(a)\right] +$$

$$\left[\frac{\left.\frac{g}{v}\right|_{j+1}^{n+1} - \left.\frac{g}{v}\right|_{j+1}^n}{\Delta t}(1\text{-}b) + \frac{\left.\frac{g}{v}\right|_j^{n+1} - \left.\frac{g}{v}\right|_j^n}{\Delta t}(b)\right] =$$

[8.19]

$$(1\text{-}b)\ I_{j+1}^{n+1} + bI_j^{n+1} + (1\text{-}b)\ I_{j+1}^n + bI_j^n$$

$$+ (1\text{-}b)\ R_{j+1}^{n+1} + bR_j^{n+1} + (1\text{-}b)\ R_{j+1}^n + bR_j^n$$

where a = the space weighting factor, and b = the time weighting factor. Δx = the space increment, Δt = time increment, and g_j^n is the quantity g at grid point x = $j\Delta x$ and t = $n\Delta t$. The weighting factors are $0 \leqslant a \leqslant 1$ and $0 \leqslant b \leqslant 1$. When a and b are both zero, equation [8.19] is a fully implicit scheme. When a and b equal 1/2, equation [8.19] is a central implicit scheme (Li, 1977). Given initial and boundary conditions, g_{j+1}^{n+1} is the only unknown in equation [8.19]. The other values are known from either a previous computation, initial and boundary conditions, or are values given by the hydrology model driving the erosion model.

Several steps are required to solve equation [8.19].

Step 1: Compute potential sediment load, g_{j+1}^{n+1}, from equation [8.19] assuming no rill detachment at x_{j+1} and t_{n+1}, i.e., $R_{j+1}^{n+1} = 0$.

Step 2: The potential load, g_{j+1}^{n+1} from Step 1 is the minimum amount of sediment available for transport from upslope and from interrill delivery within Δx. Compute transport capacity, T_{cj+1}^{n+1}. If $T_c > g$, rill deposition occurs, and go to Step 5 for the next step.

TABLE 8.2. TYPICAL CHARACTERISTICS OF SEDIMENT IN
OVERLAND FLOW BEFORE DEPOSITION FOR A TYPICAL
MIDWESTERN SOIL

Particle type	Size, μm	Specific gravity	Fall velocity, mm/s	Fraction of sediment load	Reaction coeff. α m^{-1}
Clay	2	2.60	0.00311	0.05	0.0089
Silt	10	2.65	0.0799	0.08	0.074
Small aggregate	20	1.80	0.381	0.50	0.31
Large aggregate	500	1.60	34.7	0.31	32.0
Sand	200	2.65	23.1	0.06	22.0

α = fall velocity /5.38 × 10^{-4} m^2 /s.

Step 3: Compute g_{j+1}^{n+1} from equation [8.19] assuming that rill detachment occurs at its capacity rate which will be designated by F.

Step 4: If $T_c > g$, rill detachment R_{j+1}^{n+1} at x_{j+1} and t^{n+1} occurs at its capacity rate F and g = the computed load. If $T_c < g$, rill detachment rate is computed as that which will just fill transport capacity, and therefore sediment load $g_{j+1}^{n+1} = T_{cj+1}^{n+1}$. Go to next iteration.

Step 5: Since $T_c < g$, deposition occurs at the rate given by equation [8.3]. Replace R_{j+1}^{n+1} in equation [8.19] with $\alpha(g_{j+1}^{n+1} - T_{cj+1}^{n+1})$ and solve for g_{j+1}^{n+1}. Go to next iteration. If the interaction among deposition, sediment load, and transport capacity, i.e., equation [8.3], is neglected, set $g_{j+1}^{n+1} = T_{cj+1}^{n+1}$.

3. Sediment Mixtures

Sediment is composed of both primary particles of sand, silt, and clay and aggregates, conglomerates of primary particles. Sizes range from less than 0.002 mm for the clay to greater than 1.0 mm for large aggregates. Specific gravity ranges from about 1.6 for the largest aggregates to 2.65 for the primary particles.

The sediment mixture is divided into classes according to density and diameter. Table 8.2, developed from a review of the literature by Young (1978), gives a typical distribution for a midwestern soil. The distribution is a function of soil, management, and other factors. Particle distribution is discussed in greater detail in later sections.

In this chapter, particle segregation is assumed to occur only during deposition. Detachment is assumed to add sediment having the given distribution, e.g., that shown in Table 8.2.

Equations [8.1] and [8.3] are solved for each particle type designated in the mixture. This requires a scheme to distribute transport capacity among the various particle types. A scheme is discussed in the section on Transport Capacity of Flow in Rills. The method used should prevent deposition of one particle type simultaneously with detachment of another type. This constraint is a result of the assumption that if deposition occurs, then rill detachment does not; if rill detachment occurs, then deposition does not; and that particle segregation occurs only during deposition.

4. Modeling Component Processes

Equations [8.1] and [8.3] or their simplifications are the framework of the model. The next step is to add relationships for interrill delivery rate, D_i, rill detachment capacity, D_{rc}, and transport capacity, T_c. These relationships also require hydrologic inputs which must be generated by an appropriate hydrologic model.

Two approaches to modeling the component processes are presented; one is empirically based and the other is more fundamentally based. The fundamental approach is based on recent concepts and theory from erosion mechanics and provides more information on variability of erosion and sediment load over both space and time during a storm than does the lumped empirical Universal Soil Loss Equation (USLE) and some of its modifications.

EROSION ESTIMATES WITH THE UNIVERSAL SOIL LOSS EQUATION

The Universal Soil Loss Equation (USLE) is the most widely used empirical overland flow or sheet-rill erosion equation (Wischmeier and Smith, 1978). The equation was originally developed as a tool for soil conservationists to use in developing farm management plans to control erosion and maintain soil productivity. More recently, it has been used to estimate sediment yield for design of small reservoirs. As awareness of water quality problems has grown, it has been increasingly used to estimate sediment yield and erosion's contribution to nonpoint source pollution. The equation is simple. It is based on a large data set of over 10,000 plot-years of data from natural runoff plots and the equivalent of 1,000 plot-years of data from field plots under rainfall simulators.

The USLE is given by:

$$A = RKLSCP \dotfill [8.20]$$

where A = soil loss averaged over the slope length, λ (mass per unit time period of R), R = combined erosivity of rainfall and runoff (EI units per unit time which is usually average annual), K = soil erodibility factor (soil loss, mass, from unit plot* on a specified soil per unit area per EI unit), L = a slope length factor [dimensionless; $L = (\lambda/\lambda_u)^n$ where λ = slope length, λ_u = length of unit plot (22.1 m) and n = slope length exponent (usually 0.5)], S = slope steepness factor [$S = (65.4s^2 + 4.56s + 0.065)$ where s = sine θ and θ = the slope angle], C = cover-management factor (dimensionless, ratio of soil loss with a given management practice to that from the unit plot), and P = supporting practices factor (dimensionless, the ratio of soil loss where contouring or other supporting practice is used to that from the unit plot). Note that only R and K have units. All other factors are dimensionless and express that factor's effect on erosion when all other factors are identical. The unit plot is a defined reference. Refer to Wischmeier and Smith (1978) for a working definition of the factors.

The USLE, which lumps iterrill and rill erosion together is a regression equation with nonhomogenous units which requires special consideration when it is converted from its original English units to metric units.

The base variable in the USLE is the R factor. It is expressed in English

---

*A unit plot is defined as a plot 22.1 m long on a 9 percent slope maintained in continuous fallow and tilled up and downhill periodically to prevent weed growth and to break the crust.

units of (100 ft·tons/acre)·(in./h), which is defined as a Wischmeier English EI unit. Common values range from 50 to 550 for the Eastern US (Wischmeier and Smith, 1978). No single metric EI unit for R has been accepted. The one given below is consistent with modeling convenience and the SI metric system.

Multiplication of a Wischmeier English EI from Wischmeier and Smith's (1978) definition and map values by 1.702 gives an SI metric EI having units of Newtons per hour. Example: R = 125 from the English EI map gives R = 213 N/h.

The English unit for K is tons/acre·EI. Typical values from Wischmeier et al. (1971) English soil erodibility nomograph range from 0.05 to 0.60. Multiplication of an English K by 0.1317 gives a metric K having units of kilograms per Newton times hour per square meter. Example: K = 0.40 from English erodibility nomograph gives K = 0.053 kg·h/N·m² = 0.53 Mg·h/N·ha. Combining, A = R·K = N·kg·h/h·N·m² = kg/m². Note that 1 kg/m² = 0.1 Mg/ha. While metric tons per hectare is perhaps a more common measure of soil loss, kg/m² is satisfactory for modeling, is less confusing, and is in keeping with the SI system.

Three major limitations of the USLE restrict its application in many modeling analyses. First, it is not intended for estimating soil loss from single storm events. Second, it is an erosion equation, and consequently it does not estimate deposition (Wischmeier, 1976). Third, it does not estimate gully or channel erosion.

The USLE is intended to estimate average soil loss over an extended period, e.g., average annual soil loss. Errors are large in the estimated soil loss from a single storm from substituting storm EI for R in equation [8.20], primarily because the great variation in runoff which can occur from rainfall to rainfall for a given rainfall amount is not considered. However, an improved erosivity factor for a single storm is (Foster et al., 1977b):

$$R_m = 0.5 \, R_{st} + 0.35 \, V_u \, \sigma_{pu}^{1/3} \quad \ldots \ldots \ldots \ldots \ldots \ldots \ldots \ldots \ldots \quad [8.21]$$

where R_m = a modified erosivity factor to replace R when the USLE is used to estimate soil loss from a single storm soil loss, R_{st} = the EI_{30} (N/h) for the storm (E = total energy of the storm and I_{30} = the storm's maximum 30 min intensity), V_u = runoff volume (mm), and σ_{pu} = peak rate (mm/h) of runoff from a unit plot of the same soil assuming that the given storm had occurred on the test plot. The C and P factors are selected based on conditions at the time of the storm. They already account for the effect of cover-management and supporting practices' on runoff as compared with runoff from unit plots.

Also, the slope length exponent n for the slope length factor $L = (\lambda/\lambda_u)^n$ varies from storm to storm (Foster et al., 1977b). It is greater when rill erosion is greater—for example, a storm occurring on a bare, wet soil produces greater runoff and thus more rill erosion. Conversely, n is smaller for a rain on a dry soil where runoff is smaller. Data are inadequate to estimate how much n changes. A conservative change would be to increase n by 0.1 when rill erosion is considerably more than normal and decrease n by 0.1 when rill erosion is considerably less than normal.

A similar variation may also exist in the slope steepness effect (Foster and Meyer, 1972a). However, information is inadequate for a recommendation.

The USLE was developed from plots of uniform steepness, soil, and cover. Generally no deposition other than local deposition in microdepressions occurs on uniform slopes, especially those greater than 3 percent, the slope of the flatest USLE plot. Therefore, the USLE is an erosion equation, that does not estimate deposition (Foster and Wischmeier, 1974). However, nonuniformities that do not cause deposition including slope shape, soil, and cover-management can be analyzed (Foster and Wischmeier, 1974).

Since A in equation (8.20) is the average soil loss for the slope length λ, the sediment load q_s at any location x downslope is therefore:

$$q_s = R \, K \, x^{n+1} \, S \, C \, P/\lambda_u^n \dotfill [8.22]$$

Assuming quasi-steady conditions and differentiating equation [8.22] according to equation [8.2] gives the USLE as a detachment equation applying at location x (Foster and Wischmeier, 1974).

$$D = (n+1) \, R \, K \, (x/\lambda_u)^n \, S \, C \, P \dotfill [8.23]$$

where K, S, C, and P are factor values at location x. Note that rill and interrill erosion, $D_r + D_i$, are lumped together as D. If the slope is divided into segments, the average soil loss on a segment is:

$$A_j = R \, K_j \, (x_j^{n+1} - x_{j-1}^{n+1}) \, S_j \, C_j \, P_j/[\lambda_u^n \, (x_j - x_{j-1})] \dotfill [8.24]$$

The sediment load at location x is:

$$q_{sj} = (x_j - x_{j-1}) \, A_j + q_{sj-1} \dotfill [8.25]$$

This procedure is not applicable to slope segments where deposition occurs.

If deposition occurs, a transport relationship is required in addition to the USLE. Total sediment transport capacity of overland flow for a storm may be estimated from (Neibling and Foster, 1977):

$$T_c = 138 \, V \, q_p \, s^{1.55} \, C_T \dotfill [8.26]$$

where T_c = total transport capacity for a storm, mass per unit width (g/m), V = total discharge per unit width (m³/m), q_p = peak discharge per unit width (m³/s·m), s = sine of slope angle, and C_T = a factor reflecting the direct influence of soil cover on the flow's hydraulic forces. A value for C_T may be taken from Fig. 8.4. Equation [8.26] and Fig. 8.4 represent conditions typical of most aggregated soils. The coefficients and exponent in equation [8.26] depend on the particle distribution. See Neibling and Foster (1977) for additional discussion of parameter values.

When transport capacity decreases below the sediment load, the coarser and denser particles are deposited within a short distance. Fine particles, like clays, travel a considerable distance before settling out. This lag effect may be described by equation [8.3].

Deposition and sediment load can be calculated using equations [8.6] through [8.11], [8.13], and [8.16]. Since rill and interrill erosion are lumped together in the USLE, the interrill detachment variable D_i is set equal to zero

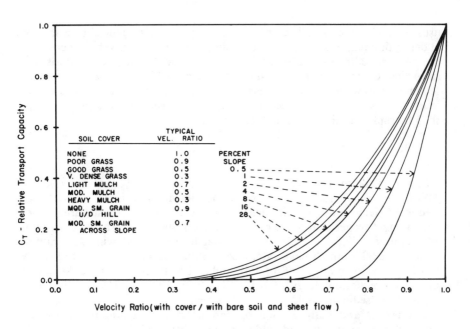

FIG. 8.4 Relative transport capacity factor C_T (Neibling and Foster, 1977).

in the deposition equation, which is equivalent to the assumption that inter-rill detachment does not occur during deposition. The rill erosion variable D_r is the deposition rate. The sum of rill and interrill detachment $D_i + D_r$ is equal to total detachment D in equation [8.23]. The equations also require choosing a representative proportionality constant α for deposition for the sediment mixture or else treating various particle types separately.

V. SEDIMENT YIELD ESTIMATES WITH THE MODIFIED UNIVERSAL SOIL LOSS EQUATION

Sediment yield is sometimes estimated by estimating gross erosion with the USLE and then multiplying by a delivery ratio to obtain sediment yield (ASCE, 1975). For small watersheds, especially fields, this method is often inadequate and can lead to totally false conclusions. Thus, it should be used only as a first approximation. The following example illustrates the problem.

Assume a terraced field in conventionally tilled corn that produces a given runoff for a given storm. A typical delivery ratio for terraces is 0.2 (Wischmeier and Smith, 1978) meaning that 80 percent of the sediment produced on the interterrace interval is trapped in the terrace channel. Now, assume that no-till corn is planted next year. Probably runoff does not significantly decrease. Consequently, sediment transport capacity in the terrace channel is not greatly reduced although crop residue in the channel may slightly reduce it. With the incoming sediment load being greatly reduced, however, and no corresponding reduction in transport capacity, deposition may not occur in the terrace channel. The fraction deposited in the terrace channel depends on the amount of sediment entering the flow relative to the transport capacity of the flow. Consequently, the delivery ratio is not constant as is often assumed.

In many watersheds, especially those larger than fields, some deposition usually occurs; the overall sediment yield response is influenced by a variety of deposition features rather than by a single major feature. When deposition does occur, sediment yield is highly correlated with runoff characteristics, since flow controls sediment transport capacity which is closely related to sediment load when deposition occurs. Williams (1975a) modified the USLE to estimate sediment yield for individual runoff events from a given watershed by replacing the USLE R factor with:

$$R_w = 9.05 \ (V{\cdot}Q_p)^{0.56} \quad \dots\dots\dots\dots\dots\dots\dots\dots\dots\dots\dots \quad [8.27]$$

where V = volume of runoff (m³) and Q_p = peak discharge rate (m³/s). The USLE with this R factor is referred to as the Modified USLE or MUSLE. Sediment yield is now given in megagrams for the total watershed area rather than kilograms per square meter when K has units of Mg h/ha N. For example, assume a 40.5 ha (4.05x10⁵ m²) watershed, a storm giving 25.4 mm of runoff at a 50.8 mm/h peak rate, a soil with a K factor of 0.53 Mg h/ha N (corresponds to an English K of 0.4), and an LSCP product of 1.0. Sediment yield from equations [8.20] and [8.27] is 9.05[(10290)(5.715)]⁰·⁵⁶ (0.53) = 2248 Mg of sediment yield.

Channel and gully erosion or deposition in impoundments are accounted for separately and added to or subtracted from the equation's estimate (Williams, 1978).

Although the MUSLE assumes that deposition occurs in the watershed, it only gives an estimate of total sediment yield and not an estimate of the yield of individual particle classes. Deposition segregates particles. The more easily deposited particles settle out early after they leave their source area while the smaller and lighter ones travel further through the watershed before depositing. An exponential decay function can be used to route sediment through the watershed to estimate this segregation (Williams, 1975b; Williams, 1978). The relationship is a function of travel time and particle diameter and is similar to equation [8.11].

V. FUNDAMENTAL MODELS

Fundamental models have several advantages over empirical equations. (1) They are generally more physically based and consequently can be more accurately extrapolated; (2) they more accurately represent the processes, for example, rill and interrill erosion are considered separately rather than being lumped; (3) they are more accurate for single storm events; (4) they can consider more complex areas; (5) they consider deposition processes directly; and (6) they can consider channel erosion and deposition.

The importance of fundamental principles in the erosion process was recognized as early as the 1930's (Cook, 1936). In the 1940's, Ellison (1947) presented an extensive analysis of several erosion subprocesses which was important background for more recent erosion modeling. Meyer and Wischmeier (1969) formularized Ellison's and other more recent concepts in a model. They and Negev (1967), who added an erosion component to the Stanford Watershed Model, demonstrated the potential of such models for understanding and estimating the behavior of soil erosion.

Like early models, most recent models have no established parameter values for a variety of situations. Values were assumed or were obtained by optimization from observed data. Even though 'handbook' parameter values are not readily available for most fundamental models, these models will become increasingly important tools in evaluation of erosion and sedimentation as experience with the models and erosion research provide parameter values.

The modeling relationships presented below are as fundamentally based as seems practical. The relationships are designed so that they should require relatively little calibration using observed data. However, the modeler should recognize that this is ideal and seldom occurs. Where calibration is required, the functional forms of the equations are believed to be valid, and the given parameter values should be good starting points for optimization.

Relationships are presented below for: interrill and rill processes that occur on overland flow areas, channel processes, and impoundment processes. Detachment, transport, and deposition relationships are required for interrill, rill, and channel processes. Deposition is the major process in impoundments. Also, sediment characteristics are discussed since they greatly affect transport capacity and deposition. Storage of deposited sediment on overland flow areas and analysis of some supporting practices like contouring and stripcropping are discussed separately.

INTERRILL PROCESSES

Both detachment and transport of soil particles occur on interrill areas. Detachment is almost entirely by raindrop impact. The detached soil particles are transported to the rills by the combined action of the thin, interrill sheet flow and raindrop impact. Alone, the flow can transport only the smallest particles, but raindrop impact entrains larger particles, significantly increasing the thin flow's transport capacity. Most transport to the rills is by the interrill flow while only a small fraction of the interrill sediment is splashed directly to the rills (Young and Wiersma, 1973; Meyer et al., 1975b). Likewise, net downslope transport by raindrop splash is negligible.

At small slope steepnesses, delivery of interrill sediment to the rills may be limited by transport capacity. This is especially true if depressions or roughness 'pond' flow and causes deposition. On steeper slopes, detachment limits delivery of interrill sediment as suggested in Fig. 8.5 (Foster and Meyer, 1975).

Detachment

Ideally a model of soil detachment by raindrop impact considers raindrop size and mass, drop impact velocity (speed and direction), and depth of water over the soil surface. Given these variables, and the Navier-Stokes hydrodynamic equations, the fluid forces at the soil boundary could be calculated for each raindrop impact. Mutchler's (1970) experimental data would be valuable in development of the procedure. Mutchler and Young (1975) suggested modeling detachment of soil using shear stresses at the soil surface caused by a drop impact. A model based on the forces from each typical drop and the probability distribution of drops in a rain could be developed to more fundamen-

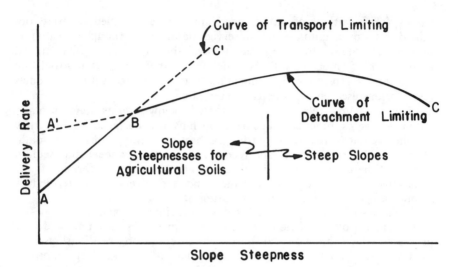

FIG. 8.5 Conceptual model of the delivery rate of detached particles from interrill areas to rill flow.

tally describe the erosivity of rain than does the energy times intensity (EI) parameter. Nevertheless, the state of the art requires that we rely on gross parameters like EI.

1. Interrill Erosivity

Total interrill soil loss for a storm is a function of the storm's total energy and intensity. Free's (1960) data indicated that interrill detachment in proportional to EI_{30}, as Wischmeier and Smith (1958) found for 22 m plots. For a constant rainfall intensity, total energy for a storm is $E = e \cdot i \cdot t$ where e = energy per unit area per unit depth of rainfall, i = rainfall intensity, and t = time. Unit energy of natural rainfall is (Wischmeier and Smith, 1958):

$$e = 11.9 + 8.73 \log_{10} i \quad \dots\dots\dots\dots\dots\dots\dots\dots\dots\dots\dots\dots\dots \quad [8.28]$$

where e = unit energy [joules/(m^2 of area·mm of rainfall)], and i = intensity, (mm/h). For intensities between 10 and 250 mm/h, unit energy is approximately proportional to $i^{0.14}$. Combining the factors gives interrill detachment rate as being proportional to $i^{2.14}$ (Foster and Meyer, 1975).

This basic relationship based on Laws and Parsons' (1943) data from Washington, D.C., differs with the rainfall region. In northern Mississippi, unit energy is essentially constant for rainfall intensifies above 20 mm/h (McGregor and Mutchler, 1977). The general shape of the e vs. i relationship is the same for different regions of the world (Hudson, 1971), but rainfall energy in Japan, for example, is about 70% of that in the U.S. for a similar intensity. However, equation [8.28] applies to the Palouse region in Washington, Idaho, and Oregon where raindrops are small and rainfall intensity is low (McCool et al., 1977; Bubenzer, 1979).

Laboratory experiments using soils and simulated rain of uniform drops also suggest that interrill detachment is proportional to i^2 (Meyer and Wischmeier, 1969; Bubenzer and Jones, 1971; Moldenhauer and Long, 1964; Foster and Meyer, 1975). This relationship has been used successfully in several erosion models (David and Beer, 1975; Fleming and Leytham, 1976; Smith, 1977; Curtis, 1976; Beasley, 1977).

An interrill erosivity parameter is therefore rainfall intensity squared (i^2) which may be "calibrated" by fitting ai^2 to the storm energy times maximum 30 min intensity (EI_{30}) from the USLE relationship for storms assumed to have constant intensities. However, first, the EI_{30} values from the USLE are divided by 2 because the USLE includes both interrill and rill erosion. Here, the interest is only in interrill erosion. Apparently, interrill erosion equals rill erosion on "average" USLE unit plot conditions (Foster et al., 1977b). The division by 2 reflects this assumed equality. Fitting of ai^2 to the EI/2 vs. i USLE relationship gives $a = 0.0138 \text{ N/m}^2$ for i in mm/h and $i = 63.5 \text{ mm/h}$ as a typical intensity. A more accurate value for 0.0138 coefficient may be obtained by calibration with observed erosion data.

The rate of particle detachment by raindrop impact is time dependent even for a constant rainfall intensity (Moldenhauer and Koswara, 1968). The pattern is not consistent, and generally the time effect must be ignored until further research defines the relationships.

2. Interrill Erodibilty

Soils differ in their susceptibility to detachment by raindrop impact due to different inherit physical, chemical, and minerological properties. Soil properties known to affect erodibility include primary particle size distribution, organic matter content, soil structure, content of iron and aluminum oxides, electro-chemical bonds, initial moisture content and aging (Wischmeier and Mannering, 1969; Wischmeier et al., 1971; Grissinger, 1966; Romkens et al., 1977; Parthmiades, 1972; Bubenzer and Jones, 1971).

A basic equation for interrill detachment is:

$$D_1 = 0.0138 \, K_1 \, i^2 \qquad\qquad\qquad\qquad\qquad\qquad\qquad\qquad [8.29]$$

where D_i = detachment rate (kg/m²·h), K_1 = soil erodibility factor for detachment by raindrop impact (kg·h/N·m²), and i = rainfall intensity (mm/h). Note very carefully the specified units. Since no tested parameter is available for K_1, equation [8.29] was written so that the USLE soil erodibility factor K may be used. However, K_1 may be greater than or less than the USLE K because K reflects both rill and interrill erosion susceptibility. A soil's susceptibility to detachment by raindrop impact is difficult to judge. Therefore, using rill erosion as a guide, if a particular soil seems especially susceptible to rill erosion, K_1 might be decreased by 1/3 from the USLE K value. Conversely, if the soil is not susceptible to rilling, K_1 might be increased by 1/3 (Foster et al., 1977b).

Equation [8.29] is the basic equation for interrill detachment. It applies to 9% slopes to be consistent with the USLE K. Parameters must now be added to account for other factors that influence interrill detachment. One variable, slope length, is not added because interrill erosion is assumed to be independent of location on the slope when all other factors are the same.

3. Slope

The effective slope is the slope of the interrill area rather than the average land slope. For example, the interrill slopes on a ridged cotton field (row side slopes) may be many times that of the average land slope in a Mississippi Delta field, but on a construction site, the interrill slope is usually the same as the slope of the land. In a plowed corn field, the slope of roughness elements left by tillage (especially primary tillage) may be more important than the land slope itself. The increase in interrill side slopes from tillage increased soil loss (Young and Mutchler, 1969b) which is consistent with the above concept.

Data of Meyer et al. (1975b) and Lattanzi et al. (1974) were used to develop an interrill slope factor term:

$$S_i = 2.96 \, (\sin\theta)^{0.79} + 0.56 \dotfill [8.30]$$

where S_i = interrill slope steepness factor and θ = slope angle.

This equation uses a base slope of 9 percent for compatibility with the USLE soil erodibility factor K in equation [8.29]. The data are from soil pans 0.6 m by 0.6 m exposed to simulated rainfall of 64 mm/h intensity for 2 h. Slopes ranged from 0 to 30 percent. The soil surface was relatively smooth. Later data of Harmon and Meyer (1979) confirm the shape of the relationship given in equation [8.30].

The increase in detachment with an increase in slope is much less than that reflected in the slope factor S of the USLE. However, the USLE S factor also reflects the effect of slope on runoff and rill erosion over a variety of storm types—some that produce small amounts of runoff; others large amounts. Although adjustments might be needed in equation [8.30] to give greater increases in soil loss for increases in slope, the form of the equation should be adequate.

4. Cover and Management

Combining equations [8.29] and [8.30] and adding a cover-management factor, the interrill detachment equation is now:

$$D_1 = 0.0138 \, K_1 \, i^2_{\text{eff}} \, [2.96(\sin\theta)^{0.79} + 0.56] \, C_i \dotfill [8.31]$$

The term i^2_{eff} represents a crop canopy's effect on the erosivity of rainfall and C_i is a cover-management factor for interrill detachment. A USLE supporting practice factor P is not included because, primarily, a supporting practice affects only rill erosion or overland flow transport capacity, both of which are discussed later.

Relationships for i_{eff} and C_i are based on Wischmeier's (1975) Type I, II, and III effects. Type I is an above ground effect primarily from crop canopy; Type II is a soil surface cover effect, (e.g., plant residue); and Type III is a subsurface effect due to grass roots, improved soil structure and incorporated residue. The Type I effect is reflected in i_{eff} whereas the Type II and III effects are in C_i. Subfactor values are multiplied together to obtain a composite C_i value.

a. Canopy. The effect of canopy is described by modifying the rainfall intensity to an effective rainfall intersity as:

$$i^2_{\text{eff}} = i^2 [a + (1-a) \, (m_{ca}V^2_{ca}/m_p V^2_p) \, (i_{can}/i)] \dotfill [8.32]$$

where i^2_{eff} = the effective rainfall erosivity; i = rainfall intensity above the canopy; a = fraction of open area where drops may strike the ground unintercepted by the canopy; m_{ca} = mass of the drops falling from the canopy; m_p = mass of the drops passing unhindered through the canopy; V_{ca}

= impact velocity of the drops falling from the canopy; and V_p = impact velocity of the unhindered drops; and (i_{can}/i) = the fraction of the rainfall at a given time reaching the ground by falling from the canopy as reformed drops. Crop canopy intercepts some of the raindrops; others pass directly through the canopy unhindered. These detach soil particles at the rate they would if there were no canopy.

The drops intercepted first fill initial storage requirements. This water remains attached to the plants to be evaporated during and after the storm. Part of the intercepted water becomes stemflow and causes no detachment by drop impact although it contributes to overland flow. The remaining water reforms drops which may be larger than the original raindrops (Chapman, 1948), but rarely do drops regain the velocity of the original raindrops. These reformed drops generally have less energy than the original raindrops, although this depends on the height of the canopy. In a tall canopy, the energy of the drops may be increased (Chapman, 1948).

The adjustment made in equation [8.32] to account for canopy assumes that the effective intensity varies directly with the energy of the drops reaching the soil surface which is accounted for in terms for ratios of the kinetic energy and intensity.

Drop size from the canopy may be taken as 3.4 mm while fall velocity can be estimated from Laws and Parsons' data (Wischmeier and Smith, 1958). Alternatively, the drop impact velocity can be estimated by assuming that the drops are spheres and by applying common drag relationships from fluid mechanics.

b. Cover in Direct Contact with Soil Surface. The effect of cover in direct contact with the soil surface is given by:

$$C_{i\,II} = \xi \exp[-0.21\,(y_c/y_b - 1)^{1.18}] \quad \dotsb \quad [8.33]$$

where $C_{i\,II}$ = subfactor due to soil surface cover, ξ = fraction of the surface left exposed to direct raindrop impact, and y_c/y_b = the ratio of the flow depth with cover to that without cover. The ratio y_c/y_b is given by:

$$y_c/y_b = q_c v_b / q_b v_c \quad \dotsb \quad [8.34]$$

where q_c and q_b = discharge rate for cover and bare conditions respectively and v_c and v_b = flow velocity for cover and bare conditions respectively. The functional form of the last term of equation [8.33] is similar to that used by David and Beer (1975) and Smith (1977).

Soil surface cover includes mulches (straw on highway embankments), crop residue (corn stalks left on the surface by conservation tillage), gravel (desert pavement which develops from selective erosion), and grass. Cover is a key element in many erosion control practices.

Since surface cover dissipates the energy of raindrops striking the cover directly, a first approximation of detachment by raindrop impact is to take D_i as proportional to ξ.

Surface cover also reduces interrill flow velocity, because cover generally increases the hydraulic roughness of the flow surface, and thereby increases the flow depth. Water depth greater than a critical depth cushions the impact of raindrops and reduces the drops' hydrodynamic impact forces at the soil boundary. This reduces detachment by raindrop impact (Mutchler and

TABLE 8.3. EFFECT OF STRAW MULCH
COVER ON SOIL DETACHMENT BY
RAINDROP IMPACT ON INTERRILL
AREAS

Mulch rate	Fraction of soil left exposed	$\overset{\cdot}{C}_{i\,II}*$	
		Observed	Fitted
kg/m^2			
0.05	0.75	0.61	0.61
0.20	0.39	0.22	0.23
0.50	0.10	0.023	0.031

*$C_{i\,II}$ = Ratio of interrill detachment with cover
to that without cover. Observed was from
Lattanzi's (1973) data. Fitted is from equation
[8.33].

Young, 1975). The effect was empirically evaluated using data from Lattanzi's (1973) study of the effect of mulch rate on interrill erosion. His data showed no slope effect although shallower flows and thus less cushioning are expected on steeper slopes. The slopes of his 0.6 m by 0.6 m soil pan exposed to simulated rainfall ranged from 0 to 30 percent.

Lattanzi's experimental variation in $C_{i\,II}$ is given in Table 8.3. Although equation [8.33] was developed from straw mulch data, it should be applicable to other covers like corn stalks and gravel. Corn stalks, for example, should give a greater flow depth for a given discharge than does straw, and consequently they should be a more effective mulch for control of interrill erosion based on a given fraction of the soil covered.

In many situations where the soil is bare, a significant water depth, either in a continuous layer over a large area or in roughness and tillage depressions is an effective soil cover. Mutchler and Young (1975) suggested that 6 mm or more of water essentially eliminated detachment by raindrop impact. Consequently, surface roughness is important. Interrill detachment occurs on the soil protruding above the water line, not at all where water depth is greater than 6 mm, and at a reduced rate where the water is shallower than 6 mm in the depressions. The fraction ξ in equation [8.33] then represents the protruding areas. A further adjustment is required if the protruding areas have cover.

On very flat land, ridges from crop rows protrude above the waterline. Interrill erosion can be great on these ridges (Meyer and Harmon, 1979). The effective slope in equation [8.31] is the slope of the ridge side slopes. At this point, our only concern is with detachment. Whether or not sediment detached on the row ridges leaves the field depends on the transport capacity of the flow in the row middles.

Detachment by raindrop impact on smooth, flat soil surfaces may be greatly reduced by a continuous layer of water. The exp( ) term of equation [8.33] can be used to describe the effect, but since no value can be suggested for the parameters, calibration is required.

c. **Incorporated Plant Residue.** Annual incorporation of plant residue builds the soil's organic matter and improves soil structure, both of which reduce erosion (Wischmeier and Smith, 1978). Estimated subfactors for this effect range from 0.75 for large amounts of corn residue incorporated to 1.0 for continuous tillage with no incorporation like the USLE unit plot. A one time incorporation when a meadow is plowed out, for example is not credited. This is credited as a land use residual effect.

Large pieces of buried residue have no effect on detachment until erosion or tillage exposes them. Once they are exposed, treat them as cover in direct contact with the soil surface if they are stable and are not carried away by runoff. Exposed grass roots and gravel are also treated as cover in direct contact with the soil surface.

d. Residual Land Use. Land is much less erodible immediately after it is plowed out of meadow than it is when continuously tilled. Soil plowed out of meadow has good soil structure and many roots left from the meadow, both of which reduce erosion. With continuous tillage, however, the effect disappears in about 3 years or less. The following values are based on soil loss ratios from Wischmeier and Smith (1978).

The subfactor ranges from 0.25 good meadow to 0.4 poor meadow for land just plowed out of established meadow that is part of a crop rotation or permanent pasture. At seedbed time in the second year, the range is from 0.70 for good meadow to 0.80 for poor meadow if corn was grown the previous year. By seedbed time of the third year, the effect of the meadow is gone, but the continuous corn will have developed a residual effect that is estimated to vary from 0.82 for high production to 0.86 for low production.

Soybeans leave the land more erodible than does corn. For a season following soybeans, the above values should be multiplied by 1.4 (Moldenhauer and Wischmeier, 1969). If the present crop is soybeans and the previous crop was corn, erosion does not increase during the soybean crop. For continuous tillage without crop production like on the USLE unit plot, the subfactor value is 1.0.

Less information is available to estimate the land use residual of crops like permanent pasture. As an estimate, use 0.25 to 0.40 for established meadow.

e. Tillage. Tillage is assumed to have no effect on interrill erosion but a great effect on rill erosion. Bulk density apparently affects interrill detachment but the relationship has not been satisfactorily defined (Foster and Martin, 1969; Meeuwig, 1971).

f. Double Accounting. The values for effects of incorporated plant residue and residual land use are based on soil loss ratios for the USLE (Wischmeier and Smith, 1978). Therefore, they reflect both interrill and rill erosion. In some cases, the reduction in erosion may be entirely due to a reduction in runoff which is represented by these soil loss ratios. In such situations, the above values will reflect an excessive decrease in erosion which can be accounted for entirely with the rill erosion equations and reduced runoff.

2. Simplification

In some modeling analyses, consideration of all the above factors may prove cumbersome. Foster (1976) and Beasley (1977) simplified equation [8.31] to:

$$D_i = 0.0138\, i^2\, K\, C_{slr} \quad \dotfill \quad [8.35]$$

where C_{slr} is the soil loss ratio from the USLE. Since equation [8.35] contains no slope effect, the model will likely not reproduce the USLE slope relationship, but neither will equation [8.30]. Also, the 0.0138 coefficient can be improved by calibration.

Transport

Sediment delivery from interrill areas is the lesser between transport ' capacity of the interrill flow and the amount of detached particles available for transport.

Interrill flow is generally a broad, sheet flow. If flow is concentrated, like in a row middle, it is considered rill flow regardless of whether or not erosion occurs in the concentrations. The transport capacity of interrill flow is greatly enhanced by impacting raindrops that lift and splash particles up into the flow so that the flow can more easily move them toward a rill.

Transport on interrill areas is difficult to model. In most models, any transport effect and particle sorting effect on interrill areas is included with the interrill detachment relationship and is referred to as interrill sediment delivery. Although the modeler may wish to directly ignore interrill transport, he should consider several important factors before doing so.

1. Hydraulics

Interrill flow length is assumed to be short--less than about 5 m. However, on relatively flat slopes, 2% and less, interrill areas may become so long that transport capacity relationships for rill flow apply. Transport of particles by interrill flow should be directly related to flow characteristics like velocity and depth. Therefore, interrill transport capacity depends on excess rainfall rate, interrill slope length and steepness, and depth of flow. If flow is ponded by depressions or obstacles like corn stalks, transport capacity of the interrill flow is greatly reduced. Also, interrill transport capacity is assumed to be greatly enhanced by raindrop impact (Foster and Meyer, 1975).

Unfortunately, a meaningful interrill transport capacity equation is not available. A general relationship without validation or parameter values is suggested below. The basic relationship might be a typical sediment transport equation form of:

$$T_{cl} = A_t(\tau - \tau_{cr})^{1.5} \dots\dots\dots\dots\dots\dots\dots\dots\dots\dots\dots\dots \quad [8.36]$$

where T_{cl} = the transport capacity of flow on interrill area (mass per unit width per unit time), τ = shear stress, τ_{cr} = critical shear stress, and A_t = a coefficient. The coefficients A_t and τ_{cr} are functions of particle diameter and density. The shear stress τ has two components: a flow component and a raindrop induced component; it can be written as:

$$\tau = \gamma y_b s[(y_b/y_p) \cdot a\, i_{eff}^2\, C_{it}] \dots\dots\dots\dots\dots\dots\dots\dots\dots \quad [8.37]$$

where a = a coefficient to be estimated, y = flow depth assuming laminar flow, y_b/y_p = the ratio of the flow depth on a smooth surface to that in the ponds from depressions and "dams," i_{eff} = effective rainfall intensity from equation [8.32], and C_{it} is taken from equation [8.33] as:

$$C_{it} = \exp \left\{ -0.21[(y_p/y_b) - 1] \right\}^{1.18} \quad \ldots\ldots\ldots\ldots\ldots\ldots \quad [8.38]$$

The flow depth would be based on a discharge rate calculated from $q = \sigma x_l$ where x_l = flow length on the interrill area and σ = excess rainfall rate. Given the short flow lengths of interrill areas, overland flow dynamics can be neglected.

As depressions fill with deposited sediment, sediment transport rates increase and larger and denser particles are transported. Equation [8.36] estimates an increased transport capacity as storage of deposited sediment reduces the ratio of y_p/y_b. Thus storage of deposited sediment and its effect on flow depth must be accounted for.

While use of equations [8.36] through [8.38] may not be practical, an alternative method of estimating the effect of roughness on interrill sediment delivery is to estimate the amount of sediment detached on interrill areas with equation [8.31], and then multiply by a roughness factor. The values given in Table 8.4. for such a factor are based on soil loss ratios given by Wischmeier and Smith (1978). These values increase as depressions fill with deposited sediment.

The factors given in Table 8.4 are for total sediment load. Obviously, the largest and heaviest particle are most likely to deposit. A roughness factor of 0.3 may catch all but the primary silt and clay particle while a factor of 0.92 may catch only the largest sand particles with the lighter aggregates passing through. The fractions of the different particle type passing through various roughness elements were estimated using equations [8.6], [8.7], and [8.9], no interrill detachment (i.e., $D_l = 0$), values for the deposition proportionality constant α from Table 8.2, and the assumption that total T_{cl} is distributed among the particle types in the same proportions as the particle types in the interrill sediment before deposition. The computed fractions are given in Table 8.5.

Since interrill sediment is a mixture of particle sizes and densities, roughness is random, and raindrops are distributed over a range of sizes;

TABLE 8.4. ROUGHNESS FACTOR VALUES FOR INTERRILL
SEDIMENT DELIVERY. BASED ON SOIL LOSS RATIOS GIVEN
BY WISCHMEIER AND SMITH (1978)

Condition	Roughness factor
1. Large scale roughness like from turn plowing of a well aggregated soil from meadow (depressions > 150 mm)	0.3
2. Moderate to large scale roughness like from turn plowing in highly productive soil in second year row crop out of meadow (depressions 100 to 150 mm)	0.5
3. Small to moderate scale roughness like from turn plowing in highly productive soil, continuous cropping (depressions 70 to 100 mm)	0.65
4. Small scale roughness like from turn plowing in poorly productive soil 2nd year out of meadow (depressions 50 to 70 mm)	0.75
5. Slight roughness, like turn plowing in poorly productive soil in continuous tillage (depressions 20 to 50 mm)	0.85
6. None to slight roughness, like disking (depressions 0 to 20 mm)	0.92
7. Smooth surface (a finely disked field following an intense rain)	1.00

TABLE 8.5. ESTIMATED FRACTION OF VARIOUS
PARTICLE TYPES PASSING THROUGH INTERRILL
ROUGHNESS DEPRESSIONS

Interrill roughness factor (Table 4)	Fraction of original load for each particle type				
	Clay	Silt	Small aggregate	Large aggregate	Sand
0.30	0.91	0.79	0.37	0.00	0.00
0.50	0.97	0.93	0.75	0.00	0.00
0.65	1.00	0.99	0.98	0.07	0.17
0.75	1.00	1.00	0.99	0.32	0.46
0.85	1.00	1.00	0.99	0.58	0.69
0.92	1.00	1.00	1.00	0.78	0.84
0.95	1.00	1.00	1.00	0.86	0.90
0.98	1.00	1.00	1.00	0.94	0.96
1.00	1.00	1.00	1.00	1.00	1.00

particles may move when transport estimates based on average shear stress in equation [8.36] would indicate no transport. The problem should be analyzed as a stochastic process.

2. Characteristics of Interrill Sediment Particles

The characteristics of particles available for interrill transport depend on the sizes produced by interrill detachment. Generally, raindrop impact detaches a mixture of primary particles of sand, silt, and clay and aggregates that are conglomerates of primary particles (Long, 1964). Specific gravity of the aggregates is about 2.0 and that of primary particles 2.65.

Sediment characteristics are a function of soil properties; tillage; soil history since tillage; particle selectivity during detachment and transport; and cover (Swanson et al., 1969; Alberts et al., 1980; Yoder, 1936; Moldenhauer, 1978; Meyer et al., 1978).

Although information on sediment characteristics is somewhat lacking, the following is suggested as a guide in choosing particle sizes and specific gravities.

Many soil particles detached by raindrop impact are aggregates especially for agricultural topsoils and for many subsoils high in clay

TABLE 8.6. SIZE DISTRIBUTION OF ERODED SEDIMENT FROM
RAINDROP IMPACT ON FOUR IOWA SOILS (Moldenhauer, 1978)

Soil	Fraction by weight in size class				
	<2 μm	2-50 μm	50-250 μm	20-1000 μm	>1000 μm
Marshal silty clay loam (Meadow)	0.08	0.35	0.15	0.08	0.34
Marshal silty clay loam (Corn)	0.10	0.55	0.20	0.04	0.11
Luton silty clay (Corn)	0.18	0.50	0.12	0.11	0.09
Ida silt loam (Corn)	0.04	0.68	0.24	0.02	0.02
Hagener fine sand (Corn)	0.03	0.11	0.48	0.36	0.02

TABLE 8.7. SIZE DISTRIBUTION OF DISPERSED SURFACE SOIL, ERODED SEDIMENT, AND DISPERSED SEDIMENT ERODED FROM INTERRILL AREAS FOR 20 SOILS (Meyer et al., 1978)

	Percent by weight in size class														
	Grenada #1*			Cascilla			Sharkey			Bruin			Vicksburg		
Size class	Ds So	Er Sd	Ds† Sd	Ds So	Er Sd	Ds Sd	Ds So	Er Sd	Ds Sd	Ds So	Er Sd	Ds Sd	Ds So	Er Sd	Ds Sd
μm															
>1000	0	5	T	0	2	T	0	2	0	0	1	T	0	0	T
500-1000	1	9	0	1	6	0	0	13	0	0	2	T	1	1	0
250-500	2	10	1	4	14	4	0	21	0	0	4	0	2	3	1
125-250	1	6	1	5	8	4	0	8	0	0	3	0	3	4	3
63-125	1	5	1	1	5	1	1	4	1	12	34	13	1	3	1
31- 63	6	15	8	16	18	18	1	1	3	47	31	44	19	22	20
16- 31	50	28	48	37	28	38	8	9	8	16	15	15	45	43	45
8- 16	16	12	18	14	11	17	19	20	18	6	6	7	16	16	17
4- 8	5	4	5	6	1	2	16	10	15	3	1	3	4	3	4
<4	18	6	18	16	7	16	55	12	55	16	3	18	9	5	9

	Lexington			Arkabutla			Grenada #8			Memphis			Morganfield		
Size class	Ds So	Er Sd	Ds Sd	Ds So	Er Sd	Ds Sd	Ds So	Er Sd	Ds Sd	Ds So	Er Sd	Ds Sd	Ds So	Er Sd	Ds Sd
μm															
>1000	0	1	0	0	1	0	0	0	0	T	1	T	T	0	T
500-1000	1	5	1	1	3	1	1	2	0	0	6	0	0	0	T
250-500	4	14	4	4	9	4	2	6	2	0	13	0	0	3	0
125-250	5	10	4	10	14	11	3	5	3	0	7	0	0	2	0
63-125	2	4	2	8	9	9	1	3	1	0	3	0	7	6	4
31- 63	13	18	15	13	17	12	22	26	22	19	21	22	54	56	56
16- 31	31	24	31	23	21	24	40	37	42	34	28	34	20	22	23
8- 16	15	12	17	15	14	15	13	13	13	14	10	14	5	6	5
4- 8	5	4	3	7	5	7	3	3	3	6	4	5	1	1	2
<4	24	8	23	19	7	17	15	5	14	27	7	25	13	4	10

*Soil name
†Ds So = Dispersed Surface Soil, Er Sd = Eroded Sediment, Ds Sd = Dispersed Sediment.
‡Unreplicated plot.

(Long, 1964). On sandy soils and others where aggregate stability is low, the soils erode more as primary particles (Young and Onstad, 1978). Also, management practices that build aggregate stabilty probably also increase the amount of aggregates in the sediment (Meyer et al., 1978). Table 8.6 shows how management and soil texture influenced interrill sediment sizes from four Iowa soils. Table 8.7 shows the observed interrill particle distribution for several Mississippi soils.

Given this variety of particle sizes and densities along with limited transport capacity, considerable selective sorting of the sediment potentially occurs. The large aggregates and sands are deposited readily in depressions, whereas they might not be deposited on a smooth surface. Usually interrill sediment is enriched in clay and deficient in sand because of selective sorting (Alberts et al., 1980; Monke et al., 1977). In some cases, however, interrill sediment is deficient in clay probably because the clays are washed into the soil pores. Clay washed into pores is also a likely cause of surface sealing (Young and Onstad, 1978). Surface seals are often enriched in clay (Long, 1964).

Particle size may be a function of rainfall intensity (Long, 1964) due to the higher probability of repeated raindrop impact. When Long increased simulated rainfall intensity from 29 mm/h to 72 mm/h, the sand sized fraction decreased from about 34% to 15% while the silt-sized fraction increased from 56% to 74% and the clay sized fraction increased from 10% to 11%. When Meyer et al. (1978) increased rainfall intensity from 25 mm/h to 104 mm/h, the fraction of particles smaller than 4 μm approximately doubled. Their tests were on steeper slopes than were Long's.

As cover increased, size of eroded particle decreased in Yoder's (1936) study. The decrease may have been due to deposition since Meyer et al. (1978) did not observe a similar decrease on slopes where there was no opportunity for deposition.

Detachment and transport on interrill areas is usually more selective than is rill erosion (Meyer et al., 1975b). Probably, smaller particles come from interrill areas because of greater particle breakdown from the intense hydrodynamic forces of a raindrop impact, further particle breakdown by repeated raindrop impact before the particles reach a rill, and selective sorting during transport (Meyer et al., 1975b; Alberts et al., 1980).

RILL EROSION PROCESSES

Rill erosion is the most identifiable indicator of serious erosion. Excessive interrill erosion can go unnoticed because it removes sediment in a uniform layer. However, a soil susceptible to rill erosion is immediately obvious because flow concentrates in many small eroded channels (rills). Rills are most obvious where the hazard is greatest--for example bare, freshly tilled agricultural fields and steep, bare roadway embankments. Flow in rills is characteristically narrow and incised in contrast to the broad and shallow flow where deposition occurs.

Almost all natural soil surfaces where flow occurs are irregular causing shear stress concentrations. If stress at these concentrations is greater than the soil's critical shear stress, erosion occurs. Shear stress is greatest in the bottom of the flow, which tends to incise the rill channels.

Many rills are initially formed by the upslope advance of a gully-like headcut where erosion is particularly intense. Rate of advance of headcuts and their dimensions are functions of slope, discharge, soil, and incorporated material like crop residue (Meyer et al., 1975a).

After an initial headcut passes, other headcuts may form. The rills erode more deeply until a layer less susceptible to erosion restricts them. When this occurs, the rills widen and the erosion rate decreases. Other gully erosion processes such as undercutting and sloughing of the side walls, also occur in rills.

Rill erosion potentially occurs if the incoming sediment load from the interrill areas is less than the flow's transport capacity. If the sediment load is greater, deposition occurs. For example, deposition frequently occurs in row middles on a relatively flat slope (Meyer and Harmon, 1979). On steep slopes, rill erosion instead of deposition may occur in the middles.

Rill erosion is assumed to occur at a capacity rate if no sediment is present in the flow. If the flow's transport capacity is partially filled, a corresponding reduction may be assumed for rill erosion rate (Simons et al., 1977; Foster and Meyer, 1972a). Or since much rill erosion occurs at headcuts, all rill erosion can be assumed to always occur at a capacity rate. The relationships presented in this section are for rill erosion capacity rates.

Total rill erosion on an area can be modeled by describing erosion in each individual rill (Foster and Meyer, 1975). At first, this seems impractical because of the typically large numbers of rills and the varied geometry of the rills. However, in the special case of row middles, analysis of erosion in a few selected rills is quite feasible and is in fact advisable. Regardless of the modeling techniques, examination of erosion in a single rill provides insight into relationships that might be used to describe gross erosion.

Erosion in a Single Rill

Erosion in a single rill is assumed to be a function of flow hydraulics, specifically shear stress. As discharge or slope increases, rill erosion is expected to increase because shear stress increases. In a field study, Meyer et al. (1975a) found rill erosion rate to be proportional to $(Q-Q_c)$, where $Q =$ discharge rate, and $Q_c =$ discharge rate below which rill erosion is negligible. The USDA-Agricultural Research Service, (ARS), Lafayette, Indiana obtained similar results in a more recent unpublished but similar field study. The soils in these two studies were tilled just before the experiments and were about the same looseness as a seedbed prepared for corn or soybeans by moldboard plowing and disking at least twice. Rill erosion seems to behave differently on untilled, consolidated soils (Alberts et al., 1980). Alberts et al. found that erosion rate was constant over a 10:1 ratio of highest to lowest flow rate. Rill erosion rate was significant, i.e., it was not negligible. If a typical number of rills with their observed erosion rate had been in a 4 m by 23 m plot, the rills would have contributed about 0.5 kg/m²·h out of a total 2.0 kg/m²·h measured on the same soil. Rill erosion concepts suggest that even if the soil had a high critical shear stress, erosion rate should increase with increases in flow rate once the flow exceeds a critical level. Apparently, in Albert et al.'s situation, if the flow's shear stress exceeds the soil's critical shear stress, the soil erodes at a rate independent of flow hydraulics but controlled entirely by the soil itself; i.e., by how rapidly soil releases particles.

Tillage can greatly increase rill erosion. When a soil lies idle, it apparently becomes more resistant to rill erosion than it is immediately after tillage. In another unreported field test with simulated rainfall, USDA-ARS, at Lafayette, Indiana observed a constant erosion rate of 1.7 g/s·m of rill length from a test area 0.9 m by 10.7 m under 64 mm/h of simulated rainfall over a range of discharge from 4.5×10^{-4} to 3.8×10^{-3} m³/s. The soil had lain undisturbed since the previous crop year in a corn field that had not been moldboard plowed for at least 3 yr before the tests.

Immediately after tillage with a rototiller, the erosion rate increased to 2.6 g/s·m at a discharge of 3.8×10^{-4} m³/s and increased as discharge increased. Erosion rate was 48 g/s·m at a discharge of 4.9×10^{-3} m³/s. Apparently, as the soil consolidates over time after tillage, the critical shear stress increases significantly, which corresponds with observations for flow in larger channels (Graf, 1971).

Undisturbed soil under the tilled zone may therefore be much less erodible than the tilled layer. When a rill erodes through the tilled layer to the undisturbed soil, its downward growth may rapidly slow with the rill rapidly becoming wider, as was observed in the previously mentioned unpublished rill erosion field tests similar to those of Meyer et al. (1975a).

If headcuts are present, they are active before the rills reach the resistant boundary. A constant erosion rate during this period may be assumed, and an exponential decay may be assumed once the rill strikes the boundary. These relationships are discussed later in the section on Concentrated Flow.

An equation for rill erosion rate was developed for this chapter from analysis of Meyer et al. (1975a) data. Since they did not estimate shear stress, observations from the unreported rill erosion study were used to estimate shear stress. Rills were performed with a field cultivator in both studies. A "typical" cross section for a typical furrow left by the field cultivator was developed from approximately 25 cross-sections obtained with a "rill meter" having pins spaced 6.4 mm apart. The equation for hydraulic radius as a function of flow area was: $R = 0.70A^{0.64}$ where R = hydraulic radius (m) and A = area (m²). This, along with the velocity-discharge relationship given by Meyer et al., allowed computation of shear stress for each discharge rate. The resulting equation fitted to the data for rill erosion rate under a 64 mm/h simulated rainfall and no canopy cover was:

$$D_{rc} = 2.76(\bar{\tau} - 2.87)^{1.17} \qquad \dotfill \qquad [8.39]$$

while the equation with a canopy cover was:

$$D_{rc} = 2.34\,(\bar{\tau} - 4.16)^{0.93} \qquad \dotfill \qquad [8.40]$$

where D_{rc} = rill erosion detachment capacity rate per unit channel area (g/m of rill length·m of wetted perimeter·s) and $\bar{\tau}$ = average shear stress (N/m²). The values 2.87 and 4.16 are critical shear stress τ_{cr} values. The fit of the equation to the data is shown in Table 8.8. The rill erosion equation from the

TABLE 8.8. COMPARISON OF OBSERVED EROSION RATES
WITH EROSION RATES FROM EQUATION FITTED TO
DATA FROM RILL EROSION STUDY OF MEYER ET AL.
(1975a)

Discharge X 10⁴	Velocity*	Shear stress	Rill erosion rate	
			Observed	Fitted
m³/s	m/s	N/m²	g/m rill length · m wetted perimeter · s	
1.85	0.27	3.76	2.44	2.41
3.51	0.33	4.97	6.50	6.58
5.49	0.39	6.06	10.74	10.43
7.97	0.44	7.12	15.02	15.59
4.36†	0.36	5.48	2.88	3.02
8.22†	0.44	7.23	6.63	6.19
10.78†	0.48	8.17	8.50	9.56

*From Meyer et al. (1975a) velocity vs. discharge regression equation fitted to measured data.
†A three layer screen canopy just above the soil covered these rills.

unpublished rill erosion study with 64 mm/h simulated rainfall and no canopy was:

$$D_{rc} = 11.4 \, (\bar{\tau} - 4.78)^{1.05} \quad \dots\dots\dots\dots\dots\dots\dots\dots\dots\dots\dots\dots \quad [8.41]$$

which is similar to results of Meyer et al. except that the critical shear stress is almost twice as large and the proportionality constant is more than four times as large. This illustrates how parameter values in a rill erosion equation can vary without apparent reason for similar soils.

Gross Rill Erosion

In most modeling applications, erosion in the many single rills is lumped and described as gross rill erosion. Rill erosion and flow are assumed to be uniformily distributed across the slope, although physically the flow and erosion are concentrated in small channels.

With this assumption, the equation assumed for rill erosion is:

$$D_{rc} = a(\tau - \tau_{cr})^b \quad \dots\dots\dots\dots\dots\dots\dots\dots\dots\dots\dots\dots\dots \quad [8.42]$$

where D_{rc} = rill erosion detachment capacity rate (mass per unit total surface area per unit time) and τ = the flow's shear stress assuming broad shallow flow, and τ_{cr} = a critical shear stress.

Tests results presented earlier for erosion in a single rill support this form. However, τ_{cr} is especially difficult to evaluate. Values suggested by equations [8.39] through [8.41] are not applicable because the shear stress of broad sheet flow is much less than the shear stress of the flow concentrated in rills. The term τ_{cr} is, in effect, "fictitious" and is a function of factors other than soil properties. It depends on number of rills, distribution of the discharge among the rills, variation of shear stress both in time and space in the rills, and other nonuniform factors. The greater the nonuniformity, the smaller is the apparent τ_{cr} when it is calculated from an average shear stress computed assuming broad sheet flow.

Although the apparent τ_{cr} will be less, sometimes much less, than obtained in single rill measurements, single rill measurements should indicate the variation in the apparent τ_{cr} as a function of compaction and other factors. Furthermore, under 64 mm/h simulated rainfall rate, rills have been observed within a meter of where overland flow originates on soils susceptible to rill erosion indicating a small τ_{cr} (Foster and Meyer, 1975). On soils not susceptible to rill erosion, rills may hardly develop and hardly move even a short distance upslope.

If τ_{cr} values from single rill experiments are used in an erosion model assuming broad shallow flow, either τ_{cr} or τ must be adjusted to compensate for the flow being concentrated in the rills. If the modeler wishes to include a critical shear stress, equation [8.41] is suggested as a form with b set to 1.10. The parameter a and τ_{cr} must be obtained by calibration.

In many modeling applications, τ_{cr} can be assumed to be zero. For this chapter, data from 3.7 by 10.7 m rainfall simulator plots used by Wischmeier et al. (1971) to develop a soil erodibility nomograph were analyzed to derive the rill erosion equation:

$$D_{rc} = 83.7 \, K_r \tau^{1.5} \, C_r \quad \dots\dots\dots\dots\dots\dots\dots\dots\dots\dots\dots\dots \quad [8.43]$$

where D_{rc} = rill erosion detachment capacity rate (kg/m² of total area·h), τ = average shear stress assuming broad shallow flow (N/m²), K_r = soil erodibility factor for rill erosion (kg·h/N·m²), and C_r = a cover-management factor for rill erosion. Data were analyzed from each of three simulated storms for each of 55 soils.

Assuming steady kinematic flow and the Darcy-Weisbach uniform flow equation, the equation for total rill erosion for the slope length x is (Foster et al., 1977a):

$$q_{src} = a\gamma^{1.5} \, (f/8g)^{0.5} \, s \, \sigma \, x^2 \, K_r \, C_r/2 \quad\quad\quad\quad\quad\quad [8.44]$$

where q_{src} = sediment load for slope length x when rill erosion occurs at the detachment capacity rate, γ = weight density of water, f = Darcy-Weisbach friction factor, g = acceleration due to gravity, s = sine of slope angle, and σ = excess rainfall rate. Soil erodibility K_r for rill erosion was taken to be equal to the K value of the USLE, and C_r was taken to be equal to the soil loss ratio value of the USLE which accounted for the effect of previous cropping history on erosion. Rill erosion q_{src} was estimated by subtracting an estimate of interrill erosion obtained from equation [8.31] from the measured total erosion. Values for the coefficient a in equation [8.44] was computed for each simulated storm assuming a coefficient of friction f of 0.4. The values were combined with constant factors and were averaged to obtain the 83.7 number in equation [8.43]. The 83.7 coefficient could be refined by calibration.

The analysis did not indicate how K_r varies with soil properties, although some soil conditions are more susceptible to rill erosion than are others (Meyer et al., 1975b). As with interrill erodibility K_i; there is no proven measure of K_r. Consequently, equation [8.43] was written so that USLE K values can be used for K_r. The following adjustments may be made where applicable. If the soil seems especially susceptible to rill erosion, K_r should be increased from K by 1/3, and, conversely, reduce K by 1/3 if the soil does not seem susceptible to rilling.

The exponent of τ was increased from 1.05 or 1.17 for a single rill to 1.5 for overland flow with τ_{cr} = 0 for two reasons. When an equation of the form of equation [8.43] is fitted to data having the form of equation [8.42], the exponent increases to partially account for dropping of τ_{cr}. To illustrate: the relationship τ^b fits the data in Table 8.8 very well with an exponent of 3. This seems much too large because it would give too large of a slope length effect in comparison with the USLE (Foster et al., 1977a, b). Other modeling analyses have satisfactorily used either 1.5 (Foster et al., 1977a), or 1.0 (Meyer and Wischmeier, 1969; Curtis, 1976; David and Beer, 1975; Beasley, 1977). Regardless of the wide usage of the 1.0 power, 1.5 seems better because it better fits observed slope length exponents (Foster et al., 1977b). Furthermore, 1.5 facilitates simpler mathematical solutions when the Darcy-Weisbach flow equation is used in analytical analyses (Foster and Meyer, 1975; Lane and Shirley, 1978).

1. Cover and Management

A number of cover-management factors influence rill erosion and are treated within the framework of Wischmeier's (1975) Type I (canopy), II (cover in direct contact with the soil surface), and III (subsurface) effects.

The canopy and subsurface effects are described by the C_r factor in equations [8.43] and [8.44]. The effect of cover in direct contact with the soil surface is described separately by adjusting for the effect of cover on the flow's shear stress τ. The factor C_r is the product of subfactors for canopy, incorporated residue, residual land use, and tillage.

a. Canopy. Studies by Meyer et al. (1975b) and Alberts et al. (1980) indicated that canopy intercepting rainfall immediately above flow in rills decreases rill erosion in addition to greatly reducing interrill erosion. The reasons are not obvious from very detailed measurements of rill flow hydraulics (Foster, 1975). Significant changes in flow hydraulics caused by rainfall that might affect rill erosion were undetectable. Similarly Foster and Huggins (1977) and Davis (1978) found little or no rainfall effect on the transport of sediment by shallow overland flow.

If the effect is due to flow turbulence, the greatest increases in turbulence with an increase in rainfall intensity is at low rainfall rates with the rate of increase of turbulence diminishing at high intensities (Yoon, 1970). Based on Meyer et al. (1975a) results, the 83.7 factor in equation [8.43] should be 44.5 for a complete canopy close to the flow. The effect should also be related to effective rainfall intensity in equation [8.31]. Putting these suppositions together, the C_{rI} subfactor for canopy would be:

$$C_{rI} = 44.5 + 39.2 \left[1 - \exp(-0.074 \, i_{eff}^2) \right] \quad \dots\dots\dots\dots\dots\dots\dots \quad [8.45]$$

The -0.074 factor was selected to give 95 percent credit to the reduction of rill erosion when effective rainfall intensity is 64 mm/h.

A word of caution—equation [8.45] has not been validated. In fact, the influence of the canopy on rill erosion has not been positively identified. However, if the modeler chooses to include the effect, equation [8.45] is a functional form for consideration.

b. Cover in Direct Contact with the Soil Surface. This effect is included directly in τ rather than as a subfactor in C_r. Although material in direct contact with the soil surface increases the flow's total shear stress, it reduces the stress acting on the soil surface. The shear stress acting on the soil surface is:

$$\tau_{cs} = \gamma \, v_c^2 \, f_s / 8g \quad \dots\dots\dots\dots\dots\dots\dots\dots\dots\dots\dots\dots\dots \quad [8.46]$$

where τ_{cs} = shear stress acting on the soil, γ = weight density of the runoff, v_c = flow velocity with cover, f_s = friction factor due to the soil, and g = acceleration due to gravity. Development of equation [8.46] follows that used to express drag due to grain resistance and form resistance in channel flow (Graf, 1971). Total friction factor is:

$$f = f_c + f_s \quad \dots\dots\dots\dots\dots\dots\dots\dots\dots\dots\dots\dots\dots\dots\dots \quad [8.47]$$

where f = total friction factor and f_c = the friction factor due to cover.

The value for τ_{cs} is used instead of τ in equation [8.43] when cover is present.

Sometimes cover will fail allowing excessive rill erosion. The shear stress:

$$\tau_{cc} = \gamma \, v_c^2 \, f_c / 8g \quad \dots\dots\dots\dots\dots\dots\dots\dots\dots\dots\dots\dots\dots \quad [8.48]$$

is a measure of flow forces on the cover. When τ_{cc} exceeds a critical shear

TABLE 8.9. CRITICAL SHEAR STRESS FOR MULCH
TO MOVE BY OVERLAND FLOW. SHEAR STRESS IS
THAT PORTION OF TOTAL SHEAR STRESS THAT
ACTS ON THE MULCH

Mulch type and rate	Critical shear stress (acting on mulch)	Total friction factor (soil & mulch)	Total Manning's n (soil & mulch)
	N/m^2		
Corn*			
Bare	—	0.05	0.010
0.25 kg/m^2	0.6-1.0†	0.23	0.019
0.50 kg/m^2	2.1	0.38	0.032
1.00 kg/m^2	5.2	2.00	0.071
Straw*			
Bare	—	0.22	0.024
0.12 kg/m^2	0.6	0.28	0.024
0.25 kg/m^2	3.0	1.07	0.055
0.50 kg/m^2	14.0	5.90	0.150

*Corn stalks were on plots in corn fields which had not been dis-
turbed since the previous year's crop. Rows were up and down
hill. The row ridges concentrated the flow. Values given are
based on assumption of broad shallow flow and measured velocities in row middles. Consequently roughness factors are lower than normally associated with broad sheet flow. Straw mulch
was placed on a soil that had been recently tilled with a rototiller.

†Failure of heavier rates was generally by enmasse movement.
The 0.25 corn and 0.12 kg/m^2 straw rates failed gradually with
mulch being carried away piece by piece rather than in enmasse.
Failure could not be precisely defined.

stress required for stability, the cover moves. This type of mulch movement
can be seen on highway embankments and other construction slopes.

During unreported studies by USDA-ARS, Lafayette, Indiana on the
stability of corn stalk residue, typically, larger rates of nonincorporated
residue floated in place on top of the flow. As flow discharge increased, the
residue abruptly floated away when a critical discharge was reached. The
failure was enmasse movement. For mulch low rates, 0.1 kg/m^2, the residue
floated away piece by piece. Estimated shear stress values acting on the
mulch when abrupt failure occurred are given in Table 8.9. These values are
approximate because the exact failure point is difficult to define.

It can also be shown from the Darcy-Weisbach equation that (Foster
and Meyer, 1975):

$$(\tau_{cs}/\tau_b) = (v_c/v_b)^2 \qquad\qquad\qquad\qquad\qquad\qquad [8.49]$$

where τ_b = shear stress for no cover and v_b = flow velocity for no cover.
Equations [8.43] and [8.46], measured velocity and cover data, and equations [8.31] and [8.33] without the exp( ) term in equation [8.33] were applied to experimental erosion data for straw mulch (Foster and Meyer, 1975).
The results, given in Table 8.10, indicated that this method of accounting for
surface cover works reasonably well.

Table 8.11 gives typical velocity ratios for use in equation [8.49] based
on measured velocities from several erosion experiments (Neibling and
Foster, 1977). The velocity ratios shown in the table do not account for any
increase in infiltration with mulches. This must be accounted for separately.

TABLE 8.10. COMPARISON OF PREDICTED SOIL LOSS
WITH OBSERVED SOIL LOSS FROM 11 m EROSION
PLOTS COVERED WITH WHEAT STRAW MULCH
(Foster and Meyer, 1975)

Mulch rate	Fox loam, 15% slope		Xenia silt loam, 3% slope		Wea silt loam, 5% slope	
	Ob-served	Pre-dicted*	Ob-served	Pre-dicted	Ob-served	Pre-dicted
(kg/m²)						
0.06	0.32	0.47	0.40	0.39	0.25	0.45
0.11	0.31	0.34	0.25	0.27	0.16	0.27
0.22	0.19	0.19	0.12	0.14	0.029	0.088
0.45	0.040	0.064	—†	—	—	—
0.90	0.024	0.024	—	—	—	—

*Predicted and observed values are ratio of soil loss from the mulch treatments to that from no-mulch.
†The 0.45 and 0.90 kg/m² mulch rates were not includes in these studies.

c. Incorporated Plant Residue. Incorporated and decay of crop residue in the soil builds soil structure and the soil's organic matter content which reduces erosion. The subfactors for this effect are those given for the same effect on interrill detachment.

Large pieces of buried residue and grass roots exposed to the flow reduce the flow's shear stress acting on the soil, and they also act like grade control structures in channels. However, they are not ef-

TABLE 8.11. MEASURED VELOCITY RATIOS* FOR SEVERAL
COVERS (Neibling and Foster, 1977)

Treatment	Velocity† ratio	Treatment	Velocity† ratio
Cornstalk residue applied to fallow surface		Crushed stone mulch	
0.2 kg/m²	0.7	3 kg/m²	0.9
0.4 kg/m²	0.4	13 kg/m²	0.6
0.9 kg/m²	0.3	30 kg/m²	0.4
		54 kg/m²	0.3
		84 kg/m²	0.3
Cornstalk residue disk-harrow incorporated		Woodchip mulch	
0.2 kg/m²	0.9	0.4 kg/m²	0.7
0.4 kg/m²	0.7	0.9 kg/m²	0.5
0.5 kg/m²	0.6	2.0 kg/m²	0.4
		3.0 kg/m²	0.3
		6.0 kg/m²	0.3
		Rough surface depressions	
Wheat straw mulch			
0.06 kg/m²	0.8	100-150 mm deep	0.5
0.10 kg/m²	0.7	50-100 mm deep	0.7
0.20 kg/m²	0.5	20- 50 mm deep	0.9
0.40 kg/m²	0.3	No depressions	1.0
0.90 kg/m²	0.3		

*Ratio of velocity with treatment to that for a bare, fallow unrilled soil surface.
†Does not account for a reduction in velocity caused by increased infiltration with heavy mulch covers.

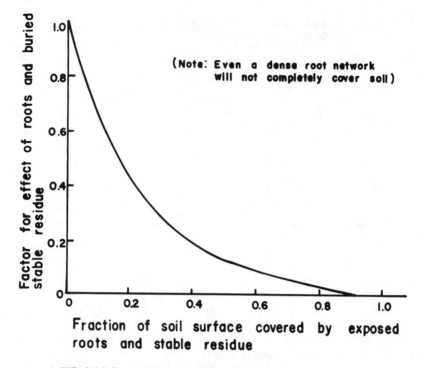

FIG. 8.6 Influence of buried residue and grass roots on rill erosion.

fective until erosion exposes them. Consequently, erosion often decreases over time due to their influence. Fig. 8.6, which gives values
for this effect, is based solely on intuition and has no basis other
than that effectiveness must be greater than linear for an increase in
cover. The fraction of the soil covered is that at the time of the
erosion estimate. This fraction can increase greatly during a storm
occurring immediately after tillage. Perhaps a more rigorous accounting could be developed by considering the material's effect on the
flow's shear stress.

   d. Residual Land Use. The values suggested for this effect on interrill erosion can be used for the rill erosion effect also.

   e. Tillage. Tillage increases a soil's susceptibility to rill
erosion as confirmed by limited field test by USDA-ARS, at Lafayette,
Indiana. Erosion on a plot packed with a lawn roller and exposed to
simulated rainfall was as great as that from an adjacent disked plot.
Little or no rilling occurred on the packed plot, which indicated that
consolidation does not reduce and, in fact, may increase detachment by
raindrop impact. Increased bulk density similarly increased detachment by raindrop impact in Foster and Martin's (1969) study. Erosion
on undisturbed plots at Zanesville, Ohio decreased in 5 years to 0.44
of what it had been just after the last tillage on the plots
(Wischmeier, 1975). All of the reduction is credited to a reduction
in rill erosion.

   The effect is also assumed to be a function of type of tillage and
moisture content at tillage. Plowing, for example, leaves large ag-

TABLE 8.12. ESTIMATED REDUCTION IN RILL
EROSION OVER TIME AFTER TILLAGE

	Ratio of erosion to that just after tillage		
Years after tillage	Conventional seedbed	Chisel plowing and disking as primary tillage	Turn plowing
0	1.00	0.80	0.60
1	0.60	0.55	0.45
2	0.40	0.38	0.32
3	0.30	0.28	0.25
5	0.22	0.22	0.22

gregates and does not produce as many readily erodible fine particles as does tillage for a conventional seedbed. Also, the aggregates from tillage when the soil is too wet may be more resistant to rill erosion. Conversely, freezing and thawing over the winter probably makes the soil more susceptible to rilling. The subfactor values in Table 8.12 are unvalidated estimates for soil tilled in the spring at optimum moisture.

Donigian and Crawford (1976) used a concept of soil consolidation and reduced erodibility. Their parameter requires calibration.

The effect of roughness from tillage is not included in Table 8.12; it is accounted for separately in shear stress τ, critical shear stress τ_{cr}, and velocity ratios from Table 8.11.

Rill erosion decreases if the rills reach a dense, restricting layer like a plow sole. Thereafter, erosion decreases exponentially. This decrease is not a function of time directly but is a function of the amount of erosion since the last tillage. Bruce et al. (1975) modeled a decrease in erosion using an exponential decay function. The influences that should be described are: time to describe the consolidation effect and amount of previous erosion to describe the influence of a restricting layer. The function should be reset following each tillage that obliterates previously developed rills. Equations are discussed in the section on Concentrated Flow that can be used to describe these effects.

2. Simplifications

The relationships for rill erosion and its subfactors are complex and somewhat cumbersome. A simpler alternative to equation [8.43] and its subfactor relationships is (Foster, 1976; Beasley, 1977):

$$D_{rc} = C_B \, q \, s \, K \, C_{slr} \quad \dots\dots\dots\dots\dots\dots\dots\dots\dots\dots\dots\dots \quad [8.50]$$

where D_{rc} = rill erosion detachment capacity rate, C_B = a coefficient to be determined from data by calibration, q = runoff rate, s = sine of slope angle, K = soil erodibility factor from the USLE, C_{slr} = the soil loss ratio from the USLE. The soil loss ratios include both rill and interrill erosion in the USLE and the influence of cover and management on runoff. Consequently, there may be a double accounting where runoff rate q from hydrologic considerations is also a function of cover and management. Also, D_{rc} will be in error when erosion for the conditions represented by a given C_{slr} is mainly interrill erosion.

Particle Characteristics of Sediment Eroded in Rills

Little selective erosion of particles occurs with rill erosion except in special cases (Meyer et al., 1975b). If the flow has enough capacity to detach particles, it has capacity to transport the detached particles away from their local point of origin. The occasional deposition of sands observed in rills may be deposition during flow recession after the end of rainfall. Large channels, however, can develop an armor layer due to selective erosion (Graf, 1971) which may also occur in rills in a highly gravelled soil. If it does occur, the exposed gravel is treated as a mulch.

Particles eroded from rills seem to be larger than those eroded from interrill areas (Meyer et al., 1977b; Alberts et al, 1980). Since information on particle sizes detached by rill erosion is limited, however, the particle distribution assumed for the sediment detached from interrill areas is also assumed for that detached from rills.

Transport Capacity of Flow in Rills

Flow in rills transports most of the detached soil particles downslope. A basic erosion modeling concept is that sediment load in flow is limited by either the sediment available for transport or by the flow's transport capacity. If sediment load exceeds the flow's transport capacity, deposition occurs. In contrast to the eroding flow that forms incised channels, flow that is depositing sediment tends to be broad and shallow and to extend over broad areas. A typical example is deposition at the toe of concave slopes. When deposition occurs in row middles, the flow is as broad and shallow as the row sideslopes allow.

Although overland flow that is depositing sediment is typically broad and shallow, it is still referred to as rill flow simply to distinguish it from interrill flow. Rill flow denotes an accummulation of runoff over a greater distance from upslope than is normally associated with interrill flow.

In general, transport capacity is a function of the flow's hydraulic forces and the transportability of the sediment.

1. Modes of Transport

Two distinct modes of transport can be observed--bedload and suspended load. Bedload sediment moves along the bottom of the flow and is readily deposited when transport capacity decreases to less than the bedload component of the sediment load. Deposition of the coarse bedload is often evident where flow had been ponded.

The suspended load is more evenly distributed throughout the flow depth and is much less readily deposited, especially the very fine particles. As a consequence, suspended load generally travels considerably further than does bedload before it is deposited when the transporting force is removed.

Fine suspended clay particles are deposited very, very slowly. In some instances, deposition occurs because the small particles form flocs. In other cases, deposition may be entirely by mechanical settling. The chemistry of both the flow and the sediment probably plays a major role that researchers have almost totally neglected in upland erosion. See Partheniades (1972) for a discussion of the factors that affect deposition of fine particles.

2. Transport Relationships

The equation for transport capacity iş a very fundamental part of an erosion model. Whether or not deposition is calculated depends directly on the amount of transport capacity relative to the sediment load made available by the detachment processes.

Sediment is generally composed of particles having a variety of sizes and densities. For purposes of simplification, a characteristic size and density is often used. Sediment transport capacity is computed assuming that the sediment is uniform. However, in problems where calculation of segregation of sediment during deposition is important, the transport capacity equation must be modified to accommodate nonuniform sediment.

a. Uniform Sediment. Various relationships have been used in erosion models to describe transport capacity by overland flow. These include simple relationships like that of Meyer and Wischmeier (1969):

$$T_c = a\, s^{5/3}\, q^{5/3} \qquad \text{...} \quad [8.51]$$

where T_c = transport capacity, s = sine of slope angle, q = discharge rate per unit width, and a = coefficient dependent on soil transportability and the effect of soil roughness and cover on the flow's transporting forces. Other equations that have been used are the DuBoys (Young and Mutchler, 1969b; Foster and Huggins, 1977); the Meyer-Peter and Muller (Li, 1977); the Einstein (Li, 1977; Barfield et al., 1977); the Yang (Smith, 1977); the Yalin (Foster and Meyer, 1972b); and the Bagnold in a HYDROCOMP model‡. Deposition modeling to date indicates no advantage of one equation over another for deposition of sands (Davis, 1978). All basically have an adequate functional form, and given proper parameter values, most can be used to adequately simulate deposition. All transport equations require some "calibration" for overland flow.

Two factors are important in choosing a transport equation. (1) Use of or neglect of a suspended load equation is not critical if the equation has been calibrated with typical data. Even the DuBoys bedload equation can be used to describe suspended load if calibrated (ASCE, 1975). (2) The equation should be able to deal with particles having specific gravities of about 1.6 to 2.0 and diameters as small as 2 μm.

Observation of deposition in the field definitely indicates a critical shear stress for the coarse particles. They are deposited immediately upon ponding of the flow, and there is usually an abrupt lower edge to the end of deposition of the coarse particles. Critical shear stress can probably be neglected for the fines that move as suspended load.

'Textbook' equations and parameters may not fit observed data for several reasons. Overland flow hydraulics are poorly defined. Flow depth is not uniform across the slope, and the slope of the energy gradeline is difficult to estimate, especially where slopes are relatively flat or where the flow is ponded. Furthermore, sediment transport equations for streamflow generally fit poorly when applied to a

‡Walker, R. A. 1978. Personal communication.

TABLE 8.13. OBSERVED LARGE RATES OF SOIL LOSS FROM FIELD EROSION PLOTS UNDER SIMULATED RAINFALL (Wischmeier et al., 1971) These values establish a lower limit for transport; an overland flow sediment transport equation should give rates at least as large. Since detachment limited sediment load on these plots, these data are not a measure of the upper limit of transport capacity.

Slope	Discharge rate $\times 10^4$	Sediment load
%	m^3/m·s	g/m·s
1.8	1.72	6.40
3.9	1.41	3.91
4.3	1.69	5.04
4.6	1.47	4.91
6.0	1.57	9.41
7.7	1.28	7.23
8.7	1.38	16.37
9.5	1.25	12.98
10.1	1.52	16.98
12.0	1.66	22.80
14.0	0.92	4.87
15.0	1.51	10.77
20.0	1.88	51.53

variety of situations (ASCE, 1975). Most streamflow equations were derived from data where the sediment particles were larger and heavier than those encountered in erosion modeling.

A chosen equation should be checked to make sure it is reasonable under typical overland flow conditions. These conditions are almost always on the edge or outside of the data range used to develop streamflow transport equations. Some equations turn sharply at these extremes. An example is the Ackers and White equation (Ackers and White, 1973), which fits well for channel flow but is invalid for most overland flow. Strict regression equations developed from streamflow data and primary particles, for example, an early version of the Yang equation (Yang, 1972), should be avoided.

Data available to develop or check a sediment transport equation for overland flow are quite limited. However, data from erosion plots can be used as check points. Transport capacity on uniform erosion plots must be at least as large as the observed soil loss. Values in Table 8.13 define minimum values for transport capacity observed from several plots of Wischmeier et al. (1971) erodibility study under simulated rainfall. Transport capacity could be considerably larger than these values.

Table 8.14 give a few data, available from deposition studies, which can be used to measure the suitability of a particular equation. These data represent maximum values. Sediment load can lag behind a decrease in transport capacity since the fines do not respond immediately to a decrease in transport capacity. The lag was assumed to be small for the data in Table 8.14.

Each erosion modeler has a bias to a particular sediment transport equation. My preference is the Yalin (1963) equation. Of the Ackers and White, DuBoys, Yang, Bagnold, and Graf (Graf, 1971), the Yalin best fits the data in Table 8.14. However, that is a very limited test.

The Yalin equation is given by the following series of equations (Yalin, 1963):

TABLE 8.14. SEDIMENT YIELD IN OVERLAND FLOW FROM CONCAVE SLOPES

Sediment			Transport rates	
Sedimentation diameter	Specific gravity	Shear stress	Observed	Calculated by Yalin eq.
μm		N/m²	g/m·s	g/m·s
342*	2.65	0.52	5.6	4.2
342*	2.65	0.76	19.7	13.4
150*	2.65	0.55	5.2	9.0
150*	2.65	0.70	18.8	17.6
342†	2.65	0.40	2.2	1.4
342*	2.65	0.60	12.8	6.6
342†	1.60	0.30	3.5	6.0
342†	1.60	0.42	13.7	14.4
156†	1.67	0.30	3.8	6.1
156†	1.67	0.40	13.3	12.7
Eroded from barnes loam, Field plots‡		0.33 §	3.3	2.8
Eroded Miami‖ silt loam		0.51 #	4.8	7.0
Eroded Miami‖ silt loam		0.35**	2.5	3.1
Eroded Miami‖†† silt loam		—	1.4	—

*From Foster and Huggins (1977)
†From Davis (1978)
‡From Young and Mutchler (1969a)
§Shear calculated from $\tau = \gamma(3\nu q/g)^{2/3} s^{2/3}$ where $\nu = 1.12 \times 10^{-6}$ m²/s, q = 2.82 × 10⁻⁴ m²/s, and s = 0.02. Particle distribution in Table 1 assumed.
‖Unreported data. Concave field plots having a slope varying continuously from 0.18 to 0.0 over 10.7 m. Sediment yield was measured at 7.0 m and 8.8 m on separate plots.
#Shear stress calculated from $\tau = \gamma (3\nu q/g)^{2/3} s^{2/3}$ where $\nu = 1.12 \times 10^6$ m²/s, q = 1.17 × 10⁻⁴ m²/s, and s = 0.06. Particle distribution in Table 1 assumed.
**Shear stress calculated from $\tau = \gamma (3\nu q/g)^{2/3} s^{2/3}$ where $\nu = 1.12 \times 10^{-6}$ m²/s, q = 1.47 × 10⁻⁴ m²/s and s = 0.03. Particle distribution in Table 2 assumed.
††Plot had zero slope at end. Relatively large transport rate represents lag of sediment load with a decrease in transport capacity.

$$P = (W_s/S_g\rho_w dV_*) = 0.635 \, \delta \; [1-(1/\sigma) \, Ln(1+\sigma)] \quad \ldots\ldots\ldots \text{[8.52]}$$

$$\sigma = A\cdot\delta \quad \ldots\ldots\ldots \text{[8.53]}$$

$$\delta = (Y/Y_{cr}) - 1 \;(\text{When } Y < Y_{cr}, \delta=0) \quad \ldots\ldots \text{[8.54]}$$

$$A = 2.45 \, S_g^{0.4} \, Y_{cr}^{0.5} \quad \ldots\ldots \text{[8.55]}$$

$$Y = V_*^2/[(S_g-1)gd] \quad \ldots\ldots \text{[8.56]}$$

$$V_* = (gR_f s)^{1/2} = (\tau_{cs}/\rho_w)^{1/2} \quad \ldots\ldots \text{[8.57]}$$

where P = a nondimensional sediment transport capacity, W_s = the transport capacity (mass per unit width per unit time), S_g = particle specific gravity, ρ_w = mass density of water, d = diameter, V_* = shear velocity, Y_{cr} = ordinate from the Shields Diagram, g = acceleration due to gravity, R_f = hydraulic radius, s = slope of the energy gradeline, and τ_{cs} = shear stress acting on the soil. Other variables like Y, σ, and δ are defined by equations [8.53] through [8.57]. Transport capacity T_c is assigned directly to W_s for uniform sediment. The constant 0.635 was empirically derived by Yalin from laboratory flumes where flow was much deeper than it is for overland flow. Davis (1978) found that 0.88 was better as a value for the constant for sand with d = 342 μm and S_g = 2.65; he found that 0.47 was better for coal with d = 342 μm, S_g = 160 and d = 156 μm, S_g = 1.67. The equation described especially well the interaction of particle size and density for Davis' data. The Shields Diagram as extended by Mantz (1977) for small particles, Fig. 8.7, is used to estimate Y_{cr}.

Other modelers including Khaleel et al. (1979) and Li (1977) have added the Einstein equation to a bedload equation to estimate suspended load transport capacity. Given the uncertainties in estimating flow and sediment characteristics, this may be an unnecessary refinement. Details of this approach can be found in Khaleel et al. (1979) and Li (1977).

In stream channels, the bed supplies most of the sediment. Transport capacity for an individual particle type is assumed to be proportional to the fraction of the surface bed material made up of that type (Graf, 1971). Armoring occurs if a stream bed has particles larger than the flow can transport which requires modification to the above assumption (Thomas, 1976).

In stream channels, particles are continually interchanged between the bed and the flow. Such does not occur in upland erosion because the shear stress required to detach a particle is often considerably greater than that required to transport the particle, for example, the critical shear stress for detachment by rill erosion is about 2.9 N/m^2 from equation [8.39] while the critical shear stress for transport is less than 0.5 N/m^2 for 342 μm sand (Foster and Huggins, 1977). Therefore, a flow range exists where transport may occur with no rill erosion.

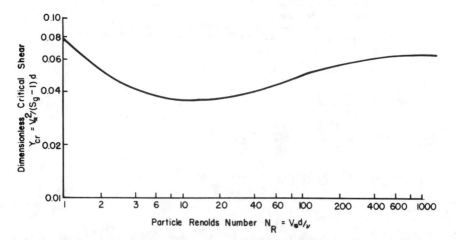

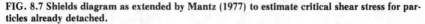

FIG. 8.7 Shields diagram as extended by Mantz (1977) to estimate critical shear stress for particles already detached.

b. Nonuniform Sediment. Sediment in overland flow is from: interrill areas, rill areas, and flow arriving from upslope. The sediment is a mixture of particles having various sizes and densities. The Yalin sediment transport equation is modified to accommodate mixtures.

The sediment load may have fewer particles of a given type than the flow's transport capacity for that type. At the same time the sediment load for other particle types may exceed the flow's transport capacity for those types. The excess transport capacity for the deficit types is assumed to shift to increase the transport capacity for the types where available sediment exceeds transport capacity.

The Yalin equation is accordingly modified to accommodate this shift in transport capacity. The procedure worked well for deposition of a sand-coal mixture where both particles had the same sedimentation diameter of 342 μm and the sand had a specific gravity of 2.65 while the coal had a specific gravity of 2.65 while the coal had a specific gravity of 1.60 (Davis, 1978). However, the procedure did not work well for a sand-coal mixture of the same sand but a coal with a sedimentation diameter of 156 μm. Wherever the sand was deposited, it trapped the small coal even though the critical shear stress of the coal was only 2/3 that of the sand. No explanation was given for the trapping. However, because of the good results for the sand-large coal mixture, the procedure is presented here. The procedure is an adaptation of that used by Foster and Meyer (1972b), Davis (1978), and Khaleel et al. (1979). Khaleel et al. (1979) discussed the procedure for the Einstein and Yalin equations combined.

c. Large and Small Sediment Loads. For large sediment loads, where sediment loads for each particle type are clearly in excess of the respective transport capacities for each particle type; or for small sediment loads, where sediment loads for each particle type are clearly less than the respective transport capacities for each particle type; the flow's total transport capacity is distributed among the available particle types based on particle size and density and flow characteristics and not on the makeup of the sediment load. Foster and Meyer (1972b) modified the Yalin equation to give these transport capacities.

Yalin (1963) assumed that sediment transport rate is equal to the number of particles in transport over a unit area times the mass and velocity of each particle. Foster and Meyer (1972b) assumed that mixture reduced the number, but not the velocity, of particles of a given particle type in transport. Yalin assumed that the number of particles in transport is proportional to δ. Therefore, for a mixture, the number of particles of a given type i was assumed to be proportional to δ_i. Values for δ_i for each particle type in a mixture were calculated and summed to give a total:

$$T = \sum_{i=1}^{n} \delta_i \quad\dotfill\quad [8.58]$$

where n = number of particle types. The number $(N_e)_i$ of transported particles of type i in a mixture was taken as:

$$(N_e)_i = N_i \, (\delta_i/T) \quad\dotfill\quad [8.59]$$

where N_i = number of particles transported in sediment of uniform type i for a δ_i.

As derived by Yalin, nondimensional transport capacity P of equation [8.52] is proportional to the number of particles in transport. Then, let $(P_e)_i$ be:

$$(P_e)_i = P_i \, (\delta_i/T) \quad\dotfill\quad [8.60]$$

where $(P_e)_i$ = the effective P for a particle type i in a mixture and P_i is the P calculated for uniform material of type i. The transport capacity W_{si} of each particle type in a mixture was then expressed by:

$$W_{si} = (P_e)_i \, S_{gi} \, \rho_w \, d_i \, V_* \quad\dotfill\quad [8.61]$$

This is the transport capacity where the availability of all particle types is either greater than or less than their respective W_{si}. In this case, transport capacity T_{ci} is assigned directly to W_{si}.

d. Shift of Transport Capacity. When availability of some particle types is greater than their W_{si}, transport capacity is assumed to shift so that all of the total transport capacity is used.

The steps given below (from Davis, 1978) are followed to redistribute the transport capacity when excesses and deficits occur.

1. For those particles where $W_{si} \geq q_{si}$, (q_{si} = sediment load for particle type i), compute a required P_{ireq} from equation [8.52], i.e.:

$$P_{ireq} = q_{si}/[(S_{gi}) \, \rho_w d_i V_*] \quad\dotfill\quad [8.62]$$

The transport capacity for these particles is:

$$T_{ci} = q_{si} \quad\dotfill\quad [8.63]$$

2. For those particles type where $W_{si} > q_{si}$, compute the sum:

$$SPT = \sum_{i=1}^{n} (P_{ireq}/P_i) \quad\dotfill\quad [8.64]$$

The sum SPT represents the fraction of the total transport capacity used by those particle types where sediment availability is less than transport capacity.

3. The excess expressed as a fraction of the total to be distributed is:

$$E_{xc} = 1 - SPT \quad\dotfill\quad [8.65]$$

4. For those particle types where $W_{si} < q_{si}$, sum the δ_i as:

$$SDLT = \sum_{i=1}^{n} \delta_i \quad\dotfill\quad [8.66]$$

5. The excess is distributed among the particle types for $W_{si} < q_{si}$ according to the distribution of δ among the particle types, i.e.:

$$T_{ci} = (\delta_i/SDLT) \, (E_{xc}) \, (P_i) \, (S_g)_i \, \rho_w \, d_i \, V_* \quad\dotfill\quad [8.67]$$

6. Repeat steps 1-5 until either all $T_{ci} \leq q_{si}$ or all $T_{ci} \geq q_{si}$. If the former

occurs, the proper T_{ci} have been found. If the latter occurs, one particle type will have had excess transport capacity. The excess for this one should be equally distributed among all of the particle types. This is done by:

$$\text{SMUS} = \sum_{i=1}^{n} (P_{ireq}/P_i) \quad \cdots\cdots\cdots\cdots\cdots\cdots\cdots\cdots\cdots\cdots \quad [8.68]$$

$$T_{ci} = (1.0/\text{SMUS}) \cdot q_{si} \quad \cdots\cdots\cdots\cdots\cdots\cdots\cdots\cdots\cdots\cdots \quad [8.69]$$

Khaleel et al. (1979) used this procedure with the Einstein equation for suspended load transport. They assumed that all parameters of the Einstein equation were unaffected by a mixture except for the reference concentration. The computed suspended load was subtracted from q_{si} in each pass through the above steps.

3. Effect of Surface Cover, Roughness, and Rainfall on Transport Capacity.

Grass, mulch, and other similar surface cover reduces the flow's shear stress acting on the soil surface, which reduces the flow's transport capacity in the same way it reduces the flow's detachment capacity. Shear stress acting on the soil is computed by equation [8.46]; it is the same as that for rill detachment. This shear stress is used to compute shear velocity in equation [8.57].

Grass and mulch strips most effectively reduce transport capacity when the flow is uniformly spread across the width of the strip. This is ideal but may not occur often. Flow in concentrations generally has greater transport capacity because of a greater submergence of the grass or mulch. This can be accounted for by adjusting the flow depth and shear stress as they are affected by the degree of concentration.

Roughness also reduces flow transport capacity. The flow's shear stress can be modified based on a ratio of the average flow depth across the slope to the average flow depth in the depressions. As the depressions fill with sediment, the flow depth in the depressions is reduced and the flow's transport capacity increases. As an alternative, the effect of roughness on the velocity ratio can also be used to compute the effective shear stress and the resulting effect of roughness on transport capacity.

The effect of roughness on interrill transport was discussed in the section on transport on interrill areas. The distinction between interrill and rill areas is not always clear. Generally, a reduction in transport capacity by roughness should not be accounted for twice, once on interrill and once on rill areas. No definite rule can be given on when to include a reduction on both areas.

Most roughness has a distribution of depressional sizes. Some depressions will fill before others. Consequently, an analysis based on an average depression size may underestimate gross transport capacity when there is great variability in depression sizes. Mitchell and Jones (1976), and Huggins and Monke (1966) described some measured roughness relationships.

The effect of rainfall rate on transport capacity of flow in rills is not definite. Perhaps the rainfall effect identified for interrill

TABLE 8.15. INFLUENCE OF DEPOSITION ON A CONCAVE SLOPE ON THE PARTICLE SIZE DISTRIBUTION OF THE SEDIMENT (FRACTIONS EXPRESSED AS A PERCENT) (Neibling and Foster, 1980)

Plot length and slope at end*	Size classes (μm)							
	>2000	2000-1000	1000-500	500-210	210-50	50-35	35-2	<2
7.0 m; 6%†	7.6	18.8	16.8	9.3	4.8	3.4	33.0	5.3
8.8 m; 3%	6.9	14.0	11.6	7.3	5.1	4.1	44.1	6.9
10.7 m; 0%	1.0	1.4	1.0	0.8	1.4	2.3	82.1	10.0
Primary particles original soil	Sand-19%, silt-55%, clay-26% (USDA classification)							

*Plots were concave in shape and described by equation $S_* = 2(1-x_*)$ where S_* = slope at a point divided by average slope (equal to 9%), and $x_* = x/10.7$ (x measured from top of plot). Erosion and flow produced by 64 mm/h simulated rainfall on untilled uniform subsoil.
†Approximate location where deposition began.

erosion applies. However, Foster and Huggins (1977) and Davis (1978) found that rainfall had a negligible effect. Consequently, it is neglected.

A zero sediment transport capacity does not necessarily mean that sediment load is zero. Bedload responds immediately to a reduction in bedload transport capacity. If transport capacity is zero, bedload transport is zero. However, suspended load does not respond immediately to a change in transport capacity, but lags behind. This is important for grass strips because wider grass strips give the suspended load more time to respond. Also, sediment from interrill erosion is assumed to enter the flow as suspended sediment. Consequently there will be a sediment load on a rough surface even though transport capacity might be zero. Equation [8.3] is used to describe this lag.

4. Particle Distribution after Deposition

No particle sorting is allowed during detachment. Any change of the particle distribution occurs during deposition. The primary particle size distribution of sediment from bare, tilled uniform slopes is close to that of the original soil although the clay is slightly enriched (Young and Onstad, 1976). Thus, any major enrichment of clays comes from selective sorting during deposition, although cover will enrich the clays slightly (Yoder, 1936). Table 8.15 shows the effect of deposition on short (7 to 10.7 m) concave slopes on particle size distribution (Neibling and Foster, 1980), and Table 8.16 shows the effect of deposition in a mulch strip on particle size distribution (Alberts, 1979). As expected, the coarser particles were most likely to be deposited. However, the fraction of clay as primary clay is still small, indicating that most of the sediment passing through the depo-

TABLE 8.16. INFLUENCE OF DEPOSITION BY OVERLAND FLOW IN A MULCH STRIP (CORN STALKS) ON THE PARTICLE SIZE DISTRIBUTION OF THE SEDIMENT (FRACTIONS EXPRESSED AS A PERCENT) (Alberts, 1979)

Plot	Size classes (μm)							
	>2000	2000-1000	1000-5000	500-210	210-50	50-35	35-2	<2
Check, 10.7 m bare, 6% slope	0.7	2.7	21.9	25.5	10.3	9.0	26.0	3.9
Strip, 0-6.1 m bare, 50% residue cover on 6.1-10.7 m, 6% slope	0.3	2.0	9.9	8.7	5.1	9.7	54.9	9.4
Primary particles original soil	Sand-29%, silt-54%, clay 17%, (USDA classification)							

sition area is still aggregated. Since most of the deposited sediment was aggregated, considerable clay was deposited. The assumption that clay is not deposited on upland slopes is false; aggregates containing clay are easily deposited.

Storage of Sediment

When deposition occurs, sediment is stored. Some models like those of Curtis (1976), Li (1977), and Donigian and Crawford (1976) account for stored sediment and assume that it is available for subsequent erosion if either incoming sediment supply decreases below transport capacity or transport capacity increases above the supply rate.

Much of the eroded sediment is composed of aggregates. The large aggregates arc deposited much like noncohesive sediment. Immediately after deposition, they are highly erodible much like sands. Over time, however, natural processes bond the aggregates together as infiltration carries fines and other cementing agents into the matrix of these particles. Traffic and tillage may consolidate or break up the soil mass producing more intermixed fines which hastens the consolidation process. Consequently, over a time period that may be short if tillage or traffic occurs, the stored sediment essentially becomes part of the original soil mass, requiring the same forces to re-detach the sediment once again.

Fines (clays) seem to attach themselves immediately to the soil mass as they are deposited and thus are much less erodible than the aggregates. (Partheniades, 1972).

When overland flow is depositing sediment, it deposits the sediment over a fairly wide area. Overland flow over deposited sediment is probably more like broad shallow flow than at any other location in the watershed. However, if the flow is detaching sediment, it tends to concentrate in incised channels and cover only a portion of the total width, perhaps as little as 20%. The previously deposited sediment in between the rills is effectively unavailable for subsequent erosion by flow. Also, since the soil layer under the deposited sediment is probably much less erodible, the influence of the nonerodible layer decreases erosion rates. A typical situation is at the toe of a concave slope where flow has deposited sediment over a broad area during the seedbed period. After cover develops, sediment supply may be reduced much more than runoff. Thus while potential for erosion of the previously deposited sediment may exist, actual erosion rates will be reduced because the flow concentrates in rills. In effect much of the previously deposited sediment is unavailable for erosion.

Before runoff begins, raindrops detach sediment. Generally, this sediment fills the depressions. Even after runoff begins, the transport capacity through depressions can be very low if the depressions are deep and considerable deposition will continue. As this storage fills, flow moves more sediment through the depressions.

The practical significance of this concept relates to fall plowing. Farmers in many areas in the midwest use primary tillage in the fall, which gives large depressional storage. Sediment yield from these fields is low from the first few storms after tillage because of local deposition in the depressions. As the depressions fill with sediment, however, sediment yield increases because transport capacity of the flow through the depressions increases as deposition reduces the depth of flow in the depressions.

The previously deposited sediment is not available for transport even though it may be highly erodible. The ridges of soil around the depressions act as grade control structures. Erosion is controlled by the rate of downward erosion of these ridges. Previously deposited material is effectively removed at a rate no faster than the rate that the original soil erodes.

Only a fraction of all the depressions will be directly connected by rills. Unless a rill cuts through a depression, most of the stored sediment in the depressions will not be eroded because interrill flow does not have the capacity to erode them. Therefore, a large portion of the previously stored sediment in the depressions is generally unavailable for transport. However, on a smooth surface with no depressional storage, if raindrop impact detaches more sediment than flow at the time can transport, the excess is available for transport when sufficient transport capacity develops.

The accounting of previously stored sediment and its subsequent erosion on regularly tilled agricultural land can usually be neglected.

Supporting Practices

Supporting practices like tillage across slope (contouring), stripcropping, and terraces supplement cropping-management practices to control erosion. These are treated in the USLE with the P factor. Generally, the practices control erosion by reducing rill erosion, transport capacity of runoff, or both. In previous sections, parameter values have been adapted from the USLE, but here the USLE P factor is not adapted for all supporting practices because of its inconsistency with basic erosion modeling concepts. Use of the P factor on a single storm basis can cause large errors; it is useful only under certain circumstances.

Conventional terraces behave as channels. Newer terrace systems, like parallel tile outlet terraces, behave as both channels and impoundments. Stripcropping, including the use of buffer strips along streams, use thick vegetation to slow the runoff and induce deposition. Although contouring is the most difficult of the P factor effects to decribe, the USLE P factor values for contouring can be used in modeling if used with care.

1. Contouring

Contouring consists of tillage marks and ridges on the contour. It reduces the effective slope gradient, which reduces the flow's detachment capacity and transport capacity. In fact, transport capacity may be reduced below sediment delivery rate from interrill (row sideslopes) areas. Deposition then occurs, which eliminates rill erosion. This can be modeled by using the effective slope along the contour to describe erosion and transport by rill flow.

Contouring stores more excess rainfall than does tillage up and down hill. Excess rainfall collects at low points since tillage marks are seldom exactly on the contour. When storage becomes filled, the ridges overtop. Storage depends on the height of the ridges and the profile shape along the tillage mark as the mark approaches low points. If excess rainfall is less than the available storage, little or no runoff occurs, and thus little or no erosion occurs.

When the ridges overtop, they erode rapidly much like breeched dam embankments. The overtopping cascades downslope with each overtop unleashing a flush of water. During the storm that causes overtopping, the ridges are assumed to erode down to the bottom of the furrows within minutes of the overtop. Subsequent erosion is assumed to occur at normal rill erosion rates, or it can be analyzed using the concentrated flow erosion relationships given in the section on Concentrated Flow.

Whether or not deposition occurs in the row middles depends on the row gradient, runoff rate, cover, and interrill erosion rate. Although deposition may occur at the upper end of a row middle, as the middle steepens and as flow accumulates, rill erosion may occur in the middle before the flow reaches the low point.

A field with rows on any degree of contouring can be analyzed with these concepts. However, definition of the flow patterns and their complexity may make the method impractical. The USLE P factor values may be used with caution giving attention to when breakover occurs and its effect on subsequent storms.

2. Stripcropping and Buffer Strips

Stripcropping is an effective erosion control practice in two ways: (1) erosion is minimal on the areas having the close growing crop like grass, and (2) the close growing crop induces deposition as flow from the row crop area enters the vegetation. Buffer strips along streams do not significantly reduce total erosion if their area is small relative to the total area. Their effectiveness is due to deposition. Only the deposition characteristics of grass or mulch strips will be examined.

Strips of grass and mulch of cornstalks, straw, crushed stone, etc. cause deposition by reducing transport capacity of the flow below usual sediment loads. The process is illustrated in Fig. 8.8. The following sections in a strip can be identified based on studies by Barfield et al. (1977). Section A-B is a ponded flow area caused by the large

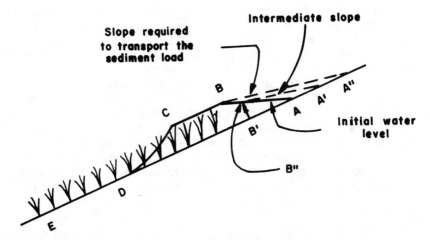

FIG. 8.8 Deposition zones in a grass or mulch strip. See text for definition of symbols.

hydraulic resistance of the grass relative to the small hydraulic resistance on the upslope bare area. Coarse sediment readily deposits in the pond, which may account for much of the effectiveness of the strip for removing sediment.

Once the pond fills, the entire sediment load is carried into the grass. The final slope A″-B will be the steepness required to transport the incoming load.

As the sediment moves into the grass, a deposition face C-D develops which moves downslope as deposited sediment accumulates. If the process continues, the entire grass width will become filled with sediment like section B-C. The slope of B-C is the same as the land slope. The amount of grass exposed will be just that to give a transport capacity equal to the entire sediment load. Deposition does not occur on section B-C at this stage.

The deposition face section C-D is linear for coarse noncohesive sediment (Barfield et al., 1977). By point D, deposition of coarse material has essentially ceased. If a significant fraction of the sediment load is suspended, deposition may occur beyond D, decreasing exponentially with distance. For the strip to be most effective, it must be as a minimum as long as B-D. If a large quantity of the sediment load is suspended, the strip may need to extend far beyond D for the sediment load to decay below the desired level. Where grass is sparse, the baseline transport capacity through the grass may be greater than the desired sediment yield. If so, even an infinitely wide strip will not reduce the sediment load to the desired level.

Three approaches are given for estimating the amount of sediment passing through a filter strip of grass or mulch assuming steady runoff and sediment inflow.

The first approach is to neglect the "pond" (A-B) and to assume that deposition begins at the upper edge of the strip. First, the likely maximum depth of deposition (H) in the strip should be estimated. This depth of deposition will just leave sufficient grass exposed so that transport capacity on B-C at the land slope will just balance the incoming sediment load. An approximate estimate is the top of mulch or grass with due accounting for any flattening of the grass by flow.

Next, divide the strip width into segments so that the change in transport capacity with distance dT_c/dx can be assumed constant over each segment. Estimates of deposition rate and sediment load for each segment can be estimated by applying equation [8.6] through [8.12] sequentially downslope and treating the flow as quasi-steady.

At the upper edge of the strip, the flow is assumed to abruptly lose transport capacity. Within the strip, transport capacity may increase if infiltration is not so high as to cause a decrease in discharge like an undisturbed forest floor does downslope from a disturbed area. Assuming that transport capacity increases within the strip, a point is reached where deposition ends, and erosion occurs downslope. The point that deposition ends is given by equation [8.13]. Since the increased flow depth in the grass is likely to eliminate interrill detachment, D_i can be set to zero in equation [8.13].

If transport capacity T_c is assumed constant over the strip, the equations reduce to:

$$q_{so} = T_c - (T_c - q_{sin}) \exp[-\alpha \, L_w] \quad \dots\dots\dots\dots\dots\dots\dots\dots \quad [8.70]$$

where q_{so} = sediment outflow rate (mass per unit width per unit time), q_{sin} = sediment inflow (mass per unit width per unit time), α = first order reaction coefficient for deposition, and L_w = width of the strip.

The depth of deposition, Y_d, at each point along the strip can be calculated from:

$$Y_d = (1/\rho_{ds}) \int D_r dt \dots \dots \dots \dots \dots \dots \dots \quad [8.71]$$

where ρ_{ds} = the effective mass density of the deposited sediment taking into account the displacement of the grass or mulch, D_r = deposition rate from equation [8.6], and t = time. Once T_d reaches the maximum possible depth of deposition, H, the segment length is shortened accordingly. A refined analysis would consider the effect of Y_d on T_c. Transport capacity increases as depth of deposition approaches its maximum depth.

The second approach includes an analysis of the pond. As before, the maximum possible depth of deposition is determined. This establishes the depth of the pond at the grass. Assume that the pond is level and that the transport capacity in the pond is zero.

Deposition occurs in the pond and extends upslope from the pond as a concave slope that soon becomes almost linear (Foster and Huggins, 1977). A uniform slope is assumed equal to the slope required to transport the incoming sediment load.

This slope can be estimated given the discharge, sediment inflow rate, and the particle size and density. Assuming that $T_c = 0$ in the pond, at time zero, the amount of sediment leaving the pond is:

$$q_{so} = q_{sin} \exp(-\alpha L_p) \dots \dots \dots \dots \dots \dots \dots \quad [8.72]$$

where q_{sin} = inflow sediment rate, q_{so} = outflow rate, and L_p = length of the pond (initially A-B, but decreases to B-B'). The volume of sediment V_{dp} deposited in the pond over a time interval Δt is:

$$V_{dp} = \Delta t (q_{sin} - q_{so})/\rho_{sp} \dots \dots \dots \dots \dots \dots \dots \quad [8.73]$$

where ρ_{sp} = mass density of sediment deposited in the pond. The area A'-B'-B'' contains this volume of deposited sediment. Line A'-B'' is the slope required to transport the incoming sediment and B'' is located on the initial watersurface. Deposition in the grass is analyzed as before using q_{so} as q_{sin} in equation [8.70].

For the next time step, equations [8.72] and [8.73] are repeated with L_p having been shortened from B-B to B-B'.

The third approach is abstracted from Barfield et al. (1977) and Hayes and Barfield (1977).

The deposition face C-D in Fig. 8.8 is assumed to be uniform. Sediment load at point D is assumed to be equal to the transport capacity. Sediment transport capacity at D is given by:

$$\Psi = 1.08 \, \phi^{-0.28} \dots \dots \dots \dots \dots \dots \dots \quad [8.74]$$

where:

$$\Psi = [(\rho_s - \rho)/\rho](d/s \, R_s) \dots \dots \dots \dots \dots \dots \dots \quad [8.75]$$

$$\phi = q_{sd}/\rho_s \left\{ [(\rho_s - \rho)/\rho] g d^3 \right\}^{1/2} \dots \dots \dots \dots \dots \dots \quad [8.76]$$

where q_{sd} = sediment load at D, ρ_s and ρ = mass density of the sediment and water respectively, g = acceleration due to gravity, d_p = particle diameter, s = slope of bed, and R_s = a spacing hydraulic radius defined by:

$$R_s = S_s \, y_f/(2y_f + S_s) \dots \dots \dots \dots \dots \dots \dots \dots \dots \dots \quad [8.77]$$

where S_s = spacing of media elements and y_f = flow depth. Equations [8.74] through [8.76] are a modified Einstein sediment transport equation. Flow depth d_f can be estimated from the Manning equation with n = 0.0072.

$$q = (1/n) \, R_s^{2/3} \, s^{1/2} \, d_f \dots \dots \dots \dots \dots \dots \dots \dots \dots \dots \dots \quad [8.78]$$

where q = discharge rate. Equations [8.72] and [8.73] can be used to estimate q_{sc}, the sediment load at C. Although Hayes and Barfield (1977) give equations for the time before the deposition builds to H, the depth of deposition is assumed to be at its maximum depth H at point B initially.

The fraction of the sediment load trapped on the face C-D is:

$$f_d = (q_{sc} - q_{sd})/q_{sc} \dots \dots \dots \dots \dots \dots \dots \dots \dots \dots \dots \quad [8.79]$$

and the sediment load at the midpoint on the face is:

$$q_{sm} = (q_{sc} + q_{sd})/2 \dots \dots \dots \dots \dots \dots \dots \dots \dots \dots \dots \quad [8.80]$$

Given q_{sm}, q, and equations [8.74] through [8.78], the slope of the face C-D can be calculated. The new location of C after Δt is:

$$x_{cn} = x_{co} + \Delta t \, (f_d \, q_{sc}/H \, \rho_{sg}) \dots \dots \dots \dots \dots \dots \dots \dots \quad [8.81]$$

where x_{cn} and x_{co} = the new and old positions of C, respectively, and ρ_{sg} = the mass density of the deposited sediment accounting for the displacement of the media.

Hayes and Barfield (1977) reported that deposition from point D can be described by:

$$(q_{sd} - q_{se})/q_{sd} = \exp[-1.05 \times 10^{-3} \, (vR_s/\nu)^{0.82} \, (L_{DE} \, v/V_s y_f)^{-0.91}]$$

$$\dots \dots \dots \dots \dots \dots \dots \dots \dots \dots \dots \dots \dots \dots \dots \dots \dots \dots \quad [8.82]$$

where q_{sd} = sediment discharge at point D, q_{se} = sediment discharge rate at E, v = flow velocity, ν = viscosity of the water-sediment mixture, L_{DE} = the distance between points D and E in Fig. 8.8, and V_s = particle fall velocity. The length L_{DE} decreases as point C moves downslope.

Equation [8.82] gives a sediment yield that approaches zero as D-E $\rightarrow \infty$. Equation [8.70] assumes that there is a transport capacity below which the sediment load will not decrease even for $L_{DE} \rightarrow \infty$. However, for very thick media, T_c can be zero, in which case sediment yield approaches zero for $L_{DE} \rightarrow \infty$.

None of the approaches to deposition in mulch or grass strips have been checked against actual field data. However, these fundamental relationships can serve as the basic component in a model for evaluating these processes.

CHANNEL PROCESSES

Distinguishing between channels and rills is difficult. By definition, rills become gullies or channels when they can not be obliterated by normal tillage (Hutchinson et al., 1976). The smallest gully today is by definition larger than the smallest gully in the 1930's simply because modern farm equipment can farm over larger rills. By another definition, a rill becomes a gully when it exceeds a certain depth. While such definitions may be quite satisfactory for erosion surveys, they are unworkable for erosion modeling. The definition must be related to the processes.

Most erosion models have sufficient degrees of freedom that channel and rill erosion can be lumped together. However, lumping distorts model parameter values (Lane et al., 1975) requiring more model calibration resulting in less transferability of parameter values from gaged to ungaged areas. Since an objective of this chapter is to minimize calibration, a special attempt should be made to separately identify and analyze channels and their processes.

Rather than attempt a rigorous definition of a channel, examples of channels will be given and discussed. While such an ambiguous definition is undesirable, a more rigorous one is not obvious.

Concentrated Flow

If overland flow is eroding the soil, it is concentrated in many small definable channels. However, topography of most farm fields further converges overland flow into a few major flow concentrations before the overland flow leaves the field. If these concentrated flow areas erode, a grass waterway may be installed to control the erosion problem.

Erosion in these areas when unprotected is most obvious in the spring when a large storm occurs on a freshly prepared seedbed. These concentrated flow areas will erode down to a less erodible layer which may be the depth of tillage by a secondary tillage tool like a disk. Once the bottom of the channel strikes the nonerodible layer, erosion rate decreases and the channel widens.

The following equations for erosion in nonvegetated channels developed by Lane and Foster (1980) describe the effect of a nonerodible layer on rill and concentrated flow erosion.

Shear stress distribution around a channel varies depending on channel shape and aspect ratio of width to depth (Graf, 1971).

Given a particular shear stress distribution around the channel, a critical shear stress, discharge, slope, and roughness, a channel will erode to a particular equilibrium shape if the nonerodible layer is deep enough. Although the shear stress distribution in an actual channel can be quite irregular (Foster, 1975), the shear stress distribution given by equations [8.83] and [8.84] was fitted to observed shear distributions in smooth channels (Graf, 1971).

$$(\tau/\overline{\tau}) = \exp[0.127 - 0.516 \ \mathrm{Ln} \ x_* - 0.408 \ (\mathrm{Ln} \ x_*)^2 - 0.0344 \ (\mathrm{Ln} \ x_*)^3]$$

$$x_* \geqslant 0.02 \ \dots\dots\dots\dots\dots\dots\dots\dots\dots\dots\dots\dots\dots\dots \ [8.83]$$

and

$$(\tau/\overline{\tau}) = 0.13 \cdot x_* / 0.02 \ x_* < 0.02 \quad \dots\dots\dots\dots\dots\dots\dots \quad [8.84]$$

where τ = shear stress at x_*, $\overline{\tau}$ = average shear stress for the cross-section, and x_* = distance from water surface along wetted perimeter to point of interest divided by wetted perimeter, WP. The curve has the properties of: area under the curve equals 0.5 for $0 \leqslant x_* \leqslant 0.5$, slope at $x_* = 0.5$ is 0.0, and the maximum $\tau/\overline{\tau}$ is 1.35. Equations [8.83] and [8.84] were validated by fitting them and the following erosion rate equations to data from 16 rills at eight discharge rates (two reps) and using the erosion rates at the beginning and end of the 40 min tests at continuous, steady flow (Lane and Foster, 1980). The fit is shown in Fig. 8.9.

A channel is assumed to reach an equilibrium shape if allowed to erode over a long period with steady flow and with no restricting subsurface layer. The important geometric properties of the equilibrium eroded channel were calculated and plotted in Fig. 8.10.

In application, the channel is assumed to be rectangular until it reaches the nonerodible layer with a width obtained from Fig. 8.10. The solution requires finding a value for x_c, the x_* where $\tau = \tau_{cr}$. Given the discharge Q, Manning's n, weight density of water γ, critical shear stress of the soil τ_{cr}, and slope s, a value $g(x_c)$ is calculated from:

$$g(x_c) = [Q \ n/s^{\frac{1}{2}}]^{3/8} \ \gamma \ s/\tau_{cr} \quad \dots\dots\dots\dots\dots\dots\dots\dots \quad [8.85]$$

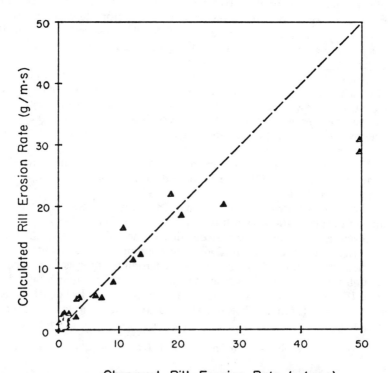

Observed   Rill   Erosion   Rate   (g/m·s)

FIG. 8.9 A comparison of calculated rill erosion rates vs. observed rates.

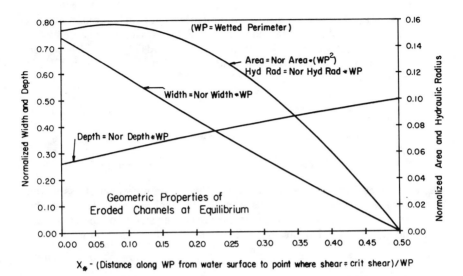

FIG. 8.10 Geometric properties of an eroding channel at equilibrium.

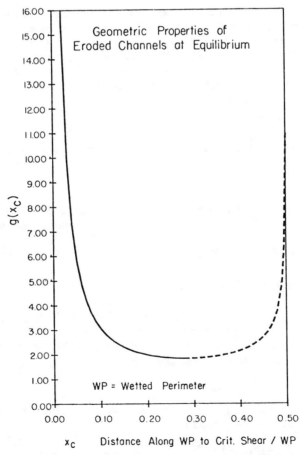

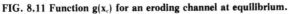

FIG. 8.11 Function $g(x_c)$ for an eroding channel at equilibrium.

The function $g(x_c)$ is entirely a function of geometry of the channel. Given a value $g(x_c)$, a value of x_c is obtained from Fig. 8.11. Having x_c, a value for R_* = hydraulic radius divided by wetted perimeter and W_* = width/wetted perimeter is read from Fig. 8.10. The width of the equilibrium channel W_{eq} is then calculated from:

$$W_{eq} = (Q \, n/s^{1/2})^{3/8} \, W_*/R_*^{5/8} \quad \dotfill \quad [8.86]$$

The channel is assumed to move downward at the rate d_{ch}:

$$d_{ch} = e_m/\rho_{soil} = K_{ch}(1.35\,\bar{\tau} - \tau_{cr})^{1.05}/\rho_{soil} \quad \dotfill \quad [8.87]$$

where e_m = erosion rate calculated using the maximum shear stress at the middle of the channel, K_{ch} = soil erodibility for channel erosion, ρ_{soil} = the mass density of the soil in place, $\bar{\tau}$ = average shear stress for the cross section, and τ_{cr} = critical shear stress. The erosion rate in the channel is:

$$E_{ch} = W_{eq} \, K_{ch} \, (1.35\bar{\tau} - \tau_{cr})^{1.05} \quad \dotfill \quad [8.88]$$

where E_{ch} is the soil loss per unit channel length (mass per unit time per unit length).

Once the channel hits a nonerodible boundary below the surface, erosion rate decreases with time as the channel widens even with a constant discharge. The rate that the channel widens is equal to the rate that the channel perimeter erodes at the nonerodible layer. Let x_b be the distance from the water surface to the nonerodible layer divided by the wetted perimeter. Shear stress τ_b at x_b can be calculated from equations [8.83] and [8.84]. The rate that the channel widens is:

$$d \, W_{ch}/dt = 2 \, K_{ch} \, (\tau_b - \tau_{cr})^{1.05}/\rho_{soil} \quad \dotfill \quad [8.89]$$

which, multiplied by the depth to the nonerodible layer, d_{ne}, gives an erosion rate of:

$$E_{ch} = 2 \, K_{ch} \, (\tau_b - \tau_{cr})^{1.05} \, d_{ne} \quad \dotfill \quad [8.90]$$

As the channel widens, the erosion rate decreases. Erosion rates were computed for several values of Q, n, s, and τ_{cr} and nondimensionalized as:

$$W_* = (W - W_{in})/(W_f - W_{in}) \quad \dotfill \quad [8.91]$$

$$t_* = [t \, (dW/dt)_{in}/(W_f - W_{in})] \quad \dotfill \quad [8.92]$$

where $(dW/dt)_{in}$ is the rate that the channel widens at the beginning of the time period, W = width of the channel at time t, W_{in} = the initial width of the channel, W_f = the final width of the channel, and W_* and t_* = respectively normalized width and time. The curve:

$$dW_*/dt_* = \exp(-1.04 \, t_*) \quad \dotfill \quad [8.93]$$

fits the data reasonably well as shown in Fig. 8.12. The nondimensional width is the integral of equation [8.93] as:

$$W_* = [1 - \exp(-1.04 \, t_*)]/1.04 \quad \dotfill \quad [8.94]$$

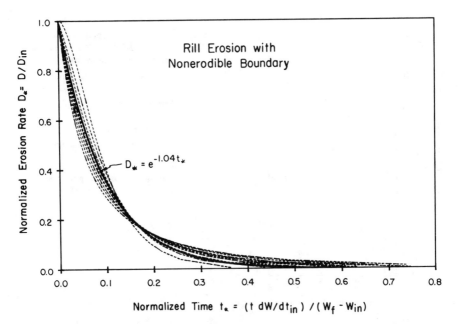

FIG. 8.12 Normalized rill erosion rates after the bottom of the rill reaches a nonerodible layer.

Theoretically, the coefficient 1.04 should be 1.00 if $W_*= 1$ for $t_* \to \infty$ which it should according to the definition of W_*. The soil volume $[W-W_{in}] \cdot d_{ne}$ is the amount eroded over time t.

The final width W_f is the width that gives $\tau = \tau_{cr}$ at x_b. This x_b is defined as x_{cf} which can be found by solving:

$$(Qn/s^{1/2})^{3/8} \, (\gamma s/\tau_{cr}) = 1/ \left\{ [x_{cf}(1-2x_{cf})]^{3/8} \, f(x_{cf}) \right\} \quad \cdots\cdots\cdots [8.95]$$

where $f(x_{cf})$ is the shear stress distribution function (i.e., equations [8.83] and [8.84]) evaluated at x_{cf}. The final width is calculated from:

$$W_f = [(Qn/s^{1/2}) \, (1 - 2x_{cf})/x_{cf}^{5/3}]^{3/8} \quad \cdots\cdots\cdots\cdots\cdots\cdots [8.96]$$

Erosion in a channel with a nonerodible boundary depends on previous erosion even for steady flow, as assumed in this analysis. If a flow larger than the one that forms a channel is put in the previously formed channel, erosion rates will be large until the channel readjusts itself. Conversely, if flow is less than the forming flow, erosion will be reduced.

Critical shear stress in a function of soil properties, disturbances by tillage, compaction, moisture at tillage and compaction, and aging. Even though much information exists on critical shear stress (Graf, 1971), much of it is conradictory. Smerdon and Beasley (1959) related τ_{cr} to dispersion ratio as:

$$\tau_{cr} = 10.2/d_r^{0.63} \quad \cdots\cdots\cdots\cdots\cdots\cdots\cdots\cdots\cdots\cdots\cdots\cdots\cdots\cdots [8.97]$$

where dispersion ratio d_r is expressed as a percentage and τ_{cr} as N/m^2. This equation seems to give reasonable results for rill erosion in freshly tilled agricultural soils prepared for a seedbed (Foster and Meyer, 1975). Values

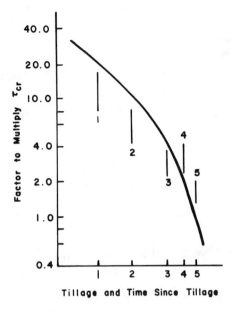

FIG. 8.13 Effect of tillage on critical shear stress.

for dispersion ratio ranged from 5 to 24 for the 55 Indiana soils that Wischmeier et al. (1971) used to develop their soil erodibility nomograph. Most values were about 15.

Critical shear stress increases with compaction and with aging. Experimental observations clearly show that a soil is much more susceptible to erosion by flow just after tillage than after an undisturbed period. One can estimate critical shear stress by equation [8.97] and assume that the value applies to a typical freshly prepared seedbed. Fig. 8.13 may be used to adjust τ_{cr} depending on the type of disturbance and length of time since the disturbance.

While much information is available on critical shear stress (Graf, 1971), almost none exists on channel erosion rate. The functional form of equation [8.39] should apply to many soils. However, channel erosion rate, especially for consolidated soils, may not be related to flow hydraulics but is more related to the rate that the soil releases particles (Alberts et al., 1980). Factors such as moisture content at which the soil was compacted are important (Grissenger, 1966).

Soil cover like plant residue from a conservation tillage system reduces the shear stress acting on the soil. If a stable mulch cover is present, the shear stress acting on the soil is computed like it is for rill erosion. However, if shear stress acting on the mulch exceeds a critical value, the residue moves by floating off enmasse. At lower residue rates, the residue may float away piece by piece. If the mulch fails, then erosion of the channel flow for corn stalks and straw lying on the soil surface in a channel are given in Table 8.17.

If the tillage system leaves large, stable clods, they might be considered as soil cover. The shear stress acting on the soil is reduced accordingly.

Soil cover like grass in a grass waterway or even mulch may reduce the shear stress acting on the soil and effectively reduce sediment transport

TABLE 8.17. CRITICAL SHEAR STRESS FOR MULCH
MOVEMENT BY CHANNEL FLOW. SHEAR STRESS IS
THAT ACTING ONLY ON MULCH, NOT TOTAL
SHEAR STRESS

Mulch type and rate	Critical shear stress (acting on mulch)	Total Manning's n (soil & mulch)
	N/m^2	
Corn*		
Bare	—	0.030
0.25 kg/m^2	2.0-3.0†	0.050
0.50 kg/m^2	5.0	0.075
1.00 kg/m^2	11.0	0.140
Straw*		
Bare	—	0.03
0.12 kg/m^2	0.6†	0.03
0.25 kg/m^2	3.0	0.05
0.50 kg/m^2	14.0	0.15

*Corn stalks were on plots in corn fields that had not been
disturbed since the previous year's crop. Rows were up
and down hill. The row ridges concentrated the flow.
Straw mulch was placed on a soil that had been recently
tilled with a rototiller.
†Failure of heavier rate was generally by enmasse movement. The 0.25 corn and 0.12 kg/m^2 straw rates failed
gradually with mulch being carried away piece by piece
rather than enmasse. Failure could not be precisely defined.

capacity to the point that deposition occurs. The transport capacity in the
concentrations may be computed using the transport equations discussed
earlier.

Field borders along roads and ditches often result in a depressed
area about 3 to 5 m out into the field. Flow will move down the slope
as overland flow, collect in concentrated flow along the field border,
and move parallel to the border to a field outlet. The potential for
erosion and deposition must be calculated for these areas. Deposition
is common.

Ridges and heavy vegetation around the edges of many fields pond the
runoff and create backwater. The reduced flow velocity will often induce considerable deposition. This can remove most of the coarse sediment and some of the fines, depending on the length of the backwater
and the flow gradient in the backwater.

Gullies

Gullies are usually more incised channels than the ones discussed
above. Usually the gully bottom is below any tillage layer. Gullies
are frequently formed by the upslope advance of a headcut with subsequent widening by sidewall sloughing (Piest et al., 1975).

Gully erosion is complex and is seldom included in erosion models.
Some of the major processes are discussed below (Piest et al., 1975),
but the modeler should consult geomorphology texts and *Sedimentation
Engineering* (ASCE, 1975) for a more thorough discussion of gully
processes and techniques for estimating gully erosion.

Gully erosion in general is unsteady and occurs in pulses even during a steady inflow. The most steady part is probably the intense erosion that occurs at headcuts as they advance upslope. Flow in the gully may erode the channel boundary and produces some erosion, but in many cases this may not be major. If this erosion occurs, it may undercut the side walls of the gully, and when the weight of the overhang exceeds the soil's strength, the overhang sloughs off into the flow. Sediment yield increases while the flow 'cleans out' the sloughed material. In some situations, the banks of the gully experience slope stability type failures. Consequently, factors like internal moisture flow in the banks, overburden loads, and soil strength are important. When these slope stability type failures occur, material sloughs into the flow and is 'cleaned out' if the flow has adequate transport capacity. Just after a failure, sediment yield can greatly increase. If flow is too small to remove the sloughed material, the sloughed material stabilizes the bank against further slope failures.

Consequently, the main gully erosion processes to model are advance of the headcut; sloughing of the side walls from undercutting, slope stability type failures, or both; and cleanout of sloughed material.

Terrace Channels

Terraces reduce sediment yield by: (1) reducing the slope length of overland flow thereby reducing the quantity of sediment produced on the overland flow areas and (2) if the grade is flat enough, inducing deposition in the terrace channel. The amount of deposition depends on the slope of the channel, flow rate in the channel, roughness of the channel, and sediment inflow rate. If the channel is too steep, it will erode instead of inducing deposition.

Detachment and transport capacity in a terrace channel are calculated using previously described relationships. The major problem with terraces is determination of the slope of the energy gradeline, especially in very flat or level terraces. Flow in a terrace is spatially varied for steady flow; and for unsteady conditions, the kinematic assumptions are often invalid. Three possible controls exist: (1) Flow depth in the outlet channel (this is unlikely if the outlet channel is properly designed); (2) critical depth at the terrace outlet which is likely if the outlet channel has no cover to restrict the flow leaving the terrace channel; or (3) the depth required to discharge the water through grass or other cover at the channel outlet. The modeler should refer to hydraulic texts for information on modeling terrace hydraulics.

Deposition in terraces usually occurs at the water's edge in the terrace channel where flow and sediment enter laterally. The lateral inflow requires a change in momentum. Also, flow is shallow and shear stress is small at the water's edge. The sediment is effectively being added in a narrow section giving a very great sediment load per unit width in that section of the terrace channel. Deposition occurs in this local area even though flow could transport the incoming sediment load if it were distributed evenly across the channel. The same effect occurs where sediment moves down row side slopes into flow in the row middles and in other shallow channels receiving lateral inflow.

A consequence is that usual application of sediment transport equations may underestimate deposition. However, no information is available for a suitable adjustment to the equations.

Defined Stream Channels

Defined stream channels are channels where intermittent or continuous streamflow occurs. Stream channels are either sources or sinks of sediment; the difference depends primarily on upland inputs. If the sediment load from the uplands exceeds the transport capacity in the stream, deposition occurs and the stream is a sink. If at a later date, the incoming sediment load is reduced below the flow's transport capacity, the stream may become a source with erosion of the previously deposited sediment. If no sediment was previously deposited, the channel boundaries will erode unless they are protected by an armor layer, vegetation, or a nonerodible soil. Sediment yield from a channel may continue at large rates for several years due to erosion of previously deposited sediment even after a cutoff of incoming sediment from the upland areas (Trimble, 1975).

Channels in many agricultural watersheds have three major flow areas: (1) main channel, (2) banks, and (3) overbank. The main channel may or may not have vegetation and the boundary may or may not be noncohesive. Coarse particles tend to be transported in the main channel. The banks are usually of cohesive soil and may be covered with vegetation. Vegetation on the banks can trap fines. The overbank flow tends to be shallow and to deposit fines (ASCE, 1975).

Flow in channels is often nonuniform due to curves and variable local channel gradients. For example, shear stress on the outside of bends is high and may cause local erosion.

Considerable information is available in the literature that allows an estimate of whether or not erosion occurs in a cohesive channel but little information is available on rate of erosion (Graf, 1971). The basic concepts discussed for concentrated flow might be applied for small channels until better information is available.

Aggradation and degradation models are available for noncohesive channels that armor (Thomas, 1976; Chang and Hill, 1976; Hales et al., 1970). The basic concept of these models is that sediment load equals transport capacity, and erosion unless, limited by armoring or deposition, occurs at the rate required to keep the transport capacity filled.

Basic relationships and techniques for modeling stream channels are described in sediment transport texts (Graf, 1971; ASCE, 1975) and by the models of Li (1977), Chang and Hill (1976), and Thomas (1976).

Continuity

The continuity equation for sediment transport in channels is:

$$\partial Q_s/\partial x + \rho_s \, \partial(cA)/\partial t = D_{ch} + D_L \quad \dotfill \quad [8.98]$$

where Q_s = sediment load (mass per unit time), $\partial Q_s/\partial x$ = channel erosion (or deposition) rate per unit channel length x (mass per unit time per unit channel length), $\rho_s \, \partial(cA)/\partial t$ is the storage rate of sediment in flow, ρ_s = mass density of the sediment particles, t = time, c = sediment concentration by volume, A = flow cross sectional flow area, D_{ch} = erosion rate or deposition rate from the channel boundary per unit channel length (mass per unit time per unit channel length), and D_L = lateral inflow rate of sediment per unit length of channel (mass per unit time per unit channel length).

The modeler has the same option as with upland erosion of using the interrelation between channel erosion rate and sediment load, equation [8.3], or ignoring it. The first order reaction coefficient, α, for channel flow is (Einstein, 1968):

$$\alpha = V_s/q \dots\dots\dots\dots\dots\dots\dots\dots\dots\dots\dots\dots\dots\dots\dots\dots \quad [8.99]$$

where V_s = fall velocity of the sediment particle and q = discharge per unit width. Equation [8.3] can be ignored with bedload transport but may be significant for the transport and deposition of fine particles.

The logic used for the overland flow areas is used for the channels to account for particle mixtures and to prevent simultaneous erosion and deposition. Equation [8.98] is solved using the same finite difference scheme and algorithms used to solve equation [8.1], the continuity equation for overland flow. A hydrology and hydraulics model provides the necessary inputs for the erosion and sediment transport computation. Degradation or aggradation of the channel changes its slope and thus flow hydraulics requiring updating during the simulation. Given an erosion or deposition rate D_{ch} (mass per unit area per unit time), the change in elevation ΔE over a time step Δt is:

$$\Delta E = D_{ch}\, \Delta t/\rho_{sd} \dots\dots\dots\dots\dots\dots\dots\dots\dots\dots\dots\dots\dots\dots \quad [8.100]$$

where ρ_{sd} = the density of the soil mass as it is either eroded or deposited. Numerical analysis texts and description of other models extensively discuss methods to solve the equations.

IMPOUNDMENT PROCESSES

Impoundments such as tile outlet terraces and sediment basins control sediment yield by inducing deposition in the impoundments. These structures usually have withdrawal pipes that drain the ponds at a controlled rate. Deposition is a function of the opportunity for settling of the particles. Curtis and McCuen (1977), Laflen et al. (1978), and Ward et al. (1977) have modeled this process with settling tank theory.

Laflen et al. (1978) developed a relative simple model for deposition in an impoundment terrace. They assumed that initially the mixture of water and sediment is homogeneous in the impoundment, i.e., storm runoff instantaneously fills the impoundment and is uniformly mixed. No mixing is assumed after the initial filling. Sediment of a given size moves downward as plug flow which leaves a clear water layer at the top of the impoundment.

Water is assumed to exit from the bottom of the impoundment. The proportion, T_d, of the initial amount of a given sediment type that is discharged is:

$$T_d = V_d/V_b \dots\dots\dots\dots\dots\dots\dots\dots\dots\dots\dots\dots\dots\dots\dots\dots \quad [8.101]$$

where V_d = the volume of water discharged while the sediment is in suspension and V_b = the initial volume of water at t = 0. The volume discharged is:

$$V_d = \int_0^{t_{dt}} Q \, dt \qquad \ldots\ldots\ldots\ldots\ldots\ldots\ldots\ldots\ldots\ldots\ldots\ldots\ldots\ldots \quad [8.102]$$

where Q = discharge rate from the impoundment and t_{dt} = the time required for the volume containing sediment of size d and its associated density to reach zero.

Particles are lost from the impoundment volume in three ways: (1) out the discharge pipe, (2) to the bottom of the impoundment by infiltration, and (3) to the bottom of the impoundment by settling. At a given time and for a given particle, assume that the depth from the bottom of the basin to the clear water is D_d and that the surface area at D_d is A_d. The flux m_d that particles are lost at this time is:

$$m_d = c_d Q + c_d I A_d + c_d V_{sd} A_d \qquad \ldots\ldots\ldots\ldots\ldots\ldots\ldots\ldots \quad [8.103]$$

where m_d = mass rate that the given particle type is lost from the impoundment either by outflow or reaching the impoundment bottom, c_d = concentration of the given particle type (mass sediment/volume water), I = infiltration rate, and V_{sd} = fall velocity of the given particle type. The initial total mass of particle type d in an elemental volume is $c_d A_d \cdot dD_d$ where dD_d is the elemental depth. The time required for the elemental volume to become clear is $m_d \cdot dt_{pf} = c_d A_d \cdot dD_d$ is:

$$t_{df} = \int_0^{D_o} [A_d/(Q + I A_d + V_{sd} A_d)] \, dD_d \qquad \ldots\ldots\ldots\ldots\ldots \quad [8.104]$$

where D_o = the initial depth. The proportion D_R that is discharged of the total initial amount of sediment is given by:

$$D_R = \int_0^{\infty} T_d \, h(d) \, dd \qquad \ldots\ldots\ldots\ldots\ldots\ldots\ldots\ldots\ldots\ldots\ldots \quad [8.105]$$

where $h(d)$ = the frequency distribution of the sediment initially in suspension and d = the particle sedimentation diameter.

Generally, the functions for Q and A_d are too complex to solve analytically. Hence, the equations are solved numerically. Computed results compared reasonably well with experimental observations from impoundment terrace systems in Iowa (Laflen et al., 1972; Laflen et al., 1978).

In a similar but more detailed analysis, Ward et al., (1977) developed a model to describe sedimentation in sediment basins. They routed the inflow hydrograph through the basin by dividing the flow into plugs and assuming no mixing between plugs, i.e., first in-first out. They then divided each plug into four layers in the basin and, using settling theory, they described the transfer of particles from one layer to the next accounting for traping on the impoundment sides and selected withdrawal from various layer within the basin.

Curtis and McCuen (1977) used settling tank theory by Camp (1945) to describe deposition in sediment basins. They assumed that if settling velocity of a particle takes it to the basin bottom before forward velocity of the flow takes it to the outlet, the particle is trapped.

Fig. 8.14 shows that all particles settling with a velocity, V_s, greater than a velocity, V_o, will be removed. The parameter V_o can be defined as:

$$V_o = h_b/t_b \cdot\ldots\ldots\ldots\ldots\ldots\ldots\ldots\ldots\ldots\ldots\ldots\ldots\ldots\ldots\ldots \quad [8.106]$$

V_s = Settling Velocity

V_o = Critical Settling Velocity

V_h = Horizontal Velocity

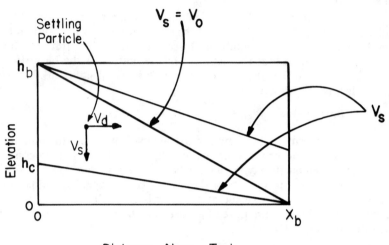

FIG. 8.14 Paths taken by descrete particles in a settling basin.

where h_b = the settling height and t_b = basin detention time which is defined by:

$$t_b = V_b/Q \qquad\qquad [8.107]$$

where V_b = volumetric capacity of the basin and Q = volumetric flow rate through the basin.

Particles are assumed to be evenly distributed over the entrance cross section to the basin. Particles entering a basin have a variety of sizes and densities and hence a distribution of fall velocities. Let $(1-f_o)$ equal the fraction of the total particles that have fall velocities greater than the critical velocity V_o. The fraction $(1-f_o)$ is totally removed.

The remaining fraction, f_o, has fall velocities less than the critical velocity V_o. There is a critical elevation h_c for each of these particle types so that if particles enter the basin at an elevation less than h_c, they will be trapped within the basin. The fraction of these particles is h_c/h_o or:

$$h_c/h_o = V_s/V_o \qquad\qquad [8.108]$$

the fraction f_r removed from a size class where $V_s < V_o$ is:

$$f_r = V_s/V_o \qquad\qquad [8.109]$$

where fall velocity V_s is a function of the size and density of the class.

Summed over all of the size classes, the fraction of the total that is removed is:

$$R_T = (1-f_o) + \sum_{i=1}^{n_s} (V_{si}/V_o) f_{pi} \quad \dots \dots \dots \dots \dots \dots \dots \dots \quad [8.110]$$

where R_T = fraction of the total that is removed, i = particle class index, n_s = number of particle classes where fall velocity V_s is less than the critical velocity V_o defined by equations [8.106] and [8.107] and f_{pi} = the fraction of the total made up of a particle class i.

During a runoff event, R_T is a function of time as f_o and V_o are functions of time.

Although impoundments are usually designed structures, a number of natural impoundments may exist in farm fields and on other irregular terrain. A road with or without a culvert that crosses a depression is one example. Flow leaves most fields from only a few points. Often a ridge or grass around most fields ponds the flow and induces deposition.

If the flow gradient through the pond is steep enough that flow has transport capacity, the problem should be analyzed using channel relationships.

INTERFACING THE EROSION MODEL
WITH A HYDROLOGY MODEL

A hydrology model is required to drive the erosion-sediment yield model. Usually the model is some form of a distributed kinematic model that provides the required hydrologic-hydraulic inputs at the required points in time and space. Closed form analytical solutions for erosion have been obtained for special conditions of either steady state or uniform slope and uniform excess rainfall rate (Foster and Meyer, 1975; and Lane and Shirley, 1978). However, these have limited applications for complex areas.

The numerical solution is usually based on finite difference equations written for a rectangular grid. The scheme may be either explicit or implicit. The explicit method is simpler and requires less computer space, but the size of distance and time steps must be chosen carefully to ensure stability and accuracy. The implicit method is much more stable and allows larger time and distance steps. Although the implicit method is more difficult to program, algorithms for the method are widely available. The method of characteristics can also be used and the finite element method is just being developed that might be useful in some situations (Ross et al., 1978). The methods of characteristics and finite elements are more complex to understand and program than finite difference methods.

Time Scale

Fundamental erosion models generally provide output throughout the

**TABLE 8.18. VARIATION IN THE RELATION OF SEDIMENT
YIELD TO SOIL LOSS ON A STORM BY STORM BASIS**

Storm	Soil loss	Transport capacity	Sediment yield
1	100	25	25
2	10 (Added cover)	25 (Runoff unchanged)	10
TOTAL	110	50	35

runoff event. In that way, they are continuous, but since runoff is not continuous on most small watersheds between events, the models are event based. If flow in the channels continues between storm events, however, the models are fully capable of being continuous.

In general, erosion and sediment delivery processes are nonlinear, and consequently, sediment yield is best analyzed on a storm by storm basis. However, if deposition occurs, the erosion produced with each storm must be compared with the transport capacity of that storm. Correct results cannot be obtained by summing the soil loss for the year and comparing it with the total transport capacity for the year as Table 8.18 illustrates. Total erosion for the two assumed storms in Table 8.18 was 110. Total transport capacity was 50. Comparing total transport capacity with total erosion would suggest deposition of 60. In reality, the deposition was 75, or total erosion less sediment yield. Erosion can be estimated on an average annual basis using the linear USLE erosivity-erodibility, EI-K, relationship, but sediment yield can not be estimated with a USLE-type linear relationship for a watershed where deposition controls sediment yield during some storms and detachment controls it during other storms.

Some equations and models estimate erosion on an event basis without a continuous simulation during the event (Foster et al., 1977b; Simons et al., 1977; Foster et al., 1980). These equations use factors like volume of runoff and peak discharge for the storm and an effective intensity and duration for the storm. Generally, these relationships do not take into account changes that might occur during a storm, such as failure of cover or interaction between deposition and detachment control.

The time scale chosen for the model depends on its intended application. If an estimate of long term erosion is acceptable, then the USLE is probably satisfactory. If long term sediment yield estimates are required, a storm-by-storm analysis is required for accurate estimates. If accurate estimates are required for a given storm, the fundamental model is potentially much more accurate. Furthermore, it has considerably more power for analyzing the combined influence of terrace channels, grass waterways, and field boundaries, for example, than do simple relationships like the USLE-delivery ratio concept.

Segmenting

Any model is a representation of the real watershed. Several schemes have been used to represent the watershed. These include a streamtube concept (Onstad and Foster, 1975); a system of planes and channels (Curtis, 1976); a system of converging surfaces, planes, and channels (Smith, 1977); and a uniform grid (Beasley, 1977). Each has it's own advantages; no particular one is best for all situations. The uniform grid can provide much detail about characteristics over the watershed, and it is quite adaptable to collecting input data on a regular pattern with remote sensors. On the other hand, collection of the large mass of data may be prohibitively costly and time consuming in applications requiring a quick answer with minimum effort.

By careful selection of the watershed elements with a system of planes and channels, almost as much information as a grid provides can be obtained with a minimum of resources for data preparation and com-

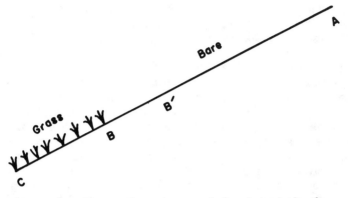

FIG. 8.15 Sketch used to illustrate proper selection of segment lengths.

puter operation.

A major objective should be to choose a system that minimizes distortion of parameter values. Many models can fit observed output if proper parameter values are known. Calibration can be minimized by choosing a model type that preserves model parameter values obtained from small area, unit source measurements. The effect of model representation on model parameters can be estimated for some hydrologic variables (Lane et al., 1975).

Segment size should be distinguished from step size required for the numerical solution. Generally, the step size is smaller. For example, the segment length of a uniform slope can be the entire slope length but the step size required for an accurate numerical solution to the differential equations might be 1/50 of the segment length.

Generally, segments are chosen so that erosion properties over a segment can be assumed to be uniform. Also, segments are chosen so that they are singled process, i.e., the flow is either depositing or detaching over the element but not both on separate parts of the same element. The scheme needs to allow flexible segment sizes to obtain good representation of the processes yet still maintain computational efficiency. Selection of segments is easier for field sized areas than for larger watersheds where lumping and averaging may be a necessity.

The first step in selecting segments is to examine the area. Fig. 8.15 shows two distinct areas: an upslope bare area that produces considerable sediment and a grass area which potentially induces deposition. This slope would be segmented as A-B and B-C. Much smaller distance steps than either A-B or B-C may be required in the numerical solution of the equations.

A problem with fixed grid sizes is that a grid line will not necessarily fall exactly at B. If a grid line falls at B', a problem exists on the B'-C segment because of mixing detachment on B'-B with deposition on B-C. Use of the segments A-B' and B'-C would considerably distort parameter values. The parameter values become event dependent when they can be kept constant with a proper choice of segments such as A-B and B-C.

A model using a single relationship to represent erosion-sediment yield together can not give results for the slope in Fig. 8.15 that are as good as those obtainable by the more fundamental concept. Taking the USLE as an example, the USLE might be applied to this slope using a P factor to reflect the influence of the grass strip. Assume that the bare area produces 150 kg/m of width of sediment but only 75 kg/m passes through the grass. This indicates a P factor value of 0.5. Now assume that the same grass is on a different soil that is much less erodible but produces the same runoff. In this case, assume that erosion produces 40 kg/m of sediment and that multiplied by the P factor indicates 20 kg/m sediment yield by standard USLE procedure. However, this is incorrect. The grass can pass 75 kg/m of sediment and since the available sediment, 40 kg/m, is less than the transport capacity through the grass, 75 kg/m, no deposition actually occurs.

This same type error potentially exists with the delivery ratio concept. In most analyses, the value of the delivery ratio is assumed to be constant regardless of the practice on the watershed. By the delivery ratio concept, if erosion is reduced by 75%, sediment yield is also assumed to be reduced by 75%. This will not be true unless transport capacity is reduced by 75%. If transport capacity is not reduced by 75%, delivery ratio effectively increases. Furthermore, reducing upland erosion by a given amount may be offset when the channels become a source rather than a sink (Trimble, 1975). The USLE and the delivery ratio concept is considered a poor choice of a model for accurate evaluation of the effect of a change in land use on sediment yield.

An alternative to use of the USLE is to replace the rainfall erosivity variable with a runoff factor (Williams, 1975a). Assume Williams' modification to the USLE, and that it gives the correct answer for the first case just described where erosion produced 150 kg/m. In the second case, the soil erodibility or some other factor must be reduced to reflect the lower erosion rate. The ratio of erosion factors for the two cases times the runoff component that is unaffected in the two cases gives 20 kg/m as an estimate for sediment yield in the second case. This illustrates that lumped models lack sensitivity especially for small areas where control of sediment yield may alternate between detachment and transport capacity. In larger watersheds where deposition and thus sediment transport capacity and flow hydraulics alone control sediment yield, the Williams method is a major improvement over the USLE-delivery ratio concept as a simple tool for estimating watershed sediment yield.

Longer segments are normally used for larger watersheds. As a result, overland flow lengths may become excessively large. For example, the side of a 4.0×10^4 m^2 grid would be 20 m. Three grids cumulatively draining across each other give a slope length of 603 m. With the exception of flat, mechanically graded uniform fields, such long overland flow lengths probably occur only rarely. The flow concentrates before reaching such a length. Perhaps the last two or even all three segments should include a channel regardless of whether or not a contour map shows a channel. Hydraulically, flow behaves as a channel in the flow concentrations. This is especially important for fields containing a grass waterway.

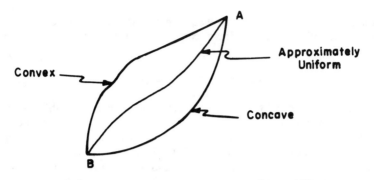

FIG. 8.16 Slope shape influences erosion and sediment yield.

Most models have sufficient degrees of freedom to give 'right answers' but will require distortion of the parameter values to describe sediment yield for these excessive overland flow lengths. If no data are available for calibration, use of parameter values from small source areas can lead to large errors. Overland flow slope length and steepness parameters should be defined and used so that they are independent of grid or segment size.

Averaged or lumped parameters should be used with great care. All three slopes in Fig. 8.16 have the same average slope, yet their sediment yield characteristics are greatly different. Such differences are compounded when soil or cover varies along the slope.

Optimization

Many models require calibration to obtain parameter values. Several optimization schemes are available that may be used to formally optimize parameters (Overton and Meadows, 1976; Pickup, 1977), but different optimization schemes sometimes give different values. Also, since most models have many degrees of freedoms, the optimized parameter values may not be unique, i.e., more than one set of values could give the same results.

Parameter values obtained by optimization should be inspected for reasonableness. Erosion and sediment yield data are often 'noisy' which may lead to false values. Use of a data record that is too short or from a single location may also lead to poor values. With some erosion data, after a large initial reduction in the objective function (e.g., sum of squared deviations between observed and estimated), large and sometimes very unreasonable changes in parameter values are necessary for final reductions in the objective function. In such cases, it is better to stop with more reasonable parameter values which will have greater transferability to ungaged areas or to alternate management practices.

When a functional relationship is selected to be fitted to observed data, the modeler should choose a function that is 'well behaved' on the extremes such as very flat slopes, very steep slopes, very short slope lengths, or very long slope lengths. Most erosion functions should tend toward an asymptote when extrapolated to extremes. Also, the relationships should be formulated to minimize absurd answers like erosion increasing when cover increases. Although an optimization or regression may give such answers, they should be rejected. Often a more reasonable equation form can be developed with a better fit to the data.

EXAMPLES OF MODELS

A variety of erosion-sediment yield models are available. A model user is encouraged to select one of these and modify if necessary rather than develop one from scratch. Most models are sufficiently modular that component relationships can be changed to meet the specific needs of the user. Some models require calibration using previously observed data; others do not require calibration although most could benefit from some parameter optimization. Some examples of erosion-sediment yield models are given below.

1. Universal Soil Loss Equation (USLE) (Wischmeier and Smith, 1978):
   Type: Simple, empirical equation developed from regression analyses of 10,000 plot years of data from natural runoff plots and plots under artificial rainfall simulators.
   Estimates: Long term, average annual sheet-rill erosion
   Strengths: Simple, large data base, parameter values readily available, widely used by agencies like the USDA-Soil Conservation Service, adaptable to nonuniform areas where deposition does not occur.
   Limitations: Does not estimate deposition, sediment yield, channel erosion, or gully erosion; is not accurate for a single storm event.
2. Onstad and Foster (1975):
   Type: A modification of the USLE where the rainfall erosibity factor has been replaced with one having separate terms for rainfall and runoff.
   Estimates: Erosion for single storm event on either a uniform slope or a watershed.
   Strengths: Simple, easy to apply, uses the USLE data base and parameter data set.
   Limitations: No information on distribution of erosion during event; does not estimate deposition, sediment yield, or any form of channel erosion.
3. Modified Universal Soil Loss Equation (MUSLE) (Williams, 1975a):
   Type: A modification of the USLE where the R factor has been replaced with a runoff erosivity factor.
   Estimates: Sediment yield from watersheds for an individual storm event.
   Strengths: Simple, easy to apply, uses the USLE parameter data set.
   Limitations: Provides no information on time distribution of sediment yield during a runoff event, is strictly a sediment yield equation and should not be used where detachment controls sediment yield.
4. Negev (1967):
   Type: Based on relationships for erosion subprocesses and driven by Stanford Watershed Model (See David and Beer and ARM models for additional discussion of this type). This was an early application of using a detailed hydrology model to drive an erosion model.
5. Meyer and Wischmeier (1969):
   Type: Has relationships for each of the major erosion subprocesses occurring on overland flow areas. Was an early model which formularized fundamental erosion concepts. Curtis (1976) described application of this model.
6. Lane and Shirley (1978):
   Type: Analytically derived model based on fundamental erosion mechanics and kinematic overland flow assumptions.
   Estimates: Erosion from uniform slopes for single storms.
   Strengths: Potential for development into a practical erosion equation based on fundamental erosion processes, relatively simple, can be adapted to nonuniform slope shapes.
   Limitations: Restricting hydrologic assumption like uniform rainfall excess and simple overland flow slopes, parameter data set not available.
7. David and Beer (1975), ARM (Donigian and Crawford, 1976; Donigian and Davis, 1978; Fleming and Leythan, 1976):

Type: Has relationships for major erosion subprocesses for both overland flow and channel areas except ARM which does not consider channels, driven by Stanford Watershed Model or one of its variations, continuous simulation.

Estimates: Erosion and sediment yield for watershed.

Strengths: Considers the erosion-sediment yield subprocesses and uses hydrologic inputs for both rainfall and runoff to get interaction effects.

Limitations: Lumps parameter values over the watershed, requires historical data to calibrate, questionable transferability to ungaged areas and to land uses significantly different those used during model calibration.

8.   Curtis (1976):

Type: Uses Meyer and Wischmeier's (1969) erosion relationships and is driven by a kinematic hydrology model using a system of overland flow and channel segments.

Estimates: Erosion and sediment yield distribution in time and space for a given event.

Strengths: Has relationships to reflect interactions between detachment and transport by rainfall and runoff, is a distributed model able to reflect interactions due to spatial variability.

Limitations: Oriented primarily to urban watersheds (Meyer and Wischmeier's relationships have more general application), requires calibration, includes no channel erosion processes.

9.   Smith (1977):

Type: Based on fundamental erosion and sediment transport relationships and is driven by a kinematic runoff model. Uses a system of a converging overland flow section, overland flow planes, and a channel. An event based model.

Estimates: Erosion and sediment yield distributed in time and space.

Strengths: Is adaptable to small watersheds like farm fields; is a distributed model; and is fundamentally based.

Limitations: Must be calibrated, relationships need to be developed for use as a practical model.

10.   Bruce et al. (1975):

Type: Is a two stage convolution model similar to instantaneous unit hydrograph theory but model operates nonlinearly, driven by a two stage convolution scheme. An event based model.

Estimates: Erosion and sediment yield distributed in time and space.

Strengths: Can fit a variety of areas complex in size, shape, and land use.

Limitations: Model is abstract and thus difficult for the user to understand, requires historical data to calibrate, transferability to ungaged areas or to new land uses may be limited at present.

11.   CSU—(Li, 1977):

Type: Based on equations for separate erosion and transport processes on overland flow and channel areas, driven by a kinematic overland flow model, uses a system of grids and channels. An event based model.

Estimates: Erosion and sediment yield distribution in time and space, particle distribution of sediment.

Strengths: Adaptable to the variety of erosion processes occurring on a variety of overland flow and channel areas. Complex and large areas can be represented. Grids can be combined to eliminate some redundancy in input.

Limitations: Although values are available for most parameters, some calibration is required for a few parameters. Although the model can represent complex areas, there may be distortion of parameters depending on how grid size and channel network are chosen to represent watershed. Also, see limitations for ANSWERS model, for additional discussion of problems due to location of grid lines.

12.   ANSWERS—(Beasley, 1977):

Type: A distributed model that uses separate equations for detachment and transport on overland flow areas and transport in channels. Uses a regular square grid and channels to represent watershed.

Estimates: Erosion and sediment yield distributed in time and space for single events.

Strengths: Well adapted to remote sensing and other inventory surveys where observations are on a regular grid to determine parameter values, layout of grid is straight forward, represents a variety of land use, soils, and topographic features over the watershed. Model is designed for little or no calibration by using several of the USLE parameters.

Limitations: Model currently allows no erosion in channels, model requires great effort to assemble input data. Grid boundaries may not correspond to boundaries of soil or land use, for example, the edge of a grass buffer strip. Or, grid elements may be larger than a subwatershed feature which has a major effect, thereby requiring parameter distortions to avoid errors in the estimates.

13. CREAMS—(Foster et al., 1980; See Simons et al., 1977 for similar model of this type that does not consider channels or impoundments.):

Type: Event based model that uses storm EI, volume of runoff, and peak runoff rate with fundamental erosion relationships to compute detachment and transport on overland flow areas and channels in field sized areas. Uses typical overland flow profile, typical channel, and typical impoundment elements to represent watershed. Model can be used for single events, or for long term simulation.

Estimates: Erosion, sediment yield, and distribution of sediment particles from each element.

Strengths: Inexpensive simulation of 10 to 30 yr of record. Can describe a broad range of management practices. Does not require calibration since model uses USLE and other readily available parameter data sets. Can represent complex field sized watershed with minimum input detail.

Limitations: Can represent variability only in downslope direction, does not provide information during the storm. Flow hydraulics are approximate for gradually varied flow since regression equations are used. Model not as powerful as the complete models like ANSWERS and CSU.

References

1 Ackers, P. and W. R. White. 1973. Sediment transport: New approach and analysis. Journal of the Hydraulics Division, Proc. of ASCE 99(HY11):2041-2060.

2 Alberts, E. E. 1979. The nitrogen and phosphorus content of eroded soil aggregates and sediment. Ph.D. Thesis. Purdue University. West Lafayette, IN. 100 pp.

3 Alberts, E. E., W. C. Moldenhauer, and G. R. Foster. 1980. Soil aggregates and primary particles transported in rill and interrill erosion. Soil Science Society of America Journal 44(3):590-595.

4 American Society of Civil Engineers (ASCE). 1975. Sedimentation Engineering. American Society of Civil Engineering, New York, NY. 745 pp.

5 Apmann, R. P. and R. R. Rumer, Jr. 1970. Diffusion of sediment in developing flow. Journal of the Hydraulics Division, Proc. of the ASCE 96(HY1):109-123.

6 Barfield, B. J., E. W. Tollner, and J. C. Hayes. 1977. Prediction of sediment transport in grassed media. ASAE Paper No. 77-2023. ASAE, St. Joseph, MI 49085.

7 Beasley, D. B. 1977. ANSWERS: A mathematical model for simulating the effects of land use and management on water quality. Ph.D. Thesis, Purdue University, West Lafayette, IN, 266 pp.

8 Bennett, J. P. 1974. Concepts of mathematical modeling of sediment yield. Water Resources Research 10(3):485-492.

9 Bruce, R. R., L. A. Harper, R. A. Leonard, W. M. Snyder, and A. W. Thomas. 1975. A model for runoff of pesticides from small upland watersheds. Journal Environmental Quality 4(4):541-548.

10 Bubenzer, G. D. 1979. Rainfall characteristics important for simulation. In: Proc. from the Rainfall Simulator Workshop. ARM-W-10, USDA-Science and Education Administration. pp. 22-34.

11 Bubenzer, G. D., and B. A. Jones. 1971. Drop size and impact velocity effects on the detachment of soils under simulated rainfall. TRANSACTIONS of the ASAE 14(4):625-628.

12 Camp, T. R. 1946. Sedimentation and the design of settling tanks. Trans. of the ASCE 111:895-958.

13 Chang, H. W. and J. C. Hill. 1976. Computer modeling of erodible flood channels and deltas. Journal of the Hydraulics Division, Proc. of the ASCE 102(HY10):1461-1477.

14 Chapman, G. 1948. Size of raindrops and their striking force at the soil surface in a red pine plantation. Trans. of the American Geophysical Union 29:664-670.

15 Cook, H. L. 1936. The nature and controlling variables of the water erosion process. Soil Science Society American Proc. 1:487-494.

16 Curtis, D. C. 1976. A deterministic urban storm water and sediment discharge model. In: Proc. of National Symposium on Urban Hydrology, Hydraulics, and Sediment Con-

trol. University of Kentucky. Lexington, KY. pp. 151-162.

17 Curtis, D. C. and R. H. McCuen. 1977. Design efficiency of storm water detention basins. Journal of the Water Resources Division, Proc. of ASCE 103(WR1):125-141.

18 David, W. P., and C. E. Beer. 1975. Simulation of soil erosion—Part I. Development of a mathematical erosion model. TRANSACTIONS of the ASAE 18(1):126-129, 133.

19 Davis, S. S. 1978. Deposition of nonuniform sediment by overland flow on concave slopes. M.S. Thesis. Purdue University. West Lafayette, IN, 137 pp.

20 Donigian, A. S., and N. H. Crawford. 1976. Modeling nonpoint source pollution from the land surface. EPA-600/3-76-083. U.S. Environmental Protection Agency, 279 pp.

21 Donigian, A. S. and H. H. Davis. 1978. User's manual for Agricultural Runoff Management (ARM) Model. EPA-600/3-78-080. U.S. Environmental Protection Agency, 163 pp.

22 Einstein, H. A. 1968. Deposition of suspended particles in a gravel bed. Journal of the Hydraulics Division, Proc. of the ASCE 94(HY5):1197-1205.

23 Ellison, W. D. 1947. Soil erosion studies. AGRICULTURAL ENGINEERING 28:145-146, 197-201, 245-248, 297-300, 349-351, 402-405, 442-444.

24 Fleming, G. and K. M. Leytham. 1976. The hydrologic and sediment processes in natural watershed areas. In: Proc. of the Third Federal Inter-Agency Sedimentation Conference. Water Resources Council, Washington, DC. pp. 1:232-246.

25 Foster, G. R. 1971. The overland flow process under natural conditions. In: Biological Effects in the Hydrological Cycle. Proc. of the Third International Seminar for Hydrology Professors, Purdue University. West Lafayette, IN, pp. 173-185.

26 Foster, G. R. 1975. Hydraulics of flow in a rill. Ph.D. Thesis, Purdue University, West Lafayette, IN, 222 pp.

27 Foster, G. R. 1976. Sedimentation, general. In: Proc. of National Symposium on Urban Hydrology, Hydraulics, and Sediment Control. University of Kentucky, Lexington, KY. pp. 129-138.

28 Foster, G. R. and L. F. Huggins. 1977. Deposition of sediment by overland flow on concave slopes. In: Soil Erosion Prediction and Control. Special Publication No. 21. Soil Conservation Society of America, Ankeny, IA, pp. 167-182.

29 Foster, G. R., L. J. Lane, J. D. Nowlin, J. M. Laflen, and R. A. Young. 1980. A model to estimate sediment yield from field sized areas: Development of model. In: CREAMS— a field scale model for Chemicals, Runoff, and Erosion from Agricultural Management Systems. Volume I: Model Documentation. Chapter 3. USDA-Science and Education Administration Conservation Report No. 26. pp. 36-64.

30 Foster, G. R. and L. D. Meyer. 1972a. A closed-form soil erosion equation for upland areas. In: Sedimentation (Einstein). H. W. Shen (ed.). Colorado State University. Fort Collins, CO. Chapter 12.

31 Foster, G. R. and L. D. Meyer. 1972b. Transport of soil particles by shallow flow. TRANSACTIONS of the ASAE 15(1):99-102.

32 Foster, G. R. and L. D. Meyer. 1975. Mathematical simulation of upland erosion by fundamental erosion mechanics. In: Present and Prospective Technology for Predicting Sediment Yields and Sources. ARS-S-40. USDA-Agricultural Research Service, pp. 190-207.

33 Foster, G. R., L. D. Meyer, and C. A. Onstad. 1977a. An erosion equation derived from basic erosion principles. TRANSACTIONS of the ASAE 20(4):678-682.

34 Foster, G. R., L. D. Meyer, and C. A. Onstad. 1977b. A runoff erosivity factor and variable slope length exponents for soil loss estimates. TRANSACTIONS of the ASAE 20(4):683-687.

35 Foster, G. R. and W. H. Wischmeier. 1974. Evaluating irregular slopes for soil loss prediction. TRANSACTIONS of the ASAE 17(2):305-309.

36 Foster, R. L., and G. L. Martin. 1969. Effect of unit weight and slope on erosion. Journal of Irrigation and Drainage Division, Proc. of the ASCE 95(IR4):551-561.

37 Free, G. R. 1960. Erosion characteristics of rainfall. AGRICULTURAL ENGINEERING 41(7):447-449, 455.

38 Graf, W. H. 1971. Hydraulics of sediment transport. McGraw-Hill Book Co., New York, NY. 544 pp.

39 Grissinger, E. H. 1966. Resistance of selected clay systems to erosion by water. Water Resources Research 2(1):131-138.

40 Hales, Z. L., A. Shindala, and K. H. Denson. 1970. Riverbed degradation prediction. Water Resources Research 6(2):549-556.

41 Harmon, W. C. and L. D. Meyer. 1978. Cover, slope, and rain intensity affect interrill erosion. In: Proc. of the Mississippi Water Resources Conferences. Mississippi State University. Mississippi State, MI, pp. 9-16.

42   Hayes, J. C. and B. J. Barfield. 1977. Filtration of non-homogeneous sediment by simulated vegetation. ASAE Paper No. 77-2513, ASAE, St. Joseph, MI 49085. 18 pp.

43   Holeman, J. N. 1968. The sediment yield of major rivers of the world. Water Resources Research 4(4):737-747.

44   Hudson, N. H. 1971. Soil conservation. Cornell University Press. Ithaca, NY. 320 pp.

45   Huggins, L. F., and E. J. Monke. 1966. The mathematical simulation of the hydrology of small watersheds. Technical Report No. 1. Water Resources Center. Purdue University. West Lafayette, IN, 130 pp.

46   Hutchinson, D. E., H. W. Pritchard, and others. 1976. Resource conservation glossary. In: Journal of Soil and Water Conservation 31(4). 63 pp.

47   Khaleel, R., G. R. Foster, K. R. Reddy, M. R. Overcash and P. W. Westerman. 1979. A nonpoint source model for land areas receiving animal wastes: III. A conceptual model for sediment and manure transport. TRANSACTIONS of the ASAE 22(6):1353-1361.

48   Laflen, J. M., H. P. Johnson, and R. O. Hartwig. 1978. Sedimentation modeling of impoundment terraces. TRANSACTIONS of the AS AE 21(6):1131-1135.

49   Laflen, J. M., H. P. Johnson, and R. C. Reeve. 1972. Soil loss from tile outlet terraces. Journal Soil and Water Conservation 27(2):74-77.

50   Lane, L. J. and G. R. Foster. 1980. Concentrated flow relationships. In: CREAMS—a field scale model for Chemicals, Runoff, and Erosion from Agricultural Management Systems. Volume III: Supporting Documentation. Chapter 11. USDA-Science and Education Administration Conservation Report No. 26 pp. 474-485.

51   Lane, L. J. and E. D. Shirley. 1978. Mathematical simulation of erosion on upland areas. USDA-Agricultural Research Service. Tucson, AZ.

52   Lane, L. J., D. A. Woolhiser, and V. Yerjevich. 1975. Influence of simplification in watershed geometry in simulation of surface runoff. Hydrology Paper No. 81. Colorado State University. Fort Collins, CO. 50 pp.

53   Lattanzi, Alfredo. 1973. Influence of straw-mulch rate and slope steepness on interrill detachment and transport of soil. M.S. Thesis. Purdue University. West Lafayette, IN, 90 pp.

54   Lattanzi, A. R., L. D. Meyer, and M. F. Baumgardner. 1974. Influence of mulch rate and slope steepness on interrill erosion. Soil Science Society American Proc. 38(6):846-950.

55   Laws, J. O. and D. A. Parsons. 1943. The relation of raindrop-size to intensity. Trans. of the American Geophysical Union. 24:452-460.

56   Li, R. M. 1977. Water and sediment routing from watersheds. Proc. of River Mechanics Institute. Colorado State University. Fort Collins, CO. Chapter 9.

57   Long, D. C. 1964. The size and density of aggregates in eroded soil material. M.S. Thesis. Iowa State University, Ames, IA, 119 pp.

58   Mantz, P. A. 1977. Incipient transport of fine grains and flakes of fluids—extended Shields diagram. Journal of Hydraulic Division, Proc. of the ASCE 103(HY6):601-615.

59   McCool, D. K., M. Molnau, B. L. Papendick, and F. L. Brooks. 1977. Erosion research in the dryland grain region of the Pacific Northwest: Recent developments and needs. In: Soil Erosion: Prediction and Control. Special Publication No. 21. Soil Conservation Society of America. Ankeny, IA, pp. 50-59.

60   McGregor, K. C. and C. K. Mutchler. 1977. Status of the R factor in northern Mississippi. In: Soil Erosion: Prediction and Control. Special Publication No. 21. Soil Conservation Society of America. Ankeny, IA, pp. 135-142.

61   Meeuwig, R. O. 1971. Soil stability on high elevation rangeland in the intermountain area. Research Paper INT-94. USDA-Forest Service, 10 pp.

62   Meyer, L. D., G. R. Foster, and S. Nikolov. 1975a. Effect of flow rate and canopy on rill erosion. TRANSACTIONS of the ASAE 18(5):905-911.

63   Meyer, L. D., G. R. Foster and M. J. M. Romkens. 1975b. Source of soil eroded by water from upland slopes. In: Present and Prospective Technology for Predicting Sediment Yields and Sources. ARS-S-40. USDA-Agricultural Research Service, pp. 177-189.

64   Meyer, L. D. and W. C. Harmon. 1979. Multiple-intensity rainfall simulator for erosion research on row sideslopes. TRANSACTIONS of the ASAE 22(1):100-103.

65   Meyer, L. D., W. C. Harmon, and L. L. McDowell. 1978. Sediment sizes eroded from rowcrop sideslopes. ASAE Paper No. 78-2518, ASAE, St. Joseph, MI 49085, 20 pp.

66   Meyer, L. D. and W. H. Wischmeier. 1969. Mathematical simulation of the process of soil erosion by water. TRANSACTIONS of the ASAE 12(6):754-758, 762.

67   Mitchell, J. K. and B. A. Jones. 1976. Micro-relief surface depression storage: Analysis of models to describe the depth-storage function. Water Resources Bulletin 12(6):1205-1222.

68   Moldenhauer, W. C. 1978. Sizes of soil particles detached by raindrop impact. Personal communication.

69   Moldenhauer, W. C. and J. C. Koswara. 1968. Effect of initial clod size on characteristics of splash and wash erosion. Soil Science Society of America Proc. 32(6):875-879.

70   Moldenhauer, W. C. and D. C. Long. 1964. Influence of rainfall energy on soil loss and infiltration rates: I. Effect over a range of textures. Soil Science Society of America Proc. 28(6):813-817.

71   Moldenhauer, W. C. and W. H. Wischmeier. 1969. Water erosion following soybeans. Crops and Soils 21(6):20.

72   Monke, E. J., H. J. Marelli, L. D. Meyer, and J. F. DeJong. 1977. Runoff, erosion, and nutrient movement from interrill areas. TRANSACTIONS of the ASAE 20(1):58-61.

73   Mutchler, C. K. 1970. Size, travel, and composition of droplets formed by waterdrop splash on thin water layers. Ph.D. Thesis. University of Minnesota. St. Paul, MN, 205 pp.

74   Mutcher, C. K. and R. A. Young. 1975. Soil detachment by raindrops. In: Present and Prospective Technology for Predicting Sediment Yields and Sources. ARS-S-40. USDA-Agricultural Research Service. pp. 113-117.

75   Negev, M. 1967. A sediment model on a digital computer. Technical Report 76. Department of Civil Engineering. Stanford University. Stanford, CA. 109 pp.

76   Neibling, W. H. and G. R. Foster. 1977. Estimating deposition and sediment yield from overland flow processes. In: Proc. International Symposium on Urban Hydrology, Hydraulics and Sediment Control. (D. T. Koa, ed.). University of Kentucky. Lexington, KY. pp. 75-86.

77   Neibling, W. H. and G. R. Foster. 1980. Sediment transport capacity of overland flow. In: CREAMS—a field scale model for Chemicals, Runoff, and Erosion from Agricultural Management Systems. Vol. III: Supporting Documentation. Chapter 10. USDA-Science and Education Administration Conservation Report No. 26, pp. 463-473.

78   Onstad, C. A. and G. R. Foster. 1975. Erosion modeling on a watershed. TRANSACTIONS of the ASAE 18(2):288-292.

79   Overton, D. E. and M. E. Meadows. 1976. Stormwater modeling. Academic Press. New York, NY. 358 pp.

80   Partheniades, E. 1972. Results of recent investigations on erosion and deposition of cohesive sediments. In: Sedimentation (Einstein). (H. W. Shen, ed.). Fort Collins, CO, Chapter 20.

81   Pickup, G. 1977. Testing the efficiency of algorithms and strategies for automatic calibration of rainfall-runoff models. Hydrological Sciences Bulletin. XXII, 26:257-274.

82   Piest, R. F., J. M. Bradford, and R. G. Spomer. 1975. Mechanisms of erosion and sediment movement from gullies. In: Present and prospective technology for predicting sediment yields and sources. ARS-S-40. USDA-Agricultural Research Service. pp. 162-176.

83   Robinson, A. M. 1976. The effects of urbanization on stream channel morphology. In: Proc. of National Symposium on Urban Hydrology, Hydraulics, and Sediment Control. University of Kentucky. Lexington, KY. pp. 115-127.

84   Romkens, M. J. M., C. B. Roth, and D. W. Nelson. 1977. Erodibility of selected clay subsoils in relation to physical and chemical properties. Soil Science Society of America Journal 41(5):954-960.

85   Ross, B. B., V. O. Shanholtz, and D. N. Contractor. 1978. A finite element hydrologic model to determine the effect of land management practices on erosion and sedimentation in a watershed. ASAE Paper No. 78-2507, ASAE, St. Joseph, MI 49085.

86   Simons, D. B., R. M. Li, and T. J. Ward. 1977. A simple procedure for estimating on-site erosion. In: Proc. of International Symposium on Urban Hydrology, Hydraulics, and Sediment Control. University of Kentucky, Lexington, KY. pp. 95-102.

87   Smerdon, E. T. and R. P. Beasley. 1959. Tractive force theory applied to stability of open channels in cohesive soils. Research Bulletin No. 715. Agricultural Experiment Station, University of Missouri. Columbia, MO. 36 pp.

88   Smith, R. E. 1977. Field test of a distributed watershed erosion/sedimentation model. In: Soil Erosion: Prediction and Control. Special Publication No. 21. Soil Conservation Society of America. Ankeny, IA, pp. 201-209.

89   Swanson, N. P., A. R. Dedrick, and H. E. Weakly. 1969. Soil particles and aggregates transported in runoff from simulated rainfall. TRANSACTIONS of the ASAE 8(3):437-440.

90   Thomas, W. A. 1976. Scour and Deposition in rivers and reservoirs. HEC-6. Hydrologic Engineering Center, US Army Corps of Engineers.

91   Tollner, E. W., B. J. Barfield, C. T. Haan, and T. Y. Kao. 1976. Suspended sediment filtration capacity of simulated vegetation. TRANSACTIONS of the ASAE 19(4):678-682.

92   Trimble, S. W. 1975. Denudation studies: Can we assume stream steady state? Science 188:1207-1208.

93   Ward, A. D., C. T. Haan, and B. J. Barfield. 1977. Simulation of the sedimentology of sediment basins. Technical Report 103. University of Kentucky. Water Resources Institute. Lexington, KY.

94   Williams, J. R. 1975a. Sediment-yield prediction with Universal Equation using runoff energy factor. In: Present and prospective technology for predicting sediment yields and sources. ARS-S-40, USDA-Agricultural Research Service, pp. 244-252.

95   William, J. R. 1975b. Sediment routing for agricultural watersheds. Water Resources Bulletin 11(5):965-974.

96   Williams, J. R. 1978. A sediment yield model routing model. In: Proc. of the Specialty Conference on Verification of Mathematical and Physical Models in Hydraulic Engineering. American Society of Civil Engineers. New York, NY. pp. 602-670.

97   Wischmeier, W. H. 1960. Cropping-management factor evaluations for a universal soil-loss equation. Soil Science Society of America Proc. 24(4):322-326.

98   Wischmeier, W. H. 1975. Estimating the soil loss equation's cover and management factor for undisturbed areas. In: Present and prospective technology for predicting sediment yields and sources. ARS-S-40. USDA-Agricultural Research Service. pp. 118-124.

99   Wischmeier, W. H. 1976. Use and misuse of the Universal Soil-Loss Equation. Journal of Soil and Water Conservation 31(1):5-9.

100   Wischmeier, W. H., C. B. Johnson, and B. V. Cross. 1971. A soil erodibility nomograph for farmland and construction sites. Journal of Soil and Water Conservation 26(5):189-193.

101   Wischmeier, W. H. and J. V. Mannering. 1969. Relation of soil properties to its erodibility. Soil Science Society of America Proc. 33(1):131-137.

102   Wischmeier, W. H. and D. D. Smith. 1958. Rainfall energy and its relationship to soil loss. Trans. of the American Geophysical Union 39(2):285-291.

103   Wischmeier, W. H. and D. D. Smith. 1978. Predicting Rainfall Erosion Losses. Agriculture Handbook No. 537, USDA-Science and Education Administration, 58 pp.

104   Yalin, Y. S. 1963. An expression for bed-load transportation. Journal of the Hydraulics Division, Proc. of the ASCE 89(HY3):221-250.

105   Yang, C. T. 1972. Unit stream power and sediment transport. Journal of the Hydraulics Division, Proc. of the ASCE 98(HY10):1805-125.

106   Yoder, R. E. 1936. A direct method of aggregate analysis of soils and a study of the physical nature of erosion losses. Journal of the American Society of Agronomy 28(4):337-351.

107   Yoon, Y. 1970. The effect of rainfall on the mechanics of steady spatially varied sheet flow on a hydraulically smooth boundary. Ph.D. Thesis. University of Illinois. Urbana-Champaign, IL.

108   Young, R. A. 1978. Sizes and densities of eroded soil particles. Personal communication.

109   Young, R. A., and C. K. Mutchler. 1969a. Effect of slope shape on erosion and runoff. TRANSACTIONS of the ASAE 12(2):231-233, 239.

110   Young, R. A., and C. K. Mutchler. 1969b. Soil and water movement in small tillage channels. TRANSACTIONS of the ASAE 12(4):543-545.

111   Young, R. A. and C. A. Onstad. 1976. Predicting particle size composition of eroded soil. TRANSACTIONS of the ASAE 19(6):1071-1075.

112   Young, R. A. and C. A. Onstad. 1978. Characterization of rill and interrill eroded soil. TRANSACTIONS of the ASAE 21(6):1126-1130.

113   Young, R. A. and J. L. Wiersma. 1973. The role of rainfall impact in soil detachment and transport. Water Resources Research 9(6):1629-1639.

XIII. LIST OF SYMBOLS

a	Coefficient in rill erosion equation,
a	Coefficient in transport capacity equation,
a	Fraction of open area in a crop canopy,
a	Space weighting factor in finite difference equation for continuity,
A	Flow area,
A	Soil loss from USLE per unit area averaged over slope segment for time period of erosivity factor (mass/area · time period of erosivity factor),
A_d	Surface area of impoundment for uppermost layer of particle of given type,
A_t	Coefficient in sediment transport equation for interrill areas,
$A_{x_1 - x_2}$	Average soil loss over segment $x_1 - x_2$ (mass/area · time),
b	Exponent in rill erosion equation,
b	Time weighting factor in finite difference equation for continuity,

c	Sediment concentration in runoff (volume sediment/volume runoff),
c_d	Sediment concentration of a given particle in an impoundment (mass sediment/volume water),
C	Cover-management factor for USLE,
C'	Constant of integration,
C_B	Rill erosion coefficient to be determined by calibration,
C_i	Cover-management factor for interrill erosion,
C_{iII}	Interrill subfactor for effect of cover in direct contact with soil,
C_{it}	Interrill subfactor for effect of raindrop cushioning,
C_r	Cover-management factor for rill erosion,
C_{slr}	Soil loss ratio from the USLE,
C_T	Transport factor for effect of cover in direct contact with soil surface,
d	Particle diameter,
d_{ch}	Downward erosion rate of eroding channel at equilibrium (depth/time),
d_{ne}	Depth of soil above nonerodible layer,
d_r	Dispersion ratio expressed as a percent,
D_*	Ratio of channel erosion rate at t_* to that at $t_* = 0$,
D_{ch}	Channel erosion rate (mass/length · time),
D_d	Depth from top layer of particle of given type to bottom of impoundment,
D_1	Delivery rate of sediment from interrill areas (mass/area · time),
D_L	Lateral inflow rate of sediment (mass/length · time),
D_0	Initial depth in impoundment,
D_r	Deposition rate (mass/area · time),
D_r	Rill erosion detachment rate (mass/area · time),
D_{rc}	Rill erosion detachment capacity rate (mass/area · time),
D_{ru}	Deposition rate at upper end of segment (mass/area · time),
D_R	Proportion of sediment initially in impoundment that is discharged from impoundment,
e	Rainfall energy per unit of rainfall (force · distance/area · depth),
e_m	Erosion rate at middle of eroding channel at equilibrium (mass/area · time),
E	Total storm energy (force · distance/area),
EI	Erosivity unit, product of storm energy times an intensity (force · distance/area) · (depth/time),
E_{ch}	Erosion rate per unit length of channel (mass/length · time),
E_{xc}	Excess nondimensional transport capacity,
f	Darcy-Weisbach coefficient of friction,
$f(x_c)$ or $f(x_{cf})$	Distribution of $(\tau/\bar{\tau})$ around wetted perimeter,
f_c	Contribution of cover in direct contact with soil to friction factor,
f_d	Fraction of sediment load trapped on disposition face in grass strip,
f_0	Fraction of particles having a fall velocity less than the critical velocity V_0,
f_p	Fraction of total sediment made up of particles of a given class,
f_r	Fraction of a particle class removed in a sedimentation basin,
f_s	Contribution of soil to friction factor,
F	Rill erosion detachment capacity rate at x_{j+1} and t^{n+1} (same as D_{rc} at that point).
g	Acceleration due to gravity,
g	Sediment load per unit width (mass/width · time),
$g(x_c)$	A function describing geometry of an eroded channel at equilibrium,
h(d)	Frequency distribution of sediment initially in impoundment,
h_c	Maximum elevation that a particle having a fall velocity less than the critical velocity V_0 can enter sedimentation basin and still be trapped,
h_0	Maximum depth of sedimentation basin,
H	Maximum depth of deposition in a grass strip,
i	Particle class index,
i	Rainfall intensity (depth/time),
i_{can}	Rainfall intensity under crop canopy (depth/time),
i_{eff}	Effective rainfall intensity (depth/time),
I	Average rainfall intensity over a time period (usually 30 minutes),
I	Delivery rate of sediment from interrill areas (mass/area·time),
I	Infiltration rate through bottom of impoundment (depth/time),
I_{30}	Maximum 30 minute rainfall intensity,

j	Slope segment index,
j	Space index in finite difference equation for continuity,
K	Soil erodibility factor for USLE (mass/area·erosivity unit),
K_{ch}	Soil erodibility factor for channel erosion (mass/area·erosivity unit),
K_1	Soil erodibility factor for interrill erosion (mass/area·erosivity unit),
K_r	Soil erodibility factor for rill erosion (mass/area·erosivity unit),
L	Slope length factor for USLE,
L_{DE}	Distance from lower edge of a deposition face in a grass strip to lower edge of strip,
L_p	Length of pond above a grass strip,
L_w	Width of grass strip,
m_{ca}	Mass of a drop falling from a canopy,
m_d	Mass removal rate of sediment from impoundment,
m_p	Mass of raindrop,
n	Manning's n,
n	Number of particle types in a mixture,
n	Slope length exponent in USLE,
n	Time index in finite difference equation for continuity,
n_s	Number of particle classes having fall velocities less than V_o,
N	Number of particles transported in uniform sediment,
N_e	Number of particles in a particle class,
P	Nondimensional sediment transport capacity,
P	Supporting practices factor for USLE,
P_e	Nondimensional sediment transport capacity for a particle class in a sediment mixture,
P_{ireq}	Nondimensional sediment transport capacity required to transport a given load of a particular particle type,
q	Discharge rate per unit width (volume/width·time),
q_b	Discharge rate per unit width on bare areas (volume/width·time),
q_c	Discharge rate per unit width on covered area (volume/width·time),
q_p	Peak discharge rate per unit width (volume/width·time),
q_s	Sediment load per unit width (mass/width·time),
q_{sc}	Sediment load per unit width just above deposition face in a grass strip (mass/width·time),
q_{sd}	Sediment load per unit width just below deposition face in a grass strip (mass/width·time),
q_{se}	Sediment load per unit width at lower edge of grass strip (mass/width·time),
q_{sin}	Sediment inflow rate per unit width (mass/width·time),
q_{sm}	Sediment load per unit width at midpoint on deposition face in a grass strip (mass/width·time),
q_{so}	Sediment outflow rate per unit width (mass/width·time),
q_{su}	Sediment load per unit width at upper end of a segment (mass/width·time),
q_{sxl}	Sediment load per unit width at location x_1 (mass/width·time),
Q	Discharge rate (volume/time),
Q_c	Critical discharge rate below which rill erosion is negligible (volume/time),
Q_p	Peak discharge rate (volume/time),
Q_s	Sediment discharge rate (mass/time),
R	Detachment rate by rill erosion (mass/area·time),
R	Erosivity factor from USLE (erosivity units/time),
R_*	Ratio of hydraulic radius of flow in an eroding channel at equilibrium to wetted perimeter,
R_f	Hydraulic radius due to soil,
R_m	Modified erosivity factor,
R_s	Spacing hydraulic radius for flow through grass,
R_{st}	Storm EI value,
R_t	Fraction of particles trapped in sedimentation basin,
s	Sine of slope angle θ,
S	Slope steepness factor for USLE,
S_g	Specific gravity of a sediment particle,
S_i	Slope factor for interrill erosion,
S_s	Spacing of media elements in a grass strip,
SDLT	Summation of nondimensional excess shear stress,

SMUS	Summation of ratios of required nondimensional transport capacity to nondimensional transport capacity of a particle type,
SPT	Summation of ratios of required nondimensional transport capacity for a particle class to total nondimensional transport capacity,
t	Time,
t_*	Nondimensional time for channel erosion,
t_d	Detention time in sedimentation basin,
t_{df}	Time for impoundment to clear of given particle type,
T	Summation of nondimensional shear stress for a group of particles,
T_c	Transport capacity per unit width (mass/width·time),
T_{cl}	Transport capacity per unit width on interrill areas (mass/width·time),
T_{cu}	Transport capacity per unit width at upper end of a segment (mass/width·time),
T_d	Proportion of a given particle type discharged through impoundment,
USLE	Universal Soil Loss Equation,
v	Flow velocity,
v_b	Flow velocity over bare soil,
v_c	Flow velocity with cover in direct contact with soil,
V	Runoff volume (volume),
V	Depth of runoff from a land slope,
V_*	Shear velocity,
V_b	Initial volume of water in impoundment,
V_b	Volume of sedimentation basin,
V_{ca}	Impact velocity of a drop falling from a canopy,
V_d	Volume of water discharged from impoundment while sediment is in suspension,
V_{dp}	Volume of sediment deposited in pond above grass strip,
V_o	Critical fall velocity for trapping a given particle type in sedimentation basin,
V_p	Impact velocity of an unhindered rain drop,
V_s	Fall velocity of a sediment particle,
V_u	Depth of runoff from USLE unit plot,
W	Width of channel,
W_*	Ratio of width of eroding channel at equilibrium to wetted perimeter,
W_{ch}	Width of channel,
W_{eq}	Width of eroding channels at equilibrium,
W_f	Final channel width,
W_{in}	Initial channel width,
W_s	Sediment transport capacity before adjustment for nonuniform sediment (mass/width·time),
WP	Wetted perimeter,
x	Distance or location,
x_c	Ratio of distance along wetted perimeter from water surface to point where shear stress at a point = critical shear stress to wetted perimeter,
x_{co}	Old location of the upper edge of a deposition face in a grass strip,
x_{cn}	New location of the upper edge of a deposition face in a grass strip,
x_{cf}	x_c value when channel has eroded to its maximum width,
x_{de}	Location within a segment where deposition ends,
x_u	Location of upper end of a segment,
x_*	Distance along wetted perimeter from water surface to a given point divided by wetted perimeter,
x_1, x_2	Location of ends of a segment,
y	Flow depth,
y_b	Interrill flow depth on bare soil,
y_c	Interrill flow depth with cover in direct contact with soil,
y_f	Flow depth in a grass strip,
y_p	Interrill flow depth with depressions and dams on soil,
Y_{cr}	Ordinate from Shields Diagram,
Y_d	Depth of deposition,
α	First order reaction coefficient for deposition (length^{-1}),
γ	Weight density of water (force/volume),
δ	Nondimensional excess shear stress,
ΔE	Change in elevation for a time step,
Δt	Time interval,
Δx	Distance interval,

θ	Angle of a land slope,
λ	Slope length,
λ_u	Length of unit plot for USLE (22.1 m),
ν	Kinematic viscosity (distance^2/time),
ξ	Fraction of soil surface left exposed by cover in direct contact with soil,
ρ	Mass density of water (mass/volume),
ρ_s	Mass density of sediment particles (mass/volume),
ρ_{sd}	Mass density of soil either in place or as it is deposited (mass/volume),
ρ_{sg}	Effective mass density of sediment deposited in grass (mass/volume),
ρ_{soil}	Mass density of soil in place (mass/volume),
ρ_{sp}	Effective mass density of sediment deposited in pond above a grass strip (mass/volume),
σ	Excess rainfall rate or runoff rate (depth/time),
σ_{pu}	Maximum rate of runoff from USLE unit plot (depth/time),
τ	Shear stress (force/area),
$\underline{\tau}$	Shear stress at a point along wetted perimeter (force/area),
$\bar{\tau}$	Average shear stress over wetted perimeter of rill or broad sheet flow (force/area),
τ_b	Point shear stress in channel at nonerodible layer (force/area),
τ_b	Shear stress acting on soil when no cover is present (force/area),
τ_{cc}	Shear stress acting on cover when cover is present (force/area),
τ_{cr}	Critical shear stress (force/area),
τ_{cs}	Shear stress acting on soil when cover is present (force/area).

chapter 9 █████████████

MODELING THE QUALITY OF WATER FROM AGRICULTURAL LAND

9

9

MODELING THE QUALITY OF WATER FROM AGRICULTURAL LAND

by   Maurice H. Frere, Soil Scientist, USDA-ARS,
      Chickasha, OK 73018; Edward H. Seely,
      Hydraulic Engineer, USDA-ARS, Oxford, MS
      38655; Ralph A. Leonard, Soil Scientist, USDA-
      ARS, Agricultural Research, Watkinsville, GA
      30677.

INTRODUCTION

Water flowing from land contains dissolved and suspended material as a natural consequence of fluvial and geochemical processes. Man's activities alter this flow by delaying or accelerating and increasing or decreasing the natural transport rates and by adding material from outside the watershed. We must understand the natural transport processes so that we can better utilize resources to meet the growing demands for food, water, energy, and space. These demands will lead to watershed management with consequent changes in water and material transport. To best use our resources, we must also understand how such management affects the transport processes.

To minimize repetition, we assume that the reader is aware of material in other chapters of the monograph. Some repetition is needed because of the unique problems of chemical transport. For example, although watershed runoff might be modeled with little attention to the actual flow paths, understanding chemical transport requires knowledge of these paths. Similarly, a knowledge of total sediment movement may be enough for some purposes, but in understanding adsorbed chemical transport, the size distribution of the sediment is also important.

In this chapter, modeling and different types of models are discussed in the context of chemical transport. The processes that affect chemical transport from small watersheds are described, and then constituents of runoff are discussed. Table 9.1 shows a matrix of the different chemical constituents and transport processes and shows how important they are currently considered in water from small watersheds. The chapter closes with a review of some specific models.

MODELING

The goals of modeling, types of models, sources of uncertainty, parameter estimation, and model evaluation are discussed in this section in the context of chemical transport modeling. Other chapters of this monograph, particularly those dealing with model calibration and testing, should be reviewed.

TABLE 9.1. THE IMPORTANCE OF VARIOUS CHEMICAL CONSTITUENTS AND
TRANSPORT PROCESSES IN WATER QUALITY FROM SMALL WATERSHEDS

			CHEMICAL CONSTITUENTS					
	Sediment	Salinity	Nutrients N	P	Pesticides	Oxygen deficit DO & BOD	Heavy metals	Micro-organisms
Convection	x	$\underline{x}$	$\underline{x}$	x	$\underline{x}$	x	x	x
Suspension	x		$\underline{x}$	$\underline{x}$	$\underline{x}$	x	x	x
Deposition	x		$\underline{x}$	x	$\underline{x}$	x	x	x
Dispersion	?	?	?	?	x	x	x	x
Diffusion		?	$\underline{x}$	?	x		?	
Tillage	x		$\underline{x}$	x	$\underline{x}$		?	?
Sorption			$\underline{x}$	$\underline{x}$	$\underline{x}$		$\underline{x}$	?
Ion exchange		$\underline{x}$	$\underline{x}$				?	
Crystalization		$\underline{x}$		x			x	
Hydrolysis					$\underline{x}$		x	
Oxidation-reduction			$\underline{x}$		$\underline{x}$	x	x	
Photochemical					$\underline{x}$			
Biochemical			$\underline{x}$	x	$\underline{x}$	$\underline{x}$	?	x

☐ – process not important in explaining transport of constituents
? – process of uncertain importance
x – process is important
$\underline{x}$ – process is important and discussed in paper

Modeling Goals

The goal of chemical transport modeling is to describe the rate of chemical transport from a watershed under specified conditions. There may be an interest in real-time forecasting so that the short-term impact of acute problems such as pesticide transport can be estimated. There may be an interest in statistical characteristics of chemical transport processes (such as average annual transport) so that the chronic or long term impact of a watershed treatment can be estimated.

To choose an adequate model type, one must clearly understand goals for the model and the resources available to meet the goal. The need for model performance dictates certain types of models, whereas the money and time available limits the choice. For some sets of constraints, a model may not be available.

Types of Models

Models range from very complex research tools to relatively simple planning tools. As a research tool, the model should incorporate the best understanding of the processes being modeled. Its primary goal is to reveal gaps in knowledge that must then be filled. Such models are useful in planning additional experiments for testing, verification, and further model development. The simpler models for such applications as planning may be developed directly, or the more complicated models can be simplified.

Many different types of models have been developed. In classifying them, such terms as statistical, stochastic, deterministic, process-oriented, theoretical, conceptual, and parametric are used. Clarke (1973) and Freeze (1975) have provided useful model classifications. Unfortunately, no unanimity exists as to the meaning of many of these terms. One person's theoretical or conceptual model may be someone else's statistical or "black-box" model. An illustration is the use by Beck and Young (1976) of the Streeter-Phelps formulation for variation of dissolved oxygen in a stream. Although some might call the Streeter-Phelps equation theoretical, Beck and Young used it in a statistical state-space model. Their approach is certainly statistical, but it isn't a black-box approach; it includes some material that could be considered deterministic. We will use these terms in our discussion even though their meaning in the literature is sometimes ambiguous.

Many types of models have been used to predict water quality variables at the watershed outlet. If the watershed response and its time variability is of interest, then complicated models may not be needed; simple statistical models may be adequate. The simplest type of statistical model for this purpose is a frequency model in which the data are represented by a probability distribution. This could be an empirical distribution (a histogram), or a mathematical probability density function, such as the normal distribution. Examples of applications of frequency models to water quality data are given in Hem (1970). One must use or interpret frequency distributions cautiously. Because data from a process appear to fit a particular distribution does not mean that the process is completely random. The process may have dependence or it may have trend, periodicity, or other types of nonstationarity or nonrandomness. Ideally such dependence or nonstationarity should be removed from the data and modeled separately. The remaining component is then modeled as a completely random process.

Models that can represent dependence include the autoregressive, integrated, moving-average (ARIMA) models (Box and Jenkins, 1976). Data are needed to calibrate such models, and the models are not suited to nonstationarity of a general form. While not particularly suitable for answering questions about the impact a change will have, these models can represent an observed stationary process for analysis of statistical characteristics, or they can provide input to other models. Examples of such models of water quality are given in Huck and Farquhar (1974) and McMichael and Hunter (1972).

The state-space model common in control theory and the multivariate ARMA (or ARMAX) model (Young and Whitehead, 1977) are two types of stochastic models. The state-space model is commonly written in a discrete form as

$$X_k = F\,X_{kl} + G\,U_{kl} + W_{kl} \quad\dots\dots\dots\dots\dots\dots\dots\dots\dots\dots\dots\dots\dots\dots\quad [9.1]$$

$$Y_k = H\,X_k + V_k \quad\dots\dots\dots\dots\dots\dots\dots\dots\dots\dots\dots\dots\dots\dots\dots\quad [9.2]$$

where X is a state vector of finite dimension, U is an input vector, Y is a response vector, W and V are random vectors, and F, G, and H are parameter matrices.

The multivariate ARMAX (for ARMA with exogeneous variable) can be written as

$$A(D)\,Y_k = B(D)\,U_k + C(D)\,e_k \quad\dots\dots\dots\dots\dots\dots\dots\dots\dots\dots\dots\dots\quad [9.3]$$

where Y and U are defined as for equations [9.1] and [9.2], e is a random vector usually assumed to have a zero mean and to be serially uncorrelated, and A(D), B(D), and C(D) are parameter matrix polynomials in the delay operator D. The univariate Box-Jenkins model is a special case of equation [9.3]. Although these two forms, state space and ARMAX, have been little used in water quality modeling, they have tremendous potential because of their capacity to model a system with multivariate output, a characteristic of the chemical response of a watershed.

The regression model could even be considered as a special case of equation [9.3]. However, the regression model is usually confined to a univariate response analysis, which may be a marginal analysis if there is actually interest in a multivariate response. This model is commonly written as

$$y_i = \sum_{j=1}^{N} a_j x_{ij} + e \quad \dots\dots\dots\dots\dots\dots\dots\dots\dots\dots\dots\dots\dots\dots \quad [9.4]$$

where y_i is the ith observation of a univariate response, x_{ij} is an independent variable input to the system, a_j is the linear coefficient of the jth independent variable, and e is the random component. When the regression model is used in analysis of chemical transport, y is often a mass per unit time period. If x_{ij} is area of land use, then a_j would be interpreted as mass per unit area per unit time. Physical definition of the coefficients is usually possible. Where the y_i are not independent and where the x_{ij} are intercorrelated, the model does not satisfactorily approximate the complex watershed transport processes.

Many models are of the lumped storage and process type, similar to the Stanford watershed model (Crawford and Linsley, 1966). These types have been called explicit soil moisture accounting (ESMA) models (Todini and Wallis, 1977). They are much more complicated than simple linear models but are still coarse approximations to the real processes on watersheds. This type of model has value if the added cost and structure can be justified. The greatest difficulty with very complicated models is that the complexity limits usage, which in turn limits understanding of the performance of the model, thus increasing the uncertainty associated with its use.

In reviewing models or considering model types, certain characteristics are important: (a) the presence or absence of stochastic components; (b) the nature of the physical and chemical processes represented in the model and how they are represented; (c) the overhead, or time and computer requirements; and (d) the type of inputs required.

The presence of stochastic components is important in considering transferability and in evaluating the model. If a chemical characteristic or process is represented as a stochastic component, the model may not be suitable for forecasting in real time, but might be appropriate for predicting statistical properties. If the stochastic components have parameters that can be estimated or physically defined, the model may be transferred more readily to watersheds with different characteristics. Formal treatment of the model error provides better understanding of the uncertainty associated with model use.

Model structure also affects transferability. If, in a watershed to be modeled, an important process is occurring that is not represented in the model, using the model would be inappropriate. The model structure gives insight into whether a particular physical system can be adequately represented.

The overhead and input requirements may prevent the use of certain models without any consideration of model structure. Models, as computer programs, may not be readily adaptable to some computers and if modification is needed, adequate description of the program may be limiting.

Model Errors

Perhaps the most important need in model use is knowledge of errors and sources of uncertainty. The principal error categories are model error, input error, and output error.

Common sources of model error include modeling a distributed system as a lumped system, omitting processes that are important but not of interest, and representing nonlinear processes as linear ones. Model error is always present, for the very nature of modeling is abstraction. Knowledge of model error is important in evaluating results from model use. The results always include uncertainty due to model error, and evaluation of these results must be tempered by knowledge of that error.

Input error is a second major source of error, especially in hydrologic modeling because one of the main inputs, precipitation, can be quite variable over an area. If erroneous input data are used to calibrate the model, the estimated parameters will contain error. Input error also makes estimation of the model error more difficult because the difference in model prediction and observed watershed response can be due partly to input error.

Output error (that is, error in the measured responses of interest) will usually be less serious than input error, but it is still important. Its major source in small watershed chemical transport comes from infrequent sampling. Although spatial variability is not usually important because a stream sample is a point sample relative to the size of the watershed, there may still be problems with unrepresentative samples from a river cross section.

Spatial Variability

Physical, chemical, and biological characteristics are rarely uniform across a watershed. Recent studies (Biggar and Nielsen, 1976) have shown the variability of leaching, even in an apparently uniform field. When obviously different soils and land uses are considered as one unit, what determines the integrated value observed at the outlet? Will a single value be adequate to represent a given characteristic? Some of these difficulties for ground water flow have been the subject of recent analysis (Freeze, 1975).

One approach to modeling spatial variability is to use a cumulative frequency distribution of a characteristic or process across the watershed. The Stanford watershed model uses a linear approximation to the cumulative frequency distribution for infiltration, whereas the ARM model (Donigian and Crawford, 1975a) arbitrarily divides the watershed into five equal parts based on infiltration capacity and uses the zones to represent the known spatial variability. The zones of the ARM model are not necessarily contiguous. Another approach is to divide the watershed into subunits. The USDAHL model (Holtan and Lopez, 1971; Frere et al., 1975) divides the watershed into three or four zones of approximately uniform hydrologic response. A model developed at Colorado State University (Simons et al., 1975) uses a grid system to divide the watershed into subunits. This approach has possibilities if the subunits have suitable uniform properties.

Time Variability

Sources of error due to time variability arise because of model representations and sampling problems. Model representation refers to considering some condition, characteristic, or process during an interval as constant, as sampled only once, or as interacting with other processes only once. Large time intervals during which processes are nonlinear can introduce very significant errors.

The sampling error arises because of the difficulty of collecting and analyzing chemical samples continuously. Only characteristics (such as electrical conductivity) that can be sampled by some means such as a probe are commonly sampled continuously. The individual chemicals in solution or suspension are not routinely analyzed because of cost. Because processes with very different time scales, such as diurnal, storm, or seasonal, make up the total variability of a system, the frequency of sampling limits the ability to detect such variability. However, some inorganic ions show a relatively stable relationship with electrical conductivity, which can serve as a continuous source of information about the ion.

Parameter Estimation

Many models contain parameters that have physical meaning, but that in application to a watershed or stream require estimation from real data. An example is the deoxygenation coefficient in the Streeter-Phelps equation. Parameter estimation or fitting may be the best way to get information for a parameter value, but great caution must be exercised. Different parameter values can be obtained from the same set of data, and errors in the data also affect the parameter value selected. The approaches used for estimation include least squares, method of moments, maximum likelihood, and Bayesian techniques. The choice depends on the error distribution and model form.

Model Evaluation

The model building loop is usually to (a) choose a model or model structure, (b) estimate the parameters, and (c) evaluate the model. The importance of model evaluation cannot be overstressed. This last step gives information to modify the first step in the next loop. If application rather than model development is important, then information from the model evaluation step is necessary for deciding if the model will meet the need.

Model error is important in judging whether a model is worth the cost. A very elaborate model may not justify the cost difference over a simpler model. It is not true that bigger is better in modeling. One source of problems in fitted models is the tendency for the estimated parameters to reflect errors in the input and output data. Unless carefully controlled, the model will not only be overfitted, but also will create an illusion of very low uncertainty in prediction.

Commonly, a model is evaluated based on how much of the variance in the observed response it explains. The pattern of the unexplained variance also should be considered. The apparent unexplained variance can be unreasonably low when the model is fitted. Split-sample testing is one way to guard against this. Any pattern in the difference between observed and calculated results is an indication of a model weakness, for example, a process not included in the model

TRANSPORT PROCESSES

The processes involved in the transport of chemicals from a watershed are very complex. A theoretical model that represents simultaneously all of the processes does not exist and is unlikely to be a useable tool in the foreseeable future. However, even if a complete theoretical model is not practical, an examination of many of the processes is useful in understanding the models that have been developed. For discussion here, the processes are organized into physical, chemical, and biological groups, although considerable interaction and some overlap occur.

Physical Processes

Convection is the process in which the transporting fluid carries the constituent. Water is the principal carrier. It occurs as rainfall, overland flow, and subsurface movement. These mechanisms are described in considerable detail in other chapters of this monograph. Constituents important to water quality are either dissolved or suspended in the water.

Suspension and deposition are the processes by which solid particles are moved into and returned from the water. Rainfall and overland flow are major factors that detach and suspend soil and organic particles. How much material can be held in suspension depends upon the turbulence of the flow. When the turbulence is reduced, the particles begin to settle out with the heavier particles being deposited first. Because various chemicals are attached to organic and inorganic particulates, these processes are very important in chemical transport.

Dispersion is the result of irregular or unequal transport. Eddies and other turbulences in streams cause some parcels of water to move ahead or lag behind the main flow. Also, the movement of water through porous media, some pathways are longer than others. In both cases, some of the constituents in the water move ahead or lag behind the main flow. The result is an increase in the volume of water containing the constituents, and eventually, a reduction in the peak concentration of the constituent. The amount of mixing or dispersion is proportional to the square root of the distance moved or to the square root of time if the flow is constant.

Diffusion is the net movement of a constituent in response to a concentration difference or gradient. Diffusion processes in the water soil are slow and relatively unimportant in comparison with the previously discussed processes. But volatilization, the movement of a constituent from the liquid phase into the gaseous phase, can be a primary path for dissipation of volatile chemicals. The turbulent action of wind can maintain a very low concentration of the chemical at the soil and water interface, so that diffusion to the surface becomes the factor that limits the rate of volatilization.

Tillage affects chemical transport indirectly by modifying water and sediment movement. Seedbed preparation, planting, and cultivation usually increase infiltration during the first part of a storm. The loosened soil, however, is more susceptible to erosion. The impact of a tillage operation decreases with time, making the time between tillage and the storm important.

Chemical Processes

Sorption is the general term for the movement of a constituent between the solid and solution phases. Adsorption, which may also be considered a physical process, occurs when the chemical leaves the solution and adheres to some solid. Desorption is the reverse process. At equilibrium, a balance between the processes is achieved. The relation between the concentration of a chemical in solution and that on the solid is usually described by a power function; a coefficient times the solution concentration to a power. Often, a single equation will not adequately describe both the adsorption and desorption processes.

Ion exchange is the exchange of an ion in solution for an ion of similar charge on the surface of an oppositely charged solid. Clays usually are negatively charged and thus attract cations. However, clays and hydrous oxides of iron and aluminum can be positively charged under some conditions and thus hold anions. In the pH range of most soils, the charge on organic matter is generally negative and attracts cations.

Crystallization occurs when the concentration of a chemical in solution exceeds its solubility. The concentration in solution is reduced by the formation of the compound in the solid phase. Although solubility relations are well defined for many pure mineral-water systems, these relations can deviate widely in the dynamic soil-water system.

Hydrolysis is the reaction of a chemical with water to form a different compound. Chemical bonds of both the chemical and water are broken and new bonds form.

Oxidation-reduction reactions occur when one chemical loses an electron and is oxidized while another compound gains the electron and is reduced. Oxygen is often involved, but it is not essential.

Photochemical reactions occur when energy from light promotes cleavage of chemical bonds, causing new compounds to form.

Biochemical Processes

Enzymes that various microorganisms contain can greatly accelerate reaction rates. Thus, many organic chemicals can be transformed into other chemicals by oxidation, reduction, hydrolysis, and other chemical reactions occurring in the microorganism.

CHEMICAL CONSTITUENTS

Water even when it falls on land in the form of rain, is not pure; it contains varying amounts of various constituents. Water quality standards are established on the basis of water use. Thus, standards for drinking water are much higher than standards for other uses such as irrigation. The following section discusses the most common constituents that become pollutants when their concentration exceeds standards and describes the efforts that have been made to model them.

Sediment

Sediment is the largest pollutant in terms of volume. Sediment deposits reduce the storage capacity of reservoirs and ponds and the carrying capacity of waterways and channels. Sediment muddies rivers and lakes, reduces aesthetic appeal, and causes turbid conditions that interfere with the normal processes of the aquatic ecosystem.

In addition, sediment carries chemicals, nutrients, pesticides, and metals that can be released to the surrounding water under certain conditions. Thus, accurate measurement of the sediment load in the water and of the chemical content of the sediment is important.

Because sediment has been recognized as a problem for many years, some standards for erosion from cropland have been discussed by Moldenhauer and Onstad (1975). However, these standards (typically allowable loss of 3 to 5 tons of soil per acre per year) were based on the loss of a soil resource and not on the downstream environmental impact. Standards for downstream pollution from sediment have not yet been developed.

The process of soil erosion is selective in terms of particle size and weight. Raindrop splash and flowing water first move the smaller and lighter particles. In addition, the larger particles drop out first during deposition. Consequently, the suspended sediments tend to contain more of the finer and lighter particles, which usually contain higher concentrations of adsorbed chemicals. Therefore, the enrichment process must be predicted by the erosion model (Young and Onstad, 1976) or may be inversely related to the sediment yield (Massey and Jackson, 1952; Massey et al., 1953).

Salts

Most of the problems with salts (inorganic dissolved solids) in the United States occur west of the Mississippi River because of lower precipitation in that area. The limited precipitation does not leach soluble salt from the soil, nor does it supply adequate water for crop production. Therefore, irrigation water containing salts is used; some of the water is transpired by the crop, and the rest can accelerate the leaching process and return large volumes of salts to the rivers. Natural salt sources, such as saline springs and salt areas, also contribute salt to our rivers.

Measurement of electrical conductivity (EC) is a common method of monitoring salinity. The EC can be continuously measured. Measuring total dissolved solids by evaporation of a sample of water is another method used. Determining what individual ions are in water is often needed for complete evaluation. Calcium, magnesium, and sodium are the principal cations of significance for irrigation and industrial uses. High salt content increases the cost of treating the water for municipal and industrial users and limits the types of crops that can be irrigated (U.S. Salinity Laboratory Staff, 1954). A limit of 250 parts per million chloride (Committee on Water Quality Criteria, 1973) and a limit of 500 parts per million total dissolved solids (Public Health Service, 1962) are recommended for public water supplies. Water for agricultural use is classified according to EC and the sodium to calcium and magnesium ratio (U.S. Salinity Laboratory Staff, 1954).

There are numerous functional relationships (Lane, 1975) between specific ions or aggregates of ions and flow. Although the models are not formal statistical models, parameters usually are fitted to observed data by a regression-type approach.

The most common model is of the form

$$C = aQ^b \dots\dots\dots\dots\dots\dots\dots\dots\dots\dots\dots\dots\dots\dots \quad [9.5]$$

where C is concentration, Q is flow, and a and b are parameters. C is often taken to be electrical conductivity or total dissolved solids. Lane (1975) summarized a number of these models. O'Connor (1976) also derived some of these relationships by considering very simple ideal cases of systems that are described by partial differential equations. Hallam (1976) gave several such relationships for experimental catchments in Australia that also included copper and iron on one catchment. Pionke and Nicks (1970) and Pionke et al. (1972) studied salinity in the southwestern U.S. as related to several hydrologic variables, including flow. Most of these models are a components-of-flow type relating total concentration to the concentration in surface flow, concentration in groundwater flow, or the respective flow rates. With the components-of-flow model there is usually difficulty in drawing a line between base flow or groundwater contribution and surface flow.

Several models or studies relate specific ions to EC. Lane (1975), Steele and Matalas (1971), and Steele (1976) all give examples. Relating specific ions to EC in modeling watershed response is useful because EC is relatively easy to measure continuously. If a fairly constant relationship is established between EC and another ion of interest, then fewer analyses are needed. Hem (1970) gives results that show strong correlation. O'Connor (1976) also looked at some simple cases of variation in total dissolved solids concentration with time of year and cited the work of Gunnerson (1967).

Because salinity has been a problem for many years, a number of models have been developed for predicting chemical movement down through the soil by leaching (Alfaro and Keller, 1970; Boast, 1973; Burns, 1974; Kolenbrander, 1970; Lai and Jurinak, 1972; Shaffer and Robbens, 1977; Tanji, 1970; Terkeltoub and Babcock, 1970; and Warrick et al., 1971). The more sophisticated models recognize the exchange of calcium, magnesium, sodium and potassium between the solution and the clay minerals. They also incorporate the dissolution and crystallization of calcium and magnesium sulfates, carbonates, phosphates, and silicates. The models divide the soil into layers, calculate the equilibrium concentrations in the layer, and move part of this new solution to the next layer where a new equilibrium is calculated.

Nutrients

The nutrients nitrogen and phosphorus can cause a water quality problem. Cultivated land is generally fertile, has had fertilizers applied, and is susceptible to surface erosion. Although nitrates can be a health hazard in concentrations above 10 parts per million nitrogen, a more common problem is accelerated eutrophication. Eutrophication is the profuse growth of aquatic organisms in fertile waters. Aquatic plants require most of the same elements as crop plants. Under certain conditions any of several elements may be limiting, but concerns with nitrogen and phosphorus are those most frequently voiced.

Several forms of each nutrient are significant: inorganic ions; nitrate (NO_3), ammonium (NH_4), and orthophosphate (PO_4), which are easily measured; and numerous organic compounds containing nitrogen and phosphorus, which are difficult to measure. Ammonium and orthophosphate are also adsorbed to the mineral particles in the sediment by various ion exchange and sorption reactions. Transport of inorganic and organic forms with sediment is important on many watersheds, and enrichment from the deposition and resuspension of sediment must be recognized.

All the nutrients in solution are considered available to plants, but only a small part of the forms insoluble in water is available. Usually, the amount of insoluble forms far exceeds the amount of soluble forms. The availability of the insoluble forms varies with environmental conditions such as temperature, pH, and oxidation-reduction status. Because there are no procedures for accurately predicting the availability of nutrients in the insoluble forms, total phosphorus and total nitrogen are usually specified.

Some statistical modeling of the inorganic nutrients ammonia, nitrate, nitrite, and orthophosphate has been done. Haith (1976) indicated that 60 to 70 percent of the variation in nitrate could be explained by land use with agricultural land use explaining about 35 percent. However, land use did not explain significant variation in the phosphates.

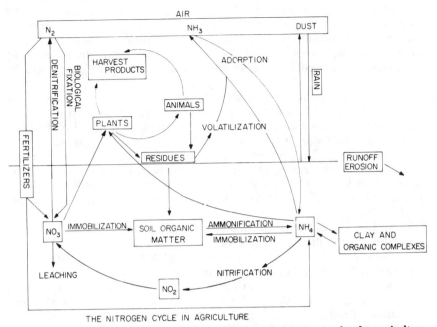

THE NITROGEN CYCLE IN AGRICULTURE

FIG. 9.1 The interrelation of the various nitrogen forms and processes as related to agriculture.

The pickup of nitrate in overland flow is not considered a major problem unless fertilizer or animal wastes are spread on the surface. Nitrate is not adsorbed by the soil. Therefore, rainwater that infiltrates during the first part of a storm should leach most of the nitrate below the soil surface and keep it from entering direct runoff water. The nitrate content of surface runoff from irrigation is similar to that of the water applied (Bondurant, 1971). Part of the nitrate in runoff undoubtedly comes from the rain (Viets and Hageman, 1971). Another part may be from infiltrated water that moves through the soil and returns to the surface as runoff in larger watersheds (Jackson et al., 1973).

Fig. 9.1 (Frere, 1976) illustrates the numerous transformations of nitrogen in the soil-water-air-plant environment, collectively called the nitrogen cycle. "Soil Nitrogen" is a comprehensive review of the subject (Bartholomew and Clark, 1965). A number of models have been developed to predict the behavior of nitrogen in the soil-plant-water system (Beek and Frissel, 1973; Duffy et al., 1975; Dutt et al., 1972; Frere et al., 1970; Hagin and Amberger, 1974; Mehran and Tanji, 1974; Reuss and Cole, 1973).

One of the most important processes that must be considered is mineralization—the production of nitrate from soil organic matter. This can be described by a first-order rate equation:

$$N = N_0 \left[1 - \exp\left(MC \times t\right)\right] \quad \dots \dots \dots \dots \dots \dots \dots \dots \dots \dots \dots \dots [9.6]$$

where N is the amount of nitrate produced from the potential mineralizable nitrogen, N_0, in time, t. The rate constant, MC, is sensitive to temperature and moisture (Smith et al., 1976). Another important process is nitrogen uptake by plants. Generally, plants remove from 40 to 80 percent of the nitrate and ammonium supplied by fertilizer or mineralization. The uptake process varies with the plant species and with growth as controlled by the environment. A general relation has not been developed, although several models are under development (Davidson et al., 1977). Leaching removes nitrate and ammonium from the root zone. Leaching equations for salinity or pesticides (equations [9.9], [9.10], [9.11]) can be used to predict leaching of nitrates and ammonium, assuming an adsorption coefficient of zero for nitrate and from 0.1 to 5.0 for ammonium.

In many soils, the conditions conducive to leaching are also conducive to denitrification, which is the conversion of nitrate to N_2 and N_2O gases by chemical reduction or biochemical reactions. A good model of denitrification is not available. Nitrate in rainfall may be one of the major sources of nitrogen in nonfertilized watersheds. Biological conversion of nitrogen gas, N_2, to organic forms by plant-microbe systems is the other major source. Ammonia is lost by volatilization when ammonium compounds are applied to the soil, particularly alkaline soils (Fenn and Kissel, 1973; Miyamoto et al., 1975).

Davidson et al. (1978) have put a number of the water-nitrogen processes together to predict the fate of nitrogen in the root zone. They developed both a detailed research-type model and a conceptual management-type model. Processes they considered in both models were downward transport of water and dissolved nitrogen as a result of irrigation or rainfall, equilibrium adsorption-desorption of ammonium, microbiological transformations of nitrogen, and uptake of water, nitrate, and ammonium.

Their research model uses an explicit-implicit finite difference scheme to calculate the water and solute movement. They used first-order kinetics to describe nitrification, denitrification, mineralization, and immobilization. They examined a number of relations for root growth and plant uptake of water and nitrogen before finally selecting some relatively simple empirical equations.

Because the research model is complex and needs a large number of input parameters that are seldom available, a simpler model is needed for management situations. They assumed a "piston displacement," described later in equation [9.9], for water and solute movement. The total amount rather than concentration distributions in the root zone is calculated for the various nitrogen forms. These assumptions limit this management model to homogeneous well-drained soil profiles. The research model can simulate a heterogeneous or layered soil profile, but neither model can consider loss of nitrogen in surface runoff.

A number of situations have been simulated with both models, using "realistic" input data. However, the lack of a reliable data base has prevented complete verification of either model. Some data from a field experiment with corn showed the management model overpredicted N uptake by about 14 percent. Results from the management model were in general agreement with results from the research model. In a limited sensitivity test, a 100 percent increase in the nitrogen transformation rate coefficients increased the nitrate concentration only 17 percent.

The phosphorus cycle, illustrated in Fig. 9.2 (Frere, 1976), is not as complicated as the nitrogen cycle. The major reaction is the equilibrium between the orthophosphate (PO_4^{-3}) in solution and that absorbed to the soil. However, no clear distinction exists between surface adsorption and precipitation in various mineral forms, and therefore not all the phosphate removed from solution by the solid phase is readily exchangeable. In run-

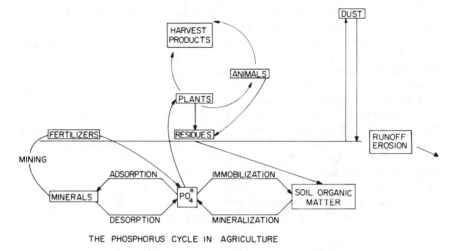

THE PHOSPHORUS CYCLE IN AGRICULTURE

FIG. 9.2 The interrelation of the various phosphorous forms and processes as related to agriculture.

off, sediment with high phosphate adsorption capacity, like subsoil from bank and gully erosion, can remove phosphate from the solution phase (Kunishi et al., 1972). The nonlinear equation

$$S = AC \times C^n \qquad\qquad\qquad\qquad\qquad\qquad\qquad\qquad [9.7]$$

is often used to describe the adsorption isotherm where S is the concentration of exchangeable phosphate on the soil, C is the solution concentration, and AC and n are coefficients to be determined. For phosphate, AC ranges from less than 100 to several thousand and n from 0.5 to 1.0. Three recent papers describe models of phosphorus in the soil system (Enfield and Shew, 1975; Helyar and Munns, 1975; Shah et al., 1975).

Pesticides

Organochlorine pesticides, which are stable and persistent, are being replaced by readily degradable organophosphate and carbamate compounds. A major concern with organochlorines is their biomagnification to toxic concentrations in the higher trophic levels of the ecosystem (vertebrates). The less persistent chemicals are often more toxic and can create an acute toxicity hazard from a single runoff event immediately downstream from a treated area.

Very sophisticated equipment, such as gas, liquid, and thin-layer chromatography, are needed for quantitative pesticide analysis. Interferences from naturally occurring compounds usually make accurate determinations at low levels difficult. Because of the great variety of chemicals sold and their different toxicities (more than 1,800 biologically active compounds in over 32,000 formulations) recommended limits for drinking water range widely. The limits range from 1,000 parts per billion for methoxychlor to a low of 1/10 of a part per billion for heptachlor compounds (Committee on Water Quality Criteria, 1973).

Most pesticides are synthetic organic compounds. The amounts applied are low, 1 or 2 kg/ha, so that concentrations in runoff and sediment are low. Total seasonal losses are commonly 2 to 3 percent or less of the amount applied (Leonard et al., 1976). Some pesticides are found principally in the solution phase; others are very highly adsorbed to the sediment and organic matter. We know of no examples of statistical models for response of pesticides from small watersheds.

Degradation is the major pathway of pesticide loss. The mechanisms involved depend upon the chemical and the environment. There are chemical reactions such as hydrolysis and oxidation or reduction, photochemical reactions with sunlight, and biochemical reactions carried on in microbial metabolism. Obviously, one equation cannot perfectly describe all chemicals in every environment. However, the first-order rate equation appears to be an adequate first approximation for many chemicals (Frere, 1975). The amount of chemical remaining, A, after time, t, is:

$$A = A_0 \exp(-BC \times t) \quad \dots\dots\dots\dots\dots\dots\dots\dots\dots\dots\dots\dots\dots\dots\dots \quad [9.8]$$

where A_0 is the amount at time zero and BC is a breakdown coefficient in reciprocal time units. This coefficient is related to the half-life, $t_{1/2}$, (BC = $0.693/t_{1/2}$), which is reported for many compounds in various environments (Menzie, 1972). A second approximation would be to make BC a function of environmental conditions such as temperature, moisture, and accessibility to sunlight. Pesticide volatilization, another mechanism of dissipation, is also subject to many environmental factors such as temperature, wind speed, and moisture content (Farmer and Letey, 1974; Harper et al., 1976).

The need to predict movement and redistribution of agricultural chemicals and constituents from waste effluents has stimulated development of several models (Davidson et al., 1975; Lindstrom and Boersma, 1973; Oddson et al., 1970; and Shah et al., 1975). Most of these models divide the soil into layers and compute movement from one layer to another. A simple concept that eliminates the need for layers (Frere, 1975) is that the location of the peak chemical concentration in the soil lags in the water front in proportion to the degree of adsorption to the soil. The concentration of the peak decreases with the square root of the distance moved because of dispersion. This concept is expressed mathematically as

$$D = \frac{IN}{FC} \times \frac{FC}{[AM + (BD \times AC)]} \quad \dots\dots\dots\dots\dots\dots\dots\dots\dots\dots\dots \quad [9.9]$$

$$C = \frac{A \times U}{(4\pi \times DF \times D)^{1/2}} \quad \dots\dots\dots\dots\dots\dots\dots\dots\dots\dots\dots\dots \quad [9.10]$$

$$U = 1/[SM + (BD \times AC)] \quad \dots\dots\dots\dots\dots\dots\dots\dots\dots\dots\dots\dots\dots \quad [9.11]$$

where D is the depth of chemical movement, IN is the amount of water infiltered in depth units, FC is the volumetric field capacity, AM is the average moisture content between field capacity and saturation, BD is the bulk density of soil, AC is adsorption coefficient (ratio of the concentration on the soil to the concentration in the solution, see equation [9.7]) C is the concentration in solution at depth D (amount per unit volume), A is the application rate in amount per unit area, DF is the dispersion distribution factor in depth units, U is the units conversion factor, and SM is the soil moisture (volumetric) at D.

Pesticide placement determines concentrations at the soil surface, and, therefore, runoff concentrations for surface-applied chemicals are potentially much higher than for those placed in or mixed with the soil. If pesticides are sprayed on the plant cover, part of the application reaches the ground and part is washed from the plant surfaces during rains.

The process by which runoff extracts chemicals from the soil is complicated and ill-defined (Bailey et al., 1974) and necessary measurements and experiments have yet to be conducted. Several predictive approaches have been suggested. One (Frere, 1975) is to assume leaching and runoff are equally effective in moving chemical. The leaching algorithm (equations [9.9], [9.10], and [9.11]) are used with total rainfall and with infiltration to give two concentrations at the soil surface assuming a guassian distribution about the peak. The mean value between these surface concentrations is assumed to be the mean concentration of the chemical in the runoff water.

Bruce et al. (1975) used a simple extraction coefficient. Kang et al. (1970) used a model of a stirred tank with a constant rate of injection for feedlot runoff. The ARM model (Donigian and Crawford, 1975a) uses a modified Freundlich adsorption curve to equilibrate pesticides with the soil and water in the upper zone. The NPS model (Donigian and Crawford, 1976) assumes that the pesticide comes from the suspended sediment. The weight of soil in the surface layer that equilibrates with surface runoff has been estimated as the ratio of the watershed area to the specific surface area of the soil $(m^2)/(m^2/g)$, (Huff and Kruger, 1967). This can be deduced from the observation that a large part of the adsorption capacity and surface area of soils is a result of plate-shaped clay particles. Assuming that the surface runoff reacts with one layer of clay particles, then the particles would have a surface area twice the watershed area. Not all the surface area is from plates, some is from other particles, so a factor of 2 can be dropped.

For any chemical adsorbed to the soil, erosion is a major transport process. When the chemical is applied to the surface, the amounts of rill and interrill erosion are important (Bruce et al., 1975; Frere, 1975; Rogowski and Tamura, 1970). When the chemical is mixed into the soil, then a single composite process called surface erosion is probably sufficient (Donigian and Crawford, 1975, 1976). On larger watersheds, sediment from gully and bank erosion, which is probably free of pollutants, must be considered because it can adsorb pollutants from the solution phase (Taylor and Kunishi, 1971).

Oxygen-Demanding Material

The microbial oxidation of organic matter in water uses dissolved oxygen. A low level of dissolved oxygen is detrimental to many aquatic organisms, including fish. Municipal and industrial effluents are often principal sources of organic matter, but runoff from land and aquatic growth also contribute.

An electrode can be used to continuously measure the concentration of oxygen dissolved in water. The ambient oxygen concentration does not always reflect the concentration downstream because of potential oxygen uptake during oxidation of organic matter. Potentially degradable organic matter is usually estimated in a 5-day biological laboratory test called the biochemical oxygen demand (BOD). The pioneering work of Streeter and Phelps (1925) has been used for many years to relate dissolved oxygen to BOD. Several more rapid chemical methods have been developed to estimate oxygen demand and are commonly called chemical oxygen demand (COD).

Little has been done with statistical models of watershed responses to dissolved oxygen (DO) or biochemical oxygen demand (BOD), although organic responses have been modeled extensively for channel systems with point inputs. One reason is the importance of organics in larger streams with points of waste discharge. Beck and Young (1976) give an example of use of a state-space model to estimate the reoxygenation coefficient and reaeration coefficient.

Heavy Metals

Before the use of synthetic organic pesticides became widespread, inorganic compounds containing copper, lead, and arsenic were used extensively. Although while they are seldom used today, runoff from land where large amounts of these chemicals were used might be contaminated. Other sources of heavy metals are drainage from landfills, runoff from surface application of municipal sludge, runoff from urban areas, and atmospheric fallout from power plants and industries. Most heavy metals are highly adsorbed to soil, so sediment is the principal transport mechanism. Only limited modeling has been attempted with heavy metals (Patterson et al., 1976).

Microorganisms

One of the most important qualities in any public water supply is the concentration and type of microscopic organisms in the water. The largest source of most microbes is the sewage effluent from municipalities and industries. Runoff from watersheds with large numbers of animals, either domestic or wild, is also a source. Apparently no modeling of microorganism movement has been attempted.

Water Temperature

Although it is not a chemical constituent, water temperature is included here because it is often considered a water quality characteristic and because it is important in modeling many of the chemical transport processes, particularly those involving biochemical activity. Temperature of small streams has received little modeling attention, but several statistical models have been used for temperature in larger streams. McMichael and Hunter (1972) represented daily water temperature as a linear function of a cosine term and a first-order autoregressive term for the Ohio River. Song et al., (1973) found a structurally similar model in a Minnesota study.

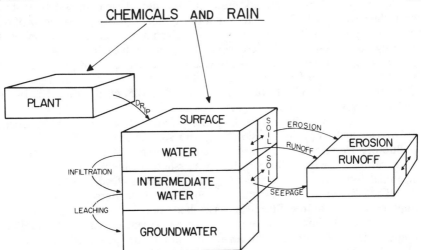

FIG. 9.3 The compartments and processes of a model for chemical movement in watersheds.

COMBINED MODELS

As the preceding description indicates, much information about hydrology and sediment is needed to model chemical transport. Fig. 9.3 (Frere, 1975) illustrates some of the interactions of chemicals, water, and sediment. A number of mathematical models have been prepared that combine models of various processes.

Models have been developed to describe water quality in streams (Beckers et al., 1976; Crim and Lovelace, 1973; Masch and Associates, 1971; Systems Engineering Division, 1970a, 1970b; O'Conner et al., 1973; Water Resources Engineers, Inc., 1973; Harleman et al., 1977). Models also have been developed for urban water quality problems (Donigian and Crawford, 1976; U.S. Corps of Engineers, 1975; Metcalf and Eddy, Inc. et al., 1971). Most of the urban-type models relate water quality parameters to the dust and dirt volume transported. Brandsetter et al. (1976) has a good list of various urban-type models available. Some of the models, such as storm water management model (SWMM), have been modified in recent years (Diniz et al., 1976).

Betson and McMaster (1975) constructed one of the simplest models for stimulating mineral loads in the Tennessee Valley. They used the TVA daily flow model to simulate streamflow, Q, from a watershed of drainage area, DA, and then used the empirical relation, $C = a(Q/DA)^b$, to predict the concentration, C, of various mineral constituents in the water. The coefficients a and b were related by regression techniques to the fraction of the watershed in forest, to four geologic rock types on 66 watersheds, and to 15 standard mineral constituents. The average standard error in fitting was about 40 percent. Testing the model on 12 other watersheds in the region showed overall errors ranged from about 30 percent for some constituents to 100 percent for others.

The most tested combined model for agricultural lands is EPA's agricultural runoff model (ARM) (Donigian and Crawford, 1975a; Crawford and Donigian, 1973). The hydrology section is essentially the Stanford watershed (Crawford and Linsley, 1966). The algorithms for sediment were initially derived by Negev (1967) and subsequently modified. Basically, the model calculated by empirical equations the detachment of soil fines and then their transport. The pesticide subroutine is basically one of adsorption and desorption to the soil. Options are given for a single function or a shifting function that gives increasing adsorption with each cycle of sorption. A simple first-order decay process is used for degradation. The nutrient section uses first-order rate equations for most of the nutrient reactions. Only calibration results have been published, although the model is being tested at several locations.

The nonpoint pollutant loading model (NPS) (Donigian and Crawford, 1976) uses hydrology and erosion programs similar to those of ARM. Other pollutants are related to the sediment by a potency factor. The model has been calibrated with data from four watersheds in metropolitan areas and two small agricultural watersheds (Donigian and Crawford, 1977).

The Wisconsin hydrologic transport model (Patterson et al., 1974), another version of the Stanford watershed model, is being used at Oak Ridge National Laboratory to predict the movement of heavy metals. They combine it with other subroutines for a unified transport model (Patterson et al., 1976).

An agricultural chemical transport model (ACTMO) (Frere et al., 1974, 1975) has been developed to trace chemical movement from one field of a complex watershed. In this model, the chemical submodel (Frere, 1975) uses data calculated by a sediment submodel (Onstad and Foster, 1975; Onstad et al., 1976) and the USDA Hydrograph Laboratory model of watershed hydrology (USDAHL) (Holtan and Lopez, 1971). The hydrology model divides the watershed into several hydrologic zones. Water from the upper zones cascades over the lower zones or goes to a channel. The erosion model further subdivides the watershed into cascade paths over which the sediment is routed to the channel. Consequently, if one of the hydrologic zones is a chemically treated field, the impact of water and sediment from the rest of the watershed on the chemical transport can be evaluated.

The most recent combined system (Williams and Horn, 1978) is a set of models for runoff volume, runoff peak, sediment, phosphorus balance, nitrogen balance, and the routing of sediment, phosphorus, and nitrogen from small watersheds through a large watershed. A modified SCS curve number model simulates the volume of individual storm runoff. Peak flow for the storms is determined by convolving source runoff with an instantaneous unit hydrograph. A modification of the Universal Soil Loss Equation, using runoff volume and peak flow in place of the rainfall factor, is used to predict the sediment yield.

Williams's phosphorus and nitrogen yield models are adapted to individual storm prediction by simulating daily nutrient concentrations in the soil and then associating them with the daily sediment prediction by using loading functions and enrichment ratios. Enrichment ratios are determined from sediment routing, using the entire particle size distribution. The concentration of nitrate in runoff is assumed to be the same as that of the top 2.5-cm soil layer diluted with the volume of rainfall.

The model has not been tested with a complete data set, but realistic results were obtained when a 100-km^2 watershed was simulated. Results of the chemical transport system of models can be used in a linear programming model to obtain optimal land use within constraints imposed by sediment, phosphorus, and nitrogen yield.

Finally, submodels for chemical transport are combined with other models for farm management analysis and evaluation. An example is a model for nutrient management on a dairy farm (Coote et al., 1975). It was designed to determine the economic and environmental consequences of various farm practices and the impact of certain regulatory restrictions. Nutrient inputs are rainfall, fertilizer, and feed. Losses are volatilization, denitrification, leaching, runoff, erosion, and crop and animal products. Very simple relations were used in the calculations.

DEVELOPING A MODEL

The preceding material illustrates the complexity of modeling water quality and chemical transport. Many combinations of processes and chemicals could be considered. Therefore, it is important to clearly define the objectives for using the model. Depending upon the objectives, a number of processes and/or chemicals can be neglected. No one model is universal.

The development of models can be approached from two directions. One way is to start with a high degree of detail and to eliminate process that appear less important. An example of this is the first-order rate equations for many nutrient transformation reactions in the ARM model. A subsequent version has reduced the number of reactions considered. The other approach is to start with simple relations and increase the complexity as necessary. An example of this approach is illustrated in the models of Williams and Hann (1978) where an average annual sediment loss was refined to storm event losses with storm runoff.

It seems that nutrient problems are chronic, or long-term problems, Therefore, seasonal or annual estimates may be adequate. An exception to this would be washoff of surface-applied fertilizer, because the time and amount of rainfall between application and the first runoff event can significantly affect the observed concentration of nutrients in solution. Pesticides in use today cause acute, or short-term, problems. As with surface-applied fertilizer, storm event information is needed for accurate evaluation of pesticide losses.

SUMMARY

Water quality is a many-faceted problem. The pollutants that lower water quality are sediment, salts, nutrients, pesticides, heavy metals, organic matter, and microorganisms. Sources of these pollutants are also numerous and varied. They range from point sources like municipal and industrial waste treatment plants to nonpoint sources like runoff from urban and rural lands.

Planning for future development and correction of today's problems requires the ability to predict the quantity and quality of water resources under various management conditions. The problem is complex; mathematical models are needed for predictions. Because knowledge of whether some chemical characteristic is a pollutant depends on the given situation, the emphasis must be on understanding and modeling the chemical transport process. The models that reflect this understanding can then be used for a particular situation to help in making decisions.

The models range from simple models for first approximations to highly complex research tools, and from statistical relations to process-oriented or deterministic models. No one model is adequate for all jobs, and none has been documented well enough even for a few uses. But we hope that identifying areas of strength or weakness will lead to renewed research efforts. Perhaps this overview will result in more effective use of water quality models.

References

1 Alfaro, J. F. and J. Keller. 1970. Model theory for predicting process of leaching. TRANSACTIONS of the ASAE 13(3):362-368.

2 Bailey, G. W., R. R. Swank, Jr., and H. P. Nicholson. 1974. Predicting pesticide runoff from agricultural land: A conceptual model. J. Environ. Qual. 3:95-102.

3 Bartholomew, W. V., and F. E. Clark (Ed.). 1965. Soil nitrogen. Am. Soc. of Agron., Madison, WI.

4 Beck, B., and P. Young. 1976. Systematic Identification of DO-BOD model structure. J. Environ. Eng. Div., ASCE 102:909-927.

5 Beckers, C. V., P. E. Parker, R. N. Marshall, and S. G. Chamberlain. 1976. RECEIV-II, a generalized dynamic planning model for water quality management. In Environmental Modeling and Simulation. Edited by W. R. Ott. Environmental Protection Agency Technol. Ser. EPA-600/9-76-016, pp. 344-349.

6 Beek, J., and M. J. Frissel. 1973. Simulation of nitrogen behavior in soils. Center for Agr. Pulbishing and Documentation, Wageningen, The Netherlands. 67 pp.

7 Betson, R. P., and W. M. McMaster. 1975. Nonpoint source mineral water quality model. J. Water Pollut. Contr. Fed. 47(10):2461-2473.

8 Biggar, J. W. and D. R. Nielsen. 1976. Spatial variability of the leaching characteristics of a field soil. Water Resour. Res. 12:78-84.

9 Boast, C. W. 1973. Modeling the movement of chemicals and soils by water. Soil Sci. 115(3):224-230.

10 Bondurant, J. A. 1971. Quality of surface irrigation runoff water. TRANSACTIONS of the ASAE 14:1001-1003.

11 Box, G. E. P., and G. M. Jenkins. 1976. Time Series Analysis. Holden-Day, San Francisco, CA.

12 Brandsetter, A., R. Field, and H. C. Torno. 1976. Evaluation of mathematical models for the simulation of time varying runoff and water quality in storm and combined sewage systems. In Environment Modeling and Simulation. Edited by W. R. Ott. Environmental Protection Agency Technol. Ser. EPA-600/9-76-016, pp. 548-552.

13 Bruce, R. R., L. A. Harper, R. A. Leonard, W. M. Snyder, and A. W. Thomas. 1975. A model for runoff of pesticides from small upland watersheds. J. Environ. Qual. 4(4):541-548.

14 Burns, I. G. 1974. A model for predicting the redistribution of salts applied to fallow soils after excess rainfall or evaporation. J. Soil Sci. 25(2):165-178.

15 Clarke, R. T. 1973. A review of some mathematical models used in hydrology, with observations on their calibration and use. J. Hydrol. 19:1-20.

16 Committee on Water Quality Criteria. 1973. Water Quality Criteria. 1972. Environmental Standards Board, National Academy of Science. EPA-R3-73-003.

17 Coote, D. R., D. A. Haith, and P. J. Zwerman. 1975. Environmental and economic impact of nutrient management on the New York dairy farm. Search Agriculture 5(5): 27 pp. Cornell University, Ithaca, NY.

18 Crawford, N. H., and A. S. Donigian, Jr. 1973. Pesticide transport and runoff model for agricultural land. Environmental Protection Agency Technol. Ser. EPA-660/2-74-013. 211 pp.

19 Crawford, N. H., and R. K. Linsley. 1966. Digital simulation in hydrology: Stanford Watershed Model IV. Department of Civil Engineering, Stanford University, Stanford, CA. Tech. Rept. No. 39. 210 pp.

20 Crim, R. A., and N. L. Lovelace. 1973. AUTO-QUAL modeling systems. Environmental Protection Agency Technol. Ser. EPA-440/9-73-003.

21 Davidson, J. M., G. H. Brusewitz, D. R. Baker, and A. L. Wood. 1975. Use of soil parameters for describing pesticide movement through soils. Environmental Protection Agency Technol. Ser. EPA-660/2-75-009, 149 p.

22 Davidson, J. M., D. A. Graetz, P. S. C. Rao, and H. M. Selim. 1978. Simulation of nitrogen movement, transformation, and uptake in plant root zone. Environmental Protection Agency EPA-600/3-78-029.

23 Davidson, J. M., S. C. Rao, and H. M. Selem. 1977. Simulation of nitrogen movement, transformations, and plant uptake in the root zone. In Proc. of the National Confer-

ence on Irrigation Return Flow Quality Management. Edited by J. P. Law and G. V. Skogerbor. U.S. Environ. Protection Agency and Colorado State Univ., Ft. Collins, CO. pp. 9-18.

24 Diniz, E. V., D. E. Holloway, and W. G. Characklis. 1976. Modeling urban run-off from a planned community. In Environmental Modeling and Simulation. Edited by W. R. Ott. Environ. Protection Agency Technol. Ser. EPA-600/9-76-016, pp. 367-371.

25 Donigian, A. S., Jr., and N. H. Crawford. 1975. Modeling pesticides and nutrients on agricultural land. Environmental Protection Agency Technol. Ser. EPA-600/2-76-043.

26 Donigian, A. S., Jr. and N. H. Crawford. 1976. Modeling nonpoint pollution from the land surface. Environmental Protection Agency Technol. Ser. EPA-600/3-76-083.

27 Donigian, A. S., Jr., and N. H. Crawford. 1977. Simulation of nutrient loadings in surface runoff with the NPS model. Environmental Protection Agency EPA-660/3-77-065.

28 Duffy, J., C. Chung, C. Boast, and M. Franklin. 1975. A simulation model of biophysiochemical transformations of nitrogen in tile-drained corn belt soil. J. Environ. Qual. 4(4):477-486.

29 Dutt, G. R., M. J. Shaffer, and W. J. Moore. 1972. Computer simulation model of dynamic biophysiochemical process in soil. Technical Bulletin No. 196. Agr. Expt. Sta., Univ. of Arizona, Tucson, AZ.

30 Enfield, C. G., and D. C. Shew. 1975. Comparison of two predictive nonequilibrium one-dimensional models for phosphorus sorption and movement through homogeneous soils. J. Environ. Qual. 4(2):198-202.

31 Farmer, W. J., and J. Letey. 1974. Volatilization losses of pesticides from soils. Environmental·Protection Agency Technol. Ser. EPA-660/2-74-054.

32 Fenn, L. B., and D. E. Kissel. 1973. Ammonia volatilization and surface applications of ammonium compounds on calcareous soils: I. General Theory. Soil Sci. Soc. Am. Proc. 37:855-859.

33 Freeze, R. A. 1975. A stochastic-conceptual analysis of one-dimensional ground-water flow in nonuniform homogeneous media. Water Resour. Res. 11:725-741.

34 Frere, M. H. 1973. Adsorption and transport agricultural chemicals in watersheds. TRANSACTIONS of the ASAE 16(3):569-572 and 577.

35 Frere, M. H. 1975. Integrating chemical factors with water and sediment transport from a watershed. J. Environ. Qual. 4(1):12-17.

36 Frere, M. H. 1976. Nutrient aspects of pollution from cropland. In Control of Water Pollution from Cropland. An Overview. II(4):59-90. USDA Rept. No. ARS-H-5-2.

37 Frere, M. H., M. E. Jensen, and J. N. Carter. 1970. Modeling water and nitrogen behavior in the soil plant system. Proc. 1970 Summer Computer Simulation Conf., pp. 746-750.

38 Frere, M. H., C. A. Onstad, and H. N. Holtan. 1974. Modeling the movement of agriculture chemicals. Proc. 1974 Summer Computer Simulation Conf., pp. 271-274.

39 Frere, M. H., C. A. Onstad, and H. N. Holtan. 1975. ACTMO, an agricultural chemical transport model. ARS-H-3. ARS, USDA, Washington, DC. 54 pp.

40 Gunnerson, C. G. 1967. Streamflow and quality in the Columbia River basin. J. Sanitary Eng. Div., ASCE 93:1-16.

41 Hagin, J., and A. Amberger. 1974. Contribution of fertilizers and manures to the N- and P-load of waters. Final Report to Deutsche Forschangs Gemeinschaft, Technion Haifa, Israel.

42 Haith, D. A. 1976. Land use and water quality in New York Rivers. Journal of the Environmental Engineering Division ASCE 102(EE1):1-15.

43 Hallam, P. M. 1976. Water quality studies on experimental catchments and an ecosystem. In hydrologic techniques for upstream conservation, p. 73-87, FAO Conservation Guide 2, Rome.

44 Harleman, D. R. F., J. E. Dailey, M. L. Thatcher, T. O. Najarian, D. N. Brocard, and R. A. Ferrara. 1977. User's manual for the M.I.T. transient water quality network model—including nitrogen cycle dynamics for rivers and estuaries. Environmental Protection Agency Ecol. Res. Ser. EPA-600/3-77-010, 231 p.

45 Harper, L. A., A. W. White, R. R. Bruce, and R. A. Leonard. 1976. Soil and microclimate effects on trifluralin volatilization. J. Environ. Qual. 5:236-242.

46 Helyar, K. R., and D. N. Munns. 1975. Phosphate flux in the soil plant system: A computer simulation. Hilgaradia 43(4):103-130.

47 Hem, J. D. 1970. Study and interpretation of the chemical characteristics of natural water. USGS Water Supply Paper 1473, U.S. Government Printing Office, Washington, DC.

48 Holtan, H. N., and N. C. Lopez. 1971. USDAHL-74 model of watershed hydrology. Tech. Bull. No. 1435, ARS, USDA.

49 Huck, P. M., and G. J. Farquhar. 1974. Water quality models using the Box-Jenkins method. J. Environ. Eng. Div. 100:733-752.

50 Huff, D. D., and P. A. Kruger. 1967. A numerical model for the hydrologic transport of radioactive aerosols from precipitation to water suplies. Isotope techniques in the hydrologic cycle, Geophys. Monogr. (11):85-96.

51 Jackson, W. A., L. E. Asmussen, E. W. Hauser, and A. W. White. 1973. Nitrate in surface and subsurface flow from a small agricultural watershed. J. Environ. Qual. 2: 480.

52 Kang, F. F., L. T. Fan, E. S. Lee, and L. E. Erickson. 1970. Modeling feedlot runoff pollution. I. Analog simulation. TRANSACTIONS of the ASAE 13(6):859-863.

53 Kolenbrander, G. J. 1970. Calculations of parameters for the evaluation of leaching of salts and under field conditions, illustrated by nitrate. Plant and Soil 32:439-453.

54 Kunishi, H. M., A. W. Taylor, W. R. Heald, W. J. Gburek, and R. H. Weaver. 1972. Phosphate movement from an agricultural watershed during two rainfall periods. J. Agr. Food Chem. 20:900-905.

55 Lai, S. H., and J. J. Jurinak. 1972. Cation adsorption in one-dimensional flow through soils: A numerical solution. Water Resour. Res. 8(1):99-107.

56 Lane, W. L. 1975. Extraction of information on inorganic water quality. Hydrology Paper 73. Colorado State University, Ft. Collins, CO.

57 Leonard, R. A., G. W. Bailey, and R. R. Swank, Jr. 1976. Transport, detoxification, fate, and effect of pesticides in soil and water environments. In Land application of waste materials. Soil Conserv. Soc. Am., Ankeny, IA, p. 48-78.

58 Lindstrom, F. T., and L. Boersma. 1973. A theory on the mass transport of previously distributed chemicals in a water saturated, sorbing porous medium: III. Exact solution for first order kinetic sorption. Soil Sci. 115(1):5-10.

59 Masch, F. D. and Assoc. 1971. Simulation of water quality in streams and canals. Texas Water Development Board Rept. No. 128, Austin, TX.

60 Massey, H. F., and M. L. Jackson. 1952. Selective erosion of soil fertility constituents. Soil Sci. Soc. Am. Proc. 16:353-356.

61 Massey, H. F., M. L. Jackson, and O. E. Hayes. 1953. Fertility erosion on two Wisconsin soils. Agron. J. 45:543-547.

62 McMichael, F. C., and J. S. Hunter. 1972. Stochastic modeling of temperature and flow in rivers. Water Resour. Res. 8(1):87-98.

63 Mehran, M. and K. K. Tanji. 1974. Computer modeling of nitrogen transformations in soil. J. Environ. Qual. 3:391-396.

64 Menzie, C. M. 1972. Fate of pesticides in the environment. Annual Review of Entomology 17:199-222.

65 Metcalf and Eddy, Inc., University of Florida, and Water Resources Engineers, Inc. 1971. Storm water management model. U.S. EPA, Washington, DC. Rept. Nos. 11024 DOC 07/71, 08/71, 09/71, 10/71.

66 Miyamoto, S., J. Ryan, and J. L. Stroehlein. 1975. Sulphuric acid for the treatment of ammoniated irrigation water: I. Reducing ammonia volatilization. Soil Sci. Soc. Am. Proc. 39(3):544-548.

67 Moldenhauer, W. C. and C. A. Onstad. 1975. Achieving specified soil loss soils. J. Soil and Water Conserv. 30(4):166-168.

68 Negev, M. A. 1967. Sediment model on a digital computer. Dept. of Civil Engineering, Stanford Univ., Stanford, CA. Tech. Rept. No. 39. 109 pp.

69 O'Connor, D. J. 1976. The concentration of dissolved solids and river flow. Water Resour. Res. 12(2):279-294.

70 O'Connor, D. J., R. V. Thonnan, and D. N. DiToro. 1973. Dynamic water quality forecasting and management. Environmental Protection Agency Technol. Ser. EPA-660/3-73-009.

71 Oddson, J. K., J. Letey, and L. V. Weeks. 1970. Predicted distribution of organic chemicals in solution and adsorbed as a function of position and time for various chemical and soil properties. Soil Sci. Soc. Am. Proc. 34(3):412-417.

72 Onstad, C. A., and G. R. Foster. 1975. Erosion modeling on a watershed. TRANSACTIONS of the ASAE 18(2):288-292.

73 Onstad, C. A., R. F. Piest, and K. E. Saxton. 1976. Watershed erosion model validation for southwest Iowa. Thrid Federal Inteagency Sedimentation Conf. Proc., Water Resour. Coun., Washington, DC. pp. 1-22, 1-34.

74 Patterson, M. R., C. L. Begovich, and D. R. Jackson. 1976. Environmental transport modeling of pollutants in water and soil. Symposium on Nonbiological Transport and Transformation of Pollutants on Land and Water, National Bureau of Standards, Gaithersburg, MD.

75 Patterson, M. R., J. K. Munro, D. E. Fields, R. D. Ellison, A. A. Brooks, and D. D. Huff. 1974. A users manual for the FORTRAN IV version of the Wisconsin hydrologic transport model. ORNL/NS/EATC-7.

76   Pionke, H. B., and A. D. Nicks. 1970. The effect of selected hydrologic variables on stream salinity. International Association of Scientific Hydrol. Bull. 25:13-21.

77   Pionke, H. G., A. D. Nicks, and R. R. Schoof. 1972. Estimating salinity of streams in the southwestern United States. Water Resour. Res. 8(6):1597-1604.

78   Public Health Service. 1962. Public Health Service Drinking Water Standards, revised. Public Health Service Publication No. 956, Government Printing Office, Washington, DC. 61 pp.

79   Reuss, J. O., and C. V. Cole. 1973. Simulation of nitrogen flow in a grassland ecosystem. 1973 Summer Computer Simulation Conf. Proc., Montreal, Quebec, Canada. pp. 762-768.

80   Rogowski, A. S., and T. Tamura. 1970. Erosional behavior of Cesium-137. Health Physics 18:467-477.

81   Shaffer, M. J., and R. W. Robbens. 1977. Practical applications of irrigation return flow quality models to large areas. In 'Proceedings of a National Conference on Irrigation Return Flow Quality Management". Edited by J. P. Law and G. V. Skogerboe. U.S. Environmental Protection Agency and Colorado State Univ., Fort Collins, CO. pp. 217-223.

82   Shah, D. B., G. A. Coulman, L. T. Novak, and B. G. Ellis. 1975. A mathematical model for phosphorus movement in soils. J. Environ. Qual. 4(1):87-92.

83   Simons, D. B., R. M. Li, and M. A. Stevens. 1975. Development of models for predicting water and sediment routing and yield from storms on small watersheds. Civil Engineering Dept. Colorado State Univ., Fort Collins, CO. CER 74 75DBS-RML-MAS24.

84   Smith, S. J., L. B. Young, and G. E. Miller. 1976. Field evaluation of soil nitrogen mineralization potentials. Soil Sci. Soc. Am. Proc. (in press).

85   Song, C. C. S., A. F. Pabst, and C. S. Bowers. 1973. Stochastic analysis of air and water temperatures. J. Environ. Eng. Div. ASCE 99:785-800.

86   Steele, T. D. 1976. A bivariate-regression model for estimating chemical composition of streamflow or groundwater. Hydrol. Sci. Bull. 21:149-161.

87   Steele, T. D., and N. C. Matalas. 1971. Principal-component analysis of streamflow chemical quality data. Paper presented at Int. Symp. on Math. Models in Hydrology. IASH. Warsaw, Poland.

88   Streeter, H. W., and E. B. Phelps. 1925. A study of the pollution and natural purification of the Ohio River. U.S. Public Health Service, Public Health Bull. 146, 75 p.

89   Systems Engineering Division. 1970a. DOSAG-I Simulation of water quality in streams and canals. Texas Water Development Board, Austin, TX.

90   Systems Engineering Division. 1970b. QUAL-I Simulation of water quality in streams and canals. Texas Water Development Board, Austin, TX.

91   Tanji, K. K. 1970. A computer analysis on the leaching of boron from stratified soil columns. Soil Sci. 110(1):44-51.

92   Taylor, A. W., and H. M. Kunishi. 1971. Phosphate equilibria on stream sediment and soil in a watershed draining an agricultural region. J. Agr. Food Chem. 19:827-831.

93   Terkeltoub, R. W., and K. L. Babcock. 1970. A simple method predicting salt movement through soils. Soil Sci. 111(1):182-187.

94   Todini, E. and J. R. Wallis. 1977. Using CLS for daily or longer period rainfall-runoff modeling. In Mathematical models for surface water hydrology. Edited by T. A. Ciriani, U. Maione, and J. R. Wallis. John Wiley and Sons, London, England, 1977. pp. 149-168.

95   U.S. Corps of Engineers. 1975. Urban storm runoff-STORM. U.S. Army Corps of Engineers, Davis, CA. The Hydrologic Engineering Center. Computer Program No. S23-SB-L2520. 140 pp.

96   U.S. Salinity Laboratory Staff. 1954. Diagnosis and improvement of saline and alkali soils. Agri. Handb. 60, USDA (Reprinted 1969).

97   Viets, F. G., Jr., and R. H. Hageman. 1971. Factors affecting the accumulation of nitrate in soil, water, and plants. U.S. Dept. Agr., Agr. Res. Serv., Agr. Handb. No. 413, Washington, DC.

98   Warrick, A. W., J. W. Biggar, and D. R. Nielson. 1971. Simultaneous solute and water transfer for an unsaturated soil. Water Resour. Res. 7(5):1216-1225.

99   Water Resource Engineers, Inc. 1973. Computer program documentation for the stream quality model QUAL-II, Walnut Creek, CA.

100   Williams, J. R., and R. W. Hann, Jr. 1978. Optimal operation of large agricultural watersheds with water quality constraints. Texas Wat. Res. Inst., Texas A&M Univ., College Station, TX, TR No. 96.

101   Young, R. A., and C. A. Onstad. 1976. Predicting particle-size composition of eroded soil. TRANSACTIONS of the ASAE 19(6):1071-1075.

chapter 10

SOME PARTICULAR WATERSHED MODELS

10

SOME PARTICULAR WATERSHED MODELS

by Curtis L. Larson, Professor of Agricultural
    Engineering, University of Minnesota, St. Paul,
    MN; Charles A. Onstad, Agricultural Engineer,
    USDA, ARS, Morris, MN; Harvey H. Richardson,
    Hydraulic Engineer, Soil Conservation Service,
    Glenn Dale, MD, and Kenneth N. Brooks,
    Assistant Professor of Forestry, University of Min-
    nesota, St. Paul, MN.

Several frequently-used, deterministic watershed models are discussed in this chapter. In each case, the principal features and components of the model are described in general terms and some examples of model application are given. The various models are characterized as to general structure, scope, parameters and applicability and compared in these terms. Special purpose, partial and distributed watershed models are also considered briefly.

The principal objective of this chapter is to provide some insight into how watershed models in general are structured and how they work internally and how these characteristics relate to model application. Several representative watershed models are used as a basis for study, comparison and generalization. It is suggested, therefore, that while proceeding the reader consider such questions as "How do the various models differ?" and "In what ways are they similar?" Also, "Do the common aspects represent essential features?" "Are the differences useful in providing a choice of watershed models for various needs and applications?" The insights gained will be enhanced further if the reader has studied the modeling of individual hydrologic processes as described in previous chapters.

Three possible approaches to a modeling application are: using an existing model, modifying an existing model and developing a new model. In general, they should be considered in that order. The act of choosing one of these approaches is itself an important decision. If the decision is to use an existing model, one should choose the model best suited to the particular application. Similarly, if an existing model is to be modified, choosing a model amenable to the particular modification(s) is, of course, necessary. Developing a new model should be recognized as a major undertaking, probably requiring several years of intensive work for a complete watershed model. Applying an existing model may involve several months of effort and significant modification of the model would require considerably more time.

The decision about the best approach to a particular modeling application should be made on the basis of knowledge of both modeling principles and available watershed models. This chapter is an attempt to combine or integrate these two aspects of watershed modeling. The earlier chapters have concentrated on the "building blocks", i.e., component models, and modeling principles. On the other hand, Chapter 13 provides, without discussion, an inventory of existing watershed models.

To fully understand the principles of watershed modeling one needs to work with one or more particular watershed models. Studying about watershed models is a poor substitute, but can be very worthwile as a preparatory step. Applying a watershed model is by far the best way to learn it's capabilities and limitations. By using the model for a number of watersheds and/or watershed conditions, one also becomes familiar with the sensitivity of it's parameters. If the objective is only to study the effects of various inputs, one can apply the model without a detailed understanding of its inner workings. In most applications, however, a good understanding of the model is highly desirable if not absolutely essential.

MODEL STRUCTURE

A deterministic watershed model usually includes the following elements:

1 Input parameters representing the relevant physical characteristics of the watershed.

2 Input of precipitation and other meteorological data.

3 Calculation of water flows, both surface and subsurface.

4 Calculation of water storages, both surface and subsurface.

5 Calculation of water losses.

6 Watershed outflow and other outputs, if desired.

Elements 3, 4 and 5 are the working portion or "heart" of a deterministic watershed model. Most models include a number of water flows, storages and losses which are shown in a flow chart of the model. (Figs. 10.1 and 10.3). In general, the greater the detail of the model, the greater the number of flow pathways and storages.

A deterministic watershed model consists of a series of submodels each representing a particular hydrologic process (infiltration, overland flow, etc.) and usually is structured accordingly. The submodels utilize the above types of elements as needed. Each submodel represents basically a flow of water and usually includes a storage. The submodel output is either an outflow to the next submodel or a water loss. Water losses, mainly to the atmosphere, are in reality outflows from the system.

Water storages are essential parts of the model, since they play key roles in regulating flow in the watershed itself. Most flows in a model are into or out of a storage. The flow is often related to the amount of water in storage as well as other factors, as in nature. In some cases, the storage is not represented separately in the model but is a part of the flow relationship, for example, in dynamic channel routing.

Model building is a process of choosing appropriate submodels, linking them together to form a watershed model, and making the resulting watershed model work. Each of these steps if important and requires considerable effort. Which submodels are appropriate? The answer to this question depends mainly on the purpose or intended use of the overall model. Is the model intended purely for predicting watershed outflow, or for other purposes also? Are low flows important or not? Is the model intended for a particular type of watershed in terms of size, topography or land use e.g., urban watersheds? Or is it intended for use on any type of watershed?

How much detail should be used in each submodel? In choosing or developing a submodel, one's instinct is to choose the most detailed submodel available or to add some "improvements" to an existing submodel. Coming later to assembling the submodels, one may find that the resulting watershed model is entirely too cumbersome or too costly to operate. The next step is to reduce the detail wherever it can be done without serious loss of accuracy, if possible. Thus, in studying existing models or submodels, one should be aware that the model developer probably went through this process and made some tradeoffs of this type to obtain a practical model.

If the model is intended for purposes beyond streamflow prediction, the structure and amount of detail may need to be adjusted to suit the application. If the objective is to study the hydrologic effects of some land use modification, the model needs to be appropriately sensitive to the corresponding factor(s) and process(es). This may require special emphasis and detail in one or more of the submodels. At the same time, if the model is intended for this purpose only, it may be possible to reduce the detail in some other submodel(s). Similarly, if the watershed model is to be the basis for a transport model, its emphasis may need to be directed accordingly. For example, if the overall objective is modeling soil erosion and sediment delivery, special attention will undoubtedly need to be given to the overland flow submodel.

We see then that watershed models can vary in structure, amount of detail and emphasis on individual hydrologic processes. Their basic nature also varies, as indicated in Chapter 1 and further in the following pages. It is evident that the potential for model development is unlimited and that new or modified watershed models will continue to be developed.

CHARACTERIZING WATERSHED MODELS

It was noted in Chapter 1 that certain descriptive terms are frequently applied to hydrologic and other mathematical models and that these can be applied to either component models or watershed models. Some additional descriptive terms will be utilized here, since they are quite useful in characterizing watershed models. Such terms, if well defined*, enable one to indicate by a word or a short phrase how one model differs from another in character scope, purpose, operation or application. It will be convenient and useful to use these terms in discussing the several particular models described in this chapter.

Watershed models can be characterized also as event models or continuous models. An event model is one that represents a single runoff event occurring over a period of time ranging from an hour, more or less, to several days. The initial conditions in the watershed for each event must be assumed or determined by other means and supplied as input data. The accuracy of the model output may depend on the reliability of these input conditions. A continuous watershed model is one that operates over an extended period of time determining flow rates and conditions during both runoff periods and periods of no (surface) runoff. Thus, the model keeps a continuous account of the basin moisture condition and, therefore, determines the initial conditions applicable to runoff events. However, at the beginning of the run, the

---

*Some terms are well understood and accepted, e.g., deterministic model, but useage varies for certain others.

initial conditions must be known or assumed. Most continuous watershed models utilize three runoff components, direct runoff, shallow subsurface flow (interflow) and groundwater flow, while an event model may omit one or both of the subsurface components and also evapotranspiration.

In terms of scope, there are complete models and partial models. A complete or comprehensive watershed model is one for which the (primary) input is precipitation and the output is the watershed hydrograph. The model represents in more or less detail all hydrologic processes significantly affecting runoff. A partial model represents only a part of the overall runoff process. A water yield model gives runoff volumes but no discharges.

It is useful also to characterize watershed models as fitted parameter models or measured parameter models. A fitted parameter model is one which has one or more parameters that can be evaluated only by fitting computed hydrographs to the observed hydrographs. Fitted parameters are usually necessary if the watershed model has any conceptual component models, which is true for most presently used watershed models. Thus, with a fitted parameter model, a period of recorded flow is needed, usually several years, for determining the parameter values for a particular watershed. In general, therefore, fitted parameter models can be used only on gaged watersheds, except for a few special applications.

A measured parameter model, on the other hand, is one for which all the parameters can be determined satisfactorily from known watershed characteristics, either by measurement or by estimation. For example, watershed area and channel lengths can be determined from existing maps. Two examples of direct measurement would be field measurements of channel cross-sections and lab measurements of soil characteristics. Channel roughness is often estimated. A measured parameter model can be applied to totally ungaged watersheds and, therefore, is highly desired. The development of such a model that is also continuous, acceptably accurate and generally applicable is, however, a very difficult task. In fact, it is a goal that has not yet been attained.

Watershed models can be classified also as general models and special purpose models. A general model is one that is acceptable (without modification) to watersheds of various types and sizes. The model has parameters, either measured or fitted, that adequately represent the effects of a wide variety of watershed characteristics. Unfortunately, it is difficult to do this without resorting to conceptual submodels, which usually have parameters that require fitting. A special purpose watershed model is one that is applicable to a particular type of watershed in terms of topography, geology or land use, e.g., an urban runoff model. Usually, such models can be applied to watersheds of different sizes, as long as the character of the watersheds are the same.

Watershed models or submodels are sometimes referred to as distributed models or lumped models. A distributed model is one in which areal variations in watershed characteristics, e.g., soils and land use, can be utilized directly in applying the model. In a lumped model, this cannot be done and, therefore, representative or mean values of land slope, slope length, soil characteristics, etc. are usually used. Distributed models are, of course, more desirable, but they have an added price in terms of model complexity, input data requirement and operating (computer) costs. As a result most watershed models to date are lumped models.

With this background, we proceed to review and compare several frequently used watershed models. The models selected for this purpose are all complete and general watershed models, but differ in other respects. Beyond this, the choice was somewhat arbitrary. For example, there are several good Australian watershed models (Moore and Mein, 1976), none of which are included here.

STANFORD WATERSHED MODEL

The Stanford Watershed Model was developed by Crawford and Linsley (1966) and is frequently cited in the literature, being one of the first comprehensive watershed models.† The model has been widely used in water resource studies and has undergone numerous modifications, additions and revisions. Perhaps the best known of these is the Kentucky version of the model (James, 1970). Revisions have been reported also by Ligon et al. (1969), Claborn and Moore (1970), Ricca (1974) and others.

The Stanford Model is a complete and general watershed model, being intended for application to watersheds of all types and sizes. It is a continuous model and is usually operated over a period of years. The model utilizes a number of fitted parameters and, therefore, requires several years of flow records for most applications.

In the Stanford Model, the various hydrologic processes are represented mathematically as flows and storages (Fig. 10.1). In general, each flow is an outflow from a storage, usually expressed as a function of the current storage amount and the physical characteristics of the subsystem. Thus, the overall model is physically based, although many of the flows and storages are represented in a simplified or conceptual manner. Although this requires the use of fitted parameters, it has the advantage of avoiding the need for giving the physical dimensions and characteristics of the flow system. This greatly reduces input requirements and, more importantly, gives the model its generality.

The model employs various surface and subsurface water storages which, in most cases, are not defined explicitly. The lower zone storage, for example, represents soil moisture storage, but neither the depth of the zone or the soil moisture characteristics are specified. Instead, a fitted parameter, LZSN, is utilized as an index value of water storage in the zone and the current storage, LZS, varies widely over time from a low value to amounts well above LZSN. Similarly, for the upper zone, a parameter, UZSN, and a variable, UZS, are utilized. All rainfall or snowmelt (except on impervious areas) goes into shortterm, limited storage in the upper zone, which includes interception and depression storage. Thus, UZS is the supply of water available for overland flow or for infiltration to the lower zone, except for minor losses.

One key feature of the Stanford Model is that the infiltration, interflow, and ET are varied over the watershed area, but arbitrarily. Infiltration capacity, for example, is assumed to be linearly distributed over the watershed area from zero to a maximum value, f_p (Fig. 10.2). A portion of this, f_r, is retailed in the soil and the remainder becomes interflow. Both f_p and f_r are transient, each varying (differently) with the relative water content of the lower zone, LZS/LZSN, according to a fixed empirical relationship.

---

†A report on the first version of the model was published in 1962.

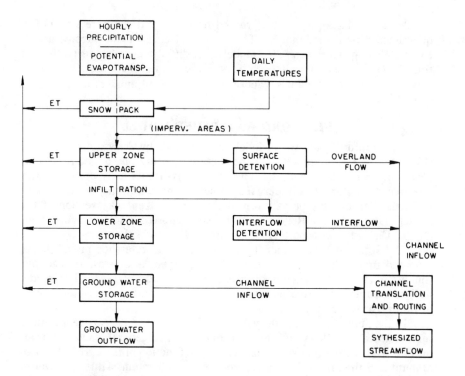

FIG. 10.1 General form of Stanford Watershed Model IV, showing principal storages and flows (adapted from Crawford and Linsley, 1966).

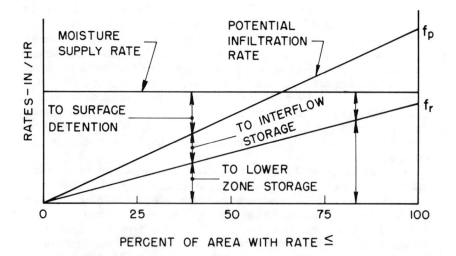

FIG. 10.2 Schematic of areal distribution for infiltration and interflow submodels, Stanford Watershed Model IV (adapted from Crawford and Linsley, 1966).

Somewhat similar relationships are used to calculate actual ET from potential ET, which is based on lake evaporation values or other input data.

The model has three different inflows to the channel system (Fig. 1). In each case, the relative volume of the flow over a period of time varies according to a parameter that controls the inflow to the corresponding storage. Another parmeter controls the timing of the outflow (channel inflow). Channel routing is in two steps. First, a time-area histogram is used to represent the effect of translation time from various parts of the watershed and their relative areas. Secondly, a conceptual reservoir at the watershed outlet represents the effects of channel storage. In the routing portions of the model, fitted parameters are utilized for interflow, groundwater flow and the conceptual reservoir.

The snowmelt subroutine, developed by Anderson and Crawford (1964), was a major addition to the Stanford Model. It utilizes daily temperature data and a number of parameters, some of which can be estimated, others fitted. Another addition was the sediment model developed by Negev (1967).

Primary data inputs to the Stanford Model include hourly and daily precipitation and daily maximum and minimum temperatures (for snowmelt only). Several rainfall stations may be used to improve the accuracy, one (or more) of which must have hourly data. Potential evapotranspiration can be input directly or as lake evaporation and, in either case, on a daily or semi-monthly basis. Observed daily streamflows, if available, are input for comparison to calculated values. Input parameters include various measured land and watershed characteristics and trial values of the fitted parameters. The Model IV version (Crawford and Linsley, 1966) has 16 land surface, channel system and groundwater parameters, of which 12 are clearly fitted parameters. Using their own version of the model, Herricks et al. (1975) listed nine measured parameters (watershed characteristics), six parameters estimated from historical records and eight estimated by trial and error, plus six initial moisture conditions.

In applying the Stanford Model to watersheds with a number of rainfall stations, the watershed is often divided into subareas. Each subarea needs a recording rainfall station. This improves the accuracy of simulation, of course, for medium-size or large watersheds. According to Crawford and Linsley (1966), the availability of good precipitation data is a major factor affecting the accuracy of simulation. The study by Herrick et al. (1975) illustrates, among other things, this limitation in applying the model.

In most cases, four or five years of observed runoff data are sufficient for fitting the Stanford Model. A parameter optimization procedure for the Kentucky verision of the Stanford Model was developed by Liou (1970) and was utilized by Shanholtz and Carr (1975). Most users, however, fit the model by making a series of trial runs. This is possible because the effects of the major fitted parameters (about 7) are to a large extent separable. The annual runoff volume, for example, is influenced mainly by the evapotranspiration parameter. Storm runoff volumes are controlled mainly by the infiltration and interflow parameters, etc. Once the runoff volumes are about right, the flow rate (routing) parameters can be fitted. Nevertheless, many trial runs are needed to complete the fitting process, unless the initial parameter values are chosen wisely. Crawford and Linsley (1966) have shown how the key parameters vary in importance from one watershed to another and have given some guidelines for choosing their initial values. Shanholz and Carr (1975), using the Kentucky version of the model, studied parameter stability, selec-

TABLE 10.1. SOME APPLICATIONS OF THE STANFORD WATERSHED
MODEL (MODEL IV) BY CRAWFORD AND LINSLEY (1966)

Stream and gage location	Approx. area,	No. of subareas	Annual runoff,	Years simulated	Corr. coeff. daily flows
	mi^2		in.		
Russian R. Hopland, CA	232	3	18	8	0.971
Russian R. Healdsburg	791	3	18	8	0.978
Russian R. Guerneville	1342	4	17	8	0.981
French Broad R. Blantrye, NC	296	3	43	6	0.963
South Yula R. Cisco, NV	55	6	46	5	0.945
Napa, R. Helena, CA	81	1	14	5	0.979
Beargrass, Cr. Louisville, KY	18	1	14	4	0.946

tion criteria for parameters, and sensitivity of the model to key parameters.

Some applications of the Stanford Model are summarized in Table 10.1. Further details, including computed vs. observed hydrographs, were presented by Crawford and Linsley (1966). Visual comparison of the hydrographs indicates good to excellent agreement most of the time, excellent for the Russian River. This area in northern California is well suited to modeling, being characterized by steep topography and winter rainfall occurring mainly in large, cyclonic storms. Larson (1965) applied the Stanford Model III to an 88 square mile watershed in the same area over a 20-yr period, using the first five years for fitting the parameters (Table 10.2). The results were quite good, but show that peak flows are simulated with less accuracy than other flow rates and runoff volumes.

Application of the Stanford Watershed Model to ungaged watersheds is possible in some cases but, at best, is uncertain. Herricks et al. (1975) applied the model to small, ungaged watersheds by using parameters obtained by fitting the model to adjoining, gaged watersheds. Several efforts have been made toward relating key parametes to measurable watershed characteristics empirically, notably studies by Ross (1970) and Magette et al. (1976). The Kentucky version of the Stanford Model was used in both cases. Although some of the parameters were predicted satisfactorily, it appears that considerably more effort is needed to achieve the goal of generalizing the model parameters.

Perhaps the most common applications of the Stanford Watershed Model have been to obtain hydrographs for unusual rainfall events and to ex-

TABLE 10.2. STANFORD MODEL III RESULTS VS. OBSERVED
VALUES FOR DRY CR. NEAR CLOVERDALE*, CA,
1944-1963 (Larson, 1965)

	Number of cases	Mean deviation[2]	Mean ratio: Model/observed
		percent	
Annual runoff	20	10.0	0.99
Storm runoff volume	39	13.8	1.04
Peak discharge	39	19.6	0.96

tend a short flow record sufficiently for hydrologic analyses. In spite of its reliance on fitted parameters, the Stanford Model can, under certain circumstances, be used for studying the effects of watershed modifications, e.g., James (1965), Fleming (1971) and Herricks et al. (1975). In general, however, physically based, measured parameter models, if available, are better suited to studying such effects (Larson, 1973).

USDA HL-74 MODEL OF WATERSHED HYDROLOGY

The United States Department of Agriculture Hydrograph Laboratory (USDAHL) Watershed Model (Holtan et al., 1975) is intended especially for small, agricultural watersheds, but is used for various types of watersheds. Model development began in the early 1960's with the introduction of Holtan's infiltration function (Holtan, 1961, 1965). The first version of the model, USDA HL-70, was reported by Holtan and Lopez in 1971. The model, still undergoing refinement (Holtan and Yaramanoglu, 1977), consists of a series of empirical expressions or submodels selected to provide a hydrologic continuum from watershed divide to outlet.

USDA HL-74 can be classified as a complete model since it considers the entire hydrologic cycle for a watershed. The model can also be classified as continuous in that it simulates the hydrologic processes that occur between storms as well as during storms. It is also a general model designed to simulate the effects of agricultural on any of the hydrologic processes. The model utilizes many parameters, most of which are measurable. Those that require existing flow records for evaluation are the routing coefficients for the channel flow and the subsurface flow regimes.

In applying the USDA HL-74 model, the soils of the watershed are grouped by land capability classes to form hydrologic response zones which serve as basic units for all calculations. Three zones representing the natural elevation sequence of uplands, hillsides, and bottomlands are used. This sequence tends to combine areas of similar soil and land use characteristics.

The general structure of the current model is shown in Fig. 10.3. Input precipitation for the entire watershed consists of a continuous record of rainfall or snowfall. Weighted values are used if there is more than one weather station. Rainfall amounts can be handled for regular time intervals or by breakpoint tabulations. Any snow accumulation is dispersed as daily snowmelt for each zone as follows:

$$\text{MELT} = c \, (T\text{-THAW}) \, (1\text{-}0.5 \, \text{VEG}) + 2 \, P \quad \dots\dots\dots\dots\dots \quad [10.1]$$

where

$\quad$ MELT $\quad=$ potential daily snowmelt in zone (depth)
$\quad$ T $\qquad=$ weekly average air temperature
$\quad$ THAW $\quad=$ temperature at which snowmelt starts
$\quad$ VEG $\qquad=$ weighted average zone vegetative density
$\quad$ P $\qquad=$ rainfall for given day (depth)
$\quad$ c $\qquad=$ a coefficient (0.15 for depth in inches and with Fahrenheit temperatures)
$\quad$ c $\qquad=$ a coefficient (0.15 for depth in inches and with Fahrenheit temperatures)

Infiltration capacity in the model is represented by the following equation (Holtan, 1961):

$$f = GI \, a \, S_a^{1.4} + f_c \quad \dots\dots\dots\dots\dots\dots\dots\dots\dots\dots\dots\dots\dots \quad [10.2]$$

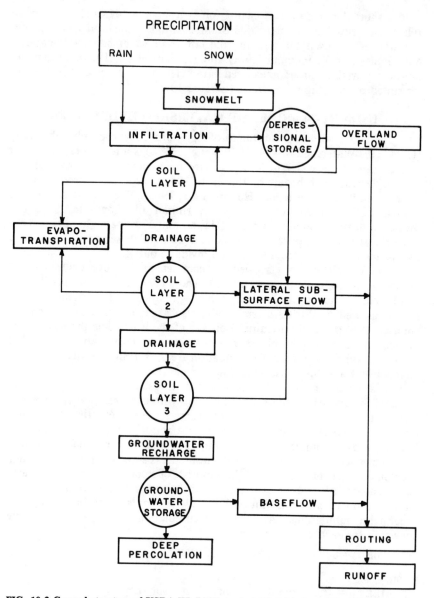

FIG. 10.3 General structure of USDA HL-74 Watershed Model (adapted from Holtan et al., 1975).

where
f = infiltration capacity (depth/time)
GI = growth index of crop
a = index of surface connected porosity
S_a = available storage in surface layer (depth)
f_c = constant rate of infiltration after prolonged wetting (depth/time)

The term "a" is a vegetative parameter and GI is used as a seasonal modifier of "a". Initially S_a is obtained from initial moisture conditions and total soil porosity. Values for f_c can be locally determined values or the generalized values of Musgrave (1955). In equation [10.2], infiltration capacity depends on the total voids in the soils which are diminished as infiltration occurs and recovered by drainage and evapotranspiration. Depressional storage can be considered also in this treatment. Precipitation or snowmelt in excess of infiltration capacity is subject to further infiltration as it moves from zone to zone of the watershed.

Precipitation excess is routed downslope across each soil zone enroute to the channel using continuity:

$$P_e - Q_O = \Delta D \quad \dots\dots\dots\dots\dots\dots\dots\dots\dots\dots\dots\dots\dots\dots\dots \quad [10.3]$$

and

$$q_O = (ova) \, D^{1.67} \quad \dots\dots\dots\dots\dots\dots\dots\dots\dots\dots\dots\dots\dots\dots \quad [10.4]$$

where

P_e	=	precipitation excess (depth/time)
Q_o	=	outflow (depth/time)
ΔD	=	increment of flow depth
q_o	=	overland flow rate (depth/time)
ova	=	roughness coefficient

The roughness coefficient can be estimated from vegetative density, slope steepness and flow path length as shown by Holtan et al. (1975). Channel flows and subsurface return flows are routed using an outflow function for the recession:

$$q_t = q_O e^{-t/m} \quad \dots\dots\dots\dots\dots\dots\dots\dots\dots\dots\dots\dots\dots\dots\dots \quad [10.5]$$

where

q_o	=	flow rate at start of time increment (depth/time)
q_t	=	flow rate one time increment later (depth/time)
t	=	time increment (time)
m	=	routing coefficient (time)

Storage coefficients for each flow regime are derived using a method where successive flow regimes are represented by linear segments of a semilogarithmic plot of the hydrograph recession (Onstad and Jamieson, 1968). Time steps for the rising limb of the hydrograph are those defined by the input precipitation distribution.

Subsurface flow regimes are considered to be regulated; that is, seepage from a given regime is inflow to the next regime and so on (Fig. 10.3). Seepage is computed as a function of the amount of gravitational water present at each time increment and must be adequate to supply the maximum flow rate experienced in the next regime.

For crops at a given stage of growth, potential evapotranspiration (PET) is estimated from pan evaporation using a coefficient and a crop growth index (GI). The latter depends on crop growth cardinal temperatures and reflects amount of crop foliage or stage of growth as it relates to transpiration.

Thus:

$$PET = GI \, k \, E_p \quad \dots\dots\dots\dots\dots\dots\dots\dots\dots\dots\dots\dots\dots\dots\dots \quad [10.6]$$

where
   PET = potential evapotranspiration (depth/day)
   GI = growth index (percent of maturity)
   k   = pan coefficient
   E_p = pan evaporation (depth/day)
The ratio k varies with the type of vegetation from 1.0 to 2.0 (Holtan et al., 1975). Evapotranspiration continues down to the wilting point of the soil and is expressed as the potential evapotranspiration modified by the existing soil moisture condition when the cardinal temperature conditions are met, as follows:

$$ET = PET\,[(S\text{-}SA)/AWC]\,^{AWC/G} \qquad \dots\dots\dots\dots\dots\dots\dots\dots\dots\dots \quad [10.7]$$

where
   ET = predicted evapotranspiration (depth/day)
   S   = total soil porosity (depth)
   SA = available soil porosity (depth)
   AWC = water content removable only by ET (depth)
   G   = gravitational water (depth)
Model output can range from monthly values to an overland flow hydrograph for a storm. Recently, an output subroutine was added to indicate daily status of soil moisture and increments of water movement in each layer of each watershed zone.

   Results in terms of monthly runoff values are presented in Table 10.3 for four watersheds in differing physiographic areas. These limited results seem to indicate that monthly water yields are predicted more accurately in humid climates.

SCS TR-20 WATERSHED MODEL

   The TR-20 watershed model was developed in 1964 for use by the Soil Conservation Service in project formulation and design (U.S. Soil Conservation Service, 1965). For individual storm events, the model determines peak discharges, their time of occurrence and water surface elevations. It can also provide complete hydrographs when desired. Discharges at selected locations can be determined both without and with various combinations of reservoirs and channel modifications, as desired. The model is widely used by SCS and others in planning and design of small watershed projects, also in flood plain studies.

   TR-20 can be classified as a complete, event-type model. It is a general, measured parameter model, being easily applied to most agricultural and ur-

TABLE 10.3. SUMMARY OF RESULTS FOR SOME APPLICATIONS
OF THE USDA HL-74 WATERSHED MODEL, 1956-1964
(Holtan et al., 1975)

Watershed	Location	Size, ha	No. of months, mo	Avg. mo. runoff, mm	Standard error mm	%
W-97	Coshocton, OH	1854	96	24.4	14.5	59
W-11	Hastings, NE	1413	96	6.9	5.3	78
W-3	Ft. Lauderdale, FL	4069	60	34.8	14.5	42
W-G	Riesel, TX	1773	90	8.6	6.6	76

ban watersheds, including ungaged watersheds, using only readily obtainable measured or estimated input parameters. The model is available from the U.S. Department of Commerce, National Technical Information Service.

The general structure or organization of the TR-20 model is shown in Fig. 10.4. The model includes two types of operations (in addition to input and output): (a) hydrograph computations and (b) control operations. The latter makes it possible to obtain, in a single computer run, outputs for many combinations of storm rainfall and watershed conditions, including variations in reservoir number, size and location, in channel characteristics and in land use practices. The control instruction for a specific storm can apply to one subarea, a group of contiguous subareas or the entire watershed.

The hydrograph computations include several steps or subroutines, which will be summarized. The first one (RUNOFF) calculates subarea flood hydrographs from rainfall data. The well-known SCS runoff curve number method is used to compute rainfall excess, which is applied incrementally to a dimensionless unit hydrograph to obtain subarea hydrographs (Soil Conservation Service, 1972). The curve number (CN) for each subarea is based on the land use, associated management and hydrologic condition, and hydrologic soil group and is entered as input to the model.

Another subroutine, RESVOR, routes a flood hydrograph through a reservoir or other type of water storage area by the storage-indication method (Soil Conservation Service, 1972). Reservoirs can be located on the main stem or on any of the tributaries, in any combination.

A subroutine REACH routes flood hydrographs through stream reaches

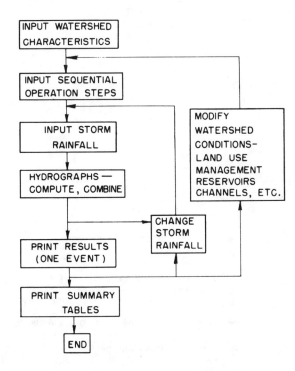

FIG. 10.4 General structure of SCS TR-20 Watershed Model (adapted from U.S. Soil Conservation Service, 1965).

by the convex method (U.S. Soil Conservation Service, 1972):

$$O_2 = (1 - C) O_1 + CI_1 \quad \dotfill \quad [10.8]$$

$$C = \frac{\bar{V}}{\bar{V} + 1.7} \quad \dotfill \quad [10.9]$$

where

O_1 and O_2 = outflow at start and end of a time interval
I_1 = inflow rate at the start of time interval
C = routing coefficient
$\bar{V}$ = average velocity for reach

Hydrographs for subareas are combined by another subroutine, making allowance for differences in timing. The model also provides for flow diversions, if any.

A schematic map similar to that in Fig. 10.5 is helpful in preparing the sequence of operational steps for the watershed and in coordinating the development of the subwatershed input data. The input parameters required are subwatershed drainage areas, times of concentration, runoff curve

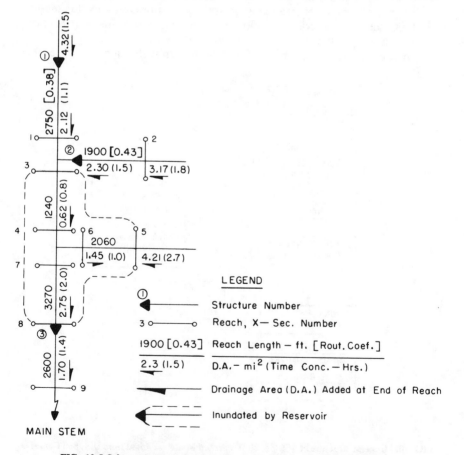

LEGEND

①◄—— Structure Number

3 o———o Reach, X— Sec. Number

1900 [0.43] Reach Length — ft. [Rout. Coef.]

2.3 (1.5) D.A.— mi² (Time Conc.—Hrs.)

———— Drainage Area (D.A.) Added at End of Reach

◄— — — Inundated by Reservoir

MAIN STEM

FIG. 10.5 Schematic map of a typical watershed for use with SCS TR-20.

numbers, reach lengths for stream routing, routing coefficients, baseflow or triangular interflow hydrograph data, and initial reservoir elevations. The input requirements for the control instructions are the main time increment (Δt); storm rainfall depth, duration, and starting time; and the antecedent moisture condition (AMC). Tabulated input data for the program include the following:

1 storm rainfall distribution — actual or synthetic
2 channel and valley cross-sections
3 reservoir characteristics, including spillways
4 dimensionless hydrograph (if other than SCS standard)
5 observed flood hydrographs (if to be combined with computed hydrographs)

A number of output options are provided in the model, including a summary table for comparison of alternate designs and inputs.

The watershed model should be calibrated using high water marks (HWM's) or observed peak flows within the watershed or downstream. Comparisons can usually be made between: (a) an elevation of a routed storm discharge and a historical storm HWM; (b) model vs. observed hydrographs, and (c) the routed discharge-frequency relation vs. the gaged discharge frequency curve. Critical measured and estimated parameters need to be reevaluated, adjustments made, and the input revised and rerun until the results are verified.

The TR-20 model is structured so that it can accommodate numerous reservoirs and channel reaches. It can process as many as nine rainfall distributions and an unlimited number of rainstorms. There are some limitations in input data and in control cards. To yield satisfactory results, the rainfall increment must adequately define the most intense rainfall and the main time increment must be small enough to define the hydrograph in the smallest subwatershed. Also, the routing coefficient must be properly related to the main time increment and the reach length to obtain correct distribution of the volume and time of the routed hydrograph.

The TR-20 program is designed primarily for small watersheds where thunderstorms or other intense rainstorms of short duration cause peak flows. Snowmelt runoff is usually considered as baseflow or interflow. The assumption of uniform rain depth and distribution over an area can also be used in large watersheds if varied by subwatersheds. The areal distribution of a given frequency of rainfall may, however, limit the program when discharge-frequency relationships from the headwaters to the outlet of a large watershed are desired. Application typically has been on watersheds ranging from 2 to 400 mi² with subareas from 0.1 to 10 mi².

SSARR MODEL

The Streamflow Synthesis and Reservoir Regulation (SSARR) Model was originally developed by the U.S. Corps of Engineers (Rockwood, 1958, 1964) for the planning, design and operation of water control projects in the Columbia River Basin. Further development in cooperation with the National Weather Service (Schermerhorn et al., 1968) resulted in a model suitable for operational river forecasting. The model is somewhat unique because it has evolved largely as a result of operational needs. The philosophy behind development of the model has been to add complexity only as it is needed.

The SSARR Model consists of a watershed model, a river system model and a reservoir regulation model (U.S. Army Corps of Engineers, 1975). Although this discussion will focus on the watershed model, the other submodels are described because each can be used separately or in any combination, which allows one to model a variety of hydrologic systems. The river system model provides the linkages between watersheds, rivers, lakes and reservoirs. Channel routing, special routines for three variable routing relationships, summing points for any location in a basin for printing or plotting purposes, and local inflow routines are contained in the river model. The reservoir submodel allows one to specify reservoir characteristics and operations. Often an artificial reservoir is used in watershed modeling to determine and accumulate differences between computed and observed streamflow volumes for some time interval.

The SSARR watershed model is a complete, general, continuous simulation model with fitted parameters. Although originally designed for large watersheds, its application is constrained primarily by availability of streamflow data needed for parameter fitting and model verification. The watershed model represents conceptually processes and relationships involved from rainfall or snowfall to the resultant streamflow (Fig. 10.6). Either SI or English units may be used.

Precipitation data for 0.1 to 24 h periods can be entered for one or more stations. If precipitation can occur as snow, the user must indicate a base temperature for separating rainfall from snowfall events. Daily means or maximum temperatures must be entered as input for snowmelt computations. Area-evalation relationships can be specified for mountainous areas with snowfall so that temperatures can be lapsed from the stations to appropriate elevations. Options are available to follow snow accumulation and snowmelt on a zonal (elevation) basis or more simply, on a snow covered and snow free basis. Snowmelt can be calculated by either a degree-day method or by generalized snowmelt equations (U.S. Army Corps of Engineers, 1956).

Once rainfall and/or snowmelt are computed, the total moisture input enters the Soil Moisture Index (SMI) function (Fig. 10.6). Runoff is determined as a percent of moisture input on the basis of the soil moisture status indexed by SMI and, if desired, by a third variable, rainfall intensity. This general watershed-runoff response was developed and used instead of the more traditional infiltration-runoff approach. The lack of infiltration data plus the extreme variability of infiltration rates over large watersheds favor the use of this approach. Initial estimates of SMI-runoff relationships are obtained by comparing computed and observed stream-flow volumes over periods of varying soil water conditions. That part of the moisture input which is not runoff is added to the existing SMI which is depleted by evapotranspiration:

$$SMI_2 = SMI_1 + (WP - RGP) - (\frac{PH}{24} * KE * ETI) \dots \dots \dots \dots [10.10]$$

where
SMI_1 = soil moisture index at beginning of time increment (depth)
SMI_2 = soil moisture index at end of time increment (depth)
WP   = weighted input from rainfall and/or snowmelt (depth)
RGP   = runoff generated for the time increment (depth)
PH   = time increment (hours)

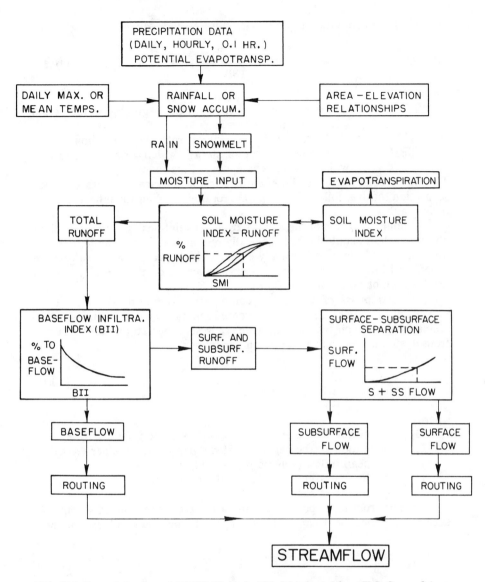

FIG. 10.6 General structure of SSARR Watershed Model (adapted from U.S. Corps of Army Engineers, 1975).

ETI = evapotranspiration index (depth per day)

KE = factor which reduces ETI for rainy periods or for low soil moisture conditions

Although baseflow, surface and subsurface components cannot be physically separated for an observed streamflow event, the SSARR developers recognized the importance of different flow pathways in determining the complete streamflow hydrograph. All moisture in excess of that which replenishes the SMI is separated into these three components of flow. Baseflow is determined as a percent of runoff from a Baseflow Infiltration Index (BII) and can be bounded by a maximum percolation rate. The BII for the end of the computation period (BII_2) is determined from:

$$BII_2 = BII_1 + (24 * RG - BII_1)\left(\frac{PH}{TSBII + PH/2}\right) \dots\dots\dots\dots [10.11]$$

where

BII_1 = baseflow infiltration index at the beginning of the period (depth per day)

RG   = RGP/PH which is the runoff rate (depth per hour)

TSBII   = time delay or time of storage which governs the rate at which BII can change over time (hour).

The water not diverted to baseflow enters the Surface-Subsurface (S/SS) separation routine, followed by separate routings to determine the watershed hydrograph.

Although all three of the above parameter relationships are fitted, their ultimate values should be hydrologically reasonable. For example, forested watersheds with deep soils usually exhibit a high percentage of subsurface runoff and little surface runoff. Impervious areas, on the contrary, should exhibit little or no subsurface flow.

The last phase of streamflow computation is routing the three components of flow. Each component is routed separately through successive increments of reservoir type storage which represent the natural delay of runoff from upstream to downstream points as follows:

$$O_2 = O_1 + \left(\frac{I_m - O_1}{T_s + t/2}\right)t \dots\dots\dots\dots\dots\dots\dots\dots\dots [10.12]$$

where

O_2 = outflow at the end of the period (volume per second)

O_1 = outflow at the beginning of the period (volume per second)

I_m = mean inflow (volume per second)

t   = time duration of the computation period

T_s = time of storage

Channel routing is performed similarly except the time of storage for each routing increment can be related to discharge in a nonlinear manner:

$$T_s = \frac{KTS}{Q^n} \dots\dots\dots\dots\dots\dots\dots\dots\dots\dots\dots\dots\dots\dots [10.13]$$

where

T_s = time of storage per increment

KTS = a constant estimated either by trial and error or from known discharge-routing time relationships

Q   = discharge (cfs)

n   = coefficient typically between 0.1 and 0.5.

The application of the SSARR watershed model usually requires at least four or five years of data for parameter fitting or model calibration. The variability of hydrologic responses is important for this process; a few years with extreme high and extreme low runoff sequences are of greater value then ten years of rather constant flows. Without a few periods of high flows, especially, one may get a false sense of accuracy. Model verification should

TABLE 10.4. SOME APPLICATIONS OF THE SSARR WATERSHED MODEL*

| | Approximate area | Applications | |
Stream or watershed	$10^3 \, km^2$	Operational use	Study purposes
1. Columbia River Basin to Bonneville, USA (37 watersheds, 47 channel reaches, 28 reservoirs	622	Yes	Yes
2. Chena River at Fairbanks, Alaska	5.26	No	Yes
3. Upper Paraguay River, South America	370	No	Yes
4. Nam Mune River, Thailand	269	No	Yes
5. South Saskatchewan River Basin, Canada	145	Yes	Yes
6. Castro Valley California	0.0126	No	Yes (R^2=0.99)†
7. Bird Creek, Oklahoma	2.34	No	Yes (R^2=0.93)‡
8. Salt River Basin, Arizona	11.2		
Lower Basin		No	Yes (R^2=0.84)†
Upper Basin		No	Yes (R^2=0.94)†
Near Roosevelt		No	Yes (R^2=0.76,0.70)§

*Sources: Beschta (1974), U.S. Army Corps of Engineers (1956, 1972, 1976) and Water Survey of Canada (1974).
†For mean monthly flows.
‡For annual volumes (10 years).
§ For seasonal volumes (Nov.-May), R^2 for calibration and validation, respectively.

include several events and two or three years of streamflow not used for calibration, i.e., for independent testing.

The SSARR Model has been tested and applied on watersheds and river basins worldwide (Table 10.4). For most of these watersheds, the model was applied by subwatershed units, as indicated for the Colombia River. Most applications have involved project design or operation studies and development of flood forecasting procedures. An exception, the Castro Valley example, was the result of an urban hydrology study where rainfall and runoff data were available for the watershed over short time increments. The SSARR Model has been used extensively on large watersheds where snowmelt is a major component of the watershed runoff, especially in the Pacific Northwest.

One of the principle limitations of applying the SSARR Model to a new area is the lack of information or methods relating parameters to measurable watershed characteristics. In the case of the Columbia River Basin, enough watersheds have been modeled that some regionalization of parameters has taken place. For other regions, initial parameter relationships are difficult to estimate.

The model cannot be used directly to investigate the hydrologic effects of modifying watershed characteristics such as vegetative cover types, soil conservation practices, and other similar land management activities. Hydrologic changes associated with altering storages on a watershed or changing characteristics such as the percent of impervious area can be simulated.

COMPARISON OF MODELS

The four watershed models described in the preceding pages are seen to have certain similarities but also some major differences. All four are general models and are complete models also.

The Stanford, USDA HL-74 and SSARR Models are continuous watershed models. They are designed for operation over long periods of time with actual weather sequences. With the SCS TR-20 model, being an event model, the initial conditions for each event must be specified. Its main purpose is to evaluate alternative systems of structural measures (reservoirs, channels, etc.). The HEC-1 watershed model (not described here), developed by the Corps of Engineers (1973) is another well known event model and is frequently used to generate hydrographs for project design.

With respect to parameters, the three models vary considerably. With the Stanford and the SSARR Models, both land phase and channel phase parameters are evaluated by fitting. Only the channel phase (routing) and groundwater flow parameters need fitting for the HL-74 Model. The SCS TR-20 model was developed for application to ungaged watersheds. Accordingly, it utilizes only parameters that can be evaluated directly from observable watershed characteristics. Referring again to the HEC-1 model, its parameters are evaluated almost entirely by fitting the flow records. Thus, with respect to parameters, it is quite different from the TR-20 model, though both are event models.

In terms of specific methods of representing the individual hydrologic processes, e.g., infiltration, the various models are quite different. The amount of detail and the emphasis on various parts of the runoff process vary considerably between models. Most event models, including the TR-20 and HEC-1, use direct, shortcut methods for estimating runoff amount or volume. Most continuous models, on the other hand, including the Stanford and HL-74 models determine infiltration, soil moisture storage, interflow and groundwater flow daily (sometimes more often) and use these values in determining runoff amounts.

DISTRIBUTED MODELS

In a distributed watershed model, the spatial variations of key land characteristics, e.g., soil type, vegetation and topography, can be utilized directly in determining runoff. In general, the watershed area is divided into a number of elements and runoff volumes are first calculated separately for each element. Since the related parameters need to be specified as input for each element, such a model is sometimes referred to as a "distributed parameter" model.

The more common "lumped parameter" models are usually structured so that average values of the watershed characteristics affecting runoff volume are utilized. Averaging a certain parameter "averages" (implicitly) the process being represented. Because of nonlinearity and threshold values, this can lead to significant error. A distributed model removes this as a constraint on simulation accuracy.

Huggins et al. (1977) cited several advantages of using a distributed parameter model. The primary advantage is the potential for more accurate simulation of the runoff process. Greater accuracy is not automatic, however. It accrues only if the model is well designed and operated, i.e., to take advantage of its capacity for spatial representation of the processes involved. A significant aspect of this is the fact that geographic position within a watershed is preserved in a distributed model, and is sometimes important. A second advantage of distributed models is that they are well suited to use on ungaged watersheds, with measured parameters, making it possible to model the influence of projected modifications in land use within a watershed. A third important advantage is that distributed models are well suited to simulating water quality on a watershed basis. The source areas for various types of water pollutants are seldom uniformly distributed and, moreover, may need to be identified.

The principal disadvantages of distributed parameter models are increased complexity, data requirements and computing time. The importance of these points depends on various factors, including watershed size, number of subareas required and the model structure. In the final analysis, the deciding factor is probably whether or not a distributed model is needed to accomplish the objective(s) of the study.

It is not surprising that most of the existing watershed models are lumped parameter models. None of the models described earlier in this chapter are distributed models. Distributed models are relatively new and, at present, are subject of considerable developmental effort.

One approach to distributed parameter modeling is the use of a grid system to delineate watershed elements. The initial development of this concept was reported by Huggins and Monke (1968) and was applied to two small areas (about one ha each) in Indiana using a grid size of 25 by 25 ft. The slope direction for each element was used to route the runoff from one element to two adjoining elements. To facilitate application to larger, watershed size areas, an improved method of incorporating channel flow effects was added by Burney (Huggins et al., 1973) along with various other improvements.

This work at Purdue University led to the development of the more comprehensive ANSWERS model by Beasley (1977). The original, basically hydrologic model was greatly expanded to include tile flow, channel flow, soil erosion and sediment transport. ANSWERS is intended for individual storm events and, therefore, does not have an evapotranspiration submodel. The model parameters are all physically based, making it possible to measure or estimate their values and apply the model to ungaged watersheds for both present and future conditions. The grid size is varied to suit the accuracy required and the nonuniformity of soils and topography in the watershed.

Applications of the ANSWERS Model to two Indiana watersheds having areas of 714 and 942 ha was described by Huggins et al. (1977). An element size of 2 to 5 ha was found to be satisfactory in this area. U.S. Geological Survey Topographic maps and County Soil Survey maps were used to compile the data file for the numerous elemental areas. Flow records were available for the two basins. Comparison of simulated to recorded values for several complex storms in 1975 and 1976 indicated that the results were generally within 30 percent of the observed values. The model was then used to predict the effects of improved tillage methods on sediment delivery from the two watersheds.

Gupta and Solomon (1977) have developed a distributed parameter model for predicting both runoff and sediment discharge. The model utilizes square elements as in the ANSWERS Model. Runoff and sediment loads are calculated separately for each element and are discharged to the north, south, east or west into an adjoining element. Channels are identified for channel routing and sediment transport calculations. The model is intended for use on the river basin scale with elements of any size, but usually 1 km² or larger.

The finite element method has recently come into frequent use in modeling groundwater flow (Pinder and Gray, 1977). This technique could be very useful in developing a distributed parameter surface runoff model because it enables one to use elemental areas of various shapes, e.g., triangles or quadrilaterals. The watershed could be delineated into source areas that are hydrologically homogeneous (in terms of soil type and land use), which vary widely in both shape and size. It remains to be seen whether the additional detail and calculation required for a finite element, areally distributed watershed model will prove to be worthwhile.

Ross et al. (1978) developed and tested a distributed parameter model for predicting watershed runoff, erosion and sedimentation. The model was applied to six small watersheds in Virginia varying in size from 74 ha (183 acre) to 428 ha (1,058 acre). The watershed area is divided into hydrologic response units (HRU's) each having a certain combination of soil type and land use. Runoff volumes are calculated for each HRU. As an example, one of the watersheds had 65 HRU's. These were combined into 17 overland flow strips varying in size from under 2 ha to about 9 ha and assumed to be rectangular. The dynamic flow equations, solved by means of finite elements, were used for channel routing. All model parameters were measured or estimated from watershed characteristics. Results with the model were described as "poor to excellent."

There are alternative ways of considering areal variations in modeling runoff, i.e., other than an areally distributed model. The most common way is to divide the watershed into subwatersheds, apply the watershed model separately to each major subwatershed, and combine (and route) the subwatershed hydrographs. This was done quite successfully on the Russian River in California with the Stanford Watershed Model (Crawford and Linsley, 1966). This procedure is possible with other watershed models also. With the SCS TR-20 model, for example, a different runoff curve number can be used for each subarea (Fig. 10.5). Each of these examples represents a compromise between using a truly distributed parameter model and a single application of a lumped parameter model.

Moore and Larson (1978) developed a model for small depressional watersheds in which runoff was areally distributed according to the type of drainage. Four combinations of surface and subsurface drainage, both natural and constructed, and land slope were utilized for "elemental watersheds", typically about 40 ha (100 acre) in size. Various percentages of such areas were used to represent the area contributing runoff to each channel reach for the original, present and projected conditions of the watershed. Other watershed characteristics, however, were not distributed nor were the meteorological inputs.

Another approach is to incorporate an areal distribution into one or more of the submodels of individual hydrologic processes. An example of this is the arbitrary distribution of infiltration capacities used in the Stanford Model described earlier (Fig. 10.5). Similarly, some other type of distribution, e.g., a normal distribution can be applied to any of the parameters (or inputs) of a watershed model. In most cases, however, the geographical distribution of the values within the watershed is not accounted for. Thus, such a procedure does not satisfy the definition of a distributed model.

Some Special Purpose Watershed Models

Some watershed models, referred to here as special purpose models, are created to provide a better representation of the runoff (as compared to general watershed models) for watersheds of a certain class or type. By designing the model for a given type of topography, geology or land use, one can devote more detail in the model to the key hydrologic processes for that type of watershed. At the same time, less detail can be used in modeling the subprocesses known to be of less importance in such areas. The overall result will be a watershed model that can be either more complex or less complex than the general models previously described.

One example of special purpose watershed models is the modeling of runoff from flat, depressional watersheds in a series of studies at Iowa State University culminating with that of Campbell and Johnson (1975). A similar approach was used by Moore and Larson (1978). In these models, special attention was given to the natural storage of runoff in topographic depressions and also to the routing of runoff through both ditches and tile drainage systems. These models are of course intended only for this type of topography.

Another example of special purpose watershed models is the development of various urban runoff models. In general, these models are applicable to urban areas only, since the watershed is delineated into pervious and impervious areas. In some cases, pervious area runoff is neglected. Relatively close attention is usually given in the models to routing through street gutters and storm sewers. Many urban models are event models and utilize only physical parameters than can be measured or estimated to permit modeling of ungaged areas. This is possible in urban watershed modeling which is based largely on routing of runoff from impervious areas. Some well-known urban runoff models are described, compared and tested by Heeps and Mein (1974).

Some Partial Watershed Models

A partial watershed model is one that represents only a part of the watershed runoff process. Most partial models fall into one of two categories, water yield models and routing models. Since the former is used to predict runoff amounts only, the model includes mainly such "land phase" processes as infiltration, soil moisture storage, evapotranspiration, snowmelt and groundwater storage.

A good example of a water yield model was reported by Haan (1976). The model represents the key processes of infiltration, soil water storage and evapotranspiration, but in a simplified manner. The model utilizes only four parameters which are evaluated by fitting. The model can be applied to an ungaged watershed by first evaluating the parameters for nearby watersheds having similar land characteristics. Along similar lines, but utilizing the SCS runoff equation, Williams and LaSeur (1976) developed a water yield model that has only one fitted parameter. Stochastic techniques can be useful also in developing water yield models, as shown by Bonné (1971) and by Majtenyi (1972).

Routing models are used to determine the runoff hydrograph, given the amount and duration of runoff. This can be done in various ways. Although not usually considered a model, the unit hydrograph is actually a conceptual routing model and, therefore, a partial watershed model. Being originated by Sherman (1932), it is one of the oldest hydrologic models. It is clearly a fitted parameter model, but dimensionless hydrographs are intended to serve as measured parameter models. Other conceptual routing models or methods are used, for example, as in the Stanford Model (1966). Many other models utilize a more direct, physical or hydraulic approach to routing through the channel system, dividing it into reaches and applying either storage routing or a method based on the unsteady flow equations. An example of the latter that is also a partial watershed model is the study by Machmeier and Larson (1968) and a subsequent study by Wei and Larson (1971). In each of these studies, a detailed routing model of a specific but hypothetical watershed was developed and used experimentally.

References

1 Anderson, E. A. and N. H. Crawford. 1964. The synthesis of continuous snowmelt hydrographs on a digital computer. Stanford Univ. Dept. of Civil Eng. Tech. Report No. 36.

2 Beasley, D. B. 1977. Answers: A mathematical model for simulating the effects of land use and management on water quality. Ph.D. Thesis. Purdue University.

3 Beschta, R. L. 1974. Streamflow hydrology and simulation of the Salt River Basin in central Arizona. Ph. D. Dissertation (unpublished). University of Arizona, Tucson.

4 Bonné, Jochanan. 1971. Stochastic simulation of monthly streamflow by a multiple regression model utilizing precipitation data. J. of Hydrology, Vol. 12.

5 Campbell, K. L. and H. P. Johnson. 1975. Hydrologic simulation of watersheds with artificial drainage. Water Resources Research 11(1).

6 Claborn, B. J. and W. L. Moore. 1970. Numerical simulation of watershed hydrology. University of Texas, Department of Civil Engineering. Tech. Report HYD 14-7001.

7 Crawford, N. H. and R.K. Linsley. 1966. Digital simulation in hydrology: Stanford watershed model IV. Stanford Univ. Dept. of Civil Eng. Tech. Report No. 39.

8 Fleming, G. 1971. Simulation of water yield from devegetated basins. J. of Irrig. and Drainage Div. Am. Soc. Civil Engrs. 97(IR2).

9 Gupta, S. K. and S. I. Solomon. 1977. Distributed numerical model for estimating runoff and sediment discharge of ungaged rivers. I. The information system. Water Resources Research 13(3).

10 Haan, C. T. 1976. Evaluation of a monthly water yield model. TRANSACTIONS of the ASAE 19(1):55-60.

11 Heeps, D. P. and R. G. Mein. 1974. Independent comparison of three urban runoff models. J. Hydr. Div., Am. Soc. Civil Engrs. 100(7).

12 Herricks, E. E., V. O. Shanholtz and D. N. Contractor. 1975. Models to predict environmental impact of mine drainage on streams. TRANSACTIONS of the ASAE 18(4):657-663, 667.

13 Holtan, H. N. 1961. A concept for infiltration estimates in watershed engineering. United States Department of Agriculture-Agricultural Research Service No. 41-51.

14 Holtan, H. N. 1965. A model for computing watershed retention from soil parameters. J. Soil and Water Conservation 20(3).

15 Holtan, H. N. and N. C. Lopez. 1971. U.S. Department of Agriculture HL-70 model of watershed hydrology. U.S. Department of Agriculture-Agr. Research Service Tech. Bulletin No. 1435.

16 Holtan, H. N., G. J. Stittner, W. H. Hanson, and N. C. Lopez. 1975. USDAHL-74 revised model of watershed hydrology. U.S. Department of Agriculture-Agr. Research Service Tech. Bull. No. 1518.

17 Holtan, H. N. and M. Yaramanoglu. 1977. A user's manual for the Maryland version of the USDA-HL model of watershed hydrology. Univ. of Maryland Agric. Exp. Sta. MP 918.

18 Huggins, L. F. and E. J. Monke. 1968. A mathematical model for simulating the hydrologic response of a watershed. Water Resources Research 4(3).

19 Huggins, L. F., J. R. Burney, P. S. Kundu and E. J. Monke. 1973. Simulation of the hydrology of ungaged watersheds. Water Resources Research Center, Purdue University Tech. Rept. 38.

20   Huggins, L. F., D. Beasley, A. Bottcher and E. Monke. 1977. Environmental impact of land use on water quality: Sec. 4.9 Modeling. Environmental Protection Agency Report EPA-905/9-77-007-B.

21   James, L. D. 1965. Using a digital computer to estimate the effects of urban development of flood peaks. Water Resources Research 1(2).

22   James, L. D. 1970. An evaluation of relationships between streamflow patterns and watershed characteristics through the use of OPSET, a self-calibrating version of the Stanford watershed model. University of Kentucky Water Resources Institute Research Report No. 36.

23   Larson, C. L. 1965. A two-phase approach to the prediction of peak rates and frequencies of runoff for small ungaged watersheds. Stanford University Dept. of Civil Eng. Tech. Report No. 53.

24   Larson, C. L. 1973. Hydrologic effects of modifying small watersheds—Is prediction by hydrologic modeling possible? TRANSACTIONS of the ASAE 16(3).

25   Ligon, J. T., A. G. Law and D. H. Higgins. 1969. Evaluation and application of a digital simulation model. Clemson Univ., Water Resources Research Institute Report No. 12.

26   Liou, E. V. 1970. OPSET-Program for computerized selection of watershed parameter values for the Stanford watershed model. Univ. of Kentucky Water Resources Institute Research Report No. 34.

27   Machmeier, R. E. and C. L. Larson. 1968. Runoff hydrogrpahs for mathematical watershed model. J. Hydr. Div. Amer. Soc. Civil Engrs. 94(6).

28   Magette, W. L., V. O. Shanholtz and J. C. Carr. 1976. Estimating selected parameters for the Kentucky watershed model from watershed characteristics. Water Resources Research 12(3).

29   Majtenyi, S. I. 1972. A model to predict mean annual watershed discharge. J. Hydr. Div. Amer. Soc. Civil Engrs 98(7).

30   Moore, Ian D. and R. G. Mein. 1976. Evaluating rainfall-runoff model performance. Am. Soc. Civil Engrs. J. Hydraulics Div. 102(9).

31   Moore, Ian D. and C. L. Larson. 1978. Effects of drainage projects on surface runoff from small depressional watersheds in the North Central Region. University of Minnesota Water Resources Research Center Bulletin 99.

32   Musgrave, G. W. 1955. How much of the rain enters the soil? Water, U.S. Dept. of Agric. Yearbook of Agriculture.

33   Negev, M. 1967. A sediment model on a digital computer. Stanford Univ. Dept. of Civil Engr. Tech. Report No. 76.

34   Onstad, C. A. and D. J. Jamieson. 1968. Subsurface flow regimes of a hydrologic model. Second Seepage Symposium Proc. U.S. Dept. of Agric.-Agric. Research Service No. 41-147.

35   Pinder, G. F. and W. G. Gray. 1977. Finite element simulation in surface and subsurface hydrology. Academic Press, New York, NY.

36   Ricca, V. T. 1974. The Ohio State version of the Stanford streamflow simulatin model. Ohio State Univ. Water Resources Center.

37   Rockwood, D. M. 1958. Columbia Basin streamflow routing by computer. J. Waterways and Harbors Division, Am. Soc. Civil Engrs. 84(1874) Part 1.

38   Rockwood, D. M. 1964. Streamflow synthesis and reservoir regulation. U.S. Army Engr. Div., North Pacific, Portland, Oregon, Engineering Studies Project 171, Technical Bulletin No. 22.

39   Ross, B. B., V. O. Shanholtz, D. N. Contractor and J. C. Carr. 1978. A model for evaluating the effect of land uses on flood flows. Virginia Water Resources Research Center Bulletin 85.

40   Ross, G. A. 1970. The Stanford watershed model, the correlation of parameters selected by a computerized procedure with measurable physical characteristics of the watershed. Univ. of Kentucky Water Resources Inst. Research Report No. 35.

41   Schermerhorn, V. P. and D. W. Kuehl. 1968. Operational streamflow forecasting with the SSARR model. In: The use of analog and digital computers in hydrology. Symposium, International Association of Scientific Hydrology, UNESCO, Tucson, AZ. Vol. 1.

42   Shanholtz, V. O. and J. C. Carr. 1975. Optimizing parameters for a watershed model. TRANSACTIONS of the ASAE 18(2):307-311.

43   Sherman, L. K. 1932. Streamflow from rainfall by the unit graph method. Eng. News Record 108:501-505.

44   U.S. Army Corps of Engrs. 1956. Snow hydrology. Summary Report of the Snow Investigations, North Pacific Division, Portland, OR.

45   U.S. Army Corps of Engrs. 1972. Application of the SSARR model to the upper Paraguay River Basin. North Pacific Division, Portland, OR.

46   U.S. Army Corps of Engrs. 1973. HEC-1 flood hydrograph package - users' manual. U.S. Corps of Engineers Hydrologic Engineering Center, Computer Program No. 723-010.

47   U.S. Army Corps of Engrs. 1975. Program description and user manual for SSARR model. North Pacific Division, Portland, OR.

48   U.S. Army Corps of Engrs. 1976. Development and application of the SSARR model, summaries of technical reports. North Pacific Division, Portland, OR.

49   U.S. Soil Conservation Service.1965. Computer program for project formulation-hydrology. Technical Release No. 20 (also Supplement No. 1 1969).

50   U.S. Soil Conservation Service. 1972. Hydrology. National Engineering Handbook, Section 4.

51   Water Survey of Canada. 1974. Streamflow forecasting, South Saskatchewan River. Technical Report to the PPWB Committee on Hydrology, Department of Environment.

52   Wei, T. C. and C. L. Larson. 1971. Effect of areal and time distribution of rainfall on small watershed runoff hydrographs. Univ. of Minn. Water Resources Research Center, Bull. No. 30.

53   Williams, J. R.and W. V. Laseur. 1976. Water yield model using SCS curve numbers. J. Hydr. Div. 102(9).

SELECTION, CALIBRATION, AND TESTING OF HYDROLOGIC MODELS

chapter 11 ▮▮▮▮▮▮▮▮▮▮▮

11

SELECTION, CALIBRATION, AND TESTING OF HYDROLOGIC MODELS

by   L. Douglas James, Director, Utah Water Research Laboratory, Utah State University, Logan, UT 84322, and Stephen J. Burges, Associate Professor, Department of Civil Engineering, University of Washington, Seattle, WA 98195.

INTRODUCTION

Hydrologic modeling is an important tool for estimating and organizing quantitative information for water resources planning, design, and operation. The first two chapters of this monograph provide background on how to model by presenting the principles of deterministic and stochastic system synthesis. The next five chapters apply these principles to modeling precipitation, infiltration, runoff, evapotranspiration, and subsurface flow. Chapter 10 describes various ways these process models can be combined into a general hydrologic model, and chapter 13 inventories currently available models.

Planners or designers who require hydrologic information can choose from a variety of modeling alternatives. They can follow the principles outlined in the preceding chapters to develop a new model to meet their needs, or they can select from among available models. The purpose of this chapter is to provide guidance on how to select a model for a given application, how to calibrate the model selected to get the best information, and how to test the adequacy of the results. The guidelines begin with qualitative aids for screening to determine which models are conceptually sound for a given use and follow with quantitative measures for completing the selection, calibration, and testing.

THE BASIC PRINCIPLE OF MODEL SELECTION

The goal in hydrologic modeling is to estimate rates of water movement overland, underground, or within streams; amounts of water stored in the soil or in natural water bodies; or how these rates and amounts vary with time. Engineers and water planners see the careful representation of hydrologic processes necessary for hydrologic modeling as promising better

Acknowledgment: The authors appreciate the help of Courtney Bates, Boeing Computer Services, Kent, Washington, in preparing this paper. He generously agreed to having his work on time series error analysis directly included in the text. The authors are also grateful for the review comments received on earlier versions from David Bowles, David Dawdy, Willard Snyder, C. T. Haan, and an anonymous reviewer.

estimates of hydrologic quantities for management decisions. Those who attempt to model, however, soon find that the physical laws that govern these water movements and storages are so complex and that the parameters that must be measured for their representation are so variable in space and time that construction of a reliable model is no easy matter. Consequently, considerable research must go into developing understanding of physical laws and acquiring data on physical situations. At the present time, hydrologic science still falls far short of a universal model that can be generally recommended for all user applications, and a user must consider alternatives in deciding how best to model for a given application.

As users make these applications, the science of hydrology is also advanced. One of the most important contributions of model building toward advancing hydrologic science is through the discipline of data collection, system representation, and expression of results required for quantitative representation of complex hydrologic processes. When model results are compared to measured data, careless work quickly becomes evident as results prove to be scientifically invalid and unreliable for practical application. Through careful modeling, the scientist seeks better understanding of the causes of observed physical events, and the planner seeks more reliable estimates of design flows and of how those flows are affected by planning alternatives. The scientist wants to explain observed patterns of infiltration, overland flow, and channel flow; the planner wants to design reservoirs, delineate flood plains, and size culverts.

The fundamental criterion for the planner in selecting, calibrating, and testing hydrologic models must be how well the model performs as a sound basis for planning and management decisions. The fundamental criterion for the scientist must be how well the model contributes to a hydrologic understanding that will eventually help planners make even better decisions. By applying scientific contributions, those making planning and management decisions are helped as they can be surer of the hydrologic consequences of the alternatives they consider and can have greater confidence in the hydrologic estimates for the technical designs they recommend. The primary decision-makers, hence the primary users of hydrologic estimates, have been professional planners and design engineers. Recently, shifts toward public participation in selecting government projects, and toward individual implementation of many small-scale (flood proofing for example) and nonstructural measures, are increasing the need for hydrologic models that can produce information for specific locations (flood hazard on land parcels for example) whenever someone wants it, yet be easily understood by the less technically sophisticated public (James, 1973).

A hydrologic model represents runoff processes in a manner that can be used to estimate (a) how the prototype physical system would respond to sequences of external stimuli (usually precipitation), (b) the frequency distribution of responses of interest (high or low flows), or (c) how changes to the system would alter the response. The representation may be a physical model providing scaled-down duplication of the prototype system, an analog model using another physical system that is more economically constructed but has similar response characteristics, or a mathematical model that represents the physical processes by a set of equations programmed for a digital computer. Physical and analog models have definite advantages where governing physical laws cannot be expressed by succinct and readily-solvable equations (or the precision desired exceeds that of the equations; e.g., hydraulic modeling of spillways) or where the analogy is inexpensive and accurate. Digital computer modeling, however, now dominates hydrology because of: (a) its relatively low cost while skilled labor required by other model types is scarce and expensive, (b) its ease of transferability from one computer or from one prototype configuration to another, (c) greater flexibility for modelers who would like to make changes. This chapter therefore is restricted to digital computer models.

A FRAMEWORK FOR COMPARING DIGITAL MODELS

Application of a digital computer model to meet a given planning need requires an inventory and evaluation of available models, adopting or adapting (few can afford to start from scratch) the one judged most suitable in terms of reliability and cost (both factors depend highly on user familiarity), and calibrating the selected model to estimate the hydrologic information of interest. Chapter 13 provides an inventory of currently available models and general information for preliminary screening. To establish screening criteria, it is helpful to review the alternatives in model development because the choices a modeler makes on these alternatives govern the suitability of his product for any given use.

Hydrologic modeling requires (a) identification of the hydrologic quantities important to the user and therefore to be estimated by the model, (b) identification of hydrologic processes within the prototype system that need to be modeled to estimate the desired quantities adequately, (c) selection of equations to represent each identified component physical hydrologic process (chapters 3 to 7), (d) structuring the equations to differentiate coefficients treated as constants in all model applications from parameters which are varied in calibrating the model for specific watersheds, (e) synthesizing the selected process equations into a computational framework (the mathematical model) adequately reproducing the desired hydrologic responses for the system as a whole (chapter 10), (f) selecting values for the parameters that provide the best estimates of hydrologic response for a specific watershed, (g) testing the adequacy of the model estimates in the desired applications, and (h) communicating the results to decision-makers.

The first five subtasks produce the model; the sixth calibrates it; the seventh tests it; and the eighth, the often overlooked aspect of depicting technical information so that the user can understand and will believe it, is critical to making the modeling effort worthwhile.

A person, selecting from among a set of models programmed by others, needs to review the decisions made by the modelers during the first five subtasks. **Selection** should be based on the user's determination that (a) the model provides the kinds of information needed, (b) the watershed characteristics represented by the model parameters indeed govern watershed response in the intended application, (c) the equations used are correct in light of the state-of-the-art, available data, and available computer facilities, and (d) the model will provide results, which are suitable for the intended use, of acceptable quality at a reasonable cost within a required time frame. **Calibration** should seek an economical and reproducible method for estimating parameters. **Testing** should judge the adequacy of the model for decision-making.

The decisions made by the modeler that a potential user should consider in model selection, calibration, and testing may be classified into the areas of (a) modeling strategy, (b) model conceptualization, (c) model structure, (d) model calibration, (e) model testing and verification, (f) model development dynamics, and (g) display and communication of model results. These seven issue areas are explored qualitatively in the next seven sections of this chapter.

ISSUES IN MODELING STRATEGY

The issues in modeling strategy relate to basic goals of model construction and to the best type of model for achieving those goals. The four broad strategy alternatives are:

1 Simulation of water movement through the component physical processes and then integrating the results through water accounting within a general hydrologic model. The Stanford Watershed Model (Crawford and Linsley, 1966), as an example, provides continuous information on water storages and movements over time. Some of the hydrologic event models (chapter 10) provide this kind of accounting during storm periods.

2 Simulation of the total flow (or soil moisture, evapotranspiration, or some other water movement or storage) for a selected hydrologic event or events (a given date and given location) through relationships derived by statistical techniques seeking maximum correlation between observed inputs (e.g., precipitation, antecedent moisture, and basin size) and output, (e.g., streamflow). Traditional procedures for estimating storm runoff from information on storm characteristics and antecedent moisture (Linsley et al., pp. 265-274), a variety of statistical approaches (Beard, 1962), and some of the "event" models (chapter 10) are examples.

3 Estimation of the statistical properties of the time series of events through relationships derived by statistical techniques seeking maximum correlation of the selected statistics (e.g., the mean or standard deviation of a recorded series of annual floods, computed 10- or 100-yr flood peaks, etc.) with watershed characteristics (drainage area, forest cover, slope, soil type, etc.). The procedures developed by Santa Clara County, CA, for estimating flood peaks on ungaged watersheds (Saah et al., 1976) and by Fletcher et al. (1976) for estimating flood flows for desired frequencies for highway culvert design are illustrations. Flow statistics estimated in this manner are used in stochastic methods (chapter 2) to estimate reservoir yield.

4 Optimization of system design or operation by programming the model to integrate hydrologic information with relevant economic, social, and environmental factors and produce comparisons of management alternatives. This modeling strategy is illustrated in models selecting the optimum combination of structural and nonstructural flood control measures (James, 1970) or facilitating other aspects of hydrologic design (Fleming, 1975, pp. 257-312).

The first strategy, simulation based on component physical processes, requires subdivision of the watershed into separable spatial units and subdivision of the period of analysis into discrete time units. Data must be collected to depict the precipitation and potential evaporation stimulating hydrologic activity in each spatial unit by time period and to depict the physical characteristics controlling the response of each spatial unit. Such modeling is limited by the impossibility of obtaining complete information on the small space-time grid required for comprehensive physical representation and by the computer time required for repeated solution (once for each space-time unit) of the differential equations that provide accurate process representations. Consequently, operational models use areas of a size matching rain gage density rather than small homogeneous areas and use time aggregations of total water movement over hours or days rather than continuous instantaneous flow rates. The greater grid coarseness in time and space, however, causes the parameters in the equations to be less correlated with directly measurable physical watershed characteristics. Values for the parameters, therefore, have to be estimated by statistical methods based on criteria of best match of model results to measured data. A model calibrated in this way can only be used for conditions covered by the data used to calibrate it; it cannot be used to extrapolate beyond the range of the calibration data.

The second strategy provides the user a simpler model by sacrificing replication of water movement through physical processes. The statistical techniques used to estimate output (streamflow) from correlations with input (precipitation) and watershed characteristics are tested on the basis of goodness of match of the end results without any provision for intermediate process checks. A typical example is to use streamflow measured at scattered gages to develop a regional relationship between flows and watershed characteristics to estimate flows at ungaged sites. Greater separation of these methods from physical processes suggests greater difficulty in obtaining reliable estimates for watersheds not well represented in the data base and greater scatter between predicted and measured results.

Examples of the third strategy (a regional relationship to estimate a design parameter such as a 100-yr flood instead of a flow during a dated historical event) are found in estimating reservoir yield (Haan and Allen, 1972) and in regional flood studies. The Santa Clara County flood study used records from 23 gaging stations in and near the county to derive the relationship between the 100-yr flood peak and watershed characteristics:

$$Q_{100} = 19.4 \, A^{0.95} \, P^{0.58} \, S^{-0.25} \quad \dots\dots\dots\dots [11.1]$$

where Q_{100} is the 100-yr peak in cfs (0.0283 m³/s), A is the drainage area in square miles (2.59 km²), P is the mean annual precipitation in inches (0.0254 m), and S is the slope of the main stream (Saah et al., 1976, p. 36). The equation has a coefficient of determination (R^2) of 0.904 and a standard error of estimate for Q_{100} of 0.218. The information on the design parameter or dependent variable used to derive such a relationship is ideally estimated from long sequences of measured flows but can be approximated from data series constructed through one of the first two strategies.

While equation [11.1] is very helpful to Santa Clara County officials needing to estimate flood peaks at ungaged locations, it also provides a good example to illustrate cautions required in using this sort of model. Obviously equation [11.1] should not be applied outside the county, except perhaps at locations just across its borders. In addition, a location map showing the 23 gaged watershed shows virtually all the gages to be in the western half of the county, and the eastern portion is significantly different in climate, geology, and topography. Even within the western half, many ungaged watersheds fall outside the gaged range of the dependent variables or are influenced by other variables which do not appear in the equation because they did not happen to vary much among the watersheds that were used. All of these issues illustrate dangers in extrapolating outside the range of available data, and all of them should be carefully considered.

The fourth strategy integrates hydrologic modeling with various information on the physical, economic, and environmental consequences of water management alternatives to help decision-makers understand (a) the consequences of physical changes, occurring within the watershed, on runoff (Lumb and James, 1976) or (b) the benefits and costs of structural changes under construction. The integration expands the scope of modeling to portray implications of hydrologic change rather than have the user look to other methods for applying the output of the hydrologic model.

The first strategy has its primary application when one wants a time series of hydrologic responses or information on how hydrologic responses will be altered by watershed changes. It is enhanced by quantitative information on physical watershed characteristics and becomes progressively more attractive as estimates of more types of hydrologic response (floods, low flows, runoff volumes, soil moisture, etc.) are desired. The second strategy has its primary application in estimating a single type of hydrologic response for specific events (e.g., flood peaks on a given date) and becomes progressively more attractive as estimates are required for a number of storms on the same watershed or for the same storm on a number of adjacent watersheds. The third strategy is more economical than the first two for producing design estimates but achieves the economy at a greater risk of error because of the further separation of the approach from physical causes. The fourth strategy extends modeling by interfacing with non-hydrologic factors but does so at the risk of becoming too broad (interdisciplinary) to be easily understood and of combining data of greatly varying reliability and precision without explicit recognition of the uncertainties resulting. Progression from the first to the fourth strategy moves the modeling effort from scientific hydrology through statistical analysis to multiple objective planning; a potential user needs to select a model that matches where he needs to be on this spectrum.

ISSUES IN MODEL CONCEPTUALIZATION

The basic issue of model conceptualization is the degree of detail to use in making model results reflect physical watershed characteristics within the framework of the selected modeling strategy. Specific examples, strategy by strategy, are (a) which physical processes to model, the detail and level of sophistication to use for those selected, and the accounting detail to use in routing water through the model, (b) which outputs to have the model estimate (for flood hydrology the scale may vary from peak flows to complete flood hydrographs), the storm characteristics and watershed conditions to use as independent variables, and the statistical techniques to use, (c) which distribution to use to represent a hydrologic time series and which parameters of that distribution to estimate, and (d) which economic, environmental, and social considerations to combine with the hydrology to guide decision-making.

The scientific bias in modeling strategy is to assume that any effort that will make a model theoretically more correct or empirically more reliable is desirable. The planning reaction is to ask whether the extra effort is justified. The practical justification is in terms of contribution to better water resources planning and management decisions. Specifically, will the value received from the additional information justify the additional cost of a more comprehensive model? Factors relevant to this determination include the contribution the additional or more reliable results will make to better planning decisions or more economical engineering design, the strength of the theory and the reliability of the data required for the additional computations, the cost of assembling any additional data in the required form, and the capacity of available computer facilities to handle additional computations at a reasonable cost. A user selecting a model should carefully review the data and funds he has available and the objectives that he is trying to achieve to avoid either a greater level of sophistication than can be justified by his need or an approach that does not produce key inputs to his decision-making.

A number of examples might be used to illustrate the care that should go into selecting an appropriate level of model sophistication; one is the selection of a method of streamflow routing. Methods available range from using time-area historgrams, adding linear reservoirs, applying Muskingum routing parameters derived from recorded hydrographs, to computing from kinematic or full dynamic routing equations. Hydraulic theory supports dynamic routing as the most accurate, but the additional accuracy is only gained at the cost of collecting additional data and executing a more complex model. Justification of these additional costs depends on the model application. As examples, justification is highly likely for simulating flood hydrographs for urban drainage design but very unlikely for estimating reservoir yield for water supply design; vastly different time increments are involved.

The tendency has been to add theoretical advances to hydrologic models without first exploring the advantages and disadvantages. One result has been models that have an order of magnitude of greater precision in representing some processes than in representing others. This lack of balance can only be justified if the results desired from the model are sensitive to the more precisely represented hydrologic process by a comparable order of magnitude. The sensitivity of the results should be explored before adding theoretically justified but computationally more expensive model elements.

Coleman and DeCoursey (1976) built on previous work by McCuen (1973) to provide a methodology for employing model sensitivity analysis to estimate the reduction in variance achieved by model modification; the achieved reduction in variance provides a basis for determining whether the modification is justified. The method defines sensitivity (S) as the derivative of model results (R) with respect to a parameter (P) of interest. Therefore,

$$S = \partial R / \partial P \qquad \dotfill [11.2]$$

Relative sensitivity (S_r) is defined as

$$S_r = \frac{\partial R}{\partial P} \frac{P}{R} \qquad \dotfill [11.3]$$

A number of numerical measures of model performance are presented later in this chapter. P may be taken as a defined model parameter or as a discrete change to the model (shifting from Muskingum to kinematic routing).

These sensitivity estimates can be applied at various levels of sophistication. Relative sensitivity provides a basis for comparing various parameters and concentrating research and data collection on the more sensitive. Such comparisons contribute a great deal toward logical priorities in making model changes and working toward a product that does not consume a great deal of computer time in refined calculations whose contribution is negligible because the model combines the results with very rough estimates from other computations. Equation [2] can be combined with the rules of economic optimization (James and Lee, 1971) to make explicit modeling choices. For this purpose, the economic sensitivity (S_e) can be defined by

$$S_e = \frac{\partial R}{\partial P} \frac{M_b}{M_c} \quad \dots\dots\dots\dots\dots\dots\dots\dots [11.4]$$

where M_b is the marginal benefit of better results to the model user and M_c is the marginal cost of parameter refinement. A value of S_e exceeding unity indicates a profitable change. A user may find a model change that he can justify solely from his intended application ($S_e > 1$ with only M_b to himself counted). Modelers often would consider marginal benefits to all users to justify additional work. In a completely balanced model, one would achieve equal marginal rates of substitution among parameters and equal marginal rates of transformation among results (James and Lee, 1971, pp. 74-82). Such refinement, however, should be taken as more of a conceptual ideal than a working guide.

Other considerations in tying model results to physical watershed characteristics are the extent to which those characteristics can be expected to change over time and the control the user has over those changes. If watershed changes result from influences outside the user's control, the model can be used in advance to estimate flow sensitivity to these changes. A flood control planning agency, concerned that upstream ubranization and channelization will increase design flows for downstream structures, needs a model that will relate upstream land use and channel changes to downstream flow for flood control plan formulation. If the user regulates certain watershed characteristics (e.g., channel dimensions or detention storage capacity), the more directly those characteristics are used as input data to the model, the easier it will be for him to use the model for planning. A user who thinks in terms of specific watershed characteristics should select a model whose parameters relate to those characteristics.

ISSUES IN MODEL STRUCTURE

The basic issue of model structure is which method to use in putting the conceptualized model components together. Specific issues under this general heading are (a) how the level of aggregation (the size of the spatial units and the length of the time intervals) used in the model match the spatial and time detail at which information is required by the user, (b) how well the equations and computational framework contained within the model represent the state-of-the-art for estimating the hydrologic responses of interest to the user, (c) the robustness of the model as reflected by its ability to make reliable estimates if the user faces limited data availability, and (d) the capability of the user to collect and manage data for model calibration and testing. Most hydrologic models are structured with particular users in mind. As additional users apply a model, the structure becomes generalized.

A person desiring to use a hydrologic model to obtain needed information may either start from scratch and build a specialized model or adopt a more general model. There is some chance of finding a general model that will work directly, but, more likely, it will have to be modified to handle the peculiarities of the new special situation. A new specialized model can often produce better estimates of a few selected hydrologic responses but requires much greater expertise and cost. The total process of developing a general model requires much greater investment in research and development but generates net savings if the investment is divided among more applications. A major component of a general model is its data management structure. Many special purpose models are poorly programmed, and little thought is given to the development of data files for easy manipulation within the model. Developers of more general models have generally been forced to recognize that as much as 80 percent of the effort involved in modeling a watershed is spent in data management; consequently, they have made considerable effort to simplify data management for the user. The quality and scope of the data management component of a model is an extremely important factor in model selection and use. Development of a few general models would therefore seem to be more in the interest of hydrologic science and practice than for each user to develop his own specialized one.

A user in the process of selecting the model with the best structure for a particular application normally has in mind a minimum acceptable level of accuracy. He also would like to improve on that minimum level to the degree better results justify the extra time and cost (equation [11.4]). For example, a user that needs to know flood peaks on a small watershed needs to identify models (e.g., from those in chapter 13) with a fine enough spatial grid to represent that watershed and a fine enough time grid not to miss the flow peak by a significant amount. A selection can then be made among qualifying models on the bases of theoretical reputability, computational economy, probable public credibility of the modeling approach, and the time required to become familiar with the model and establish the necessary data files.

Model builders generally major on theoretical reputability with a minor in computational economy. They are less likely to have structured their models to minimize user difficulties in making applications. One user difficulty modelers are very likely to overlook is that many water resources planners are required by law or by administrative regulation to incorporate certain considerations in their analysis and cannot use a model whose programming they do not understand well enough to know for sure that it meets those requirements. Other users encounter difficulty in running a computer program or in interpreting the results and will return to a more familiar method even though theoretically it will not meet their needs as well. A great deal more attention needs to be given to the technology trans-

fer of complicated hydrologic models; one survey could not find one user
that was able to apply a complex model successfully without first taking a
course on the model from someone who was previously trained (James et al.,
1975, pp. 157-160).

ISSUES IN MODEL CALIBRATION

Once a model is selected, it must be calibrated for a watershed. There
are two calibration criteria: model results should match recorded data, and
the estimates of parameter values should be consistent with watershed characteristics. The second criterion should not be interpreted too literally. For
example, conceptual watershed models often represent infiltrated water
movement by means of several conceptual soil moisture storages. These
storages cannot be tied to any specific watershed characteristic; they represent integrated, areally averaged conceptual approximations to subsurface
moisture storage.

A model that produces only an estimate of the 100-yr flood peak is
almost impossible to check without a long history of gaged records. A model
that produces annual runoff volumes provides one value to check per year.
A continuous streamflow model provides a continuous time series of flows
for comparison. A model that replicates the total runoff process provides
the possibility of checking soil water content, depression storage, and other
observable watershed responses. A model whose parameters are related
to physical watershed characteristics allows the user to compare the parameter estimates that do the best job of simulating hydrologic output with
such measurable physical watershed characteristics as impervious area,
soil permeability, and channel flow times. Such models provide greater
opportunity to gain confidence in the results.

The calibration process requires a procedure to evaluate the success
of a given calibration and another procedure to adjust the parameter estimates for the next calibration. The criterion of success may be a subjective
judgment on adequacy, some statistic selected as measuring goodness of
fit, or some multi-objective function combining several statistics. The adjustment procedure may be a subjective determination of what parameter
changes seem likely to be desirable, a set of rules derived from sensitivity
studies (equation [11.2] or [11.3]) on the various parameters, or a systematic
variation of parameter values designed for efficient examination of a response surface (James and Lee, 1971, pp. 486-488). The statistical models
are more likely to use a systematic search because their objective function
is more easily defined whereas the many items for which synthesized results can be compared with measured values in the more general models
make selection of criteria of best fit more difficult. At the present state-
of-the-art, users wanting to estimate flood peaks, low flows, and soil water
content may legitimately make three different calibrations of the same
general model for the same watershed.

Statistics that might be examined in deciding if a given calibration
is acceptable include (a) statistics computed from the complete set of simulated flows (e.g., minimum sum of the squares of daily flow differences),
(b) statistics computed from only those flows of particular interest (e.g.,
minimum sum of the square of daily flow differences during low flow periods
for a waste water dilution study) (c) statistics on other types of measurements such as soil water content or known physical characteristics of the
watershed such as impervious area, (d) statistics on changes in flow from

one time period to the next, (e) magnitudes and patterns of systematic and random "errors," and (f) sensitivity data on the impacts of uncertainty in initial conditions, of errors in precipitation and evaporation data (Dawdy and Bergman, 1969), or of defective modeling equations. Any one of these statistics might be selected to guide the model user to an acceptable calibration, or several might be combined in a more complicated objective function. No matter which statistic or combination of statistics is chosen, the calibration goal is to minimize errors (differences between recorded and simulated values), and alternatives error measures are discussed in a later section.

Certain model parameters are more appropriately obtained by direct measurement before beginning the calibration than by statistical criteria of goodness of fit. Watershed drainage area, the impervious fraction of the watershed, and channel hydraulic capacity are specific examples. As models become more sophisticated and the relationships between model parameters and watershed characteristics become better known, the number of parameters that have to be estimated by minimizing error statistics become fewer, and model calibration will be able to make greater use of field data. For his selected model and application, the modeler should give careful thought in deciding which parameters to estimate from data on watershed characteristics and which to estimate by adjusting values to minimize errors. The parameters to estimate from field information are those which the model structure ties to physical watershed characteristics on which reliable descriptive data are available.

Presently, very few parameters can be identified directly from field measurements. Watershed area can be readily obtained for rural watersheds; however, delineating the watershed boundary on a topographical map can lead to substantial errors in urban watersheds if field checks are not made to adjust for human activities that have altered drainage patterns. If variable Muskingum-type coefficients are required, they can be obtained readily from stream-gage measurements. Unless one is modeling an extremely small area (about a square yard or a square meter per measurement) field infiltration data are virtually worthless for direct estimation of model parameters. The enormous spatial variability of infiltration, land slopes, etc., necessitate using some average values representative of the level of the process. Similarly, use of an average permeability for groundwater flow is necessary; the permeability coefficient has been known to range over three orders of magnitude in a distance as short as 200 ft (61 m) in materials that are geologically uniform. The modeler should be very careful in using physical field measurements for most parameter values.

Calibration can simultaneously deal with the full set of parameters or can separate out subsets that are relatively independent of one another and deal with each subset separately as is done in one self-calibrating version of the Stanford Watershed Model (Liou, 1970). The chief advantage of dealing with subsets separately is that some watershed characteristics have much greater effect on certain flows than on others. For example, recorded information on the shape of the flood hydrograph can be used to calibrate parameters related to channel hydraulics but is of little worth in calibrating parameters related to subsurface flow. The parameter subsets used by Liou are those dealing with:

1   Streamflow recession for which parameters are calibrated on flow sequences between storm periods.

2   Division of precipitation between surface runoff and infiltration and of infiltration between that contributing to evapotranspiration and that contributing to interflow or baseflow. Liou calibrates this parameter subset on annual runoff volume and the distribution of that volume among the months of the year.

3   Flood routing as calibrated by the shape and timing of the rising and crest portions of flood hydrographs.

4   Interflow as calibrated by flows in periods immediately after larger flood events.

After deciding which parameters to assign values directly from information on watershed characteristics, the user should group the remaining parameters into relatively independent subsets for joint calibration. The recession rates of Liou's first group can be estimated directly from recession data; two major parameter subsets for estimation by calibration remain: (a) parameters that determine runoff volume and (b) parameters that determine flood hydrograph shape. These two subsets should be calibrated separately.

One method for calibrating these subsets of parameters is by the systematic pattern search method presented by Hocke and Jeeves (1961), applied to hydrologic model calibration by Munro (1971), and refined by Lumb et al. (1975). Some error measurement (possible equations given later in this chapter) is selected for minimization as a criterion of goodness of fit. A set of initial (X_0) for the parameters to be calibrated is established by arbitrarily selecting plausible values for each, and a simulation is made. The results are associated with some error (E_0). The value of the parameter to which the error measurement is most sensitive is then increased by a relatively small amount Δ while holding all other parameter values constant. If the error increases with a positive Δ, a negative Δ is tried. After these two trials, the first parameter is returned to its X_0 value, and the process is repeated for each of the remaining parameters one at a time until one or two of these local excursions have been made for each parameter. The search then makes a pattern move from X_0 to a new set (X_1) by changing the value for each parameter in the direction found to reduce the error measurement. The amount of change for a parameter is increased as repeated local excursions indicate adjustment in the same direction. The search continues in this fashion from one set of parameters to the next $(X_0, X_1, X_2 \ldots X_n)$ until the error measurement is no longer being reduced appreciably $(E_n \cong E_{n-1})$.

An alternative adjustment procedure is to use either the judgment developed through model building experience or a sensitivity analysis to determine which particular flows (or other simulated output) vary most with a change in a given parameter. Each parameter is then only adjusted as indicated by error measurements originating from related sensitive flows. Factors to consider in choosing between the two approaches include: (a) systematic search takes more computer time for many trials and is therefore impractical for a large number of parameters; (b) judgment search depends on adjustment rules that must be gained by experience, vary with local hydrologic conditions, are much more difficult to program, and are more sensitive to data errors; and (c) systematic search will lead to minimum error measurements while judgment search will lead imperfect models to parameter values that make better sense when compared with known watershed characteristics. Either method can be programmed into a model, but repeated trial simulations are expensive, and one should try to keep the cost as low as possible by beginning from a good first approximation and by using a simulation algorithm that is as economical as possible.

One very important goal in calibration is that the results be reproducible and independent of the person performing the calibration. Subjective calibration works reasonably well for a one time application by an individual user but becomes quite unsatisfactory when separate calibrations are used to compare hydrologic responses among watersheds or time differences in response of a given watershed. Deterministic errors caused by judgment differences dominate physical differences.

ISSUES IN MODEL TESTING AND VERIFICATION

Once the calibration process has been used to estimate the best values for the model parameters, the outcome needs to be evaluated to determine if the results provide adequate information for answering the questions facing the decision-makers. Answers may be unsatisfactory either because the model provides faulty estimates of needed hydrologic quantities or because the selected outputs do not provide information the decision-makers consider relevant. The accuracy problem is more widely discussed by hydrologic model builders, but the relevancy problem may well generate greater potential-user skepticism. Hydrologic information is imperfect. The acceptability of results from a given calibration generally depend on whether the insufficiencies justify additional effort to upgrade the model, to improve the calibration, or to turn to an alternative method for estimating the desired information.

Faulty results may stem from a variety of causes with the appropriate remedial action (where remedial action is possible) depending on the problem. Common problems and possible remedial measures include:

1 Errors in the data used in calibration. Both the data used as input to the model and the data used to check model output should be checked. Application of correlation techniques (Haan, 1977, pp. 222-235) to identify cases where a relationship among data departs from its normal pattern is one approach, and such graphical techniques as the double mass curve (Linsley et al., 1975, p. 81) are often a practical substitute. Data with large errors should not be used for calibration, particularly with computerized search techniques that do not temper results with hydrologic judgment. The effects of smaller data errors can be balanced over time by using a longer calibration period. Seldom are records of concurrent precipitation, stream flow, evapotranspiration, etc., complete; therefore, some gaps in the records exist. If one is calibrating a continuous simuluation model, these gaps must be filled in. The user should not be too concerned if simulated and observed streamflow do not match very well during periods when filled-in data have been used; he should not use the filled-in portion of the record (fill-in techniques are very crude) to influence his assessment of the model calibration. As another warning, streamgage records for overbank flow are less accurate than within channel flow estimates. Flow rates for large floods are seldom measured but rather extrapolated from stage-discharge relationships. Difficulties in matching recorded high flows cannot necessarily be blamed on the model.

2 Use of a period of record that does not contain enough events with the physical processes needed to calibrate key parameters. For example, the hydraulic characteristics of overbank flow differ substantially from those

of main-channel flow; consequently, overbank flow parameters cannot be estimated from a period of record during which no such flows occurred. The calibration period should be reviewed to make sure that all important event types were recorded.

3 Inadequate or misrepresentation by the model of hydrologic processes found in the watershed (for example, a failure to represent the impervious characteristics of frozen ground in watersheds where significant storms occur after freezing periods). Model results should be compared visually with recorded data series to look for consistent variations. Possible physical causes of those detected should be explored, and the model should be corrected to deal with problems where the effort seems justified.

4 Insufficient output for decision-making. Any failure to develop desired information normally becomes obvious when model results are presented to users. Sometimes the additional information can be obtained by outputing quantities already computed internally, but often the modeling process itself must be revised.

The basic issue in model testing is to determine if the hydrologic estimates (residual error) achieved by the calibration are acceptable. The basic process is to run the calibrated model for a time period other than that used for calibration and evaluate the results. The modeler would normally test with the same error measurements used for calibration, but a new user may consider different sorts of error more important and select different statistics to evaluate a previous calibration.

The user is interested in the expected error, the distribution of possible errors, the consequences of using erroneous information, and the prospects for improving the estimates. The acceptability of a calibrated model ultimately depends on judgment as to whether or not the estimates can be improved (a) for a cost justified by reducing the consequences of using erroneous information and (b) before the critical decisions must be made. Hydrologic modelers can contribute to better water resources planning through frank discussion of these issues with decision-makers.

ISSUES IN MODEL DEVELOPMENT DYNAMICS

Many hydrologic modelers are more familiar with the issues in model selection, calibration, and testing than they are with the issues in communicating model results to users to provide a useful water resources planning tool. These issues include how best to (a) transfer an understanding of the technology of applying a complicated model to others, (b) organize libraries of available models and keep them updated for ready access and reference by users, (c) facilitate communication of user-discovered model deficiencies to researchers to take corrective action, (d) facilitate the exchange of experiences among model builders to minimize duplication of effort, and (e) decide when to use a previously developed model and when to develop a new one.

Because these issues have not been studied in anywhere near the depth given to the topics addressed in the previous sections, criteria for efficient model development dynamics have not been established. Basic principles of effective communication, however, suggest needs for (a) carefully documented user manuals and other descriptive material on each model so users can make informed decisions whether a particular model is applicable for a situation and make that application should the decision be favorable,

(b) libraries where users can go for manuals, source programs, and contacts with experts who can provide detailed help, and (c) effective feedback channels for exchanging modeling experiences. Development of specific guidelines for achieving effective programs in all three areas would be very worthwhile.

Model documentation should include a frank presentation of model strategy, conceptualization, and structure and specific recommendations to facilitate model calibration and testing. The reader needs to learn model strengths and weaknesses with respect to the application that he has in mind. He needs to be told of the theoretical and empirical constructs incorporated within the model so that he can decide whether he concurs, if they also hold for the use he has in mind, and if they are in harmony with the design policies of his agency. He needs a flow chart to understand how the program is organized, a listing for detailed analysis, and a dictionary defining the major variables so that he is in a position to make changes that he feels desirable. He needs guidance on the sensitivity of model output to input data so that he can concentrate his data collection efforts productively and on sensitivity to parameter values so that he can calibrate more effectively.

Two items of concern to all model users are learning and implementation time. Most model developers do a poor job of conveying this information. The lack of a concise manual which states what the model can and cannot do, its accuracy, data needs, user training time, implementation time, etc. is a strong recommendation against use of the model. Model builders who do not provide this information are only permitting their models to be used by a few skilled persons. User demand for a careful summary of model capabilities from model salespersons will improve the overall level of practice.

ISSUES IN DISPLAY AND COMMUNICATION OF MODEL RESULTS

Most hydrologic models have been designed to communicate to scientific hydrologists or to design engineers, and very little effort has been spent in developing the potential of modeling for displaying hydrologic information to land use planners, property managers, water users, and others not trained in water resources engineering. Such user groups require more explanatory labeling of model output, conveyance of that output in a manner that generates credibility through its intuitive reasonableness, greater ability to produce information at specific spots of special interest to particular individuals (translation of streamflow measurements to a graphic portrayal of what the flood will look like as it crosses a specified land parcel), and quick response to information needs whenever they arise. These needs contrast with the common operating scenario in which hydrologists communicate a single set of design information to a design group.

Hydrologic models have great potential for communicating hydrologic information to the public. One can imagine a videoscreen portraying a reach of a river and adjacent buildings in three dimensions. By interacting with a computer terminal, one might ask to see the 100-yr flood moving through the reach and be shown the dynamics of the rising and falling hydrograph and the damage left in its wake. He might then ask how this hydrograph (or any other historical storm hydrograph) would be affected by new upstream development, a storage reservoir, a culvert enlargement, or any other factor of interest. The potential for communicating to the public is tremendous and untapped. Complex models need not create communication barriers.

Nevertheless, the modeler needs to keep in mind the importance of conveying the uncertainties inherent in his work as well as the results. All models are imperfect. It is important to show and explain the uncertainty bounds on all outputs. Display techniques might range from plotting levels of confidence on both sides of prediction curves to showing the low, most probable, and high estimates on a videoscreen system.

ORGANIZING FOR MODEL CALIBRATION

General Principles

Once the user has selected a hydrologic model based on the principles outlined above, he needs to calibrate it. Space does not permit discussion of the specific intricacies of calibrating all the various types of models discussed above and catalogued in Chapter 13, but deterministic rainfall-runoff model calibration will be discussed in some detail and used to provide a foundation for some general principles. These models were chosen for illustration because they are probably the most difficult to calibrate and because the principles described can generally be extended readily to other model types. The intent is to describe a general approach to rainfall-runoff model calibration and avoid becoming involved in such specialized issues as modeling snowmelt, river freezing and thawing, groundwater recharge, interbasin tranfers, flash flood events, and desert storms. No matter what aids to calibrate are programmed into a model or recommended in user manuals, the user should follow a systematic calibration approach based on general principles.

Model calibration should begin by deciding what information will be important when the calibrated model is applied. The user needs to translate these decisions into criteria of goodness of fit, data to collect, and pitfalls to avoid. These issues are extremely well articulated by Clark (1971); his paper should be read along with this chapter before applying any model.

The calibration process should begin from a clear realization that calibration is data demanding. The less frequent a given hydrologic event, the more difficulty will be encountered in calibrating a model for that type of event. For example, extreme flood events are more difficult to replicate than are ordinary flows.

A Philosophy for Dealing with Error

No hydrologic modeler nor model user can afford to forget the errors inherent in mathematical representation. Rainfall-runoff models convert a precipitation time series into a series of stream flows. Error exists in precipitation measurement and in the use of gaged data to estimate precipitation over a watershed area. Any model contains error in its representation of hydrologic processes; and the time series of recorded flows, against which model-simulated events are compared, also contains measurement errors.

Ideally, the modeler can best serve the model user by incorporating within the programming means for computing both (a) the error associated with the estimated values of the parameters, particularly for assessing the calibration, and (b) the error associated with the quantities estimated by the model, particularly for assessing the results. Few hydrologic models, however, are programmed with either capability. Hydrologists need to pursue application of state estimation techniques, specifically Kalman and Extended Kalman filters (Gelb, 1974) for these purposes. Estimates of both parameters and flows and their respective associated errors could with such a system be updated as new data become available.

The crux of the Kalman filter technique (Kalman, 1960) is a combination of two independent estimates of system state to produce an optimal or minimum variance estimate. The measurements of the prototype and the predictions from the model provide the two independent estimates. The weighting used for combining the two estimates is based on the relative uncertainties in the two processes. For the measurements, this uncertainty is represented by the vector $\underline{V}$ (t) for values for m measurement items. For the model, the uncertainty is represented by estimation error propagated by the system model and specified by vector $\underline{W}$(t). Larger model uncertainty necessitates placing less weight on model predictions and more on the measurements.

A simple form of the Kalman filter represents the model of the system by the first order differential equation:

$$\frac{dX}{dt} = \underline{f}\ (\underline{X},t) + \underline{W}(t) \quad \dots \dots \dots \dots \dots \dots \quad [11.5]$$

where $\underline{X}$ is a vector of n state variables (perhaps different moisture storages or flows), $\underline{f}$ is a driving function for estimating values for the n state variables at time t given their values at time t-1, and $\underline{W}$(t) represents model error with respect to each state variable. $\underline{W}$(t) thus accounts for such varied modeling errors as neglected parameters, linearization of nonlinear functions, incorrect input data, etc. Measurements of the system are represented by:

$$\underline{Y}\ (t) = \underline{h}\ (\underline{X},t) + \underline{V}\ (t) \dots \dots \dots \dots \dots \dots \quad [11.6]$$

where $\underline{Y}$(t) is a vector of m measured variables (those of the n state variables that are measured, $\underline{h}$ is function for estimating variables from measurements of the m variables, and $\underline{V}$(t) is the noise vector for the m measurement variables. For hydrologic modeling, the m measurements will be less than the n states because of storages or flow points included in the model but for which no measured data are available for comparison.

Equation [11.6] could, for example, represent estimation of metered flows $\underline{Y}$ from stage-discharge relationship $\underline{h}$, where $\underline{V}$ represents the uncertainty involved in converting stage to discharge. Equation [11.5] could then represent a modeling of flows $\underline{X}$ by function f from input parameters, initial conditions, and precipitation, where $\underline{W}$ represents model uncertainty. Given $\underline{h}$, one could estimate $\underline{X}_1$ the vector of flows at time t $= 1$, from equation [11.6] with error $\underline{V}$. Given parameter values and input data, one could estimate $\underline{X}_2$ from equation [11.5] by integrating over the time interval with error W. These two estimates would then be weighted according to respective error magnitudes for an estimate of $\underline{X}$. From these results, one could obtain, through equation [11.5], associated errors in estimated parameter values.

As examples of successful applications of models of the form of equations [11.5] and [11.6], considerable success has been achieved in flood forecasting using relatively simple (Todini and Wallis, 1978) and more complicated models (Kitanidis and Bras, 1978). These applications use measurements of precipitation and streamflow as they become available to update model parameters, noise component estimates, and short-term forecasts. Models may be calibrated using, e.g., recorded precipitation and streamflow; the model error covariance matrix is automatically obtained. Predictions with this type of model using a reduced measurement vector (e.g. precipitation) yield streamflow plus a measure of prediction error. Lettermaier and Burges (1976) and Bowles and Grenney (1978) report other applications. Traditional approaches do not provide comparable prediction errors. Much work is underway with these types of models.

The conventional approach to model calibration does not account for uncertainties included in the filter models explicitly; values for coefficients (called parameters) in deterministic models are estimated by assuming no error in any of the inputs, in the model, or in the quantities compared with model output. One, for example, calibrates the Stanford Watershed Model (Crawford and Linsley, 1966) by choosing a time period having concurrent measurements of model input and output time series (precipitation, evapotranspiration, streamflow, etc.) and forcing the model output to as close a match as possible with the measured physical system output. The quality of the calibration can then be determined via model testing, i.e., examining differences between measured and predicted outputs for a different period of record. It is this testing that measures the validity of the calibrated model.

Practical Help

The model user should seek about five consecutive years of continuously recorded hydrologic and meteorologic data which include low flow and high flow events reflecting the range of flow and storm phenomena experienced by that watershed. Experience and observations in nearby watersheds are useful when shorter records are all that is available at a site of interest or when unusual events of interest have not been recorded.

The user next needs to decide whether he wants to calibrate the model to represent the watershed as a whole or if it would be better to divide the total area into parts for separate calibration. If subdivision is desired, how many subwatershed divisions should be used? Recorded outputs are needed from each (or most) of the subwatersheds for calibration. Quite often a modeler is forced to treat hydrologically diverse subwatersheds as one lumped system simply because there is no practical way to estimate parameters satisfactorily in more homogeneous subwatershed units. If division of the watershed is required, at least one or two more years of record reduces compensating errors which could give erroneous parameter estimates. The art of hydrology can be used, of course, as a substitute for some additional measurements.

To begin a calibration, it is necessary to estimate initial values of water stored in various compartments of the model as well as to make initial estimates for the parameters. Starting values for initial conditions can be estimated by assigning numerical values based on observable phenomena. For example, in models having conceptual water storages representing interception, surface runoff, water in the top few inches of soil, etc., the initial values will usually be zero if it did not rain during the preceding week. An antecedent precipitation index, API, is helpful in estimating the initial moisture content of deeper storages. Starting values for the parameters are best estimated from previous calibrations on other watersheds with similar physical characteristics. With these initial storage values and parameter estimates, runoff is simulated from precipitation, simulated runoff is compared with recorded runoff, and the quality of the simulation is evaluated.

The quality of a simulation depends on the following requirements:

1   Annual flow volume for each water year should agree with the recorded values.

2   Seasonal flow volumes should agree with the corresponding recorded values.

3   Weekly and daily volumes should agree with recorded values.

4   Simulated and recorded hydrographs corresponding to specific precipitation events should have similar shapes, the same peak values, and the same time of occurrence to peak flow.

When calibrating, initial emphasis is placed on the first two requirements. Finer tuning concentrates on items 3 and 4. When all four requirements have been satisfied, further checks must be made to see that the model has not given the right answers for the wrong reasons. Such a situation is likely to result for models with multiple peaked objective function response surfaces when the selected calibration is taken from the wrong peak. Greater model credibility results if:

5   Predicted evapotranspiration (ET) is less than potential evapotranspiration for the area.

6   Modeled water storage contents fluctuate with precipitation patterns.

7   The values estimated for model parameters are in accord with physically observed watershed characteristics.

8   The modeled division between surface runoff and base flow is reasonable in light of known watershed soil and geological conditions.

It might be possible, for example, to satisfy requirements 1 to 4 yet drastically mismatch actual and simulated ET. Peak flows, for example, may have been matched by synthesizing too much surface runoff and too little base flow.

When calibrating flood hydrographs, time distributions as well as flows should be compared. If, for example, the simulated agrees with the recorded hydrograph in shape and volume but comes either earlier or later in time, one needs to look to possible causes. They are of two sorts. The rain gage, either because of improper synchronization with the stream gage, or because of its juxtaposition to the watershed and prevailing storm patterns, may be providing a faulty time relationship. The model parameters may represent channel travel times inadequately. If the model is calibrated to match recorded flows during a period of improper synchronization, major problems will occur if the results are tested for another period without that timing problem.

The most important factor in obtaining a good calibration is the representativeness of the precipitation data. It is desirable to have precipitation gages located within the watershed boundary but possible to use gages located nearby. What distance constitutes nearby and how should these gages outside the watershed be used? The answers depend on precipitation areal and temporal variability patterns in the region. For example, a recording gage at the Seattle-Tacoma International Airport is not representative of precipitation amounts ten miles to the northwest. Therefore, it is not possible to use precipitation amounts measured at the airport to calibrate accurately many of the small watersheds that drain into Lake Washington. How does one proceed in such circumstances? The most common approach is to use locally measured daily storage gage totals and the recording gage data to distribute that total over periods between storage gage readings. Precipitation at the master gage is scaled (by a different factor for every day if necessary) to reflect actual precipitation totals on the watershed.

Which storms should be used to match recorded and simulated hydrographs? Storms resulting from major frontal activity usually provide the best results because proportional precipitation over a large area is more likely. Lesser frontal storms differ markedly in areal variability. Consistent matching of hydrographs resulting from convective storms is made hopeless by the spatial and temporal variability of such storms. The only way to overcome this problem is through a dense network of precipitation gages or, in the future, combination of one or more precipitation gages with indirect precipitation measurement techniques.

The most likely sources of data error are inoperable or non-operating equipment, erroneous transcribing of measured quantities, and systematic errors in the measurements. Precipitation data should be examined for large events. For example, the data during the calibration period should be compared with maximum hourly, 6 hourly, 24 hourly, etc., precipitation records. Moderate events should be compared with regional precipitation records and weather maps for the same date. Even after these checks, some important errors may not be recognized until the simulation is effected. For example, if a large precipitation amount is not matched with a large hydrograph, both records should be checked for the events in question. Often, a mismatch between simulated and recorded events in a model, that is otherwise doing well, points to an error in either the recorded precipitation or streamflow. For example, in one situation, it was impossible to obtain agreement between recorded and simulated flows during winter months because the recorded streamflow data had been incorrectly adjusted for the stream icing over.

GRAPHICAL CALIBRATION AIDS

Since there is no unique criterion that defines a good calibration, several summary statistics that might be compared are discussed below. The problem is compounded because shortcomings in the model or data can be accommodated by the parameters during calibration. For example, a seemingly good calibration may result from parameters adjusted in a way that compensates for a systematic measurement error. Such a calibration can be expected to prove quite poor when tested over some other time period when the measurement error did not occur.

It is advisable that many calibration aids be employed. Graphical comparisons are extremely useful, and in fact, some form of computer graphics is almost essential. Four particular displays are recommended:

1 Continuous time series plot of simulated flow superposed on the recorded flow. (A plot on cartesian paper emphasizes differences for high flows whereas a plot with flow on a log scale normalizes for easy comparison of both high and low flows).

2 Continuous time series plot of the difference between recorded and simulated series. (This may be normalized by, say, recorded flow for nonzero flows, to show relative errors.)

3 Plot of cumulative sum of departures from the mean for the simulated series superposed on the cumulative sum of departures of recorded flow. (The recorded flow mean should be used in both instances.)

4 A scattergram of recorded data plotted against simulated flows as shown on Fig. 11.1 (Bates, 1976). While this method does not preserve the flow sequences contained in the time series plots, differences between a

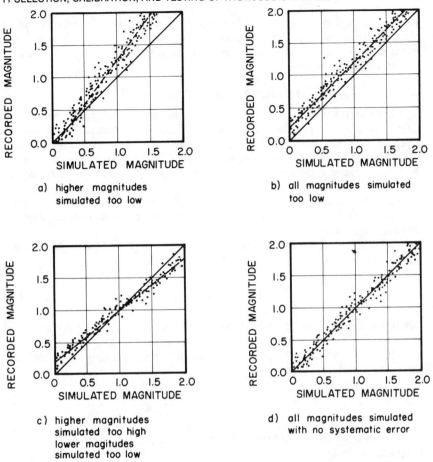

FIG. 11.1 Scattergrams showing presence of systematic errors.

linear regression line through the plotted points and the equality line of the scattergrams help identify errors that cannot be detected as easily from time series plots.

Any desired time aggregation can be used with these four graphical displays, but average daily flow is most common.

If the calibration is only for one watershed at one stream gage location, the graphical displays are easily interpreted. If, however (as is the case in many design situations), numerous basins are being calibrated simultaneously and many of the points of comparison represent the combined runoff from several, careful organization of the displays is required to develop a viewing system for judging the quality of simultaneous simulation at a series of points. Comparison of daily data at many sites along a channel is often physically impractical. Longer periods of aggregation may help the viewer to absorb relevant information. Weekly information for a 3 to 5 yr period gives 150 to 250 observations per site to compare. One suggestion is to plot, one below the other, information at corresponding times at the several sites.

These graphical techniques stimulate very important man-machine interaction in model calibration. Difficulties in objective measurement of goodness of fit have caused some modelers to rely almost entirely on subjective evaluation of agreement between time series. On the other hand, a rigid application of objective measures can replace good hydrologic judgment to the detriment of model performance. Balanced man-machine interaction avoids both extremes.

NUMERICAL CALIBRATION AIDS

Several types of statistics provide useful numerical measures of the degree of agreement between modeled and recorded quantities. Basically, one can compute and display comparisons for each item or develop and use summary statistics for groups of items. Selection requires choices on how to measure differences and on how to aggregate groups of measured differences in a single statistic.

For evaluating the results of hydrologic simulation, one is normally comparing time series. Bates (1976) defined three ways of measuring errors in time series data as

A Absolute errors in magnitudes of flows or other items in the time series as defined by:

$$eA(i) = S(i) - R(i) \quad \ldots \ldots \ldots \ldots \ldots \ldots \ldots \quad [11.7]$$

where the S(i) are the i items in the simulated and the R(i) are the recorded series.

B Relative errors in time series magnitudes with respect to the raw data origin as defined by:

$$eB(i) = (S(i) - R(i))/R(i) \quad \ldots \ldots \ldots \ldots \ldots \ldots \quad [11.8]$$

C Relative errors in time series magnitudes with respect to some other origin as defined by:

$$eC(i) = (S(i) - R(i))/(R(i) - g) \quad \ldots \ldots \ldots \ldots \quad [11.9]$$

where g is a constant equal to the value of the series at the point of the other origin. One example of where a modeler might perfer another origin would be in modeling surface runoff and only caring about runoff above the baseflow.

The i can be defined for any suitable time period such as day, month, or year. The denominators in equations [11.8] and [11.9] must be nonzero.

If a model user is governing his calibration on minimizing departures between recorded and synthesized flow (equation [11.7]), the results will be weighted so heavily toward accurate reproduction of the larger flows that the determined optimum calibration may miss the low flows by an order of magnitude. One approach to overcoming this problem is to normalize by dividing each synthesized flow by the corresponding recorded flow (equation [11.8]). Two difficulties surface with this method. Extremely low flows may be associated with large ratios even though the magnitude of the difference may be small. Second, a flow synthesized at one tenth the recorded value will have a departure of 0.9 and hence be given much less weight than a flow synthesized at ten times the recorded value and having a departure of 9. To overcome these difficulties, Liou (1970, pp. 99-102) proposed the calibration statistic:

D
$$eD(i) = \frac{S(i) + a}{R(i) + a} - 1 \quad S(i) > R(i)$$

$$eD(i) = 1 - \frac{R(i) + a}{S(i) + a} \quad S(i) \leqslant R(i) \quad \cdots [11.10]$$

where a is a constant set according to the desired emphasis in calibration, a larger value gives greater weight to matching higher flows.

Bates (1976) defined two other ways for measuring errors based on the pattern of change within a time series.

E Absolute errors in the magnitude of differences between consecutive items in a time series as defined by:

$$eE(i) = \Delta S(i) - \Delta R(i) \quad \cdots \cdots \cdots \cdots \cdots [11.11]$$

where $\Delta S(i) = S(i) - S(i\text{-}l)$; and $\Delta R(i) = R(i) - R(i\text{-}l)$

F Relative errors in time series differences as defined by:

$$eF(i) = (\Delta S(i) - \Delta R(i))/\Delta R(i) \quad \cdots \cdots \cdots \cdots [11.12]$$

The above error series may be computed either directly from numerical data or from some transform such as the logarithm of the data. After they are computed, the error series may be used directly or transferred by squaring or raising to some other power. The log series generally provide a better comparison of relative error.

If errors at higher magnitudes (e.g., flood hydrographs) are more important, absolute errors (A) are of interest. If errors near some other level are more important, then relative errors with respect to an origin at that level (B or C) are of interest. For symmetrical treatment of relative errors around the origin, equation [11.10D] provides an option. For errors in differences between consecutive time series items, if higher rates of change are important, the absolute errors (E) are of interest. If all rates of change are equally important, then the relative errors (F) are of interest.

Selection among the expressions must take into account such computational difficulties as zero occurring in the denominator of a relative error or when the mean or other statistic is extracted (equation [11.9]) by substraction from the recorded value. If zeros are absent, no problem will be encountered with the relative errors; extraction of a value of a size within the range of the process may, however, cause a zero denominator. Rejection limits should be set on the term R(i)-g such that no zero values are obtained. The rejection limit is arbitrary; a logical value would be some multiple (typically 2 or 3) of the standard error of the value R(i). If negative data are encountered and relative errors are of interest, all data should be transferred to positive values by addition of a constant; this gives a new arbitrary origin.

A number of alternatives can be used to condense these error series into more compact effectiveness measures. Clarke (1973) gave a thorough discussion of the alternatives. As an illustration of the variety of opinion on the subject and the danger of choosing a single promising effectiveness measure, Aitken (1973) illustrated a number of alternatives and favored a residual mass curve coefficient (similar to equation [11.33]). Later, Wallis and Todini (1975) showed how the residual mass curve coefficient is functionally analogous to the adjusted range (Rodriguez-Iturbe et al., 1972) and indicated that the presence of a weak seasonal cycle in the cumulative sum of departures series makes the residual mass curve coefficient inconclusive. Their comments serve to emphasize the elusiveness of a single effectiveness measure to judge model performance.

Some of the problems that can result from using a single coefficient as a measure of performance can be illustrated by considering a simple linear regression equation. If the linear relationship y = mx has a coefficient of determination, D, of unity, all data fall on a straight line. If m equals unity, simulated flows equal recorded flows rather than some constant multiple of recorded flows. Neither number alone tells how good a calibration is because departures of m from unity indicate systematic error and departures of D from unity indicate random error.

McCuen and Snyder (1975) proposed weighting the Pearson product-moment correlation coefficient by the ratio of the standard deviations as a simple index for comparing hydrographs of specific events. If R(i) are values read off the recorded hydrograph at some selected time increment and S(i) are corresponding simulated values, the Pearson moment is

$$r = \frac{1}{N} \sum_{i=1}^{N} \left(\frac{R(i) - \overline{R}}{S_R} \right) \left(\frac{S(i) - \overline{S}}{S_S} \right) \quad \ldots \ldots [11.13]$$

where $\overline{R}$ and $\overline{S}$ are the means and S_R and S_S are the standard deviations of the N values in the recorded and simulated hydrographs respectively. The weighted moment is cr where c equals S_S/S_R if $S_S < S_R$ and c equals S_R/S_S if $S_S \geqslant S_R$. The weighted moment is thus always smaller than the Pearson moment and approaches unity with perfect agreement between $R_{(i)}$ and $S_{(i)}$.

The error series (eA(i) to eF(i)) defined by equations [11.7] to [11.12] can be represented by summary statistics, mean (me), standard deviation (se), and serial correlation coefficient (re) as follows:

$$me = \sum_{i=1}^{N} e(i)/N \quad \ldots \ldots \ldots \ldots \ldots \ldots \ldots [11.14]$$

$$se = \left\{ \sum_{i=1}^{N} (e(i) - me)^2/(N-1) \right\}^{1/2} \quad \ldots \ldots [11.15]$$

$$re = \left\{ \sum_{i=1}^{N} (e(i) - me) * (e(i-1) - me) \right\} /se^2$$

$$\ldots \ldots \ldots \ldots \ldots \ldots \ldots \ldots \ldots \ldots \ldots \ldots \ldots \ldots [11.16]$$

Equation [11.16] is only defined for continuous series. The summary statistics are measures of aggregate agreement of the simulated with the recorded time series and can be used to evaluate the performance of a model. For summary statistics calculated using the magnitude errors (equations [11.7] to [11.10]), the mean indicates if the model is under- or over-simulating; a non-zero value suggests a probable systematic error with respect to magnitude. The standard deviation gives a measure of the range of errors in the probability distribution of the error occurrence. The serial correlation gives a measure of the impact that an error in previous periods has on subsequent periods (systematic errors with respect to time). For the difference errors (equations [11.11] and [11.12]), the statistics indicate the ability of the model to predict rates of process change instead of the magnitudes of the process. The serial correlation gives an indication of the effect of error persistence since a low correlation means errors are damped out rapidly.

All these statistics are useful in evaluating the adequacy of a given calibration. If, however, one needs to choose between models instead of just between calibrations of a given model, it is important to explore the distribution of results or the variation within the process. To allow for the process variation, the statistics of the error magnitudes may be standardized to a zero-mean-unit-variance process with the error series denoted as

$$e(i) = (S(i) - R(i))/S_R \quad \ldots \ldots \ldots \ldots \ldots [11.17]$$

where s_R is the standard deviation of the recorded process, $R(i)$.

The lag serial correlation can be used for processes which are periodic (monthly streamflows are a good example). A periodic process has less variation from one time period to the next than a process which is not periodic, even if both have the same overall variance. The effect of periodicity on the statistics can be removed if the ability of the model to account for differences in the process, normalized by the variance of the differences of the process, is considered. The error series is:

$$e(i) = (\Delta S(i) - \Delta R(i))/s\Delta R \quad \ldots \ldots \ldots \ldots [11.18]$$

where $s\Delta R$ is the standard deviation of the series $\Delta R(i)$.

All the statistics and summary statistics of the above error series give an indication of disagreement between two time series. All parameters approach zero (except for the weighted Pearson moment which approaches unity) as the two time series approach complete agreement. For example, a model is judged to be well calibrated when $eF(i)$ tends toward zero, and the calibration is judged unbiased when the values of $eF(i)$ follow a pattern of white noise around the origin.

A common method for evaluation of time series agreement is by examination of the sum of the squared differences. Limitations of this approach have been discussed by Clark (1973) and Wallis and Todini (1975) among others. The respective equations for the six error measurements presented in equations [11.7] to [11.12] are

$$CP_A = \sum_{i=1}^{N} eA(i)^2 \quad \ldots \ldots \ldots \ldots \ldots \ldots [11.19]$$

$$CP_B = \sum_{i=1}^{N} eB(i)^2 \quad \ldots \ldots \ldots \ldots \ldots \ldots [11.20]$$

$$CP_C = \sum_{i=1}^{N} eC(i)^2 \quad \ldots \ldots \ldots \ldots \ldots \ldots [11.21]$$

$$CP_D = \sum_{i=1}^{N} eD(i)^2 \quad \ldots \ldots \ldots \ldots \ldots \ldots [11.22]$$

$$CP_E = \sum_{i=1}^{N} eE(i)^2 \quad \ldots \ldots \ldots \ldots \ldots \ldots [11.23]$$

$$CP_F = \sum_{i=1}^{N} eF(i)^2 \quad \ldots\ldots\ldots\ldots\ldots\ldots\ldots [11.24]$$

CP_A is used to designate "coefficient of performance, error series A." If desired, any of the above terms may be divided by the length of the series to obtain a measure of the error in individual values within the series. To compare models of processes having different degrees of variation, equations [11.19] to [11.21], [11.23] to [11.24] are divided by the variation of the process:

$$CP'_A = \frac{CP_A}{\sum_{i=1}^{N} (R(i) - mR)^2} \quad \ldots\ldots\ldots\ldots\ldots [11.25]$$

$$CP'_B = \frac{CP_B}{\sum_{i=1}^{N} (R(i)/mR - 1)^2} \quad \ldots\ldots\ldots\ldots [11.26]$$

$$CP'_C = \frac{CP_C}{\sum_{i=1}^{N} [R(i)/(R(i) - g) - g/(R(i) - g)]^2} \quad [11.27]$$

$$CP'_E \frac{CP_E}{\sum_{i=1}^{N} (\Delta R(i) - m\Delta R)^2} \quad \ldots\ldots\ldots\ldots [11.28]$$

$$CP'_F = \frac{CP_F}{\sum_{i=1}^{N} (\Delta R(i)/m\Delta R - 1)^2} \quad \ldots\ldots\ldots [11.29]$$

All of the above indices of error approach zero as two time series reach complete agreement. The indices may be arranged to approach any value p by adding or subtracting the index from p. The most commonly used constant (p) is unity, as shown below the error type A (equation [11.19]):

$$CP'^*_A = 1 - CP'_A, \text{ or}$$

$$CP'^*_A = \frac{\sum_{i=1}^{N} (R(i) - mR)^2 - \sum_{i=1}^{N} (S(i) - R(i))^2}{\sum_{i=1}^{N} (R(i) - mR)^2}$$

$$\ldots\ldots\ldots\ldots\ldots\ldots\ldots\ldots\ldots\ldots\ldots\ldots\ldots [11.30]$$

Equation [11.30] is similar to the coefficient of efficiency presented by Nash and Sutcliffe (1971).

If the simulated values are replaced by values, SR(i), estimated from the regression of R(i) on S(i), and the simulated differences by values, ΔSR(i), estimated from the regression of ΔR(i) on ΔS(i), the preceding equations may be used to determine the degree of systematic errors in simulated magnitudes and rates given by the model procedure. If model errors of the type exposed in a coefficient (eA to eF) are completely random in magnitude, that type of error will plot randomly about a 45 deg line on a scattergram, and the values of equations [11.19] to [11.29] will be equal to those with regressed values substituted for the simulated values. Equation [11.30] with the regressed values substituted is similar to the coefficient of determination given by Aitken (1973).

Differences in the magnitudes of the six coefficients (equations [11.7] to [11.12]) indicate the amount of systematic error in the model. Depending on which coefficients are larger or smaller, it is possible to determine if relative or absolute error dominates. Likewise, in the statistical evaluation of the error, if differences (ΔS(i) or ΔR(i)) rather than magnitudes (S(i) or R(i)) are examined, the effect of periodic processes is removed to give equal evaluation of process models.

Accumulated errors may be considered by examining differences in the residual mass curves. The equations are:

$$CP''_A = \sum_{j=1}^{N} \left\{ \sum_{i=1}^{j} S(i) - \sum_{i=1}^{j} R(i) \right\}^2 \quad \ldots \ldots [11.31]$$

$$CP''_B = \sum_{j=1}^{N} \left\{ \frac{\sum_{i=1}^{j} S(i) - \sum_{i=1}^{j} R(i)}{\sum_{i=1}^{j} R(i)} \right\}^2 \quad \ldots \ldots [11.32]$$

$$CP''_C = \sum_{j=1}^{N} \left\{ \frac{\sum_{i=1}^{j} S(i) - \sum_{i=1}^{j} R(i)}{\sum_{i=1}^{j} (R(i) - mR)} \right\}^2 \quad \ldots \ldots [11.33]$$

Equation [11.33] is similar to that Aitken (1973) termed the residual mass curve coefficient. Similarly as for the previous coefficients, regressed values of S(i) with the mean error removed, can be substituted into the coefficients to determine the degree of systematic error in the residual mass of the simulated process.

SYSTEMATIC APPROACH TO CALIBRATION AND TESTING

A systematic approach to model calibration and testing is outlined in Fig. 11.2. Three stages are involved: preliminary calibration, refined calibration, and model testing and evaluation. The first stage uses a preliminary inspection followed by a more refined comparison using the model to obtain the best possible data for the model. The second stage uses the resulting meteorological inputs and streamflows to achieve the best possible calibration. In the third stage, data measured at the same stations, but for a different time period than used for calibration, are used to test the calibrated model and determine its accuracy.

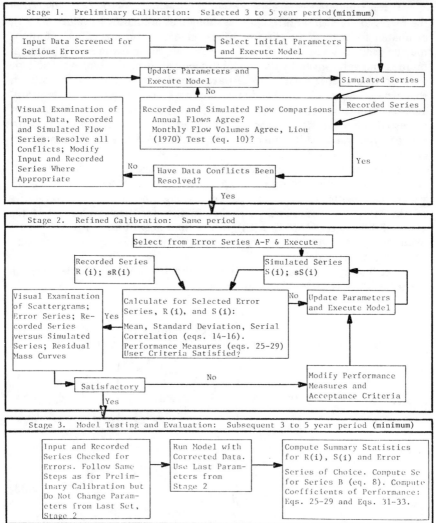

FIG. 11.2 Steps involved in model calibration and testing.

At the start of the preliminary calibration stage, input data (precipitation, evapotranspiration, etc.) and the recorded streamflow series (at all locations of interest) need to be screened for obvious errors. The two major checks are for (a) recorded hydrographs whose volume exceeds recorded rainfall, or is such a high fraction of recorded rainfall as to be highly improbable, a condition usually associated with major storms over the watershed but largely missing the precipitation gages, and (b) large recorded rainfalls simultaneous with little runoff, a condition usually associated with intense rainfalls registered at the gage not being representative of precipitation over the watershed. If storms with these properties produce a major portion of the annual runoff in a given year, it is normally best to use other, better years for calibration. When such storms occur during years used for calibration, adjustment of the precipitation data to values the model suggests as commensurate with recorded streamflow is recommended in order to avoid a major upset in antecedent moisture conditions for the next storm, but the time period covered by the adjusted data should not be used in calculating test statistics for parameter optimization.

Actual modeling begins as initial conditions and initial parameter values are assigned, and streamflows are simulated for the input data. The recorded and simulated series are compared for agreement between annual and seasonal flow volumes. Usually it is desirable for monthly and perhaps weekly flow volumes to agree at this stage too. Liou's (1970) test statistic (equation [11.10]) is useful here. The mean and standard deviation of daily flow are computed and compared to ensure that the simulated and recorded flows have comparable low order moments. Model parameters are updated and calibration continued until the preliminary calibration criteria have been satisfied. Parameters may be changed manually or by programmed rules.

When acceptable preliminary agreement is achieved (e.g. recorded and simulated annual flow values agree to within 10 percent), visual examination of input data and recorded and simulated streamflow should be made to detect remaining conflicts, e.g. recorded data being in error, incompatibility between precipitation and runoff events, etc. Conflicts must be resolved by correcting the input and recorded series; even a relatively crudely calibrated model is very effective in identifying errors in recorded data.

Once the preliminary calibration has developed compatible data series, the calibration needs to be refined to obtain the best possible matching of daily hydrographs; shorter time scales are of interest for certain flood events. The quantification of best is based on selection by the user of one or more of the error series and performance measures discussed above. After a calibration achieves the user's criteria with respect to the numerical performance measures, it is important to use graphical aids to assess visually the quality of the calibration.

A scattergram of recorded and simulated flow is the simplest method to view the calibration quality in one convenient graph. Stochastic information is lost but the user can determine immediately if high and low flows are being modeled equally well or systematic errors are present (Fig. 11.1). It is often useful to plot the scattergram of the logarithms of flow to look at poor model performance at low flows. Overall stochastic behavior is exhibited best by plotting one or more of the error series as well as the residual mass curve. Most users prefer to plot recorded and simulated flow against time. Additionally, it is valuable to plot series B (equation [11.8]) for a visual display of relative error. The residual mass curves of recorded and simulated flow provide an excellent means for viewing error persistence.

The user must specify error series and performance measures with desired values for each as acceptance criteria which indicate a satisfactory calibration. If, after examining a time series of simulated flows that achieves these criteria, he desires added refinement, the acceptance criteria must be made more demanding; perhaps error series and performance measures should be changed. The parameters are modified and the model is rerun; the procedure is continued until the new criteria are satisfied.

Some thought needs to be given to selecting appropriate criteria to use at the beginning of the calibration. Error series A and B (equations [11.7] and [11.8] are of most general interest. Series D (equation [11.10]) provides a means for added refinement when results seem too strongly influenced by a few points. While ideally the mean, standard deviation, and lag one correlation coefficients of series B are all zero, practical criteria are to try to attain a mean level to within 5 percent, standard deviation 5 to 10 percent, and satisfy the lag one correlation (p_1) tendency to zero. As a good calibration is approached, p_1 is normally distributed with mean zero and variance $(N-2)/(N-1)^2$ (Anderson, 1942).

For the calibration period (3 to 5 yr), there are between 1095 and 1827 daily values of recorded and simulated flow to compare, so the samples are statistically large. It should be remembered, however, that the individual series (recorded and simulated) are highly auto-correlated so their information content is associated with a much smaller number of independent events. Bayley and Hammersley (1946) give details for computing the reduced information content. For example, the effective sample size to be used when computing the standard error of the mean is N_d^* as defined by:

$$\frac{1}{N_d^*} = \frac{1}{N} + \frac{2}{N^2} \sum_{j=1}^{N-1} (N-j)\rho_j \quad \dots \dots \dots \dots [11.34]$$

with ρ_j the jth autocorrelation coefficient. Many streamflow series, after nonstationary components have been removed, follow a lag-one Markov process. For such cases N_d^* is

$$N_d^* = \frac{1}{N} + \frac{2\rho_1}{N^2 (1-\rho_1)} \left[N + \frac{(\rho_1^N - 1)}{(1 - \rho_1)} \right] \quad \dots [11.35]$$

Two other criteria are useful to set. These are values for the coefficient of efficiency (equation [11.30]) and the coefficient of residual mass (equation [11.33]). Excellent calibrations are achieved if both coefficients exceed 0.97. Generally, criteria that apply to error series B are more restrictive because the model must replicate both high and low flows satisfactorily. Minimization of the standard deviation of error series B, subject to errors in model structure, input data, and recorded flow data is desirable, but it is unrealistic to expect to achieve values lower than 5 to 10 percent.

The modeler should beware of the possibility of achieving a calibration that reduces prediction error, sSe, below the recorded series relative error, sRe. For such a calibration, the errors in modeling the process are less than the errors in measuring the process. Another danger is for the modeler to match his results too closely to the particular flow series that occurred during the calibrating period and lose generality so as actually to make results worse when the model is tested later on data for other time periods. This is one of the dangers in calibrating using a period that is either too short or that contains non-representative flow sequences.

After the model has been calibrated, a different time period is used to evaluate its performance. Use of the 3 to 5 yr immediately following the calibration period is recommended for verification and evaluation. A major reason for using data immediately following the calibration period is to make use of end conditions from the calibration stage as initial conditions for the evaluation stage. The effects of initial conditions are observable for a period of six to twelve months when using models similar to the Stanford Watershed model. Avoiding uncertainties in initialization by following the above procedure ensures maximum use of scarce data for model evaluation.

An overall statement of the quality of the calibration model can be made by determining the mean and standard deviation of series B (equation [11.8]), the series of relative errors, and the coefficients of efficiency (equation [11.30]) and the residual mass (equation [11.33]). When these coefficients exceed 0.97, very little systematic error remains. Other coefficients may be used; the above measures suffice for most situations. The standard deviation of error series B gives the most useful general measure of prediction confidence.

It is usually not possible to have a model perform uniformly well over the entire low and high flow range. Therefore, several coefficients of performance might be used. One can subdivide the total time series into several parts, e.g., wet periods, low-flow periods, etc. for each year, and compute performance coefficients for each part. For example, the mean and standard deviation (error series B), could be computed for the wet period in each year, and the computation repeated for all years used for verification to develop average summary statistics.

CALIBRATION PROCEDURE ILLUSTRATION

An example calibration with summary statistics and recorded and simulated streamflow is given in this section to illustrate measures and visual aids helpful in the refined calibration stage (Fig. 11.2). A 407-square kilometer watershed draining to USGS gage 12-1252 located on the Sammamish River, Washington, was subdivided into four sub areas and modeled via the Hydrocomp (1969) HSP rainfall-runoff digital computer model. This model did not contain pattern search parameter optimization features; parameters were changed manually after evaluating each calibration run. An initial calibration had been effected by a user who thought that a good calibration had been achieved.

A refined calibration was based on water years 1966 to 1968. Complete details of the model, parameters used, and the flow simulation (including problems of obtaining representative precipitation, etc.) are given in Bates (1976). The parameters were modified systematically to attempt the best possible calibration. The watershed experienced marked temporal and spatial precipitation variability, particularly during smaller precipitation events; reliable rain gages were not available within the watershed boundaries. Snowmelt runoff was negligible.

For the pollution control application the user had in mind, it was necessary to model high and low flow with comparable relative precision. The unfortunate location of the rain gage (outside the watershed) was a clear warning that the response of the watershed to light to moderate rain would not be predicted with much accuracy. Based on the precision needed in the required application and the constraints the precipitation data posed as to what was possible, selected model acceptance criteria were coefficient of determination, coefficient of efficiency and coefficient of residual mass should all exceed 0.97; mean daily flow in each year (series B, equation [11.8]) $\leqslant$ 5 percent; standard deviations of daily flows (series B, equation [11.8]) $\leqslant$ 15 percent; individual monthly volumes $\leqslant$ 10 percent.

Inspection of Table 11.1, which summarizes results from the preliminary calibration and three refined calibrations, indicates the criteria were too demanding. The particular situation did not lend itself to further parameter adjustment to achieve calibration better than the second refined calibration (Run 2). The statistics for the standard deviation of error series B were approximately the same in each water year for each time increment investigated; therefore, to save unnecessary computations and deluging the viewer with summary information, summaries were computed for the middle water year only for Runs 2 and 3. Added summary statistics are given in Table 11.2. The performance coefficients all exceeded the criteria, but a better calibration could have been achieved had better precipitation data been available.

TABLE 11.1. SUMMARY STATISTICS FOR SIMULATING MODELING,
USGS STREAM GAGE 12-1252

Water year	1966	1967				1968			
Flow period	Year	Day	Week	Month	Year	Day	Week	Month	Year
Preliminary	-16.7*	25.0†	21.0†	17.0†	-12.0*	27.0†	22.0†	16.0†	-15.2*
Refined calibration									
Run 1	-3.1	22.0	22.0	15.0	+0.0	23.0	22.0	14.0	+ 4.5
Run 2	5.6	17.0	16.0	12.0	4.1				- 1.8
Run 3	3.9	20.0	17.0	13.0	-1.7				- 6.4

Relative error series (equation [8]) in percent
*Mean Value (daily time increment)
†Standard Deviation (day, week, and month time increments)

Visual evaluation of the simulated flow from Run 2 can be made from Figs. 11.3 to 11.5 which contain daily flow information for water year 1967. Fig. 11.3 indicates that high flows were well modeled. Fig. 11.4, which plots error series A against recorded flow, shows that simulated low flows overestimate recorded low flows. Dawdy (personal communication, 1978) pointed out that the information could have been conveniently displayed had Fig. 11.3 been ploted to logarithmic scales. The display is a matter of personal choice and the type of error one needs to emphasize for a given application.

Most hydrologist draw comfort from examining the recorded and simulated time series on a single plot. These daily flow series are shown in Fig. 11.5 on a linear scale; use of a semi-log scale might be preferred by some users. Inspection of Fig. 11.5 clearly shows the hydrograph recessions were not well modeled and that there is substantial error in the low flow simulations. This graph clearly explains the large standard deviation statistics given in Table 11.1. The cumulative mass curves shown in Fig. 11.5 indicate that little systematic error remains, a fact supported by the three performance coefficients in Table 11.2. Use of the cumulative mass curves is not widespread; the authors find them generally useful to supplement the other summaries.

TABLE 11.2. STATISTICAL SUMMARY (DAILY) FOR CALIBRATED
MODEL AT USGS GAGE 12-1252 (SAMMANISH RIVER) FOR
RUN 2, WATER YEAR 1967

Statistics of Series	Mean	Standard deviation
Recorded	9.30*	8.71*
Simulated	9.70*	8.37*
Difference (absolute error series A equation [4])	0.4*	1.14*
Percent difference (relative error series B equation [8])	4.1	17.0
Coefficients		
Coefficient of determination (square of correlation coefficient between R and S)		0.984
Coefficient of efficiency, equation [30]		0.981
Coefficient of residual mass, CP''_A, equation [33]		0.980

*Cubic meters per second.

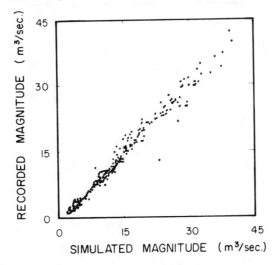

FIG. 11.3 Scattergram of recorded and simulated daily flows at USGS gage 12-1252 for water year 1967.

This illustration provides several lessons. The most important is to show that coefficients of performance are not complete measures of calibration quality. High values of performance coefficients can be attained while low flows are poorly modeled. The utility of the standard deviation of error series B, the relative errors, is clear. This statistic was not close to zero (at its optimum it should represent the accuracy of stream gaging, i.e. be about 2.5 percent for an excellent record) while the coefficients of performance were almost unity. Joint performance measures, as well as final graphical comparison, are essential to achieve physically sensible and accurate calibrations.

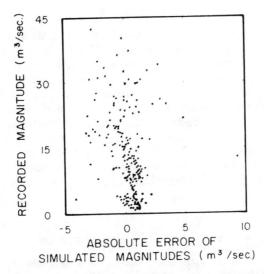

FIG. 11.4 Absolute errors of simulated flows at USGS gage 12-1252 for water year 1967.

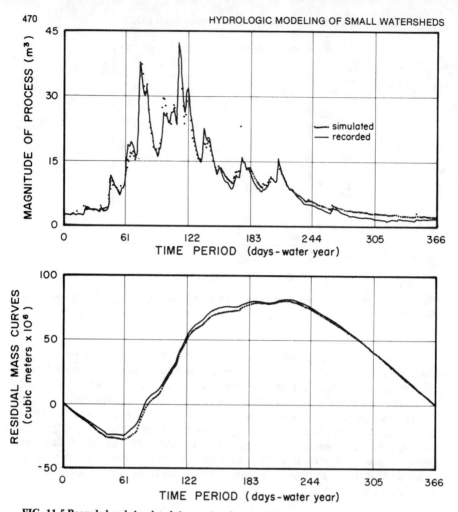

FIG. 11.5 Recorded and simulated time series plots for USGS gage 12-1252 for water year 1967.

SUMMARY

This chapter has reviewed basic issues in selection, calibration, and testing of hydrologic models. The first half describes selection of modeling strategy, conceptualization of the components to include in the selected model type, development of a model structure combining these components into a working whole, calibration to estimate parameter values in the selected model, testing the adequacy of the calibrated results, communicating modeling advances to other scientists, and displaying model results to the user public. The second half provides specific descriptions of graphical and numerical aids that can be used to obtain the best possible calibration for a given watershed and illustrates their power through an example of how they were used to achieve significant improvement over a preliminary calibration.

References

1   Aitken, A. P. 1973. Assessing systematic errors in rainfall-runoff models. Journal of Hydrology 20:121-136.

2   Anderson, R. L. 1942. Distribution of the serial correlation coefficient. Annals Math. Statistics 13:1-13.

3 Bates, C. L. 1976. Analysis of time series modeling errors with application to the Lake Sammamish hydrologic system. MSCE Thesis, Dept. of Civil Engineering, University of Washington, Seattle.

4 Bayley, G. U., and J. M. Hammersley. 1946. The effective number of independent observations in an autocorrelated time series. Journal Royal Statistical Society 8(1B):184-197.

5 Beard, L. R. 1962. Statistical methods in hydrology. Civil Works Investigations Project CW-151, U.S. Army Engineers, Sacramento, CA.

6 Bowles, D. S., and W. J. Grenney. 1978. Steady state river quality modeling by sequential extended Kalman filters. Water Resources Research, 14:84-96.

7 Clarke, R. T. 1973. A review of some mathematical models used in hydrology with observations on their calibration and use. Journal of Hydrology 19:1-20.

8 Coleman, G., and D. G. DeCoursey. 1976. Sensitivity and model variance analysis applied to some evaporation and evapotranspiration models. Water Resources Research 12(5):873-879.

9 Crawford, N. H., and R. K. Linsley. 1966. Digital simulation in hydrology: Stanford Watershed Model IV. Technical Report 39, Dept. of Civil Engineering, Stanford University, Stanford, CA.

10 Dawdy, D. R., and J. M. Bergman. 1969. Effect of rainfall variability on streamflow simulation. Water Resources Research 5(5):958-966.

11 Diskin, M. H. 1970. Objectives and techniques of watershed modeling. Proceedings ARS and SCS Watershed Modeling Workshop, Tucson, AZ, Chapter 3.

12 Fleming, G. 1975. Computer simulation techniques in hydrology. American Elsevier Pub. Co., Inc., New York.

13 Fletcher, J. E. et al. 1976. Runoff estimates for small rural watersheds and development of sound design method. Research Report and Manual, 2 volumes, Utah Water Research Laboratory, Logan.

14 Gelb, A. (Ed.). Applied optimal estimation. The MIT Press, Cambridge, MA.

15 Haan, C. T. 1977. Statistical methods in hydrology. Iowa State University Press, Ames.

16 Haan, C. T., and D. M. Allen. 1972. Comparison of multiple regression and principal component regression for predicting water yields in Kentucky. Water Resources Research 8(6):1593-1596.

17 Hooke, R., and T. A. Jeeves. 1961. Direct search solution of numerical and statistical problems. Journal of the Association of Computing Machines 8(2):212-229.

18 Huang, Y. H., and R. K. Gayner. 1977. Effects of stream channel improvements on downstream floods. Research Report No. 102, Water Resources Research Institute, University of Kentucky, Lexington.

19 Hydrocomp. 1969. Hydrocomp simulation programming operations manual. Hydrocomp, Inc., Palo Alto, CA.

20 James, L. D. 1969. Computers in flood control planning. Proc. of ASCE 95(HY6): 1859-1870.

29 Liou, E. Y. 1970. OPSET: Program for computerized selection of watershed parameter values for the Stanford Watershed Model. Research Report No. 34, Water Resources Institute, University of Kentucky, Lexington.

30 Linsley, R. K., Jr. et al., 1975. Hydrology for engineers. Second Edition. McGraw-Hill Book Co., New York.

31 Lumb, A. M., and L. D. James. 1976. Runoff files for flood hydrograph simulation. Proc. of ASCE 102(HY10):1515-1531.

32 Lumb, A. M. et al. 1975. GTWS: Georgia Tech watershed simulation model. Report ERC-0175, Environmental Resources Center, Georgia Institute of Technology, Atlanta.

33 Maass, A. et al. 1962. Design of water-resource systems. Harvard University Press, Cambridge, MA.

34 McCuen, R. H. 1973. The role of sensitivity analysis in hydrologic modeling. J. of Hydrology 18:37-53.

35 McCuen, R. H., and W. M. Snyder. 1975. A proposed index for comparing hydrographs. Water Resources Research 11(6):1021-1024.

36 Munro, J. C. 1971. Direct search optimization in mathematical modeling and a watershed model application. NOAA Technical Memorandum NWS HYDRO-12.

37 Nash, J. E., and J. V. Sutcliffe. 1971. River flow forecasting through conceptual models. Journal of Hydrology 13:297-324.

38 Overton, D. E., and M. E. Meadows. 1976. Stormwater modeling. Academic Press, New York.

39 Rodriguez-Iturbe, I., J. M. Mejia, and D. Dawdy. 1972. Streamflow simulation, 1. A new look at Markovian models, fractional Gaussian noise and crossing theory. Water Resources Research 8(4):921-930.

40   Saah, A. D. et al. 1976. Development of regional regression equations for solution of certain hydrologic problems in and adjacent to Santa Clara County. Santa Clara Valley Water District, San Jose.

41   Todini, E. and J. R. Wallis. 1978. A real time rainfall runoff model for an on-line flood warning system. Proceedings, Chapman Conference on Application of Kalman Filter to Hydrology, Hydraulics, and Water Resources, Pittsburgh, PA.

42   Wallis, J. R. and E. Todini. 1975. Comment on the residual mass curve coefficient. Journal of Hydrology 24:201-205.

43   Wolf, P. O. 1966. Comparison of methods of flood estimation. Proceedings of the River Flood Hydrology Symposium, the Institution of Civil Engineers, London.

44   Woodward, D. E. 1973. Hydrologic and watershed modeling for watershed planning. TRANSACTIONS of the ASAE 99(3):582-584.

chapter 12

APPLICATION AND SELECTION OF HYDROLOGIC MODELS

12

APPLICATION AND SELECTION OF HYDROLOGIC MODELS

by   Thomas J. Jackson, Hydrologist, USDA, ARS,
      Hydrology Laboratory, Beltsville, MD.

INTRODUCTION

This chapter is a compendium of published applications of hydrologic models to small watersheds. In addition, some general guidelines
for selecting a model for a specific problem are presented. Most of the
models referenced are described in Chapter 13.

All model applications can be divided into two categories: decision-
making and research and training. Although we cover the second category
here, we will emphasize the first category. We will first discuss general aspects of selecting and applying hydrologic models. In later sections we will
provide more detail.

Applications

Decision-Making: In a decision-making application an analyst uses
hydrologic information to select an optimal course of action. Usually,
except for the most simple, well-defined problems the analyst will combine hydrologic information with other types of information (i.e., economic,
biological, and social) by using an explicit or implicit objective function
that weighs each type of information according to its importance in the
particular situation. In this process hydrologic variates are inputs to the
decision-making model.

Decision-making applications can be subdivided several ways. One
scheme could be based on the level of decision-making, planning, design
and operation (McPherson, 1975a). Planning studies are concerned with
macro-scale problems. In such studies, the interaction of various basic
elements within the planning area must be considered, as well as how the
individual locations relate to the overall goal. At this level of decision-
making, the hydrologic variates can play a relatively minor role in the decision. In addition, there are problems in data collection due to the areal
extent of such studies. For these two reasons, less emphasis is placed on
model sophistication.

In design level studies, a decision has already been made to implement

Contribution from the U.S. Department of Agriculture, Scientific and Education Administration, Agricultural Research, Beltsville, MD.

a course of action. This may be the result of a planning level study or established policy. At this point, the analyst is usually involved in a cost-effectiveness problem where effectiveness is related to a hydrologic variate and achieved at a minimum cost. Less emphasis is placed on other types of information. A typical situation might be the design of a flood-water retarding structure that must handle the runoff from an X-year event at minimum cost. The hydrologic variates would be the peak discharge and runoff volume associated with the X-year event. Typically, more emphasis is placed on the hydrologic model. The main problem is the sizing of facilities. Many studies are exploratory or deal with problem identification. These types of analysis fall under both planning and design.

Operational level decision-making deals with problems like irrigation scheduling and detention-storage regulation. Typically, the objective function is well-known. The decision-maker's problem is to assess the current condition, anticipate future events and select a course of action that optimizes the objective. The model is a tool for incorporating the system condition and anticipating events with hydrologic transfer functions to produce readily useful information that can be used in making the decision.

At all levels of decision-making, the analyst requires a reasonably accurate prediction of the system response to a specified input, subject to cost considerations. For operational studies another factor, lead time, is very important. As described in U.S. Army Corps of Engineers (1972), the utility of a forecast depends upon its accuracy and timeliness. The value of even a perfect forecast approaches zero as the time between the forecast and the event becomes zero.

Operation level models are usually application specific because of the wide diversity of management practices, the problems encountered, and the actual system configurations. Lindahl and Hamrick (1970) discussed additional factors, including costs, which must be considered when using hydrologic models for operational level decision-making.

In this chapter, we subdivided model applications by subject into five major categories: agriculture, forest and rangeland, surface mining, urban and minor structures. Agricultural applications are further divided into irrigation, drainage and land-treatment applications.

In general, there is a gap between procedures actually used to generate hydrologic information and the current state-of-the-art of hydrologic modeling. Several factors contribute to this gap — one of the most important is related to the economics of small watershed decisions and modeling.

Most decision-makers realize that some procedures they currently use to generate hydrologic information are much less than optimal hydrologically. They also realize that in some watershed problems the net benefits are relatively small and that efforts to increase these returns by using better information in the decision-making will yield minimal additional net benefits. Thus, usually the use of costly hydrologic models is not justified.

Hydrologic models will have greater application only if their developers make a concentrated effort to make them easier to use. This may require creative thinking on the part of the model developers. One technique that can work is to take advantage of economy-of-scale situations. These are situations in which several small scale problems of the same type are encountered, such as culvert design, in a jurisdiction. On a case-by-case basis, the use of a hydrologic model could not be justified. However, on a cumulative basis, efforts to develop better procedures can be justified. Crawford (1973a) suggested two methods which would work.

1   Use the model to develop a set of design tables and/or graphs.

2   Precalculate information that will be used in all the problems and then provide a simple technique for the balance of the analysis.

Such techniques show the greatest promise for more widespread use of hydrologic models. Several applications using this approach will be presented.

Application of models could also be increased if the model is thoroughly tested and documented, a well-written user's manual is available, the user can obtain a useable copy of the model, and training is available.

Research and Training: The second important type of hydrologic model application is as a research and/or training tool where the goal is a better understanding of the hydrologic cycle. An essential difference between this category and decision-making is that research and training deal with knowledge whereas decision-making involves information.

As described by Diskin (1970), when a researcher constructs a model, he is explicitly defining his concepts of how the physical processes occur. If he then tests the model by comparing its output against data from observed events, he can make statements about the model's validity. Good agreement substantiates his ideas, whereas poor agreement leads to rejection. Johnson (1973) pointed out that one indirect benefit of modeling can be that the abstraction of the researcher's concepts can in itself raise questions that may otherwise be unnoticed. In addition, information gaps and areas of needed research can be defined. The researcher can also gain important insights concerning the components of the hydrologic cycle under particular circumstances that will guide him in constructing simplified and more practical models. This process of sensitivity analysis can be very useful.

Another important application of hydrologic models in research is that they can serve as a focal point for research in multidisciplinary units, thus providing coordination (Engman, 1970).

A few years ago, the use of hydrologic models was limited primarily to the research area. However, today's analysts are expected to be able to operate these models routinely. This trend is reflected in the revisions of two popular texts on hydrology. Earlier editions of Linsley et al. (1975) and Viessman et al. (1977) contained very little information on linked process or simulation-type hydrologic models. Recent editions have been expanded to include more information on these models. In addition, two other texts, Overton and Meadows (1976) and Fleming (1975), have been published which deal exclusively with hydrologic modeling.

A student spends a considerable amount of time studying the individual processes of the hydrologic cycle and through laboratory experiments gains an appreciation of each process. The use of a model lets the student examine the interaction of the individual processes. When the models are implemented on an interactive computer system, a student can perform experiments very quickly. Also, as Moore (1971) pointed out, the use of models in training gives the student experience and an appreciation of the problems of data assembly and processing.

Model Selection

In the process of identifying an optimal course of action, decision-making uses information on several variates. The optimality of the decision is based upon specific criteria, like the net monetary benefit.

Inaccurate information can cause the decision-maker to choose a course of action that yields less than optimal returns or a loss of net benefits. With more accurate information derived using models or other techniques, the decision-maker avoids losing these net benefits. Each procedure will have a different value. Economically, the best procedure is that which provides the maximum positive difference between its value and the cost of obtaining the information.

It would be very useful to a decision-maker if he could afford to perform the analyses required to determine the value and cost of various hydrologic models in each problem he encounters. However, these analyses usually require more resources than he can commit. As a result, the decision-maker uses approximate techniques and hopes that they yield nearly the same result.

A variety of procedures have been presented in the literature for use in model selection and these will be described in a later section. Based upon these procedures and additional considerations, we suggest a general framework for model selection — a sliding cost-effectiveness analysis. The technique consists of the following five steps:

1   Explicitly define the problem and specify the information required to reach a decision.

2   Identify the available models.

3   Specify the criteria and limits that will be used and define the values for each available model (effectiveness analysis).

4   Estimate costs by item for each model.

5   Rate candidate models and select.

This is a sliding evaluation system because it is up to the analyst to determine exactly how much effort he should put into it. Item 1 may require some effort; however, this should be the first step of the analysis, even if a model has already been chosen.

A few years ago, item no. 2 might have been a considerable effort. However, today several surveys like Chapter 13 of this monograph list the available models and their attributes.

Effectiveness analysis is concerned with specifying minimum levels of performance. Does the model provide the needed information in time and space with specified accuracy? This step is discussed by Grimsrud et al. (1976). It is their opinion, as well as mine, that this item should not require an excessive effort if the necessary information is available. However, this type of information is not usually available. McCuen et al. (1977) reviewed many techniques for determining flood-frequency and found that information on accuracy was usually not given or was presented in incompatible formats. Thus, often the decision-maker would have to use a less meaningful evaluation or conduct his own tests. This later alternative, while desirable, is impractical and expensive.

Next, he would perform a cost analysis to compare estimates of model cost to funding limits. He can make these estimates but presently he has very little information available on which to base a decision.

By the time the decision-maker reaches item on. 5, most models will have been eliminated. The rating scheme can be as sophisticated as desired. Grimsrud et al. (1976) presented a procedure that uses two levels of rating. At one end of the scale, very arbitrary assignments of weights could be used, while at the other end Decision Theory could be used.

These general guidelines still leave undetermined how much effort should be devoted to the analysis. The level of effort varies with the problem. At one extreme, a firm might be working on a very unique project with relatively small potential economic benefits associated with it. Under these circumstances, a major analysis to evaluate models would not be justified. However, a state highway administration involved in designing several hydraulic structures each year should carefully consider its choice of a model. On a project-by-project basis such an analysis would not be justified but from a cumulative viewpoint it would be.

In this section, we presented a general set of guidelines for model selection whose purpose was to make two points. First, the value of a model is derived from the fact that it helps to avoid incorrect decisions that reduce the net benefits of a project. If this value can be quantified and the costs are known, then a net return for each model can be estimated which would in turn identify a best model.

Second, elaborate model evaluation are often not practical or possible; the effort put into these studies should reflect the consequences of the decision that will be made and its sensitivity to the hydrologic information. A decision-maker should have some idea of these factors a priori. Whether the application will be used repetitively should be considered. Although many effectiveness criteria and cost constraints can be specified with relatively little effort, only sparse information is available with which to evaluate data without conducting independent tests.

MODEL APPLICATIONS

Agriculture

Irrigation. The planning, design, and operation of irrigation systems is aimed at maximizing crop returns. Irrigation practices should also strive to maximize water-use efficiency. Jensen (1972) pointed out that the irrigator is concerned with the overall net return from his efforts and that other factors, besides water use must be considered. Fortunately, as Jensen (1972) noted, water-use efficiency is usually achieved in reaching the goal of maximizing returns. Whether the question at hand is determining the overall irrigation water requirements for a season or scheduling the next application of water, the decision-maker can benefit from information describing the soil water as a function of time and climatic variables. Hydrologic models can be used to generate this information.

With irrigation scheduling, the problem is to control the status of the soil water reservoir so that it is never depleted enough to significantly reduce crop yield (Kincaid and Heerman, 1974). This reduces to determining how much and when to apply supplemental water. What the decision-maker needs is a prediction or forecast of when the soil water reservoir will reach a critical state. To generate this forecast, the crop type, its stage of growth, soil type and hydraulic properties, soil water status, preceeding climate and projected climatic variables must be taken into account. One way to do this is by using a hydrologic model.

An example of the application of hydrologic models to irrigation scheduling is presented by Jensen (1972) and Kincaid and Heerman (1974). Jensen (1972) developed a model to predict the date and amount of irrigation. His model includes all of the variables mentioned earlier. Of course, the model does not include all of the hydrologic processes because many are not important in this type of application.

Jensen (1972) recognized that the individual farmer would be unlikely to use this procedure on his own. Therefore, the emphasis of his follow-up work was to develop a means for getting the model into use. The most feasible approach was to put the responsibility for developing irrigation schedules into centralized agencies or companies which could maintain the necessary staff and equipment. Jensen (1972) discussed several cases where this approach is used with success. Based upon the data presented in his report, apparently such as service is both valuable and low cost. Estimates of cost range from 4 to 10 dollars per hectare per year.

A more elaborate example of the application of a hydrologic model in irrigation was conducted by Carr (1973). In his investigation he used the Stanford Watershed Model with a management model to define the difference in crop yield and water use between traditional practices and those which could be used if a project was constructed and new practices initiated. His results indicated that improvements in yields would be obtained if the proposed project and new practices were introduced.

Another study that was conducted using a hydrologic model is described by Dragoun et al. (1972). In this investigation, an irrigation district concerned with stabilizing the groundwater table, providing water to obtain maximum crop yield, alleviating drainage problems, and maintaining the environment, used the model as a diagnostic and a predictive tool. They analyzed corrective measures and studied the effects of additional irrigation and irrigated lands on the various decision variables.

Drainage. Drainage of agricultural lands using a combination of surface and subsurface methods increases root aeration, improves soil trafficability, promotes soil warming, and aids in controlling salts accumulation in the root zone. As a result, farmers obtain higher crop yields, higher quality crops and/or are able to plant higher value crops.

Several factors must be considered in drainage design — soil properties, climate, management practices and drain features are all important. Equally important are the plant characteristics — rooting depth and plant tolerance to waterlogging.

Procedures for drainage design have been available for many years; however, these methods are based on simplifications and assumptions. Today, better designs are possible by using hydrologic models that take into account more of the factors involved.

Bhattacharya et al. (1977) presented an excellent example of how a hydrologic model can be used with economic data to optimize drainage design. A model was used that divided the soil profile into homogeneous zones. A water balance was continuously maintained in each zone using precipitation records as input. The evapotranspiration processes were simulated for each zone to determine available soil water. Transient water was simulated along with the formulation of the groundwater table. Simulated tile drains would remove the transient water at computed rates which would in turn affect the water table. Different spacings and depths of drains were simulated and related to drainage coefficients, the rate of water removal in millimeters per day.

The model was operated with 27 yr of precipitation data using specified soil properties to develop relationships between the drainage coefficient and the number of successive days the water table was within a specified distance from the surface. Then, using this data along with a specified depth and tolerance, a frequency of waterlogging relationship was established for each drainage rate. Fig. 12.1 shows one example of such a relationship.

Bhattacharya et al. (1977) carried the analysis one step further. Using the estimated crop price, interest rate, amortization period, and drainage system installation costs, they developed a frequency-net benefit relationship shown in Fig. 12.2. The optimal design is based upon the maximum net benefit which occurs at 10 percent. Of course, as the authors noted, their analysis does not take into account all of the economic factors. However, results show the potential of the technique.

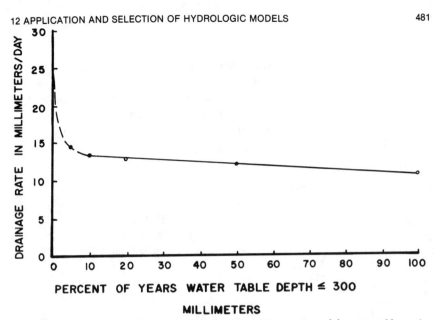

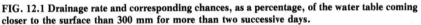

FIG. 12.1 Drainage rate and corresponding chances, as a percentage, of the water table coming closer to the surface than 300 mm for more than two successive days.

Another application of hydrologic modeling to drainage is presented in a series of investigatins, using the Iowa State University Hydrologic Model. These studies were concerned with an area of the midwest United States that is characterized by depressional areas and thus most of the region is drained. Recent flooding downstream from this region prompted a controversy over the impacts of drainage. One opinion was that the installation of drainage eliminated natural storage and accelerated the removal of soil water, thus increasing flood peaks. The other school of thought was

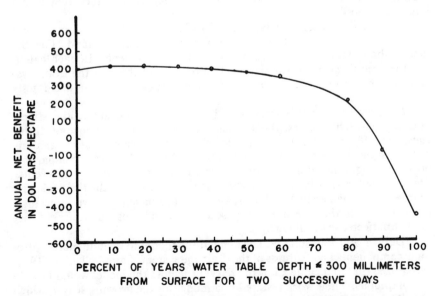

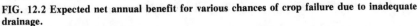

FIG. 12.2 Expected net annual benefit for various chances of crop failure due to inadequate drainage.

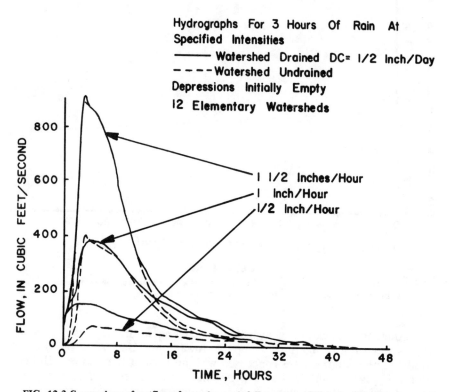

FIG. 12.3 Comparison of outflows for various rainfall excesses with and without drainage.

that, by eliminating storage in the depressions, the chance that they might be full when a storm occurred was eliminated. If the depressions were full, the runoff would be accelerated. However, if they were drained they would intercept runoff.

Haan and Johnson (1968a) and (1968b) analyzed the problem using a hydraulic model designed specifically for the problem at hand. For the model, the watershed is divided into elemental catchments. In each catchment the emphasis is on simulating the flow to and through the drain system and to the channel system for specific events. They conducted tests to verify the model.

Simulated watersheds were used in the model to evaluate the effects of drainage-ditch features, the drainage coefficient, the influence of drainage on runoff, and the effects of the storm pattern. The results of the analysis of the last two items are of particular interest. Fig. 12.3 shows a comparison of the hydrographs with and without drainage for different storm events. They concluded that for long duration, low intensity rainfall, the peak discharge from a watershed will increase with drainage. However, for high intensity storms that are likely to produce flooding, peak discharge is virtually unaffected by drainage.

DeBoer and Johnson (1971) extended the model to include more hydrologic components and features of the drainage system. Campbell et al. (1974) recognized that to include all of the relevant factors the model would have to be continuous. Their work resulted in a model for the growing season which simulates runoff, drainage, and the soil moisture status of the root zone.

Land Treatment and Other Applications. Agricultural land management is aimed at improving the onsite conditions to increase returns and conserve the land. Besides these onsite effects, changes in the land cover also have offsite impacts. It is important to quantitatively evaluate these practices so that better techniques can be suggested or corrective measures taken.

Some land-surface modifications associated with agriculture include modifying the vegetative cover, inhibiting evaporation and transpiration, modifying the soil condition by tillage and residues, and modifying the surface geometry (Larson, 1973). The hydrologic effects of these actions will include the water yield in all cases and in some cases the peak flows, low flows and water quality.

Researchers have been concerned with evaluating the effects of land treatment on hydrologic variables for many years. The Soil Conservation Service Hydrology Handbook (1972) includes techniques for analyzing these effects.

The USDA-SEA Hydrograph Laboratory developed a model (USDAHL) for watershed hydrology. Holtan and Lopez (1970), Holtan et al. (1975), Langford and McGuinness (1976) and Glymph et al. (1971) demonstrated how the model could be used to evaluate a variety of land treatments. The model has the potential for many other applications. Since it includes components and parameters reflecting crops, soils, land cover, and management, it can be used in many types of investigations. This model has also been used in a more elaborate model for simulating water quality characteristics (Frere et al., 1975).

A series of investigations were conducted by Haan (1975), Shanholtz and Carr (1975) and Shanholtz et al. (1972) to evaluate a number of simulation models for agricultural watershed in the Southeastern States.

Another application of increasing interest is the effects of conservation or minimum tillage and residues on water yield and runoff. An analysis of the soil-water-balance effects of no tillage was conducted by Shanholtz and Lillard (1970), using a hydrologic model. The model allowed analysis of the soil water status for conventional and no till practices for each soil zone.

In response to increased awareness and legislation, we need better information on the fate of pesticides and nutrients applied to agricultural lands, especially those factors involving the hydrologic system. Donigian and Crawford (1976) have developed a model for simulating the fate of pesticides and nutrients which utilizes the Hydrocomp hydrologic model as a component.

Forests and Rangelands

Awareness of the importance of wildlands in the U.S. is increasing. The pressure is increasing on those involved in making decisions on the management of these areas. Forest and rangeland areas are typically multipurpose and, therefore, several objectives must be considered. Fogel (1971) listed some of these objectives as timber production, forage and grazing, water production (quantity and quality), wildlife habitant and recreation. Proper management requires the integration of all these factors, which leads to the adoption of an ecosystem or general approach (Huff, 1971; Carder, 1976).

To evaluate alternative management plans, the decision-maker can use a hydrologic model. Using a hydrologic model is an attractive alternative to using some of the other available techniques, like paired watersheds.

Activities that influence the water quantity and quality of wildland watersheds are presented in the following list taken from U.S. Forest Service (1977).

1   Manipulation of vegetation
2   Roads and trails construction
3   Fire
4   Grazing
5   Timber harvesting
6   Application of pesticides
7   Recreation
8   Forest fertilization
9   Waste disposal
10 Impoundments and diversion

Other practices, like weather modifications, could be added to the list. These activities cause changes in water yield, erosion, flooding and water quality.

In forest hydrology, most research has been related to increasing water yield and controlling erosion. Most techniques used for increasing water yield were described in Dortignac (1967).

Shih et al. (1972) used the Utah State University Watershed Model to analyze a small watershed in a coniferous forest. They observed good results in matching hydrographs during the non-snow periods. Further investigations were conducted using a revised model in the Entiet Experimental Watersheds in Washington (Bowles et al., 1975). The goal of this investigation was to study the effects of forest fires on runoff characteristics. A forest fire burned three experimental watersheds which had been gaged for several years. The gage was maintained after the fire. Pre- and post-fire hydrographs were used to calibrate the model. Post-fire increases in water yield were noted and attributed to reduced evapotranspiration and infiltration. Similar studies were conducted on a much larger scale by Fleming (1971) using the Hydrocomp Model.

The Rocky Mountain Forest and Range Experiment Station has sponsored several studies in conjunction with an investigation of Beaver Creek in Arizona which involves multiple-use management of forested watersheds (Carder, 1976). Hydrologic models play an important role in these studies. Forest-management practices designed for increased water yield are being evaluated in terms of their impacts on sediment transport, flooding, timber harvesting yields, and wildlife. The results of these studies are being used by the watershed managers.

Simons et al. (1975) developed a model for predicting water and sediment on a single event basis. The model can be used to simulate the effects of clear cutting and burning. These vegetation manipulation actions are simulated by changing parameters reflecting the canopy cover and ground cover density. Figs. 12.4 and 12.5 show the effects of changing the canopy and ground cover densities on hydrographs for a 313.6-acre watershed. The watershed was calibrated for a clear-cut condition and then the parameters were changed to reflect increased cover. Simulations were performed for both large and small storms. The model and a continuous simulation model of water balance (Rogers, 1973) were combined to develop a model called ECOWAT (Carder, 1976).

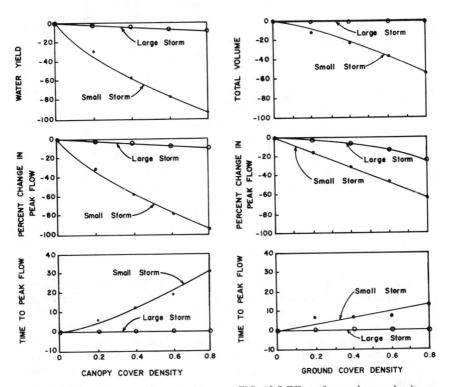

FIG. 12.4 Effect of canopy cover density on   FIG. 12.5 Effect of ground cover density on-
the water hydrograph from watershed 1   the water hydrograph from watershed 1

Leaf and Brink (1972) developed a model to predict the changes in both the rate and seasonal distribution of snowmelt if clearcutting small openings in old growth was initiated. This model was further refined to simulate the short term effects of partial cutting and other practices on water yield and sediment yield (Leaf and Brink, 1973). From the short term model, a long term simulation model was developed for evaluating long range effects of various land-management systems (Leaf and Brink, 1975).

The effects of thinning vegetation on water balance in small drainage areas in pine hardwood forests were studied by Rogerson (1976) using a hydrologic model.

Riley and Hawkins (1976) investigated the use of hydrologic modeling on rangeland watersheds. An example application is presented which involves the effect of converting a pinyon juniper woodland to grassland or a grass shrub mixture on water yield and discharge rates. The hydrologic model was calibrated for a small forested watershed. Parameters were then adjusted to reflect a change to a rangeland condition. After this, the model was run for several storms to evaluate the impacts.

Ardis (1973) utilized the Tennessee Valley Authority Storm Hydrograph Model to evaluate the effects of timber harvesting on the discharge hydrographs of two small forested watersheds. Fig. 12.6 shows the observed and computed hydrographs of one storm for the existing 100 percent forest condition of one watershed. Model parameters were varied to simulate forest clearing. Fig. 12.6 also shows the model hydrographs for the same storm if the watershed was 95 and 50 percent cleared.

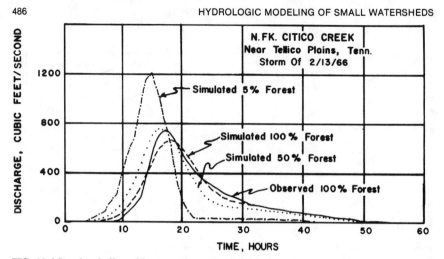

FIG. 12.6 Simulated effect of forest cutting at North Fork Citico Creek Watershed for storm of 2/13/66

Surface Mining

Surface mining alters the hydrologic regime of an area and disrupts or destroys the environment. In the past, the conflict over surface mining was environment versus profit; however, from now on this conflict will be energy versus the environment. Recognizing this fact, the decision-maker's attention has been directed toward developing reasonable controls on mining methods. To meet these regulations they must preplan their operations; this requires the ability to assess a variety of alternatives for before, during, and after mining.

Spoil piles of overburden materials are the principal sources of acid drainage in many surface-mining operations. Sternberg and Agnew (1968) used a hydrologic model to study the water contribution of spoil piles to surface waters.

Herricks et al. (1975, 1976) used the Stanford Watershed Model to develop a tool for evaluating the environmental effects of various surface mining systems. The model was calibrated for a large watershed and used to generate a continuous discharge record. This record was interfaced with models which simulated sulfate production and sediment yield. Finally, the model information was combined with biological samples to predict the impact of mine drainage on stream biological communities.

The effects of contour-surface mining for coal on the hydrology of a watershed were studied by Tung (1975). He used the TVA continuous daily stream flow model to study the hydrology as a function of the degree of stripping. Data from a gaged watershed were used in the study. As a result of the model investigations he developed relationships between the model parameters and the percent of the watershed disturbed.

The most complete effort to model the hydrologic impacts of mining is presented in a report by Shumate et al. (1976). They developed a comprehensive model which simulates the water quantity and quality effects of mining and includes an optimization procedure to allocate resources. There are two important elements in the hydrologic portion. One portion is a set of unit source models to simulate the flow and acid production for deep draft mining, strip-mining, and refuse piles. These individual units are linked through the other important feature, the Stanford Water Model, to generate continuous traces. These authors point out that presently the model is probably too complex for practical use. However, further studies, using test data, may lead to valid simplifications. A model like this has great versatility and would be very useful in preplanning mining operations.

Urban Areas

A wide variety of water-related problems are encountered in urban areas (McPherson, 1975a). Here, we will discuss only those involving stormwater runoff. Most of these problems originate from one of the following:

1 Urban growth. Increased volumes and rates of runoff brought about by increased imperviousness and channelization. Also, the occupation of flood-prone areas.

2 Previous design philosophy. Many existing storm drainage systems were built with the purpose of removing the stormwater from the site without regard for offsite effects.

3 Increased public awareness and legislation. Years ago no one was really concerned with the water quality aspects of urban runoff.

The complexity of the urban system, the economics and the politics involved in decisions regarding stormwater control and management, require that the hydrologic information used in design be reliable and complete. Thus, it is not surprising that hydrologic models have been used in many studies. The examples which follow include studies conducted on small watersheds and regional studies in which the effects of small watershed decisions are related to downstream impacts.

Hydrologic models are being used on a daily basis in many jurisdictions for stormwater management. Lumb and James (1976) developed a procedure for DeKalb Co., Georgia that retains most of the advantages of sophisticated hydrologic modeling while minimizing costs. They used the Stanford Watershed Model to generate unrouted runoff files for a wide range of watershed characteristics. Hydrologic frequency information was then developed using a routing model.

Hartigan and Bonuccelli (1977) presented an application of a version of the Stormwater Management Model (Huber and Heaney, 1977) in Virginia. They presented an example which involves a planned unit development which would add 48 acres of impervious cover to 50.5 km² (19.5 mi²) watershed. After establishing the predevelopment and postdevelopment hydrographs, a variety of stormwater control alternatives were analyzed. Several onsite controls, including parking lot storage, rooftop storage and porous pavement, were modeled. The effects of these controls, simulated using the model, are illustrated in Fig. 12.7 for the design storm selected.

Perhaps, the most widely used urban hydrologic model is the Stormwater Management Model (SWMM) developed under the sponsorship of the U.S. Environmental Protection Agency (Huber and Heaney, 1977). SWMM has been applied in several investigations in the U.S., Canada, and other countries. These applications include storm sewer design, infiltration/inflow analysis, evaluation of existing systems, overflow analysis, facilities planning and regional planning (Anderson, 1976; Cole and Shutt, 1976; Jewel et al., 1974; and Meinholz et al., 1974). One particularly informative application is a study guide which presents a step by step example of how to use the model and includes all of the necessary data and explanations of each procedure (Jewell et al., 1977).

Several studies have been conducted to demonstrate how hydrologic models can be integrated with economic data to generate optimal designs for urban drainage systems. Crawford (1973b) made this type of investigation which included a comparison of conventional drainage and a system

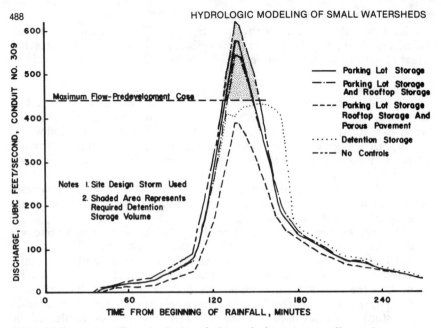

FIG. 12.7 Comparison of post-development hydrographs for various runoff control measures at Skyline Center Planned Unit Development.

utilizing retention basins for a watershed in Santa Maria, California. His objective was to select the most cost-effective system for reducing local flooding. Design variables included the conduit and channel slope, conduit size, retention basin size, and runoff magnitude (an indicator of the degree of development) and the land value.

Shih et al. (1976) developed a procedure for the optimal design of urban drainage systems that incorporates a hydrologic model and economic data. The hydrologic model is used to generate discharge frequency curves for the existing conditions and also for various increases in urbanization which are incorporated in the model through an urbanization factor. For a particular alternative control measure, the model is used to generate the same information. Then, for the particular watershed, flood-damage data are related to the degree of urbanization. The pattern of urbanization is projected over time and a discharge-damage-time relationship is developed. Hydrologic and economic data are then integrated to determine the average annual damages for the existing conditions and those under each alternative. Then using cost data, the optimal project is selected. In their report, they presented a numerical example.

Control of urban runoff can be incorporated in the design of new subdivisions. Several authors have used hydrologic models to assess different development patterns and control alternatives. McCuen and Piper (1975) studied the effects of Planned Unit Developments (PUD). These are completely planned developments, like townhouse communities, which are not constrained by internal lot subdivision. Several alternative development patterns were generated and related to the Land Use Intensity Index (LUI) used by the Federal Housing Administration as a measure of land use. Using the model and design storms, peak discharge data for various return periods were generated for each layout. Shown in Fig. 12.8 in a summary of this information. These curves are considered reliable for areas under 2 km² (0.78 mi²) without very flat slopes. In the same study, the effects of rooftoop detention storage were evaluated and found to be relatively ineffective.

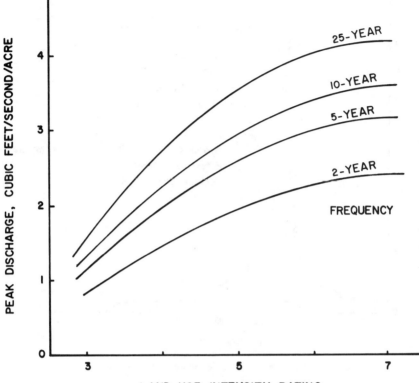

FIG. 12.8 Peak discharge versus land use intensity.

Lumb et al (1974) conducted a similar study of the Clairmont Watershed in Georgia with a preliminary version of the UROS4 model. In their study the effects of reducing the slopes of pervious area, increased channel roughness, storage and "disconnecting" impervious areas were studied in relationship to peak discharge and volume of runoff. Their tests indicated that the most effective measures might be increased roughness and "disconnecting" impervious areas. In another recent Canadian investigation, Henry and Ahern (1976) evaluated the effects of rooftop ponding, onsite storage, catch basin storage and holding reservoirs on the runoff from a proposed residential subdivision. Their analysis used a hydrologic model that combined concepts used in the SWMM with other model features. Results of these tests indicated that when both the hydrologic and economic information was considered that the most effective control measure was a centralized holding reservoir.

Jackson and Ragan (1974) examined the potential of using porous pavements to control the runoff from large parking lots. A hydrologic model was formulated to simulate the system for a variety of design variables. Fig. 12.9 shows the hydrographs which would be obtained on a typical area with and without porous pavement. In Fig. 12.9, the symbol OLF represents overland flow and INF represents infiltration. The analysis was taken a step further to develop easy to use design aids which would allow an analyst to evaluate several alternatives without resorting to the model. General equations and charts were developed.

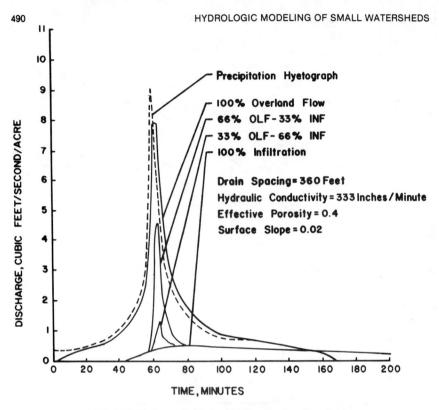

FIG. 12.9 Hydrographs for overland and subsurface flows.

Bras and Perkins (1975) examined an interesting problem using this model. A commonly stated principle of urban hydrology is that the increased imperviousness and other aspects associated with urban development increase the peak discharge and total volume of runoff while decreasing time of concentration. However, for catchments in Puerto Rico these changes could have a different impact because the soils have low infiltration rates and normally have a high moisture content, the land is naturally hilly and urbanization would flatten the slopes, and housing in the area is constructed with flat roofs with storage areas and drains. To resolve this conflict, Bras and Perkins (1975) used a model to simulate runoff for natural conditions and residential development on a small catchment. Development was simulated in great detail. The results of the tests showed that urbanization did increase peak discharge and reduce the time of concentration. They found that if the rooftop drainage rate was decreased, the peak discharge from the development could be maintained at the pre-development level.

Minor Structures

Small or minor structures design is one of the most common problems that decision-makers encounter. These structures include small detention ponds, highway culverts, dam spillways, drainage inlets, and others. Although the hydrologic variable most often used in design is peak discharge, some designs use the entire hydrograph.

There are several examples in which hydrologic models have been used to generate design information. However, as stated earlier, the use of hydrologic models for this purpose has been hindered by the relative numbers and economics of the problems involved. In this section, we would emphasize applications in which a hydrologic model was used to generate easier-to-use and less costly analysis tools like equations, charts, and monographs.

This type of investigation was conducted by Clark (1968) and followed up by Miller (1968). The purpose of the study was to develop more reliable peak-discharge estimates for culvert design in Kentucky. As a first step, the Stanford Watershed Model was calibrated for a small watershed and then the calibrated model was used with continuous rainfall data to generate a runoff record. Model parameters were related to watershed characteristics and then a range of parameter sets was used with the rainfall record to generate runoff records. For each record a flood-frequency curve was determined. These data, for a specific frequency were related to the watershed characteristics through a coaxial correlation technique. Results were extended to watersheds of different sizes, other locations, and different return periods. Using the graphs developed, a decision-maker can very rapidly determine the peak discharge for a particular watershed and return period.

Fleming and Franz (1971) outlined a procedure for estimating peak discharge in the design of highway culverts and bridges on small watersheds. Their procedure was developed with the goals of reliability, wide geographic applicability, low data requirements, minimum subjectivity and compatibility with the amount of time and money normally devoted to projects of this scale. In the method, the Hydrocomp model is calibrated over a region and parameters at the various calibration sites plotted on maps to develop contour lines. Relatively homogeneous areas in terms of soil, cover, and precipitation, are defined. Channel inflow for a long period is generated for each region and stored. A designer would input the channel characteristics for a particular watershed into the model. By routing the stored channel inflow, a flood frequency curve is produced.

A procedure similar to that described above was developed for a county in Michigan (Crawford, 1973a). After developing the data base and operational program, the package was implemented on an interactive remote terminal computer system. Crawford (1973a) presented an example of how the interactive drainage design program operates.

A flood-frequency estimation technique (based on a hydrologic model) was developed by Hauth (1974) for Missouri. His method was comprised of three steps. First, the U.S. Geological Survey hydrologic model (Dawdy et al., 1972) was calibrated for 43 gaged watersheds throughout the state. These watersheds ranged in size from 0.33 to 20 km² (0.14 to 8.36 mi²) with an average size of about 4.8 km² (2 mi²). Second, data from four continuous precipitation records with an average length of 70 yr were used to synthesize runoff for each of the 43 watersheds. These data were used to develop a flood frequency curve for each site. The final step of the procedure was to utilize regression techniques to relate the peak discharge for return periods to watershed characteristics in the region.

Equations were developed for return periods of 2, 5, 10, 25, 50, and 100 yr (Table 12.1). The area of the watershed, A, is in square miles, and S is the main channel slope. Also shown in the table are the standard errors for the equations. The equations can be applied rapidly using easily obtained data.

Ragan et al. (1975) developed a rapid noncomputer-based method for use in inlet design on very small drainage areas. A complex hydrologic model was used as a tool. They conduct 100 numerical experiments for drainage areas of varying length, width, total area, percent impervious and

TABLE 12.1. SUMMARY OF REGRESSION ANALYSIS
(FROM HAUTH, 1976)

Recurrence interval of flood peak	Equation	Standard error of estimate, percent
2-year	$Q = 53.5 A^{0.851} A^{-0.02} S^{0.356}$	38.6
5-year	$Q = 64.0 A^{0.886} A^{-0.02} S^{0.450}$	34.7
10-year	$Q = 67.6 A^{0.905} A^{-0.02} S^{0.500}$	34.5
25-year	$Q = 73.7 A^{0.924} A^{-0.02} S^{0.543}$	35.0
50-year	$Q = 79.8 A^{0.926} A^{-0.02} S^{0.560}$	33.3
100-year	$Q = 85.1 A^{0.964} A^{-0.02} S^{0.576}$	33.3

Notation: $Q =$ Discharge in cubic feet/second.
            $A =$ Area in square miles.
            $S =$ Main channel slope in feet/mile.

slope using design storms for 2, 10, and 25 yr return periods in the Washington, DC area. The hydrographs generated were analyzed to identify any basic relationships that existed.

The result of the analysis of the numerical experiments was a Dimensionless Inlet Hydrograph Model which is very easy and inexpensive to use, while retaining the high degree of accuracy. Two charts are used in the procedure. The first, shown in Fig. 12.10 for a 2-yr return period storm, relates dimensionless peak discharge to the slope and percent of impervious area in the drainage area. Peak discharge is obtained by multiplying the dimensionless value by the peak intensity of the design storm. Next, the cutoff flow for the hydrograph is calculated by multiplying the final rainfall intensity of the design storm by the percent of impervious area. Fig. 12.11 is the dimensionless inlet hydrograph. Using these data the design hydrograph is obtained. Ragan et al. (1975) presented a numerical example of the method.

Marsalek (1976) reported on an investigation similar to that conducted by Ragan et al. (1975). In this study, the Stormwater Management Model developed by the U.S. Environmental Protection Agency served as the generator of the dimensionless hydrograph data. Chen (1976) also conducted research aimed at developing a similar technique.

Overton and Tsay (1974) have developed a procedure for obtaining the time of concentration and the peak discharge for small watersheds based upon the combination of kinematic wave theory and the SCS curve numbers. Using the general formulation, sets of design curves can be generated for an area with the same rainfall intensity-duration-frequency relationship which relate the peak discharge to a factor called the lag modulus and the curve number. The lag modulus is described by Overton and Meadows (1976) as a factor that represents the geometry and roughness of the flow paths.

Recent water-quality regulations require cattle feedlot operators to control runoff of contaminated water from their lands. The most common solution to this is a storage pond which is emptied by pumping to land application sites and/or by evaporation. A good design depends upon many factors which can be coordinated by using a hydrologic model. The most useful approach is to use a continuous simulation model which can keep track of precipitation, runoff, soil moisture, storage volume, evaporation from the pond and pumping operations. Examples of the application described above are presented in Wensink and Miner (1975, 1977), Koelliker et al. (1975) and Zoune et al. (1977).

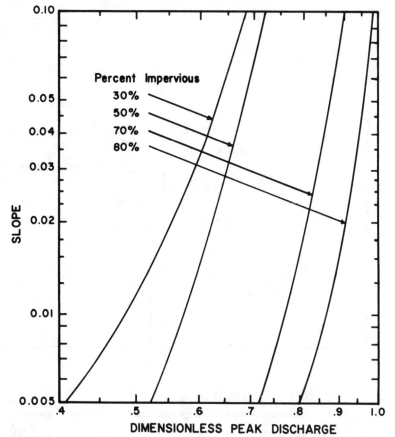

FIG. 12.10 Dimensionless peak discharged as function of average watershed slope and percent imperviousness for a 2-year storm.

MODEL SELECTION TECHNIQUES
Why Should the Decision-Maker Use a Model?

As a prelude to this section on model selection we would present a general scenario for decision-making using a very simplified example. The problem that is to be solved is the sizing of a highway culvert. It is stipulated that all benefits and costs are monetary. Benefits are based upon the re-

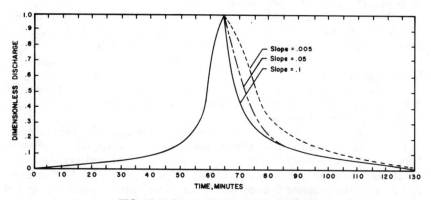

FIG. 12.11 Dimensionless inlet hydrograph.

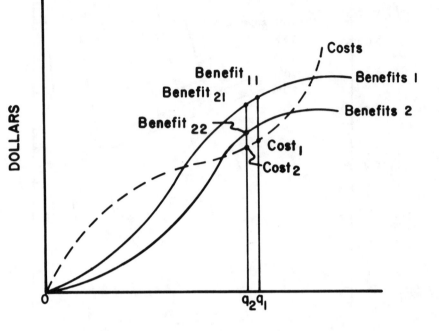

DISCHARGE (q)

FIG. 12.12 Relationship between discharge and benefits and costs of a design.

duction in property damages, and they increase as the size of the culvert increases. Costs are based upon size, installation, and maintenance, of the culvert; it is assumed that all values are converted to uniform annual series. The decision-maker must choose the size culvert, specified by a design discharge, that provides the maximum net benefit (benefits minus costs) for all of the alternatives including a do-nothing alternative. If the benefits were plotted as a function of design discharge (q) a relationship resembling curve 1 in Fig. 12.12 might be obrained. As the design level increases, the benefits increase, up to a point since the probability of the larger flows occurring becomes very small.

The costs of the projects for each design level are also shown in Fig. 12.12. There will be certain fixed costs which make the relatively small designs expensive; however, as the size is increased the marginal increase in cost decreases up to a certain point at which it becomes necessary to use a different type of control.

A decision-maker who has information like that in Fig. 12.12 available is able to define the optimal level of design by identifying the discharge which yields the maximum net benefit, q.

Part of the information that is needed to generate the benefit curve in Fig. 12.12 is a relationship between discharge (q) and frequency. Different benefit curves can be obtained which depend upon the technique used in developing the discharge-frequency relationship. Shown in Fig. 12.12 are two different curves. Assume that curve 1 is the "true" benefit relationship and a method called technique 2 was used to obtain curve 2.

If curve 2 was used to select the optimal level of design, 2 would be chosen because, under the assumption that curve 2 is correct, this value yields the maximum net benefits. Actually, the optimal level was where the net benefit was Benefit 11-Cost 1. The return from choosing q is really Benefit 21-Cost 2 which is less than Benefit 11-Cost 1. Therefore, a loss of net benefits has occurred. Now suppose that a model is used and the information on discharge frequency it provides results in Curve 1, the true relationship. The value of the model over technique 2 is the loss of net benefits that is avoided.

A decision-maker should use a model to reduce the loss of net benefits due to incorrect decisions which may result if they use less accurate methods. A net gain will be obtained through modeling if the reduction in the loss of net benefits minus the cost of obtaining the model information is positive. The best approach to generating the information is that which provides the maximum net gain. However, possibly all of the modeling techniques could result in negative net gains in which case modeling should not be used.

If the decision-maker can easily perform the analyses required to evaluate the models, his selection of a model would be straightforward. However, the investigations necessary for these analyses usually require resources well beyond those that can be devoted to the process of model selection. As a result, the decision-maker must use approximate techniques. In the following selections some of the procedures that have been used in model selection are reviewed.

Cost-Effectiveness Analysis

Cost-effectiveness analysis involves the specification, measurement, and comparison of performance and cost criteria for several alternative methods for achieving a final goal. The selection of the most suitable alternative is based upon either choosing the method with the lowest cost for a fixed minimum level of effectiveness or choosing the method with the maximum effectiveness for a fixed maximum level of costs. Using a cost-effectiveness approach in model selection assumes that the decision to use a model has already been made.

One of the first steps in the analysis is the specification of the criteria that will be used in evaluation. Cost items are usually the easiest to define. Some factors to consider are listed in Kisiel and Duckstein (1972) and Grimsrud et al. (1976). These include the costs of model acquisition, model setup or development, equipment acquisition, data acquisition and processing, computer operation time and maintenance and associated manpower costs for time and training. It is also necessary to estimate and maintain accounts for time. In some cases, the collection of data, training and manpower or model development may require more time than is allowed for under the project requirements.

Effectiveness analysis is more complex than cost analysis because the criteria may not be quantitative or commensurable. Many factors will be problem specific. Some measures that can be used are listed by Kisiel and Duckstein (1972) as bias, variance, consequences or errors, transferability to ungaged sites, creditability, fidelity, simplicity, sensitivity of the results to spatial and temporal description of input variables and parameters. Grimsrud et al. (1976) utilized all of these factors and others in their approach.

After specifying all of the relevant variables, the value for each item and model must be estimated. Then, the overall values can be compared based upon fixed cost or fixed effectiveness to select the best model.

Model selection procedures utilizing cost effectiveness analysis have been developed by Kisiel and Duckstein (1972) and Grimsrud et al. (1976). Kisiel and Duckstein (1972) utilized a 10-step procedure developed by Kazanowski (1968):

1 Define desired model goals, objectives, or purposes.

2 Identify model requirements (specifications) that are essential to the attainment of the desired goals.

3 Develop alternative models for realizing the goals.

4 Establish criteria (measures) for model evaluation so that model capabilities can be compared with model specifications.

5 Select a fixed-cost or fixed-effectiveness approach (this will be dictated by the circumstances of the practical problem but is usually a non-trivial task).

6 Determine capabilities of all alternative models in terms of evaluating criteria.

7 Generate an array that classifies models in terms of the criteria.

8 Analyze the merits of alternative models.

9 Perform sensitivity analysis.

10 Document the rationale, assumptions, and analyses underlying the previous nine steps.

Application of this technique has been illustrated by Kisiel and Duckstein (1972) for selecting a forecasting model and Fogel et al. (1972) for selecting a model for evaluating urbanization on Southwestern semiarid watersheds.

A more complete presentation of how cost-effectiveness analysis is applied is included in Grimsrud et al. (1976). Although the emphasis of this report is on instream water quality, the general technique is widely applicable and the examples most instructive.

The technique consists of four phases:

Phase I: Model Applicability Tests
Phase II: Cost Constraint Tests
Phase III: Performance Index Rating-Simplified
Phase IV: Performance Index-Rating-Advanced

The model applicability tests are designed to evaluate the suitability of a model to the specific problem under consideration. An analyst specifies limits and specific criteria. Table 12.2 is a summary of some of the factors considered. Phase II, cost estimation, is also straightforward and some of the items used are summarized in Table 12.2.

Models which remain after the elimination processes of Phases I and II are subjected to performance index ratings. The more important items are considered in Phase III, the simplified analysis. Attributes of each model defined in Phases I and II are rated on a scale of 0 (poor) to 10 (excellent) performance. Next each attribute is assigned a weight according to its relative importance. The performance index for a particular model is calculated by multiplying the rating by its weight for each attribute and summing the values over all attributes and then dividing by the sum of all the attribute weights. If desired the analysis can be expanded to Phase IV to include the advanced rating and items listed in Table 12.2.

Final selection of a model can be based upon fixed costs, fixed effectiveness or other criteria. Grimsrud et al. (1976) presented an example of the application of this procedure.

Other Techniques and Guidelines

The cost-effectiveness analysis approach to model selection presented earlier in this is one example of a comprehensive framework for evaluating alternative models. Other procedures have been suggested which are not as comprehensive. These include general guidelines, techniques developed for special problems, and methods for evaluating specific criteria. All of these additional procedures could be incorporated into a cost-effectiveness analysis.

A fairly sophisticated technique for model selection was developed by Lovell (1975). He viewed the model-choice problem as one between information retrieval and optimization. He presented a formal methodology for performing the analysis; however, he did not perform the actual application of the technique to hydrologic model selection.

TABLE 12.2. SUMMARY OF COST-EFFECTIVENESS EVALUATION TABULATIONS (FROM FINNEMORE AND GRIMSRUD, 1976)

Cost-effectiveness evaluation categories	I Applicable	I Applic. limitations	II Time	II Cost/run	II Cost	II Time OK?	II Cost OK?	III Rating	III Weight	IV Rating	IV Weight	All PI rating
Applicable situations												
Water body	A							R	W			
Time variability	A							R	W			
Discretization, etc.	A							R	W			
Constituents modeled												
Constituents modeled	A							R	W			
Driving forces, boundary factors	A							R	W			
Data requirements for model inputs												
Hydrologic and geologic	A							R				
Water quality	A	A						R				
Effluent	A	A						R				
Other	A	A						R				
Data requirements for calibration and verification												
Hydrologic and hydrodynamic	A	A						R				
Water quality	A	A						R				
Overall data rating	A							R	W			
Initiation costs												
Model acquisition			A		A							
Equipment requirements			A		A							
Data acquisition			A		A							
Utilization costs												
Machine costs			A	A	A							
Manpower costs			A		A							
Total costs			A	A	A							
Cost constraint tests						A	A	R	W			
Advanced PI rating												
Internal factors accounted for										R	W	
Model representation accuracy										R	W	
PI rating, stage 2												
Numerical accuracy										R	W	
Sufficiency of available documentation										R	W	
Output form and content										R	W	
Updateability										R	W	
Ease of modification												
Overall PI rating												R

A = Answer (yes, no, $, weeks, etc.); R = Rating on scale 0-10; W = Weight, normalized about 1.0.

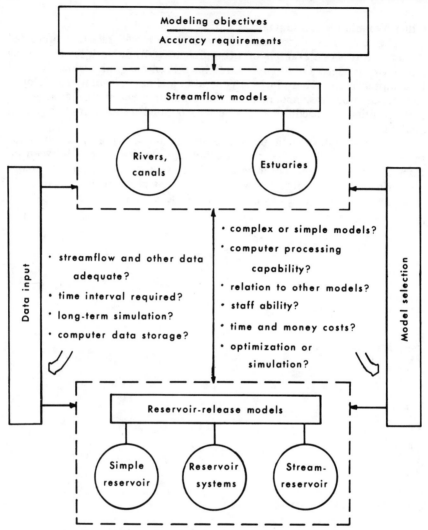

FIG. 12.13 Model selection process by use of a question-choice diagram.

General guidelines for model selection have been presented by several authors (Linsley, 1971; Weber et al., 1973; Duckstein, 1974; Walesh, 1976; Wisner et al., 1976; Lager, 1977; U.S. Forest Service, 1977; and Alley, 1977). Some include tables which summarize the properties of specific types of models. Additional material on model properties is summarized in Chapter 13 and several of the references presented there. These summary tables are very useful in any model-selection procedure.

Examples of model selection procedures designed for special classes of decision-making were presented in Jennings et al. (1976), Baker and Carder (1976), Debo and Lumb (1975) and McCuen et al. (1977). Jennings et al. (1976) developed a technique to select models for use in streamflow and reservoir-release studies to be conducted on the Willamette River Basin. The models were used in the evaluation of various basin development plans in terms of their effects on river quality. The model selection problem was viewed as an interative question-choice process, as shown in Fig. 12.13.

**TABLE 12.3. BASIC CRITERIA FOR EVALUATING
MODELS (FROM BAKER AND CARDER, 1976)**

1. Ease of use — includes:
   — ease of use by field level user
   — skills required
   — ease of interpreting results
   — type of results display
   — assumptions required by models

2. Availability of data—includes:
   — ability to use readily available or estimated data rather
     than exotic parameters
   — ability to handle small and variable time increments
   — ability to substitute data parameters
   — kinds of input data needed
   — data accuracy
   — data resolution

3. Availability of models — includes:
   — ease of accessibility of system and support to train users
   — cost to operate and number of runs needed to provide
     data necessary to make management decisions

4. Applicability to forest management activities — includes:
   — ability of models to represent common alternative man-
     agement activities
   — sensitivity to change in management activities
   — number of parameters predicted

5. Broad geographical areas—includes:
   — ability of a model to operate in diverse hydrologic areas
   — extrapolation of model

6. Accuracy of prediction—includes:
   — ability to predict relative change and absolute effects
   — need to calibrate model
   — ability to estimate recovery rates of various types of
     disturbances
   — accuracy in predicting range of events, i.e. high and low
   — precision or repeatability of model predictions
   — percent error between actual and predicted values for
     volumes, peak discharge, and time to peak for both
     water and sediment

Baker and Carder (1976) described an investigation which is under-way to develop information that can be used by decision-makers in select-ing a model. The area of interest is the relationship between forest man-agement and water and soil yields. In this program, various models will be tested and evaluated using the criteria listed in Table 12.3.

Another program to evaluate alternative models, or more precisely procedures, for estimating flood frequencies at ungaged sites is underway by the U.S. Water Resources Council. As described in McCuen et al. (1977), a set of procedures will be selected which can be applied to drainage areas of all sizes and geographic locations. Three criterias are defined which will be used in the evaluations: accuracy (precision and bias), reproduci-bility, and practicality. McCuen et al. (1977) also discussed indices which could be more to measure the performance of a model with respect to these three criteria.

Specific requirements have been placed on studies which are performed to analyze areawide waste-treatment alternatives which make modeling the only practical procedure for generating the necessary information. Debo and Lumb (1975) discussed the requirements of these studies and suggested the following general criteria for selecting water quality models: broad ap-plication, representation of the actual processes, flexibility, planning capa-bilities and cost-effectiveness.

Another technique that could be useful in certain model selection problems is Bayesian Decision Theory (Jackson and Ragan, 1977). Bayesian Analysis can be performed to determine the value of the additional information which a model provides. The technique has been successfully applied evaluating the worth of data and alternative data sources. This procedure requires considerable effort to apply. It could be very useful as a component of a more comprehensive model-selection procedure.

References

1　Alley, W. D. 1977. Guide for collection, analysis, and use of urban stormwater data. American Society of Civil Engineers. New York.

2　Anderson, J. C. 1976. Storm water management for the Merivale industrial area — Township of Nepean. pp. 593-608. In Environmental Aspects of Irrigation and Drainage. American Society of Civil Engineers. New York.

3　Ardis, C. 1973. Storm hydrographs using a double-triangle model. Research Paper No. 9. Tennessee Valley Authority. Knoxville, TN.

4　Baker, M. B., and D. R. Carder. 1976. An approach for evaluating water yield and soil loss models. Presented at the Earth Sciences Symposium. Fresno, CA.

5　Betson, R. D. 1976. Urban hydrology a systems study in Knoxville, TN. Water Systems Development Branch. Tennessee Valley Authority, Knoxville, TN.

6　Bhattacharya, A. K., N. Foroud, S. T. Chieng, and R. S. Broughton. 1977. Subsurface drainage cost and hydrologic model. Journal of the Irrigation and Drainage Division of ASCE 103(IR3):299-308.

7　Bock, P., I. Enger, G. P. Malhotra, and D. A. Chisholm. 1972. Estimating peak runoff rates from ungaged small rural watersheds. National Cooperative Highway Research Program Report 136. Highway Research Board, Washington, DC.

8　Bowles, D. S., J. P. Riley, and G. B. Shih. 1975. An application of the Utah State University Watershed simulation model to the Entiat Experimental Watershed, Washington State, PRW6126, Utah Water Research Laboratory. Utah State University, Logan, Utah.

9　Bras, R. L., and F. E. Perkins. 1975. Effects of urbanization on catchment response. Journal of the Hydraulics Division of ASCE 101(HY3):451-466.

10　Campbell, K. K., H. P. Johnson, and S. W. Melvin. 1974. Mathematical modeling of drainage watersheds. American Society of Civil Engineers Meeting Preprint 2373, ASCE Annual and National Environmental Engineering Convention, Kansas City, MO.

11　Carder, D. R. 1976. Development and application of a prototype family of ecosystem component simulation models for land and water management. Presented at the Earth Sciences Symposium, Fresno, CA.

12　Carr, D. P. 1973. A computer study of water management of rice paddy in Korea. United Nations Food and Agriculture Organizations Internal Publication, Rome, Italy.

13　Chen, C. L. 1976. Urban storm runoff inlet hydrograph study Vol. 1. Computer analysis of runoff from urban highway watersheds under time- and space-varying rainstorms. Report No. FHWA-RD-76-116. Federal Highway Administration. Washington, DC.

14　Clarke, K. D. 1968. Application of the Stanford Watershed Model concepts to predict flood peaks for small drainage areas. HPR-1(3) KYHPR-64-23. Division of Research. Kentucky Department of Highways. Lexington, KY.

15　Cole, G. D., and J. W. Shutt. 1976. SWMM as a predictive model for runoff. pp. 193-202. In Barfield, B. J. (ed.). National Symposium on Urban Hydrology, Hydraulics and Sediment Control. University of Kentucky, Lexington, KY.

16　Crawford, N. H. 1973a. Flood frequency determination on ungaged watersheds simulation network newsletter. Hydrocomp, Inc. Palo Alto, CA.

17　Crawford, N. H. 1973b. Computer simulation for design criteria for urban flow storage systems. Hydrocomp, Inc. Palo Alto, CA.

18　Dawdy, D. R., R. W. Lichty, and J. M. Bergmann. 1972. A rainfall-runoff simulation model for estimation of flood peaks for small drainage basins. Geological Survey Professional Paper 506-B. U.S. Government Printing Office, Washington, DC.

19　Debo, T. N., and A. M. Lumb. 1975. Criteria for selecting a water quality model for 208 planning. Simulation Network Newsletter 6(2). Hydrocomp, Inc. Palo Alto, CA.

20　DeBoer, D. W., and H. P. Johnson. 1971. Simulation of runoff from depression characterized watersheds. TRANSACTIONS of the ASAE 14(4):615-620.

21　Diskin, M. H. 1970. Objectives and techniques of watershed modeling. In Proceedings of ARS-SCS Watershed Modeling Workshop. U.S. Department of Agriculture. Tucson, AZ.

27 Donigian, A. C., Jr., and N. H. Crawford. 1976. Simulation of agricultural runoff. American Society of Civil Engineers Meeting Preprint 2670. ASCE National Water Resources and Ocean Engineering Convention. San Diego, CA.

28 Dortignac, E. J. 1967. Forest water yield management opportunities. pp. 579-592. In Sapper, W. E., and H. W. Lull (eds). International Symposium on Forest Hydrology. Pergamon Press, New York.

29 Dragoun, F. J., J. A. Robertson, and R. D. Dirmaiger. 1972. Changing conditions in an irrigated watershed. pp. 230-235. In Csallany, S. C., T. G. McLaughlin, and W. D. Striffler. Watersheds in Transition. American Water Resources Association, Urbana, IL.

30 Duckstein, L. 1974. Trade-off between models and information in river basin planning. Presented at the Fall Annual Meeting of the American Geophysical Union. San Francisco, CA.

31 Engman, E. T. 1970. Watershed models as a research tool. In Proceedings of ARS-SCS Watershed Modeling Workshop. U.S. Department of Agriculture. Tucson, AZ.

32 Finnemore, E. J., and G. P. Grimsrud. 1976. Evaluation and selection of water quality models: A planners guide. pp. 391-395. In Ott, W. R. (ed). Environmental Modeling and Simulation. EPA 600/9-76-016. Environmental Protection Agency. Washington, DC.

33 Fleming, G. 1971. Simulation of water yield from devegetated basins. Journal of the Irrigation and Drainage Division of the ASCE 97(IR2). pp. 249-262.

34 Fleming, G., and D. D. Franz. 1971. Flood frequency estimating techniques for small watersheds. Journal of the Hydraulics Division of the American Society of Civil Engineers 97(HY9):1441-1460.

35 Fleming, G. 1975. Computer simulation techniques in hydrology. American Elsevier Publishing Company, Inc., New York.

36 Fogel, M. M. 1971. Evaluating the effects of water yield management. pp. 303-314. In Monke, E. J. (ed). Biological Effects in the Hydrological Cycle. Purdue University, West Lafayette, IN.

37 Fogel, M. M., L. Duckstein, and C. C. Kisiel. 1972. Choosing hydrologic models for management of changing watersheds. pp. 118-123. In Csallany, S. C., T. G. McLaughlin, and W. D. Striffler (eds). Watersheds in Transition. American Water Resources Association, Urbana, IL.

38 Frere, M. H., C. A. Onstad, and H. N. Holtan. 1975. ACTMO, an Agricultural Chemical Transport Model. ARS-H-3. Agricultural Research Service, U.S. Department of Agriculture, Beltsville, MD.

39 Glymph, L. M., H. N. Holtan, and C. B. England. 1971. Hydrologic response of watersheds to land use management. Journal of the Irrigation and Drainage Division of the ASCE 97(IR2):305-318.

40 Grimsrud, G. P., E. J. Finnemore, and H. J. Owens. 1976. Evaluation of water quality models a management guide for planners. EPA-600/5-76-004. Environmental Protection Agency, Washington, DC

41 Haan, C. T., and H. P. Johnson. 1968a. Hydraulic model of runoff from depressional areas. Part I. General considerations. TRANSACTIONS of the ASAE 11(3):364-367.

42 Haan, C. T. and H. P. Johnson. 1968d. Hydraulic model of runoff from depressional areas. Part II. Development of the model. TRANSACTIONS of the ASAE 11(3):368-376.

43 Haan, C. T. 1975. Evaluation of a model for simulating monthly water yields from small watersheds. Southern Cooperative Series Bulletin 201, Kentucky Agricultural Experiment Station, Lexington.

44 Hartigan, J. P., and H. A. Bonuccelli. 1977. Management of urban runoff in a multi-jurisdictional watershed. pp. 33-58. In Kao, T. Y. (ed). International Symposium on Urban Hydrology, Hydraulics and Sediment Control. University of Kentucky, Lexington.

45 Hauth, L. D. 1974. Model synthesis in frequency analysis of Missouri floods. Geological Survey Circular 708. U.S. Geological Survey, Reston, VA.

46 Hendricks, J. R., Jr., and J. T. Ligon. 1973. Application of a digital hydrologic simulation model to an urbanizing watershed. Report No. 35. Water Resources Research Institute. Clemson University, Clemson, S.C.

47 Henry, J. G., and P. A. Ahern. 1976. The effects of storage on storm and combined sewers. Research Report No. 34. Environmental Protection Service. Environment Canada. Ottawa, Canada.

48 Herricks, E. E., V. O. Shanholtz, and D. N. Contractor. 1975. Models to predict environmental impact of mine drainage on streams. TRANSACTIONS of the ASAE 18(4):657-663, 667.

49 Herricks, E. E., and V. O. Shanholtz. 1976. Predicting the environmental impact of mine drainage on stream biology. TRANSACTIONS of the ASAE 19(2):271-274, 283.

50 Holtan, H. N., and N. C. Lopez. USDAHL-70 model of watershed hydrology. Technical Bulletin No. 1435. Agricultural Research Service, U.S. Department of Agriculture.

51   Holtan, H. N., G. J. Stiltner, W. H. Henson, and N. C. Lopez. 1975. USDAHL-75 Revised model of watershed hydrology. U.S. Department of Agriculture Technical Bulletin No. 1518.

52   Huber, W. C., and J. P. Heaney. 1977. Introduction to the EPA stormwater management model (SWMM). pp. 34-73. In DiGiano, F. A., D. D. Adrian, and P. A. Mangarella (eds). Short Course Proceedings Applications of Stormwater Management Models 1976. EPA-600/2-77-065. Environmental Protection Agency, Cincinnati, OH.

53   Huff, D. D. 1971. Hydrologic simulation and the ecological system. pp. 18-30. In Monke, E. J. (ed). Biological effects in the hydrological cycle. Purdue University, West Lafayette, IN.

54   Jackson, T. J., and R. M. Ragan. 1974. Hydrology of porous pavement parking lots. Journal of the Hydraulics Division of the American Society of Civil Engineers. 100(HY12): 1739-1752.

55   Jackson, T. J., and R. M. Ragan. 1977. Value of landsat in urban water resources planning. Journal of the Water Resources Planning and Management Division of the American Society of Civil Engineers. 103(WRI):33-46.

56   James, L. D. 1965. Using a digital computer to estimate the effects of urban development of flood peaks. Water Resources Research 1(Z):223-234.

57   Jennings, M. E., J. O. Shearman, and D. P. Bauer. 1976. Selection of streamflow and reservoir-release models for river-quality assessment. Geological Survey Circular 715-E. U.S. Geological Survey. Reston, VA.

58   Jensen, M. E. 1972. Programming irrigation for greater efficiency, pp. 133-161, in Hillel, D. (ed), Optimizing the Soil Physical Environment Toward Greater Crop Yields. Academic Press, New York.

59   Jewell, T. K., D. A. Mangarella, and F. A. DiGiano. 1974. Application and testing of the EPA stormwater management model to Greenfield, MA. pp. 61-72. In Kao, T. Y. (ed). National Symposium on Urban Rainfall and Runoff and Sediment Control. University of Kentucky, Lexington.

60   Jewell, T. K., P. A. Mangarella, F. A. DiGiano, and D. C. Adrian. 1977. SWMM Application Study Guide, pp. 93-238. In Digiano, F. A., D. D. Adrian, and P. A. Mangarella (eds). Short course proceedings applications of stormwater management models-1976. EPA-600/2-77-065. Environmental Protection Agency. Cincinnati, OH.

61   Johnson, H. P. 1973. Hydrologic and watershed modeling—A summary. TRANSACTIONS of the ASAE 16(3):585-586.

62   Kazanowski, A. D. 1968. A standardized approach to cost-effectiveness evaluations. pp. 113-150. In English, J. M. (ed). Cost-effectiveness — the Economic Evaluation of engineered systems. John Wiley and Sons, Inc. New York.

63   Kincaid, D. C. and D. F. Heerman. 1974. Scheduling irrigations using a programmable calculator. ARS-NC-12, Agricultural Research Service, USDA.

64   Kisiel, C. C., and L. Duckstein. 1972. Economics of hydrologic modelling: A cost-effectiveness approach. pp. 319-330. In International Symposium on Modelling Techniques in Water Resource Systems. Ottawa, Canada.

65   Koelliker, J. K., H. L. Manges, and R. I. Lipper. 1975. Modeling the performance of feedlot-runoff-control facilities. TRANSACTIONS of the ASAE 18(6):1118-1121.

66   Lager, J. A. 1977. Criteria for selection of stormwater management models. pp. 239-258. In DiGiano, F. A., D. A. Adrian, and P. A. Mangarella (eds). Short Course Proceedings Application of Stormwater Management Models. EPA-60012-77-065. Environmental Protection Agency, Cincinnati, OH.

67   Langford, K. J., and J. L. McGuinness. 1976. Using a mathematical model to assess the hydrological effects of land use change. Agricultural Research Service ARS-NC-31. USDA.

68   Larson, C. 1973. Hydrologic effects of modifying small watersheds is prediction by hydrologic modeling possible. TRANSACTIONS of the ASAE 16(3):560-564, 568.

69   Leaf, C. F., and G. E. Brink. 1972. Simulating effects of harvest cutting on snowmelt in Colorado subalpine forest. pp. 191-196 in Csallany, S. C., T. G. McLaughlin, and W. D. Striffler (eds), Watersheds in Transition. American Water Resources Association, Urbana, IL.

70   Leaf, C. F., and G. E. Brink. 1973. Hydrologic simulation model of Colorado subalpine forest, U.S. Department of Agriculture Forest Service Research Paper RM-107.

71   Leaf, C. F., and G. E. Brink. 1975. Land use simulation model of the subalpine coniferous forest zone. U.S. Department of Agriculture Forest Service Research Paper RM-135.

72   Lindahl, L. E., and R. L. Hamrick. 1970. The potential practicality of watershed models in operational water management. Presented at the National Water Resources Engineering Meeting. American Society of Civil Engineers, Memphis, TN.

73   Linsley, R. K., Jr. 1971. A critical review of currently available hydrologic models for analysis of urban stormwater runoff. Hydrocomp, Inc., Palo Alto, CA.

74 Linsley, R. K., Jr., M. A. Kohler, and J. L. Paulhus. 1975. Hydrology for engineers. McGraw-Hill, New York.

75 Lovell, R. E. 1975. Hydrologic model selection in a decision-making context. Technical Report No. 26. Department of Systems and Industrial Engineering. University of Arizona, Tucson, AZ.

76 Lumb, A. M., J. R. Wallace, and L. D. James. 1974. Analysis of urban land treatment measures for flood peak reduction. ERC-0574. Environmental Resources Center. Georgia Institute of Technology, Atlanta, GA.

77 Lumb, A. M., and L. D. James. 1976. Runoff files for flood hydrograph simulation. Journal of the Hydraulics Division of the American Society of Civil Engineers 102(HY 10):1515-1532.

78 Michel, H. L., and W. D. Henry. 1974. Flood control and drainage planning in the urbanizing zone: Fairfax, County, VA. pp. 119-139. In Whipple, W., Jr. (ed). Urban Runoff Quantity and Quality. American Society of Civil Engineers. New York.

79 Marsalek, J. 1976. Discussion of dimensionless inlet hydrograph model. Journal of the Hydraulics Division of the American Society of Civil Engineers 102(HY12):1773-1776.

80 McCuen, R. H., and H. W. Piper. 1975. Hydrologic impact of the planned unit developments. Journal of the Urban Planning and Development Division of the American Society of Civil Engineers 101(UP1):93-102.

81 McCuen, R. H., W. J. Rawls, G. T. Fisher, and R. L. Powell. 1977. Flood flow frequency for ungaged watersheds: A literature evaluation. ARS-NE-86. U.S. Department of Agriculture. Agricultural Research Service, Beltsville, MD.

82 McPherson, M. B. 1975a. Regional earth science information in local water management. American Society of Civil Engineers, New York.

83 McPherson, M. B. 1975b. Urban hydrological modeling and catchment research in the U.S.A. Urban Water Resources Research Program Technical Memo IHP-1. American Society of Civil Engineers, New York.

84 Meinholz, T. L., C. A. Hansen, and V. Novotny. 1974. An application of the storm water management model. pp. 109-114. In Kao, T. Y. (ed). National Symposium on Urban Rainfall and Runoff and Sediment Control. University of Kentucky, Lexington, KY.

85 Miller, C. F. 1968. Evaluation of runoff coefficients for small natural drainage areas. Research Report No. 14. Water Resources Institute. University of Kentucky, Lexington, KY.

86 Mills, W. C., W. M. Snyder, T. K. Woody, R. B. Slack, and J. D. Dean. 1976. Use of a piecewise linear model with spatial structure and input for evaluating agricultural to urban hydrologic impact. pp. 215-224. In Barfield, B. J. (ed). National Symposium on Urban Hydrology, Hydraulics and Sediment Control. University of Kentucky, Lexington, KY.

87 Moore, W. L. 1971. New aids and methods for teaching hydrology. pp. 379-391. In Monke, E. J. (ed). Biological Effects in the Hydrological Cycle. Agricultural Experiment Station. Purdue University, West Lafayette, IN.

88 Overton, D. E., and G. G. Tsay. 1974. A kinematic method of urban peak runoff design rates using SCS curve numbers for Knoxville, TN. Research Series No. 25. Department of Civil Engineering. University of Tennessee, Knoxville, TN.

89 Overton, D. E., and M. E. Meadows. 1976. Stormwater modeling. Academic Press. New York.

90 Ragan, R. M., M. J. Root, and J. F. Miller. 1975. Dimensionless inlet hydrograph model. Journal of the Hydraulics Division of the American Society of Civil Engineers 101(HY9): 1185-1196.

91 Riley, J. P., and R. H. Hawkins. 1976. Hydrologic modeling of rangeland watersheds. pp. 123-138. In Heady, H. F., D. H. Falkenborg, and J. P. Riley. Watershed Management on Range and Forest Lands. Utah Water Research Laboratory, Utah State University, Logan, UT.

92 Rogers, J. J. 1973. Design of a system for predicting effects of vegetation manipulation on water yield in the Salt-Verde Basin. PhD Dissertation, University of Arizona, Tucson, AZ.

93 Rogerson, T. L. 1976. Simulating hydrologic behavior on Ouachita Mountain drainages. U.S. Department of Agriculture Forest Service Research Paper SO-119.

94 Rovey, E. W., D. A. Woolhiser, and R. E. Smith. 1977. A distributed kinematic model of upland watersheds. Hydrology Paper No. 93. Colorado State University, Fort Collins, CO.

95 Shanholtz, V. O., and J. H. Lillard. 1970. A soil water model for two contrasting tillage systems, Bulletin 38. Water Resources Research Center, Virginia Polytechnic Institute and State University, Blacksburg, VA.

96 Shanholtz, V. O., J. B. Burford, and J. H. Lillard. 1972. Evaluation of a deterministic model for predicting water yields from small agricultural watersheds in Virginia. Research Division Bulletin 73, Department of Agricultural Engineering, Virginia Polytechnic Institute and State University, Blacksburg, VA.

97   Shanholtz, V. O., and J. C. Carr. 1975. Evaluation of a model for simulating continuous stream flow from small watershed. Southern Cooperative Series Bulletin No. 200, Virginia Agricultural Experiment Station, Blacksburg, VA.

98   Shih, G. B., R. H. Hawkins, and M. D. Chambers. 1972. Computer modelling of a coniferous forest watershed. pp. 433-452. In Age of Changing Priorities for Land and Water. American Society of Civil Engineers. New York.

99   Shih, G. B., E. K. Israelsen, R. N. Parnell, Jr., and J. P. Riley. 1976. Application of a hydrologic model to the planning and design of storm drainage systems for urban areas. PRWG 86-1. Utah Water Research Laboratory. Utah State University, Logan, UT.

100   Shumate, K. S., E. E. Smith, V. T. Ricca, and G. M. Clark. 1976. Resources allocation to optimize mining water pollution control. EPA-600/2-76-112. Environmental Protection Agency, Cincinnati, OH.

101   Simons, D. B., R. M. Li, and M. A. Stevens. 1975. Development of models for predicting water and sediment routing and yield from storms on small watersheds. Report to the U.S. Department of Agriculture Forest Service Rocky Mountain Forest and Range Experiment Station, Flagstaff, AZ.

102   Soil Conservation Service. 1972. Hydrology Section 4. SCS National Engineering Handbook. USDA.

103   Sternberg, Y. M., and A. F. Agnew. 1968. Hydrology of surface mining—A case study. Water Resources Research 4(2):363-368.

104   Terstriep, M. L., and J. B. Stall. 1974. The Illinois urban drainage area simulator, ULLUDAS. Bulletin 58. Illinois State Water Survey. Urbana, IL.

105   Terstriep, M. L., M. L. Voorhees, and G. M. Bender. 1976. Conventional urbanization and its effect on urban runoff. Illinois State Water Survey. Urbana, IL.

106   Tung, H. 1975. Impact of contour coal mining on steamflow, A case study of the New River Watershed, TN. PhD Dissertation. University of Tennessee, Knoxville, TN.

107   U.S. Army Corps of Engineers. 1972. Program description and user manual for SSARR model streamflow synthesis and reservoir regulation. Program 724-K5-G0010. North Pacific Division of the U.S. Army Corps of Engineers. Portland, OR.

108   U.S. Forest Service. 1977. Non-point water quality modeling in wildland management: A state-of-the-art assessment (Volume 1—Text), EPA-600/3-77-036, Environmental Protection Agency, Athens, GA.

109   Viessman, W., Jr., J. W. Knapp, G. L. Lewes, and T. E. Harbaugh. 1977. Introduction to hydrology. IEP Dun-Donnelley. New York.

110   Walesh, S. G. 1976. Models: Practical tools in urban water resources planning. Presented at the Spring Annual Meeting of the American Geophysical Union, Washington, DC.

111   Weber, J., C. C. Kisiel, and L. Duckstein. 1973. On the mismatch between data and models of hydrologic and water resources systems. Water Resources Bulletin 9(6):1075-1088.

112   Wensink, R. B., and J. R. Miner. 1975. A model to predict the performance of feedlot runoff control facilities at specific Oregon locations. TRANSACTIONS of the ASAE 18(6): 1141-1145, 1150.

113   Wensink, R. B., and J. R. Miner. 1977. Modeling the effects of management alternatives on the design of feedlot runoff control facilities. TRANSACTIONS of the ASAE 20(1):138-144.

114   Wisner, P. E., A. F. Ashamalla, and P. A. Ahern. 1976. Selection of models for urban drainage problems: Technical aspects and nontechnical constraints. pp. 246-263. In Environmental Aspects of Irrigation and Drainage. American Society of Civil Engineers. New York.

115   Zoune, J. J., T. A. Bean, J. K. Koelliker, and J. A. Anschutz. 1977. Model to evaluate feedlot runoff control systems. Journal of the Irrigation and Drainage Division of the American Society of Civil Engineers 103(IR 1):79-92.

chapter 13 ▮

CURRENTLY AVAILABLE MODELS

13

CURRENTLY AVAILABLE MODELS

by K. G. Renard, Director, Southwest Watershed Research Center, USDA, ARS, Tucson, AZ 85705; W. J. Rawls, Hydrologist, USDA, ARS, Beltsville, MD 20705; M. M. Fogel, Hydrologist and Professor, School of Renewable Natural Resources, University of Arizona, Tucson, AZ 85721

Users of hydrologic models for small watersheds are generally faced with the problem of selecting from among the many models available in technical literature. Many of the models are site specific (simplifications and assumptions made preclude their use universally), and, therefore, the user is faced with the problem of selecting the model which will most efficiently provide the answers needed. Although we made no comparisons herein of the simulation ease or accuracy of simulation against a common data base, we attempted to pull all of the models of the hydrologic cycle (or subcomponents of the cycle) into one reference. A summary table is presented which references readily available models on the basis of land use, geographic region, and hydrologic cycle portion to be simulated.

In reviewing the literature, we utilized computer literature searches, manual literature searches, and a survey questionnaire widely distributed to people and groups who were felt might have input. The computer data bases searched were those included in the Water Resources Scientific Information System (WRSIS), National Technical Information Service (NTIS), and the Science and Education Administration — Agricultural Research (SEA-AR, formerly Agricultural Research Service) Current Awareness Literature Search.

About 300 survey questionnaires soliciting information on available models were distributed to the following: Federal agencies involved in water, universities (agricultural engineering, civil engineering, and forestry departments), water resources research centers, selected State water agencies, and selected private consultants. We made no effort to include models developed outside of the United States, although some are included because of developments on these models within the U.S. The following information was requested in the questionnaire:

1 Model name.
2 Author's name(s).
3 Address of the senior author.
4 Hydrologic process simulated.
5 Model description.
6 Time scale of simulation.
7 List of major input variables.

    8 List of major output variables.
    9 Optimization routine.
  10 Status of model.
  11 Geographic and land use areas where the model has been used.
  12 Computer requirements.
  13 Pertinent development references.

Within the space and time allowed, it would be impossible to completely list all hydrologic models mentioned by those answering the questionnaire. Also, we felt a listing would serve no useful purpose since many of the models identified in response to the questionnaire were in various preliminary stages of development and were not ready for immediate use. Without a brief model description, the user would not be able to choose between models. Therefore, we decided to include only computer models that were ready for distribution and for simulating the total or a major land phase portion of the

TABLE I SUMMARY OF CURRENTLY AVAILABLE MODELS

Model Number	PROCESS SIMULATED									GEOGRAPHIC AREA						LAND USE			
	Total Watershed	Precipitation	Snowmelt	Infiltration	Evapo Transpiration	Surface Runoff	Subsurface Flow	Chemical Movement	Erosion / Yield	Northeast	Southeast	Midwest	Southwest	Northwest	Other	Forest	Pasture & Range	Agriculture	Urban
1	O			O		O				O									O
2	O	O		O		O	O					O				O		O	O
3	O	O			O	O	O	O	O		O					O		O	O
4	O	O		O	O	O				O			O						O
5		O		O	O	O	O								O	O	O		
6									O	O		O				O	O	O	O
7	O	O	O	O	O	O	O							O		O	O	O	O
8						O				O		O	O					O	
9				O								O	O					O	
10				O		O							O				O		
11	O	O		O	O	O	O					O				O		O	
12	O	O	O	O	O	O	O	O	O	O	O	O	O	O	O	O	O	O	O
13		O		O	O	O				O	O	O	O	O					O
14		O				O									O				
15	O			O	O	O	O	O	O		O	O		O				O	O
16	O			O	O	O	O	O	O		O	O						O	
17						O				O	O					O			
18		O									O					O	O	O	O
19				O	O	O	O				O	O				O	O		
20	O										O					O		O	
21				O		O					O					O			
22		O								O	O					O			
23	O		O			O	O	O					O	O				O	
24	O		O	O	O	O	O			O	O	O	O	O	O	O		O	O
25		O		O	O	O	O				O					O	O	O	
26	O		O	O	O	O	O	O			O				O	O		O	
27	O		O	O	O	O	O	O	O	O	O					O		O	O
28	O	O		O		O	O		O		O							O	
29	O		O	O	O	O	O			O	O	O	O			O		O	O
30	O			O	O	O	O			O	O	O	O			O		O	O
31			O			O		O		O	O	O	O	O					O
32						O							O				O		
33						O	O									O		O	O
34		O	O										O	O		O			
35	O	O	O		O	O			O				O	O		O			
36	O	O	O		O	O							O	O		O			
37					O										O			O	
38	O				O	O						O				O		O	
39					O							O				O			
40	O			O	O	O				O	O		O	O	O	O	O	O	

hydrologic process. All models meeting these criteria are given in Appendix 13-A. Generally, the following information is included for each model:

1 Name of the model developer(s). (Models are listed alphabetically according to developer's name.)

2 Model name.

3 Address of the senior model developer.

4 Abstract. (Brief description of what the model does, including computer requirements and general geographic and land use for which the model has been used.)

5 Development reference.

Table 1 summarizes the data of each model included in Appendix 13-A, and lists the hydrologic process simulated, and the general geographic location and land use for which the model has been used or should be used. This table should serve to help direct potential users to the model(s) that best fit their requirements.

TABLE I CONT'D

Model Number	Total Watershed	Precipitation	Snowmelt	Infiltration	Evapo Transpiration	Surface Runoff	Subsurface Flow	Chemical Movement	Erosion / Yield	Northeast	Southeast	Midwest	Southwest	Northwest	Other	Forest	Pasture & Range	Agriculture	Urban
41					O								O					O	
42	O	O	O	O	O	O	O	O	O			O						O	O
43	O	O		O	O	O	O								O	O	O		
44	O					O	O	O				O							O
45	O	O	O	O	O	O	O							O		O	O	O	O
46						O					O	O				O	O	O	O
47	O			O	O	O	O	O					O				O	O	O
48	O			O	O	O	O	O	O				O				O	O	O
49		O										O	O			O	O	O	O
50					O							O	O					O	
51					O	O					O	O	O			O	O		
52	O	O	O	O	O	O	O			O	O	O	O	O	O	O	O	O	O
53	O	O				O	O						O			O			
54					O			O	O			O						O	
55			O			O				O	O	O	O	O	O	O	O	O	O
56					O					O								O	
57			O			O			O			O				O			
58					O					O	O	O	O	O	O	O	O	O	O
59			O			O		O	O			O	O					O	O
60	O	O		O	O	O	O					O						O	
61	O	O	O	O	O			O						O		O			
62						O					O		O			O	O	O	O
63		O		O		O	O			O	O	O	O	O		O	O	O	O
64		O	O	O		O	O			O	O	O	O	O		O	O	O	O
65		O		O		O		O	O	O	O	O	O	O					O
66				O									O					O	
67				O											O			O	
68		O			O										O			O	O
69	O	O		O	O	O		O	O	O									O
70		O	O	O	O	O		O	O	O	O	O	O	O		O	O	O	O
71									O				O					O	O
72									O		O	O	O	O		O	O	O	
73					O					O	O	O	O	O	O	O	O	O	O
74					O						O	O	O				O	O	O
75		O	O	O		O						O	O						O
76																			
77																			
78																			
79																			
80																			

During the literature search, we found several comprehensive listings of annotated bibliographies on hydrologic models (Table 2). The reader looking for a developed model for his problem should refer to these for additional summaries on hydrologic models. Several references in Table 2 also compared the predicted results using different models on a common watershed data base. Future efforts along this line are needed to assist users in deciding between models. Such efforts will undoubtedly include requirements for data, as well as computer costs which can vary greatly.

TABLE 2: HYDROLOGIC MODELING REFERENCES

1   Agricultural Research Service. 1977. File of agricultural research models. Agricultural Research Service, National Agricultural Library, Beltsville, Maryland.

2   Bowers, C. E., A. F. Pabst, and S. P. Larson. 1972. Computer programs in hydrology. Bulletin 44, Water Resources Research Center, University of Minnesota, Minneapolis, Minn.

3   Brandstetter, A. 1976. Assessment of mathematical models for storm and combined sewers. Environmental Protection Agency, EPA-600/2-76-175a, Washington, DC. 510 pp.

4   Brown, J. W., M. R. Walsh, R. W. McCarley, A. J. Green, Jr., and H. W. West. 1974. Models and methods applicable to Corps of Engineers urban studies. Miscellaneous Paper H-74-8, U.S. Army Engineers Waterways Experiment Station, Vicksburg, Miss. 300 pp.

5   Chu, Chung Sang, and C. Edward Bowers. 1977. Computer programs in water resources. Bulletin 97, Water Resources Research Center, University of Minnesota, Minneapolis, Minn.

6   Clarke, R. R. 1973. Mathematical models in hydrology, irrigation, and drainage, Paper #19, Food and Agriculture Organization of the United Nations, Rome. 282 pp.

7   Fleming, G. 1975. Computer simulation techniques in hydrology. Elsevier Environmental Series. 333 pp.

8   McCuen, R. H., W. J. Rawls, G. T. Fisher, and R. L. Powell. 1977. Flood frequency for ungaged watersheds: A literature evaluation, ARS-NE-86, Agricultural Research Service, Beltsville, Maryland. 140 pp.

9   U.S. Forest Service. 1976. Non-point water quality modeling in wildland management: A state-of-the-art assessment. EPA-600/3-77-075, Environmental Protection Agency, Washington, DC.

10   World Meteorological Organization. 1975. Intercomparison of conceptual models used in operational hydrological forecasting. WMO Operational Hydrology Report No. 7, Geneva, Switzerland.

APPENDIX 13-A
CURRENTLY AVAILABLE MODELS, AUTHORS, ABSTRACTS, AND REFERENCES

MODEL NUMBER   **Authors**

1   Aron, Gert, and David F. Lakatos, Penn State urban runoff model, 212 Sackett Bldg., University Park, PA 16802.

ABSTRACT: The model was constructed specifically for urban watersheds of the Northeast ranging in size from 0.5 to 10 sq mi, with possible application to areas up to 20 sq mi. The model tracks only water quantity for periods from 30 minutes to 2 days. The program is written in Fortran IV, and requires 280-K storage.

REFERENCE: None.

2   Beasley, D. B., E. J. Monke, and L. F. Huggins, (ANSWERS) Areal non-point source watershed environment response simulation, Department of Agricultural Engineering, Univ. of Arkansas, Fayetteville, AK 72701.

ABSTRACT: The model is a distributed parameter event-oriented watershed model applicable to forest, agriculture, and urban areas of the Midwest. It simulates the hydrologic processes of interception, infiltration, surface and subsurface flow, and detachment and transport of sediment on a spatial basis. A variety of input and output options exist to tailor the model to the particular user's needs. The program is written in Fortran IV using GASP iv and requires 150 K storage.

REFERENCE: Beasley, D. B. 1977. ANSWERS: A mathematical model for simulating the effects of land use and management on water quality. Unpublished PhD Thesis, Purdue University, 266 p.

3   Betson, Roger P., and Harold E. Pratt, TVA Streamflow simulation and analysis model (SSAM), Tennessee Valley Authority, 410 Evans Building, Knoxville, TN 37902.

ABSTRACT: The model package consists of a continuous daily streamflow model and a storm hydrograph model. These two models can be combined in a simulation version which stochastically generates precipitation and simulates evapotranspiration, surface runoff, subsurface flow, sediment and conservative water quality constituent transport for forest, agricultural and urban land use in the Southeast. The package has an optimization routine. The program is written in Fortran IV and requires 170 K storage.
REFERENCE: Betson, R. P. "Storm hydrographs using a double-triangle model," TVA Research Paper No. 8, Feb. 1972, Knoxville, TN 37902.

4 Boning, Charles W., U.S.G.S. Peak flow synthesis rainfall/runoff model, U.S. Geological Survey National Center, Mail Stop 415, Reston, VA 22092.

ABSTRACT: The model was developed for urban areas of the Northeast and Southwest. The model uses daily rainfall and evaporation moisture conditions to compute infiltration and rainfall excess for selected flood events. The rainfall excess is routed through the basin using translation hydrographs and the attenuation of the hydrograph is accomplished using distributed linear storage reservoirs. The time scale of simulation is from 1 to 60 min. An optimization routine is also included. The program is written in PL/1 and requires between 356 to 756 K storage.
REFERENCE: Charles W. Boning. 1974. Users guide for a US Geological Survey rainfall-runoff model: U. S. Geol. Survey open-file report 74-33, 252 p.

5 Boughton, W. C., The Boughton Model, Griffin University, Nathan, Brisbane Queensland, Australia 4111.

ABSTRACT: Several versions exist (McMahon-Mein version is perhaps the best). The model operates on a daily basis, in three cycles, namely, wetting, drying, and drainage, the former cycle operating only on days with recorded rainfall, while the latter two operate each day. The model, written in Fortran IV, consists of three moisture stores (interception store and upper and lower soil stores), and requires 11 parameters and 4 estimated or assumed moisture states for its complete specification. The model has no routing routine.
REFERENCE: Boughton, W. C. 1968. A mathematical catchment model for estimating runoff. J. of Hydrol. (New Zealand), 7:75-100.

6 Boyce, R. C. SEDEL Sediment Delivery, SCS, CTU, 269 Federal Center Building, Hyattsville, MD 20782.

ABSTRACT: The model estimates river basin sediment yield by sub-basins, sheet erosion by Universal Soil Loss Equation, channel types of erosion by unit rates. Routes through existing or proposed impoundments, computes sediment storage requirements for proposed dams. Parallel computations for suspended load and bedload. The model has been used in the Northeast and Midwest for all types of land use. The program is written in Fortran and requires 37-K storage.
REFERENCE: Boyce, R. C. 1975. Sediment routing with sediment delivery ratio, ARS-S-40, pp. 61-66.

7 Boyd, Donald W., and Theodore T. Williams, State Water Planning Model, 318 Roberts Hall, Montana State University, Bozeman, MT 58415.

ABSTRACT: A system of linear simultaneous solution equations with temperature/time varying coefficients; models primary data base with zero prediction error; expands data base via generation of secondary data; is validated via the method of perturbation; proceeds from macro to micro (relative to space and time) in degree of simplicity to complexity; metric format for ease of linking the other models; linearity permits linear programming solution technique when coupled to an objective function. The program is written in Fortran IV and requires 10-K storage.
REFERENCE: Development of a State Water Planning Model, Parts I, II, III (models), Parts IV, V (data preparation of data bank), Montana University Joint Water Resources Research Center, Montana State University, Bozeman, MT 58415.

8 Brakensiek, D. L., Kinematic flood routing, N.W. Watershed Research Center, USDA-SEA-AR, P.O. Box 2700, Boise, ID 83701.

ABSTRACT: This is a flood routing model that routes inflow as overload flow or channel flow with time scales as specified in the program which is written in Fortran IV.
REFERENCE: Brakensiek, D. L. 1966. Storage flood routing without coefficients, ARS-41-122.

9 Brakensiek, D. L., Green and Ampt infiltration into a layered soil, N.W. Watershed Research Center, USDA-SEA-AR, P.O. Box 2700, Boise, ID 83701.

ABSTRACT: The model calculates depth to wetted front, time to reach that depth, total infiltration amount and rate. The program is written in Fortran IV.
REFERENCE: None.

10 Chery, D. L., Jr., WATSHED, Southeast Watershed Research Center, USDA-SEA-AR, P.O. Box 5677, Athens, GA 30604.

ABSTRACT: The model used kinematic solution of overland and channel flow. Distributed lateral inflow from triangular planes to channel flow and uniform lateral inflow to channel flow can be represented. An interactive infiltration model operates on both plane and channel flow. The model has been applied to range conditions in the Southwest. The program is written in Fortran and requires 51-K storage.
REFERENCE: Chery, D. L. 1976. An approach to simplification of watershed models for application purposes. PhD dissertation, Utah State University, Logan UT 84321.

11   Claborn, B. J., and W. L. Moore, University of Texas Watershed Model/Texas Watershed Model, Department of Civil Engineering, Texas Tech. University, Lubbock, TX 79409.

ABSTRACT: This is a general, continuous, accounting-type of watershed model in which an attempt is made to simulate, as realistically as possible, physical processes occurring in the watershed. Most of the parameters have a physical meaning, and some of them are independently measurable. It emphasizes the importance of soil moisture movement and simulates runoff at a time interval appropriate to the conditions. The model uses many of the same algorithms as the Stanford Model. Major difference is in infiltration (Holtan's equation is used), evaporation, and time scale. The model has been applied to areas in the Midwest and Southwest under all types of land use. The program is written in Fortran and requires 160-K storage.
REFERENCE: Claborn, B. J., and W. L. Moore. 1970. Numerical simulation of watershed hydrology, Tech. Rept. HYD 14-7001, University of Texas, Austin, TX 78712.

12   Crawford, N. H., R. K. Linsley, D. D. Franz, et al., Hydrocomp Simulation Programming (HSP), HYDROCOMP INC., 1502 Page Mill Road, Palo Alto, CA 94304.

ABSTRACT: The HSP system simulates hydrologic processes (including snow accumulation and melt) and water quality processes for as many as 20 water quality variables. Channel processes and reservoirs are also simulated. HSP is a continuous simulation model, and has been used in all sections of the U.S. for all types of land use. The time scale of simulation varies from 5 min to hourly, depending on the process. Statistical analysis of continuous output time series is used to produce data for economic analysis of alternate water management plans. The program is written in PL/I and requires about 250-K storage.
REFERENCES: 1. Hydrocomp 1976. Hydrocomp Simulation Programming Operations Manual, Hydrocomp Inc., Palo Alto, California. 2. Hydrocomp 1977. Hydrocomp Water Quality Operations Manual, Hydrocomp Inc., Palo Alto, CA.

13   Dawdy, David, John Schaake, and William Alley, Dawdy-Schaake Urban Stormwater Model, Dames and Moore, Suite 700, 7101 Wisconsin Ave., Washington, DC 20014.

ABSTRACT: The model computes intermediate and outfall hydrographs for urban or partially urban basins of variable land-use type. The model uses a kinematic method of land surface and has a conduit routing provided for detention reservoir routing. The model uses USGS-type infiltration model with optimization of parameters. The program is written in Fortran IV and requires 250-K storage.
REFERENCE: D. R. Dawdy, John Schaake, and William Allen. 1977. Distributed routing rainfall-runoff model for urban planning, U.S. Geological Survey Computer Contribution (In press).

14   Dingman, S. Lawrence, Snowmelt-runoff model for the U.S. Tundra biome (SNOR03), Institute of Natural and Environmental Resources, University of New Hampshire, Durham, NH 03824.

ABSTRACT: The model simulates a small tundra watershed of low slope as a linear reservoir. In present revision, snowmelt due to solar radiation only is simulated. Distribution of water equivalent on watershed is important to results, and is accounted for in model. Can be modified to nonlinear reservoir, if appropriate. The program is written in Basic language.
REFERENCE: "Development of a Snowmelt-Runoff Model for the U.S. Tundra Biome — Progress Report," by S. Lawrence Dingman, U.S. IBP Tundra Biome Report 73-3, 1973. Available from author or from Dr. Jerry Brown, Director, U.S. Tundra Biome Program, USA CRREL, P.O. Box 282, Hanover, NH 03755.

15   Donigian, A. S., Jr., and N. H. Crawford, Nonpoint Source Pollutant Loading (NPS) Model, HYDROCOMP INC., 1502 Page Mill Road, Palo Alto, CA 94304

ABSTRACT: The NPS Model simulates hydrologic processes (including snow accumulation and melt), erosion processes, and surface nonpoint source pollutants. The hydrologic model is based on the Stanford Watershed Model. The model can simulate up to five different user-specified pollutants from up to five different land uses in a single operation. All pollutants are simulated as a function of the eroded sediment. Pervious and impervious land surfaces within each land use are simulated separately. Channel processes are not simulated. The program is written in Fortran IV and requires 150-K storage.

REFERENCES: 1. Donigian, A. S., Jr., and N. H. Crawford. Modeling nonpoint pollution from the land surface. Office of Research and Development, U.S. Environmental Protection Agency, EPA-600/3-76-083, July, 1976. 2. Donigian, A. S., Jr., and N. H. Crawford. Simulation of nutrient loadings in surface runoff with the NPS model. Office of Research and Development, U.S. Environmental Protection Agency, November, 1976. 109 p. (In press)

16   Donigian, A. S., Jr., and N. H. Crawford, Agricultural Runoff Management (ARM) Model, HYDROCOMP INC, 1502 Page Mill Road, Palo Alto, CA 94304.

ABSTRACT: The ARM Model simulates hydrologic processes (including snow accumulation and melt), erosion processes, pesticide-soil interactions, and soil nutrient transformations to model runoff, sediment loss, and pesticide and nutrient content of runoff from small agricultural watersheds. The hydrologic model is based on the Stanford Watershed Model. No channel processes are simulated. The ARM Model is a continuous simulation model. The program is written in Fortran IV and requires 360-K storage.

REFERENCES: 1. Crawford, N. H., and A. S. Donigian, Jr. Pesticide transport and runoff model for agricultural lands. Office of Research and Development, U.S. Environmental Protection Agency. EPA-660/2-74-013. December, 1973. 211 p.
2. Donigian, A. S., Jr., and N. H. Crawford. Modeling Pesticides and Nutrients on Agricultural Lands. Office of Research and Development, U.S. Environmental Protection Agency. EPA-600/2-76-043, February, 1976. 263 p.
3. Donigian, A. S., Jr., D. C. Beyerlein, H. H.Davis, Jr., and N. H. Crawford. The Agricultural Runoff Management (ARM) Model Version II: Testing and Refinement. U.S. Environmental Protection Agency, June, 1977. (In preparation.)

17   Douglass, James E., Streamflow modification, U.S. Forest Service, Coweeta Hydrologic Lab., Box 601, Franklin, NC 28734.

ABSTRACT: Curves or equations are used to predict magnitude and duration of streamflow change after cutting of hardwood forests in Appalachian highlands of eastern U.S. The time scale of simulation is annual and the simulation uses an algebraic expression for changes in basal area, land slope, and aspect.

REFERENCE: Douglass, J. E., and W. T. Swank. 1975. Effects of Management Practices. In Municipal Watershed Management Symposium Proceedings, USDA For. Serv. Gen. Tech. Rept. NE-13:1-13.

18   Eli, Robert N., II, and Thomas E. Croley, II, IIHR Hourly Precipitation Model, Department of Civil Engineering, West Virginia Univ., Morgantown, WV 26506.

ABSTRACT: A stochastic data generation model for producing a time series of hourly precipitation accumulations at a point. Related wet time intervals, corresponding to an independent storm event, are scheduled by an inter-arrival time model using a fitted exponential distribution. Intra-storm structure is described in terms of "storm segments," correponding to the passage of a storm rainfall cell or group of cells. The location in time and the duration of storm segments can be entirely specified by independent random variables. The intensity and distribution of precipitation within storm segments are modeled by fitted log-normal intensity probability distributions and by cataloguing sample storm segment shapes. The program is written in Fortran and requires 120-K storage.

REFERENCE: Eli, R. N., and T. E. Croley. 1976. "An hourly precipitation model for Ralston Creek," IIHR Report No. 192, Iowa Institute of Hydraulic Research, The University of Iowa, Iowa City, IA.

19   Goldstein, R. A., and J. B. Mankin, PROSPER, Electric Power Research Institute, P.O. Box 10412, Palo Alto, CA 94304.

ABSTRACT: Daily evapotranspiration, calculated by combination equation, is in steady state with liquid water flow through vegetation and soil. Liquid water flow is simulated by network equations (potentials, resistances). Darcy flow equation used for water flow between soil layers. Roots occur in the upper two (A and B horizons) of up to five soil layers. The model has been used in the Southeast and Midwest for forest and range conditions. The program is written in Fortran IV.

REFERENCE: Goldstein, R. A., J. B. Mankin, and R. J. Luxmore. 1974. "Documentation of PROSPER: A model of atmosphere-soil-plant-water flow," EDFB-IBP-73-9, Oak Ridge National Laboratory, Oak Ridge, TN.

20   Haan, C. T., Monthly Water Yield Model, Agricultural Engineering Department, University of Kentucky, Lexington, KY 40506.

ABSTRACT: The model simulates monthly water yield based on daily precipitation and average daily potential evapotranspiration. Three types of runs can be made: (1) parameter optimization runs (there are four parameters), (2) simulation runs with four parameters known and with observed monthly runoff, and (3) simulation runs without observed runoff. The model has been primarily used in forest and agricultural areas of the Southeast. The program is written in Fortran IV and requires 115-K storage.

REFERENCE: Haan, C. T. 1975. A monthly water yield model computer program documentation. Agr. Eng. Tech. Rept. 6, Agr. Eng. Dept., University of Kentucky, Lexington, KY.

21 Helvey, J. D., Soil Moisture, U.S. Forest Service, 1133 N. Western Ave., Wenatchee, WA 98801.

ABSTRACT: The model consists of a series of equations which predict soil moisture content in Southern Applachian mountains. The model can be solved easily on any computer by solving some algebraic equations.

REFERENCE: Helvey, J. D., J. D. Hewlett, and J. E. Douglass. 1972. Predicting Soil Moisture in the Southern Appalachians, Soil Science Society of America Proceedings 36(6):954-959.

22 Helvey, J. D., Canopy and litter interception — Hardwoods and pines, U.S. Forest Service, 1133 N. Western Ave., Wenatchee, WA 98801.

ABSTRACT: The model is a series of predictive equations for canopy, streamflow, and litter interception for mixed hardwood forests throughout the eastern U.S. Eastern White Pine in the southern Appalachian Mountains, and Loblolly Pine in the South Carolina Piedmont. The model, consisting of some algebraic equations, simulates on either a storm, season, or annual basis.

REFERENCE: Helvey, J. D. 1967. Interception by Eastern White Pine. Water Resources Res. 3(3):723-729.

23 Hill, Robert W., A. L. Huber, E. K. Israelsen, and J. P. Riley, HYDSM, Utah State University, Department of Agriculture and Irrigation Engineering, Logan, UT 84322

ABSTRACT: River basin hydrology-salinity flow simulation model related to agricultural crop use. The model has been used in the agricultural areas of the Southwest and Northwest. The program is written in Fortran IV and requires 32-K storage.

REFERENCE: None furnished.

24 Holtan, H. N., University of Maryland version of USDAHL Model, Shriver Lab., University of Maryland, College Park, MD 20742.

ABSTRACT: The model uses linear dimensions available from soil survey to compute storage volumes on the soil surface and in layers of soil profiles. Watersheds are zoned by soils, by land use, by slope or whatever feature is important to the problem. Water balances are computed for each layer of each zone to produce watershed outflow. This model has been applied to all types of land use in all geographic parts of the U.S. The program is written in Fortran IV and requires 99-K storage.

REFERENCE: Holtan, H. N., G. J. Stiltner, W. H. Henson, and N. C. Lopez. 1975. USDAHL-74 model of watershed hydrology, USDA Tech. Bull. No. 1518, ARS, Beltsville, MD.

25 Huber, W. C., J. P. Heaney, and P. B. Bedient, HLAND, Department of Environmental Engineering Sciences, Univ. of Florida, Gainesville, FL 32611.

ABSTRACT: The model combines Thornthwaite and Mather soil moisture accounting procedure with SCS runoff method for obtaining soil moisture storage. T-M procedure compiles change in soil storage, areal ET, and surface runoff. A base flow relationship is included. Surface overland flow is routed in a manner equivalent to use of a linear reservoir. Streamflow is routed via the Muskingum method. The model has been used for all types of land use in the Southeast. The program is written in Fortran IV and requires 37-K storage.

REFERENCE: Huber, W. C., J. P. Heaney, P. B. Bodient, and J. P. Bender. "Environmental resources management studies in the Kissimmee River Basin," Final Report No. ENV-05-76-3 to Central and Southern Fla. Flood Control Dist., West Palm Beach, Fla., Dept. of Env. Engr. Sciences, Univ. of Florida, Gainesville, May 1976. 379 p.

26 Huff, D. D., R. J. Luxmoore, J. B. Mankin, and C. L. Begovich, TEHM: A terrestrial ecosystem hydrology model, Bldg. 3017, Oak Ridge National Laboratory, P.O. Box X, Oak Ridge, TN 37830.

ABSTRACT: The TEHM is a process oriented, mechanistic model for watershed hydrology and the role of water in transport of nutrients and contaminants. It is designed to interface with an atmospheric transport model, a soil chemistry model, a primary productivity model, and models for the uptake and cycling of materials by basin vegetation. Its core is a soil-plant-atmosphere water dynamics model. Snowmelt is included, but not tested. The model has been used for forest and agricultural areas of the Southeast. The program is written in Fortran IV and requires 540-K storage.

REFERENCE: Huff, D. D., R. J. Luxmoore, J.B. Mankin, and C. L. Begovich. 1977. TEHM: A terrestrial ecosystem hydrology model, ORNL/NSF/EATC-27, EDFB/IBP 76-8, Oak Ridge National Laboratory.

27 Huff, D D., Wisconsin hydrologic transport model, Bldg. 3017, Oak Ridge National Laboratory, P.O. Box X, Oak Ridge, TN 37830.

ABSTRACT: This hydrologic transport model is based on the Stanford Watershed Model and forms a major component of the Unified Transport Model developed at ORNL. It includes the hydrologic transport of a trace contaminant by entrainment in overland flow, infiltration, impervious area runoff and subsurface flow. Chemical exchange is designed to interface with atmospheric transport and sediment transport modules. The model has been used for all types of land use for the Southeast and Midwest. Optimization is included. The program is written in Fortran IV and requires 540-K storage.
REFERENCE: Patterson, M. R. et al. 1974. A user's manual for the FORTRAN IV version of the Wisconsin hydrologic transport model, ORNL/NSF/EATC-7, EDFB/IBP/74-9, Oak Ridge National Laboratory.

    28 Huggins, L. F., D. B. Beasley, E. J. Monke, and J. R. Burney, ANSWERS, Agricultural Engineering Department, Purdue University, W. Lafayette, IN 47907.

ABSTRACT: The model uses a distributed parameter approach to characterize behavior of all points throughout the catchment. Watershed is subdivided into a grid of elements for simulation. Model generally applicable to areas less than 20 sq mi. Time scale of simulation is variable, but usually resolution to 1 min. The model has been used for agricultural areas of the Midwest. The program is written in Fortran and storage depends on number of watershed elements.
REFERENCES: 1. Beasley, D. B. 1977. ANSWERS: A mathematical model for simulating the effects of land use management on water quality. PhD Thesis, Purdue University. 2. Huggins, L. F., and E. J. Monke. 1968. A mathematical model for simulating the hydrologic response of a watershed. Water Resour. Res. 4(3):529-539.

    29 James, L. Douglas, Kentucky Watershed Model, Utah Water Research Laboratory, Utah State University, Logan, UT 84322.

ABSTRACT: This is Fortran translation and modification of the Stanford Watershed Model providing continuous simulation of streamflow and other hydraulic responses. The model has been used for all types of land use and in all geographic areas of the U.S., except the Northwest. The program includes an optimization routine and requires 150-K storage.
REFERENCE: James L. Douglas. 1972. Hydrologic modeling, parameter estimation, and watershed characteristics. J. of Hydrol. 17:283-307.

    30 James, L. Douglas, OPSET, Utah Water Research Laboratory, Utah State University, Logan, UT 84322.

ABSTRACT: This is a self-calibrating version of the Stanford Watershed Model. The model will proceed from default initial values to estimate values for each parameter that best matches simulated to recorded flows. Time scale of simulation is 15 min. The model has been used for all types of land use and in all geographic parts of the country, except the Northwest. The program is written in Fortran IV and requires 90-K storage.
REFERENCE: Liou, E. Y. 1970. OPSET: Program for computerized selection of watershed parameter values for the Stanford Watershed Model. Research Report 34, Water Resources Institute, University of Kentucky, Lexington, KY.

    31 Jennings, Marshall E., QWILLUDAS, U.S. Geological Survey, Gulf Coast Hydro Science Center, Bay St. Louis, MS 39529.

ABSTRACT: The model is basically the urban stormwater model ILLUDAS, developed by the Illinois State Water Survey with additions for detention reservoir flow and QW routing of land-use pollutants. The model has been used in all geographic sections of the U.S. The program is written in Fortran IV and requires 280-K storage.
REFERENCE: Tenstreip, Michael L., and John B. Stall. 1974. The Illinois urban drainage area simulator, ILLUDAS. Illinois State Water Survey, Bull. 58, 90 p., Urbana, IL.

    32 Lane, L. J., Southwest Watershed Research Center, USDA-SEA-AR, 442 East Seventh Street, Tucson, AZ 85705.

ABSTRACT: A stochastic runoff model was developed for describing intermittent and independent runoff events in arid/semiarid areas of the Southwest. A probability distribution is used to describe variables for the start of the runoff season, number of events per season, time interval between events, beginning time of the runoff event, and runoff volume and peak discharge. The mean and standard deviation used to describe each distribution are expressed as functions of the watershed area. The program is written in Fortran and requires 50-K storage.
REFERENCES: 1. Diskin, M. H., and L. J. Lane. 1972. A basinwide stochastic model for ephemeral stream runoff in southeastern Arizona. Bulletin IAHS 17(1):61-76. 2. Lane, L. J. and K. G. Renard. 1972. Evaluation of a basinwide stochastic model for ephemeral runoff from semiarid watersheds. TRANSACTIONS of the ASAE 15(1):280-283.

    33 Larson, N. M., and M. Reeves, No model name. Oak Ridge National Laboratory, Oak Ridge, TN 37830.

ABSTRACT: This model predicts coupled movement of water and trace contaminants through a layered and unsaturated soil-moisture zone. Rapid computation speed is achieved via approximation of moisture properties as exponential functions of pressure head, allowing analytical solution of the resulting equations. The model depends on site-specific parameters. The program is written in Fortran IV and requires 270-K storage.

REFERENCE: Larson, N. M., and Reeves, M. Analytical analysis of soil-moisture and trace-contaminant transport, Oak Ridge National Laboratory Report, Oak Ridge, TN ORNL/NSF/EATC-12.

    34 Leaf, Charles F., and Glen E. Brink, Snow melt model (MELTMOD), 4412 E. Mulberry #113, Fort Collins, CO 80521.

ABSTRACT: The model simulates daily snowmelt in Colorado subalpine watersheds for all combinations of aspect, slope, elevation, and forest cover composition and density. The model simulates winter snow accumulation, the energy balance, snowpack condition, and resultant melt in time and space. The model has been used in the Southwest and Northwest. The program is written in Fortran IV and requires 50-K storage.

REFERENCE: Leaf, Charles F., and Glen E. Brink. 1973. Computer simulation of snowmelt within a Colorado subalpine watershed. USDA For. Serv. Res. Pap. RM-99, 22 p. Rocky Mt. For. and Range Exp. Stn., Fort Collins, CO.

    35 Leaf, Charles F., and Glen E. Brink, Land use model (LUMOD), 4412 E. Mulberry #113, Fort Collins, CO 80521.

ABSTRACT: This model simulates the short- and long-term hydrologic impacts of combinations of timber harvesting and weather modification to develop management strategies for planning intervals which can vary from a few years to the rotation age of subalpine forests (120 yr and longer). The model contains time trend functions which compute changes in evapotranspiration, soil water, forest cover density, reflectivity, interception, snow redistribution, and sediment yield as the forest stands respond to timber harvesting. The program is written in Fortran IV and requires 60-K storage.

REFERENCE: Leaf, Charles F., and Glen E. Brink. 1975. Land use simulation of the subalpine coniferous forest zone. USDA For. Serv. Res. Pap. RM-135, 42 p. Rocky Mt. For. and Range Exp. Stn., Fort Collins, CO.

    36 Leaf, Charles F., and Glen E. Brink, Water Balance Model (WBMODEL), 4412 E. Mulberry #113, Fort Collins, CO 80521.

ABSTRACT: This model is specifically designed to determine the probable hydrologic changes resulting from watershed management in the Colorado subalpine zone. It simulates the total water balance on a continuous year-round basis and compiles the results from individual hydrologic response units into a "composite overview" of an entire drainage basin. The program is written in Fortran IV and requires 100-K storage.

REFERENCE: Leaf, Charles F., and Glen E. Brink. 1973. Hydrologic simulation model of Colorado subalpine forest. USDA For. Serv. Res. Pap. RM-107. 23 p. Rocky Mt. For. and Range Exp. Stn., Fort Collins, CO 80521.

    37 Makkink, G. F., and H. D. J. van Heemst. ROTTEGAT. Agricultural University, Wageningen, Netherlands.

ABSTRACT: ROTTEGAT is a computer program which simulates the water balance of the soil and the depth of the shallow water table. The model which operates continuously is based on macrometeorological data, the physical properties of the soil, the hydrological situation of the field, and some pertinent data on the crop cover throughout the year. The program is written in CSMP language and has been used in the Netherlands.

REFERENCE: Makkink, G. F., and H. D. J. van Heemst. 1974. Simulation of the water balance of arable land and pastures. Simulation Monographs, Centre for Agricultural Publishing and Documentation, Wageningen, Netherlands.

    38 Molz, Fred J. Practical simulation models for the subsurface hydrologic system, Civil Engineering Department, Auburn University, Auburn, AL 36830.

ABSTRACT: The model consists of the groundwater flow equation with a source term to allow for groundwater recharge. The model has national application under all types of land use. The program is written in Fortran with variable storage provisions.

REFERENCE: Molz, F. J. Practical simulation models of the subsurface hydrologic system. W.R.R.I. Bulletin 19, Water Resources Research Inst., Auburn University.

    39 Moore, Allen, LEM: Litter evaporation model, Biology Department, Western Carolina University, Cullowhee, NC 28723.

ABSTRACT: The model predicts daily water content and evaporative losses in the litter of a mixed deciduous forest. Model incorporates throughfall and litter delay functions. The model has been used for forested areas of the Southeast. The program is written in Fortran.

REFERENCE: Moore, A., and Swank, W. T. 1974. A model of water content and evaporation for hardwood leaf litter. In *Mineral cycling in Southwestern ecosystems,* F. G. Howell, J. B. Gentry, and M. H. Smith eds., ERDA Symposium Series CONF-740513, pg. 58-69.

40 National Weather Service Hydrologic Research Laboratory, National Weather Service River Forecast System, National Weather Service, W23, NOAA, Silver Spring, MD 20910.

ABSTRACT: This is an operational model for real time simulation for river forecasting. It contains many models including catchment (Sacramento) snow accumulation and ablation, dynamic wave routing, reservoir operation and extended streamflow prediction. Also contains procedures for data processing and analyses for calibration and forecast models. The model has been used in all sections of the country for all types of land use. The program is written in Fortran and contains an optimization routine.

REFERENCE: Staff, Hydrologic Research Laboratory, "National Weather Service river forecast system, forecast procedures," *NOAA Tech Memo NWS HYDRO-14 and HYDRO-17*, U.S. Dept. of Commerce, Silver Spring, MD December 1972.

41 Nimah, M. N. and R. J. Hanks. No model name. Utah State University, Department of Soil Science and Biometeorology, Logan, UT 84321.

ABSTRACT: A model to predict soil water content profiles, evapotranspiration, water flow from or to the water table, root extraction, and root water potential under transient field conditions.

REFERENCE: Nimah, M. N., and R. J. Hanks. 1973. Model for estimating soil water, plant and atmospheric interrelations: I. Description and sensitivity. Soil Sci. Soc. of Am. Proc. 37(4):522-527.

42 Novotny, Vladmir, LANDRUN, Department of Civil Engineering, Marquette University, 1515 W. Wisconsin Place, Milwaukee, WI 53233.

ABSTRACT: This program models the total hydrologic cycle. The kinematic wave theory is used for the flow routing. Erosion modeling is based on the Universal Soil Loss Equation and chemical pollution is based on absorption theory. The model has been used for agricultural and urban areas of the Midwest. The program is written in Fortran IV and requires 30-K storage.

REFERENCE: Novotny, V., J. G. Mahoney, and J. Konrad. 1976. Land use effect on water quality. An overload non-point continuous model. Nat. Conf. on Env. Eng., ASCE, Seattle, WA.

43 Porter, J. W., and T. A. McMahon, The monash model, Melbourne and Metropolitan Board of Works, Melbourne, Victoria, Australia.

ABSTRACT: This model is applicable to any catchment to synthesize daily (or hourly) discharges on a continuous basis using rainfall and evaporation data. Infiltration is based upon an adaptation of a simplified equation derived from diffusion theory by Philip, and nonlinear routing techniques were used in both the daily and hourly versions of the model. Spatial and temporal variations in rainfall can be considered by dividing the catchment into sub-areas, and up to four hydrologic regimes may be specified to model spatial variations in physical characteristics. The model is written in Fortran IV.

REFERENCE: Porter, J. W., and T. A. McMahon. 1975. Application of a catchment model in southeastern Australia. J. Hydrol. 24:121-134.

44 Preul, H. C., and C. Papadakis, Storm water management. Division of Water Resources, Civil Engineering Dept., University of Cincinnati, Cincinnati, OH 45221.

ABSTRACT: Two mathematical models of urban runoff are presented: One simulates the rate of runoff, and the other simulates the rate of pollution transport. The reference also reviews urban runoff models. The model has been tested using watershed characteristics and runoff quantity and quality data for a combined sewer watershed in Cincinnati.

REFERENCE: Pruel, H. C., and C. Papadakis. 1970. Urban runoff characteristics. EPA Water Pollution Control Research Series 11024 DQU 10/70. 339 p.

45 Quick, M. C., and A. Pipes, UBC Watershed Model, Department of Civil Engineering, University of British Columbia, Vancouver, B.C., Canada.

ABSTRACT: The model is designed for forecasting runoff from mountain catchments and for this reason the model is divided into area-elevation bands. The model estimates snowpack accumulation and depletion, and operates entirely from meteorological inputs of daily maximum and minimum temperatures and precipitation. Soil moisture and groundwater characteristics are used to control the sub-division into fast, medium, and slow components of runoff. These various components of runoff are routed to the stream system by using unit hydrograph and storage routing techniques. Additional facilities are available in the model to describe lake storage and lake routing. The model has been used for all types of land use in the Northwest. The program is written in fortran IV and requires 300-K storage.

REFERENCE: Quick, M. C., and Pipes, A. "Daily and seasonal forecasting with a water budget model," Proceedings of the International Symposium on the Role of Snow and Ice in Hydrology, UNESCO, WMO, and NRC, Banff, Canada, September 1972, pp. 1017-1034.

46 Reeves, M., and J. O. Duguid, Model name - none, Oak Ridge National Laboratory, Oak Ridge, TN 37830.

ABSTRACT: The model provides solution to the nonlinear saturated-unsaturated flow equations for two-dimensional flow under transient conditions. The model depends on site specific parameters. The program is written in Fortran IV.

REFERENCE: Reeves, M., and Duguid, J. O. Water movement through saturated-unsaturated porous media: A finite-element Galerkin model, Oak Ridge National Laboratory Report, Oak Ridge, TN ORNL-4927, 1975.

> 47   Ricca, Vincent T., The Ohio State University version of the Stanford streamflow simulation model, The Ohio State University, 1790 Neil Avenue, Columbus, OH 43210.

ABSTRACT: This is a deterministic model which generates continuous watershed hydrographs in response to precipitation data. The program is written in Fortran IV and requires 300-K of storage.

REFERENCES: 1. Ricca, V. T. 1972. "The Ohio State University version of the Stanford streamflow simulation model," Office of Water Resources Research, USDI, Projects #B-005-OHIO, and B-019-OHIO. 2. Warns, J. C. 1971. "User's Manual for The Ohio State University version of the Stanford Streamflow Simulation Model IV." M.S. Thesis, The Ohio State University.

> 48   Ricca, Vincent T., The deep mine source model and the refuse pile and strip mine pollutant source model, The Ohio State University, 1790 Neil Avenue, Columbus, OH 43210.

ABSTRACT: These models produce a time trace of acid load and flow rate from acid drainage sources as a function of climatic conditions, watershed status, and mine situations. The model, written in Fortran IV, requires 300-K and has been used on Midwestern watersheds.

REFERENCES: 1. North, A. H. 1971. "Acid mine drainage: A mathematical model." PhD Dissertation, The Ohio State University. 2. Blemel, G. D. 1975. "Watershed evaluation and data needs for hydrologic and acid mine drainage modeling." M.S. Thesis, The Ohio State University.

> 49   Richardson, C. W., Time-area rainfall generation, USDA-SEA-AR, Box 748, Temple, TX 76501.

ABSTRACT: This model generates daily rainfall amounts at multiple points in an area or watershed with the same statistical properties as observed rainfall. The model has been used in the Midwest and Southwest. The program is written in Fortran IV and requires 32-K storage.

REFERENCE: Richardson, C. W. "A model of stochastic structure of daily precipitation over an area," PhD dissertation, Dept. of Civil Engineering, Colorado State University, 1976.

> 50   Richardson, C. W., and J. T. Ritchie, Water balance model, USDA-SEA-AR, P.O. Box 748, Temple, TX 76501.

ABSTRACT: The model predicts daily components of the water balance of an agricultural watershed. The model has been used for range and agricultural conditions in the Southeast, Midwest, and Southwest. The program is written in Fortran and requires 40-K storage.

REFERENCE: Richardson, C. W., and J. T. Ritchie. Soil water balance for small watersheds, TRANSACTIONS of the ASAE 16(1):72-77. 1973.

> 51   Ritchie, Joe T. No model name. Grassland-Forage Research Center, USDA-SEA-AR, Box 748, Temple, TX 76501.

ABSTRACT: Models the daily evaporation rate from a row crop canopy situation in which the soil water supply to the plant roots is not limited. The crop evaporation rate is calculated by adding the soil surface and surface components (based on a leaf area index), the potential evaporation, the rainfall, and the net radiation above the canopy.

REFERENCE: Ritchie, J. T. 1972. Model for predicting evaporation from a row crop with incomplete cover. Water Resources Research 8(5):1204-1213.

> 52   Rockwood, David M., Streamflow synthesis and reservoir regulation (SSARR), Army Corps of Engineers, North Pacific Division, 220 N.W. 8th Avenue, Portland, OR 97209.

ABSTRACT: This model simulates the runoff process in complex river basins. The three major components of the model are: a generalized watershed model which translates rainfall/snowmelt into runoff according to continuous soil moisture accounting indices; a river routing model; and a reservoir regulation model. It can be operated in a forecasting mode to predict future streamflows. The model has been used in all sections of the country for all types of land use. The model is written in Fortran and requires 32-K of storage.

REFERENCE: Rockwood, D. M. 1975. SSARR, Streamflow synthesis and reservoir regulation model, U.S. Army Corps of Engineers, North Pacific Division, Portland, OR.

> 53   Rogerson, Thomas L., Ouachita HYDROSIM, Southern Forest Experiment Station, 830 Fairview Street, Fayetteville, AR 72701.

ABSTRACT: This is a simple simulation model to predict the water balance and hydrologic changes resulting from thinning small pine-hardwood drainages in central Arkansas. The program is written in GPSS and requires 100-K storage.
REFERENCE: Rogerson, T. L. Simulating hydrologic behavior on Ouachita Mountain Drainages. USDA, FS Research Paper SO-119.

54 Saxton, Keith E., AET2-NUT, USDA-SEA-AR, Smith Agricultural Engineering Building, Washington State University, Pullman, WA 99164.

ABSTRACT: Part one, AET2, is a detailed daily budget of evapotranspiration and soil moisture considering atmospheric, plant, and soil characteristics. Daily relationships of plant canopy, phenological development, rooting, and moisture stress are used. Soil water movement in a 6-ft profile is calculated by tension and conductivity relationships. Part two, NUT, calculates daily nitrate budgets in the soil profile by considering fertilizer addition, plant uptake, and water movement. The model has been used in agricultural areas of the Midwest. The program is written in Fortran and requires 140-K storage.
REFERENCE: Saxton, K. E., H. P. Johnson, and R. H. Shaw. 1974. Modeling evapotranspiration and soil moisture. TRANSACTIONS of the ASAE 17(4):673-677.

55 Schaake, John C. Jr., Deterministic urban runoff model, Hydrologic Research Laboratory, W23, National Weather Service, NOAA, Silver Spring, MD 20910.

ABSTRACT: The model uses kinematic wave equations and a selection of infiltration equations to route surface runoff overland and through a channel system. Model allows distributed precipitation inputs and distributed parameters. Model is similar to MIT Catch-Model. The model has been used for all types of land use in all areas of the country. The program is written in Fortran IV and requires 8-K words of storage.
REFERENCE: 1. Schaake, J. C. 1971. Deterministic urban runoff model, Chapter VIC, in Treatise on Urban Water Systems. Ed. by M. L. Albertson et al., Colorado State University, pp. 357-383. 2. Leclere, G., and J. C. Schaake. 1973. Methodology for assessing the potential impact of urban development on urban runoff and the relative efficiency of runoff control alternatives, MIT Ralph M. Parsons Laboratory for Water Resources and Hydrodynamics, Report 167.

56 Showcroft, R. W. and E. R. Lemon. The soil-plant-atmosphere model, USDA-SEA, Cornell University, Bradfield Hall, Ithaca, NY 14853.

ABSTRACT: The model sequence is: (1) to define the response of leaf and soil surfaces to a given microclimate; (2) to calculate the immediate microclimate of the leaf and soil surface from the gross meteorological boundary conditions; (3) to calculate the specific response of leaf and soil surfaces to this immediate microclimate; and (4) to sum this response from the soil surface to the top of the crop by layers. The program is written in Fortran and simulates on a 1/2- or 1-hr interval.
REFERENCE: Showcroft, R. W., E. R. Lemon, L. H. Allen, D. W. Stewart, and S. E. Jensen. 1974. The soil-plant-atmosphere model and some of its predictions. Agr. Meteor. 14:287-307.

57 Simons, D. B., R. M. Li, and M. A. Stevens, WASED, Civil Engineering Department, Engineering Research Center, Colorado State University, Fort Collins, Co 80523.

ABSTRACT: The model allows user to stratify watershed into homogeneous land and channel units. It is an individual storm model which includes water balance, loose soil detachment by raindrop impact and by moving water, and water and sediment routing for both overland and channel flow systems. Flow routing is by nonlinear kinematic wave approximation. The model has been used for forested areas of the Southwest. The program is written in Fortran with the storage requirement proportional to the watershed size and number of simulation units.
REFERENCES: 1. Simons, D. B., R. M. Li, and M. A. Stevens. 1975. Development of a model for predicting water and sediment routing and yield from storms on small watersheds. USDA Forest Service, Rocky Mountain Forest and Range Expt. Station, Flagstaff, AZ. 2. Li, R. M., R. K. Simons, and L. Y. Shiao. 1977. Mathematical modeling of on-site soil erosion. Proc. Int. Symp. on Urban Hydrology, Hydraulics and Sediment Control, University of Kentucky, Lexington, KY. p. 87-94.

58 Soil Conservation Service, U.S. Department of Agriculture, Computer program for project formulation hydrology (TR), Central Technical Unit, Room 269, Federal Building, Hyattsville, MD 20782.

ABSTRACT: This model computes surface runoff resulting from any synthetic or natural rain storm; develops flood hydrographs; routes through stream channels and reservoirs; combines hydrographs with those from tributaries and provides peaks and/or flood hydrographs, their time of occurrence and water surface elevations at any desired cross-section or structure. Up to nine storm rainfall distributions can be used for continuous analyses of a watershed under present conditions and with combinations of land cover/use, structural and/or channel modifications. The model has been used for all types of land use all over the country. The program is written in Fortran IV and requires 256-K storage.

REFERENCE: Soil Conservation Service — Technical release-20 (TR-20) computer program for project formulation hydrology, May 1965, Supplement 1, March 1969.

59   Smith, R.E., and D. A. Woolhiser, KINEROS, USDA-SEA-AR, Engineering Research Center, CSU Foothills Campus, Fort Collins, CO 80521.

ABSTRACT: The model uses kinematic approximation and mass balance for runoff from infiltrating planes. Watershed topography is approximated by sequences of cascading planes and branching channels. Water quality and quantity simulated on storm runoff using transfer function assumptions. Erosion quantities totaled and erosion sedimentation depths calculated (optional). The model has been used in the Midwest and Southwest on range and urban conditions. The program is written in Fortran and requires 70-K storage.

REFERENCE: Smith, R. E. 1977. Field test of a distributed watershed erosion/sedimentation model. In *Soil erosion: Prediction and control*, Proc. Nat'l Conf. on Soil Erosion. SCSA Special Publ. #21, pp. 201-209, Ankeny, IA.

60   Smith, R. L., and Ernest C. Pogge, Kansas water budget model, University of Kansas, Civil Engineering Department, Lawrence, KS 66044.

ABSTRACT: The KWBM takes as input hourly and daily precipitation, and maximum and minimum daily temperatures. Simulation of the land phase of the hydrologic cycle is performed. Moisture accounting on various zones of soil profile is performed. Surface runoff, interflow and baseflow are outputted on a daily basis. The program has been used in agricultural areas of the Midwest. The program is written in Fortran.

REFERENCE: Smith, R. L., and A. M. Lumb. 1966. Derivation of basin hydrographs. Kansas Water Resources Research Institute Contribution No. 19, Lawrence, KS.

61   Sollins, Phillip, G. Swartzman, and Al Brown, CONIFER, USFS Forest Sci. Laboratory, 3200 Jefferson Way, Corvallis, OR 97331.

ABSTRACT: CONIFER consists of about 40 nonlinear difference equations, and is designed to predict effects of perturbations (e.g., thinning, defoliation, fertilization, climatic change) on productivity, water yield, and rates of N circulation. Water and N flux in through fall, litter, and soil drainage are considered as are evaporation from canopy surfaces, transpiration, and evaporation from litter. Many hydrologic processes are keyed to leaf area index and percent canopy cover, both of which are calculated from carbon state variables (foliage and stem carbon mass) of the model. Decomposition processes are also modeled. The model has been used in the Northwest. The program is written in Fortran.

REFERENCE: CF Modeling Group 1977. CONIFER: A model of carbon and water flow through a coniferous forest (Documentation). Bulletin No. 8, Coniferous Forest Biome, Univ. of Washington, Seattle.

62   U.S. Army Corps of Engineers, HYDPAR — Hydrologic parameters, The Hydrologic Engineering Center, 609 Second Street, Davis, CA 95616.

ABSTRACT: This model computes SCS and Snyder unit hydrograph and precipitation loss rate parameters from a grid cell data bank of spatial geographic characteristics. The model has been used for all types of land use in the Southeast and Southwest. The program is written in Fortran IV and requires 27-K storage.

REFERENCE: U.S. Army Corps of Engineers. 1977. HYDPAR user's manual, The Hydrologic Engineering Center, Davis, CA.

63   U.S. Army Corps of Engineers, Unit hydrograph and loss rate optimization, The Hydrologic Engineering Center, 609 Second Street, Davis, CA 95616.

ABSTRACT: The model computes optimal unit graph and loss rate coefficients for a watershed from historical rainfall and runoff data. Several storms may be used to determine overall optimal parameters. The model has been used for all types of land use in all geographic areas of the U.S. The program is written in Fortran IV and requires 20 K-storage.

REFERENCE: U.S. Army Corps of Engineers. 1966. Unit hydrograph and loss rate optimization, The Hydrologic Engineering Center, Davis, CA.

64   U.S. Army Corps of Engineers, HEC-1 Flood hydrograph package, The Hydrologic Engineering Center, 609 Second Street, Davis, CA 95616.

ABSTRACT: Simulates single event rainfall/snowmelt runoff processes in complex watersheds. Automatic optimization may be made for loss rate and unit graph or routing parameters. Sophisticated hydrologic analysis of basin wide flow-frequencies and analysis of expected annual flood damages may also be accomplished. The model has been used for all types of land use and in all geographic areas of the U.S. The program is written in Fortran IV and requires 35-K storage with four input-output units.

REFERENCE: U.S. Army Corps of Engineers. 1973. HEC-1 flood hydrograph package user's manual, The Hydrologic Engineering Center, Davis, CA.

65   U.S. Environmental Protection Agency, Storm Water Management Model (SWMM), Municipal Pollution Control Division OR&D, Environmental Protection Agency, Waterside Mall, Room 3828, Washington, D.C. 20460.

ABSTRACT: The model gives detailed analysis of urban storm runoff, combined sewer systems, diversions, storage, treatment and receiving waters. Time scale for simulation is single events using short time steps. The program is written in Fortran IV and requires 325-K storage.
REFERENCE: Metcalf & Eddy, Inc., University of Florida, and Water Resources Engineers, Inc., Storm water management model. U.S. Environmental Protection Agency, Report No. 11024DOC07/71, October 1971.

    66   van Bavel, C. H. M., and J. Ahmed. No model name. Texas A&M Univ., Dept. of Soil and Crop Sciences, College Station, TX 77843.

ABSTRACT: The joint effect of the distribution of soil water potential and root mass upon the water uptake by the crop is represented by a single equation. The expression is used to join a layered crop canopy model for finding the evapotranspiration, as controlled by stomatal action and weather, with a hydraulic flow model for the root zone and the underlying soil. The program is written in CSMP language.
REFERENCE: van Bavel, C. H. M., and J. Ahmed. 1976. Dynamic simulation of water depletion in the root zone. Ecological Modeling 2:189-212.

    67   van Kenlen, H. ARID CROP. Department of Theoretical Production-Ecology, Agricultural University, Wageningen, Netherlands.

ABSTRACT: ARID CROP calculates the course of dry matter production for a crop and the distribution of soil water below that crop from basic or derived physical and physiological properties of plant and soil as well as from meteorological observations from standard weather stations. The model assumes that adequate nutrients are available and that growth is determined mainly by the availabililty of water. The program is written in CSMP and was developed in the Netherlands.
REFERENCE: van Kenlen, H. 1975. Simulation of water use and herbage growth in arid regions. Simulation Monographs, Centre for Agricultural Publishing and Documentation, Wageningen, Netherlands.

    68   Wang, Ru-Yih, I-Pai Wu, and L. Stephen Lau, Instantaneous unit hydrograph model, Department of Agricultural Engineering, National Taiwan University, Taipei, Taiwan, Republic of China.

ABSTRACT: A short duration unit hydrograph has been used to develop an instantaneous unit hydrograph by using Nash's method and the method of moment for the Hawaiian small watershed. The instantaneous unit hydrographs have been developed for 29 small watersheds on Oahu using a computer program. The two instantaneous unit hydrograph parameters, Gamma function arguments, N, and reservoir constant, K, were found to correlate with the drainage area with assumed triangular shape for hydrographs. Program is written in Fortran IV.
REFERENCE: Wang, R., I. Wu, and L. S. Lau. Instantaneous unit hydrograph analysis of Hawaiian small watersheds, Technical Report No. 42, pp. 54, Water Resources Research Center, University of Hawaii, Honolulu, Hawaii 96822, USA.

    69   Wanielista, Martin, Diversion Storage, Florida Tech University, Box 25000, Orlando, FL 32816.

ABSTRACT: The model determines BOD, SS, N, and P efficiencies for a diversion basin where percolation rates, inventories on soil moisture, routing using Muskingum pollutant transport by exponential function, and impervious and pervious load areas are considered. The program, written in Fortran, requires 120-K storage and was developed for nonpoint pollution work in Florida.
REFERENCE: None provided.

    70   Water Resources Engineers/Hydrologic Engineering Center, USCE, Storage, Treatment, Overflow Runoff Model (STORM), Water Resources Engineers, 710 South Broadway, Walnut Creek, CA 94596.

ABSTRACT: The model provides continuous analysis of quantity and quality of storm runoff from urban and non-urban watersheds. Two main uses are:
1. Prediction of wet-weather pollutographs for use in receiving water assessment models.
2. Preliminary sizing of detention reservoirs and treatment plant capacities. The model has been used for all types of land use all over the country. The model is written in Fortran and requires 50-K storage.
REFERENCE: Storage, treatment, overflow runoff model, generalized. Computer Program, User's Manual, July 1976, The Hydrologic Engineering Center, Davis, CA.

    71   Williams, J. R. Sediment routing, USDA-SEA-AR, Blackland Research Center, Box 748, Temple, TX 76501.

ABSTRACT: The model routes sediment yield from small watersheds through streams and valleys to the outlet of large watersheds. The technique is based on MUSLE and a first-order decay function of travel time and particle size. Sediment routing allows determination of subwatershed contributions to the total sediment yield. Also, the locations and amounts of floodplain scour and deposition can be predicted. The model has been used for agricultural and range areas of the Southwest. The program is written in Fortran IV and requires 50-K storage.

REFERENCE: Williams, J. R. Sediment routing for agricultural watersheds, AWRA Water Resources Bulletin, Vol. 11, No. 5, Oct. 1975, pp. 965-974.

72   Williams, J. R., Modified Universal Soil Loss Equation (MUSLE), USDA-SEA-AR, Blackland Research Center, Box 748, Temple, TX 76501.

ABSTRACT: The USLE was modified by replacing the rainfall energy factor with a runoff factor. MUSLE does not require a delivery ratio and is applicable to individual storms. Daily sediment yield is predicted for ungaged watersheds by attaching MUSLE to the SCS curve number water yield model and HYMO. The model has been used in forest, range, and agricultural lands in all parts of the country, except the Northeast. The program is written in Fortran and requires 100-K storage.

REFERENCE: Williams, J. R. Sediment yield prediction with universal equation using runoff energy factor. Proceedings of the Sediment Yield Workshop, Oxford, MS Nov. 28-30, 1972, ARS-S-40, June 1975, pp. 244-252.

73   Williams, J. R., and R. W. Hann, HYMO, USDA-SEA-AR, Blackland Research Center, Box 748, Temple, TX 76501.

ABSTRACT: HYMO is a problem-oriented computer language that is useful in flood control planning, flood forecasting, and water quality modeling. It was designed to transform rainfall into runoff hydrographs and to route these hydrographs through streams and valleys or reservoirs. HYMO will also predict sediment yield for an individual storm at any point on a watershed. The model has been used under all types of land use in all sections of the country. The program is written in Fortran IV and requires 73-K storage.

REFERENCE: Williams, J. R., and R. W. Hann. HYMO: Problem-oriented computer language for hydrologic modeling, User's Manual, USDA ARS-S-9, May 1973, 76 p.

74   Williams, J. R., and W. V. LaSeur, SCS curve number water yield model, USDA-SEA-AR, Blackland Research Center, Box 748, Temple, TX 76501.

ABSTRACT: The model is based on the SCS runoff curve number technique and a soil moisture accounting procedure. It predicts daily runoff from agricultural watersheds with areas up to about 2500 km^2. The model is calibrated on a gaged watershed, and can be used to extend short periods (3-5 yr) of record into long-term periods for the calibrated watershed or to predict water yield for nearby ungaged watersheds. The model has been used in most areas of the country under all types of land use, except forest. The program is written in Fortran and requires 90-K storage.

REFERENCE: Williams, J. R., and W. V. LaSeur. 1976. Water yield model using SCS curve numbers. ASCE J. Hyd. Div. 102(HY9):1241-1253.

75   Yen, Ben Chie, and Ven Te Chow, IUSR: Illinois Urban Storm Runoff Model, Department of Civil Engineering, University of Illinois, Urbana, IL 61801.

ABSTRACT: The model consists of three submodels: a surface runoff quantity and quality model, a channel-sewer system quantity (ISS) model, and a channel-sewer system quality model. They can be run separately. The surface routing is by nonlinear kinematic wave method. The channel-sewer routing is by solving numerically the complete St. Venant equation accounting for backwater effects and reversal flow in networks. The model has been used for urban areas of the Midwest and Southwest. The program is written in Fortran and PL-1 and requires 300-K storage.

REFERENCE: Yen, B.C., A. O. Akan, V. T. Chow, and A. S. Sevuk. 1976. "Prediction model for urban storm runoff," *Utility of urban runoff modeling*, Proceedings of a special symposium of the Am. Geophys. Union 1976 Spring Annual Meeting, ASCE Urban Water Resour. Res. Prog. Tech. Memo. No. 31, pp. 108-117.

SUBJECT INDEX